Classified

Classified is a fascinating account of the British state's long obsession with secrecy, and the ways it sought to prevent information about its secret activities from entering the public domain. Drawing on recently declassified documents, unpublished correspondence and exclusive interviews with key officials and journalists, Christopher Moran pays particular attention to the ways that the press and memoirs have been managed by politicians and spies. He argues that, by the 1960s, governments had become so concerned with their inability to keep secrets that they increasingly sought to offset damaging leaks with their own micro-managed publications. The book reveals new insights into seminal episodes in British post-war history, including the Suez Crisis, the D-Notice Affair and the treachery of the Cambridge spies, identifying a new era of offensive information management, and putting the contemporary battle between secret-keepers, electronic media and digital whistle-blowers into long-term perspective.

Christopher Moran is a British Academy Postdoctoral Fellow in the Department of Politics and International Studies at the University of Warwick. His previous publications include *Spooked: Britain, Empire and Intelligence* (as co-editor, 2009).

Classified

Secrecy and the State in Modern Britain

Christopher Moran

CAMBRIDGE
UNIVERSITY PRESS

10 0681257 8.

CAMBRIDGE UNIVERSITY PRESS
Cambridge, New York, Melbourne, Madrid, Cape Town,
Singapore, São Paulo, Delhi, Mexico City

Cambridge University Press
The Edinburgh Building, Cambridge CB2 8RU, UK

Published in the United States of America by
Cambridge University Press, New York

www.cambridge.org
Information on this title: www.cambridge.org/9781107000995

© Christopher Moran 2013

First published 2013

Printed and bound in the United Kingdom by the MPG Books Group

A catalogue record for this publication is available from the British Library

Library of Congress Cataloguing in Publication Data

Moran, Christopher R.
  Classified : secrecy and the state in modern Britain / Christopher Moran.
    p. cm.
  Includes bibliographical references and index.
  ISBN 978-1-107-00099-5 (Hardback)
  1. Official secrets–Great Britain. I. Title.
  JN329.S4M67 2012
  352.3'79–dc23

                                                                    2012020422

ISBN 978-1-107-00099-5 Hardback

CONTENTS

ILLUSTRATIONS

FOREWORD
Chapman Pincher

During my sixty-five years of investigative writing, thirty-four of them as a Fleet Street journalist, there were many occasions when I knew that I was being secretly subjected to the Leak Procedure – a systematic Whitehall inquiry to discover the source of my offending information. I also assumed that the inquiries had failed but had seen none of the evidence until 2007 when the author of this book, who was researching official documents, consulted me in connection with his Ph. D. thesis. He had managed to secure declassified Cabinet papers and other documents which described my Leak Procedure cases in detail, along with the consoling news that not one of them had ever been successful. Now, in this remarkably detailed and entertaining account of the machinations of the 'Secret State' to prevent intrusion into its activities, he has produced documentary evidence of its ruthless attempts to have me, and others, prosecuted as criminals for giving the public information which was being withheld to avoid political or official embarrassment rather than because of genuine national security concerns.

My respect for security classification was sullied on a pitch-black night of torrential rain in 1942 when an army dispatch rider, soaked to the skin, arrived at my unit, near Newark, where I was the officer on duty. I had to sign for an envelope marked 'Secret' and, on opening it, read 'Tinned sausages are now available.' As we were in the heartland of Bomber Command, we had been warned that German paratroopers might drop near us any time so I imagined that it might be a coded message requiring urgent action. I made immediate telephone inquiries only to find that the message meant what it said – our unit could now get access to this welcome addition to our rations.

This experience may have conditioned my rather cavalier attitude to the Whitehall concept of secrecy when, after becoming a Fleet Street defence reporter in 1946, I was loftily told by a civil servant that an official secret is 'official information of any kind which has not been officially released'. To me this was a challenge to assault the bastions of the Secret State by methods which I have since expressed in my *Who's Who* entry, concerning my hobbies, as 'fishing, shooting, ferreting in Whitehall and bolting politicians'.

As someone who was deeply aware of the relentless threat posed by Soviet espionage, I remained so conscious of the need for genuine security that I have always had a golden rule that I would never touch or look at any classified documents. So, through Dr Moran's enterprise, it is especially interesting to see some of them now they have been released. (What might be considered as the sole breaking of my rule concerns my private briefing before I travelled to an Australian desert to observe a test of Britain's first useable atomic bomb in 1953. Sitting at a large desk opposite a senior Supply Ministry official, I noticed that the folder he was about to open bore the word 'TOTEM'. Clearly, it was the code name of the operation and when I used it in my dispatch describing the successful test there was a second explosion, both in Whitehall and Australia, to discover the source of the leak. It failed, as did so many other inquiries, wasting the time of so many senior officials and Forces' chiefs. Another released document shows that, as far back as 1958, the Permanent Secretary of the Defence Ministry had advised his minister against any more time-wasting 'witch hunts' of me (which were to include having me watched), stating 'I believe that we must live with the man and make the best of it. We can console ourselves that his writings, though embarrassing at times to Whitehall, disclose nothing that Russian intelligence does not already know.' That sage advice was ignored and in good *Yes Minister* style the security 'mandarins' insisted on continuing their sterile activities.

Some of Dr Moran's discoveries have astonished me. The serious concept in the minds of some security officials that I would put my head on a block by disguising myself and using a false name to gain entry to a secret establishment beggars my belief.

As someone who witnessed most of the action described here, being personally involved in much of it, and has a full, quickly consultable record of most of it in my forty thick volumes of newspaper cuttings, I congratulate Dr Moran on producing an accurate and enthralling read which captures the excitement, the conspiracy and the tragedy of historic events like the 'D-Notice Affair' while providing a reliable work of reference on events which impacted on the nation's history.

ACKNOWLEDGEMENTS

While writing this book, I have necessarily accumulated a good many debts to colleagues, friends and institutions. I have the greatest admiration for my doctoral supervisor, Professor Patrick Major, to whom I am most indebted. Patrick was the first to give academic substance and direction to my enthusiasm for studying the hidden history of the British state. This book would not exist without his imagination, encouragement and timely interventions. With his breadth of knowledge, editorial acumen and willingness to reply to emails in the early hours of the morning, Professor Richard J. Aldrich has been an excellent post-doctoral supervisor. I have greatly enjoyed working alongside him, together with Matthew Jones, Trevor McCrisken, Paul McGarr, Kaeten Mistry and Simon Willmetts on the successful 'Landscapes of Secrecy' project funded by the Arts and Humanities Research Council. I have learned much from them and their influence on my career has been significant. Further gratitude is extended to my Ph.D. examiners, Professors Philip Murphy and Christopher Read, together with all my colleagues in History and Politics at Warwick who have provided such a stimulating research environment over some ten years of study.

Thanks go to the espionage writer Chapman Pincher, who, as well as being gracious enough to write a foreword to this book, welcomed me into his home in Kintbury to discuss my project. It was in this setting – with a 'Gone Fishing' placard hanging disingenuously on the front door – where *Classified* really took shape. I wish to express my gratitude to Pincher for the insight, colourful vignettes and access to private papers he gave me, but also for reminding me of Gibbon's apothegm that history should not only educate, but amuse. The history of British secrecy has moments of genuine high comedy, and it is thanks to Pincher's wise counsel that I did not resign these moments to the cutting-room floor.

For astute suggestions, incidental kindnesses and much else besides, I should like to thank a number of academic friends and colleagues: Christopher Andrew, Peter Gill, Andrew Hammond, Michael Herman, Robert Johnson, Christopher Murphy, David Robarge, William Rupp, and Nicholas Wilkinson. I should also like to acknowledge Sir Harold Evans, whose knowledge of the Crossman Affair – imparted to me during an extended interview in the back of a New York taxi – is unsurpassed. Sadly, I have not had the opportunity to meet in person a number of scholars whose work I frequently cite in this book. My understanding of certain episodes would have been greatly reduced without the earlier studies of John Naylor, David Reynolds, Andrew Suttie and David Vincent, in particular.

A host of institutions warrant special praise, not least the libraries and archives from which the primary materials of my book were located. Honourable mention should go to the following for permission to quote from their collections: Academy of Motion Picture Arts and Sciences, Los Angeles; Bodleian Library, Oxford; Churchill College, Cambridge; Harry Ransom Center, Texas; House of Lords Records Office, London; Howard Gotlieb Archival Research Center, Boston; Lauinger Library, Washington, DC; Library of Congress, Washington, DC; Liddell Hart Centre for Military Archives, London; Lilly Library, Indiana; London School of Economics, London; Modern Records Centre, Coventry; National Archives (UK), London; National Archives (US), College Park; National Library of Wales, Aberystwyth; Seely G. Mudd Manuscript Library, Princeton; Trinity College, Cambridge; Worcester College, Oxford; University of Birmingham Special Collections; Warner Bros. Archives, Los Angeles; and West Sussex Record Office, Chichester. I am deeply grateful for the assistance of the staff at these institutions, whose willingness to go beyond the call of duty in search of documentary jewels and nuggets was often remarkable.

At Cambridge University Press, Michael Watson has been unfailingly helpful, offering sage advice about content, argument and style, as well as providing much-needed reassurance when the going got tough. At the Press, Chloe Howell has been instrumental in escorting this work through to publication. The end product has also benefited from the astute comments of several anonymous reviewers and the copy-editing skills of Pat Harper. Finally, I should like to thank my parents who have endured my obsession about this book with admirable patience.

ABBREVIATIONS

BSC	British Security Coordination
CIA	Central Intelligence Agency [US]
DG	Director General [MI5]
DNI	Director of Naval Intelligence
D-Notice	Defence Notice
FBI	Federal Bureau of Investigation [US]
FO/FCO	Foreign Office/Foreign and Commonwealth Office
GC&CS	Government Code and Cypher School
GCHQ	Government Communications Headquarters
GRU	Soviet military intelligence
HMG	His/Her Majesty's Government
HMSO	His/Her Majesty's Stationery Office
HO	Home Office
humint	human intelligence
JIC	Joint Intelligence Committee
JSM	Joint Services Mission
KGB	Soviet secret service/security police
MI5	The Security Service
MI6	The Secret Intelligence Service
MI9	Wartime Evasion and Escape Service
MoD	Ministry of Defence
NATO	North Atlantic Treaty Organisation
NSA	National Security Agency [US]
OIA	Official Information Act
OSS	Office of Strategic Services [US]
PRO	Public Record Office
PWE	Political Warfare Executive

RAF	Royal Air Force
sigint	signals intelligence
SIS	Secret Intelligence Service [MI6]
SOE	Special Operations Executive
TNA	The National Archives
TSR2	Tactical Strike/Reconnaissance 2 aircraft

INTRODUCTION

In 2010, governments that ruled in secret faced a new enemy: WikiLeaks. Set up by the Australian hacker Julian Assange, the once-fringe whistle-blowing website shot to world fame with a string of monumental 'document dumps', in what was called the largest government leak in history. Philosophically opposed to state secrecy, the Internet-based watchdog organisation first grabbed the headlines in April 2010 when it posted harrowing video footage of US Apache helicopter pilots killing a dozen men in Baghdad in 2007, including two unarmed employees of the Reuters news agency. In July, it published 75,000 battlefield reports, spanning six years, from the US military in Afghanistan. The huge cache of documents, which were made available to the *Guardian*, *Der Spiegel* and the *New York Times*, painted a devastating picture of the failing war in the country, revealing unreported civilian casualties, soaring Taliban attacks, and the fear among NATO commanders that the neighbouring states of Iran and Pakistan were aiding the insurgency. Three months later, a further 400,000 war logs were published, this time about the conflict in Iraq. With simultaneous coverage again provided by the newspapers, the documents detailed the deaths of thousands of Iraqi civilians, and suggested that the US military had ignored evidence of torture committed by Iraqi security forces against suspected insurgents. The White House condemned the website, with US Secretary of State Hillary Clinton proposing that the releases put the work and even lives of coalition forces at risk. Hawks branded Assange a 'cyber-terrorist' and called for his arrest, trial and possible execution. Unbowed, in late November he began unleashing a torrent of some 250,000 diplomatic cables from US embassies and consulates around the world, providing an unprecedented look at the hidden world of backstage international relations. The material contained brutally candid, and often unflattering, assessments of foreign statesmen, with British officials among those targeted. Cables revealed that President Obama, no less, thought Prime Minister David Cameron (then in opposition) a 'political lightweight' after their first meeting in 2008.[1]

In the maelstrom that was WikiLeaks, governments, institutions and individuals considered important normative questions about foreign policy, free speech, secrecy and openness. The core of the debate was the age-old question of what constitutes the 'public interest'. WikiLeaks had touched on one of the fundamental and incompatible tensions in any democratic system: the need of governments to keep secrets weighed against the right of citizens to know and criticise the policies carried out in their name. For supporters, the public interest had been served by exposing the contradictions between what officials had been prepared to tell the public about their actions, especially with respect to the costly wars in Iraq and Afghanistan, and what they knew and said in private. Accordingly, Assange is lionised, and WikiLeaks is heralded as a glorious chapter in the history of freedom of information.

Detractors argued differently. Washington insisted that the disclosures not only endangered lives and threatened US operations abroad, but undermined its ability to do business with allies who would now be more wary of cooperating with the US in the fight against terrorism. Criticism of WikiLeaks was by no means limited to a red-faced US administration. Discerning commentators questioned the logic of casually dumping troves of documents onto the Internet seemingly with no regard for the content. Is the public interest really served by knowing that a US diplomat has likened the Russian prime minister Vladimir Putin and the Russian president Dmitry Medvedev to 'Batman and Robin', or that a junior State Department official discovered, apparently in total shock, that Italian premier Silvio Berlusconi had a penchant for 'late nights' and 'partying hard'? Professor Frank Furedi has suggested that, whatever Assange or high-minded newspapers might claim, such decontextualised and tawdry scraps of information amount to voyeurism, not good journalism.[2] Following the law of unintended consequences, there is a strong possibility that the end result of WikiLeaks will be more, not less secrecy. If officials suspect that Assange or someone like him will shortly tout their private intimacies on the Internet, they will adopt practices and behaviour that are against the public interest. What they said in correspondence, they will now say in hushed tones; what they said in hushed tones, they will now not say at all. For future generations of historians, the end to a private sphere in government would spell disaster, since they would discover archives conspicuously lacking in documentary material.

WikiLeaks is not the subject of this book, but it does provide a useful touchstone by which to introduce the fundamental interrogative of this study: information control – defined by sociologist Richard Wilsnack as 'the processes used to make sure that certain people will or will not have access to certain information at certain times'.[3] WikiLeaks marked a stunning defeat of the US government's ability to control classified information. For all its power and reach, Washington was undone by a disillusioned army intelligence analyst, Bradley Manning, said to have copied thousands of files from military servers onto blank CDs. To avoid detection, the lowly private first-class allegedly labelled the discs 'Lady Gaga' after the American pop singer, and pretended to sing along whilst performing the download. Significantly, the US was caught cold by technology. Assange's skill was to harness technology to develop a system for disclosing secrets which, for now at least, the most powerful nation in the world appears unable to control. A truly transnational organisation, WikiLeaks is headquartered not in one country, but on the World Wide Web, thus rendering it immune from the laws of most countries. The site – a 'digital drop box' – allows anyone to post sensitive information under the cloak of anonymity.[4] Moreover, the post hoc removal of leaked material is virtually impossible such is the speed with which the Internet spreads information. Despite talk of a cyber clampdown – perhaps in the form of extrajudicial financial blockades by sympathetic corporate intermediaries such as Amazon or MasterCard – for now the likelihood of Washington wresting back control is slim.

The core problem facing the US – how to keep sensitive material out of the public domain – is one that UK officials have grappled with throughout the last hundred years or so with varying degrees of success. In the post-1945 period, the issue became an obsession and all-consuming. In late 1945, as world war evolved into a precarious peace, and the Labour Party settled into office on a promise of welfare reform, the new prime minister, Clement Attlee, moved the matter to the front and centre of his government's programme. In a private directive to colleagues, he underlined: 'No government can be successful which cannot keep its secrets.'[5] According to noted intelligence historian Richard J. Aldrich, Britain fought two 'imperial' campaigns after 1945: one was to defend its empire of colonies and protectorates; the other was to protect its 'empire of secrecy'.[6] The means by which this second empire was protected is the central concern of this book. Analogous to the pitched battles and bitter rearguard actions that accompanied the extinguishing of colonial fires after 1945, it is a story of struggle. Several key questions are addressed by this study. What secrets, if any, were exposed and by whom? To borrow Aldrich's expression (and continue the imperial analogy), who were the most effective 'shock troops' that rolled back the frontiers of secrecy? What mechanisms existed to prevent disclosure? How successful were these mechanisms? Moreover, how did they evolve over time? In tracing the development of the British state's obsession with shielding its programmes and activities from the gaze of public scrutiny, this book puts in long-term perspective the present-day battle between secret-keepers, electronic media and digital whistle-blowers.

The central argument of this book is twofold. First, the British state has generally been loath to preserve secrecy by taking offenders to court, preferring instead to use informal mechanisms of control. As Attlee explained in 1945, 'the problem of secrecy cannot be solved by rules, however carefully drawn'.[7] Typically, when confronted with an individual threatening the security of its classified information, the state has relied on making deals and devising pragmatic solutions behind the scenes. In most cases, it has tried to appeal to personal honour and conscience, in the hope of securing restraint. For example, in 1963 Her Majesty's Government (HMG) discovered that David Irving, not then a controversial historian, had a chapter in his forthcoming book, *The Mare's Nest*, which contained a stunning scoop: namely, the Ultra secret, the decryption of German communications by British codebreakers during the Second World War. Concerned that Ultra's disclosure would undermine peacetime signals intelligence (sigint), officials invited Irving for a chat at the Cabinet Office where they asked him to consider the nation, be an 'English gentleman' and self-censor; he did so and the secret remained unrevealed until 1974.[8] Such appeals were believed to be far more effective than the legal hammer. Most people, it was assumed, would sacrifice the self for the greater good when the strings of patriotism and gentlemanly spirit were gently pulled. Of course, this is not to contend that legislative action was never taken. The first five years of Margaret Thatcher's premiership saw the sweeping powers of Section 2 of the Official Secrets Act activated once every eighteen weeks.[9] Overt censorship, however, tended to happen at the request of headstrong individuals, such as Thatcher, rather than the system as a whole. In short, it was not the Whitehall way.

Second, by the 1960s the state had concluded that maintaining absolute secrecy with respect to some of its work was not only impossible but also counterproductive. Although informal controls were effective in many cases, they were far from perfect, meaning that damaging disclosures – sensationalised and presented out of context – slipped through the cracks. With this, the state moved into the realm of 'offensive' information management, putting 'secrets' into the public domain on its own terms. The traditional 'defensive' approach of saying and releasing nothing was seen as too rigid. What was needed was flexibility. This shift led the state to sponsor official intelligence histories, written with the aid of classified material, as well as to sanction reminiscences by trusted veterans. Micro-managed by government departments so as not to injure national security or cause political embarrassment, such works were designed to offset the damage of leaks, as well as to pre-empt future revelations by unscrupulous individuals over whom the departments had little or no control. Carefully manicured accounts allowed governments to boost their standing in the public eye, since works were presented as emblematic of increased liberalisation. Moreover, they helped to deflect calls for potentially more revealing, more wide-ranging and ultimately more radical open government initiatives. In making this argument, this book builds on the work of Peter Gill, who, in an excellent article surveying changes in the oversight of the UK intelligence community in the 1990s, contends that the changes did not amount to a unilateral reduction of secrecy, but were instead a variation of information control from secrecy to 'persuasion'.[10] Where this book differs from Gill's analysis is in saying that the shift began much sooner.

Who, then, had made life so difficult for the secret state that it felt compelled to retaliate with its own releases? In an age before web-based information clearing houses, it will be suggested, the biggest challenge to official secrecy came from 'insiders' and their memoirs. In the twentieth century, especially after 1945, it became increasingly common for retired public servants to want to leave a record of their careers. As we shall see, the motives were often transparently banal, pertaining to personal ambition and pecuniary gain. Politicians were the chief producers, but also getting in on the act were civil servants and even retired intelligence officers. Armed with privileged information, few were content to leave out critical details about their lives, especially if those details allowed them to burnish their reputations or set the record straight. Moreover, with publishers and newspapers offering vast sums for the revelation of secrets and first-class gossip about colleagues, authors had an added incentive to open up. The problem for officialdom was that many were simply too eminent to control. They comprised individuals who possessed impeccable Establishment credentials and who could name prestigious educational institutions as their alma mater. They included figures (nay, 'Great Britons') who had held the highest office and successfully led the country through the two defining conflicts of the modern era. Persons of such distinction commanded enormous respect from their institutional successors, propitiously the very people who were supposed to censor them. For reasons not hard to discern, the new generation was loath to crack the whip. Problematically, it was also the case that authors of status *expected* to get their own way. Stubborn and not easily intimidated, they acted as if the rulebook did not apply, comforted by the realisation that no one had the nerve to take stiffer action against them.

Investigative journalists provided the other main opposition to the strictures of official secrecy. In a departure from much of the existing literature on the British press in this period, I will argue that Fleet Street was far more challenging to the secret state than has been acknowledged. At the monographic level, the words of legendary Labour Foreign Secretary Ernest Bevin, who once famously said of UK journalists 'why bother to muzzle sheep?', have resonated strongly and the overall picture is one of press submission to information controls.[11] The media's complicity in the Defence Notice (D-Notice) system is frequently taken as evidence of this. A compact in which journalists voluntarily receive guidance from the government on the suitability of publishing stories with national security implications, the century-old system, critics claim, is akin to 'back-door' censorship and goes against the very idea of a free press. According to Leonard Downie, a former editor of the *Washington Post*, such an arrangement would not be tolerated in the United States; indeed, it would be unconstitutional.[12] Scholarship has also entrenched the view that UK reporters, as well as being deferential to authority and enfeebled by controls, have struggled to match the detective skills and ferreting ability that are such distinctive features of muckraking political hacks in the United States. In the words of Anthony Sampson, the best-selling anatomist of modern Britain, 'they find themselves severely restricted as to how much they can uncover; partly because of commercial limitations, but more importantly because of the growing difficulty of extracting the most crucial information from the secret recesses of government'.[13]

In what follows, a different assessment of media–state relations will be made. After 1945, it will be argued, the press gave Whitehall's business managers a torrid time. Official files denied to earlier investigators, but now available at the National Archives, reveal a government machine at its wits' end about how to stop mainstream journalists from finding sensitive information and breaking headline-grabbing stories. In this period, reporters devised ways of unearthing secrets that bypassed legal controls. They cultivated sources so senior and so distinguished that no government had the stomach to censor these conduits for fear of causing a scandal. With advances in air travel and communications, they prised information out of overseas contacts and libraries, especially in the United States where a tradition of openness was built into the polity. Certain journalists also possessed scientific education and training, allowing them to piece together remarkably accurate stories about top-secret matters, including atomic bomb development and signals intelligence. The notable American investigative journalists of recent times – Bob Woodward, Carl Bernstein and Seymour Hersh, to name but a few – are objects of hero worship, while their sources, such as the notorious garage-dweller known as Deep Throat, are the stuff of legend. Now is the moment to acclaim their counterparts across the pond – trailblazers such as Chapman Pincher, Duncan Campbell and Sir Harold Evans. In the face of strong opposition, and without the same constitutional protection afforded to US reporters, their achievements are extraordinary and deserve to be applauded.

Secret Britain: historiographical considerations

This book falls into an established body of literature that attempts to identify what makes the British state, in many ways unique among Western democracies, so secretive. Traditionally, works took their cue from Max Weber, the German sociologist, who considered secrecy as endemic to all administrative institutions. 'Every bureaucracy', he claimed, 'seeks to increase the superiority of the professionally informed by keeping their knowledge and intentions secret.'[14] According to this model, secrecy insulates officials from criticism and allows them to make decisions free of external pressures, whether from individuals looking to exploit information for personal gain or newspaperman looking to trivialise it. To quote Weber, 'Bureaucratic administration always tends to be an administration of "secret sessions": in so far as it can, it hides knowledge and action from criticism.'[15] This 'structural' approach won many devotees. In their seminal work on the civil service, Peter Kellner and Lord Crowther-Hunt concluded: 'The unspoken heart of the argument for closed government is that private debate among civil servants and ministers produces more rational policies. Wise men, cogitating quietly on the nation's problems, will produce the right answers, if they are shielded from the hubbub of the political marketplace.'[16] In *Whitehall*, Peter Hennessy, the fastidious connoisseur of modern government, referred to secrecy as 'built into the calcium of a British policymaker's bones'.[17]

In the past quarter-century, there has been a proliferation of exciting work on British secrecy, much of it advancing the original frame as it was supplied by Weber. Weber had said nothing, as he later admitted, about either the causes or modes of secrecy in particular national contexts. His approach lacked historical specificity and over-estimated homogeneity between competing bureaucratic systems. In the 1980s, especially against the backdrop of Prime Minister Margaret Thatcher's failed attempt to use the courts to stop the publication of *Spycatcher*, the memoir of MI5 renegade Peter Wright, it became popular for scholars to see secrecy as a consequence of legislation. Supplanting the 'ideal type' formulations to which Weber and his followers subscribed, works explored the manifold legislative constraints that criminalised the illicit release of information, the most important being the draconian Section 2 of the Official Secrets Act which made illegal the unauthorised dissemination of any government document, no matter how old or trivial.[18] A consensus emerged that the effect of Section 2 should not be measured by the number of times it had been activated in the courtroom (an average of less than once per year since 1911),[19] but by its inhibiting effect on the behaviour of government employees. In *The Frontiers of Secrecy*, David Leigh suggested that it worked *in terrrorem*, 'frightening official[s] and inducing a "clearance mentality"' that it was best to disclose nothing unless authorised to do so.[20] A similar picture had been painted by the then Cabinet Secretary, Burke Trend, when interviewed by Lord Franks in 1972: 'I am not saying that you say to yourself "If I say something to X will I breach the Official Secrets Act?" But you are conscious that at the back of everything you say and do all day long there is a tremendous sanction.'[21] In short, Section 2 made secrecy a largely mindless reflex, with the default rule being: 'When in doubt, classify.'

Certainly, no crown servant could claim ignorance of the Act. One of the first things that a new entrant will do is 'sign the Official Secrets Act', a device of great symbolic value but which has no statutory force, since employees are bound by it whether they sign it or not.[22] As Kellner and Crowther-Hunt put it, 'The fact that tens of thousands of people each year "sign" the Act has almost nothing to do with national security; it has a great deal to do with indoctrinating civil servants into the culture of closed government.'[23] The standard declaration form – 'Estasecret' – was introduced during the Second World War. A decision was taken to keep the wording as simple as possible, inviting the reader's attention to the key points. 'It would take an experienced person a good while to get at the meaning of Section 2,' conceded a War Office official in November 1944: 'He certainly wouldn't do it while waiting to sign "on the dotted" line and, unless he were a lawyer, he would probably not arrive at the right conclusions even if he were given a copy to read at leisure.'[24] Hardly a comment to inspire confidence!

The deterrent effect of Section 2 was also achieved with posters. Posters detailing the Act's main provisions were hung in the buildings of government departments, particularly in depots, workrooms and storehouses where large numbers of industrial staff were located.[25] By the 1950s, the perceived importance of posters in 'promoting secrecy' (MI5's words) had led to the establishment of a working party to consider everything from the layout to colour schemes.[26] With this, posters became 'much shorter and much more striking'; typically, they included an image of a disciplinarian pointing the finger or gesticulating like a traffic warden.[27] One such poster stated: 'The Official Secrets Act affects you. You must not talk about or pass on information about your work unless you are authorised to do so. You must not keep or copy any drawing or document unless it is your job to do so. You must take care not to lose any drawings or other documents. You must hand them back when they are finished with or asked for. Penalties for infringing the acts may be heavy.'[28]

Studies of legislative controls eventually gave way to a much richer historiography proposing that the Official Secrets Act represented not the cause of secrecy in Britain, but a manifestation or symptom. In an important primer, Gavin Drewry and Tony Butcher argued that 'legislation tells only part of the story. The rest is embedded in British political culture, constitutional conventions and the understandings and habits of civil service behaviour.'[29] Shifting the locus of enquiry away from the law, the majority of authors toiling in this area began to think and talk in terms of a 'culture of secrecy'. The former civil servant Clive Ponting, himself the survivor of an unsuccessful prosecution under the Official Secrets Act in 1985, was the first to lend a new sharpness and depth to the debate: 'A powerful and persistent culture of secrecy – reflecting the basic working assumption that good government is closed government and the public should only be allowed to know what the government decides they should know – was carried over from the nineteenth century and refined in the twentieth century when it was given statutory backing through Britain's formidable secrecy laws.'[30] Devoting only a few passages to Section 2, Ponting sought to understand (or 'diagnose', to employ a favourite conceit of the field) this culture with reference to a raft of other official mechanisms to suppress information, including injunctions, confidentiality clauses, police search-and-seizure powers, and contempt-of-court laws.

The principal object of study for this new wave of literature was the civil service, an intensely culture-bound organisation, underpinned by almost invisible patterns of behaviour and values, but where secrecy was widely recognised as an essential feature of good government. True to the precepts of normative constitutional theory, many scholars argued that secrecy in Whitehall stemmed from the structure of the political system, principally the doctrine of ministerial responsibility which dictates that the exposition of policy is the sole responsibility of ministers and that civil servants are neither publicly identified with the work of their department, nor, when blame is apportioned, accountable for their actions. Like doctors, obligated never to breach the confidences of their patients, they are entrusted to keep the secrets to which they become privy. More adventurously, others sought to link the preference for 'closed government' to the social composition of the service. In the words of Hugh Heclo and Aaron Wildavsky, Whitehall resembled a 'village community' – private, tightly knit and where inhabitants came from the same narrow social and educational background, namely the public schools and Oxford and Cambridge.[31] In this cloistered world, people progressed in their careers by respecting and adhering to an honourable code of confidentiality. As Lord Franks explained, 'A civil servant who is regarded as unreliable, or who tends to overstep the mark, and to talk freely, will not enjoy such a satisfactory career as colleagues with better judgement and greater discretion. He may fail to win promotion, or he may be given less important and attractive jobs.'[32] In short, disclosure was not merely improper, it was impolite.

By any yardstick, the best book that moved the debate beyond Section 2 was *The Culture of Secrecy* by David Vincent, published in 1997.[33] The most comprehensive study to date, Vincent's account cast its net far wider than government, investigating secrecy in manifold areas of public life. With a cool eye and lively pen, Vincent explored a plethora of unstudied byways, such as codes of secrecy in medicine, charitable organisations, banking, and domestic households. In an important historiographical breakthrough, he revealed how the growth in formal government secrecy in the mid nineteenth century went hand in hand with the growth of professional secrecy as profound economic and social change caused by industrialisation led groups such as doctors, social workers and lawyers to consolidate their power with practices of concealment. Ironically, as Britain became more democratic, she also became more secretive. In examining the broader cultural setting for official secrecy, and in making the case for the twin and linked teleologies of 'modern' and 'secret', Vincent gave weight to Hennessy's earlier thesis that secrecy was an analogue of Britain's national character, extending through and beyond the orbit of the state to permeate society as a whole. 'Secrecy is as much a part of the English landscapes as the Cotswolds,' suggested Hennessy: 'It goes with the grain of our society. Its curtailment, not its continuity, would be aberrational. Whitehall ... is only its greatest, not its sole monument.'[34]

Vincent's account, despite being generally applauded by some of academia's most knowledgeable and discerning commentators, attracted a number of pertinent criticisms. The distinguished Cambridge historian Peter Mandler felt that the 'kitchen sink' approach of dealing with every conceivable aspect of secrecy distracted from the core narrative.[35] By conflating the experience of officials with that of non-officials, had

Vincent not fallen into the trap of over-inclusiveness, in effect brewing an academically opportunistic 'culture porridge'? The Cold War, a classic period of government secrecy, a time when departments feverishly guarded their secrets (sometimes from each other), was discussed only in two chapters. Vincent freely conceded that his concern was the processes and correlates of information control, but this meant that readers learned little about what secrets were actually kept.[36] In short, his was a history of secrecy, but without the secrets. Certain critics also pointed to the notoriously problematic and slippery concept of 'culture'. Like other important categories of historical analysis ('class', 'community', 'society' etc.), culture is difficult to define. It often possesses significations, seated in contemporary discourse, which have no relevance to their respective inferences in the past.[37] E. P. Thompson famously labelled it a 'clumpish term', whilst a recent study called it a 'dustbin' concept, used when other terms prove inadequate and too often explaining 'everything and nothing'.[38]

In many ways a sequel to Vincent's *tour de force*, my book aims to enrich our understanding of Britain's 'culture of secrecy' by trying to remedy some of the issues outlined above. It rejects the temptation to discard the term 'culture' (unconvinced by the explanatory value of more neutral anthropological catch-alls such as 'custom', 'ritual' or 'habit'), but limits the investigation to central government and dedicates the lion's share of the analysis to the period after the Second World War. One of the areas not covered by Vincent is that of memoir censorship, particularly the role played by the Cabinet Secretary in negotiating with authors and vetting accounts for public release. Falling into the category of 'book history', excellent recent works by David Reynolds and Andrew Suttie examining the origins of the war memoirs of Winston Churchill and David Lloyd George show that this is fertile ground for scholars of secrecy.[39] John Naylor, in his pathbreaking biography of the fabled Cabinet Secretary Sir Maurice Hankey, provided some fascinating detail on how, during the years between the world wars, the job of the Cabinet Secretary evolved from that of 'machine-minder', calibrating the flow of government business, into informal guardian of official secrecy.[40] It is clear, however, that a more systematic and widely sourced rendering of the subject is needed, especially for the period after 1945.

In trying to ameliorate our understanding of Britain's 'culture of secrecy', this book devotes greater attention to the day-to-day work of the D-Notice Committee than has hitherto been the case. With the exception of the recently published official history, *Secrecy and the Media* by Nicolas Wilkinson, works on the subject of press censorship in Britain have been largely preoccupied with high-profile causes célèbres – instances when journalists have fallen foul of the law.[41] Yet it is important to look beyond these episodes. Between 1945 and 1971, twenty-three prosecutions were brought under Section 2, only two of which involved journalists.[42] A better indication of the pervasiveness of the culture of secrecy is given by the many occasions where the D-Notice Committee has given advice to Fleet Street in the hope of prompting editorial self-regulation. It is striking that, whereas other voluntary censorship bodies (such as the British Board of Film Censors) have been scrutinised at length by scholars, the D-Notice system remains relatively unexplored. D-Notices – the letters of warning sent to the media – were until January 1982 headed 'Confidential' and accepted by recipients as secret communications. Little wonder that, in 1961, the great constitutional thinker Geoffrey Marshall referred to the D-Notice system as an 'unchronicled instrument of Government'.[43]

In the majority of works, secrecy is a dirty word. Commentators grounded in anti-statist or liberal traditions are suspicious of secrecy in all its forms, seeing it as a bulwark of inefficiency, violations of law, or political embarrassment. Others contend that the obsession with secrecy over the workings of state can be so pervasive that it becomes an end in itself. Put another way, it perpetuates secrecy for secrecy's sake, with little regard for whether a legitimate need to protect information really exists.[44] Interestingly, some of the harshest criticism has not always come from media or academic circles. Writing for the *New Statesman* in 1971, Richard Crossman, the Labour Party firebrand, famously described secrecy as the 'real English disease and in particular the chronic ailment of the British Government'.[45] In a private correspondence, the soldier-turned-military-theorist Captain Sir Basil Liddell Hart suggested that British secrecy had a 'bureaucratic absurdity ... conceal[ing] from Parliament and the press things that any foreign Intelligence Service can find out with very little trouble'.[46]

Ultimately, governments should be open by default, secret only when necessary. Public authorities have a duty to provide as much information as is reasonably possible on issues of national importance. They should inform citizens about what they are trying to do, why and by what means, even if this cannot always be achieved on a real-time basis. As Warren Kimball, a former Chair of the US State Department Historical Advisory Committee, has argued: 'Common sense may necessitate a longer wait in [certain] cases ... but whether the delay is 10, 20 or 30 years, accountability takes precedence.'[47] Transparency allows the public to judge elected officials and to hold them responsible for their actions. It helps to ensure that serious wrongdoing is exposed and that basic rights are not being damaged by unchecked power. Justly, it is an essential feature of democracy. Moreover, openness helps to build up public trust in government and its programmes. Secrecy often carries its own penalty, creating more problems than it is designed to prevent. By being kept too much behind a tight veil of secrecy, the work of government can be covered in misunderstanding and ignorance; conspiracy theories harden into fact. Crossman recognised this: 'One result of this secrecy is to make the British electorate feel it is being deliberately kept in the dark and increasingly to suspect the very worst of its rulers.'[48]

It will be apparent from reading this book that secrecy in Britain has not always followed the logic of necessity. Far too often the leverage of 'national security' has been misappropriated in a bid to conceal information likely to cause political embarrassment. As Chapman Pincher observed when giving evidence to the Franks Committee in 1971, in the taxonomy of secrecy 'politically embarrassing is a higher security classification than top secret'.[49] James Callaghan, then shadow Foreign Secretary, admitted as much when he too spoke to Lord Franks: 'We are not going to tell you anything more than we can about what is going on to discredit us.'[50] During the early Cold War especially, a period which involved heightened anxieties about external attack and internal subversion, 'national security' carried enormous weight and provided governments with a useful trump card over the right to information. Eventually, however, thanks to personalities such as Pincher exposing the tactic, it became much harder for governments to suppress political and administrative miscues by mere reference to security.

Yet it is not the intention of this book to leave the reader wholly opposed to official secrecy. Criticism is, of course, healthy when examining any locus of power; but, as Walter Bagehot explained in his classic study of the English Constitution, 'Nothing can be easier than to make a case ... against a particular system, by pointing out with emphatic caricature its inevitable miscarriages and nothing else.'[51] In certain fields, at certain times, secrecy was essential. It is sometimes forgotten that openness informs the enemy as well as the public. There are moments discussed in this book where information was rightly kept out of the marketplace and where strict secrecies enjoining officials were justified. Few would dispute the need to keep the identity of current intelligence agents or contacts out of the public domain; even fewer would question the logic of safeguarding the privacy of information gathered by citizens. Where successive British governments failed was in thinking only in absolutes. For too long, especially in the fields of intelligence and defence, officials clung to a belief that there was no middle ground between total secrecy and total disclosure. This antediluvian mindset was totally insensitive to the impact of time. It did not matter that governments changed, that individuals passed away, or that technologies and methods became obsolete. One of the themes of this book is how governments – not without some backsliding – gradually came to adopt a *when* not *if* approach to the release of sensitive information, and how words like 'never', 'everlasting' and 'indefinite' slowly and mercifully slipped out of usage.

Methodology

A few words about methodology and sources. The major accounts of British secrecy were written in the 1980s, a time when departments reflexively hoarded the most important records. The Thirty Year Rule – the point at which government files are transferred to the Public Record Office (now the National Archives) at Kew in London – rendered the study of the post-war period extremely difficult. Records relating to the intelligence services were particularly hard to come by. No matter how old or sensitive, the majority of documents that referred to intelligence found them in a historical 'Never-Never Land', walled off indefinitely from public view.[52] Section 3 (4) of the Public Records Act (1958, 1967), otherwise known as the 'blanket exemption', gave the Lord Chancellor discretionary powers to withhold any file relating to the intelligence services. In 1983, a House of Commons Select Committee on Education, Science and the Arts highlighted absurd examples of closed material, including postal interception files from the eighteenth century; intelligence bulletins from the Battle of Waterloo; and the journal of Captain Sir Mansfield Cumming, the first director of SIS, recording his favourite disguises for avoiding detection whilst travelling through foreign lands.[53] The difficult landscape in which scholars of secrecy were required to operate was summed up by Lord Radcliffe in December 1975: 'Government is not to be conducted in the interests of history; the historian cannot have as of right a smooth highway constructed for him through the intricate paths of public administration and statecraft.'[54]

In recent years, however, the landscape has improved. Following the high drama of 1989, with the collapse of the Soviet Empire and the ending of the Cold War, governments previously engaged in this epoch-defining conflict commenced various 'openness' initiatives. In a speech to the Oklahoma Press Association on 21 February 1992, Director of Central Intelligence Robert Gates apologised for the CIA's long-standing passion for secrecy and enthused about a 'uniquely propitious moment for change'.[55] In the months that followed, he directed the publication of classified articles from the CIA's in-house journal *Studies in Intelligence*; ordered a classification review of all documents over thirty years in vintage; and supported Congress in passing legislation requiring the release of documents pertaining to the assassination of President John F. Kennedy. Increased transparency was also inaugurated in the former Eastern bloc, with the new Russian government opening the archives of the Communist Party in Moscow, and the KGB giving television crews guided tours of its former headquarters.[56] This new age of transparency had an architectural metonym: the Berlin Wall. The wall had been the literal and symbolic epicentre of Cold War tensions, especially the super-secretive great game of espionage; by the early 1990s, it had been torn down.

Britain was not to miss out on this new wave of candour. Speaking on BBC Radio 4's *Analysis* programme on 25 June 1992, William Waldegrave, Chancellor of the Duchy of Lancaster and Minister for Open Government in the John Major administration, promised to make excessive Cold War levels of secrecy a thing of the past. In July 1993, his government went a long way to fulfilling this promise by publishing a White Paper on 'Open Government'. Under the code that was based upon it, historians were afforded the opportunity to assist in the formation of retention-and-release policy. Waldegrave had earlier vowed: 'I would like to invite serious historians to write to me . . . those who want to write serious historical works will know, probably better than we do, of blocks of papers that could be of help to them which we could consider releasing.'[57] Encouraging researchers to compile shopping lists of documents was a big step for a system that had pursued 'double secrecy' – in other words, seldom acknowledging what secrets were kept and being secretive about the existence of secrecy itself. Waldegrave's policy of glasnost resulted in the review and release of once enormously sensitive materials, including files that had been withheld beyond the normal thirty-year embargo and – for the first time – records generated by the secret services. By the millennium, some 100,000 files had been released. New sources on the atomic bomb, security vetting, the Special Operations Executive (SOE), and the formative years of MI5 inevitably grabbed the headlines, but just as valuable was the declassification of records of mainstream government departments such as the Treasury, the Foreign Office and the Ministry of Defence (MoD). Hennessy's richly documented study *The Secret State: Whitehall and the Cold War* is perhaps the best illustration of what can be now be achieved.[58]

This book is very much a product of the large volume of material released under the Waldegrave initiative. Recently opened records of the Cabinet Office and the Prime Minister's Office represent a rich seam for scholars to mine in search of the state's attitude and policies towards memoir writers. The same is true of departmental records; this is because memoirs in draft form were often sent 'round the houses' for clearance, with departments being invited to 'red-flag' objectionable passages. In certain files, there are multiple versions of manuscripts, with telltale comments in the margins and sentences struck out by the censor. Mercifully, Waldegrave's policy has led to the declassification of a host of materials pertaining to press censorship. Copies of D-Notices spanning the period 1912–71 can be found in MoD files. More important, MoD files contain minutes of meetings and associated correspondence relating to the quotidian work of the D-Notice Secretary, providing a unique insight into the articles that Whitehall attempted to suppress, choreograph or manicure.

Yet this book could not have been written from solely state records. Documents produced by the ranks of the government machine are revealing, but do not tell the whole story. Cabinet papers are intended to provide a record of decisions reached by ministers and thus fail to divulge the ideas, premeditated strategies and unconscious feelings of the personalities involved. Patrick Gordon Walker, a Cabinet minister in Harold Wilson's first Labour government, once wrote: 'Cabinet papers give no indication of the order in which the points were made: they are always marshalled pro and con. Not all the points made in argument are recorded. No indication is given of the tone or temper of the debate.[59] Richard J. Aldrich has cautioned scholars against interpreting documents from the National Archives as an 'analogue of reality', pointing out that files are meticulously weeded, cleansed and processed by the authorities before entering the public domain. The danger, argues Aldrich, is that works written purely from a 'diet of processed food' will resemble official history, albeit once removed.[60] This book, therefore, has advanced a methodological predisposition towards private papers as much as state records. Of particular value have been the collections of politicians who wrote memoirs. In the papers of prominent autobiographers, one can typically discover a host of documents detailing every stage of a book's genesis, production and reception. Correspondences with government constitute fascinating reading, but also significant are letters to friends, former colleagues, lawyers, literary agents and publishers. Here, authors show themselves to be 'sentient reflecting beings',[61] passionate and willing to speak frankly about their treatment at the hands of the state censor.

Some of the best documentary evidence used in this book was unearthed in the United States. Archivists there testify to a long-standing agreement between the State Department and the British government that allows for officials in London to request that certain categories of UK material be withdrawn from US files. Eagle-eyed researchers will spot cover notes in certain US files referring to 'attached' British reports that were obviously part of the original collection, but have since been removed. In spite of this, the United States represents a treasure trove for scholars interested in information management in Britain, rendering a passport as valuable as a reader's ticket to Kew. Admittedly, the bulk of this material is found not in official repositories but in private collections, where the scaly claw of the state fails to reach. Across the Atlantic are located the private papers of several Britons whose careers in some way intersected with that of the secret state. Housed at the Howard Gotlieb Archival Research Center in Boston, the papers of post-war media tycoon Cecil Harmsworth King, owner of Mirror Group Newspapers, contain memorandums pertaining to matters of press censorship. Nestled in the Hoover Institute at Stanford University, the papers of Kenneth de Courcy, the well-connected if dubious publisher of *Intelligence Digest*, include letters from senior UK officials concerning the government's response to the disappearance of Cambridge spies Guy

Burgess and Donald Maclean. Insights can also be gleaned from the papers of individuals who enjoyed personal relationships with members of Britain's administrative and political elite. For example, Whitehall's policy towards spy memoirs is richly detailed in the collection of the Hungarian-born military historian Ladislas Farago, held at Boston University. Farago was in regular correspondence with John Masterman, the wartime Chairman of the Double-Cross System, who by the early 1970s had become so disgruntled with official attempts to suppress his study of the system that he resorted to telling Farago all about it. The famous English historian Lewis Namier once said that to understand modern Britain, it is necessary to complete a 'cross-country paper chase', working by accretions from a variety of sources, adding a piece here and a piece there until a composite picture emerges. As a work of modern British history, this book is largely testament to this approach, although the paper chase has been cross-national as much as cross-country.

Part I

1889–1945

1 LAYING THE FOUNDATIONS OF CONTROL

> Legislation had long been desired by governments; it had been
> carefully prepared over a period of years.
>
> DEPARTMENTAL COMMITTEE ON SECTION 2 OF THE
> OFFICIAL SECRETS ACT 1911, 1972[1]

In summer 1911, an amended version of the Official Secrets
Act, first passed in 1889, was steered through Parliament. For Britain,
so long a torchbearer for freedom and democracy, the revised Act
constituted one of the most illiberal pieces of legislation ever placed
on the statute book. 'A legal monstrosity', claimed the *Washington
Post* journalist Alfred Friendly some years later, 'a burlesque of the
excellence and fairness of law and judicial procedure on which Britain
prides itself'.[2] Section 1, commonly known as the 'spying clause', made
it a criminal offence for anyone, 'for a purpose that could be prejudicial
to the safety or the interests of the state', to collect, communicate or
publish any plan, drawing or other item of official information to an
enemy.[3] The accused had no 'right to silence' and a trial could be held
in camera. Section 2, which was targeted at civil servants, politicians
and journalists, made a felony of both the unauthorised communication and the receipt of official information. It was widely drafted,
embracing all types of information without any discrimination.
A part-time clerk in the Home Office who discussed with his spouse
the department's shortage of toilet rolls was in violation of the Act, as
was a British national who betrayed critical naval plans to the
Germans. In a radical departure from English law, where generally

speaking the onus of proof is on the prosecution, the Act made the accused responsible for positive proof of innocence. In short, the wording of the Act dictated that there was no need to prove that any harm had resulted from the disclosure; guilt could be inferred simply from the circumstances of a person's actions or character.[4] Under its aegis, Section 2 was capable of generating over 2,000 offences.[5]

What was striking about the Act's passing was the pace with which it was carried out. The Act was introduced in the House of Lords on 17 July 1911. Only two members bothered to discuss it; indeed, far more attention was given to the impending Asylum Officers' Superannuation Bill. Put before the Commons on 17 August, the Bill produced scarcely a ripple of debate, the only contribution coming from Sir William Byles, who claimed that it might undo Magna Carta. The following afternoon, with the House virtually empty, the Act was rushed through its second and third readings in under an hour. The minister principally responsible for the Act, the Home Secretary, Winston Churchill, did not say a word. 'Two men got up to speak,' recollected Colonel Jack Seely (then Undersecretary for War), 'but both were forcibly pulled down by their neighbours after they had uttered a few sentences.'[6] Given the speed of events, some government departments were not even informed of what had taken place. In September, Sir John Anderson, Permanent Undersecretary at the Colonial Office, complained: 'We have no correspondence with regard to the Act.'[7]

For parliamentarians to have approved such an oppressive piece of legislation so swiftly is remarkable. Until then, official secrecy in Britain had been governed as much by convention as by the strict letter of the law. Their decision to do so has been understood by most historians as a spur-of-the-moment response to the exigencies of national security, framed on the belief that Britain would soon be at war with Germany. Parliamentary debate (or lack of) coincided with the Second Moroccan Crisis, when the Kaiser, in a striking display of gunboat diplomacy, sent the warship SMS *Panther* to the port of Agadir. In Britain at that time, there was also a widespread hysteria about German spies, said to be reconnoitring potential invasion sites and pilfering naval secrets. Against this background, it is argued, the Act was hastily put together. Those acquainted with the historiography of Whitehall will no doubt recognise this interpretation as the main thesis of Peter Hennessy: 'The real impulse towards even tighter secrecy in Edwardian times was the fear of German espionage.'[8] Other scholars, however, have advanced a different understanding of the rationale for the Act. As befits a student of the *longue durée*, Ken Robertson found its roots at a much deeper level in the politics, beliefs and social structures of the nineteenth century. While the state justified legislation as an urgent response to external threats, argued Robertson, the resort to the statute book had little to do with war fever and represented the culmination of a prolonged campaign by the ruling classes to curtail unauthorised disclosures by arrant members of the civil service.[9] Robertson's study won devotees. David Vincent has shown how, in an age of democracy marked by a more socially heterogeneous and less tractable civil service than hitherto, the Act was passed to combat failing codes of gentlemanly restraint. 'Official secrecy legislation', he asserts, 'stemmed in large part from the growing requirement to recruit to government offices those whose breeding, education, and pay excluded them from the rank of gentleman.'[10] More recently, Nicholas Wilkinson has claimed that the Act, while deliberately dressed up by the state as a critical national defence issue, was in fact designed to deter the unprincipled behaviour of the free commercial press.[11]

This chapter will re-examine the circumstances in which the Act came into existence. It will be shown that, for a long time, legalised secrecy was seen as offensive to British notions of good government and subversive of the public interest in a modern democratic age. Accordingly, although secrecy existed, it was embedded in administrative structures, regulations and *mentalités*. By the late nineteenth century, however, Whitehall would seek refuge in the panacea of the law. The rationale for this stemmed from a growing unease about unauthorised disclosures. Although in public the government made great play of the war scare and the machinations of German spies, in reality this was little more than 'strategic sleight of hand',[12] designed to engineer a smooth passage for the Act through Parliament. The growth of state bureaucracy had brought an influx of lower-class employees into government who did not embrace the gentlemanly codes that had distinguished their institutional ancestors. Products of the workplaces and as likely to have a trade union background as an old school tie, blue-collar employees and temporary clerks were believed to be beyond the reach of moral restraint. Added to this was the emergence of an inquisitive popular press, emancipated from government control and subsidy, who provided an outlet for anyone who wanted to leak information.

A further problem, unacknowledged by historians, was the rise of an embryonic memoir industry. In the Victorian era, crown servants generally did not produce memoirs. The few that did saw their reader-ship limited to learned societies and to a small clique of like-minded individuals to which they belonged both by class and occupation. In part, this was because they adhered to an ingrained belief that silence in regard to official work was golden. According to George Egerton, many potential memoirists were put off by prevailing social mores, which frowned on the act of personal political apologia. Egerton also speculates that few crown servants *needed* to produce memoirs such was the largely deferential nature of the political system.[13] It will be shown in this chapter that, by the early twentieth century, this antip-athy towards autobiographical writing had started to break down. For a number of peoples, reliving the dramas of British imperialism proved too good to refuse. The South African War (1899–1902), in particular, encouraged a flurry of works. Although the war had been won, many Britons were left wondering how the British army, numbering almost half a million soldiers, had taken nearly three years to defeat a guerrilla force of roughly sixty thousand men. In an atmosphere of national soul-searching, several of the conflict's protagonists either wrote memoirs or spoke to the press, principally to whitewash the self and blame others. For these disclosures, there was a large readership. The growth of public education and literacy had helped to bring about a greater public consciousness about affairs of state. Moreover, just as steam-powered printing had allowed for the inexpensive mass produc-tion of newspapers, so it also meant that books could now be produced at a fraction of the previous cost. In this context, Whitehall needed a mechanism to regulate what authors could reveal; that mechanism was the Official Secrets Act.

* * *

> It is not the business of a newspaper to keep secrets for an
> Administration which is unable to keep them for itself.
> *leader*, The Times, 29 *November* 1858[14]

In Victorian times, Britain prided itself on being the most 'open' of democratic powers. Irrespective of their political loyalties, statesmen spoke publicly about the virtues of transparency, which, they claimed, was a sign of progress and a bulwark against abuses of power. 'Publi-city is the fittest law for securing the public confidence,' advocated the

English jurist Jeremy Bentham.[15] Perhaps best known for his support of utilitarianism, Bentham popularised the notion that secrecy was an 'instrument of conspiracy', deployed by 'bullies, blackguards and buffoons' in the service of unenlightened Continental despotism.[16] In his seminal essay 'Of Publicity', he proposed that even the word 'secrecy' conjured up something ignoble.

Britain's liberal commitment to the free flow of information was underlined in several ways. In 1838, the state legally recognised its obligation to collect, preserve and make available the records of its operations by passing the Public Record Office Act. In an important symbolic gesture, the Act renamed public records the 'People's Evidence'; hitherto they had been known as 'Muniments of the Kingdom'.[17] The Act also decreed that records should be brought together in a single repository in Chancery Lane, London. This facility was completed in 1858. Public reading rooms were opened in 1866.

Supporting the growth of a free press was an integral part of government policy in the Victorian period. From the 1830s onwards, parliamentary reforms steadily abolished press taxation (including the Newspaper Stamp Duty in 1855 and the Excise Duty on Paper in 1861), paving the way for relatively cheap newspapers and the 'massification' of political culture. This occurred in tandem with the development of steam-powered presses and continuous newsprint rolls. The creation of a literate population also went hand in hand with Britain's liberal schema. Education Acts led to the creation of around five thousand new schools by 1876. In 1891, a Fee Grant Act guaranteed free elementary education. As a result, basic literacy grew to 97 per cent of the population by 1900.[18] Moreover, governments took steps to ensure greater public participation in the political process. In 1838, *Hansard* was sold publicly for the first time and a gallery was installed in Parliament.

Of course, governments were never as open as the public rhetoric implied. In his magnum opus *The English Constitution* (written in 1867), Walter Bagehot, the great essayist of Victorian political life, dryly commented: 'If you tell a cabman to drive to Downing Street, he most likely will never have heard of it, and will not in the least know where to take you.'[19] Details of Cabinet meetings were never disclosed; official minutes were strictly forbidden. Indeed, until the Cabinet Secretariat was established in 1916, no formal record was ever made of Cabinet proceedings. Established in 1250, the Privy Councillor's Oath committed ministers to a vow of secrecy:

> You will, in all things to be moved, treated, and debated in
> Council, faithfully and truly declare your Mind and Opinion,
> according to your Heart and Conscience; and will keep secret all
> Matters committed and revealed unto you, or that shall be treated
> of secretly in Council. And if any of the said Treaties or Counsels
> shall touch any of the Counsellors, you will not reveal it unto him,
> but will keep the same until such time as, by the Consent of His
> Majesty, or the Council, Publication shall be made thereof . . .
> So help you God.[20]

Still administered today, the oath demanded fealty to the Crown by
stipulating that ministerial advice is the property of the monarch.
In short, only with the consent of the king or queen can that advice
be disclosed. In recent times, it has become common to see the oath as
nothing more than a constitutional vestige, maintained for pomp and
tradition. Richard Crossman, who hated the ceremonial of 'trundling
off to the palace' to swear the oath kneeling before the monarch, saw
it as flummery designed only 'to camouflage stale royal authority'.[21]
For Tony Benn, battle-scarred campaigner for its abolition, the ritual
is nothing short of monarchical tyranny, imposing 'tribal magic and
personal loyalty on people whose real duty is to their electors'.[22] In
the nineteenth century, however, councillors embraced the oath as if it
were 'part campaign ribbon, part wound stripe', aware that to break
it might be considered treasonable.[23] Peter Hennessy has famously
compared it to the 'Mafia's code of *Omerta* – only the grave can bring
release'.[24]

Secrecy was an essential part of the Victorian civil service. With
few exceptions, civil servants cut a low profile, their identities seldom
mentioned outside government circles. Secrecy in the civil service
stemmed to a large extent from the structure of the political system
and the so-called 'hidden wiring'[25] that bound non-elected officials to
the ministerial executive. In the first half of the nineteenth century,
ministers and their advisers entered into a pact, now known as
the doctrine of 'ministerial responsibility', which directed that the
exposition of government was the *sole* responsibility of ministers.
From this, a minister was required to do two things. One, he had to
defend to the House the work of his department; and, two, he had
to take responsibility not only for his own actions, but for every
decision or policy that was made in his name. Put another way, he
was obligated to 'carry the can' and to be vicariously culpable for all

criticisms levelled at his department. In return, civil servants were neither publicly identified with the work of their department nor, when blame was attributed, accountable. As Gavin Drewry and Tony Butcher explain, the shield of anonymity was justified partly to preserve the rule that all actions were unequivocally taken in the minister's name, and partly because public identification of civil servants with particular government policies might lead to a scenario in which a future government of a different political party might refuse to work with them.[26]

In the early to mid Victorian period, the secrecy that accompanied ministerial responsibility was undergirded by an endemic system of patronage. At that time, academic qualifications counted for nothing; status, on the other hand, meant everything. As such, only men of the best character were placed in positions of trust. Because no post had guaranteed security of tenure, its occupant's position was theoretically at the whim of his patron. Thus, were a civil servant not to toe the line, his minister would be within his rights to fire him. According to David Vincent, civil servants gradually embraced secrecy as if it were a defining characteristic of a gentleman. As they saw it, the ability to a keep a secret was something only a gentleman possessed, on account of his superior parentage, upbringing and schooling. Interestingly, civil servants seldom referred to the ability as 'secrecy', preferring instead to clothe the practice in less morally objectionable garbs such as 'discretion', 'reticence' and 'reserve'. For example, in a letter to his wife in 1841, describing the code to which his department subscribed, the senior mandarin Sir James Stephen wrote: 'There a Christian virtue to which I have never heard an allusion from the pulpit. ... I mean the duty of silence.'[27] He continued: 'Frivolity of discourse, mere talk for talk's sake, is one of the most besetting sins of our generation.'[28] This indefinable Christian virtue is perhaps best encapsulated by Vincent, who refers to it as 'honourable secrecy'.

By mid century, the rapid development of a democratised political culture had started to create problems for Britain's secret-keepers. After centuries of snail's pace development, hamstrung by government fiscal controls, the press had changed drastically in a relatively short time. Many newspapers, not content with being mere 'sober organs' of instruction, and recognising that society was not as politically homogeneous as bourgeois metanarratives suggested, had begun adopting a distinctly party-political role.[29] As Keith Robbins argues, while some journalists proudly proclaimed their support for a particular statesman or party, others refrained from 'staking their [ideological] colours to an editorial mast' and would contentedly write a 'Tory piece in the afternoon and a Liberal piece in the evening'.[30] The press's transformation into a vehicle for political views would accelerate in the 1870s when newspapers, in order to survive, sold out to wealthy patrons, many of whom were motivated by a desire to canvass support for a political cause. The emergence of the press as a political force was confirmed by the position of *The Times*, the putative newspaper of record, which boldly claimed that it could make and unmake governments. In 1834 Lord Lyndhurst famously described its then editor as 'the most powerful man in the country'.[31] An equally significant development was the growth of an increasingly downmarket popular press. Although a far cry from the 'dumbed-down' tabloids of the twenty-first century, 'mass' dailies placed greater emphasis on scoops, sensationalism and pandering to popular prejudices about foreigners and manor-born elites.[32] Exceptional news, exceptionally presented, was the mantra of an ever more mercenary Fleet Street.

Whether popular or patrician, a key feature of 'New Journalism', as historians have since called it, was a readiness to produce revelations of highly secret matters. Even *The Times*, which was widely seen as the mouthpiece of government, was not adverse to publishing sensitive information. 'The press lives by disclosures,' declared the newspaper in 1852: 'We are bound to lend no convenient shelter to acts of injustice and oppression, but to consign them at once to the judgement of the world.'[33] 'For us,' it went on, 'publicity and truth are the air and light of existence.'[34] Not content with taking news from *Hansard*, journalists relentlessly stalked the corridors of government departments, asking questions about policy and seeking 'off-the-record' comments from officials. Journalists began referring to the 'rights of the public' – a forerunner of what we would consider to be 'the public interest'. In 1847, for example, citing the 'rights of the public' as its justification, *The Times* brushed off the government's attempts to enforce censorship and published Lord Castlereagh's correspondence at the Congress of Vienna in 1815.[35]

The need to 'scoop' market competitors meant that journalists became increasingly unethical in their pursuit of a story. Newspapers offered to pay enormous sums for sensational items, the biggest amounts being put forward by wealthy press barons themselves. To further tempt whistle-blowers into betraying their employer's confidences, journalists promised them anonymity, the most common alias being 'the unnamed source' or *nom de guerre*. The *Saturday Review* famously boasted that the nameless contributor would be 'the area of calm in the heart of the cyclone'.[36] In Whitehall, there was much anxiety about the principles of the 'New Journalism', with many officials conceding that the growth of the press had not been preceded by sufficient forethought. Unlike most of his colleagues in government, the prime minister, Lord Derby, remained calm. In theory, as a consequence of the freedoms they now enjoyed, journalists had entered a contract with the state and were expected to accept certain restrictions and surrender their prerogative powers. 'The press owes its first duty to the national interests,' Derby felt: 'If the English press aspires to the influence of statesmen, so also it [will] share in the responsibilities of statesmen'.[37] This optimism, however, would be misplaced.

Increasing bureaucratisation of the administrative system presented a further problem for secret-keepers. The Victorian period had seen a massive expansion of the state, compelling the civil service to produce more correspondence. Written communication was necessary to preserve the impartiality of public servants, while the democratic process demanded that Parliament had the right to inquire into any action taken by the state. The extent to which the civil service was now 'running to paper' was plain to see. The influential liberal thinker John Stuart Mill, who worked as an administrator in the East India Company, recalled: 'The whole government of India is carried on in writing. All the orders given, and all the acts of the executive officers, are reported in writing.'[38] In his richly detailed study of the Victorian government machine, Sir Norman Chester calculated that the number of papers registered in the Treasury averaged between 2,500 and 3,000 per year in the period 1783–93; by 1800 it was 4,812; by 1820, 22,288; and by 1849, 29,914.[39] The rapid accumulation of government business prompted departments to set up registries to process the increased stream of paperwork. Bureaucrats advanced scientific methods of filing, indexing and registration, and pioneered administrative appurtenances such as the internal memo and procedural manual. The growth in the volume of paperwork required that new staff were taken on, especially at the secretarial and menial levels. Unlike their superiors, these individuals had not been brought up in country homes or been educated at public schools and then Oxbridge.

For this reason, serious doubts existed about whether they could be trusted to maintain a judicious silence about their work.

Elite fears about the evolving social composition of the civil service were heightened by reforms targeted at the higher grades. Laid before Parliament on 23 November 1853, the Northcote–Trevelyan Report described Whitehall as a sanctuary for the 'unambitious, the indolent and the incapable', and identified 'amateurism, inefficiency and extravagance' as the inescapable consequences of patronage networks.[40] Steeped in liberal utilitarianism, the report condemned time-honoured nepotism, and called for competitive literary examinations, overseen by a Civil Service Commission, 'to test the intelligence as well as the mere attainments' of aspirants. The report's implementation was initially slow, but gathered pace following the appointment of Robert Lowe as Chancellor in December 1868. Lowe believed strongly that recruitment according to social station vitiated administrative performance. Under his watch, the Treasury became the first department to be placed on an 'open competition' footing. On 4 June 1870, he forced through a Civil Service order in council, which gave the Treasury control over recruitment policy in all departments. The incorporation of meritocratic 'bloods' into the administrative classes has been the focus of several quantitative inquiries. Henry Roseveare's examination of the Treasury's higher echelons revealed that, apart from the first three men appointed in the period 1870–1913 (who were simply leftovers of the nominated system), fifty-seven of the remaining fifty-eight were university graduates.[41]

The Northcote–Trevelyan reforms were anathema to the old nobles of Whitehall who naturally had a vested interest in the prevailing system of patronage and jobbery. Integrating second-class bureaucrats – snobbishly referred to as 'vegetables of the earth'[42] – was seen as an attack on the established order, in particular the role of the aristocrat in government. 'The more the civil service is recruited from the lower classes, the less it will be sought after until at last the aristocracy will be altogether disassociated,' was the judgement of Lord Romilly, incumbent Master of the Rolls, the second most senior judge in England.[43] The traditional elite feared that the recruitment of upwardly mobile social groups would shatter the shared spirit of gentlemanly discretion, until now successful because of the uniform congenital traits of those entrusted to work in positions of power. As they saw it, honourable secrecy would mean nothing to those not

of gentle birth and not from the public schools. In the debates
that accompanied the Northcote–Trevelyan reforms, Sir George Cor-
newall Lewis, then editor of the *Edinburgh Review*, but later Home
Secretary, emphasised that character was far more valuable than
education in the holders of permanent office: 'The honourable secrecy
which has distinguished the clerks of our superior offices, and their
abstinence from communicating information to interested parties,
cannot be too highly recommended. But this discreet reserve depends
on qualities, which cannot be made the subject of examination by a
central board, or be expressed by marks upon a paper of written
answers.'[44] Many aristocrats questioned whether the 'competition
wallahs'[45] could resist the blandishments of an ever more commercially driven and news-hungry Fleet Street. Indeed, on 20 March 1883,
the *Echo* famously boasted that payment could induce civil servants,
from any department of state, to leak information – typically, £5 for
minor news and £100 for the betrayal of 'great secrets'.[46]

Aristocratic fears about press intransigence and declining moral
standards in the civil service were confirmed by a series of high-profile
disclosures. On 23 October 1854, during the siege of Sevastopol, *The
Times* published uncensored extracts from several war correspondents'
dispatches. Following this, in a move presaging the D-Notice system,
the War Office sent a circular to editors urging them to expunge
anything 'calculated to furnish valuable information to the enemy'.[47]
Despite 'very cordial and proper replies', only three weeks later, on
12 November 1854, the *London Gazette* printed Lord Cardigan's dispatches charting the now-legendary Charge of the Light Brigade.[48]
More seriously, on 11 December 1858, two highly confidential and
politically charged dispatches, written by the Lord High Commissioner
to the Ionian Islands (Sir John Young), appeared in the Liberal-biased
Daily News. The dispatches exposed government duplicity in the
administration of the islands. On the one hand, they revealed the ruling
Tory desire to extricate Britain from Santa Maura, where 'pretensions
for patronage and expenditure showed no limits'; on the other hand,
they stressed the importance of laying claim to Corfu, which was
ready to be 'enriched by Anglicisation, British capital and enterprise'.[49]
Young initially passed off the significance of the article as 'nothing but
empty and foolish talk to catch popularity with the mob'.[50] The press,
he continued, 'has no character of reality or echo in the minds of the
people'. His mood became less forgiving when William Guernsey, who

it was discovered had stolen the dispatches from the Colonial Office library as retribution for his unsuccessful application to the department, was acquitted of charges of larceny. Guernsey, described by the judge as a 'gentleman', was condemned only in moral terms. According to *The Times*, the 'judge could not refrain from expressing his surprise that a man who had filled the position in society of Guernsey should be guilty of such an act'.[51]

In Whitehall, such was the moral obloquy attached to legislation, the preferred strategy for keeping officials in check was to try to ingrain in them a secretive state of mind. To do this, stiffly worded circulars were issued to staff likening improper communication to a form of purgatory. Imbued with moral rather than legal authority, Sir Ralph Lingen's communiqué of 3 June 1873 encapsulates the attempt to bind lesser mortals to a tacit code of silence: 'The unauthorised use of official information is the worst fault a civil servant can commit. It is on the same footing as cowardice by a soldier. It is unprofessional.'[52] Having laboured their way through a university education, which was valued for its ethical training as much as its academic tuition, topmost officials were to a large extent expected to abide by the de facto conventions. The Northcote–Trevelyan reforms, which had placed a premium on top-quality schooling for the senior civil service, had perversely made Oxford and Cambridge even better factories of honourable secrecy. In the event of an offence, Whitehall's top brass believed, it would come from the rank and file.

The aristocracy was proved painfully right in all its forebodings. On 31 May 1878, Charles Marvin, an embittered writer in the Foreign Office, decided to augment his princely wage of tenpence an hour by leaking to the *Globe and Traveller* a draft of a secret treaty between Britain and Russia, made before the Congress of Berlin, just two and half hours after it had been signed. The son of a draughtsman, with a curriculum vitae that included time as a warehouse worker, Marvin epitomised the new breed of socially inferior civil servant now making his way in government. The resultant Cabinet inquiry provided 'strong evidence' that he had been paid by the newspaper, £40 being the amount said to have changed hands.[53] Investigations also revealed that the newspaper's editor, Captain Armstrong, was 'boasting at the Clubs' that there was 'no confidential paper which he cannot buy'.[54] With nothing in the statute books prohibiting the publication of what he disclosed, Marvin was brought to trial under a charge of larceny.

Yet this could not be sustained: Marvin had memorised the document and thus had not deprived his employers of their property. Accordingly, he was acquitted. At the trial, the counsel lamented: 'There was no law which made the defendant liable to punishment, even if such an indiscretion has really been committed in the eagerness to satisfy the public craving for information.'[55] In the fallout, Lord Tenterden, Permanent Secretary at the Foreign Office, described Marvin's actions as being typical of the 'cheap and untrustworthy class of people'.[56] Legislation appeared to be the only solution. The threat of dismissal was not a threat at all to the temporary clerks and blue-collar workers who were paid peanuts, had no pension and could easily earn as much in the private sector. As Marvin would later claim, 'I was so disgusted with the Foreign Office for sucking the best years of my life for the miserable sum of £90 that I resolved to place upon the market every piece of information that chance threw my way.'[57]

By the late 1880s, incidents of unauthorised disclosure by penumbral classes in Whitehall had greatly increased, despite a further round of circulars calling on officials to be honourable and disciplined. In 1880, Marvin exacted a small measure of revenge by publishing a bestselling memoir, entitled *Our Public Offices*, in which he reiterated his argument that he had had nothing to lose by communicating the secret treaty to the *Globe*. 'It was absurd', he complained, 'for the Foreign Office to employ a Writer to copy Cabinet secrets at tenpence an hour.'[58] In 1887, Terry Young, a temporary draughtsman in Chatham Dockyard, sold confidential warship designs to a foreign power, believed to be France.[59] For his avarice, Young was dismissed. In Parliament, the First Lord of the Admiralty came under heavy fire from MPs, the most vocal being Tory backbencher Robert Hanbury, who asked, 'What classes of officials or workmen engaged at Chatham or other public dockyards are employed in positions of confidence and secrecy?'[60] Hanbury was particularly keen to know what precautions were now being taken to 'guard against a [future] breach of trust'.[61] Young's indiscretion was seen as particularly damaging since it had coincided with growing public concern that British maritime supremacy, taken for granted since Trafalgar, was again being challenged by France. In 1884, the *Pall Mall Gazette* had famously sparked a 'Navy Scare' by publishing a spate of alarmist articles on the rising strength of the French fleet and the need for enlargement and modernisation of the Royal Navy. A year later, an anonymously written novel, *The Siege of London*, envisaged a French invasion of England, culminating in the loss of India and Gibraltar. Sheepishly, the First Lord was forced to admit that de facto strategies of control had failed to stem the haemorrhaging of information. With this, he called upon HMG to consider legal coercion, a recommendation that was greeted with strong support from Hanbury and all but a few liberally minded MPs.

Government lawyers started drafting the legislation in camera in July 1887. It was divided into two sections – the first dealing with foreign espionage and the second with domestic leaks. Counteracting the work of treacherous spies was essentially a secondary concern. Lawyers spent most of their time writing and rewriting the provisions that dealt with talkative civil servants. As Anne Rogers has argued, the pre-eminence of the confidentiality issue was made clear by the various names that the legislation was known by in its formative stages.[62] Initially, it was entitled The Breach of Official Trust Bill; it was then called The Public Documents Act. However, when the Bill was brought before Parliament in 1889, there was no hint of leaks. Renamed the Official Secrets Bill, the legislation was presented as an urgent national defence issue, prepared under the direction of the Secretary of State for War to protect military secrets from foreign espionage. 'It provides', announced the Lord Chancellor, 'for the punishment of those persons who give information to the enemies of the country, or who act as spies.'[63] In the various debates, so preoccupied were they with drama-tising the threat of overseas intelligence gathering, that ministers referred to Section 2 only in passing. The Attorney General implored parliamentarians not to scrutinise the Bill too closely, claiming that it was 'an exceedingly simple one'.[64]

Parliamentarians put aside their tribal loyalties and supported the legislation *in toto*. As ministers had hoped, by invoking national security concerns they effectively precluded any sticky questions about Section 2. Although the espionage threat had been exaggerated, it was not a paper tiger. It was well known that, following the Franco-Prussian War, both France and Germany had set up permanent intelligence departments to exploit the security weaknesses of other states and map potential theatres of war. Nor was there an absence of fear about the military threat from foreign powers. In the years following Prussia's successful incursion into France in 1870, the security of Pax Britannica had become a hot topic, with the spectre of invasion engendering many harrowing works of fiction.[65] The most famous of these was *The Battle of Dorking* by George Chesney in 1871. Chesney's tale, which first appeared in *Blackwood's Magazine*, a respectable Victorian journal, was interleaved with moral warnings: 'we became wise when it was too late'; 'there, across the narrow straights, was the writing on the wall, but we would choose not to read it'.[66] As the Official Secrets Act went through the House in 1889, English fears of foreign forces arriving unopposed on its shores had not gone away. With this Act, secrecy was codified for the first time in Britain with virtually no discussion whatsoever.

* * *

> All good and sensible citizens must desire that the State should
> have ample powers to protect its real secrets and to inflict due
> punishment upon those who betray them out of malice or through
> carelessness.
>
> *leader,* The Times, *7 May 1908*[67]

The rapidity of the Bill's passing made errors inevitable. Indeed, no sooner had the ink dried on the Act than it had become obvious that serious mistakes had been made. The statute only targeted spies and crown servants; the press, unbelievably, could not be prosecuted. George Campbell MP called it a 'farce' that the Act only punished those who stole information; the real wrongdoers, he protested, were 'the receivers of the stolen goods – the newspapers'.[68] In a major oversight that would reveal itself in the coming years, the Act had practically no applicability to official memoir writers, since it was only an offence if an author was found to have printed classified information in his memoir with the deliberate intention of damaging the state. Moreover, sentences were relatively lenient, thus diminishing the Act's deterrent value. Section 1 was also poorly conceived, failing to criminalise peacetime espionage. In other words, provided the nation was not at war, a foreign spy caught red-handed stealing secret documents would walk free.

Knowing that the press would instinctively oppose anything in the way of new legislation, the Office of the Parliamentary Counsel warned against reopening 'the very difficult and delicate questions raised by the Act'.[69] Ministers agreed: 'Let this sleeping dog lie. If we find burglars pass him, we may stir him up,' was the opinion in 1895 of Sir Henry Campbell-Bannerman, Secretary of State for War.[70] However, attitudes soon changed. The inadequacies of the Act were plainly apparent during the Fashoda Incident in 1898. As this territorial dispute between France and England brought both countries to the verge of war (following the arrival of French troops in the Anglo-Egyptian Sudan), newspapers contained extensive information concerning Britain's preparations. The Director of Military Intelligence was appalled as journalists revealed the composition of garrisons stationed at or near the southern ports.[71] The press were similarly heedless of national security concerns during the South African War, printing details of troop deployments, as well as naming British transport and supply companies operating in South Africa. Lord Wolseley, Commander-in-Chief of the British Army, was disgusted: 'We cannot make war as the country expects we should, whilst our enemy is kept informed by our press of everything we do.'[72] The *Daily Mail* – Britain's first mass circulation newspaper – was among the worst offenders. In 1901, the newspaper was cut off from receiving confidential bulletins from the War Office, having been discovered offering 'pecuniary temptations' to clerks willing to provide news.[73]

During this war, the most troublesome journalist was William Thomas Stead. Stead had positioned himself at the forefront of the 'new journalism'. As editor of the *Pall Mall Gazette* (1883–90), he oversaw a series of scoops and agitations, including Andrew Mearns's famous exposé of urban housing for the poor, as well as the 1884 'Truth about the Navy' revelations discussed earlier.[74] Unapologetic when it came to mucking around in politics, Stead was an advocate of what he called 'government by journalism', the idea that legislative bodies, including Parliament, had become servants of an enlightened public opinion whose will was expressed through the medium of the press. 'The editorial pen is a sceptre of power,' he boldly proclaimed in a leading article in 1886.[75] Stead's sceptre of power, although lambasted by critics as dangerously misleading, wielded considerable influence during the conflict. From 1899 to 1902, a secret cluster of friends and associates kept him exceptionally well informed of events, sending him, inter alia, reports of apparent British atrocities against Boer women and children. (Colonel Maurice Moore, brother of the novelist George Moore, was many years later revealed as a key source.)[76] An outspoken opponent of the war, Stead delightedly recycled this material into hard-hitting broadsheets on British aggression against the Boer Republic. In 1901, he published a monograph, entitled *Methods of Barbarism*, condemning British forces for waging 'a white man's war' against helpless Boer non-combatants. Here, he provided further evidence of the British army wreaking havoc in South Africa, including examples of rape, looting and the needless destruction of property.

HMG lamented that the Official Secrets Act could not be used to punish Stead. As a 'receiver of stolen goods', Stead had not committed an offence under existing legislation. Frustrated by the Act's imperfections, but nevertheless determined to quash the wave of anti-war sentiment engulfing the public sphere (both domestically and abroad), officials agreed that the best option available to them was to find a way of discrediting the journalist's accusations. Accordingly, they surreptitiously recruited one of the nation's favourite authors, the crime novelist Arthur Conan Doyle, to write a tract advancing the government's position. Doyle was a natural choice. A staunch imperialist, he had supported the British war effort. From March through July 1900, he served as a volunteer medical officer in a military hospital in South Africa. On his return from the field, he had published *The Great Boer War*, a spirited defence of Britain's role in the controversial conflict. So keen were officials to enlist Doyle's support, they afforded him extraordinary privileges, analogous to the sort of advantages later given to official historians. Doyle was granted unprecedented access to War Office files. He was given confidential briefings from the serving Director of Military Intelligence (South Africa), Lieutenant Colonel C. V. Hume. King Edward VII personally provided £500 to defray the cost of publication and marketing.[77] The end product, a pamphlet entitled *The War in South Africa: Its Causes and Conduct* (1902), was hugely successful. Translated into many languages, it went a long way to refuting the charges levelled against the British army, arguing that Boer commandos had committed far more horrors than their European counterparts. For throwing his weight behind the British cause, Doyle received a knighthood and was appointed Deputy Lieutenant of Surrey. Delighted that the tactic of co-opting a private individual to get the government message across had worked so successfully, officials wholeheartedly supported Commander Charles Robinson's *Celebrities of the Army* (1902), providing him with portraits of military heroes to accompany his biographical sketches. The work has since been described as the finest collection of moustaches ever seen.

However, the shortcomings of the 1889 legislation could not be circumvented indefinitely. Rich in drama and incident, the South

African War provided the seedbed for a deluge of memoir literature, with many military figures writing about the stirring events in which they had been involved.[78] With no legal hold over what these individuals could say in their accounts, HMG was forced to watch, sometimes in horror, as those returning from the front line published accounts peppered with sensitive details. One of the most problematic cases was provided by a young Winston Churchill, fresh from his commission in the Light Horse regiment. Published in May 1900, *London to Ladysmith via Pretoria* told in intimate detail the story of Churchill's now legendary break-out from a prisoner-of-war camp – a daring escape that had made him a minor national hero and did much to persuade the Conservative Party to back him in his first successful bid for a parliamentary seat. Churchill's version of events caused great distress to Captain Aylmer Haldane, an officer of the Dublin Fusiliers. He too had escaped from the clutches of the Boers, albeit three months after the future premier. Haldane's complaint was twofold. Firstly, that Churchill, in a deliberate attempt to aggrandise his own ingenuity, had failed to acknowledge that his escape would not have been possible without the planning of his co-prisoners in Pretoria. (Recently discovered correspondence seems to confirm that Churchill had stolen the escape plan.)[79] More seriously, Haldane accused Churchill of being a bounder, leaving his fellow officers behind in the camp. Feeling aggrieved by Churchill's 'fiction', Haldane set hearts racing in Whitehall by threatening to retaliate with his own memoir, rich in evidence of how the newly appointed Tory MP had acted unilaterally.[80] To the relief of officials, who legally had no way of stopping such a venture, Haldane was eventually persuaded not to publish, with many of Churchill's friends personally imploring him to keep quiet.

As in 1889, the likelihood of being able to pass new secrecy legislation was contingent upon public opinion accepting that the nation needed to defend itself against dangerous external threats. Without an identifiable enemy, any new Bill would be destined for the parliamentary dustbin. In the first decade of the twentieth century, Germany became that enemy. Under Kaiser Wilhelm II, Germany aggressively pursued a policy of weltpolitik, making no secret of the fact that it wanted its 'place in the sun' commensurate with its rising industrial strength. In seeking to create a colonial empire to rival those of other powers, it embarked on a major naval arms build-up, launching some of the largest and fastest warships ever built, capable of operating at a considerable distance from the Baltic ports. In British popular culture, a defining image was that of the Kaiser – kitted out in medals, sword and polished boots – breaking champagne bottles over the bows of impressive steam-powered vessels. The emergence of Germany as an adversarial sea power aroused considerable concern. Not since the Napoleonic era had the Royal Navy's mastery of the seas, the traditional linchpin of domestic and imperial security, been seriously challenged. Against this background, Britain became gripped by invasion fears and war jitters, an atmosphere that would ultimately prove conducive to a second Official Secrets Act.

Spy fiction, although often derided as ephemeral fodder for the masses, played a key role in whipping up war hysteria and thus paving the way for new legislation. From 1900 to the outbreak of the Great War, at least 300 spy novels landed in bookshops, each with its own unique take on the German menace and the response required. Unashamedly patriotic, their political sensibilities 'finely tuned to the cadences of imperial decline',[81] authors typically wanted to see more being done by the authorities. Some demanded the creation of a domestic intelligence service and associated legal controls to combat the work of German spies; others, seeing it as their duty to highlight Britain's chronic lack of preparedness against potential invasion, sought to garner public opinion in support of new naval bases and a rapid extension of the fleet.

By any yardstick, the most famous thriller from the period was Erskine Childers's *The Riddle of the Sands*, the story of two gentlemen yachtsmen who, while cruising in the North Sea, stumble upon a secret German plot to invade England. Like many Britons, shocked at the ease with which British forces during the South African War had met their match at the hands of guerrillas, Childers had an uncomfortable feeling that the Empire was in mortal danger. In an age influenced by the doctrine of 'survival of the fittest', as much between nations as between individuals, he shared the concerns of the National Service League, a pressure group for compulsory military training, which feared that England was deteriorating physically. Germany's expanding blue-water fleet alarmed him greatly. Accordingly, upon his return from South Africa, where he had served as an artillery driver, he resolved himself to write 'a yachting story, with a purpose'. That purpose was to impress upon the government the view that its people were no longer safe.

Published in May 1903, *The Riddle of the Sands* was an instant bestseller, selling over a hundred thousand copies by the end of the year.

The book was greeted with widespread critical acclaim. The *Westminster Gazette*, which, as its title indicates, sought to be influential in parliamentary circles, called it a 'literary accomplishment of much force and originality'.[82] Childers received many letters of congratulations. In a particularly sycophantic note, a Mr K. Ward from County Durham wrote that the book had 'stirred in me a fresh desire ... to do a little for my country', prompting him to form a local rifle club presumably from where well-intentioned patriots could be trained to kill the 'Boche'.[83] Among Childers's more distinguished admirers was Rudyard Kipling, who, from the 1890s onwards was repeatedly denouncing his countrymen in the press for failing to prepare or take a firm stand against the 'Hun'. Both Childers and his publisher, Reginald Smith, were amazed by the book's success. Smith, in particular, had had little faith in it. With its forensic attention to nautical detail, the book, he felt, would bore the general reader to tears. 'My experience is that people will not take their literary publications in the close "pemmican" fare which you adopt,' he had lamented in a correspondence with the author.[84] To enliven the manuscript, Smith had insisted on a 'love interest' – a plot device that Childers found abhorrent. 'I was weak enough to "spatchcock" a girl into it and find her a horrible nuisance,' he grumbled to a friend on the eve of the book's publication.[85]

In the event, Smith need not have worried. Childers's skill as an author was to sense and to seize on glib contemporary talk about the vulnerability of Britain to overseas attack. The timing of the book's publication was in one sense brilliantly chosen to maximise the political impact of the South African War, when questions about national strength, as well as the wisdom of diplomatic isolation, dominated public discourse. At that precise moment, British eyes were increasingly turning nervously towards Germany, which had openly pronounced its support for the Boers and had taken great satisfaction from reporting the news of British military disasters on the veldt. The book's release also coincided with the first wave of real public anxiety about the intentions of Germany's rising battlefleet. Only a year earlier, in a much-publicised speech to the Reichstag, Vice-Admiral Livonius of the Germany Navy had announced the practicality of a German D-Day: '[The possibility of carrying] out a landing on the English coast has been greatly increased by the introduction of steam power. The possibility of steaming by night with lights covered in order to escape the enemy's observation, [has] much reduced the advantages of England's insular position.'[86]

Demands for the government to 'do something' were not in fact being ignored. Weeks before the book was due to go to press, the Admiralty announced that it had selected a site on the Firth of Forth for a new North Sea naval base, causing Childers to insert a hasty postscript to that effect. Pressure from backbenchers, especially those representing East Coast constituencies, eventually prompted Lord Selbourne, the First Lord of the Admiralty, to ask the Naval Intelligence Division (NID) for a detailed report on the feasibility of a seaborne assault as outlined in the book. After sending a 'couple of experts' to reconnoitre the Frisian coast, the NID concluded that an invasion was impossible, pointing out that the 'want of railways and roads, the shallowness of the water, the configuration of the coast, not to mention the terrific amount of preparation of wharves, landing-places, causeways, sheds and whatnot besides, would have rendered a secret embarkation impossible'.[87] 'As a novel it is excellent; as a war plan it is rubbish,' was the assessment of Prince Louis of Battenberg, Director of Naval Intelligence.[88]

In illustrating both the commercial rewards and the political leverage that could be had from the deceptive blending of fact and fiction – or 'faction' – *The Riddle of the Sands* set the stage for a slew of fictionalised stories that dealt with the German threat to the home islands. After Childers, as Christopher Andrew argues, an increasingly prominent feature of Edwardian spy fiction was the seditious work of German spies.[89] If not for literary style, then for success and influence, the author most associated with the devilish intrigues of the German secret service was William Le Queux. Averaging five novels a year until his death in 1927, he was among the highest-paid fiction writers of his time, earning 12 guineas per 1,000 words, the same rate as H. G. Wells and Thomas Hardy. Like Childers, he used fiction as a vehicle for political pamphleteering, designed to awaken the government to the uncomfortable truth that England had become lazy and complacent, whereas rival nation states were fast becoming virile and purposeful.

For a while, Le Queux achieved only modest success. As a self-styled amateur spycatcher, who in his spare time purportedly battled dastardly foreign nationals in the service of king and country, he regularly forwarded reports to the War Office which, taken at face value, seemed to confirm the existence of a German spy network in Britain. To his dismay, these reports were dismissed as highly fanciful.[90] By 1906, however, his fortunes as someone who could command the ear of the Establishment had changed dramatically. To lend credibility to his stories, Le Queux seductively used his immense clubability to seek, and acquire, the support of senior crown servants. By far his most important 'conquest' was Field Marshal Lord Roberts, who had served as Commander-in-Chief of the British Army between 1901 and 1904. Affectionately known as 'Old Bobs', Roberts was Britain's most popular and eminent living general; that said, the mental infirmity of old age had left him sadly vulnerable to the counsel of younger men with hidden agendas. For Le Queux, Roberts was the perfect coadjutor. Like Le Queux, he was deeply troubled by Britain's unreadiness for a major contest of arms: 'My dear William, the world thinks me a lunatic also, because, after forty years service in India, I have come home and dared to tell England that she is unprepared for war.'[91] As president and moving spirit of the National Service League, Roberts saw an alliance with Le Queux as an opportunistic way of canvassing support for conscription, opposed by many as smacking of Continental militarism.

With such a priceless ally in tow, it was not long before Le Queux hit the big time. That moment arrived with *The Invasion of 1910*, a graphic imagining of a successful invasion of England by a 40,000-strong German army. Funding for the project was provided by Lord Northcliffe, proprietor of the *Daily Mail* – by then firmly established as the most widely read periodical in England, with a circulation twice that of its nearest competitor. As a pathological Germanophobe, with an instinctive flair for a profitable story, Northcliffe was only too happy to underwrite the novel in return for exclusive serialisation rights. In violation of the extant Official Secrets Act, Le Queux received many 'off-the-record' briefings from South African War veterans, including Lieutenant Colonel Cyril Field, widely regarded as one of the best military minds of the day. Striving for realism, Le Queux and Roberts spent four months touring southern England by motor car to determine the most likely path of invasion. Their assiduousness was in vain. Northcliffe objected to the German army's invasion route on the grounds that it went through areas where *Daily Mail* readership was small. Consequently, Le Queux was forced to devise a new line of march, one where newspaper sales took precedence over accuracy!

The *Daily Mail* began serialising the story on 13 March 1906. In Oxford Street, a major thoroughfare in the city of London, peripatetic placard carriers, employed by the newspaper and dressed in spiked helmets and Prussian uniforms, bellowed at passers-by, warning them of the Hun's arrival in the nation's capital. The story centred on German troops advancing inland until they eventually reached London. As they went, the jackbooted soldiers despoiled farmland, looted churches, and bayoneted resistance fighters. Le Queux described how, prior to the assault, an army of German spies had paralysed Britain's defences by destroying bridges, rail tracks and coal staithes. *The Invasion of 1910* was explicit in agitating for a system of national service and in its denouncing of Britain's slumbering statesmen for failing to prepare for a possible invasion. Splashed across the top of each extract was the eye-catching headline, 'WHAT LORD ROBERTS SAYS TO YOU', followed by: 'The catastrophe that may happen if we still remain in our present state of unpreparedness is vividly and forcibly illustrated in Mr Le Queux's new book, which I recommend to the perusal of everyone who has the welfare of the British Empire at heart.'[92]

The *Invasion of 1910* was a huge commercial success, boosting the *Daily Mail*'s circulation and, in book form, selling over 1 million copies in twenty-seven languages. In Parliament, the prime minister labelled Le Queux a 'pernicious scaremonger' and claimed that the book risked inciting bad blood between England and Germany. Public opinion, however, was squarely with Le Queux and his clarion call against perceived complacency in Whitehall. In 1906, the naval arms race had entered a new and more alarming phase with the launch of the revolutionary HMS *Dreadnought*. The first battleship of her era to have a uniform main battery, as opposed to four large guns complemented by a second battery of smaller weapons, the *Dreadnought* rendered all other battleships obsolete, including British ones. To some, this put the nation's naval supremacy at risk. Convinced that nemesis was close at hand and saddled with xenophobic paranoia, the majority of journalists did nothing to distance themselves from Le Queux's message, instead beating the patriotic drum and whipping up popular enthusiasm for defensive measures. The Northcliffe press, which by 1908 included both the *Observer* and *The Times*, followed *The Invasion of 1910* with an explosion of admonitory articles on preparedness, focusing on how Britain had to maintain a 2:1 advantage in the crucial Dreadnought category and how it needed to strengthen the Official Secrets Act to combat German spies.

The invasion bogey alarmed journalists as much as it did statesmen. By late 1906, to the government's delight, editors of the leading London and provincial newspapers had given general approval to new legislation entitled 'Control of the Press in Time of War'. Britain's foremost publishing associations – the Newspaper Society, the Newspaper Proprietors' Association and the Institute of Journalists – had also agreed to work with the government in drafting a new Official Secrets Act. Between 1906 and early 1908, a remarkable consensus emerged on the need to ensure that naval and military matters were protected, even if this meant trampling on press liberties. In March 1908, the Newspaper Proprietors' Association wholeheartedly supported the government's condemnation of the *Morning Post* for its article 'Defenceless Dover', which gave details of the strength and disposition of artillery defences around the port.[93]

However, when the Act was finally put before the press, in May 1908, the response was hostile. Mischievously, government draftsmen had moved the goalposts, packaging journalists in the same way as spies. Clauses had been inserted to capture peacetime disclosures; official information, moreover, was taken to mean anything that was produced by government offices and not just that pertaining to national security (coastal defences, troop movements et cetera). Frank Glover, president of the Newspaper Society, was scandalised: 'We consider that no good cause has been shown for suspecting the patriotism and discretion of those who conduct the newspapers of this country.'[94] In an eleventh-hour bid to save the Bill, the Lord Chancellor appealed to Fleet Street's gentlemanly spirit, emphasising that 'anyone in the press conducting his duties honourably should be quite safe'.[95] The tactic failed; the Institute of Journalists derided the proposed legislation as a 'too wide and indefinite menace to the freedom of the press', while *The Times* castigated the attempt to 'graft upon British law some of the worst features of Continental bureaucracy'.[96]

Officials did not lose sleep over what had transpired. For them, it was only a matter of time before the German menace became so acute that no one, including the press, could oppose tougher national security measures. They were proved right. The Naval Scare of 1909 resulted in eight British battleships being ordered by a reluctant government, to counter growing German strength. With doom merchants such as Lieutenant-Colonel Charles à Court Repington on its staff, the Northcliffe press had continued to paint Germany as a cruel force, an antagonist with whom the day of reckoning was inevitable.[97] The dire prophecies of spy novelists had also continued to proliferate, stirring up a hornets' nest of tension and paranoia. By this time, Le Queux had been challenged by a host of imitators, most famously E. Phillips Oppenheim.[98] Like Le Queux, Oppenheim wrote anti-German propaganda masquerading as fiction. His novels demanded the surveillance of political suspects, the internment of enemy aliens, the introduction of compulsory military training among able-bodied men, and tougher legislation to deal with spies.

With Oppenheim et al. muscling in on the genre, Le Queux responded with his most hard-hitting story yet, *Spies of the Kaiser*. Published in May 1909, the book purported to show how England had been overrun by a 'vast army of German spies', secretly amassed over many years and craftily disguised as barbers, hairdressers and publicans. In the novel, Britain's statesmen are presented as spineless; accordingly, the fate of the nation rests squarely on the shoulders of pipe-smoking amateur Ray Raymond – 'a patriot to his heart's core' – and his gutsy fiancée Vera Vallance. Le Queux backed up his allegations by naming specific bars and clubs where he claimed German agents went to consort. In the book's introduction, moreover, he claimed: 'As a writer, I have before me a file of amazing documents, which plainly show the feverish activity with which this advance guard of our enemy is working to secure for their employers the most detailed information.'[99] The press went wild for Le Queux's yarn. The book's call for a new national security infrastructure – encompassing a revamped Official Secrets Act, a stronger control of aliens and a professional counter-intelligence service – won near-universal approval. Certain newspapers, such as the *Weekly News*, even offered prizes for anyone with information about the German hidden hand. Patriotic Britons did not disappoint; over the coming months, Fleet Street was deluged with letters telling of chance encounters with fifth columnists taking a keen interest in shipyards, fortifications and railway lines. Le Queux himself received many letters from frightened members of the public, which he earnestly forwarded to Lieutenant Colonel James Edmonds, head of MO5, the fledging counter-intelligence section of the War Office's Directorate of Military Operations. Edmonds was delighted; keen to secure funding for his own department, he had long been nagging Richard Haldane, Secretary of State for War, on the need to take the German spy menace seriously. Haldane, however, who still harboured hopes of a rapprochement with Germany, had demanded proof before initiating an inquiry. For Edmonds, therefore, Le Queux's 'evidence' was a godsend.

In spring 1909, armed with press clippings and a bundle of reports from Le Queux, Edmonds successfully managed to convince Haldane to set up a Sub-Committee of Imperial Defence to consider the 'nature and extent of foreign espionage that is at present taking place within this country'.[100] Chaired by Haldane himself, the sub-committee deliberated in secret session for several months, before submitting its report in July. Astoundingly, Le Queux's material was instrumental in persuading members to reach the conclusion: 'The evidence which was produced left no doubt in the minds of the Sub-Committee that an extensive system of German espionage exists in this country, and that we have no organisation for keeping in touch with that espionage and for accurately determining its extent or objectives.'[101] This assessment, derived not from hard facts obtained by police authorities but from information ascertained from amateur spycatchers only too eager to name and shame suspicious-looking foreigners, led directly to the formation of a Secret Service Bureau. Within a year, the Bureau would break up into a Home department responsible for counter-espionage, the Security Service (MI5), and a Foreign department in control of espionage, the Secret Intelligence Service (SIS).

The sub-committee also emphasised the urgent and 'great need' to amend the Official Secrets Act. Paradoxically, despite alerting readers to the prospect of Continental war, Fleet Street had not restrained itself from publishing military or naval secrets. The majority of journalists, lamented Major General Spencer Ewart (Director of Military Operations at the War Office), had 'forgotten entirely their duty to the nation'.[102] In the sub-committee's report, the First Lord of the Admiralty, Reginald McKenna, expressed his disgust at a recent article in the *Daily Mail* which had given detailed technical information about battleship construction; the journalist in question had broken into a military installation and copied out the text of a secret cipher onto the tail of his shirt.[103] An uncensored press, considered the sub-committee, constituted a major national security risk. Foreign intelligence services were known to read overseas publications, gleaning what they could from seemingly insignificant bits of information. Bismarck had reportedly boasted to Prince Louis of Battenberg that he had acquired all the material he needed in the Franco-Prussian War from local French newspapers.[104] 'The final result of an unchecked press', declared Ewart, 'was that a German General landing a force in East Anglia would know more about the country than any British General, and more about its town than its own British mayor.'[105]

Because Le Queux and other scaremongers had so tirelessly kept the alleged German menace in the public consciousness, the sub-committee was confident that there would be no problem in getting the revised Act through Parliament. 'At the present time', opined Haldane, 'public opinion was much more sympathetic towards a Bill of the nature proposed, and this attitude of the public should be taken advantage of.'[106] The person tasked with formally introducing the Act before Parliament was the new, 35-year-old Home Secretary, Winston Churchill. Churchill was particularly keen to see the new Bill made into statute. His first few months in office had been accompanied by a major political scandal, triggered by the unauthorised publication of a crown servant's memoirs. The furore had begun in late 1909 when extracts from the memoir of Sir Robert Anderson, a former spymaster in the Home Office, started to appear in the monthly *Blackwood's Magazine*. Entitled 'The Lighter Side of My Life', the articles revealed Anderson's part in running undercover operations against Irish Fenians. Pages were replete with examples of dirty tricks. Anderson riled Irish nationalists by expressing admiration for the Victorian super-spy Henri le Caron, who in 1889 had famously testified in court against the Irish nationalist Charles Parnell. The most controversial revelation was Anderson's confession that, in 1887, he had been the author of several articles for *The Times* called 'Parnellism and Crime'. National-ists were appalled at what they saw as confirmation of government complicity in Parnell's destruction.[107] In his memoir, Anderson had also spoken about his time as Head of Scotland Yard's Criminal Investi-gation Department. Provocatively, he claimed that the police knew the identity of Jack the Ripper, but declined to publicise it for fear of being accused of not having done enough to bring him to justice.

In the Commons, MPs called on Churchill to punish Anderson for his revelations, with many demanding the cancellation of his police pension. (Section 5 of the Police Superannuation Act of 1906 allowed for a pension to be forfeited in the event of its recipient disclosing information obtained during his or her employment with the police.)[108] Liberals and Conservatives were united in their belief that no one should be able to reveal details of secret service work. Behind the scenes, the Commissioner of Police feared that Anderson's example, if unpunished, would encourage other crown servants to write 'even more sensational autobiographies'.[109] Considering the punishment too draconian, Churchill decided against cancelling Anderson's pension. However, not wanting to be seen as a soft touch, he publicly lambasted the *Blackwood's* articles – 'they are written in the style of "How Bill Adams Won the Battle of Waterloo"' – and promised MPs that the forthcoming Act would prevent disclosures of this kind.[110] 'It would be absolutely intolerable', he announced, 'if ex-police officers and ex-agents of the secret service were to be allowed, after they retired, without fear of consequence to publish secrets.'[111]

Churchill convinced Haldane that it should be for the latter to present the Act to Parliament. As Secretary of State for War, Haldane was better qualified to emphasise that the Act was a pressing national defence issue. The long-awaited propitious moment to amend the Act finally arrived with the Agadir crisis in July 1911. As international tensions reached a fever pitch, the public's readiness to defer to the policies of government soared to an unprecedented high. Press insubordination, crucial in thwarting the abortive 1908 Bill, had been replaced by an obsequious silence. In the House of Lords, Haldane presented the draft legislation as an essential buffer against German spies. Only two members passed comment. It was then sent to the Commons where it was passed, without amendment on a sleepy summer afternoon, by 107 votes to 10. MPs accepted the assurance of the Attorney General, Sir Rufus Isaacs, that the Act represented only a minor procedural tweak to the 1889 legislation. The only person to offer more than a fleeting comment was the Undersecretary for War, Colonel Jack Seely: 'Every other country has legislation of this kind I understand, and in no case would the powers be used to infringe any of the liberties of His Majesty's subjects.'[112] As David Vincent has argued, there was something very British about the way in which the Act was approved. Whereas in most other countries the terms and conditions would have been sharply defined, the 'glory of the British constitution' ensured that as much as possible was left to interpretation.[113]

As will become clear in the remainder of this book, despite lip service being paid to the idea that there was nothing to fear from the 1911 Act, government lawyers had built a Trojan Horse. Section 2 had been extended to include the receipt as well as the communication of information, a provision that directly impinged upon the freedom of the press. Section 2 (2) dictated:

> If any person receives any . . . information, knowing, or having reasonable ground to believe, at the time when he receives it, that the . . . information is communicated to him in contravention of the Act, he shall be guilty of a misdemeanour, unless he proves that the communication . . . was contrary to his desire.[114]

In going against the grain of English law, the Act reversed the burden of proof from the prosecution to the defence. In short, the defendant was guilty until proved innocent. In its revised form, Section 2 ruled that *all* information generated by the state was 'official', regardless of its nature or importance. It provided, therefore, protection against leakages of any kind of information, and not just those connected with defence or national security. The Franks Committee, which reported in 1972, underlined its broad compass: 'The leading characteristic is its catch-all quality. It makes no distinctions of kind, and no distinctions of degree. It catches all official documents and information. A blanket is thrown over everything; nothing escapes.'[115]

    A year later, with public opinion still willing to entrust the executive with considerable latitude, the government moved to bolster its new legislative weapon with another mechanism of control: the Admiralty, War Office and Press Committee – or D-Notice Committee for short. In the first decade of the twentieth century, in parallel with deliberations about reforming the 1889 Official Secrets Act, officials had explored the idea of constituting a 'gentleman's agreement' with the press. From these discussions, the concept of the D-Notice was born. In the words of the then Director of Naval Intelligence, the idea was to 'Put the press to their honour, in the schoolboy sense of the term . . . by issuing a communiqué to the Press Association stating what is to be carried out, and asking them to cooperate in [not printing] information likely to be of value to foreign enemies.'[116] Entirely extralegal and voluntary, the arrangement hinged on the assumption that Fleet Street, for all its sins, was deep down run by decent, patriotic people who valued security above a story. Propri-etors and editors had, after all, gone to the same schools as senior officials and went to the same clubs. In effect, the voluntary code of

D-Notices was an attempt by mandarins to graft honourable secrecy onto their social peers in journalism. The system came into effect on 13 August 1912; with Anglo-German tensions running high, there was no hesitation among officials in brandishing it before a deferential Press Association. The intricacies of the system would be worked out pragmatically over time, but the basic operating procedure would involve a committee, comprised of both civil servants and editors, drafting warnings to the press specifying defence-related subjects which, in the opinion of departments, would be detrimental to the national interest if disclosed. No one from Fleet Street objected. Parliament, which had broken up for the summer recess, was not even informed.

The D-Notice Committee was the final piece in a vast architecture designed to control classified information. By 1912, with its laws and conventions, Britain was set up to protect free speech, but not free inquiry; absolute secrecy prevailed. Accordingly, the likelihood of future disclosures looked slim. Or so it was thought.

2 BENDING THE RULES: MINISTERS AND THEIR MEMOIRS 1920–1945

> The theory underlying what was done in regard to documents of
> the last war has never . . . been exactly stated, for the reason that what
> really happened was that many of the great ones took the law into
> their own hands.
>
> EDWARD BRIDGES, CABINET SECRETARY,
> *5 November 1943*[1]

In the period 1920 to 1945, British secrecy was undermined
by individuals who should have known better. During this time,
secrets entered the public domain not through investigative reporting,
but through best-selling memoirs produced by politicians of the first
rank. In their accounts, leading statesmen like Winston Churchill and
David Lloyd George exposed in unprecedented detail the discussions,
decisions and people that had been important in their careers in high
office. Works overflowed with quotations from Cabinet documents,
all of which were supposed to be inviolable and which were subject
to at least a fifty-year embargo on public release. 'This is an age of
revelation and "of the truth about" almost any occurrence in recent
history,' observed *The Times* in 1933.[2]

Since the disclosure of secrets – though laudable in a journalist –
is ostensibly counter-intuitive to the creed of a crown servant, it is
logical to ask how this situation came about. As this chapter will
discuss, the catalyst was the Great War. In the 1920s and 1930s, the
history of the war became a contested battleground, producing a flood
of writings dedicated to explaining the conduct and experience of
those who had taken part. Eclipsing all previous conflicts by its scale

of destruction, the war became the most-written-about event of modern times, as people sought to comprehend the circumstances which had led to the carnage of the Western Front. Everyone had their say. The state itself produced a grand 28-volume official history. With memoirs, the 'brass hats' upbraided the 'frocks', and vice versa. Moreover, for every soldier-poet like Wilfred Owen or Siegfried Sassoon who slammed the idiocy of the generals, there were as many writers who gave them credit for Britain's ultimate victory and attributed the losses incurred to either exceptional circumstances or the meddling of politicians back home.[3] Such was the strong feeling aroused by the war and the passion among authors to tell their side of the story, that the Victorian expectation that public officials should be treated respectfully, especially by their peers, was gradually worn away. The first generation of historiography on the war was eye-catching for the sheer ferocity of the attacks directed at some of the personalities involved.

The criticisms that were aired created an impulse for vindication, and with this came a serious challenge to the secret state. With nothing less than the perception of the war at stake – at the time regarded as the 'war to end all wars' – no politician wanted to go down in history as having made fatal mistakes. Many, therefore, chose to write a memoir as the elixir through which to achieve rehabilitation. Most were not content to tell only part of the story or describe events in general terms. In their quest for vindication they would leave nothing to chance, and this meant drawing deeply on reservoirs of classified information and bending the rules as far as official secrecy was concerned. Of course, telling the 'truth' did not come without temptation. As will become apparent in this chapter, authors were also encouraged by the lures of enterprising publishers, and by the seemingly endless appetite of the memoir consumer.

Preventing ministers from revealing too much proved a difficult task for which no easy solution was found. Prior to the war, when there were no Cabinet minutes and few Cabinet papers (save a vague summary sent by the prime minister to the sovereign after each meeting), the secret state could take comfort in the fact that, even if ministers wanted to write memoirs packed with sensitive material, they would be hamstrung in doing so.[4] This all changed with the creation of the Cabinet Secretariat in December 1916. The brainchild of Sir Maurice Hankey, Secretary to the Committee of Imperial Defence and Cabinet Secretary for nearly twenty years after the war, the Cabinet Secretariat revolutionised the way government business was recorded. Inter alia, its functions were to compile the agenda for Cabinet meetings, take down and circulate the conclusions of Cabinet meetings, and arrange for the safe keeping of Cabinet papers and minutes. The result was that the aspiring memoirist suddenly had a vast pool of information at his fingertips. As will be seen, although this material fell within the scope of the Official Secrets Act and the Privy Councillor's Oath, this did not stop authors from printing it. This happened because the authors in question were too grand to be controlled. Statesmen like Churchill and Lloyd George commanded huge respect among the very individuals in Whitehall who were charged with censoring them. If they refused to stand on ceremony, no official had the courage to confront them, still less accuse them of breaking the law. In short, they were beyond discipline and did not live in a censorious environment like everyone else. The challenge for the state was one of damage limitation – finding a way of encouraging eminent authors to self-censor without appearing to be disrespectful. In this capacity, it came to rely on the Cabinet Secretary, Hankey. As a friend of many of the memoirists concerned, and with an unrivalled knowledge of the government machine, he was uniquely qualified to act as a middleman between departments and authors. After 1918, he was all that stood between authors and their desire for full disclosure.

* * *

> I have a living to earn. After seventeen years in office, I have retired a poor man, and it is absolutely imperative that I should turn to writing as a means of livelihood.
>
> *David Lloyd George, 22 October 1922*[5]

The problem of politicians writing memoirs packed with secrets was not something that appeared suddenly, but it was an issue that exercised the collective minds of officials on several occasions during the immediate post-war years. Hankey was firmly against the idea of ex-ministers having the freedom to include Cabinet records in their reminiscences, and took steps to prevent this from happening. His argument was that, if politicians made disclosures in their memoirs, this would be destructive to the collective responsibility of the Cabinet and its successors. In short, the capacity for free discussion would be undermined if ministers and their advisers thought that their opinions might become public and, in the worst case, used against them. This was an argument that Hankey had deployed in July 1916 when, as Secretary to the War Council, he had doggedly refused to hand over his 'Secretary's Notes' to the Commission of Enquiry into the disastrous Dardanelles Campaign in 1915. The Commissioners eventually reached a compromise with Hankey, which allowed the Chairman of the Enquiry to inspect the notes, but only after a series of acrimonious exchanges which had seen the Commission threaten Hankey, presumably in the spirit of jest, with a sojourn in the Tower of London.[6] 'Whether this was serious', he recollected, 'I did not gather.'[7]

In late 1919, Hankey attempted to protect Cabinet secrecy from aspiring memoirists by drafting a set of strict 'Instructions' on the use of official papers. The instructions stipulated that Cabinet records were government property, to be returned by all ministers on retiring from office. In cases where a minister had resigned or died, the Cabinet Secretary would be responsible for regaining custody of his papers.[8] Hankey would be disappointed. In Cabinet, on 4 November, ministers refused to sanction any provision that was targeted at curtailing literary activity, arguing that Cabinet secrecy was already protected by the rule that no record could be published without the approval of the king. Accordingly, they directed that ministers could not only retain papers already in their possession, but also have access at any time to Cabinet documents generated during the period in which they had been in office.[9] In all probability, the instigators of this decision were Churchill, then Secretary of State for War and Secretary of State for Air, and Lloyd George, the prime minister (Figure 1). Both men had ambitions of writing war memoirs, not least because they had been in the firing line for criticism. In anticipation of his writing career, Lloyd George had already hired a research assistant, Major General Sir Ernest Swinton, to collect material from 'secret archives'.[10]

The government's decision to relax the rules regarding the ownership of Cabinet documents had an immediate effect. Hankey later recollected that, following this ruling, certain ministers required a pantechnicon to remove papers from their offices.[11] Lloyd George walked away with bundles of documents, including the sole copy of the Anglo-Irish Treaty of 1921. According to Frances Stevenson, Lloyd George's personal secretary, mistress and second wife, the Treaty remained in his collection until his death in 1945. 'The amazing thing', she noted in her diary, 'was that during that time it had never been asked for.'[12] Hankey observed these developments with a consternation bordering on despair. It was only a matter of time, he feared, before Cabinet papers were recycled into memoirs. In a final attempt to prevent this, he encouraged the government to remind ministers of the stiff regulations that still existed regarding the publication of Cabinet documents. The Privy Councillor's Oath imposed a special duty on all ministers to preserve the secrecy of Cabinet business to which they became party, whilst the Official Secrets Act could be called upon to prosecute anyone who without authority published classified information whose publication was proved to be 'prejudicial to the safety or interests of the State'. Once again, however, the Cabinet Secretary would be disappointed. Rather than create roadblocks for memoirists, HMG provided them with unprecedented latitude. On 30 January 1922, it was ruled that, in cases where a minister's reputation had been unfairly injured, he or she had the right to publish official documents in refutation, provided they did not damage the public interest; this became known as the 'vindicator' clause.[13] This decision was justified on the grounds that, since the end of the war, there had been a flood of partisan memoirs by military figures, in many cases quoting official sources to attack politicians. Published in June 1919, the memoir of Field Marshal Sir John French, the first Commander-in-Chief of the British Expeditionary Force (BEF) in the war, had discussed freely the frictions between the 'brass hats' and the 'frocks', including stinging criticism of the Liberal prime minister Herbert Asquith (1908–16).[14] In his memoir, Admiral John Jellicoe, who commanded the Grand Fleet at the Battle of Jutland in 1916, had fired off a number of salvos against the wartime political elite. Jellicoe's memoir also upset the Government Code and Cypher School (GC&CS), Britain's first fully integrated peacetime code-making and code-breaking unit. Vetting of the manuscript had failed to spot and delete the revelation that the wireless telegraphy set installed on the Admiralty building roof had intercepted German signals traffic. GC&CS feared that, if foreign governments picked up on this, they would at once increase the security of their cipher systems.[15]

The first individual to take advantage of the new 'vindicator' principle was Churchill, who published six volumes of self-justifying reminiscences, entitled *The World Crisis*, between 1923 and 1931.

With these works, he turned a handsome profit. In an early indication of the financial rewards that went with the disclosure of secrets in memoir format, by January 1921, before a single copy had been sold, he had contracts worth over £27,000 with London's leading literary agent, Curtis Brown.[16] Churchill epitomised the breed of memoirist most likely to cause problems. First, he possessed a sizeable private archive. After resigning his post as First Lord of the Admiralty in 1915, following the disastrous Dardanelles expedition in 1915 (for which he was blamed), he had taken away a raft of copies of minutes, memorandums and telegrams.[17] Secondly, he had a reputation as a rule-breaker, entitled to behave as he pleased. Although he was one of the prime movers behind the amendment of the Official Secrets Act in 1911, evidence seems to suggest that he never considered himself as being bound by it. Published in 1919, the diary of the English poet Wilfred Scawen Blunt shows that Churchill, as Home Secretary, had routinely kept his friends abreast of Cabinet business. The diary entry for 19 October 1912 described a visit by Churchill to Blunt's home in Sussex: 'The secrets of the Cabinet were gloriously divulged, and those of the Opposition front benches no less, from Home Rule to a reconstruction of the House of Lords.'[18] Churchill's candid discussions with Blunt are extraordinary when we consider that the latter, far from being in the inner sanctum, was an eccentric and loquacious Irish nationalist who would have had no qualms about revealing the contents of what he had heard. The final problem with Churchill was that there was no easy way of taking him to task if he stepped out of line. In 1924 he had become Chancellor. Because of his position and because of the high regard in which officials held him, there was little chance of anyone having the nerve to strong-arm him.

Churchill was granted the authority to publish direct quotations from a range of sources, including Admiralty telegrams and orders, as well as Cabinet minutes and papers. This was sanctioned on the grounds that several publications had done harm to his reputation, most notably Lord Esher's *The Tragedy of Lord Kitchener* (1921), which had accused the former First Lord of being reckless and acting without authority.[19] Since the 'vindicator' principle had been created in secret, it was no surprise that, when Volume I of *The World Crisis* was serialised in *The Times* in February 1923, people were shocked by what they read. In Parliament, Labour MPs demanded to know whether Churchill had secured permission for his disclosures. One backbencher, Captain

O'Grady, asked if the government was going to initiate legal procee-dings. When the book itself appeared in April, MPs inquired whether the appearance in the text of Admiralty telegrams had compromised naval codes.[20] The prime minister, Andrew Bonar Law, tried to diffuse the situation, explaining that the present First Lord had afforded Churchill the right of quotation, there being no danger to the security of codes. When pressed on this, Bonar Law refused to elaborate, save a glib but controversial remark that, in his opinion, Churchill had violated the Privy Councillor's Oath: 'I have taken the oath and personally I think I should consider it a breach.'[21] Away on holiday, Churchill was vexed to read the premier's statement, interpreting it as a sign that the Cabinet was determined, and secretly plotting, to bring his literary career to an abrupt end. His fear was heightened upon hearing that Bonar Law had appointed a special committee, chaired by Lord Curzon, to establish a 'code of rules' for official memoir writing.[22]

The rumpus soon passed, the Curzon Committee never met, and the proliferation of memoirs continued. 'Men are very porous,' considered Hankey (quoting Thomas Carlyle), 'weighty secrets oozing out of them like quicksilver through clay jars.'[23] As David Reynolds has shown, Churchill nevertheless learnt a valuable lesson from the events of 1923.[24] As he saw it, the row had come about because there was no procedure allowing for the official scrutiny of works before their publication. Consequently, authors were walking through a mine-field. In 1926, therefore, in advance of Volume III's publication, he submitted his chapters to relevant government departments. He also sent the entire draft to the prime minister, Stanley Baldwin. Formally, the power of approval for the publication of materials generated by privy councillors was vested in the king, advised by the premier. Acting on Churchill's advice, Baldwin delegated the responsibility of scrutinising the draft to Hankey. For many reasons, Hankey was ideal for the task at hand. He was untainted by political predisposition and was trusted by departments to make an honest assessment of what, in the public interest, should not be disclosed. His knowledge of the war was second to none. Most important for Churchill, he was increasingly sympathetic to the grievances of politicians who had been publicly criticised for their wartime conduct and who, in turn, desired a right to reply. In the absence of any prescribed guidelines, and thanks in no small measure to Churchill pulling the strings, the Cabinet Secretary thus became the 'official censor of political memoirs'.[25]

The 'vindicator' clause also paved the way for Lloyd George to write a memoir, the commencement of which was announced by the world's media in August 1922. He too had been target of criticism in the battle of the books that had broken out in the post-war period. Many of the 'brasshats' suggested that the war would have been won much sooner had it not been for the officious and amateur interference of the prime minister. Aside from the allure of self-vindication, Lloyd George had another good reason to go into print: money. George Egerton's research has shown that Curtis Brown had been goading him with the promise of untold riches from as early as January 1921.[26] Their estimate of his potential earnings far exceeded Churchill's returns for *The World Crisis*, a reflection of Lloyd George's tenure as premier not only during the critical stages of the war, but also during the difficult years of post-war reorientation and peacemaking; he was – to quote Egerton – a 'publisher's dream as a potential memoirist'.[27] Accordingly, projections started at £50,000 and did not stop, to the point where Brown was confidently predicting £75,000. Believing the hype and in a bid to get the best deal possible, Lloyd George played hard-ball with Brown for nearly eighteen months, before finally making him his agent in spring 1922. Brown did not disappoint. On 12 August 1922, newspapers reported that Lloyd George had signed contracts for a book, film and serialisation package amounting to a record sum of £90,000, more than double what Kaiser Wilhelm II had received for his memoir. It was hailed as 'the biggest deal in the history of publishing'.[28]

News of the deal caused a public outrage. In a climate of post-war hardship, the figure was seen as obscene. Lloyd George was accused of exploiting the war dead. Moreover, at a time when the press was living in fear of the Official Secrets Act, journalists were scandalised at what appeared to be a clear case of a privileged politician looking to profit from selling secrets. 'If this is honestly worth its money,' protested the journal *Outlook*, 'it will contain information which no Prime Minister can use without the gravest impropriety.'[29] (The *Sunday Times*, having acquired the UK serialisation rights, was unsurprisingly silent on the issue.) Lloyd George was shamefaced. His wife, Dame Margaret, had warned him not to take a penny from the book. In a letter to her husband she wrote with some satisfaction: 'That's a feather in my cap. You can write another book to make money, but not on the war.'[30] To assuage a guilty conscience, Lloyd George declared that all profits from the book would be donated to war charities.[31] By the end of the year, this decision haunted him. His defeat in the October general election had left him out of office and without the fortune he so desired, save a £2,000 per year gratuity left to him by the steel magnate Andrew Carnegie. Fortunately, memoirs were not the only way of making money out of secrets. An even more lucrative income could be made from the writing of newspaper columns. In November, he signed a contract with the United Press Association (UPA) to write regular articles on the war and current affairs, to the record-breaking tune of £250 per article.[32] This made him the highest-paid political journalist of the age. His first-year earnings were in excess of £30,000.[33] Over a period of six years, he banked over £150,000 from journalism, which allowed him to buy up parcels of land, as well as prime real estate in London.

Lloyd George's profitable employment as a columnist gradually dampened his enthusiasm for memoir writing. Over time, he would free himself from his various book contracts and return the advances given to him in good faith by publishers and newspapers. This was not altogether plain sailing. In December 1922, the *New York Times* and the *Chicago Tribune* threatened him with legal action, claiming that his articles for UPA would lessen the value of his reminiscences, for which they had agreed to pay £40,000 and had provided a £4,000 advance. 'At the time of making the contract,' charged solicitors, 'it never entered our client's mind that Mr Lloyd George would enter into a contract for other serial writings in competition with those which he had already sold.'[34] With this, the former premier agreed to cancel the contract and pay back the money.

Yet the idea of a memoir did not die completely. Swinton continued to work as a research assistant until 1925, when he left to become Chichele Professor of Military History at Oxford. During this time, he conducted interviews with Lloyd George's colleagues, put private papers in workable order and made copious notes from official records. A popular and trusted figure with 'marvellous contacts', he was even allocated a study space in the offices of the Cabinet, at 2 Whitehall Gardens.[35] As he saw it, his job was to 'build the trunk of the tree', as well as 'the main branches'.[36] In January 1924, so impressed was Lloyd George by his research assistant's talents and dedication that Swinton was asked if he would consider 'ghosting' the memoir. This proposal was politely turned down, Swinton arguing, 'What the world and the British public want is a subjective narrative of what Lloyd George did, written by Lloyd George, recounting his actions, motives, the working of his mind, searching of his heart, opinions and decisions.'[37] A ghosted account, he emphasised, would be 'absolutely devoid of the life, the soul, the "juice", the personality and the inside view' which Lloyd George alone could provide. Crucially, Swinton was uncomfortable with the idea that, vicariously, he would be taking the responsibility for the former prime minister's opinions. Many people were waiting for the book with 'guns and clubs';[38] with some justification, Swinton was unwilling to put himself in the firing line.

Lloyd George at last turned to writing his memoirs in 1932. Several factors led him to this. Firstly, he now had time on his hands. His career in Fleet Street had run its course, while a sudden illness and resultant operation had left him incapacitated and thus unable to join Ramsay MacDonald's National Government when it was formed in August 1931. After the general election in October, he found himself on the periphery of British politics, with little chance of a return to office. Secondly, he had become increasingly upset with the state of Great War historiography. For years he had taken a keen interest in reading what had been written about the war and about his leadership. In late 1931, while on holiday in Ceylon, he had sent to him a 'huge trunk' of books, consisting of every publication that 'had ever been written on the war by anyone of any importance'.[39] To his annoyance, many of the authors had produced their accounts without consulting him, the result being that they were wrong on crucial matters and events.

Most vexing of all was that 'history' had been kind to Field Marshal Douglas Haig, Commander-in-Chief of the BEF from December 1915 to the end of the war. In Lloyd George's eyes, Haig was a butcher and a fool. Pig-headed, strategically inept and counselled by sycophants, he had sent the flower of British youth to be cut down, while all the while he dwelled in the safety of luxurious lodgings miles behind the lines. History, however, had hitherto painted a very different picture. In the majority of works, he was lauded as a hero – an unflappable, innovative and hands-on commanding officer who had the prescience to realise the importance of tanks and who inspired his troops by regularly visiting the front line. His funeral in 1928 had been a major state occasion, with 200,000 ex-servicemen (the equivalent of 200 battalions) filing past his coffin to pay their final respects.[40] In his lifetime, Haig had been a shameless self-promoter, unwilling to let the history books take care of his reputation. He published dispatches from his field diary; meddled with the production of the *Official History of the Great War*; and even sent a 75-page memorandum on Western Front operations to people he knew were writing a history of the war.[41]

For a long time few dared to challenge the orthodoxy about Haig, partly because he was still alive, and partly because, after all, he had led a victorious army. The only dissenting voice was Churchill's, who in *The World Crisis* compared Haig to a surgeon, emotionally numb and insensitive to the fate of the patient. Elsewhere, Churchill accused Haig of using 'the breasts of brave young men' to block German machine-gun fire. For Lloyd George, this was not enough: Haig had to be destroyed – his errors as a general and his failings as a man must be put before the bar of history. The bad blood felt by Lloyd George had been heightened by a recent tour of the historic battlefields in France, which had left him with a profound sense of despair at the futility of human endeavour.[42] By 1932, the former premier had come round to the view that, unless he took pen in hand, pro-Haig publications would constitute 'the material from which the future historian of the war would draw'.[43] By extension, his own war record might be overlooked or, worse still, compared negatively to that of the Field Marshal. Perchance, with Haig dead, there would be much more freedom to challenge his status as a national hero.

A final factor behind Lloyd George's decision to write a memoir was that, in his mind, there were now few wartime secrets which he, especially as a former premier entitled to certain privileges, could not reveal. For example, had he penned his story in the early 1920s, it is improbable that even he would have been allowed to discuss Room 40 – the office of British Naval Intelligence. In September 1919, the post-war Director of Naval Intelligence (DNI), Admiral Hugh Sinclair, had ruled: 'It is just as important now as it ever was for our success to be unknown to any except those who have worked here and the few naval officers who have had the entrée in connection with this work.'[44] By 1932, however, the secrets of wartime cryptography were trickling out. On 13 December 1927, Sir James Alfred Ewing, head of Room 40 from 1914 to 1917, had startled GC&CS when he gave a lecture to the Edinburgh Philosophical Institution entitled 'Some Special War Work'.[45] Ewing escaped prosecution by a whisker, owing to the personal intervention of Lord Balfour, Lord President of the Council, who managed to convince the Admiralty that legal action represented a 'purely retrograde step'.[46] More disclosures followed. Sir Gerald Charles, DNI from 1932 to 1935, only succeeded in making minor deletions to Hugh Hoy's book *40 OB: Or How the War Was Won*.[47] Press articles on wartime cryptography grew steadily in number, to the point where William Clarke, Head of the Naval Section in GC&CS, lamented that the public knew only 'a travesty of the facts', an 'entirely erroneous and hackneyed idea of intelligence'.[48] Lloyd George watched these developments with relish, believing that it should now be possible for him to pull back the curtain not just a bit, but all the way. Whitehall had other ideas, but stopping him from doing so would prove extremely difficult.

*   *   *

> Why should the King be against my book? He can go to Hell. I owe him nothing; he owes his throne to me.
>
> *David Lloyd George*[49]

The resurrection of the Lloyd George war memoirs was Whitehall's worst nightmare. As Egerton has argued, 'Discretion and dignity had never been allowed to impede his career; neither would they impede his writing.'[50] Considering himself something of a special case as a former prime minister, and resentful of the generals and politicians who had impugned his reputation by quoting embarrassing material in their memoirs, Lloyd George had every intention of playing fast and loose with the conventions governing access to and publication of official records. The spine of his account would be documents. 'If mine were the first book in which official memoranda and information were utilised,' he wrote to Hankey, 'then I agree with you that I should be bound to go through the technical procedure.' 'But', he went on, 'I happen to be the very last of all the prominent figures of the war, except yourself, to give my account of what took place. Meanwhile a host of others have given their accounts drawn almost exclusively from secret documents which are no doubt within the purview of the Official Secrets Act.'[51] Lloyd George's blasé attitude to the rules of secrecy horrified officials. Yet there was no easy way of restraining him. In many corners of Whitehall, he was revered as one of the 'great ones' of the Edwardian era, rivalled in stature only by Churchill.[52] Acolytes were aplenty, and it is not hard to imagine him bestriding his particular world like a colossus. Moreover, it would take a brave man to challenge him. Lloyd George – famously described by A. J. P. Taylor as having no friends, nor deserving of any – was known for his volcanic temper and penchant for confrontation over conciliation.[53]

Alas, unable and unwilling to strong-arm Lloyd George, secret-keepers resorted to a less direct and less honourable mode of attack.[54] In a bid to intimidate him, an Official Secrets Act charge was brought against a lesser mortal. The individual sacrificed for the greater good of unnerving Lloyd George was Compton Mackenzie, a best-selling novelist who had served with British intelligence in the Eastern Mediterranean during the First World War. On 28 October 1932, Mackenzie published *Greek Memories*, the third instalment in a proposed four-book series of wartime reminiscences. The previous two volumes, *Gallipoli Memories* (1929) and *First Athenian Memories* (1931), had been published without reprisals from the state, despite being rich in commentary about secret service work. The second volume had reproduced a number of Foreign Office telegrams and had even disclosed that the first Chief of SIS had been known as 'C', after the first letter of his surname.[55] With *Greek Memories*, however, which covered the period when the author had been head of the British counter-espionage section in Athens, Mackenzie found himself in hot water. By 3 p.m. on the day of publication, the Director of Public Prosecutions had telephoned the publisher, Cassell, and demanded that the book be withdrawn. By early November, proceedings against Mackenzie had been instituted under the Official Secrets Act, the offence being that he had communicated to unauthorised persons, namely Cassell, 'information which he had obtained while holding office under His Majesty'.[56] The summons earned Mackenzie great sympathy. During committal proceedings, the Special Branch officer who had served it stood the author several rounds of pink gins, so ashamed was he by the prosecution.[57] Another police officer raised his glass in a toast to the unfortunate Mackenzie and announced: 'I know I'm speaking both for the Metropolitan Police and for the Old Jewry when I say we do not consider this a prosecution but a malicious persecution.'[58]

The government was the driving force behind the prosecution. Sir Reginald Lane Poole, Mackenzie's lawyer, was tipped off by a sympathetic official: 'I understand the government intend to make an example of you if they can, in order to warn Lloyd George and Winston Churchill that they can go too far in using information they could only have acquired in office.'[59] Lloyd George indicated to Mackenzie in private that HMG regarded the trial as a 'test case', designed to determine the wisdom of taking legal action against more distinguished offenders.[60] In court, the judge hinted strongly at the underlying political reasons for the case: 'It must be obvious to everybody that when confidential documents get into the hands of public servants – servants of the Crown – however long they might keep them in secret, it was not for such servants to decide when such documents were to be published.'[61] 'I hope', he emphasised, 'this case may do something to warn those whose urge to write is greater than their discretion.'[62]

This is not to say that other factors were not involved. SIS loathed the book. Within hours of its publication, someone from the organisation had written to the Director of Public Prosecutions identifying passages that 'prevent and endanger the present and future practice of the Secret Service'.[63] 'There is a scarcely a page', underlined the memo, 'which does not damage the foundation of secrecy upon which the Secret Service is built.'[64] The most destructive disclosure was judged to be the statement that a branch in the War Office, known as 'M.I.1.c', was in fact a cover for the Foreign Section of the Service. In revealing this, the book effectively disclosed the identity of three present SIS officers, whose names were printed in the *War Office List*, which was publicly available and studied by foreign general staff. Similarly, Mackenzie had blown the connection between SIS and the Passport Control Department, the latter being a cover for Heads of Station abroad. The author had also given striking pen pictures of intelligence personnel with whom he had come into contact, including the first Chief of SIS, Captain Sir Mansfield Cumming. Mackenzie told the story (now proven to be false) of how Cumming, to escape from a car wreck in France in 1914, had used a penknife to hack off his own leg.[65] Admiral Sinclair was incandescent. Several of the individuals named had been 'earmarked' for re-employment. More generally, the identity of agents was considered inviolable. The guarantee of immunity from betrayal and retribution was seen as a vital way of ensuring agent recruitment.

Held partly in camera, both the committal proceedings and the trial at the Old Bailey included some farcical moments, making an absurdity out of certain elements of the prosecution's case. 'Mr X', an anonymous witness from M.I.1.c, confirmed that not one of the sixteen agents allegedly endangered by the book was a current spy. Captain Walter Christmas, a Danish sea captain, was discovered to have passed away ten years before. Sir Clifford Heathcote-Smith, now retired, had recorded his wartime intelligence work in his *Who's Who* entry. Another person said by the prosecution to have been imperilled was Harry Pirie-Gordon – a claim which was greeted with mirth in the courtroom since Pirie-Gordon had reviewed a pre-publication copy of the book in *The Times*.[66] The prosecution's case was dealt a fatal blow when, in open court, a Foreign Office witness conceded, under intense cross-examination, that the 'public interest' had not been prejudiced by the book's disclosures.[67] This, together with press interest in the absurdities of the trial, prompted the government to offer Mackenzie a secret plea bargain. The defendant was told that the prosecution would not push for a custodial sentence provided he would change his plea to guilty, accept a comparatively small fine of £100 and make a £100 contribution towards costs. Mackenzie had little choice but to accept the deal; *Greek Memories* was packed with extensive quotations from secret documents, meaning that the likelihood of an acquittal for the Section 2 offence was slim.

The Crown's pyrrhic victory caused consternation in Fleet Street, with newspapers quick to contend that Mackenzie had paid the price for the indiscretions of persons more highly placed in public life. According to the *Statesman and Nation*, 'If the government intended to prosecute anybody it would have been better if they had started at the top with ex-Cabinet Ministers; no one would have misjudged their motives then.'[68] The weekly newspaper *Sphere* concluded that Mackenzie's only sin was his tactlessness in failing to observe the formality of Whitehall's leave. 'The Official Secrets Act', it lamented, 'has at last validated its strength by seizing one victim out of many offenders.' It went on: 'Statesmen responsible for the making of the law have driven their juggernaut coach and four through it, and galloped away unscathed. But sometimes it must happen that a victim must be found. Self-justification by war leaders has been one of our minor post-war nuisances.'[69] Journalists were not the only ones to see the double standard. In his diary, the influential military theorist Captain Basil Liddell Hart wrote that he fully understood Mackenzie's decision to take the plea bargain, but at the same time wished he had 'put up a fight'. 'For the sake of historical truth and justice', lamented Liddell Hart, Mackenzie should have taken the line:

> If you punish me it will add one more example to the
> number in which the law has made itself to be the tool of

servants of the government who have abused their power at
the prompting of injured vanity. By condemning me, you will do
far more harm to the good name of Britain, to its reputation
for honourable dealing, than any harm my book can have done.
For you will associate its present rulers with the dishonest tricks
practised by some of its minor agents fourteen years ago. And the
old charges against 'British hypocrisy' will be given a new lease of
life, to the damage of the good work and influence that Britain may
exert in the critical years that lie immediately ahead.[70]

Mackenzie got his revenge. Several months after running foul of
the authorities, he published a satirical novel, *Water on the Brain*,
mercilessly ridiculing SIS, camouflaged as MQ9 (E), the 'Directorate
of Extraordinary Intelligence'. The spoof showed the secret service to
be saddled with petty and callous rivalries, run by bumbling cuckolds
whose passion for unnecessary secrecy was matched only by their
devotion to bureaucratic drudgery. By the end of the novel, the organisation's headquarters had been converted into a lunatic asylum for
officials driven insane 'in the service of their country'. As the novel
was a work of fiction, the authorities took no action, although a close
reading of the text reveals a few genuine secrets, including the fact that
the Chief of SIS always signed his name in green ink.

In his autobiography *My Life and Times* (1968), Mackenzie
claimed that his prosecution, as an exercise in gesture politics, did have
an effect on more eminent crown servants. Some years later, Churchill
reportedly admitted to him that he had taken the precaution of burning
a number of his more sensitive papers, something he subsequently
regretted.[71] There is no evidence, however, that the trial had any impact
on Lloyd George. In the years following, there were few rules that he
did not bend or break. Throughout the period when he was writing his
memoirs, the 'Welsh Wizard' enjoyed special access to official records,
over and above his status as a 'self-vindicator'. Rather than rummage
through piles of documents himself, he cut a deal with Hankey to allow
his private secretary, Albert James Sylvester, Swinton's successor, to do
the bulk of the research for him. Hankey needed little persuasion to let
Sylvester loose in the archives. Sylvester (shown in Figure 2), who in
December 1915 had become the first person to take shorthand notes of
a Cabinet meeting, had served as Hankey's private secretary from 1916
to 1921.[72] Sylvester's diary, which is publicly available at the National

Library of Wales, provides a fascinating insight into the onerous but privileged work he carried out on Lloyd George's behalf.[73] According to the entry for 28 September 1933, he was permitted by the Foreign Office to spend two and half hours making copies of 'telegrams to and from Russia'.[74] Several days later, he was 'busily engaged digging up documents at the War Cabinet Offices'.[75] With Hankey's approval, there were few materials denied to him. 'It was open sesame for me,' he would later write: 'I used the War Cabinet Office as if I were still a member of the staff.'[76] As someone with an intimate knowledge of government records and official procedure, Sylvester came into his own when asked to find information that was uncatalogued or lost in the bureaucratic jungle of Whitehall. On one occasion, he proudly recalled, 'I got copies of plans and documents which had belonged personally to Haig and Sir Henry Wilson, which Lloyd George had never seen or known about, but which, as Prime Minister, he should have had.'[77] Where others might have balked at the idea of spending long days and late nights 'down in the bowels' of the Cabinet Office, Sylvester 'thoroughly enjoyed' it – although he did, now and again, get frustrated with his paymaster's 'never-ending demands'.[78] 'Lloyd George has no idea about the use of human effort,' he ranted on one occasion: 'He is never happy except when he is slashing his staff to bits, like a bad chauffeur who puts his foot on the accelerator when the engine is standing.'[79]

From the outset, Lloyd George found a crucial, if at first glance unlikely, ally in Hankey (Figure 3), who went beyond the call of duty to assist in the memoirs. Despite his reputation for secrecy, Hankey had grown increasingly sympathetic to Lloyd George's cause, unhappy with the way critics had savaged his reputation, in many cases with recourse to documents. More important, by the early 1930s he himself had started to think seriously about a memoir, and accordingly was reluctant to create a rod for his own back by denying authors the very same courtesies he himself would expect in the future. In a letter to Lloyd George dated 3 December 1930, Hankey explained that many of his friends had urged him to compile a record of his experiences in the war before it was too late.[80] General Smuts and Lord Lothian had implored him to devote the remainder of his life to writing a history of the conflict; Bonar Law argued that it was Hankey's 'duty' to do so for the sake of posterity.[81] Hankey was undecided. On the one hand, a memoir would represent a fundamental rejection of the culture of secrecy that underpinned the private world of the higher civil service. For Hankey, someone who prided himself on the purity of his principles and the distinction of his Whitehall 'family', this weighed heavily on his mind: 'As one who has spent his whole active life in different branches of the Public Service and has absorbed its tradition, I feel considerable repugnance in withdrawing the veil from even a portion of my official life.'[82] He went on: 'However interesting and however valuable from a historical point of view my experiences have been, I owe them exclusively to my official life.'[83] On the other hand, Hankey had been angered by the literature on the Great War and saw it as his debt to history to set the record straight:

> The war was probably the most important episode in our
> national history and will dominate our destiny for
> generations to come. Many people, including some whom one
> would expect to be rather straight-laced in these matters, have
> not hesitated to publish and record their experiences. Some
> of these memoirs and diaries were written unavoidably
> from a comparatively narrow point of view and without full
> knowledge of the facts. Consequently they sometimes
> present a very incorrect and biased picture of
> events.[84]

After much procrastination, Hankey decided that he *would* write a memoir, albeit not until he had retired. Accordingly, with one eye on this future project, he did all he could to assist Lloyd George.

Lloyd George demanded documents and Hankey gave them to him. At a time when historians had no hope of examining an official document for at least fifty years, the former premier was afforded access to tens of thousands of records, not just from the Cabinet but from a host of government departments. Hankey himself joined the paper chase, frequently visiting libraries and archives on his former master's behalf. On one occasion, at Hankey's request, the entire Cabinet Secretariat put on hold their normal duties to assist Lloyd George with his relentless pursuit of information. Sylvester noted in his diary on 29 March 1933: 'I went to see Hankey: found he had the whole Cabinet Office working hard for several days looking up facts for Lloyd George's book. How they bless Lloyd George, especially when I tell them they are only just beginning.'[85] Hankey sent bundles of documents, often originals, to Lloyd George's home in Wales. Although this was done on the strict understanding that they would be returned hastily and in perfect condition, Lloyd George rarely stuck to the rules. Documents were returned not only late, but covered in cigar burns, coffee stains and remnants of breakfast.[86] (A lot of the writing was done by Lloyd George sitting upright in bed, with the documents and gastronomic provision close to hand.) As John Naylor has shown, some documents were not returned at all – since they can now be read by researchers at the House of Lords Record Office, as part of Lloyd George's private papers.[87]

Hankey proved helpful in other respects. He arranged for Sylvester to interview a host of wartime crown servants, from Sir William Beveridge, who had been involved in the mobilisation and control of manpower, to Sir Eric Geddes, First Lord of the Admiralty between 1917 and 1919.[88] Among the most useful interviewees was Brigadier General Sir James Edmonds, the official British historian of the Great War. In a letter to Sylvester dated 19 September 1933, he included the following tranche of documents: 'Haig's order giving the objectives of the Ypres offensive in 1917; a note on the number of German divisions on the Western Front 1917–18; and a note on the use of tanks in the Passchendaele area, with extracts from the records'.[89] As head of MO5 before the war, Edmonds had played a key role in getting the Official Secrets Act revised to crack down on the haemorrhaging of official information; how things had changed.

In an inspired move, Hankey also arranged for a privately paid military 'expert', Basil Liddell Hart, to read the drafts from the perspective of tactics, strategy, and issues of command.[90] 'If there are any weak joints in your armour,' counselled Hankey, 'he will bring them to your attention.'[91] Liddell Hart was the natural choice. 'In the Himalayan range of the great thinkers about warfare he was one of the last and undoubtedly one of the pre-eminent peaks,' considered the military historian Ronald Lewin in an article for *International Affairs* in 1971.[92] In the 1920s, as military correspondent for the *Daily Telegraph*, he had become the foremost military critic of his era. Whereas Edmonds, the official historian, extolled the virtues of Britain's military leaders, Liddell Hart was of the opinion that there had been futile slaughter, brought about by heartless and incompetent commanders, the worst offender being Haig. Although

Lloyd George needed no convincing on this score, Liddell Hart, in his correspondence with the former premier, rarely turned down the opportunity to drive the point home. In one letter he wrote:

> The so-called strategy of 'killing Germans' in a stationary grapple on the Western Front was not only a mathematical fallacy, but a moral misunderstanding of human nature in war. Can't you be definite as to the General and his remark – it would carry more conviction. As so often, once he [Haig] became engaged his fighting instinct took charge of him, and he began to have super-confidence just when all hope was failing.[93]

In another, he underlined:

> The fundamental mistake of the Allied Generals was they failed to realise that war, like politics, is a two-party affair. They would never credit the enemy with an active role in opposition to theirs. Through the habit of mind induced by peace-training, with its staff and war games, they concentrated their minds on producing a plan that suited themselves without duly weighing the enemy's power to counter-act it. The importance of ensuring the enemy's distraction escaped them.[94]

For his 'advice', Liddell Hart received 100 guineas.[95]

In terms of 'vetting' the manuscript, Hankey persuaded Lloyd George to send chapters directly to him, just as he had done with Churchill, rather than go through the rigmarole of bothering the current prime minister with every twist and turn of the writing process. This put considerable strain on Hankey who, it should not be forgotten, was a busy man with many responsibilities. Lloyd George required him to scrutinise the material with breathtaking speed, a reflection of the former premier's demanding personality, but also of the tight publishing deadlines which had been agreed. Unsurprisingly, this led to the occasional conflict. Sylvester recalled one such episode in his diary:

> This morning Lloyd George asked me to find out if Hankey had read the manuscript I took to him. He was at a Cabinet meeting.

> I waited for him. He was rather narky. He said: how could Lloyd
> George expect him to have read such a lot during a weekend and
> especially when he had to read it carefully to check facts?[96]

In his self-appointed role as defender of secrecy, Hankey had several
concerns. While acknowledging that the war period was *sui generis*,
he was anxious to protect the confidentiality of Cabinet proceedings,
and this meant ensuring that the manuscript did not include wholesale
quotations from Cabinet minutes. Too many quotations would undermine the doctrine of collective responsibility, since they would expose
the opinions of particular ministers at the deliberative stages, before a
collective decision had been reached. Quotations, Hankey feared, had
the potential to inhibit freedom of expression among current ministers,
who might become chary about saying something contentious which
might later be recycled by one of their colleagues into a memoir.
Accordingly, Lloyd George was asked to keep direct quotations to a
minimum, and to use them only in cases where they were 'indispensable
to the historical presentation of the facts'.[97]

Lloyd George nevertheless refused to make sacrifices. As he
saw it, Hankey's request was unjustified. Politicians and former
members of the armed services had published memoirs replete with
documentary material, clearly with no regard to the sanctity of Cabinet
business. Many of these works reflected adversely on his conduct of
the war, and had unfairly left out relevant passages in order to build
their case against him. 'For fifteen years,' he protested, 'I have borne
with a stream of criticism polluted with much poisonous antagonism.'
He went on: 'The books published have all quoted secret documents.
My shelves groan under their mutilated bowdlerised quotations. I must
in all justice not to myself but to the public and posterity, tell the whole
truth.'[98] Such was Lloyd George's dogged determination to reveal
Cabinet documents that he threatened to send an unexpurgated version
to an American publisher, and a redacted version to a UK publishing
house. The latter, embarrassingly, would have blank passages where the
quotations should have been printed.[99] Hankey was aghast at Lloyd
George's threats and reminded him that when he, Lloyd George, was
premier, he had always respected Cabinet secrecy and had taken a dim
view of anyone who sought to undermine it by publishing documents.
In 1922, for example, when William Mackenzie King, the prime

minister of Canada, had asked for permission to quote from minutes of the Imperial War Cabinet, Lloyd George demurred to the publication of past proceedings, arguing that this would inevitably narrow the utility of future sessions.[100] Fast-forward ten years, Lloyd George was singing from a different hymn sheet.

Hankey's second concern was to ensure that the memoir did not overstep the bounds of decency in its treatment of officials and national leaders. Hankey deplored the personal attacks which, in his view, had tainted the literature of the war and which had, by extension, produced a flurry of angry authors demanding to publish evidence in refutation. No more clearly is this illustrated than in a letter sent to Lloyd George on 16 April 1934:

> I ask myself whether it is really to the public advantage that our national heroes should be hauled off their pedestals. It has somewhat the same effect as would be produced in the churches if some distinguished churchman were to marshal the historical evidence against the Saints! I also deprecate the possibility of a public controversy between the persons concerned in these events, with a competition of attack and counter-attack, involving intensive search of the official records for material.[101]

The problem for Hankey was that his job description was to protect official secrets, not official reputations. So far as the interpretive aspects of the memoirs were concerned, Lloyd George was well within his rights to tell the disapproving Cabinet Secretary to back down.

In the main, this is exactly what happened. When Lloyd George was urged to temper his polemical statements, his rejoinder was that Hankey had no right to censor the 'acerbities of truth'. Above all else, the Cabinet Secretary had wanted to lessen the obloquy heaped on the generals, particularly Haig and Sir William Robertson, the then Chief of the Imperial General Staff (CIGS). The memoir was not so much an indictment of the British High Command as a crucifixion. Inept, unimaginative and deceitful, the generals were held totally responsible for the sterile bloodbath of the Western Front. Armed with supporting documentation, Lloyd George told a harrowing story of how the fumbling generals had repeatedly launched their troops against the heavily defended German lines, in bovine deference to the antiquated military theory of the Napoleonic era, which had resulted in mass casualties, and against the better judgement of wise politicians back in London. Haig was on the receiving end of a myriad of tunnel-vision judgements designed to absolve Lloyd George from any blame for the carnage. Hankey had tried in vain to get the former premier to withdraw this material, conscious of the effect it would have on public opinion, and mindful of the potential for counter-revelation.

Hankey's struggle to spare the reputations of the generals resulted in a number of confrontations with Lloyd George, the most acrimonious relating to the book's treatment of the Third Battle of Ypres, also known as the Battle of Passchendaele. Buoyed by the comparative gains made at the offensive at Messines in June 1917, and believing that the German army was now close to collapse, Haig had conceived of Passchendaele as a 'big push', designed to force a breakthrough in the stalemate in Flanders and to capture the German submarine pens on the Belgian coast. However, what was prophesied as a decisive success became one of the most horrific attritional campaigns of the war. Within days of the launching of the drive on 31 July, the battlefield, previously idyllic countryside, resembled hell on earth. Torrential summer rain had turned the Ypres lowlands into an impassable, sodden bog, producing thick, clinging liquid mud, which coated uniforms and clogged rifles. The heavy two-week artillery barrage, which had poured more than 4 million shells into the German lines before the assault, had ground the site into potholes and dust, as well as destroying the drainage system in the area. The swamp became so cavernous that men, horses and packed mules drowned in it. As the troops thrashed about in the flooded marshland, the Germans, fortified with machine guns in concrete pill boxes, inflicted tremendous casualties. By November, three months of fierce fighting had produced gains of just eight kilometres, at the cost of 140,000 combat deaths – a ratio of approximately 2 inches gained per dead soldier.[102] In short, the campaign was a disaster on a truly epic scale, perhaps best summed up by Siegfried Sassoon's poetic epitaph, 'I died in hell – They called it Passchendaele'.

Lloyd George approached the subject of Passchendaele with a cold determination. For him, Passchendaele was to be the centrepiece of the memoir, a devastating critique of the nation's senior military figures during a period of national tragedy. He freely admitted that, when it came to the Third Battle of Ypres, he was 'not writing history

as a historian', but as a 'Solicitor in possession of the documents'.[103]
To this end, he spent a great deal of time drafting the relevant chapters.
According to Sylvester, Passchendaele 'was written, re-written and
re-written time after time'.[104] Lloyd George also interviewed countless
eye-witnesses and drew heavily on official sources. Sylvester recollected:
'Lloyd George had himself many talks with high-ranking officers: he
had masses of secret documents from CIGS and other Generals at home
and abroad, including Haig, from French sources, and from information
given daily to the Cabinet about losses. Moreover, he had a lot of
material privately coming from an official German source.'[105]

   The result was a character assassination of staggering vitriol.
Haig was presented as being in a state of constant self-deception in the
run-up to Passchendaele, learning nothing from the preceding three years
of catastrophe, which had seen the strategy of mounting massive frontal
assaults, designed to punch a hole in the German lines, fail disastrously up
and down the Western Front. 'The western strategists', claimed Lloyd
George, 'exaggerated the effect of every slight advance, and worked
themselves into a belief that the Germans were so pulverised by these
attacks that they had not the men, the guns, nor the spirit to fight
anywhere much longer ... This is no exaggeration of their illusions.
I saw them at this moment of exaltation.'[106] Haig's obstinate commitment to the flawed Western strategy was treated as an indication that he
was arrogant and, to some extent, drunk with power. 'Such is the intoxi-
cation produced by unlimited power', explained Lloyd George, even the
'slightest expression carries death or mutilation to myriads.'[107]

   In a cutting assessment, Lloyd George claimed that Haig was a
second-rate commander, possessing none of the qualities that had set
apart the great generals of the past: 'Haig was not endowed with the ...
discerning eye of a Cromwell, a Marlborough or a Stonewall Jackson.'[108] Specifically, Haig was accused of not having 'any of the elements of imagination and vision which determine the line of demarcation
between genius and ordinary'.[109] Slow of mind and stuck in the old
ways of warfare, including a blind faith in the cavalry charge, he was
simply incapable of springing a surprise on the enemy. Worst of all,
Haig was charged with lacking the personality that inspired the spirit of
sacrifice among men:

> The talk about the admiration, trust and affection felt by the
> men in the trenches for their leaders is utter nonsense. There were

> no legends of the *Petit Caporal* kind attached to any of the
> Generals. The soldiers never saw and cheered before a
> battle an impressive figure on a white horse. They hardly
> ever caught a glimpse of their Commanders except when a
> vision of burnished brass flew past in a motor car ... The legend
> of the men's faith in their leaders only flourished in the warmth
> and comfort of the home front; it never struck root in the
> trenches.[110]

Because of Haig, Passchendaele was a disaster waiting to happen. Lloyd George, who had wanted to fight defensively on the Western Front, at least until the Americans had started to arrive in Europe in decisive numbers, dedicated several chapters to describing how Haig, with customary stubbornness, scoffed at every attempt by the War Cabinet to shelve the assault; he was, it was emphasised, 'obsessed' with winning in Flanders, whatever the cost in human life. The argument was made – and backed up with documentary material – that Haig had deliberately misled the War Cabinet, hiding from its members a number of crucial details, including the French army's opposition to the offensive and the fact that the terrain in Ypres was vulnerable to rain and flooding.[111] Haig was reportedly given maps by the Tanks Corps Staff identifying the exact spots where an artillery bombardment would produce water-filled craters; his reply – 'Send no more of these ridiculous maps' – was an illustration that, in his mind, 'facts that interfered with plans were impertinencies'.[112] According to Lloyd George, Haig was asked by Hubert Gough, Commander of the Fifth Army, to put an end to the slaughter, but was pigheaded to the end.[113] With documents to prove his point, Lloyd George showed that Haig, astonishingly, had wanted to reopen Passchendaele in early 1918, a sign that the 'disastrous and costly failure' of the previous year had meant nothing to him.[114]

Hankey was shocked by the description of Passchendaele. He put it to Sylvester that Lloyd George had 'rather crabbed the general conception'.[115] The draft failed to mention that the objective had been to sweep the Belgian coast, suggesting instead that the intention, rather like at the Somme, was simply to continue 'throwing a hammer at a brick wall'.[116] Hankey was no fool and recognised that Lloyd George, in order to villainise Haig, had been selective in his use of evidence. For example, there was no mention of a telltale document which showed that Field Marshal Sir John French, Haig's predecessor as Commander-in-Chief of the BEF, had submitted a plan for a Passchendaele attack in January 1915; the draft had given the misleading impression that Haig had been the architect.[117] Hankey's main problem was that Lloyd George had been 'unnecessarily vehement' against Haig.[118] The draft was filled with insulting epithets. For example, Haig was said to be 'devoid of the gift of intelligible and coherent expression'.[119] As the Cabinet Secretary saw it, such passages had the potential to rebound negatively on Lloyd George, who would be accused by critics of having a personal spleen against Haig. Accordingly – while acknowledging that it was not his place to 'remove all the plums and spices from the cake' – he implored the former premier to temper some of the outbursts: 'my advice would be stand as far as possible on the documents and avoid any jibes. The more moderation you can show on the personal aspect – and I admit you have great provocation – the more conviction your chapter will carry, both today and before the bar of history.'[120] Lloyd George nevertheless refused to pull his punches. For him, the attack was the most important part of the book – designed to counter any suggestion that he, Lloyd George, as head of the wartime coalition government, should bear responsibility for the deaths of so many young men.

Hankey was also left frustrated in his attempts to persuade Lloyd George to curb some of the criticisms of politicians. The former premier's passion to 'tell the whole truth' had resulted in a merciless dressing down of key Liberal figures such as Herbert Samuel, Edward Grey and Reginald McKenna.[121] Vituperative comments were levelled at members of the National Government, including the former Chancellor Philip Snowden and the current prime minister, Ramsay MacDonald. MacDonald was labelled a traitor for his wartime support of pacifist activities. In a confidential letter to Sir Clive Wigram, the king's private secretary, Hankey lamented that Lloyd George, as a result of these personal attacks, 'will go down in history as lacking generosity'.[122]

Interestingly, the Cabinet Secretary did at least manage to sweet-talk Lloyd George into removing some 'frightfully damaging' remarks about Churchill. At the foot of page 24, in the first draft of Volume III, Chapter I, there was what Hankey described as a 'penetrating passage'. (Sadly, there is no record of this passage, either in the National Archives or in the Lloyd George papers; all that is known is that it began with the line: 'his mind is a powerful machine'.)[123] In

Hankey's view, the passage in question would 'always be quoted against him if he is ever in, or aspires to get into, office again'.[124] Hankey emphasised that he was not 'pleading' for Churchill on the ground that he was a 'friend', but because Churchill was 'rather down on his luck' and that the passage 'will hit him dreadfully'.[125] At the time, Britain's future leader was at a low point in his career, in a period retrospectively dubbed his 'wilderness years'. In addition to being out of office and estranged from the Conservative leadership over his opposition to Indian Home Rule, he had had several health scares and was experiencing financial hardship. In an uncharacteristic display of compassion, Lloyd George agreed to delete the offending passage.

In theory, by virtue of his position as head of the Privy Council, King George V had the final say on publication, since he could deny permission to publish Cabinet records. Although that he would do so was unlikely and without precedent, Hankey was not prepared to take any chances. In a bid to keep the sovereign sweet, he encouraged Lloyd George to interleave the memoir with 'some eulogistic references' to the king.[126] Specifically, he asked him to mention that the monarch, to set an example to the nation, had made regular visits to the front; had remained in London during air raids; and had gone 'dry', not touching a drop of alcohol, for the duration of the war. He also suggested that Lloyd George should make reference to the fact that the king had selflessly allowed his elder son to serve in the army and his younger son, the future George VI, to join the navy.[127] Lloyd George went along with Hankey's plan, not wanting to see his project scuppered by royal obstruction. This represented a major about-turn. Before, he had wanted to include a section on the build-up of an anti-monarchical movement in Britain, with several 'personal attacks upon the King'.[128] Only the strongest appeal from Hankey had dissuaded him from doing so.

The king sent word, through Wigram, that he was delighted with the material that discussed his contribution to the war effort, and he endorsed publication of the memoir. However, he also let it be known that he deplored the derogatory references to MacDonald, and demanded their deletion. Lloyd George exploded. He interpreted the king's meddling as an indication that, deep down, the monarch did not like the book and wanted to see it scythed to the point of being unpublishable. 'Why should the king be against my book?' he shouted down the phone to Sylvester.[129] George V, he continued, had 'raised no objection to what was said about me [by other writers], yet when I am about to defend myself he does not'.[130] Lloyd George, who suspected that the king had been pressured by MacDonald (the latter being a friend of the royal household), defiantly refused to be gagged: 'He can go to Hell. I owe him nothing; he owes his throne to me.'[131] According to Stevenson, interference from the Palace only served to strengthen Lloyd George's determination to attack MacDonald, so much so that he actually redrafted passages as a result, making them even 'more hostile and vehement'.[132]

The final hurdle for Lloyd George was getting political approval from HMG. Strictly speaking, he was obliged to apply to the prime minister, but as Lloyd George considered MacDonald 'a conceited, jealous fellow, [who] might try to scotch the book', he looked instead for an alternative member of the coalition.[133] Hankey arranged for Stanley Baldwin, then Lord President of the Council, to make the final judgement. Baldwin was the logical choice. He had already read large portions of the manuscript and, although he too was distressed by the petulant outbursts, had declared himself in favour of publication. On 22 June 1933, at a private meeting at the Pall Mall Club in London, he had said to Lloyd George: 'You are the last of the lot to write. You are entitled to produce your case and any document which enables you to prepare it, you may have.'[134] Moreover, by choosing Baldwin, who for some time had been de facto prime minister (on account of MacDonald's failing health), Lloyd George obviated any suspicion that he had not played by the rules. In the event, Lloyd George need not have worried about MacDonald, who finally read the memoir in April 1934. Despite calling it 'reprehensible' and 'one of the most colossal confessions of ignorance ... that I have ever read', he informed Hankey that he would take a strange pleasure from its publication, since one day he would respond with a memoir written 'with such care' that Lloyd George would be made to look a fool.[135] Alas, he passed away in 1937 without writing a word.

With Baldwin's approval, the memoirs were published in six successive volumes between late 1933 and winter 1936. As Suttie has argued, the level of anticipation was positively giddy.[136] Lloyd George was not only one of the most important statesmen of modern times, but also one of the most controversial. With the exception of Hankey, who was unknown outside government circles, he was the last major personality of the war to give his version of events. Moreover, there was no one more qualified to provide the inside story of the decision making that accompanied and drove the British war effort. Whereas Churchill, 'the other great memoirist', had spent parts of the war out of office, Lloyd George had been at the heart of the political core executive from start to finish, first as Chancellor, then as minister of munitions, next as secretary of state for war, and finally as prime minister.[137] With the public waiting with bated breadth, Lloyd George was in a strong position with potential publishers and, true to form, managed to secure lucrative contracts. Ivor Nicholson and Watson secured the British book rights with an offer of £10,000 plus royalties, Little, Brown and Company purchased the American rights for $12,000, and the *Daily Telegraph* snapped up the serialisation rights for £25,000.[138] Although small by comparison to the aborted contracts of 1922, in the depressed economic climate of the 1930s this was good money, bringing total earnings of approximately £65,000. The former premier was delighted and made a habit of boasting to friends that, at a time of unparalleled depression, he had made 'five times as much (and more)' than Churchill. The latter was said to be 'staggered' at the sums.[139]

Each volume was widely reviewed, the text scrutinised for indications of whitewashing, guilt and regret. Swinton was right when he predicted that there would be some folk awaiting the memoirs with 'guns and clubs'.[140] Hostile reviews, penned in most cases by ex-servicemen, castigated the bitter attacks directed at Haig and the High Command, branding them obscene and suggestive of an author unwilling to accept his share of the blame. No one was more vexed by these broadsides than Major-General Sir Frederick Maurice, Director of Military Operations under Robertson, who published a stream of rebuttals in the press. Maurice's condemnation was hardly surprising; he and Lloyd George had 'history'. In May 1918, Maurice had put his career on the line by writing a letter to *The Times* in which he baldly accused the premier of deceiving Parliament about the number of British troops serving on the Western Front during the German spring offensive. The letter's publication caused a storm. In Parliament, Lloyd George turned the tables on Maurice by revealing that the figures he had used had in fact come from Maurice's office, rather than the prime minister's. Following this revelation, Maurice was forcibly retired by the army for a grave breach of discipline. Other critics of the memoir included Sir Edward Carson, former First Lord of the Admiralty.

Carson took umbrage at the suggestion that Lloyd George, in the battle against German U-boats, had initiated the convoy system against the wishes of the Admiralty, calling it 'the biggest lie ever told'.[141] The memoir's blend of *suggestio falsi* and *suggestio veri* also aroused resentment from former members of the War Office, who decried the claim that Lloyd George had mobilised the country's munitions production.

At a time when most government records were walled off from public view, and when individuals like Mackenzie were taken to court for revealing classified information, the extent to which Lloyd George had quoted freely from supposedly 'secret' papers did not go unnoticed. Kingsley Martin, editor of the *New Statesmen and Nation*, was astonished by the 'crushing array of official documents' that had been included.[142] The hypocrisy was obvious, with many critics questioning how he had avoided prosecution. In public, officials refused to rise to the bait, unprepared to admit that Lloyd George, as a former prime minister with a cavalier contempt for the 'rules', was effectively above the law and impossible to restrain. Not a word was mentioned about how hard it had been to keep the uncompromising Welshman on the straight and narrow. In private, however, officials knew that the Lloyd George memoir was a dangerous precedent and a testament to the fact that they had lost a measure of control over classified information.

Inevitably, the government was soon inundated with requests from people wanting to inspect closed materials. John Maynard Keynes, who during the war had been a senior adviser in the Treasury, was baffled by the inclusion, in Volume II of Lloyd George's memoirs, of paragraphs from a minute attributed to him and allegedly shown to the War Cabinet in September 1915.[143] Keynes, who had 'little or no memory of its contents', demanded to have a copy: 'Since it has been quoted from fairly extensively in print, and made the basis of an attack on a Civil Servant by a Cabinet Minister of the day, presumably it is regarded as a public document.'[144] With this, Hankey was made to squirm, before eventually falling back on the technical argument that Keynes, as a former civil servant, was 'free neither to publish nor to defend what he wrote in an official capacity'.[145] In the 'interests' of the civil service, Keynes did not take the matter any further, although he did warn that the government was playing with fire if it persisted in allowing ministers to write abusive comments about their advisers.

Another person who appealed for access to documents was the widow of the deceased War Cabinet minister Lord Milner.[146] Her grievance was that Lloyd George had quoted extracts from a memorandum written by her late husband, giving the former prime minister the means by which to charge that Milner and his staff, while in Russia in 1917, had failed to foresee and warn HMG of the impending outbreak of the Bolshevik Revolution. Lady Milner, who was putting together a biography of her husband, asked to see the memorandum in question so that she could assess the accuracy of Lloyd George's claim. Hankey approached the request with 'very great care'.[147] By allowing a 'non-official person' access to official records, the state could find itself in the awkward position of being unable to deny the same privilege to historians. Hankey recommended that the government make a clear distinction between, on the one hand, historians who desired to see records simply in order to produce a 'better book' and, on the other hand, individuals of 'good title', like Lady Milner, who needed to vindicate the memory of a dead statesman and claimed that that memory had been injured by an authorised publication.[148] Hankey's neat bit of footwork was welcomed by the Cabinet, and Lady Milner became the first person to benefit from what was called the 'extended' vindicator principle.

The problems associated with the Lloyd George memoirs weighed heavily on Hankey's mind, and convinced him that the Cabinet Secretariat had to do something to stem the tide of revelatory political autobiographies. As he saw it, unless steps were taken, the situation was only going to get worse. Recent cases had shown that, even in cash-strapped times, publishers and newspapers were prepared to offer vast sums in order to tempt politicians into making richly documented disclosures. The *Daily Telegraph*, which claimed to have increased its circulation by 350,000 copies as a result of the Lloyd George serialisation, was so delighted with the return that it was believed to be drawing up bumper contracts for a host of potential memoirists.[149] Hankey's plan was to make life more difficult for would-be authors by creating stricter guidelines, akin to those rejected in 1919, which ruled that, on vacating office, ministers had to return all papers to the Cabinet Secretariat.

Securing political approval for this plan was always going to be difficult. Experience had shown that ministers, while in office, were chary about creating rules which might come back to bite them when they were preparing their memoirs. Luckily for Hankey, events transpired to make his plan a reality. On 6 March 1934, the danger of ministers retaining their papers was confirmed when Edgar Lansbury, the son of the Leader of the Opposition, published a biography of his father, George, which included unauthorised quotations from two Cabinet memorandums. The documents had been written by his father when he had been First Commissioner of Works in the Labour Government of 1929–31.[150] The state's reaction to this disclosure was swift and harsh. Copies of the biography were immediately pulled from bookstores, and two weeks later Edgar was convicted under the Official Secrets Act, being fined £25 and 25 guineas costs.[151] Angry recriminations followed. As with Compton Mackenzie, the government was accused of trying to frighten more eminent figures like Lloyd George and Churchill, without actually taking action against them. Some journalists speculated that the real objective had been indirect retribution against George Lansbury, who was suspected of leaking to the *Daily Herald* the names of Cabinet ministers, now in the National Government, who had blocked his social policies in 1931.[152] For many critics, the most shameful aspect of the affair was that George Lansbury himself, the person to blame for communicating the documents in the first place, was not prosecuted along with his son. The conclusion drawn from this oversight was that men of status were not bound by the same laws as everyone else.

Under fire, the National Government saw the logic behind Hankey's plan. On 21 March, the day after Lansbury's conviction, the Cabinet passed a rule requiring future ministers to return all Cabinet papers and minutes on leaving office. 'The moment', it was emphasised, 'was considered opportune for taking action owing to a recent case in the Law Courts.'[153] HMG also instructed Hankey to write to all living ex-ministers, (or, in the case of the deceased, to their representatives), requesting that they return any Cabinet papers in their possession. The task of recovering documents from the custody of former ministers was not going to be easy, because of the headstrong individuals that were involved. Howorth accepted that some would 'doubtless refuse', but hoped that many would see this as an opportunity to clear their homes of clutter.[154] Indeed, as part of the deal, former ministers were told that they could still consult their papers in the Cabinet Office. In total, 87 former ministers (or their executors) were invited to surrender their papers.[155] By November

1935, Hankey was delighted to report that the majority had complied, leaving only 8 rebels.[156] One of the hold-outs, the former Liberal Minister of Health Christopher Addison, had made the argument: 'If a man is trustworthy enough to be a Cabinet minister, he is trustworthy enough to treat his papers decently.'[157]

For Hankey, the most frustrating aspect of the attempted document retrieval was, again, that the biggest names in politics refused to adhere to the codes of practice. The most notable renegades were the 'two great memoir writers of the wartime generation' – Churchill and Lloyd George.[158] Churchill, wise to the intricacies of the law, pinned his case on the argument that, like his father, he had executed a deed specifying that no state papers in his personal collection could be printed 'without the written consent of Her Majesty's Government'.[159] Lloyd George did not even attempt to explain his refusal to relinquish his holdings, saying simply, 'I am in no mood to surrender them.'[160] Thought was given to strong-arming the 'giants', but, on reflection, nobody had the nerve to do so. On one occasion, Hankey asked a member of his staff, Lawrence Burgis, to meet Churchill at Chartwell to discuss the issue. As a near neighbour of Churchill, Burgis was seen as the ideal person to make a polite request. So in awe of Churchill was he, that it took him nearly two hours even to raise the topic, in which time he had been required to listen to a succession of monologues, clearly designed as misdirection. When Burgis finally did pluck up the courage, Churchill responded nonchalantly, 'I'll give you the abridged version of my *World Crisis* instead,' to which he had no comeback.[161]

* * *

Probably the large Civil Service element – who
have always been against the Cabinet Office and generally
obscurantist – have had something to say.
Maurice Hankey, 29 March 1945[162]

In July 1938, Hankey resigned as Cabinet Secretary and the responsibility of protecting secrecy from troublesome memoirists passed to his successor, Treasury official Edward Bridges. Bridges deplored the outpouring of secrets that had followed the end of the Great War. Unlike his predecessor, he was unsympathetic to the argument that politicians had a right to spill the beans if their reputation had been harmed in some way. As he saw it, the real motivation for most writers was to settle scores and earn enormous sums of money; in short, the vindicator clause allowed for a multitude of sins. With Bridges at the helm, an increasing number of authors were denied the opportunity to publish, starting with Admiral Lord Chatfield, Minister for the Coordination of Defence from 1939 to 1940. Submitted in late June 1941, Chatfield's memoir explored, amongst other things, the responsibility for Britain's unpreparedness for the Second World War. Written in 'the most controversial, tendentious and *ex parte* manner possible', the manuscript was filled with items considered unsuitable by Bridges, including references to the intelligence services and disparaging comments about Britain's new wartime ally, the Soviet Union.[163] In one passage, Chatfield had claimed that visitors to the East were always struck by the 'Russian smell'.[164] In briefing the War Cabinet, Bridges suggested that the effect of publication on national unity would be 'deplorable', even going as far as to argue that it 'might cause the Government to break up'.[165] The alarmism of style inherent in Bridges' assessment was enough to persuade ministers. On 21 November, the War Cabinet forbade publication on the grounds that it would be inimical to the war effort.[166] Tellingly, however, the prime minister, Winston Churchill, also emphasised that 'far greater latitude' could be given when the war was over. 'There are only a few things', he suggested, 'which should never be mentioned.'[167] As David Reynolds has argued, 'doubtless the Enigma secret lay behind Churchill's second sentence, while anticipation of his own memoirs probably prompted the first'.[168]

In a remarkable turn-up for the books, the most controversial casualty of Bridges' tough stance was none other than Hankey. On 22 September 1943, the fabled guardian of Cabinet secrecy stunned his former employers by announcing that he had written a book about the Great War, entitled *The Supreme Command*, and that he was anxious to get it vetted.[169] In a letter to Bridges, he explained that he had yet to approach a publisher, 'remembering the strain which used to be put upon me having war books thrown at my head in proof form which had to be dealt with in unseemly haste because the author had to fulfil a contract with his publisher'.[170] Bridges' kneejerk response was to prevaricate as much as possible in the hope that the problem would simply go away. Accordingly, he did not respond definitively to Hankey until March 1944; in the interim he sent the latter a succession of apologetic letters containing phoney arguments about being called away on other business. Behind the scenes, however, with Hankey in blissful ignorance, Bridges had in fact been plotting his next move, seeking advice from the Treasury solicitor, Sir Thomas Barnes, about how the government might proceed in the event that Hankey failed to take the hint. Bridges' primary concern was to stop the book for fear that it would set off a new wave of disclosures. Of course, this was no argument on which to build a case against publication; Hankey would never accept it. With this, Bridges decided that the most effective argument was to emphasise that the memoir, in its present condition, said too much about the confidential relationship between ministers and their advisers, and was therefore against the public interest and contrary to the canons of civil service tradition. Hankey, Bridges hoped, should need little convincing on this score. As Cabinet Secretary, he had prided himself on being the keeper of his own conscience; in his dealings with authors, moreover, he had routinely used the same argument.

In the event, Bridges was only successful in buying himself more time. Rather than shelve the book, Hankey spent several months making corrections and excisions in an attempt to alleviate his successor's concerns.[171] On 27 October, he resubmitted the manuscript, accompanied by a covering letter underlining that it had been decided 'long ago' that books about the Great War were to be treated as *sui generis*. By this point, he had also verbally agreed a contract with Cassells, the terms of which specified that he was to receive a £5,000 advance and a generous percentage royalty of 20 per cent.[172] (Unbeknownst to the Cabinet Office, Hankey had broken the Official Secrets Act by showing the entire draft to the publisher's proprietor, Newman Flower, who considered it 'one of the greatest books to appear from Cassells in my time'.)[173] With a publisher now in the picture, Bridges had to move more quickly. After a few weeks deliberating, he informed Hankey that publication was out of the question. Despite the changes, the book still exposed the working of the trusted relationship between civil servants and their masters.[174] In doing so, it would have a 'very unfortunate effect'; civil servants would become more self-conscious in their dealings with the Cabinet, while ministers would be 'more chary' of speaking freely to members of the Secretariat. In Bridges' view, *The Supreme Command* was particularly damaging in this respect since the general tenor stressed 'how much was done by the advisers of ministers in preparing material for them, and drafting passages for their speeches or giving them advice'.[175] The inference drawn by the public would be that the senior civil service was exercising far more power than constitutional arrangements permitted. Bridges also told Hankey that he was shocked to discover that, on a closer inspection of the manuscript, it was based on a diary that the latter had maintained, seemingly in secret, during his time in Whitehall Gardens: 'I cannot escape the conclusion that the knowledge that such a record could be kept and used as a basis for published memoirs would have a very bad effect.'[176]

Hankey was devastated. Nearly three quarters of a million words in length, the book had taken several years of hard graft to produce. In double-quick time, he wrote back to Bridges explaining that the arguments against publication were 'wholly groundless', chiefly because 'so much had been said already' by politicians and generals in their memoirs.[177] Hankey also objected to the implication that he should not have penned a diary. Always firmly bound and locked, it had been conceived during the early days of the war, serving as an invaluable record of decisions and conversations at a time when few other notes were taken.[178] Moreover, there had never been the slightest secret about its existence. Indeed, his diary had been strongly encouraged by Lloyd George, who had routinely used it to keep track of events. Tired of Bridges' stubbornness, Hankey decided to put the matter up to a higher authority, namely Churchill. In advance of this, he appealed to former colleagues, including Lloyd George, asking if they would inform the prime minister that they approved of the book.[179] On 8 December, equipped with endorsements from a host of distinguished supporters, he wrote a cleverly argued letter to Churchill stating that the events discussed in the book were at least a quarter of a century old and had passed into history. He underlined that descriptions of those same events lay scattered in the pages of countless publications, many of which had gloried in the revelation of what was said and done between ministers and advisers. He made the technical point that, during the war, his status was that of a Service Staff Officer, rather than that of a civil servant. Most cuttingly of all, he invited Churchill to remember that, 'I myself had some misgivings about *The World Crisis* and other memoirs just after the war, but on reflection I came to the conclusion that this consideration was outweighed by their contribution to history.'[180]

Irony abounded as Churchill declined to return the favour. On 23 February 1945, he sent word through Bridges that 'the War Cabinet have reached the conclusion that publication ... would not be in the public interest', principally because it 'would be destructive of the special relationship between Ministers and their chief advisers'.[181] In making this decision, the premier showed himself to be no supporter of civil servants writing memoirs. In effect, the Great War was only *sui generis* as far as ministers were concerned. Hankey was appalled and made his feelings known to a trusted former colleague, Tom Jones, an erstwhile Deputy Secretary to the Cabinet: 'It is astonishing that Churchill, who was practically the first to publish all the inner secrets with [Admiral John] Fisher, and so many intimate and confidential letters, should have the effrontery to turn me down.'[182] Hankey suspected that the real motivation for banning the book was that 'the historian who studies [it] will sometimes find that Churchill was wrong'.[183] Himself a diarist, Jones was initially sympathetic, calling the government's decision a 'bombshell'.[184] 'I hardly imagined it', he wrote on 1 March, 'because of the great freedom with which documents have been drawn upon and published by our masters, and by the present Prime Minister especially, in recent years.'[185] A month later, however, after he had read the complete typescript and not simply the 'headlines', his attitude had changed: 'I am not surprised that the Cabinet should hesitate to pass these volumes ... It is bound to have a profound effect on habits of future Secretaries to the Cabinet and Ministers, and the financial temptations for revelations will be great.'[186] 'My notion', he concluded, 'had been that only a distant posterity would see our diaries.'[187] Hankey confessed that he was 'rather shaken' by Jones' change of heart, but still maintained that Churchill was in the wrong: '27 years have elapsed since the final episode in my book.'[188]

In a final bid to get the ban lifted, Hankey sent Bridges a lengthy memorandum perfectly calculated to expose the hypocrisy in Churchill's decision. With reference to a staggering 59 volumes of memoirs and biographies published since the end of the Great War, it made the case that 'rightly or wrongly almost everything that can be revealed has been revealed'.[189] To illustrate this, Hankey skilfully drew Bridges' attention to Chapter 5 from *The World Crisis*, which contained no less than 25 quotations from official documents relating to the month of January 1915 alone. Equally damaging, Hankey reproduced a passage from Volume VI of Lloyd George's reminiscences revealing that the former premier had quoted from Hankey's diary:

'Fortunately, I had access to the most careful official diary of current events – and of the discussions that led to them – which has ever been penned, Hankey's Minutes of War Cabinets, Imperial Cabinets and Inter-Allied Conferences ... My memoirs are based on this mass of contemporaneous documents.'[190] Most devastatingly of all, Hankey quoted the following extract from the preface to *The World Crisis, 1915*: 'It is absurd to argue that the facts should not be fully published, or that obligations of secrecy are violated by their disclosure in good faith. Thousands of facts have been made public and hundreds of secret matters exposed.'[191] Hankey underlined that, although he too had had misgivings, the inter-war battle of the books had 'never caused a ripple in the relations of ministers and their civil servants' and for Churchill suddenly to make a new rule, ad hoc, applying to a single individual whose status differed from that of previous writers, involved a 'discrimination that is untenable'.[192]

The protest was in vain as the War Cabinet stuck by its decision. The matter then dropped off everyone's list of priorities because of the general election of July 1945. As we shall see later in this book, Hankey would spend the rest of his life trying to get the ban overturned; by the time it was, the story of the Great War had been crowded out by a new chapter of history and a new generation of autobiographies, spearheaded by Churchill's six-volume Second World War histories (1948–54). It is hard not to feel sorry for Hankey, especially if we consider that, throughout the Second World War, Churchill abused his position as premier to make life easy for himself when it came to the business of post-war memoir writing. Not wanting to be hamstrung by rules prohibiting the use of official papers, he took the precaution of instructing his staff to print in galley form all of the minutes and correspondence that had been written under his name.[193] These were branded explicitly the 'Prime Minister's Personal Minutes' and were kept for safe keeping in large bound volumes at his Chartwell home. Similarly, his communications with Roosevelt and Stalin were copied and labelled 'My Personal Telegrams', 'doubtless to pre-empt Cabinet Office claims that such papers were government property'.[194] Equally as self-serving, in 1943 he permitted the publication of *Wings of Destiny*, the memoir of Lord Londonderry, who had been Secretary of State for Air (1931–5) and was best remembered for his high-profile promotion of Anglo-German friendship. Bridges had wanted to see the book go the same way as Chatfield's ill-fated memoir. Considering Londonderry 'more troublesome than the scoundrel Lansbury', he put it to ministers that by allowing publication they would create a dangerous precedent, since *Wings of Destiny* would become the first memoir to go beyond 1918 and its immediate aftermath and publish documents pertaining to peacetime: 'No doubt we shall have quite enough trouble on that when the war is over, but need not anticipate it.'[195] Churchill, however, sensed an opportunity and seized it. With his 'literary' rather than 'official' hat on, he agreed to publication knowing that one day he too would want to write about appeasement and publish documents on the origins of the war. The naked self-interest was not lost on Bridges, but there was nothing he could do or say to bring an about-turn. 'I really think pre-1935 is ancient history,' ruled Churchill.[196]

The most blatant example of Churchill exploiting his power as prime minister came in May 1945 when, with the coalition on the verge of breaking up, he forced through a last-minute policy change on the guardianship of official documents. Sensing trouble, Bridges had earlier prepared a memorandum to remind departing ministers of the rule, adopted in 1934, requiring them to leave behind all official papers. Remembering the advantages of the more liberal 1919 rules, Churchill was having none of it and asked the Cabinet Secretary to draft a revised memorandum that allowed for ministers, on leaving office, to take with them copies of any document that they themselves had written. This was done and approved by Churchill himself on 23 May 1945.[197] A week later, with the coalition now at an end, giant horse boxes could again be seen parked outside government buildings loaded with bundles of papers. Following in the footsteps of Lloyd George et al., departing ministers including Hugh Dalton, Leo Amery and Anthony Eden raided countless filing cabinets, all in anticipation of producing memoirs.[198] In short, the stage was set for a repeat of the disclosure of secrets which had followed the Great War.

Part II

Secrecy and the press

3 CHAPMAN PINCHER: SLEUTHING THE SECRET STATE

> We believe that Mr Chapman Pincher, of whom you have probably heard, will try and get into your Depot to gather certain material for publication. It is most unlikely that he will arrive openly under his own name. To assist your police in recognising him, we enclose a photo. He should not, of course, be admitted and we should be grateful if you would advise us if he appears, giving as much information as you can. Ie. Date and time of 'visit', name used, names of any other persons with him or sponsoring him. It is important that this matter should be kept strictly to yourself and your police and they should be warned to this effect. We should be grateful if you destroy this letter when read.
>
> SECURITY OFFICER, MINISTRY OF SUPPLY,
> *early 1950s*[1]

The next three chapters of this book consider the extent to which the British press, during the Cold War, promoted the public's 'right to know' and rolled back the frontiers of government secrecy. Arguably, when most people think about journalists striving to unearth the secrets of state, they tend to associate that sort of activity with the American media – and with good reason. From the 1960s onwards, the ability to uncover abuses and write about highly sensitive matters became a respected dimension of the US fourth estate, a yardstick by which good journalism was measured. With the First Amendment providing journalists with an extraordinary degree of formal constitutional protection, the American press filed exposé after exposé, serving as a vital check against the unlawful exercise of state power. In his memoir *Facing Reality*, former CIA officer Cord Meyer referred to a 'drumfire of editorial denunciation ... that swept across the country'.[2] High-profile revelations began in 1967 when the muckraking California magazine *Ramparts* revealed that the CIA had been making secret subsidies to the National Student Association. In 1971, Daniel Ellsberg, a senior military analyst, made headlines around the world when he leaked to the press the Pentagon Papers – the top-secret Department of Defence history of the Vietnam War. President Richard Nixon had asked for restraining orders, only for the Supreme Court to rule otherwise. Not long after this, two young reporters from the *Washington Post*, Bob Woodward and Carl Bernstein, splashed onto the broadsheets revelations of serious wrongdoing in the White House, including the cover-up of Watergate, the Nixon-inspired burglary of the Democratic Party headquarters in Washington, DC. In their dogged attempt to unravel the scandal, Woodward and Bernstein examined telephone and bank records, followed up each and every lead, and interviewed dozens of officials, including Deep Throat – America's most famous anonymous source.[3] For their part in bringing about the President's downfall, the two men were awarded the Pulitzer Prize. In the years following, journalists such as Seymour Hersh, Jack Nelson and Daniel Schorr achieved national stardom on account of their investigative reporting.

Historiographical orthodoxy has tended to dictate that the British press, by contrast, was remarkably timid when it came to exposing secrets. According to Ann Rogers, the UK 'media have been more likely to contribute to, rather than mitigate, secrecy in Britain'.[4] This argument has a long lineage. As noted above, Ernest Bevin, Clement Attlee's straight-talking Foreign Secretary, once said: 'Why bother to muzzle sheep?' US commentators have been quick to point out that adversarial investigative journalism is not a feature of British political life. In his seminal account *The Torment of Secrecy*, Edward Shils wrote: 'The British journalist, in his dealings with the government, handles himself as if he were an inferior of the person clothed with the majesty of office.'[5] Various reasons have been given for why this has been the case. The explanation most commonly put forward is that journalists were stymied by the Official Secrets Act. Because of the Act, argued E. P. Thompson, 'in Britain a "Watergate" could not have occurred'.[6] For Rogers, the media's reluctance to dig into the workings of the secret state reflects the fact that journalists are cut from the same cloth as their governmental counterparts. Unlike American journalists, who grew up on university campuses rife with political activism and anti-Establishment rhetoric, the press corps in England were white male Oxbridge graduates with a cognitive orientation 'engendered by general class, cultural, social and financial allegiances'.[7] Out of respect for their brethren in government, therefore, they would not probe too deeply into certain areas and would gladly toe the line. Richard Crossman detected this in a leading article for the *New Statesmen* in September 1971: 'If the truth be told, the press lords are members of the closed society which ensures that so much of the information available to government remains "inside knowledge", and that well-informed discussion of the great issues of state is the privilege of a tight little oligarchy which hoards the truth as squirrels hoard their winter food supply.'[8]

Influenced by Marxist media theory, which emphasises that the press is a capitalist enterprise fatally compromised by its involvement in the profit nexus, scholars such as John Jenks have attributed the press's obedience to the so-called 'beat structure' of post–Second World War journalism.[9] Because the livelihood of a political journalist is dependent upon government departments providing him or her with a steady stream of newsworthy material, it is not in Fleet Street's interest to challenge the status quo. For a journalist to do so would put him or her out of business – unless, of course, he or she were prepared to join the ranks of the less commercially successful radical press. Other scholars suggest that the cause of Britain's deferential press is the lobby system. Established in 1884, the lobby grants a coterie of accredited journalists the licence to enter parts of Westminster that other journalists cannot reach, where they will receive 'ready to wear' briefings from MPs and ministers. The golden rule underlying this arrangement is that, while the details of the briefing might be published, lobby correspondents should never disclose the source of their information. Typically, a lobby-inspired article will report that the story came from a 'senior government figure' or a 'Whitehall source'. For many years, the engine-room of the system was a drinking den known as Annie's Bar. Given a makeover by the late Robert Maxwell in 1967, the exclusive watering hole was jokingly referred to as the only place in Westminster where MPs could escape their constituents; before major debates, Winston Churchill could often be found there taking a whiskey stiffener.[10] Criticism of the lobby takes several forms. Noteworthy critics such as Peter Kellner argue that lobby correspondents 'get sucked into ... representing the interests of an institution of government'.[11] Under editorial pressure to fill up columns of newsprint, they accept what is given to them at face value. That material, say opponents, will be supportive of executive decisions. The system, moreover, can also be used to fly kites. If, for example, a minister is uncertain whether a particular course of action or policy will sit well with the public, he or she can 'dry run' that idea by briefing the lobby. The Cabinet Secretary Robert Armstrong (1979–87) once commented that the lobby system could be wielded by officials 'to influence opinion without accepting responsibility'.[12]

It is this contention of this chapter and the next two that the British press was far more troublesome to the secret state than has hitherto been acknowledged. In recent years, many files have made their way to the National Archives that are revealing of media–state relations. The work of the D-Notice Committee is well-documented in certain MoD papers. Cabinet files include minutes of high-level meetings between ministers and their advisers on the subject of the press. The picture that emerges from these files is evocative of a shoot-out in the Wild West, with a band of gun-toting reporters at one end of the street and a frightened government at the other, protected by its bureaucracy. For many journalists, the ability to sniff out secrets became more than a vocation; it was a calling. 'Reading a Cabinet minute always induces a certain frisson in a journalist,' claimed Peter Hennessy, then Whitehall correspondent for *The Times*, in October 1978. 'Reproducing it in a newspaper', he continued, 'is even better. The sense of illicit pleasure is probably the only happy effect of the blancmange of secrecy in which Whitehall embeds itself.'[13] In the period following the Second World War, leading members of Fleet Street became less fearful of the Official Secrets Act, working on the assumption that, because their sources were men of status, no government would dare involving them in what would inevitably be a high-profile court case. Just as alarming for the guardians of official secrecy was the fact that Fleet Street became increasingly skilled and courageous in its pursuit of sensitive information. Journalists quickly learned that the best secrets could often be found in the United States and from American sources. One of the biggest challenges for the secret state was how to prevent globe-trotting hacks from publishing damaging articles based on information whose provenance was foreign, so that it was not covered by UK law. After 1945, journalists also developed a much better aptitude for 'grooming' official contacts. Just as intelligence services during the Cold War were constantly looking to exploit the character flaws of public servants, Fleet Street too had an eye for 'talent spotting'. Officials who suffered from 'peacock syndrome' (deriving pleasure from letting lesser mortals know that they possessed access to secrets)[14] would have no trouble locating a journalist to remind them how 'special' they were. Those with a weakness for alcohol would find a journalist only too willing to supply the necessary lubricant. It is important to underline that the reporter's aim was not to get the official drunk, for this could elicit false confessions, but to create an ambience of good fellowship and masculine bonhomie. *In vino veritas*!

To explore and highlight the changes that took place in Fleet Street during the post-war period, much of the early analysis will be focused on the journalistic career of Chapman Pincher (Figure 4), defence correspondent for the *Daily Express* from the end of the Second World War to 1979. A life-and-times biographical study of Pincher's career is highly revealing of the assault that was made by the press on the bastions of official secrecy. Through his eyes, one gets a real sense of just how difficult it became for the state to go about its business in silence, in the face of forceful media action. At the risk of sounding sycophantic, Pincher was Fleet Street's greatest scoop-merchant; he led the journalistic pack. Considering himself the people's watchdog, bridging the cleft between the exercise of political authority and the extent to which that authority was accountable to the public, Pincher revelled in publishing information which was meant to be secret. For his stories, Arthur Christiansen, editor of the *Daily Express* from 1932 to 1956, gave him his very own 'Column of Disclosure'. Setting the seal on Pincher's fame and earning him a considerable personal following, the column became what is known in the trade of journalism as a 'circulation prop' – a part of any newspaper that guarantees a certain amount of sales. As such, it was remarkably free of editorial interference; indeed, Christiansen's successors were told that they could tamper with anything except Pincher's column. So valuable was the column to the newspaper, editors resisted the urge to move Pincher upstairs into an executive role ('I had no interest in the mechanics of newspapers – only in the investigative role');[15] they also defended him to the hilt whenever he came under fire from outraged government departments or affronted officials.

Pincher had a truly jaw-dropping ability to get a scoop. With a generous travel budget from the *Express*, he scoured the world, especially North America, in search of sensitive information. His talent for getting secrets out through the back door of Whitehall was second to none. A sociable fellow who moved effortlessly in exalted circles, Pincher was capable of goading even the most tight-lipped of crown servants into making unauthorised disclosures. Although unaware of it at the time, he pioneered a method of journalism based on developing close personal relationships with high-placed sources. Bibulous lunches and absorptive social evenings were used to great effect, if at great personal expense (Figure 5). Pincher, moreover, was ahead of the game in realising that shooting syndicates, fishing fraternities and the like had powerful members who liked to talk shop and gossip about colleagues. In a recent interview, he recalled: 'On a shooting party, everyone's guard is down. You're chums and the conversation flows.'[16] One of the most interesting aspects of Pincher's career is that, while most individuals in the secret state deplored his investigative reporting, and put countless obstacles in his way, there was always a small coterie of indiscreet officials who could not resist feeding his ever-restless pen. Pincher's intimacy with certain groups in Whitehall has prompted some critics to label him 'less an operator than the tool of other operators'.[17] In a memorably bitter philippic, E. P. Thompson described him as an 'official urinal' where government spin-doctors queued up to leak.[18] Thompson also accused the great scoop-gatherer of colluding with right-wing elements to defame the Labour Party. Too many stories, he claimed, betrayed the hallmarks of a political vendetta against the Left. On the question of whether Pincher should have relied so heavily on 'off-the-record' leaks, the journalist has always maintained that if the information is accurate, exclusive and newsworthy, then it does not matter where it comes from. In what follows, it should become clear that Pincher was nobody's poodle and was capable of causing as many problems for the Right as for the Left.

* * *

Chapman Pincher's activities and revelations have been a source of embarrassment, particularly in the defence field, for years.
Ministry of Defence leak enquiry, September 1976[19]

Pincher joined the *Express* as a science correspondent in summer 1945. The newspaper's proprietor, Lord Beaverbrook (Figure 6), wanted someone with a scientific background to write specialist articles on the atomic bomb. Pincher was suitably qualified. A biology graduate from King's College London, in 1941 he had been posted to the Military College of Science, where he helped with the development and field testing of rocket weapons. As a serving scientific officer in the army, liable to reprisals under the Official Secrets Act, Pincher wrote his first set of articles under the guise of 'Express Science Reporter'. Only in July 1946, having been officially discharged from the army, did he dispense with his cover name and adopt the grandiloquent 'Chapman' to enrich the byline. Pincher was acutely aware that a 'nuclear beat' was likely to enrage the authorities. Atomic matters were effectively 'born secret': that is, utterly taboo from the moment of their inception, and strictly no-go areas for journalists. On the lookout for a scoop to make a name for himself, he did not let this dissuade him. Beaverbrook, moreover, was keen for his reporters to ruffle a few official feathers. As the research of John Jenks has shown, because they 'accepted the common sense about communism', the first generation of post-war reporters were fairly supine.[20] Beaverbrook, in contrast, was determined that the *Express* should not stay away from the burning topics of the day. The newspaper's reputation was that a of 'flaming sword', unafraid to cut through any political armour.

In the life of a journalist, a lucky break can be just as rewarding as a high-level leak. Pincher's breakthrough article, published on 28 September 1945, owed itself to an extraordinary slice of good fortune.[21] Earlier that month, he had ascertained from Birmingham University Professor Marcus Oliphant that the Princeton physicist Henry de Wolf Smyth had written an official history of the Manhattan Project.[22] Subsequent enquiries revealed that an advance copy of the history had been sent to the Tube Alloy headquarters in London. Pincher duly examined the report and used it as the basis for a front-page splash. Amazingly, however, it then transpired that publication of the history had been delayed – Pincher had secured a world scoop. The Americans were horrified and sent a series of angry letters to Whitehall. The MoD feared that Fleet Street would now think that stories about the bomb were fair game when, in fact, they were supposed to be completely taboo. In the months that followed, Rear Admiral George Thomson, Chief Press Censor, had to sit down with Fleet Street's top brass pleading with them not to pursue atomic matters.[23] Thomson's personal appeals had the desired effect. Editors held him in the highest regard. During the war, he had shown himself to be a person of fair-mindedness, never one to shy away from telling Whitehall if its censorship demands were unjustified. Because journalists trusted his judgement on what might, if disclosed, help to undermine the road to victory, they had desisted from publishing everything from maps to train timetables.

Pincher, however, remained the exception. In the early years of the Cold War, he made it his mission to provide the British public with as much knowledge about nuclear affairs as his detective skills could ascertain. In pursuit of information, he regularly attended international conferences on nuclear physics, something that other journalists could not do for they lacked a basic scientific understanding. 'Until I came along,' recollects Pincher, 'newspapers never had anyone before with a scientific degree. I was a freak and the authorities had no idea how to deal with me.'[24] His great skill was to accumulate and splice together otherwise unimportant scraps of information and then inject the necessary phronesis, or practical wisdom, to produce something that appeared remarkably accurate. Years later, a number of scientists privately confessed to him that he had got 'damn close' to the truth: 'The old sods used to read my column to see what they were going to do next!'[25]

Concern in Whitehall about Pincher's atomic disclosures reached fever-pitch in November 1946 when the *Express* published 'Atom Secrets Out'.[26] A week or so earlier, while enjoying a convivial evening at the world-famous music hall Player's Theatre, Pincher had been introduced to Peter 'Wilfred' Burchett, an Australian journalist who had served with American forces at Tinian air force base, the site from where the Hiroshima and Nagasaki bombs had left for Japan.[27] In conversation, it came out that Burchett had received a confidential briefing about the Manhattan Project from General Kenney, the first post-war Head of Strategic Air Command. Appreciative of Pincher's offer to buy the next round of drinks, the Australian journalist went on to claim that the Americans possessed in the region of 96 functional bombs and that each warhead weighed about 4 tons. Pincher could not believe his luck. Recognising, however, that to publish this information might break the law, he got in touch with Thomson. On account of his experience with issues of censorship and congenial relations with the press, Thomson had since become Secretary of the D-Notice

Committee, a part-time position with a modest annual salary of £500.[28] The committee itself had been resurrected, with scarcely of ripple of protest, several months after VJ Day. Astonishingly, Thomson confirmed that 'nothing could be done', provided the article attributed the leak to 'an unnamed American source'.[29] With the green light from Thomson, Pincher published the information in all its glory. Britain's North American partners were appalled. General Leslie R. Groves, head of the US atomic programme, was 'seriously disturbed'.[30] Dean MacKenzie, spokesman for the Canadian Atomic Energy Board, interpreted the story as a 'straight bit of questionable scooping', a flagrant transgression of the international agreement to formalise all releases vis-à-vis the bomb.[31] 'If it had been designed to aggravate already strained lines of co-operative effort with our neighbours,' he continued, 'it could not have been more effective.'[32]

For HMG, Pincher's article could not have come at a worse moment. On 1 May 1946, British physicist Alan Nunn May had been sentenced to ten years in prison having been found guilty of supplying atomic-bomb secrets to the Soviet Union. Resultant American fears over poor British security had led to Congress passing the McMahon Act, which imposed a strict ban on the exchange of atomic information to other powers, including British allies. Attlee's Labour government, anxious for the Americans to reconsider this position, knew that it could ill afford to be seen as 'going soft' on the *Express*. MI5 was also suspicious of Admiral Thomson's role, questioning how he had failed to nip the story in the bud. Only a few months before, to supplement his income, the D-Notice Secretary had written eight articles for the *Sunday Dispatch* on the subject of wartime press censorship. The articles were then followed by a memoir entitled *Blue Pencil Admiral*. Thomson's publishing activity had caused Britain's intelligence community great distress. To the dismay of sigint authorities, he had declined to delete references to telephone tapping; he had also mentioned that MI5 had run German double agents.[33] Moreover, when MI5 forbade him from disclosing the fact that Eamon de Valera (President of the Irish Republic) had permitted telegrams sent from the Irish Republic to Germany to be secretly routed through the UK, Thomson leaked the story to a US newspaper, the *Chicago Sun*.[34] Nevertheless, it was decided not to punish Thomson or Pincher for the atom bombs disclosure. Any indication of official disquiet, concluded officials, would not only give the article greater prominence, but might send out the message that the information contained therein was accurate.[35]

For his efforts, Pincher was promoted to the post of 'Defence and Science Reporter', a specialist position with a heavy workload for someone relatively new to the profession. 'I didn't mind the added responsibility', he said in a recent interview: 'It was an unbelievably propitious time: the start of the atomic age, the missile age, the space exploration age, and the electronic age.'[36] To succeed in his new role, Pincher knew that he needed more sources. Colleagues he had known during the war proved invaluable. Many had since remained in government employment. Wartime friends such as Solly Zuckerman and William Cook would become senior figures in the British defence industry. Zuckerman became Chief Scientific Adviser to the MoD; in the 1950s, Cook was Deputy Director of the Atomic Weapons Research Establishment at Aldermaston. Over time, Pincher found that such individuals were only too willing to provide him with titbits of news. In the Cold War, government departments had substantial budgets to defend. As they saw it, a former insider such as Pincher was the perfect vehicle for promoting their projects. The *Daily Express* readership was 11 million.[37] Another person in Whitehall with whom Pincher developed close relations was Frederick Brundrett, Deputy Scientific Adviser to the MoD, serving first under Henry Tizard and then under John Cockcroft, whom he succeeded in 1954 as Chief Scientist. Brundrett, who in his spare time was a successful farmer, had initially sought the journalist's acquaintance to tell him how much he had enjoyed *The Breeding of Farmyard Animals*, a sixpenny Penguin handbook written by Pincher in 1946. As the relationship between the two men blossomed, agricultural matters took a back seat. Brundrett believed that taxpayers had a right to know how their money was being spent; accordingly, he chose Pincher to leak that information into the public domain. Through Brundrett, Pincher also met many other senior officials. A skilled amateur sportsman, Brundrett opening the batting for the civil service cricket team. On Sundays, he sometimes brought Pincher along to watch. Predictably, the journalist paid little attention to Brundrett's innings, preferring instead to remain in the pavilion where he could gossip with Whitehall's middle to lower order.[38]

Armed with a host of new contacts, Pincher caused consternation in the defence industry. On 17 October 1947, he revealed in a leading article that flight trials of a rocket-propelled aircraft had 'failed completely'.[39] According to Pincher, scientists had expected the aircraft to break the sound barrier, but in trials it never exceeded the subsonic speed of 600 m.p.h., a velocity routinely achieved by the current jet-fighter Meteor. 'There is no specific item, which, in itself, could be described as undesirable,' asserted Squadron Leader Peel, 'but what is disturbing is the fact that the information should have been published at all.'[40] The authorities were dumbfounded as to how Pincher had learned of the aircraft's behaviour. During the trial itself, press visitations had been forbidden. The pilot, meanwhile, had been instructed by the Aerodrome's Commanding Officer at St Eval to 'be very circumspect' in talking to the press and to sidetrack technical questions into 'harmless fields of informative matter of public interest'.[41] Leak enquiries concluded that the journalist had probably overhead some 'loose talk', the aerodrome not being far from local pubs and restaurants.[42] (This deduction, Pincher assured me, was 'absolute balls' – the information came from one of his 'friends'.)[43] To the dismay of officials, Pincher followed this exposé with the equally destructive story, on 11 August 1948, that construction of a new Air Ministry research station near Bedford had fallen two years behind schedule.[44] The resultant investigation discovered that the journalist had entered the compound on 5 August, seeking an interview with 'some person in authority' and 'quoting a telephone number as a reference'.[45] Once again, however, the article could not be linked to any specific mischievous official.

With Pincher stirring up trouble, the last thing the government needed was for one of its more 'trusted' journalists to play foul. This is precisely what happened on 12 November 1947 when John Carvel, lobby correspondent for the *Star*, prematurely revealed details of the government's emergency budget, disclosing inter alia that there would be a freeze on tobacco, a penny on the price beer and a small tax increase on football pools.[46] Earlier that day, Carvel had had a 'chance meeting' in the Members' Lobby with Hugh Dalton, Chancellor of the Exchequer. On his way to the House to deliver his budget speech, Dalton had seen Carvel 'loitering' and – with his state of mind unguarded – divulged to him the principal points. Foolishly thinking that the off-the-cuff remark was given without any embargo, Carvel relayed the details to his editor, A. L. Cranfield, who proceeded to run a

'Stop Press' in advance of Dalton's speech and with the stock markets still open.[47] As a result of this episode, the Chancellor was left with no alternative but to resign.

By the late 1940s, Pincher had become less the hunter than the hunted. 'This journalist has been a thorn in our flesh for a very long time,' announced a senior Air Ministry official in December 1948.[48] Departments cottoned on to the fact that he was benefiting from discreet tête-à-tête interviews with senior personnel. In October 1948, William Penney, then Chief Superintendent of Armament Research at the Ministry of Supply, reported with great satisfaction that the Ministry's Security Section had managed to identify and 'terminate' one of his most important informants (who exactly was 'terminated' is unknown).[49] At the Ministry of Aviation, there was strong belief that Pincher was gaining access into research plants using a disguise and a false name. On 1 April 1949, therefore, the Ministry sent a Top Secret communiqué ('we should be grateful if you would destroy this when read') to all storage depots directing police to 'take particular care in checking the identity of visitors'.[50] A month later, MI5 was asked to check security systems, prepare dossiers on scientists, and 'shadow' a few staff while they were off duty.[51]

Despite their best efforts, the authorities failed to stop the disclosures. On 2 August 1949, Pincher wrote an article claiming that he had stumbled across blueprints for 'two important defence projects', housed in a deserted works unit hut in West Heath, Hampshire.[52] He followed this, on 22 September, with an exposé on the work of the Microbiological Research Facility at Porton Down in Wiltshire.[53] Once again, departments were convinced that Pincher was somehow sneaking into government buildings, sometimes posing as a contractor and on other occasions entering under cover of nightfall.[54] In a desperate attempt to stop the journalist in his tracks, both the Ministry of Supply and the Ministry of Aviation printed giant posters, or 'mugshots', likening him to a bandit in the Wild West. Each member of staff was also given a profile of Pincher's particulars. This read: 'height (5ft. 10 inches), build (medium), face (thin and angular), hair (light brown), age (looks about 35), eyes (grey), complexion (fresh), dress (smart and prefers grey)'.[55] The entrance to the Royal Ordnance factory at Foulness, Essex, even had a photograph of him with the message: 'Warning: A Person of Evil Intent'.[56]

Throughout the 1950s, Pincher had a valuable ally in the shape of the genial Admiral Thomson. Unlike his predecessors as D-Notice Secretary – retired military types who enjoyed barking out orders and laying down the strict letter of the law – Thomson employed a commonsense approach with the press. 'Everybody in Fleet Street thought Thomson the fairest chap that ever walked,' declared Pincher in a lecture in 1969.[57] Reporters liked the fact that Thomson insisted that they never address him as 'Sir'. If journalists stumbled upon an especially 'hot' story, potentially liable to reprisals under the Official Secrets Act, he would encourage them simply to ring him up, rather than go through the process of putting the matter formally before the committee. Thomson's amicable nature resulted in good working relations with both the mainstream press and the fringes, including the *Daily Worker*, organ of the Communist Party of Great Britain. In 1951, with the Korean War in full swing, Thomson was put in an extremely awkward position when service chiefs, angered by the *Daily Worker*'s pro-communist position and believing that the newspaper was aiding the enemy with the publication of military information, requested that its editors be struck off from D-Notice distribution. The *Daily Worker* was understandably upset, claiming that the request was a slight to its show of good faith in the voluntary system. Thanks to Thomson, a compromise was reached whereby the *Daily Worker* was not altogether excluded, but was denied access to new so-called 'DX Notices' covering atomic and 'other specially secret matters'.[58] For finding an acceptable middle ground, Thomson was invited out to dinner by the editor.[59]

For reasons unknown, Thomson had a particular soft spot for Pincher. According to the journalist, Thomson always did everything within his power to get an article published.[60] Sometimes he would rewrite it to make it less objectionable. On other occasions, he would invite Pincher to 'future it', in other words delay publication until a more suitable moment. More mischievously, he encouraged Pincher to cover his tracks by claming that the sensitive material in question had come from 'US sources'.[61] As Nick Wilkinson has shown, Thomson was even prepared to put his own neck on the line. In October 1950, for example, MI5's legal adviser, Bernard Hill, wrote to him grumbling about a Pincher article that mentioned telephone tapping. In reply, Thomson accepted personal responsibility, explaining that, since he had discussed the monitoring of telephone conversations in his own memoir, he (mistakenly) thought the subject was permissible to mention in print.[62]

For Whitehall, Thomson's friendship with Pincher had its benefits. If officials knew that the journalist had something embarrassing in the offing, they could ask the D-Notice Secretary to appeal to him, not as a professional, but as a friend, to kill the story. In late January 1956, for example, SIS learned that Pincher had discovered details of a botched training exercise. The episode in question was like something from a carry on film. Earlier that month, the Service had tasked some of its new intake to kidnap a fellow SIS employee, disguised as a civil servant. Recruits were informed that the SIS officer would exit the front entrance of the Home Office seconds after the Home Secretary, Lord Tenby, had left the building. Alas, the SIS man never emerged as he had missed his train. Blissfully unaware of this, the recruits shanghaied an innocent clerk who, chance would have it, had followed Tenby out of the building. When Pincher was tipped off about the incident, his instinct was to report it. His source had also informed him about the whereabouts of the safe house where the SIS recruits had taken their victim. In a comical postscript to this extraordinary episode, the journalist staked out the location not knowing that he himself was under surveillance by MI5. Thankfully for SIS, Thomson used all his powers of persuasion to convince Pincher not to publish. In agreeing to this, the journalist made a great sacrifice, for the story would have been a sensation.[63]

As Pincher's fame grew, he found himself inundated with people wanting to leak him things. With seemingly little concern for the risks involved, senior figures in Whitehall often took extended lunch breaks to join the scoop-gatherer in his preferred London haunts, which included the Écu de France, the Dorchester and Kettner's Restaurant and Champagne Bar. Knowing the journalist's fondness for traditional British field sports, other officials invited him to hunts, shoots and fishing trips. The rationale for befriending Pincher was largely self-serving. Such individuals understood the value of someone with access to mass publicity. Many went to Pincher to sell their agenda to the public, others simply to cause professional angst in their opponents. In spring 1953, for example, Sir Archibald Rowlands, the recently retired Permanent Secretary to the Ministry of Supply, asked the journalist to publish the secret codeword 'Nomination'. He did not elaborate on what it stood for. Pincher obliged, but there was no reaction. Many years later, the journalist had it confirmed to him by Professor R. V. Jones (SIS's principal wartime scientific adviser) that the disclosure had in fact triggered one of the largest witch-hunts in Whitehall history, with hundreds of civil servants being interviewed to discover who had spilled the beans. Classified above Top-Secret, 'Nomination' had been a joint CIA/SIS committee established to control and share intelligence about the Soviet Union's atomic capability. Devilishly, Rowlands had leaked it to Pincher for no other reason than to make life difficult for his successor, Sir James Helmore.[64]

Crucially for Pincher, he started to acquire high-level contacts in the Western intelligence community. As commercial air travel boomed in the mid to late 1950s, he made regular trips to the United States and ingratiated himself into East Coast high society. Regular attendance at absorbent social evenings in Georgetown, Washington DC's most exclusive neighbourhood, generated a number of key informants, the most important being FBI special agent Robert J. Lamphere. Assigned to the Bureau's Soviet Espionage Division in New York in 1945, Lamphere supervised several major espionage investigations, including those of Julius and Ethel Rosenberg, Klaus Fuchs and Kim Philby. Closer to home, Pincher became good friends with Nicholas Elliot, an extremely capable SIS field officer who after the Second World War served as Head of Station in both Berne and Vienna, before returning to London in 1956 where he became responsible for home-based operations. In 1963, Elliot was famously sent to Beirut to confront Philby and to elicit a written confession, an encounter which sparked the latter's escape to Russia. In the battles ahead, such contacts would be of great value to Pincher. During the 1950s and early 1960s, Britain's intelligence services had to endure perhaps the worst moments in their hundred-year history. What they did not anticipate was that these moments would be plastered across the front page of every newspaper.

* * *

Anything that one writes or prints gets passed from one official to another, and inevitably falls into hostile hands eventually; then one's sources are jeopardised and one's efforts sabotaged by every possible means.

Kenneth de Courcy, editor of Intelligence Digest,
14 June 1951[65]

In his richly researched history of Anglo-American intelligence during the Cold War *The Hidden Hand*, Richard J. Aldrich argued that it was not until the early 1960s – the so-called 'era of exposure' – that journalists showed any real willingness to write about British intelligence.[66] Even then, most notably during the Vassall spy case in 1962, they still refused to delve too deeply for fear of being either prosecuted or ostracised from the mainstream media for undermining the West's war against communism. This assessment is one that now deserves reconsideration. Evidence adduced in the course of writing this book shows that Fleet Street did not suffer from a case of the scruples and actively sought to discover and publish intelligence matters as far back as the end of the Second World War. By the early 1960s, many journalists were already battle-hardened when it came to the business of trying to make intelligence the object of public scrutiny. For the governing classes, the readiness of the press to bring espionage out of the shadows was anathema. The intelligence community was the 'invisible man' of government, a state within a state about which questions were never asked. Secret service work was wreathed in a miasma of secrecy; its practitioners, like members of a masonry, were spectral figures, known only to their fraternal and exclusive initiates. The peacetime existence of the security and intelligence agencies was not officially acknowledged, whilst there was a bipartisan consensus that questions should not be asked about them in Parliament. 'It is the essence of a Secret Service', declared Sir Austen Chamberlain (then Foreign Secretary) in December 1924, 'that it must be secret, and if you once begin disclosure it is perfectly obvious to me as to hon. Members opposite that there is no longer any Secret Service and that you must do without it.'[67] It was said that the British attitude to intelligence mirrored Victorian societal attitudes to marital sex; that is, everyone knew that it went on but to 'speak, write or ask questions about it' was just not the done thing.[68]

The first journalist to cause problems was Stanley Firmin, crime reporter for the *Daily Telegraph*. On 2 January 1946, he submitted a book manuscript to the War Office for security clearance. Entitled *They Came to Spy*, it purported to tell the story of the 'war behind the war', namely MI5's efforts to combat German spies who had operated in Britain. The first thing that struck the intelligence authorities was how much information Firmin had managed to acquire on the subject. The book was a truly remarkable piece of investigative journalism, consisting of over 150 pages and strangely knowledgeable about some of the most secret aspects of the Second World War. Information for the book had come to a large extent from Scotland Yard. Under the Commissionership of Sir Harold Scott (1945–63), the Metropolitan Police had been instructed to be far more open with reporters. Some senior journalists were even given their own room at the Yard, complete with hotlines direct to their Fleet Street offices.[69] It was clear to MI5 that Firmin had picked up the bulk of his material from indiscreet policemen. The manuscript also intimated that the author had been hobnobbing with certain MI5 officers. In Chapter 18, Firmin had written: 'One curious fact that baffled British Intelligence ... and is still a complete mystery to members of that service with whom I have talked.'[70]

By far and away the most serious disclosure in the manuscript was that British codebreakers had attacked enciphered radio messages used by the German armed forces and the Abwehr. 'One of the most vital of all London's secret rooms was the decoding room, the place where the German codes, no matter how intricate or ingenious, were broken down,' stated Firmin.[71] He then went on to reveal that cryptography had since become an essential part of Britain's peacetime arsenal. As Chapter 7 of this book will discuss in greater detail, the successful interception and decoding of German signals was a story that officials 'NEVER' wanted to see disclosed, not least because it had the capacity to invite questions about whether or not Britain was doing the same thing in peacetime. Only marginally less sensitive was Firmin's discussion of training schools run by the Special Operations Executive (SOE), where carefully selected trainees had been instructed in the ways of creating chaos in occupied Europe and the Far East. According to MI5 officer Major D. I. Vesey, this gave far too much away about the techniques involved.[72] Firmin had also detailed the work of Lord Victor Rothschild as Head of MI5's B1C Section, which dealt with sabotage, inventions and equipment.

Departments unanimously disapproved of the book and so began a lengthy process of negotiating with the author on an agreed set of deletions. In a strategy tantamount to keeping close to a kicking horse, MI5 set up a meeting between Firmin and Lord Rothschild on 14 May so that the latter could at least correct some of the book's inaccuracies. 'We are of the opinion', stated Major E. J. P. Cussen, 'that if the material is to be published ... it is desirable that it be of an informed character.'[73] Among the things that Rothschild set the author straight on was the suggestion that MI5 had put spies into British merchant ships to look for enemy saboteurs disguised as crew members. This was quite untrue. The German strategy was for its agents to plant explosive devices on British ships *before* they went to sea. At night, agents would tiptoe on board and deposit bombs camouflaged as innocent objects, such as thermos flasks and mess tins.[74] Agents had also been known to hide bombs in crates of oranges or onions. Quite apart from being factually erroneous, Firmin's claim that MI5 had spies on British vessels had the potential to upset such bodies as the National Seaman's Union.[75] MI5 was alarmed by the fact that Firmin, a crime reporter, had taken time out from his ordinary 'beat' to write about intelligence. As well as being known for the quality of their initiative and enterprise, crime reporters were notorious for their relentless pursuit of scandal, following the mantra 'if it bleeds, it leads'. (In his 1950 memoir *Crime Man*, Firmin recalled that a colleague had become so concerned by the absence of breaking news that he cut his own finger, soaked a handkerchief in the blood and then dumped the hankie in a tunnel where a murder had recently been committed.)[76] The last thing Whitehall wanted to see was this sort of journalist getting too interested in intelligence.

By May, MI5 had still not granted the book security clearance. Firmin and his publisher, Messrs Hutchinson & Co., were indignant. In a bid to break the deadlock, they forwarded the manuscript to Admiral Thomson. The D-Notice Secretary was anxious about the delay. As he saw it, 'the whole "D" Notice procedure' would be 'killed at birth' if the authorities did not act expeditiously.[77] 'The point I am interested in', Thomson opined, 'is that if the press are good enough to comply with D-Notices, press requirements must receive prompt attention'; failure to do so would discourage journalists from voluntarily submitting their writings.[78] As Firmin and his publisher had hoped, the level-headed Thomson settled the imbroglio. In the space of just forty-eight hours, he sat down with the author, agreed upon a reasonable number of deletions, and approved the book for release. MI5's legal adviser, Bernard Hill, was angered by Thomson's intervention, especially when he discovered that Firmin was now 'going round the public houses in Fleet Street alleging that, through the good offices of Admiral Thomson, he was able to get his book published quickly and was able to obtain a lot of inside information'.[79]

In the 1950s the British public was consumed and convulsed by episodes of scandal involving its intelligence services. Each scandal was accompanied by fevered press coverage. The first story to break was the arrest and trial of the German-born British atomic scientist Klaus Fuchs. During the war, Fuchs had worked at Los Alamos where he had played a central role in the Manhattan Project, assisting in the development of the two atomic bombs dropped on Japan in August 1945. In 1946, he had returned to Britain to take up a prestigious post at the Atomic Energy Research Establishment at Harwell, nicknamed the 'holiest of holies' on account of its passion for secrecy. By the end of the decade, it had become clear that he had been recruited by the Russian GRU military intelligence agency, to which he had passed atomic research information from as far back as 1943. In January 1950 he confessed to espionage, stating that his conscience had compelled him to come clean. On 1 March, in a trial at the Old Bailey lasting less than two hours, he was tried under Section 1 of the Official Secrets Act and sentenced to fourteen years' imprisonment, the maximum sentence permissible. Following this, Fleet Street filed story after story on the case. Reporters were critical of MI5 vetting procedures. How could Fuchs have been cleared in the first place and then allowed to spy undetected for so long? Everyone was anxious to know the full extent of the scientist's espionage. What atomic secrets had he given to the Russians? Had his treachery caused a rift in Anglo-US relations?

Pincher was quickest out of the traps with a front-page article, published the day after the trial, entitled 'Fuchs Gave the Bomb to Russia'.[80] In the *Express*, as in the rest of Fleet Street, spy cases had traditionally been handled by the resident crime reporter. Pincher, however, was chosen by the editor to break the mould since he not only possessed the necessary scientific expertise, but also had contacts in both the intelligence community and the Harwell research station. The article made it clear that Fuchs, while at Los Alamos, had been privy to most secrets and had transmitted to his courier everything from formulae to blueprints. Forbidden by a D-Notice from mentioning certain MI5 officers who he suspected of having been negligent in clearing Fuchs for secret work, Pincher laid the blame squarely on the Service's chief, Sir Percy Sillitoe, whose name was publicly acknowledged. As a recent article by Michael Goodman has shown, anxious to put an end to press attacks Sillitoe ordered his staff to prepare a summary of the case for the prime minister, Clement Attlee, which he could then use as the basis of a statement in Parliament.[81] That summary was littered with false information. It claimed that MI5 had approved Fuchs for secret work in August 1941, when in fact he had been cleared several months before. It asserted that MI5, having been tipped off by a refugee source about Fuchs's communist associations, had relayed that information to other government departments which, for whatever reason, had failed to take heed of the warning. Attlee was not told that the FBI had long had their doubts about Fuchs. He was also kept in the dark about evidence from the Venona project, the post-war decoding of wartime KGB messages, which had virtually singled out the scientist as a spy. It is unknown whether or not the MI5 officials who prepared this report made Sillitoe aware of its fraudulent content.

On 6 March 1950, Attlee went to the House and announced that there were no grounds to 'cast the slightest slur on the security services'.[82] He added that he greatly disapproved of 'loose talk in the press suggesting inefficiency' on the part of MI5.[83] As hoped, Attlee's statement calmed press interest in the matter. It did not, however, draw a line under it. Despite being unaware of the depth of the MI5-orchestrated cover-up, a number of journalists continued to try and piece together the details of the case. In August 1950, MI5 moved quickly to ask Charles Wintour, leader writer for the *Evening Standard*, if he would delete from his forthcoming history of the British Communist Party the sentence: 'Fuchs discussed with Nunn May the acceptance of a token payment of £100.'[84] According to Hill, 'This is entirely inaccurate. Fuchs at no time had any contact with Nunn May and certainly did not discuss the acceptance of money with him. There is no evidence whatever that Nunn May knew anything about Fuchs's espionage activities.'[85] In early 1954, the *Evening News* ran a series of articles on the 'Secrets of MI5'. The newspaper had wanted to dedicate a considerable portion of the series to Fuchs, but was persuaded by Thomson to focus instead on a few wartime success stories.[86] MI5 also had to dissuade filmmakers from producing films and documentaries that dealt with Fuchs. In June 1950, for example, writer and director Patrick Ryan asked the Service if it was willing to cooperate in a film about the fabled scientist. MI5 declined.[87]

By summer 1951, Fleet Street was engaged in trying to uncover the full extent of another scandal. On 6 June, news had reached the desk of the resident *Daily Express* reporter in Paris that the hunt was on for two Foreign Office diplomats who had fled the country.[88] Following up the lead, Pincher discovered that the fugitives, confirmed as being Guy Burgess and Donald Maclean, were heading for Moscow. The resultant scoop, published on 7 June, was headlined 'Yard Hunts Two Britons'.[89] Although the Foreign Office tried to quash the story by issuing a statement to the effect that Maclean had suffered some sort of breakdown owing to the pressures of his job, the media refused to be duped. 'The Great Spy Scandal', as it became known, produced countless articles assessing the lives and motivations of the two spies. Newspapers such as *The Times* – until then reluctant even to write about intelligence – began throwing brickbats instead. Journalists were quick to point out that Burgess and Maclean possessed obvious character defects which should have resulted in their expulsion from secret work. Alcohol had played a conspicuous part in the lives of both men, whether for recreation or to assuage feelings of guilt and anxiety. Burgess's violent drinking was well known in Fleet Street, as was the fact that Maclean had routinely turned up to work in the morning drunk and stuporous. At dinner parties, both men had been known to espouse the virtues of communism while intoxicated. Moreover, neither had made any effort to conceal their sexual peccadilloes: Burgess, an aggressive homosexual, was often seen at clubs and bars in London with his trousers undone. In the press, there developed a wave of anti-Establishment feeling and a clamour for housecleaning. Burgess and Maclean were archetypal gentlemen and a general thesis emerged that the Establishment had forgiven their indiscretions, so blinded had it been by class prejudice.

The press was relentless in its efforts to discover more about the case, prompting some to question if the ethics of journalism had not been compromised. In July 1952, Lady Violet Bonham Carter, daughter of the Liberal prime minister Herbert Asquith and a member of the Royal Commission on the Press from 1947 to 1949, complained to the editor of *The Times* about the way certain journalists were treating Maclean's wife Melinda. Still to join her husband in the Eastern bloc, Melinda had been subject to what is now known as 'ambush journalism', hounded by reporters soliciting unguarded remarks, wherever she went. Determined to get her side of the story, seemingly at any cost, they staked out her house, pounded on her door and inundated her with telephone calls. Bonham Carter was moved to complain about press tactics when it emerged that a major national newspaper had published an interview with Mrs Maclean which had, in fact, never taken place. 'It is deplorable and alarming to know that any member of the public may find words falsely imputed to him and reproduced to millions of readers,' protested Bonham Carter.[90] She continued: 'the repeated invasion of privacy – an invasion amounting at times to persecution – by some members of the press is surely indefensible'.[91]

Sheer good fortune played its part in ensuring that the press did not reveal further damaging information about the secret world. In July 1951, MI5 successfully censored several articles by Eric Tullet, political correspondent for the *Express*, on the subject of intelligence. Had it not been for a lucky break, however, the articles would have gone to print *without* MI5 ever having seen them. Ordinarily, this might not have mattered, but Tullet had stumbled upon a secret so big that it would have changed the course of history if revealed in 1951. The lucky break went like this: a month earlier, an inebriated Tullet had carelessly left his brown imitation leather briefcase in the Ye Old Bell public house in Fleet Street; inside the case was his prized notebook. The landlord duly handed it over to the police who, in turn, forwarded it to MI5.[92] Before returning the case to its rightful owner, officers could not resist thumbing through the notebook, which, to their amazement, included transcripts of ten interviews between Tullet and a recently retired Foreign Office security officer named Arthur Askew. In one of the interviews, Askew had informed the journalist about 'cipher machines at Eastcote', then the home of the super-secret GCHQ.[93] Upon reading this, MI5 personnel had to pinch themselves: Askew had given away what one historian has since described as the 'last great British secret'.[94] It is hardly necessary to subscribe to a methodology of 'counter-factual' or 'alternative' history to recognise that the disclosure of GCHQ's existence – in 1951 – would have had seismic repercussions.[95] Washington, at the time reeling at British security blunders in the wake of the Burgess–Maclean fiasco, would surely have taken this as further evidence of London's inability to keep secrets. Moreover, as a result of the disclosure, the work of Bletchley Park would likely have come to light prematurely. In turn, this would have had a major impact upon the historiography of the Second World War. With a modicum of understatement, a senior MI5 official commented, 'Any publicity on that point [i.e. Eastcote] would, I think, give Sir Edward Travis [Head of GCHQ] much pain.'[96] Grateful for the alcohol-induced lapse, MI5 confiscated the notebook, briefed Tullet about the importance of sigint remaining secret, and expunged the articles of offending passages.

In its struggle to keep certain reporters in check, especially those operating at the murkier, conspiratorial fringes of mainstream journalism, MI5 was not afraid to use underhand tactics. As editor and proprietor of *Intelligence Digest*, a politically accented private subscription newsletter, Kenneth de Courcy experienced this first-hand. The son of the claimant to the title of Duc de Grantmesnil, a designation he insisted on using, de Courcy led a colourful and controversial life. Before the Second World War, he was Secretary of the Imperial Policy Group, a troop of diehard conservatives who detested the Soviet Union and championed appeasement with Hitler as the best strategy for safeguarding empire. For many years, he was a confidant of the exiled Duke and Duchess of Windsor. According to royal historian Christopher Wilson, in 1949, amid the failing health of the Duke's brother, King George VI, who had succeeded him after the 1936 abdication crisis, de Courcy unsuccessfully tried to encourage his exiled friend to return to Britain to become Regent, thus sidelining the heir apparent, the then 23-year-old Princess Elizabeth.[97] As the renegade aristocrat saw it, the young princess was susceptible to the charms of the dynastically ambitious Earl of Mountbatten. In 1963, de Courcy achieved notoriety when he was convicted of fraud and sentenced to seven years' jail in Wormwood Scrubs prison, where he reportedly became a dining companion of George Blake, one of Britain's most notorious traitors. Critics maintain that the 'Duc' was a ridiculous fantasist. Later in life, he famously had his Rolls-Royce waterproofed for subaqueous motoring.

During and after the Second World War, however, the fantasist caused genuine alarm to MI5. De Courcy was powerfully connected: so well connected that, throughout his career, he was rumoured to be receiving confidential reports from intelligence officers stationed in embassies abroad. In 1983, when interviewed by the Hoover Institution, which now houses his private papers, he claimed that his most important source had been Dutch counter-intelligence officer Oreste Pinto.[98] Once described by Dwight D. Eisenhower as 'the greatest living authority on security', Pinto had worked with MI5 after the fall of France, interrogating refugees and enemy suspects entering Britain. According to the declassified diaries of Guy Liddell, MI5's wartime Director of Counter-Espionage, the Service became very concerned about how well-informed de Courcy was. In November 1942, when evidence came to light that the 'Duc' kept a confidential journal, MI5 officer Roger Fulford advocated that his 'premises should be searched and the diary confiscated'.[99]

MI5's interest in de Courcy intensified in the early 1950s when *Intelligence Digest* carried stories on Burgess and Maclean. The newsletter, which claimed to be receiving leaks from high-level sources on the Continent, relentlessly pushed for an inquiry into their disappearance. In tandem with the *Intelligence Digest*'s public lobbying, de Courcy made his case privately to a number of prominent officials, including the ex-diplomat Lord Vansittart, Lord Salisbury (Leader of the House of Lords), and Harold Macmillan (Housing Minister). De Courcy hoped that Salisbury, in particular, would use his influence in the Conservative Party to persuade the prime minister, the recently re-elected Winston Churchill, to bring the matter to a head. De Courcy's informants had provided him with sensitive biographical information about the two traitors, including details not yet publicly revealed. He knew, for example, that Burgess had been secretary to Hector McNeil, the Minister of State for Foreign Affairs.[100] He also knew that Maclean had been Head of the American Department at the Foreign Office, and had been guilty of disgraceful conduct when serving as head of chancery at the British embassy in Cairo.[101] The Conservative government, he argued, had a responsibility to investigate who had recommended these two men for such important appointments. Lord Salisbury, however, declined to take the matter to the prime minister, prompting de Courcy to label him, off the record, a 'weak fool' under the spell of the pro-Soviet Foreign Secretary Anthony Eden.[102] The government's reluctance to investigate was also seen by de Courcy as evidence of a larger conspiracy. In two handwritten notes, dated 7 November 1951 and 27 October 1952, he accused Roger Hollis (Director General of MI5 1956–65) of being a Soviet spy. The first note reads: 'Why won't [the government] investigate? The answer is that Roger Hollis of MI5 is himself a Soviet agent. And Roger Hollis is backed by the powerful [MI5 officer] Victor Rothschild who recruits the whole outfit. That is why no one can get anywhere and is stifled.'[103] The second states: 'None of them dare face up to Victor Rothschild. It is incredible that we have two top Soviet agents like Rothschild and Hollis as Establishment pets – plus many others.'[104]

Whether or not de Courcy was correct in his belief that Hollis was a traitor is not the concern of this book. (The authorised history of MI5 by Professor Christopher Andrew contends strongly that this was not the case and that anyone who claims otherwise is a conspiracy theorist.)[105] Of interest here are the measures taken by MI5 to try to hinder *Intelligence Digest*. In June 1951, de Courcy's solicitors – Messrs Churchill, Clapham and Company – complained to the War Office that members of MI5 had been harassing the staff of the newsletter, with one correspondent being pressurised to give up his sources.[106] 'I fear Roger Hollis organises this disgraceful conduct,' scribbled the 'Duc' in the margins of the solicitor's letter.[107] A few months later, de Courcy wrote to John Strachley, Secretary of State for War, accusing two MI5 officers of trying to strong-arm French security authorities into intercepting telephone conversations between the newsletter's Paris and London offices. Tipped off by the French government about MI5's 'approach', de Courcy also claimed that MI5 had requested that he and his chief Paris correspondent be put under round-the-clock surveillance.

MI5's attempts to keep a lid on the Burgess and Maclean scandal were ultimately doomed to failure when, in April 1954, the Australian prime minister, Robert Menzies, stunned the world with the revelation that Vladimir Petrov, Third Secretary of the Soviet embassy in Canberra, had defected. In the fallout, the Australian press revealed that the two Britons had been long-term Soviet agents, recruited in the 1930s while studying at Cambridge University. Until then, most newspapers had treated them as diplomats on the run. Accusations also surfaced that a so-called 'Third Man', believed to be the high-ranking officer Kim Philby, had assisted in their escape by informing them that the counter-intelligence net was closing in. The British government's response was to issue a demonstrably erroneous White Paper in September 1955. It claimed, for example, that there had been no grounds to suspect Maclean's loyalty, despite there being ample evidence from publications such as *Intelligence Digest* that the spy had been a member of certain communist associations while at university. As a result, the White Paper was derided by the press as a whitewash. Nevertheless, on the strength of that document, Harold Macmillan, now Foreign Secretary, gave Philby what the latter would describe as the happiest day of his life by announcing in Parliament that Philby was a conscientious public servant and there was no evidence of him being a traitor.

Several months later, on 11 February 1956, the Soviets paraded Burgess and Maclean at a spectacular press conference in Moscow. The outcry in Fleet Street was fierce, reigniting the question of whether or not a nation's intelligence service should be a gentleman's club for those who attended the right universities and clubs. In Whitehall, it was feared that the Russians would not stop at putting their star agents in front of the cameras and were about to launch a major propaganda campaign aimed at the West. In anticipation of this, MI5 concluded that it needed to get the message out that the KGB was feeding Burgess and Maclean a pack of lies and that any future statements by the pair should be treated as Soviet misinformation. To do this, amazingly, MI5 turned to Pincher. On 26 February, he was invited to the office of Admiral Thomson, whereupon he met Bernard Hill, MI5's legal adviser. Hill outlined the problem and solicited assistance. Pincher obliged. The following morning, the *Express* ran with the headline 'Beware the Diplomats'; Thomson promptly telephoned the journalist to tell him that MI5 was delighted.[108]

In Whitehall, word got around that Pincher had done a good job and it was not long before other departments sought his help. Pincher's greatest contribution came in April 1957 when, in league with the MoD, he published a front-page article claiming that imminent British hydrogen bomb tests in the Pacific were to be postponed on account of technical problems.[109] This was sheer poppycock. A few days before, defence chiefs had learned that Japanese anti-nuclear campaigners were making their way to the test site to prevent the explosion. As a result, Pincher was contacted and asked to write a spoof story. The deception worked: the world's media picked up on the article; the protestors kept their distance; and Britain detonated its bomb – as planned – on 15 May. That the MoD turned to Pincher for this task is remarkable when we consider that atomic authorities, only a few years earlier, had regarded him as some sort of outlaw deserving of the gallows. Indeed, a recently declassified JIC paper from September 1953 shows officials overwhelmed with anxiety when they discovered that Pincher had been selected by the *Express* to watch forthcoming atom bomb testing at Woomera, Southern Australia. 'Mr Chapman Pincher's presence at the tests would undoubtedly be viewed with grave concern by the Americans,' concluded the committee.[110] Accordingly, the JIC asked the *Express* whether it would be possible for them to send another representative instead, a request which was rejected. In 1957, by contrast, Pincher was welcomed by officials with open arms. When the situation demands it, even bandits can have their uses.

* * *

> It is absolutely essential that the finding of the body is not disclosed
> to the press.
>
> *Detective Superintendent A. Hoare, 14 May 1956*[111]

No episode better illustrates the media's appetite and ability for
uncovering intelligence scandal than the infamous Crabb Affair in
1956. Press action was instrumental in bringing the incident out into
the open when, behind the scenes, the Whitehall machine was hell-
bent on keeping it secret. As a result of press probing, there would be
a full-scale discussion in the House of Commons about the ethics and
efficacy of the intelligence agencies, something unprecedented in
British history. A prime mover in publicising not only the details of
the blunder in question, but also the official cover-up designed to
protect it, Fleet Street contributed to the unseating of the incumbent
head of SIS and unknowingly helped to bring about a root-and-
branch review of Britain's strategic intelligence and surveillance
operations.[112]

The origins of the affair go back to 1954 when the Admiralty
notified SIS of its desire for information about the noise characteristics
of Russian warships. Accordingly, SIS devised Operation Claret – code
name for a series of amphibious missions to be carried out by frogmen.
Although secret underwater inspections were typically the sort of thing
done by the Special Boat Section (SBS), there was nothing unusual
about the character of the operation. Sub-aqua espionage was an
established part of the great game on both sides of the Iron Curtain.
When British warships had visited Leningrad, seaman on board had
routinely spotted bubbles rising to the surface from the compressed-air
tanks of Russian frogmen. The first opportunity to initiate Claret came
in October 1955 when a Sverdlov class cruiser anchored in Portsmouth
harbour as part of a naval review. The resultant mission was a success,
procuring good intelligence, and SIS soon turned its attention to
mounting a follow-up dive during the goodwill visit to Britain of
Soviet leaders Nikita Khrushchev and Nikolai Bulganin in April
1956. The Russian delegation was due to arrive in Portsmouth harbour on the cruiser *Ordzhonikidze*. In Downing Street, however, the
prime minister, Anthony Eden, was adamant that nothing should
jeopardise his attempts to facilitate some measure of rapprochement
with the Soviet Union. As he saw it, the risk of blowback was too

great. On 12 April, therefore, he issued a directive expressly forbidding 'anything of this kind on this occasion'.[113]

Unfortunately for Eden, his message failed to reach its intended recipients. Michael Williams, the Foreign Office official responsible for securing clearance for the operation, had just learned that his father had passed away. In consequence, he left the office to be with his grieving family and forgot to inform the relevant people of Eden's decision. Without political approval – 'the first rule of intelligence management'[114] – the SIS officers in question should have terminated their plans. With little regard for a prime minister they viewed as 'wet', they pressed on regardless. For the dive, SIS recruited an experienced naval frogman, Commander Lionel 'Buster' Crabb (Figure 7). He was now retired, and theoretically at least afforded SIS, in the event of the operation being publicly uncovered, the defence of plausible deniability. Only too happy to help, Crabb arrived in Portsmouth on 17 April, the day before the Russian warship berthed in the harbour. He was joined by an SIS officer who went by the name Bernard Smith. Both men then checked into a local hotel, the Sallyport, foolishly writing their names and addresses in the hotel register.[115] In need of a tender – someone who remains topside during a dive – Crabb contacted a wartime diving companion, a lieutenant commander stationed at the nearby underwater weapons establishment and diving school, HMS *Vernon*. The following night, in the company of his tender, Crabb carried out a rehearsal dive and was reported to be in 'good trim'.[116] He then took a blasé attitude to operational security and went on a bibulous spree with some friends in the neighbouring town of Havant. Not known for being inconspicuous (on dry land, he always sported a monocle and carried a swordstick with a handle carved in the shape of crab), the frogman was seen by several local residents.[117] (According to later press reports, he reportedly told some of the locals that he was 'going down to take a dekko at the Russian bottoms', a task for which he would earn 60 guineas.)[118]

On 19 April, shortly before 7 a.m, Crabb slid into the water and commenced his dive. Operating instructions were restricted to an examination of the ships' rudder and propellers, and the frogman's tanks were filled with 90 minutes of oxygen, more than sufficient for the job. By 9.15 a.m, with no sign of Crabb, the tender realised that a 'serious mishap' had occurred and informed the Admiralty.[119] Naval authorities subsequently contacted SIS, which decided not to conduct a search for the body in fear of alerting the Russians. Panic swept through Whitehall. Urgent meetings were held between the Director of Naval Intelligence (Rear Admiral John Inglis), the Director General of MI5 (Dick White) and the Head of SIS (John Sinclair). Everyone recognised the severity of the situation. Were details of the illicit operation to emerge, Eden would be left shamefaced. Moreover, everyone had witnessed how the media had latched on to the Burgess and Maclean fiasco, and were determined to keep the same from happening again.

Hopes of suppressing all knowledge of the dive soon faded when, on 21 April, the Commander of the *Ordzhonikidze* let it be known to Rear Admiral Burnett, Portsmouth Naval Base chief of staff, that a frogman had been seen by three of his sailors swimming near the vessel. Several days later, the friends with whom Crabb had spent the evening in Havant contacted the Admiralty seeking news of their companion. Ruthless in their determination to cover up the blunder, intelligence authorities ruled that the Admiralty should accept responsibility and issue a statement to the effect that the frogman was presumed dead as a result of trials with underwater equipment in Stokes Bay, an area of the Solent several miles from Portsmouth near the town of Gosport.[120] Crabb's friends (and his grieving mother) were to be 'kept quiet'.[121] Moreover, it was decided that Stanley Lamport, Chief of Portsmouth Criminal Investigation Department, should visit the Sallyport, tear out the telltale pages from the logbook and threaten the hotel manager with the Official Secrets Act. In agreement with a number of senior civil servants (including Sir John Lang, the Permanent Secretary of the Admiralty, and Sir Ivone Kirkpatrick, Permanent Secretary of the Foreign Office), the intelligence authorities choose *not* to inform Eden of the botched operation or the tactics set in motion to cover it up.[122]

On 29 April, the Admiralty delivered its phoney public statement. The frogman's supposed death generated a great deal of press interest. As a war hero and recipient of the George Medal for 'gallantry and undaunted devotion to duty',[123] Crabb was the perfect 'human interest' story. Moreover, following the development of improved diving equipment, the 1950s had spawned a popular fascination with the amphibian pursuits of treasure-hunters, pearlers and combat swimmers. It did not take long, however, for journalists to realise that the Admiralty was giving them the run-around. Although a confident and decorated frogman, Crabb was a heavy smoker, even by the standards of the postwar generation, and now aged forty-six he was not in the best physical condition. It was even reported that he was only just able to swim three lengths of a 25-metre swimming pool.[124] Local journalists, some of whom were amateur divers, found it strange that Crabb had been testing equipment in Stokes Bay, a patch of water notorious for its rough tides and strong rift currents. By sheer coincidence, an officer in the SBS was staying at the Sallyport at the same time as Crabb. An expert diver, he reliably informed reporters that the bay was not a suitable location for diving exercises. The refusal of naval authorities to conduct a search for the body also aroused curiosity. Suddenly, scores of reporters descended upon Portsmouth determined to unearth conspiracies of silence. They quickly established that Crabb had stayed at the Sallyport and that someone from the local police had ripped out pages from the hotel logbook. Interviews with the hotel manager confirmed that one of the men had provided his address as 'Attached Foreign Office'. Well-informed journalists immediately recognised this as the stock cover for SIS operatives. The involvement of an intelligence authority was all but confirmed when a Soviet naval attaché, speaking to the press, claimed that one of the *Ordzhonikidze*'s crew had seen a frogman momentarily surface, seemingly struggling for air.[125]

By early May, the press was speculating wildly both about what happened to Crabb and exactly what he was doing in the water. The most common explanation was that the frogman had been sent to the *Ordzhonikidze* to gain intelligence. Journalists from local news-papers were particularly knowledgeable about naval matters and suggested that an underwater inspection could reveal details about sonar devices and submarine detection gear. Another theory was that Crabb had been patrolling the harbour after HMG had learned that a right-wing group was intent on assassinating the Russian leaders by fitting a bomb to the cruiser's keel. Admiral Thomson was quoted as saying on 5 May: 'The possibility of a daring frogman attaching a limpet mine was a security risk that had to be guarded against.'[126] On the question of Crabb's fate, press rumours run the gamut from the plausible to the ridiculous. The most likely explanation was that he had died of respiratory failure. His re-breather might have been cut on the rugged underwater terrain; it was not inconceivable, moreover, that, because of the strong tides, he had become trapped underwater by a rock or a piece of kelp, before running out of oxygen. The *Daily Express* concocted stories involving state-of-the-art equipment. These were: that

Crabb had been pinioned by a magnetic anti-frogman device until he had drowned; that he had been trapped in a television cable and died of oxygen asphyxiation; that he had been rendered cataleptic by sonar emissions; or that he had been electrocuted when a prototype flash-camera short-circuited.[127] Reporters of a conspiratorial mien suggested that Crabb had been killed by scuba-equipped sentries during an epic battle on the ocean floor.[128] Even more beguiling was the suggestion that he had been shanghaied by enemy frogmen and taken into the *Ordzhonikidze* via a 'wet compartment', where he had haemorrhaged British naval secrets under the influence of truth drugs. Escorted back to Russia, he would one day be paraded, like Burgess and Maclean, as a potent weapon of Soviet propaganda.

On 4 May, with the press indulging in conspiracy theories, Eden was finally told what had really transpired. He was understandably incensed, not only with his maverick and failure-stained secret service, but also with the tardy manner in which senior officials had notified him of events. Recognising that the press-inspired furore would almost certainly compel him to make a statement, he instructed the Foreign Office to prepare a 'defensive line'. Continuing in the spirit of the past few weeks, the Foreign Office concluded that an outright lie was still preferable to coming clean. Accordingly, it suggested making Crabb a scapegoat. The official position would be that the frogman had ignored the protests of his tender and – 'in the spirit of adventure' – had mounted an unauthorised expedition against the Russian ship.[129] To his credit, Eden was appalled by this atrocious slur. As he saw it, Crabb was a loyal and gallant patriot; to suggest that he had wantonly disobeyed orders, when in fact he had died in the line of duty, was abhorrent. In Parliament, therefore, on 9 May, he opted to confirm that there had been an unapproved mission: 'What was done was done without the authority or knowledge of Her Majesty's Ministers.'[130] He refused to go further than this, claiming that 'it would not be in the public interest to disclose the circumstances in which Crabb met his death'.[131] Hugh Gaitskell, the leader of the Labour Party, led the uproar. Five times he demanded more information and five times the prime minister refused. In the end, Eden acted in the manner of a 'command premier', ruling that 'there are certain issues which are the responsibility of the Prime Minister himself'.[132]

The media firestorm that followed Eden's statement was like nothing that had been seen before. Already angered by the intelligence community's failure to identify and then punish traitors who had sold their country down the river, the press saw the foolhardy espionage attempt as further evidence of malaise and incompetence at the heart of the Establishment. 'For boneheaded clumsiness', remonstrated the *New Chronicle*, '[the episode] would be matchable only if John Buchan were scripting the Goon Show.'[133] The *Sunday Express* accused intelligence chiefs of being utterly oblivious to the vast political consequences involved. The visit of the Russian leaders – invited at the personal behest of Eden himself – was intended as a diplomatic coup for Britain, an event unthinkable under Stalin. Yet the hamfisted operation had since caused the whole episode to be likened to 'going into the hall to search a guest's pockets, while your wife serves him a meal in the dining room'.[134] Both *The Times* and the *Daily Mail* made the case for a full inquiry into the intelligence services, suggesting that they behaved as 'laws unto themselves', completely insulated not only from democratic opinion but from ministerial supervision.[135] Also calling for heads to roll, the *Sunday Dispatch* decried the notion that Britain could ever have countenanced such an immoral and inept service.[136] Eden was also on the receiving end of the press's fury. The *News Chronicle* criticised him 'for a performance of stunning maladroitness'.[137] *The Times* accused him of shirking ministerial responsibility and failing to keep a 'tight-hand' on his secret adventurers; 'No Authority for Dive by Commander Crabb', howled the one-inch, front-page headline.[138] The insubordination of *The Times* must have been particularly galling for the beleaguered prime minister who, as D. R. Thorpe argues, 'came from that class and generation which believed [it] to be the principal newspaper of record'.[139] Press attacks could not have come at a worse time for Eden. As well as threatening to sully his efforts to thaw the Cold War, they seemed to confirm a growing suspicion among the chattering classes that he was a political 'lightweight', a bumbler who was hopelessly out of his depth and perhaps out of his time. In the much-quoted words of Donald McLachlan, deputy editor of the *Daily Telegraph* (the traditional Conservative mouthpiece), people were waiting in vain for the 'smack of firm government'.[140]

The renewed press assault brought the matter once again to the House of Commons. For nearly two hours on 14 May, MPs thrashed out all aspects of the affair. Gaitskell spoke freely about the intelligence community and speculated about its control, organisation and efficiency. Hoping to score party political points, the Opposition leader was relentless in asking Eden what disciplinary steps were being taken and against whom.[141] Others who attacked the secret services and inveighed against Downing Street's management of the case included seasoned socialist firebrands Richard Crossman and Percy Collick. They claimed that it was 'the duty of any Opposition in this democracy of ours to probe any weakness or what appear to be blunders or mistakes in government administration'.[142] Crossman was particularly eager to know who authorised the Admiralty communiqué of 29 April, which was now proven to be a manufactured falsehood.

The debate was unprecedented in the annals of British politics. Constitutional practice dictated that normal public systems of accountability, including parliamentary discussion, did not apply to the secret services. In the eyes of most MPs, the lengthy debate was inappropriate. As they saw it, it was no business of the House to speak about, let alone pillory, the intelligence services – organisations which officially did not exist. The Conservative politician Sir Patrick Spens could not hide his disapproval: 'This is the first time in my experience that a responsible Opposition has, through a most responsible leader, in a most responsible speech, none the less done what I consider to be a most irresponsible thing. I very nearly rose on a point of order when the debate began, because I believe that this debate is contrary to all our precedents.'[143] Perhaps unsurprisingly, strong protest came from Sir James Hutchison, who had been a British liaison officer with the French Resistance during the Second World War and who, in this capacity, had even undergone plastic surgery to disguise his identity from the Gestapo.[144] He declared: 'let us not persuade it [the intelligence community] to do a striptease act and cast aside one veil after another.'[145] In the light of growing press interest in espionage over the previous decade, MPs recognised that disclosures about Crabb were not an aberration, but rather were indicative of a larger epochal change in attitudes. Deference to the secret state had clearly waned and, to have any hope of restoring it, Parliament should set the standard. Accordingly, when parliamentarians were asked to vote on how to proceed with the matter, they accepted Eden's edict that there should be 'not one word more to say' about it.[146]

Ridiculed in the press, taunted in Parliament and (according to reports) teased by Khrushchev during a farewell dinner party at Claridge's hotel, Eden turned his attention to disciplinary action. At his request, Sir Edward Bridges, Head of the Civil Service, led an inquiry into how the operation had come to pass and why it had taken so long to notify ministers of its failure. (Typically well-informed, Chapman Pincher reported the inquiry's precise terms of reference in an article on 14 May.)[147] Submitted to Eden on 18 May, Bridges' report is a perfect example of the Establishment closing ranks to protect its own. Refusing to single out any one civil servant from the dramatis personae as deserving of special blame, it attributed Eden's ignorance of the whole affair to a jurisdictional misunderstanding. Apparently, investigations had shown that neither the Admiralty nor the Foreign Office had realised that it was their responsibility to inform Downing Street, both mistakenly believing that it was the job of the other department.[148] If one looks closely at Bridges' report, declassified in 2006, it is possible to see several scribbled notes in the margins. Penned by Eden in a fit of rage, they include: 'Against Orders', 'This Proves Nothing', 'Whose Business Was It', 'Forbidden' and 'Ridiculous'.[149]

Incandescent, on 26 June Eden called the Foreign Secretary (Selwyn Lloyd), the Minister of Defence (Walter Monkton), and the First Lord of the Admiralty (James Thomas) to Chequers, the Prime Minister's country residence, with the explicit intention of reprimanding guilty parties. Here Eden's abominable temper – 'one of the best kept secrets in Whitehall'[150] – boiled over. The British ambassador to Moscow, Sir William Goodenough Hayter, would later testify to a 'frightful row'.[151] In the wake of this summit meeting, the Director of Naval Intelligence, as well as the senior civil servants who had agreed to the cover-up, were told in 'no uncertain terms' that what they had done was wrong.[152] Given the seriousness of their wrongdoing, one might argue that they got off lightly. John Sinclair, Head of SIS, was not so fortunate. In what many regard as a deliberate affront to the Service, he was fired and replaced by Dick White, Director General of MI5. Eden also sanctioned a far-reaching inquiry reviewing the way future intelligence operations were to be authorised and carried out. Headed by Sir Norman Brook, the Cabinet Secretary, and Patrick Dean, Chairman of the JIC, the inquiry would bring to an end what former JIC chief Sir Percy Cradock called 'the slapdash, buccaneering' days of British intelligence.[153] Gifted amateurism, however well-intentioned, was ill suited to a new age in which intelligence operations had the capacity to cause a major rift in the international system and in which the media seemed intent on sniffing out scandal.

* * *

Can nothing be done to suppress or get rid of Mr Chapman Pincher?

Prime Minister Harold Macmillan, 4 May 1959[154]

If Whitehall learned anything from its experience with the press during the first decade of the Cold War, it was that the D-Notice Committee would, in the years to come, assume an even greater significance as a mechanism of control. By talking to officials on an unattributable basis and by getting information from overseas, journalists had found a way of writing sensitive stories without violating the Official Secrets Act (Figure 8). The likelihood of scoops being discovered in the United States was certain to increase with the advent of the jet age, which halved the flying time between New York and London from twelve to six hours at reduced cost. Pincher's carbon footprint was well known to Whitehall. Professor R. V. Jones had seen the journalist at a number of scientific conferences in the United States.[155] Against this background, the ability of the D-Notice Secretary to convince journalists to self-censor in the interests of national security would become crucial.

However, the system was about to experience some of the worst years in its existence. Whereas in the past journalists had tended to accept assurances from the government that a particular disclosure would be harmful to national security, they would now demand proof that this was in fact the case. In Fleet Street, there developed a fear that governments were misappropriating the system to prevent political embarrassment – a fear heightened by the fact that certain officials were seen to be taking too close an interest in the system's operations. Accordingly, the expression 'slapping a D-Notice on it' came into being. At the same time, officials themselves started to lose faith in the system. With every damaging disclosure came a conviction that the D-Notice Committee had failed to do its job. Ultimately, a conflict would break out over where the boundary lay between what the public had a right to know and what the state needed to keep secret. It was clear that the boundary had shifted, but neither side was going to give way on exactly how far.

In government, feelings of dissatisfaction with the D-Notice system were triggered, predictably perhaps, by Pincher. On 3 November 1958, he revealed in a leading article that Britain possessed approximately thirty atomic bombs.[156] The Air Minister, George Ward, immediately pointed the finger of blame at Thomson for failing to block the article. In the ensuing discussions, it was established that Thomson had done little wrong, for the journalist, on this occasion, had relied on his own deductions and legerdemain. Still unhappy, Ward wrote to the Minister of Defence, Duncan Sandys (Figure 9), arguing that, if the D-Notice Committee could not stop him, 'special action' should be taken to 'watch Chapman Pincher's movements'.[157] Sandys rejected the idea, claiming that were Pincher to find out, endless trouble would result.[158] A year later, it was the prime minister, Harold Macmillan, no less, who was despairing at the D-Notice Secretary. On 4 May 1959, Thomson cleared an article by Pincher explaining that the Cabinet had decided not to pursue an independent space research programme, opting instead to get its information from American satellites.[159] Appalled, Macmillan went on record as saying, 'Can nothing be done to suppress or get rid of Mr Chapman Pincher? – surely the only time in British history when a prime minister has called for a journalist to be liquidated, even if not in the literal sense.[160] Before Macmillan did something rash, the Cabinet Secretary, Norman Brook, stepped in as a calming influence. Pincher, he explained, was a 'respectable chap' and certainly not a 'danger to the nation'.[161] 'It is believed generally that he knows far more than he gives away in his stories,' explained Brook.[162] Moreover, although the article may have been politically embarrassing, it did not damage national security and thus no blame could be attached to Thomson.

Fleet Street's acceptance of the D-Notice system was thrown into jeopardy in 1961 by the government's handling of the George Blake spy case. A KGB spy and an SIS officer, who was believed to have betrayed the names of more than forty agents to the Soviets, Blake had been exposed as a traitor by Polish defector Michal Goleniewski during Christmas 1959. In advance of Blake's trial at the Old Bailey in May 1961, HMG requested that Thomson write to editors asking them not to publish that he had worked for SIS. Any mention of this would reignite media interest in secret service incompetence. Acting on orders, Thomson wrote to editors on 1 May, although the reason he gave to the press for insisting on the blanket ban was 'that the lives of MI6 employees are still in danger'.[163] According to D-Notice records, 'every editor played ball'.[164] On 5 May, however, a West German newspaper carried a story claiming that Blake had been an SIS employee. In the light of this, the British press asked Thomson to lift the ban. With further instructions from Downing Street, the D-Notice Secretary refused to do so until 8 May, resulting in a farcical situation where the rest of the world's media was free to comment while Fleet Street was gagged. The British press was understandably aggrieved, protesting that the D-Notice had been issued not to protect lives, but to cover up another fantastic security blunder. In Parliament, Macmillan faced a fusillade of questions from Labour MPs, to which he responded with the argument that time had been needed to move a number of agents to a safe location. The prime minister's explanation failed to convince Gaitskell that the government was not in fact hiding a deeper scandal. Gaitskell's persistence eventually prompted Macmillan to reveal the truth to three Labour privy councillors, who, because of their oath, would be honour-bound to remain silent on the issue. One of the chosen privy councillors was George Brown. Brown had a reputation for being something of a loose cannon and it was an open secret that he had a drink problem. True to form, a few days after being briefed, he enjoyed a bibulous luncheon with Pincher at the Écu de France where he revealed, amongst a host of other details, that Blake had compromised the existence of the Berlin Tunnel. To Macmillan's horror, Pincher duly published everything without any attribution.[165]

As a result of the Blake farce, Macmillan called for a review of the D-Notice system. On the advice of Burke Trend, then Second Permanent Secretary to the Treasury, he gave this task to the Radcliffe Committee – recently set up to investigate security procedures in Whitehall. In Trend's opinion, 'the Radcliffe Committee could take this topic in their stride with only marginal, if any, stretching of their terms of reference'.[166] As Director General during the war of the Ministry of Information, the central government department responsible for publicity and propaganda, Lord Radcliffe was particularly well-qualified to pass judgment. The Radcliffe Committee submitted its report in April 1962. Its chief conclusion was that the system made 'a valuable and effective contribution to protecting the disclosure of "military" information which needs to be concealed'.[167] The committee emphasised that the press was now acquiring 'a very considerable volume of information on secret matters'.[168] Alas, not all of that information was covered by the Official Secrets Act, coming as it did from overseas or from the unattributable lips of gossipy officials. From discussions with editors, it had also become clear that there was no 'lively expectation' in the media that Whitehall would ever be willing to prosecute for a breach of security; in effect, the Act had lost its deterrent value.[169] From the government's perspective, therefore, it was imperative that the D-Notice system remain intact.

According to Radcliffe, the 'personality of the Secretary' was, in the final analysis, the most important part of the system. For the press not to print certain stories, the Secretary had to be sensitive to the ways and needs of journalists. He also had to possess a selfless energy and dedication to his work. The job of Secretary was an exacting task. Long and unpredictable hours were common. Editors frequently required advice late in the evening, sometimes minutes before the article in question was due at the printers. It was essential, therefore, that the Secretary had the capacity to make quick and informed decisions. In Radcliffe's view, Rear Admiral Thomson personified the 'special qualifications and personality' that were required of the position.[170] Journalists viewed Thomson not as a 'faceless and forbidding censor' but as a 'talkative, endlessly affable old sailor' – someone who was on their side and who would do everything to help them.[171] Moreover, his commitment to carrying out his duties was legendary. All those who knew him spoke of his work ethic with awe. Problematically, Thomson was now in his early seventies, in poor health and looking towards retirement. Privately, key officials had already started to question his performance, believing him to be too old. Thomson's recent inability to stop the press from mentioning the redeployment by air of British troops from Cyprus to Kuwait had left Norman Brook wondering if the Admiral – 'at 80' – still had the mental faculties for the job.[172] (As Nicholas Wilkinson has observed, Brook's mistaken belief that Thomson was an octogenarian was probably a reflection of the latter's accelerated physical degeneration.)[173]

Radcliffe's report set in motion the search for a successor. That search was hastened in early 1962 when the admiral suffered a stroke. Until a permanent appointment was made, Colonel 'Sammy' Lohan stepped in as Acting Secretary. A jovial individual with a bristling handlebar moustache, Lohan had been Deputy Head of Public Relations in the army. After a honeymoon period, the Colonel soon found himself at odds with the media. Indeed, as baptisms of fire go, they do not get much hotter than the so-called Dolnytsin Affair. On 11 July 1963, the *Daily Telegraph* made an enquiry to the Aliens Department at the Home Office which revealed to MI5 that the newspaper had become aware that Anatoliy Golitsyn, a major in the KGB, had defected to the West and was now residing in the UK.[174]

Intelligence authorities were anxious that no publicity be given to the matter. Although the Russians obviously knew that Golitsyn had defected, they did not know his location. Public disclosure of his presence in the UK risked endangering the man's life. Moreover, Golitsyn was currently providing the West with intelligence of 'considerable importance'; to reveal his existence might diminish both the quality and the quantity of information he was willing to divulge.[175] Accordingly, Lohan was instructed to issue a D-Notice stating that the defection should not be reported for the aforementioned reasons. He did this at 5.30 p.m. on 11 July.

Before leaving the office, Lohan was telephoned by Sir Colin Coote, editor of the *Daily Telegraph*. Coote informed him that he was not prepared to accept the embargo since the story had come from a source in Washington, DC. The conversation ended with Lohan stating: 'the matter rests with your conscience; I've made my point, and if you wish to go ahead the best of luck'.[176] Several hours later, now back home, Lohan received a call from Pincher who said that he also knew of Golitsyn's defection and could not afford to let the *Daily Telegraph* steal a march. For the *Express*, the loss of readers was a far more terrifying prospect than the venom of Whitehall. (Lohan was unsure how Pincher had learned of the case and suspected that the scoop-gatherer had a 'planted man' in the offices of each of Fleet Street's leading newspapers.)[177] The following morning, both the *Telegraph* and the *Express* carried the story. The next day, the *Evening News* even published a purported photograph of Golitsyn, albeit with a blacked-out face and fudged background. The rest of Fleet Street was appalled. By accepting the D-Notice, they had allowed themselves to be scooped by their competitors. 'If [newspapers] cannot trust each other to respect [D-Notices],' complained William Haley (editor of *The Times*), 'then there will be a scramble to publish.'[178]

The Times' disappointment at being scooped soon turned to anger when the newspaper discovered from its own American source that the defector had been in the West for eighteen months. The wording of Lohan's D-Notice had given the impression that the defection was recent. In turn, this had created a misleading sense of urgency and importance to the whole business. Moreover, *The Times* had learned that the defector's name was not, as the D-Notice had claimed, 'Dolnytsin'. As Haley saw it, Lohan was either an idiot or he had deliberately sought to deceive editors. 'The Affair', he protested, 'has caused us to lose confidence in the whole D-Notice system.'[179] *The Times*' discoveries were soon the talk of Fleet Street. Newspapers rounded on Lohan In press attacks, it came out that the Secretary had issued the D-Notice not in a sealed envelope, but using an unprotected teleprinter, subscribed to by the Soviet news agency Tass. The *Daily Telegraph* commented that such a stupid mistake would never have happened on Thomson's watch. In Parliament on 18 July, the Conservative prime minister faced a host of questions from disgruntled Labour MPs, with some alleging that Lohan had been asked by HMG to issue a D-Notice, complete with the defector's name, in the full expectation that editors would ignore it and make great fanfare about the government's coup in securing a high-profile defection from the East.[180] Macmillan responded by underlining that the government's chief concern was to safeguard the man's life, and that the name had been given to editors in an attempt to build up confidence. Unconvinced, Haley solicited a meeting with the prime minister to discuss the matter. In advance of this, Macmillan was provided with a number of 'briefs' by his advisers. While recognising that Lohan had been required to draft and issue the D-Notice in haste to halt the *Telegraph*'s morning edition, it was emphasised that the Secretary had been careless and that his position should be 'reconsidered'.[181] In Downing Street on 29 July, Macmillan met with Haley and, to draw a line under the sordid affair, agreed that, in future, sensitive D-Notices should only be issued to editors in person.

In August, it was decided that Lohan should continue as Secretary, subject to an evaluation after six months. Richard Way, Permanent Secretary of the Ministry of Aviation, had asked each of the D-Notice Committee's eleven press members for their views on the matter. Of the eight who responded, only Harman Grisewood, Chief Assistant to the Director General of the BBC, believed that Lohan was unsuitable.[182] The justification for keeping the Colonel was threefold. Firstly, the job was difficult and any successor was bound to suffer as a result of following 'a man so experienced and respected as Thomson'.[183] Secondly, Lohan had been required to be Secretary in addition to his full-time job as Deputy Head of Public Relations in the MoD; as such, it was only fair that he be given the opportunity to do the job without the burden of another position. Thirdly, if Lohan were to be fired, it would look like the committee had found a scapegoat for the Golitsyn episode.

In the short term, the decision to keep Lohan was vindicated. On 9 August 1963, the current affairs magazine *Private Eye* identified

Dick White as 'C', the incumbent chief of the SIS. A few weeks later, *Sanity*, the official newspaper of the Campaign for Nuclear Disarmament, published a photograph of C's house together with his name and telephone number. In Whitehall, panic set in as both *Private Eye* and *Sanity* announced their intention to go further and publish everything they could find about the intelligence services. Before matters got out of hand, however, Lohan played a decisive role. He took the editors of both publications out to lunch and managed to convince them of the need to keep MI5 and SIS out of the news. The argument was put to them: 'from the point of view of national security it stands to sense that, if the movements of the Heads of the British Intelligence Services become common knowledge, then one thing leads to another. It would not be long before their associates also become known. And that, in turn, might lead to the whole structure ... of intelligence becoming known to the wrong people.'[184]

Officials were delighted with Lohan and his six-month probationary period was replaced with a full-time contract. However, such was the relief in Whitehall that *Private Eye* and *Sanity* were now on a leash, no one paid attention to the means by which Lohan had operated. In both cases, his modus operandi had been to 'go for a drink' with the editors in question.[185] In the case of the editor of *Sanity*, David Boulton, Lohan had taken him to the Savoy Grill – described by the Colonel as the 'battleground of my choosing' on account of its award-winning dessert trolley.[186] The meeting nearly did not take place when Boulton arrived without a tie and thus committed a 'sartorial misdemeanour'.[187] To Lohan's relief, the waiter was able to produce one and the meeting went ahead. With Lohan at the helm, matters of national security were being debated without formal procedure, hinging on such things as dress codes and the quality of gastronomic provision. As will become apparent, the Colonel's penchant for 'wining and dining' with journalists would prove disastrous, contributing to a political scandal in Britain that would rival any before it, or since.

4 BRITAIN'S WATERGATE: THE D-NOTICE AFFAIR AND CONSEQUENCES

> The world of the D-Notices can now never be the same again.
>
> DONALD MCLACHLAN,
> 26 September 1968[1]

The D-Notice Affair of 1967 is of critical importance when examining British secrecy. The affair, which began when Chapman Pincher published a story reporting that private cables and telegrams were being scrutinised by security authorities as a routine measure, dominated headlines and national political discourse for six months. Marcia Williams, who served as Harold Wilson's political secretary for nearly thirty years, including his eight years as prime minister (1964–70, 1974–6), commented in her memoir *Inside Number 10*: 'We all became obsessed with the matter … The whole lamentable affair had hung like a heavy cloud over us for many months. It had sapped the energies of the Prime Minister and his morale. We felt deeply concerned for him.'[2] The affair has a genuine claim to be considered the British Watergate. Rarely has a prime minister stirred as much angry reaction among not only the press but also political allies and opponents as Wilson did with his clumsy handling of the case. In an apparent personal epiphany, Wilson later observed that his behaviour had been 'gratuitous' and amounted to what he regarded as 'one my costliest mistakes of our near six years in office'.[3] His first error was to threaten the *Express* with legal action for publishing a 'sensationalised and inaccurate' story in plain defiance of D-Notices; his second was to reject the verdict of a committee of privy councillors called – by the prime minister himself, no less – to investigate the matter.[4] The consequence was a series of hostile parliamentary debates and what newspaper tycoon Cecil King estimated as the 'worst press any Prime Minister has had in my day'.[5] Behind closed doors, Wilson's Cabinet colleagues were utterly dumbfounded by what they had seen. The Minister for Transport, Barbara Castle, was 'appalled' and proposed that he had 'gone off his rocker'.[6]

Aside from the effects it had on Wilson and the Labour government, the affair was hugely damaging to the secret state. Pincher's article, a burnished page in Fleet Street's hall of fame, was confirmation, if officials needed it, that journalists were getting information about sensitive subjects and were not afraid to release that information into the public domain. Although the great scoop-gatherer failed to mention that the primary recipient of the intercepted traffic was the then still secret GCHQ, the article's subject matter – sigint – was the most closely guarded secret in Whitehall. Officials looked on in horror as Pincher, in a heroic example of press coverage under fire, challenged the will of the system and won. If, as in this case, reporters were unwilling to accept guarantees from the state that a particular publication was against the national interest, what was to stop the entire edifice of official secrecy from falling apart?

Just as alarming for the secret state was the fact that, although the D-Notice system survived by the skin of its teeth, confidence in its utility as a protector of genuine national security concerns was severely dented. Incensed by Wilson's assault on press freedom, not to mention his apparent personal vendetta against some of the personalities involved, many journalists swore never to use the committee again. 'I severed all connections,' recalls Pincher. 'The attempt to smear my reputation and that of other innocent individuals was unforgivable.'[7] As we shall see, the decision of certain reporters to operate off-piste would have profound repercussions. A further important consequence of the affair – and one thus far overlooked in existing accounts – is the part it played in Britain in creating a myth of the heroic investigative journalist.[8] The drama was a classic case of David and Goliath, with Pincher the person implacably forced to confront destiny and take on a more powerful foe. Yet it was the intrepid underdog who emerged victorious. For his efforts, Pincher became a national icon. He appeared on television and spoke on the radio. In the ultimate display of admiration for the journalist, newspapers put aside their tribal loyalties and dedicated their own precious column inches to his stand against the government. For the secret state, the ramifications of Pincher's success cannot be underestimated. Newspapers, whether driven by a thirst for fame or a righteous desire to advance the public's right to know, became ever more determined to crack an explosive story. In newsrooms and journalism schools across the country, the D-Notice Affair became an inspiration and a charter. In the eyes of many reporters, Pincher was a role model.

* * *

Our morning prayers developed into a long discussion
because I found the Prime Minister obsessed with the problem
of leaks.

Richard Crossman, 11 November 1966[9]

When Harold Wilson became prime minister in October 1964, he was determined to build good relations with the press. As leader of the Opposition, he had witnessed first-hand how the media had all but brought down the Macmillan government, most notably with their hysterical coverage of the Profumo Affair. When rumours leaked out that the Secretary of State for War, John Profumo, had enjoyed a brief but passionate relationship with Christine Keeler, a London model who it also emerged had slept with a Russian naval attaché, newspapers – hitherto straining at the leashes to report the private lives of politicians – had a field day. In his first hundred days in office, therefore, Wilson held cocktail parties for reporters at Number 10; he even invited Pincher for a chat. 'Our conversation ranged over many items,' recollected the journalist some years later.[10] In a further attempt to avoid scandal and associated media furore, the press-conscious Wilson gave George Wigg the job of Paymaster General, but with the added responsibility of being a security watchdog, responsible for monitoring rumours, leaks and general deviousness (Figure 10). A self-styled expert in matters of political intrigue – described as 'Wiggery-pokery' – Wigg was given direct physical access to Downing Street through a private door. His capacity to fuel Wilson's mania for conspiracy led Castle to call him 'Harold's Rasputin'.[11]

Wilson's swooning honeymoon with the media soon gave way to antagonism and paranoia. Predictably, it was Pincher who led the journalistic pack into battle. In early January 1965, an angry service chief leaked to him details of the government's decision to cancel a number of jet programmes, including the futuristic TSR2 bomber. Pincher, who had made no secret of his anger at Labour's looming defence cuts, duly published a headline-grabbing article on the subject.[12] Upset, Wilson called for an investigation into the leak. When interviewed by Henry Hardman, Permanent Undersecretary at the MoD, Pincher dropped into the conversation that he had recently lunched with Sir Geoffrey Tuttle, a leading figure in the British Aircraft Corporation.[13] Hardman read this for what it was – 'an attempt to bluff us about the source of the story'.[14] To the prime minister's disappointment, the leak enquiry found no evidence that any official had been guilty of impropriety. The episode left him 'thirsting for Pincher's professional blood'.[15]

Wilson's animosity towards Pincher grew to new levels in May 1965 when a remarkable slice of good fortune presented the journalist with an explosive front-page splash. On 12 May, Richard Crossman, Minister for Housing, took some work with him to dinner at Pruniers Restaurant, one of the West End's most elegant eateries. After coffee, he absentmindedly left a sheaf of Cabinet papers under the table. As chance would have it, at a nearby table was one of Pincher's acquaintances, the businessman Geoffrey Blundell-Brown. A passionate supporter of the Conservative Party ('by Christ he hated Labour's guts'),[16] Blundell-Brown gleefully retrieved the documents and passed them to his friend in Fleet Street. The following morning, Crossman reported his security lapse to Wilson. By then, Blundell-Brown had handed the documents over to the police, albeit without mentioning that he had shown them to Pincher who had made a copy. Unaware of the journalist's involvement, the prime minister laughed off Crossman's faux pas, stating 'Thank heavens you weren't dining with Christine Keeler my dear boy!'[17] Later that day, however, word reached Wilson that the *Express* knew everything, from the contents of the papers to Crossman's blunder. His mood suddenly changed. As the government had openly announced its intention to toughen up security in Whitehall, nothing could be more embarrassing to it than the revelation that one of its own had lost confidential documents. In a desperate bid to save face, Wigg telephoned Pincher, starting off by employing a softly-softly approach ('charity, Harry, charity you bugger'), before becoming devastatingly rude ('if you publish, I'll nail you to the wall').[18] Unfortunately for Wigg, although the Official Secrets Act prevented Pincher from disclosing the contents of the papers, there was nothing to stop the *Express* reporting Crossman's error, which it duly did. In the next sitting of Parliament, remembering how Wilson and particularly Wigg had vindictively pursued Profumo, Conservative backbenchers took great pleasure in taunting the government. An accomplished lord of mischief who relished smearing opponents, Wigg subsequently took it upon himself to find as much dirt on Pincher as he could, even employing a detective to dig into his private affairs.[19]

Wigg's dislike of Pincher took on a personal as well as a professional edge. In June 1966, the Paymaster General complained to the journalist that he and his wife had been harassed at home by reporters from the *Express*. According to Wigg, in the early hours of the morning on 15 June, a man had repeatedly knocked at his door. Gaining no reply, the man then woke up the next-door neighbour. The same morning, at 11.00 a.m., a reporter from the *Daily Express* returned to the property and successfully managed to obtain a statement from Wigg's wife. Minutes later, another reporter, this time from the *Sunday Express* and with a copy of an article by Pincher in his hands, came knocking. With this, Wigg gave the man a dressing-down, telling him that he considered the newspaper's behaviour an 'impertinence'.[20] Naturally, Pincher protested his innocence, stating that he 'would not dream' of getting someone on the newspaper's staff to trouble any official at their home.[21] Although content to give Pincher the benefit of the doubt, Wigg made it clear that he would not tolerate any further acts of harassment from the newspaper.

To quote Castle, in the run-up to the D-Notice Affair Wilson was 'getting pathological about leaks' (Figure 11).[22] From the *Crossman Diaries*, it is clear that almost every Cabinet meeting began with the prime minister bleating about off-the-record briefings. Wilson's paranoia about leaks led him to take drastic action. In February 1966, he issued a strongly worded circular to ministers asking them not to talk to the press unless they were in the company of a public relations officer.[23] Several months later, he instructed that ministers should be subject to exactly the same leak inquiry procedure – questionnaires, interviews with security chiefs et cetera – as civil servants. In doing this, he ignored the advice of his Cabinet Secretary, Burke Trend, who had suggested that a 'renewed oral warning' would be less 'invidious'.[24] Wilson's exasperation about leaks even led him to suggest installing a camera above the Downing Street photocopier.[25]

Yet things only got worse. In early 1965 Anthony Howard of the *Sunday Times* threw down the gauntlet by setting himself up as Fleet Street's first 'Whitehall Correspondent'.[26] The job of the 'Whitehall Correspondent' was to bypass ministers and get stories about policy direct from civil servants. Wilson interpreted this as a declaration of war. In Cabinet, he described Howard as a 'very dangerous man doing a very dangerous job' since his 'object in life' would be to ferret around Whitehall looking for clashes between ministers and their advisers.[27] Sir Laurence Helsby, Head of the Home Civil Service, was also distressed, seeing Howard's appointment as an intolerable attack on the doctrine of ministerial responsibility.[28] Wilson's response was to mount a blockade. On 25 February, he sent a letter to all ministers and permanent secretaries banning them from talking to Howard, even on an unattributable basis.[29] By July, so securely had the government machine gone into lockdown that Howard had been forced to abandon his brief. Wilson would later boast that he had 'seen off' the animal with 'his tail between his legs'.[30]

The prime minister's unhealthy obsession with the press was made worse by his concerns about Sammy Lohan. In fairness to Wilson, he was not alone in thinking that the Colonel was doing a job that was quite beyond him. In summer 1965, Roger Hollis, Director General of MI5, had made a discreet investigation into allegations that Lohan's drinking and womanising were out of control.[31] Until then, officials had always turned a blind eye to his social habits, believing that they were his business and a welcome relief from the pressures of the job. After Profumo, however, it was clear that the 'extra-curricular' activities of officials could not be ignored. The investigation found no reason to remove Lohan, although it was noted by Martin Furnival Jones, Hollis's successor-in-waiting, that the Colonel was 'sometimes fuzzy with drink' in the afternoon.[32]

Yet Wilson's anxieties about Lohan hinged on far more than whether or not the D-Notice Secretary showed up for work sober. With a conspiratorial mindset and seeing enemies all around him, the prime minister was convinced that Lohan, a hard right-winger, was colluding with rogue factions in MI5 to bring down the government. There was (and remains) no evidence to support this. Wilson's mistaken belief was fanned by the fact that Lohan, as a former section chief with the SOE and as a founding member of the Knightsbridge-based Special Forces Club (a well-known drinking den for MI5 officers), had always been close to the intelligence services. Wilson also misinterpreted the logic behind the fact that Lohan was receiving a retainer from MI5 worth in the region of £1,500 per year.[33] As he saw it, the retainer was proof that Lohan was in league with individuals who wanted to see his downfall. In reality, the retainer had two purposes. Firstly, it served as an 'entertainment allowance' for Lohan to dip into whenever he needed to take a journalist out for a meal; during his first few months as D-Notice Secretary, he had quickly discovered that lunches at the Savoy did not come cheap, and had sought a contribution from Whitehall to ensure he was never out of pocket. More mischievously, the retainer was also part of an attempt by MI5 to keep tabs on certain reporters. In the words of Laurence Helsby, it was Lohan's reward for 'bringing them small pieces of information from Fleet Street'.[34]

For Wilson, the most troubling thing about Lohan was the relationship he enjoyed with Pincher. Since the Colonel had been appointed, the two men had become the warmest of friends. Although the job of D-Notice Secretary required its holder to be pleasant with journalists and earn their trust, in Lohan's case it was apparent that he had overstepped the normal bounds of professional etiquette. The two men were frequent lunch partners at the Écu de France, the most distinguished French restaurant of its day. In Downing Street, rumours were rife that Lohan possessed a key to Pincher's second home, a flat in St James's, where he would 'entertain loose women' and enjoy nights of bacchanalian revelry.[35] ('Only on one occasion did Sammy use my flat for a bird,' Pincher told me. 'He left it in such a bloody mess that I never did it again.')[36] Such was the closeness of their friendship, the prime minister was certain that Lohan had been the source of Pincher's stories attacking defence cutbacks. Wilson's parliamentary private secretary, Charles Morris, would later write a report speculating that, over a three-year period, Lohan had inspired 26 of Pincher's articles.[37] According to Richard Way, confiding in the journalist many years later, Wilson became so obsessed with proving that Lohan was leaking information that he authorised the bugging of Pincher's telephones.[38]

This then is the background against which the cable vetting affair broke. The ingredients were explosive: a stuttering D-Notice machinery, a civil servant with character defects, a resourceful journalist with an eye for Whitehall-rocking exclusives, and a paranoid prime minister who, as well as taking every minor contretemps as if it were a cataclysm, was determined to settle some old scores.

* * *

Lohan is quite mad.

Captain Henry Kerby, 7 June 1967[39]

The affair was set in motion when, on 16 February 1967, Pincher was visited by Robert Lawson, a 'disgruntled ex-employee' of both Commercial Cables and Western Union.[40] Lawson described how every single cable and telegram handled by the two companies was collected on a daily basis by security authorities, before being returned several days later. Sensing a good story, Pincher telephoned the MoD, who told him that the information was incorrect and that the *Daily Mail* and *Manchester Evening News* had made similar inquiries the day before. Experienced enough to realise that government departments do not always tell the truth, the journalist then contacted his friend Turlough O'Brien, Post Office Director of Public Relations. A long-time fishing companion, O'Brien corroborated Lawson's claim. Pincher, the hunting dog, had seen the rabbit and was now away.

Word of an impending publication soon reached the ear of the Foreign Office. At an emergency high-level meeting on 17 February, chaired by Christopher Ewart-Biggs of the Foreign Office's Defence and Security Department, it was decided that Lohan should inform the journalists in question that the story was not suitable for public disclosure. The logic behind this decision was essentially twofold. As Richard J. Aldrich has argued, the newspapers involved had stumbled upon something very secret indeed; not only had they learned about the interception of foreign communications traffic, something that had been hidden for decades and could lead to the public exposure of GCHQ, but they had also learned about the existence of a much more sensitive state–private network.[41] Secondly, it is almost certain that there had been pressure from the Americans, in particular the National Security Agency (NSA). During the Cold War, in a clandestine programme known as Operation Shamrock, the telecommunications corporation Western Union and its associates had agreed to provide the federal government with a daily supply of copies of all cables sent to or from the United States, including telegraph messages between unsuspecting American citizens. Shamrock, which at its peak saw 150,000 messages a month being analysed by the NSA, was a flagrant violation of the US Constitution.[42]

Tasked with killing the story, Lohan was hamstrung from the outset. Crucially, he had been excluded from the meeting at the Foreign

Office on the grounds that his security clearance was insufficient. Although in the early 1950s the Colonel had been subjected to a primitive form of positive vetting, officials had avoided putting him through the updated test, knowing that his imbibing and lascivious behaviour would result in a negative outcome.[43] In his discussions with the newspapers, therefore, Lohan was not in full possession of the facts and could only emphasise in general terms that 'matters of national security were at stake'.[44] Fortunately, the *Daily Mail* and the *Manchester Evening News* quickly backed out of the picture, with the latter proposing that the story was 'too big for it'.[45] This left the old enemy – the *Express*. Knowing that Pincher would not easily back down, Lohan was instructed to emphasise to the journalist that the cable story was covered by two D-Notices. The first, 'Intelligence and Security Services', was dated 27 April 1956; the second, 'Interception of Foreign Communications', was dated 30 October 1961.

On 20 February 1967, Lohan met with Pincher at their preferred eatery, the Écu de France. For reasons unknown to Pincher at the time, the Colonel insisted that they did not dine at their regular table and should move to the front of the restaurant: 'It was bizarre – for years Sammy and I had always sat in exactly the same spot, discreetly tucked away at the back of the establishment.'[46] As a general rule of thumb, the more important you are, the deeper into the restaurant you are seated. For Lohan to forgo his power table and sit with lesser mortals was completely out of character; he had unashamedly dedicated himself to 'making it' on the *haute* eating scene. For years, Pincher could not understand why the Colonel had been so adamant that they move. Today, however, the journalist is certain that Lohan had caught wind of the fact that their beloved table was in fact bugged. In the late 1980s, Rafael Calzada (a former senior director of the Écu) informed Pincher that, at the start of the Second World War, MI5 had installed microphones behind the fabric of the banquette seats so that they could eavesdrop on the table talk of foreign diplomats.[47] With reluctance, the restaurant's management allowed the continuation of the surveillance operation after 1945 so that MI5 could eavesdrop on Russian patrons. If Calzada's revelation is to be believed, one has to assume that Downing Street had long been monitoring Pincher's conversations with Lohan. By extension, if the Colonel had discovered that his table was bugged, this would explain why he was keen to dine in the less prestigious part of the restaurant.

At the Écu de France, Lohan enjoyed a couple of aperitifs before nursing a bottle of red wine during his meal. Although this hardly qualifies as excessive drinking, especially for one so accustomed to bibulous pleasure as Lohan, it is probably fair to say that it was enough to cloud his judgement at the critical moments. According to Lohan, reporting details of the lunch some days later to Sir James 'Ned' Dunnett (Permanent Undersecretary at the MoD), Pincher had been told in no uncertain terms by him that the story was a clear infringement of two D-Notices, copies of which he had placed on the table.[48] Pincher's recollection was and remains very different. According to the journalist, Lohan kept the D-Notices in his jacket pocket at all times and stated that, while he was under strong political pressure to prevent publication, the story did not offend any D-Notice.[49] The lunch concluded with Pincher agreeing to relay the Colonel's arguments to his editor, Derek Marks. As the two men waited for a taxi outside the restaurant, the journalist emphasised that Marks was his own man – 'a fearless journalist if ever there was one'[50] – and there was no way of saying for certain what decision he would make. Pincher added that if he were in Marks' shoes, he would publish. Whether he misheard or whether he was simply too intoxicated to heed his friend's warning, Lohan hot-footed back to his office and gleefully told Ewart-Biggs not to worry, for he had it on good authority that the story would not be published.[51] Disaster averted, or so he thought, Lohan hopped on a train for his home in Kent.[52]

As Pincher had anticipated, Marks' decision was to publish and be damned. That evening, around 7.30 p.m., Marks left instructions with the night editor to send the story to the newspaper's printing houses in Manchester, Glasgow and London. Ordinarily, he would have done this himself, but he was running late for an *Express* party at the Garrick Club. At 9.30 p.m., Pincher contacted Lohan and informed him of recent developments. The poor Colonel immediately telephoned the *Express* in a desperate bid to stop the printing. The night editor delivered more bad news, saying that it was far too late to cancel the regional editions, which had now been printed and were making their way to newsstands. By this point, news of developments had reached Denis Greenhill, Chairman of the JIC. He duly notified the Foreign Secretary, George Brown (Figure 12). Brown, never at his best outside working hours, rang up the *Express* and convinced its switchboard to put him through to Sir Max Aitken, the Beaverbrook

Newspapers proprietor. His mental faculties affected by drink, Brown wrongly assumed that Aitken was speaking to him from a telephone at the *Express*. Aitken was in fact at the Garrick, along with the rest of the newspaper's senior management, and had been forced to take the call from the porter's box. The conversation between the two men was the stuff of Keystone Cops. Aitken, who was also inebriated, could not understand what the Foreign Secretary was talking about. Remarkably, this was the first time he had even heard about cable vetting. To make matters worse, Brown was deliberately speaking in riddles, conscious of the fact that he was using an open line. As a result, Aitken had no idea about the security issues at stake. The conversation ended with Aitken saying that he would speak to Marks. Foolishly, Brown took this to mean that publication had been halted. Before going to bed, he passed on the glad tidings to Greenhill. Of course, Aitken had given no such assurance. Indeed, when he returned to the party, he was told by Marks that under no circumstances could the newspaper afford to pull the story for fear of being scooped. Shortly after midnight, with Brown sound asleep, Marks told the Foreign Office that the printers had been ordered to continue rolling.[53]

On 21 February, therefore, a red-letter day in the history of British secrecy, 'sigint finally hit the headlines'.[54] Readers of the *Express* – some 11 million of them – were entertained with a thundering leader entitled 'Cable Vetting Sensation'.[55] In the article, Pincher claimed that the interception and vetting of cables was part of a much larger operation, involving telephone tapping and the unauthorised opening of mail. By shrewdly conflating the cable story with a larger Orwellian fear of intrusion into privacy, the journalist had produced an article described by one official as being written in 'napalm instead of ink'.[56] David Winnick, Labour MP for Croydon South, suggested that it 'read like something from 1984'.[57] In Downing Street, Wilson was informed by the Foreign Office that both the *Mail* and the *Express* had been warned that the story contravened two D-Notices. He hit the roof – appalled that, whereas the *Mail* had accepted the need for censorship, its great rival had gone ahead regardless. Both Wigg and the Cabinet Secretary, Burke Trend, implored Wilson not to make too big a deal out of it; they argued that public condemnation of the newspaper would undermine the authority of the D-Notice system. Wigg also claimed that, if anyone should take the blame, it should be the Foreign Secretary.[58] Thunderstruck, Wilson disagreed; as he saw it,

Pincher and his conceited, confrontational backers at the *Express* had gone too far. Against all advice, he went to the House of Commons and claimed that there had been a 'clear breach of two D-Notices', an infringement about which the newspaper had been 'repeatedly warned'.[59] He then added that the article, despite being by his own admission 'sensationalised and inaccurate', had put lives at risk, and that legal action was being considered. Wilson's parliamentary outburst was particularly striking in the light of the fact that, only weeks before, he had met Pincher at the Savoy hotel, where he had been required to present him, in full view of the cameras, with the award of Journalist of the Decade!

Over the next few days, Pincher and Wilson exchanged accusation and counter-accusation. Exhibiting remarkable courage under fire, the journalist refuted the allegations, insisting that no D-Notice had been knowingly breached.[60] In Fleet Street, newspapers echoed his scorn and rallied to defend one of their own kind. Both *The Times* and the *Telegraph* argued that, if, as Wilson had claimed, the article was inaccurate, why then was there a need to invoke D-Notices?[61] In Parliament, however, Wilson stood by his original claim. His unshakeable belief that the *Express* had been guilty of an offence was not helped by the fact that Lohan, instead of admitting that he had messed up, was steadfastly maintaining to officials that he had reminded Pincher time without number that D-Notices were relevant in this case.[62] Under pressure from Edward Heath, Leader of the Opposition, Wilson was moved to set up an inquiry. The prime minister's initial plan was that the investigation should be conducted by the D-Notice Committee itself.[63] The committee included some powerful civil servants who, he believed, would side with the government. Sadly for Wilson, the idea was thrown out when, on 23 February, during a meeting with the committee held to discuss who should conduct the investigation, Lee Howard, editor of the *Mirror*, overheard him whisper to one of the mandarins, 'you better get that chap Pincher'.[64] The next day, Howard tendered his resignation from the committee, stating that it was a 'gross abuse' of its function to sit in judgement on another newspaper.[65] In the words of the *Spectator*, Howard's abdication was a 'real kick in the shins' to the prime minister, who had confidently regarded the *Mirror* as 'the hooker in the socialist pack'.[66]

Accordingly, Wilson passed the responsibility to a committee of privy councillors under the chairmanship of Lord Radcliffe, an eminent judge with previous experience of leading public inquiries into security matters. Indeed, the regularity with which his talent as a chairman was called upon in the post-war years prompted Sir Alan Patrick Herbert, a famous novelist and playwright, to coin the phrase 'Government by Radcliffery'.[67] Party political representation on the committee was ensured by the nomination of Tory heavyweight Selwyn Lloyd and Labour stalwart Emmanuel Shinwell, chosen by their respective party leaders because they were both former ministers of defence.[68] With hindsight, Marcia Williams felt that Wilson's selection of Shinwell was 'naïve', since he had just resigned as Chairman of the Labour Party and was not on particularly good terms with George Brown whose head was, of course, on the chopping block.[69] Over the following weeks, the Radcliffe Committee took evidence from prominent figures in Fleet Street, as well as representatives from several departments of state. As it did so, acrimony between the press and the government continued to rise. On 3 March, the *Spectator* became the first publication ever to disclose the complete text of a D-Notice, when it published the two D-Notices pertaining to the case.[70] The magazine argued that the wording of the D-Notices made Pincher's story perfectly acceptable. Cable vetting was not a 'secret method' but rather a 'known method carried out in secrecy'. As such, it did not fall under the provisions of either D-Notice. Labour MPs fruitlessly attempted to turn Fleet Street against the *Express*, making the point that no other newspaper had published the story, the inference being that the *Express* was unpatriotic.

Simmering tensions between the press and certain members of the government boiled over into an ugly spat at a dinner party held at the Reform Club on 14 March by Gerald Long, general manager of Reuters. Long had arranged the meal to welcome to London the head of TASS in Moscow, Mr Goryunov. The guest list for the evening was distinguished and included the Russian ambassador, Edward Pickering (editorial director of the *Daily Mirror*), Charles Wintour (editor of the *Evening Standard*), Alastair Burnet (editor of the *Economist*), and Charles Fenby (editorial director of the *Westminster Press*). Also in attendance was George Brown. After a few pleasantries, the Foreign Secretary suddenly launched into an attack on British journalists, describing them as 'prima donnas' who, when attacked, ganged up together in order to 'do down' politicians.[71] Not wanting to offend Goryunov, guests temporarily made allowances for Brown's 'exuberance', offering mild and good-humoured protests.[72] However, Brown refused to pipe down, stating that the latest example of this 'ganging-up' was the D-Notice Affair. With this, Burnet and Pickering refused to bite their tongues any longer, intervening to say that the fault rested entirely with the prime minister. Pickering, a former editor of the *Express*, added that he would say as much to the Radcliffe Committee. Brown erupted. He argued that Pincher had ignored a third D-Notice and drummed home the point with a great deal of finger-wagging. (Where Brown got a third D-Notice from is anyone's guess!) He then announced that Pickering's appearance at the tribunal was a 'typical piece of arrogance' and that he would 'tip off Manny Shinwell tonight so that he knows the right questions to ask you'.[73] By this point, Goryunov was visibly uncomfortable and, in an effort to relieve the tension, joked that everyone would be going to prison. Brown nevertheless continued to shout abuse at Pickering: 'I am warning you.' He was even heard murmuring, 'People like this should be stuffed and put in a cage.'[74] Guests pleaded with Pickering 'to play it cool'.[75] Unbelievably, Brown then switched his venom to the other guests, lurching to his feet to call the ambassador a 'sloganist', an undignified remark which left the Russian 'deeply hurt'.[76] Thankfully, before things got even more out of hand, Pickering managed to calm everyone down by raising his glass in Brown's direction and saying, 'We have spent many evenings like this together.'[77]

By mid May, Radcliffe had finished taking evidence and had written a draft report. Until this point, Wilson had afforded the committee complete freedom; on 28 March, he had emphasised to Radcliffe: 'I need not say that I do not in the least wish to intervene.'[78] When presented with the draft report, however, he changed his tune. On 16 May, he asked Radcliffe to Chequers. Michael Halls, Wilson's principal private secretary, took detailed minutes of the meeting. According to this document, the prime minister cut straight to the chase, stating that he was unhappy with Radcliffe's conclusions. Written in 'black and white' terms, the conclusions completely exonerated Pincher and the *Express*, ruling that the cable story had not been inaccurate and had not breached any D-Notice.[79] Furthermore, the conclusions implicitly rejected the evidence of the Foreign Secretary and other key official witnesses. One of the conclusions had even postulated that a Defence Ministry spokesman, on instructions from the Foreign Office, had given false information to the press. Radcliffe did not share Wilson's concerns, claiming that the rest of the report was more balanced (written in 'varying shades of grey') and that press reaction would amount to 'something of a three day wonder'.[80] He added that it would be 'tactically unwise' for the government to continue to cast the *Express* in the role of villain, for the facts did not support such a charge. Wilson, however, was not open to persuasion, underlining that it would be the conclusions upon which Fleet Street would 'undoubtedly seize'.[81]

With both men agreeing to disagree, the prime minister started to make demands. His first request was bold in the extreme, asking if the conclusions could be deleted from the final report. To this, Radcliffe replied that Shinwell and Lloyd would never agree to it. Wilson then asked if the committee would take into consideration some new evidence which had only recently come to light. At this point, he handed Radcliffe 'certain papers relating to Lohan'.[82] According to Hall's minutes, the judge was 'deeply shocked', for the material pointed to 'gross misdemeanour' on the Colonel's part.[83] Exactly what Wilson showed Radcliffe is unknown. However, judging by the latter's subsequent comment that it could be used to prosecute Lohan under the Official Secrets Act, one has to speculate that it contained something about the Colonel's relationship with Pincher. One possibility would be that Radcliffe had been given the verbatim transcripts of the two men's lunchtime conversations at the Écu; another would be that he had been shown pictures of Lohan entering and leaving the journalist's flat with a female companion. While conceding that he had a low opinion of Lohan, and underlining that in future the D-Notice Secretary should be a person of 'much greater ability', Radcliffe claimed that it was now far too late for the committee to 'take cognisance' of the new material.[84] The prime minister's final request was that the secret evidence taken by the committee be published along with its report. This was Wilson at his most scheming, for the evidence revealed Lohan to be incompetent, prejudiced and possessing a host of character flaws. Lohan's own testimony, when cross-referenced with other statements, showed him to be a liar – for example, falsifying dates and times. The Colonel had been fighting for his professional life and had said certain things in the knowledge, or so he thought, that they would not be made public. Radcliffe consented to Wilson's final request, surely knowing that it would do untold damage to Lohan's reputation.

Following his summit with Radcliffe, Wilson became obsessed with the impending publication of the committee's report, so much so that he dedicated hour upon hour trying to get a handle on the possible fallout at the expense of other pressing issues – such as the crisis in the Middle East that led to the Arab–Israeli Six Day War in early June. According to Marcia Williams, a 'cloud of secrecy' descended on Number 10.[85] Meetings were held, but attendance was strictly limited to a small coterie of officials, the most regular attendees being Wigg, Denis Healey (Secretary of State for Defence), Gerald Gardiner (Lord Chancellor), Frederick Elwyn Jones (Attorney General), Trend and Helsby.[86] In her memoir, Williams recalled that it was the 'only period when the door between my room and the Cabinet room remained locked for very long stretches at a time'.[87] On no occasion, Williams went on, was the Political Office involved: 'We were given briefings from time to time, but it was only just enough to enable queries to be evaded and not sufficient for a balanced view to be reached on whether the thing was being handled badly or well'.[88] Endless deliberations ensured that weeks went by without any sign of Radcliffe's verdict. Pincher complained to the MoD that he had twice had to postpone his holiday and suspected that the government was looking to publish the report when other events, such as the Six Day War, were capturing the public interest.[89]

So what exactly was being discussed and why was it taking so long to reach a conclusion? One of the issues that had to be resolved was deciding what evidence from the Radcliffe Committee would be included as an appendix to the published report. This was not a simple task. A lot of the material was of an extremely sensitive nature and thus had to be vetted. The job of 'cleaning' the evidence from the perspective of national security was allocated to a working party coordinated by Ewart-Biggs. Predictably, references to GCHQ, Operation Shamrock and the like were top of the list for removal.[90] Overseeing the deletion of passages which might cause political embarrassment was Wigg.[91] A consummate dirty-trickster, Wigg took this opportunity to strengthen the government's case against Lohan, removing anything which reflected positively on the hapless Colonel. For the cutting room floor, therefore, was the opinion of Martin Furnival Jones (Director General of MI5) that 'the task of Secretary was an unenviable one', for its holder had to 'run with the hare and hunt with the hounds'.[92] Furnival Jones had also remarked, 'I doubt whether any man would be regarded as ideal at all times by all sides.'[93] Midway through the expurgation process, members of the working party started to have grave reservations about what they were doing, believing that the publication of *any* evidence 'would gratuitously provoke speculation and be damaging to security'.[94] Publication of the evidence 'might well give the Russian and other hostile intelligence services useful background material', feared one official.[95] If people were to read between the lines, as surely they would do, it would be obvious that there was an 'unspecified department' in Britain, namely GCHQ, which was concerned not only with the interception of telegrams, but with the interception of letters and telephone calls. Moreover, since GCHQ's activities were 'very closely integrated with those of the United States', any publicity to the subject was bound to have repercussions for Anglo-US relations.[96] Trend shared these concerns and told his senior Whitehall colleagues so in a private correspondence: 'Does anybody wish to raise objections, of principle or of practice, to publishing the expurgated evidence?'[97] When Wilson read this, he exploded. On Sunday 28 May, he telephoned Trend and gave him a tongue-lashing the likes of which few civil servants have known, or survived. Wilson accused him of 'backtracking' and ruled that there should be no wider ministerial consultation on the issue.[98] His ears burning, Trend replied that he had only sought to present his master with the facts, and needed to impress upon him that the publication of heavily redacted evidence would look 'a bit odd'.[99]

The next day, Wilson sent a personal minute to Trend. A cursory reading of this document would give the impression that the prime minister had finally got off his high horse and decided to listen to his advisers. He admits that the working group has made 'quite a powerful case against publication'.[100] He states that his 'inclination now is to wash my hands of the whole affair and let the machine decide how this should be handled'.[101] He apologises for his part in the feud, commenting in a handwritten postscript, 'I want you to be absolutely clear that whatever disagreements we have had … I respect your motives and concern … and [hope] this whole sad episode will make no difference whatsoever to our relationship on other and far more important issues.'[102] In the ultimate gesture of reconciliation, he remarks, 'In other words, Burke, I know when I'm beat.'[103] However, as historian Matthew Creevy astutely argues, such statements were disingenuous and amounted to a 'feigned surrender'.[104] This was because Wilson, amid all the gushing acknowledgements of defeat, had slipped in the proviso 'the last battle is fought under my direction'.[105] Trend was too long in the tooth not to realise the significance of this remark. Accordingly, on 30 May, he arranged an urgent meeting between himself, Wilson and Wigg. Here, it quickly became apparent to him that publication of the evidence was now a fait accompli. The prime minister explained (honestly) that Healey and Gardiner had given their full consent, and (untruthfully) that George Brown had too.[106] Unsurprisingly, the Foreign Secretary was violently against publication. The evidence, however carefully doctored, was bound to arouse suspicion that on the critical night in question he had overindulged. It was no secret, of course, that Brown liked a drink; *Private Eye*'s favourite euphemism for his regular condition was 'tired and emotional'. Until now, however, there had been no reason to suspect that alcohol ever impeded him in the discharge of his official duties.

On 31 May, Trend backed down and final approval for publication was granted. With this, Wilson directed his energies to the question of what response, if any, he should make to Radcliffe's report. The smart play would be to accept the committee's conclusions, apologise and let the matter rest. He opted to do no such thing. Instead, he decided that he would make an example of Pincher, the scourge of officialdom, and come down hard on Lohan in the hope of driving him out of Whitehall. As discussed earlier, evidence indicates that Wilson had long been looking for an opportunity to unseat the D-Notice Secretary, wary of the Colonel's right-wing sympathies, not to mention his supposed links with dubious elements in the intelligence community. By spring 1967, Wilson's fears about Lohan were at fever pitch. In his possession, he had several letters from disillusioned Tory MP and stoolpigeon Captain Henry Kerby, revealing that the Colonel was plotting to bring down the government. At the prompting of Wigg, Kerby had spent the previous six months cosying up to Lohan. The ploy worked. Blissfully unaware of Wigg's scheming, the Colonel mistook Kerby for a friend, someone with whom he could discuss the sins of the Labour government and devise ways of attacking it.

Lohan had first taken Kerby into his confidence on 20 December 1966 at a party in Ennismore Gardens, Knightsbridge, held by the *Sunday Telegraph*. As Kerby reported events to Wigg the next day (in a 'Most Confidential and Personal' correspondence), midway through the evening Lohan had pulled him to one side and asked, 'in [a] foghorn voice' and 'the worse for drink', whether he would be prepared to ask a series of embarrassing parliamentary questions designed to 'put that bloody bastard Wigg on the spot once and for all'.[107] The questions, Lohan continued, would be written by him personally and accompanied by one or two supplementaries which no minister could answer without 'blowing Wigg out of the water'.[108] To protect his cover, Kerby said disingenuously that he would be happy to help out and suggested lunch in the New Year. Privately, he was 'absolutely appalled by [the Colonel's] loud-mouthed and vicious indiscretions'. 'My old friend Admiral Thomson', he lamented, 'must be turning in his grave.'[109] In his letter to Wigg, he emphasised that the government had 'a sworn and most personal enemy', who would 'stop at nothing to do [Wilson] down'.[110]

Wigg encouraged Kerby to stay close to Lohan in a bid to build a case against the Colonel and discover his precise intention. This became clear when the two men met for lunch at the Danish Club in Dover Street, Westminster, on 26 January 1967. To shatter the government, announced Lohan, there must be a moral scandal, à la Profumo. Such a scandal, he enthused, was now 'on the boil'.[111] On the grapevine, Lohan had heard a rumour that Lord Chalfont, a minister in the Foreign Office, was having an affair with a communist sweetheart and had even been spotted 'with his finger up' a most attractive woman at the White Tower restaurant in Charlotte Street.[112] Lohan had no evidence of indiscretion by Chalfont, so suggested that Kerby at some expedient moment should try to flush him out by writing a secret letter to Wilson with words to the effect that 'the nation would never understand another Profumo'.[113] During the lunch, Lohan's predilection for scurrilous gossip reached new heights. He revealed that Wilson was unwell with an upper respiratory tract infection and that his doctor believed it to be serious. He also disclosed that the scientist Sir Solly Zuckerman desired a peerage and had built intimate relations with the Palace. Kerby was disgusted, reporting back to his Labour Party contacts that he considered Lohan 'mad', 'mental' and 'sinister'.[114] Over the next few months, egged on by Wigg, Kerby continued to further his contact with Lohan. On 21 February, the day of the cable story, he telephoned the Colonel and declared: 'Congrats Sammy. You really hit the jackpot this morning! Good for you ... and good for Harry!'[115] In reply, Lohan said that he had endured a 'hellish five days' and that he was 'shit scared'. During their conversation, it is interesting to note that the two men had been temporarily cut off, prompting Lohan to comment 'some bastard is monitoring us'.[116]

In view of Kerby's evidence, Wilson felt he had to act. Some years later, he reportedly held clear-the-air talks with Pincher and conceded that Lohan – 'a dreadful fellow' – had to be removed.[117] He decided therefore that the government should issue a White Paper, to be published on the same day as Radcliffe's report. Drafted in under two weeks, the White Paper represented an absolute repudiation of Radcliffe's findings, attributing all the blame to the *Express* and to Lohan. It said that the newspaper must 'bear direct responsibility for what happened' and reiterated Wilson's stance that D-Notices had been breached.[118] It upheld that the article was 'sensationalised and inaccurate', intended to convey the impression – 'in no way borne out by the facts' – that the government was inventing intrusive ways of encroaching upon people's right to privacy.[119] With subtle hints throughout the text that Lohan's judgement had been affected by drink and by his friendship with Pincher, the White Paper accused the Colonel of not having tried hard enough to stop publication. Lohan was criticised for not expressing to officials his concerns that the Foreign Office had asked him to do a job for which he had not been adequately briefed; as an appendage to this, it was alleged that he had not been positively vetted. Furthermore, it was proposed that he had had several opportunities to notify his superiors of the impending disaster, but only did so when it was too late.

Trend was extremely anxious about the White Paper. The evidence adduced by Radcliffe overwhelmingly supported the view that Wilson was wrong on several counts. Despite acknowledging that he had not seen Lohan for many years and had always found him to be a 'rather brash individual', Trend was dubious about making the Colonel a scapegoat and the target of a spin operation, fearing that this would reflect badly on Whitehall for putting him in the job in the first place. Walking on eggshells by this point, Trend warned Wilson in person that if he decided to 'go it alone', he might 'get out of the present situation only to find himself in a worse mess'.[120] Wilson, however, was in no mood to back down. On 7 June, he had received another secret note from Kerby, confirming that Lohan – a 'wild animal' not unlike a 'rogue boar' – was taking an unnatural interest in ministers' sex lives and was still looking to drop the Chalfont bombshell.[121] Kerby, who reiterated his view that the man was 'quite mad' and 'definitely not compos mentis', echoed Wilson's belief that it was essential to 'crucify' Lohan as a prelude to sacking him.

The Colonel was a Mason with friends in high places. Both MI5 and SIS were believed to be staunch supporters, seeing him as a patriot who shared their anger at the government's plans to slash defence expenditure. Unless Lohan was shamed beyond all repair, it was possible that the intelligence community would rally to his rescue and insist that he stayed on as D-Notice Secretary.

Accordingly, Wilson informed Trend that the White Paper was part of the 'political phase' of proceedings, a matter about which he would be 'intolerant of intervention by the official machine'.[122] Without wanting to suggest that Wilson was being browbeaten by Wigg, it is telling to note that the Paymaster General was maintaining throughout deliberations that he could not wait to 'square up' to Radcliffe, and gave the opinion that Trend's reservations 'made him want to spit'.[123] With Trend neutralised, the last hurdle Wilson had to overcome was getting support from his ministerial colleagues, the majority of whom had not the slightest idea of developments. Wilson, acutely aware that there would be dissenting voices, sprung the White Paper on a shocked Cabinet at the eleventh hour, on 13 June. In his diary, Crossman revealed that there was 'no chance of Cabinet amending it'.[124] The night before, Wilson had swamped his colleagues with a mountain of superfluous reading material; in Cabinet, moreover, he initiated a protracted foreign policy discussion on Rhodesia, in so doing leaving only half an hour to debate matters relating to the Radcliffe Report.[125] Although a handful of ministers did raise objections (Crossman, for example, announced that the document would 'do Harold untold harm'),[126] the wheels were already in motion. Indeed, Creevy has cleverly deduced that Wilson, several hours *before* the Cabinet had even convened, had sent a letter to Radcliffe telling him that the government was going to publish a repudiatory White Paper.[127] For Crossman, left lamenting how Wilson had bypassed his own Cabinet, 'this was the first occasion I can remember him taking the strictly presidential line'.[128] As will now be seen, both Wilson and the secret state would have to live with the consequences.

* * *

It's clear that every newspaper has been turned against Harold.
Richard Crossman, 14 June 1967[129]

When made public in the afternoon on 13 June, the Radcliffe Report sparked wild celebrations in Fleet Street. The committee's acquittal of the *Express* was seen as a major victory for press freedom. Irrespective of their professional loyalties and ideological orientations, jubilant newspapermen took great delight in casting Wilson as a man traduced, while at the same lauding Pincher as a courageous reporter who had taken a stand against the government and secured a memorable victory. In the evening, Max Aitken hosted a celebratory dinner in honour of the newspaper's heroic scoop-merchant. As Pincher remembers it, the degree of *Schadenfreude* was palpable, with every journalist and editor taking their turn to toast to Wilson's misfortune.[130] Over the next forty-eight hours, Pincher received many letters of congratulation. Several journalists wrote to him and announced that, in future, they would not be so sympathetic to government claims that national security would be imperilled if they went ahead with a particular story. A number of school leavers also contacted him, claiming that the D-Notice Affair had convinced them to follow in his footsteps and pursue a career in investigative journalism. Pincher's most cherished letter came from the legendary *Sunday Express* editor Sir John Junor, who said: 'There may have been greater triumphs in Fleet Street. But if so, I do not remember them.'[131]

Press reaction to the White Paper was vehement. 'It was the only occasion I can recall where all the newspapers presented a united front against the government,' declared Pincher in 2007.[132] The fact that the pro-Labour *Daily Mirror* branded the document a 'whitewash' must have been particularly upsetting to the prime minister, not least because, on 9 June, he had telephoned Hugh Cudlipp, chairman of the newspaper, and pleaded with him to defend the government's position. Mischievously, Wilson had even told Cudlipp a few 'not very nice' things about Lohan, in the hope that the newspaper would, through its not inconsiderable influence, turn public opinion against the Colonel.[133]

As Peter Hennessy has argued, Radcliffe was perhaps the most widely respected public servant of his generation, 'in effect the number 1 on the List of the Great and the Good'.[134] By rejecting his decision, Wilson had displayed an arrogant conviction of his own infallibility. The *Guardian* accused him of being drunk with power.[135] Fleet Street's wholehearted condemnation of the prime minister's actions was epitomised by a Michael Cummings cartoon which showed batsman Wilson, with black and heavy bags under his eyes, insisting to the umpire that he was 'Not Out', despite the sight of three stumps and bails flying in all directions. Other cartoons featured Radcliffe forcing Wilson to wear a dunce's cap for misbehaviour and asinine stupidity. The apparent smearing of Lohan evoked universal disapproval. Lohan himself gave several interviews to the press, in which he emphasised that he had been positively vetted and was convinced that someone in government was 'out to get him'.[136] As he saw it, his position as D-Notice Secretary was 'now impossible', and he doubted whether the voluntary system would survive the fallout. The publication of Radcliffe's evidence also did the government no favours in the eyes of the press. Newspapers latched on to the comic opera of the night of 20 February when everyone, it seemed, was blotto. The *New Statesman* declared, in light-hearted terms, that the 'moral of the whole business is that Foreign Secretaries should not telephone newspaper proprietors late in the evening'.[137] Other newspapers, such as *The Times* and the *Telegraph*, were not so forgiving, arguing that Brown's drink-induced errors of judgement were beyond the pale. Fleet Street, of course, had long recognised that alcohol and political life went hand in hand. Among the most famous of Westminster tipplers were former prime ministers William Pitt the Younger, Winston Churchill and Herbert 'Squiffy' Asquith. Asquith, who was often seen swaying on his feet when speaking in the House of Commons, even had his very own drinking song: 'Mr Asquith says in a manner sweet and calm – another little drink won't do us any harm'. Hitherto, journalists had tended to congratulate the conviviality of the political drinker, seeing it is as part and parcel of a hectic, stressful and sometimes lonely existence. In this case, however, they were uncharacteristically vicious.[138] The *News of the World* even suggested that, until now, the extent to which Brown had been so consistently pickled must have been hidden by a permanent D-Notice.[139]

Within hours of the first press reports being published on the morning of 14 June, Wilson knew that he had taken a heavy political risk and it had backfired. Pulled to one side after Cabinet by Crossman – who said, reassuringly, 'you're always at your best in this kind of crisis' – the prime minister lamented: 'I'm not sure I shall be on this occasion.'[140] With a parliamentary debate on the White Paper scheduled for 22 June, Wilson plotted his next move. His Cabinet colleagues were unanimous in their opinion that it was now time to 'adopt a posture of magnanimity'.[141] Journalists had exhibited an extraordinary level of opprobrium towards the government. At a

meeting of editors and selected officials held by the Newspaper Proprietors Association on 16 June, Henry James, Downing Street deputy
press secretary, noted that the 'hatred of [Wilson] personally by the
editors had to be experienced to be believed'.[142] Charles Wintour was
said to be 'pathologically hostile' to the prime minister.[143] Furthermore, it was clear that journalists were still looking for blood. 'Every
dog is allowed one bite, but a different view is taken of a dog that goes
on biting all the time,' warned the *Privateer*.[144]

Wilson, however, refused to yield. Urged on by Wigg (who by
this point had earned from Castle the sobriquet 'evil genius'),[145] he
determined that the best form of defence was attack. In a further round
of closed meetings involving the Paymaster General, it was decided
that, in Parliament, Wilson would go after the unfortunate Lohan.
The Colonel was no saint and it was believed that a few disparaging
comments would go a long way towards diverting press attention from
the embattled government. Lohan, moreover, had not yet resigned.
On 16 June, Kerby had once again written to Wigg, this time to argue
that Lohan's position could be made untenable – and his resignation
'FORCED' – if the front bench insinuated that his successor would
require higher security clearance.[146] To assist Wilson in the smear
strategy, Wigg called on Shinwell and Labour backbencher Raymond
Fletcher. Both were asked to take to the floor and blacken Lohan's
name, with Fletcher being asked to deliver a 'googly', by alleging that
the Colonel had been a major source of leaks to Pincher, the implication
being therefore that he was a traitor.[147] The irony here is that Fletcher
was himself a turncoat. In 1999, he was unmasked by Soviet defector
Vasili Mitrokhin as a former KGB spy, codenamed Peter.[148]

In Parliament, the debate lasted nearly six hours. Wilson delegated the responsibility of opening the discussion to Attorney General
Sir Elwyn Jones, a smart bit of parliamentary footwork designed to
ensure that he would speak last, without any possibility of rebuttal.
Jones spoke for forty-five minutes, in which time he repeated that there
had been a violation of D-Notices, resulting in the endangerment of
men's lives. When pressed on this, he announced that the 'government
cannot, without committing a further breach of security ... spell out
the reasons for the importance they attach to the suppression of the
Express story'.[149]

For the Conservative Opposition, Anthony Barber tabled an
alternative motion, putting forward that that the White Paper's chief

purpose was to protect the authority of an 'arrogant' prime minister who, because of sheer vanity, was unable to utter one simple sentence: 'I made a mistake.'[150] The middle portion of the debate was dominated by Shinwell and Fletcher. Shinwell labelled Lohan 'amateur', 'interesting' and 'strange', even suggesting that the Colonel could be incorporated into a James Bond film.[151] Shinwell repeatedly alluded to Lohan's heavy drinking and extravagant way of life; when describing the meal at the Écu de France, he claimed 'there was a good deal of alcoholic refreshment'.[152] Fletcher's speech, branded 'disgraceful' by one member of the House, was unadulterated character assassination. Fletcher began by underlining that the D-Notice system only works if it is administered by honourable men. He followed this by saying that neither Lohan nor Pincher, a journalist who 'ignores the ethics of the profession', had any concept of honour. Fletcher's denouement was that 'Fleet Street is buzzing with rumours to the effect that Colonel Lohan has been the source of many of Pincher's stories.'[153]

Wilson wound up the rigged debate by smearing Lohan's name still further. He accused the Colonel of maintaining an 'over-close relationship' with Pincher. This relationship, he continued, was a matter of enormous concern to the previous Conservative government, so much so that, in early 1964, consideration had been given as to whether Lohan should continue as Secretary. Wilson then declared, without qualification, that Lohan's 'shortcomings' as a man had meant that he had not been positively vetted. In saying this, Wilson delivered an appalling falsehood, for a week earlier Helsby had told him that Lohan had been put through a 'modified form' of positive vetting in 1955. Moreover, Helsby had emphasised that the 'consistent and unanimous view' of both MI5 and departmental security experts was that the post of D-Notice Secretary 'did not warrant positive vetting'.[154] After Wilson's speech, there was no time for questions and the White Paper was approved through a strictly party-line vote of confidence. In the evening, an exhausted prime minister committed to record that, with the greatest relief, the time had now come for him to disentangle himself from 'this extremely wearying subject'.[155]

Sadly for Wilson, he found himself out of the frying pan, into the fire. In the days following, every newspaper carried articles denouncing his attack upon the character and conduct of Lohan. In one of the most acerbic editorials in the newspaper's recent history, filled with pugilistic prose, The Times lambasted the 'shameful campaign of innuendo'.[156] According to the newspaper, the tactics were 'so pitiless, so adroit and so lacking in scruple' that it was plainly apparent that 'no man's character is safe'.[157] The *Daily Mirror* was no less incensed; indeed, Cudlipp told Crossman that the newspaper had 'declared war on Harold'.[158] In a caustic piece entitled 'The Love of Two Colonels', Pincher claimed that his close association with Lohan had been no different to the relationship he had enjoyed with Wigg when Labour had been out of office, suggesting that Wigg had once telephoned him and given him the rumbustious greeting, 'Is this the world's greatest journalist?'[159] Pincher went on to explain that, some years previously, after a particularly bountiful fly-fishing trip in the Scottish Highlands, he had sent Wigg a salmon as a gift. (Some months later, in a private correspondence, Wigg recollected that the salmon in question was not fit for human consumption; thus, he had it fed to a neighbouring cat – an act of cruelty, in hindsight, since the animal was never seen again!)[160] If Wilson thought things could not get any worse, he was wrong. In the House of Lords, on 6 July, Radcliffe 'took apart the government's case with the artistry of a surgeon, and at the end left it scattered about the operating theatre headless and limbless'.[161] The White Paper, he argued, was awash with 'general statements about significance to security'.[162] Its publication, he continued, was proof that the government desired 'not a free press, but a managed press'.[163] For Wilson, Radcliffe's speech was devastating. Crossman described the jurist's complaints as 'annihilating', amounting to the 'most effective quiet rebuke of a Prime Minister by a public servant of modern time'.[164]

In just under six months, Wilson had succeeded not only in alienating the most distinguished crown servant in the land, but in destroying his relations with the press. Thereafter, as Henry James lamented, 'he was not taken seriously [by journalists] – an air of cynicism entered'.[165] In her memoir, Marcia Williams similarly concluded that the impact of his harebrained antics on his meticulously constructed media image was nothing short of 'disastrous'.[166] The only crumb of comfort was the resignation of the troublesome Lohan on 26 June. Despite an outpouring of public sympathy for the Colonel, his continuation as D-Notice Secretary was impossible. Through a series of newspaper interviews, Lohan popularised the view that he had been thrown to the wolves in order to cover up failures at the highest level. In the *Spectator*, on 30 June, he claimed to have been 'slandered out of business by half-truth, untruth and innuendo'.[167]

Despite his attempts to clear his name, his reputation never recovered. An in-house Civil Service inquiry overseen by Helsby, Dunnett and Treasury solicitor Harvey Druitt concluded on 8 August that the Colonel had made 'several errors' and had allowed his long association with Pincher to cloud objective thinking.[168] Lohan, who was quizzed by Helsby's team for nearly 48 hours, asserted publicly that the inquiry was tantamount to a 'kangaroo court'. He died a broken man, stripped of his pension and denied further employment in Whitehall.[169]

Admittedly, Lohan had his flaws and was hardly the person whom one would have expected to be a guardian of national security. He drank too much, was an inveterate gossip, had a wide command of salty language, and was a self-confessed serial womaniser. When giving evidence to Radcliffe, he reportedly boasted so regularly about his sexual 'powers' that one witness doubted whether his 'performance' could match his braggadocio.[170] Yet it is hard not to feel sympathy for the Colonel. He wrongly believed the deceitful Kerby to be his friend, even referring to him in correspondence as 'my dear Bob'.[171] If, during their confabulations, the Foreign Office had allowed him on the premises, he might have had a better grasp of the broader security context. As D-Notice Secretary, he was required to maintain good relations with journalists; one might argue that his rapport with Pincher was a way of keeping close to a kicking horse. Moreover, one should remember that he and Pincher were supposedly great companions. They took lunch together at least once a month and called each other 'Harry' and 'Sammy'. Ultimately, however, when presented with a golden opportunity to deliver a political blow to the Labour government, Pincher put the scoop first. The consummate professional overcame the friend.

Along with Wilson and Lohan, the great loser of the affair was the secret state. As we have seen, in the post-1945 period journalists had shown a remarkable aptitude for unearthing secrets, which in turn had put a greater responsibility on the D-Notice Committee to maintain control. Amid the wreckage of cable vetting, a big problem facing Britain's secret-keepers was that the system had fallen into disrepute, with many reporters publicly announcing their intention to turn their back on it. Wilson's contemptuous slap in the face to Radcliffe had shown that officials expected the system to be weighted in favour of the government and all too easily confused national security with political embarrassment. Fleet Street's attitude was encapsulated by the *Weekly News* when it declared that the 'D' in *D-Notice* stood for 'Deception, Deviousness and Double-Dealing'.[172] In a bid to get the system up and running again, a new Secretary was appointed in the shape of Admiral Norman Denning, a former Director of Naval Intelligence (1960–4). To prevent a farcical situation ever again occurring where the Secretary was excluded from high-level meetings, it was ruled that the incumbent had to be vetted to the highest level.[173] In service to making the system more formal, all future D-Notice Secretaries were to be located in a secure office in MoD Main Building and denied an entertainment allowance, thus bringing to an end the days when the incumbent could be seen 'hot-desking' in the West End. One of the many lessons carried over from the Lohan era was that, in matters of national security, an abstemious way of life was absolutely essential. Despite these improvements, Whitehall knew that there were no guarantees that the system would ever again be a respected and relevant forum. For there to be any chance of trust being restored, it was important that over the coming months, perhaps years, the D-Notice Committee avoid further controversy. With a new mood of restraint, Wigg recommended 'a fairly long period of convalescence in which the patient should not be subject to violent shocks but rather should be allowed to gain health and strength in accordance with what I hope is the Will of the Lord'.[174]

This, of course, would be easier said than done. When Wilson expressed his personal censure of Pincher, the secret state's biggest irritant, he almost certainly hoped that this would put an end to the scoop-merchant's audacious brand of politically charged reporting, perhaps even force him into early retirement. Now the wrong side of fifty, Pincher had already shown an interest in pursuing a second career as a novelist, publishing two works of fiction in 1965 and 1967.[175] Wilson, however, failed to get his man. Pincher was the great victor of the D-Notice Affair. He had been vindicated very publicly by the respected Lord Radcliffe and was now, unquestionably, the grandee of investigative journalism (Figure 13). Ominously for Whitehall, he emerged from the affair more determined than ever to discover secrets, fortified by a heightened confidence that brooked no dissent: 'My career was on a peak, and with the D-Notice machinery in disarray, the future looked rosy.'[176] As a result, it was not long before he was back attacking the Labour government with damaging leaks.

On 24 June 1967, the day after the D-Notice debate, he rubbed salt into Wilson's wounds by announcing Charles de Gaulle's decision to cancel a £250 million Anglo-French project to build a variable-geometry fighter, or Swing-Wing, as a European counterpart to the American tactical strike aircraft, the F-111.[177] This premature disclosure was devastating to the government. With no time to prepare defensive lines, Wilson was forced to justify to irate MPs yet another crushing blow to Britain's ailing aircraft industry, still reeling from the cancellation of the TSR2 project. In trying to ascertain the source of the leak, officials initially considered the ludicrous possibility that Pincher had intercepted a telephone call from the MoD to the British embassy in Paris. According to Group Captain Williams, a Downing Street security officer, there were 'absolutely no existing facilities' for protecting the security of cross-channel communications.[178] In the end, it was agreed that he had probably been tipped off by a disgruntled anti-Labour employee of the British Aircraft Corporation.

For the secret state, still having Pincher to contend with was bad enough, but arguably a greater concern was the impact that the D-Notice Affair had on Fleet Street in-the-round. In summer 1967, as officials reflected on events, the big fear was that other journalists would be encouraged to join the cavalcade. The affair had shifted millions of copies of newspapers and had made a household name out of the reporter who had set it all in motion. Hitherto, defence correspondents had tended to be faceless gumshoes, content to stay out of sight in the newsroom. Over a six-month period, Pincher had given a steady stream of interviews to the BBC and ITV. Awards were aplenty. He was chosen as a Radio Industries Club 'Man of the Year' alongside the film stars Jack Hawkins and Topol – an award celebrated at a glitzy ceremony at the Savoy hotel.[179] As Trend recognised, Pincher's success and subsequent fame had gone some way to romanticising investigative reporting in Britain, and was inspiring a new wave of gutsy journalism. Suddenly, no secret seemed safe: 'There is a more cavalier attitude on the part of the press and of authors writing about sensitive subjects ... as a result of the recent Radcliffe Report.'[180] Wigg had it confirmed to him by several editors that Pincher had effectively touched off a journalistic treasure hunt.[181] Newspapers were said to be champing at the bit to crack a story so large that everyone would stand up and take notice.

* * *

These three [Burgess, Maclean, Philby] are to be x-rayed in the most searching detail ever before attempted.

Captain Henry Kerby, 20 September 1967[182]

Whitehall's fears about an emerging scoop menace were soon realised when it was discovered that the *Sunday Times* had assembled a team of investigative journalists, collectively known as the Insight team, with a view to publishing in the winter of 1967 a four-part series on Cambridge spy Kim Philby. Unlike fellow traitors Fuchs, Burgess and Maclean, at the time little was known about Philby. HMG had never admitted that he had worked for SIS. His CV was an enigma; nothing had come out on what jobs he had filled, when he was recruited by the Soviets, how he evaded detection, and, most crucially, what the consequences were of his treachery, if any. Six months after his defection in January 1963, HMG belatedly confessed that he had indeed been the person responsible for aiding the getaway of Burgess and Maclean. Apart from this, HMG kept quiet, and the assumption was that Philby had been nothing more than a low-ranking diplomat.

No newspaper had ever before embarked upon an investigation at once as expensive, far-ranging and detailed as this one. The Insight team, which had been put together by the newspaper's new crusading editor Harold Evans (Figure 14), was made up of some of Fleet Street's most bloody-minded, ambitious and brilliantly talented reporters, including Philip Knightley, Hugo Young, David Leitch, John Barry and Bruce Page. The political commentator Melvyn Bragg later described the group as the 'SAS of British journalism'.[183] With practically no documentary evidence available, in the spring and summer of 1967 the team took to interviewing hundreds of retired officials. Intelligence veterans were tracked down by combing the pages of *Who's Who*, an annual listing of prominent living Britons, in search of the gnomic reference 'attached Foreign Office' Any mysterious gaps in a person's employment history would also hint at possible involvement with the intelligence community. The majority of interviewees either spoke in circumlocutions or were incredibly guarded, offering statements such as 'leave it as that old boy, don't want to get in trouble with the Official Secrets Act'.[184] Eventually, however, the interviewing process began to pay dividends. The Insight team were struck by how many officials, when asked about Philby, had let slip a loaded comment. Lord

Chalfont, despite an overall posture of stonewalling, remarked that Philby was a 'dangerous man' and suggested that any further inquiries by the newspaper would 'help the enemy'.[185] Major General Stewart Menzies, 'C' from 1939 to 1951, refused to be interviewed but nevertheless stated in a letter to Evans: 'What a blackguard Philby was.'[186] Such comments aroused the team's curiosity. For characteristically tight-lipped men to feel compelled to say something gave the lie to the idea that Philby had been a harmless low-level diplomat.

The breakthrough arrived when the team was alerted to an espionage book entitled *British Agent* by John Whitwell, pen name of Leslie Nicholson, SIS Head of Station in Prague from 1930 to 1934.[187] Published in 1966 by William Kimber, an independent London publishing house, *British Agent* was the first memoir written by an intelligence officer describing life in SIS between the wars. It had not sold well and, indeed, by 1970 was out of print. The team soon discovered the identity of the person hiding behind the pseudonym. Further inquiries revealed that Nicholson was an emaciated, alcoholic burnout, living on a piecemeal pension in sheltered accommodation in London's East End.[188] Keen to exploit the man's prodigious thirst for alcohol, Knightley arranged a lunch and plied him with drink – brandy being the beverage of choice. As hoped, it was not long before the secrets started spilling out. 'The reason for the flip-flap', Nicholson explained, 'is that Kim was head of our anti-Soviet section.'[189] Knightley, light-headed from the brandy fumes, sought clarification: 'Let me get this straight. The man running our secret operations against the Russians after 1944 was a Russian agent himself?'[190] 'Precisely,' confirmed his lunch companion. Although this disclosure was probably occasioned by drink, one also has to consider the possibility that it was premeditated. According to intelligence scholar Nigel West, Nicholson had a grudge against SIS for refusing him financial support when his wife was diagnosed with cancer and needed treatment in America.[191] Whatever the motive, the Insight team had secured a major discovery. As head of SIS's Soviet counter-intelligence directorate, Philby would have had access to the Service's most prized secrets, including the identities of agents stationed abroad.

With Nicholson's revelation, Denis Hamilton, editor-in-chief and chairman of Times Newspapers, saw fit to give the researchers unprecedented funds, affording them the opportunity to scour the world for information. Some went to Spain, where Philby had covered the Civil War as a journalist for the *Times*; others travelled to Beirut, where he had been re-employed by SIS in 1956 as an 'informant on retainer', with the cover of Middle East correspondent for the *Economist* and the *Observer*. Following Pincher's example, the team spent nearly a month in the United States, cultivating sources from the CIA, FBI and Department of Defense. Evans even had the chutzpah to approach retired CIA Director Allen Dulles.[192] Interviews with American contacts yielded some hidden gems. Lyman Kirkpatrick, a former CIA Executive Director, confirmed that in 1949 Philby had been assigned to the British embassy in Washington as a liaison with the FBI and CIA, a highly sensitive position in which he would have been privy to most US intelligence operations.[193] With money to burn, the team pulled off a real coup when it paid for John Philby, Kim's son by his second marriage, to travel to Moscow to interview his father. John not only secured an iconic black-and-white photograph of Philby standing in Red Square in front of the Kremlin, but got from his exiled father the priceless detail that he had been a Soviet agent for the whole of his working life, dating back to 1933.

The *Sunday Times* had been desperate to keep Project X, as Evans had christened it, secret for as long as possible. The intention was to scoop the *Observer* which had bought the serialisation rights to a memoir by Eleanor Philby, Kim's third wife, entitled *The Spy I Loved* and written in conjunction with the *Observer*'s Middle East correspondent Patrick Seale.[194] By early August 1967, word of Project X had nevertheless reached Whitehall. A few weeks before, the Insight team had been put in touch with a young SIS officer named John Sackur, who had expressed an interest in leaving the Service and turning his talents to journalism. Evans' friend, the playwright and novelist Michael Frayn, knew Sackur from Cambridge University and vouched for him as someone who could be trusted and was genuine about starting a new career in Fleet Street. With this, Page took the aspiring journalist to Manzi's seafood restaurant in Soho, briefed him on the newspaper's investigation and promised him a 'flying start' in return for anything he knew about Philby.[195] Deep down, however, Sackur, had no desire to leave SIS and duly reported back to his secret bosses. As well as notifying them about the major revelations, he explained that the series was going to branch out from Philby's life story into a more general and critical consideration of the value of SIS in modern society, advancing the argument that the Service was and continued to be an upper-class racket hopelessly outclassed by its Russian adversary.[196]

Reaction in Whitehall was predictably one of sheer horror. *The Times*, still in 1967 the 'paper of record', was planning to reveal not only that Philby had been a traitor of the first rank for nearly thirty years, but that officials had suspected this and covered up his crimes. On 8 August, Trend chaired a meeting with Dunnett, Dick White ('C') and Denis Greenhill (chairman of the JIC). The consensus was that every effort should be made to halt publication. As Greenhill put it, 'what seemed to us most undesirable would be the inauguration of a general debate, or even witch-hunt, about the Secret Service which could only end up to the detriment of the organisation and the diminution of its contribution'.[197] The problem facing officials was that there was no easy way of getting the newspaper to back down. Since the 'revelations' were ipso facto already known to the Russians, it would be improper to issue a D-Notice claiming that publication would be harmful to national security. The last thing the government wanted was to assert that D-Notices had been breached and find itself 'in a public dispute with the press of much the same kind that developed over the cable vetting story'.[198] Worryingly, Sackur had also told his SIS superiors that Evans considered the D-Notice Committee morally bankrupt and would never accept its guidance, if offered.

To avoid another controversy, Trend believed that the best solution was for a minister of state, potentially Chalfont (who had previously been on *The Times*'s staff), to make a private approach to Hamilton, stressing that while publication might not damage national security, it would be injurious to the national interest, since the denigration of SIS was a 'priority purpose' of the KGB.[199] On 11 August, Trend briefed Wilson on developments: 'The incident is merely another illustration of the way in which public interest and sensational journalism are gradually eroding the safeguards by which we have hitherto managed to protect our covert agencies.'[200] The Cabinet Secretary cautioned against the government reacting 'too sharply', suggesting that this was 'one of the lessons of the recent Radcliffe Affair'.[201] Wilson accepted the advice that Chalfont was the right channel, albeit with the rider that – 'if all else fails' – stiffer sanctions might be required.[202]

Chalfont spoke to Hamilton in late August. Despite stating that the articles would be slanted in such a way as to suggest that SIS had learnt lessons from the past and things were now better, Hamilton emphasised that the newspaper was determined to expose the ineptitude of the intelligence community between 1945 and 1960, and saw no reason why the public should not be informed of how the nation had been imperilled. He also confirmed that the newspaper had no intention of consulting the D-Notice Committee.[203]

September was a month of high anxiety in Whitehall as further details about the investigation were unearthed. The ever-reliable double agent Henry Kerby informed Wigg that he had taken lunch with a member of the Insight team who had told him – in strictest confidence – that the series would name all the various heads of SIS and MI5 for the previous thirty years. 'This must be almost without precedent,' remarked the maverick Conservative MP.[204] Kerby also prised from the reporter the admission that the series was going to reveal that White's club in St James's Street had long been a hangout for SIS officers. Most alarming, officials were alerted to the fact that the Insight team had been sending letters to, as well as knocking on the door of, a certain somebody called Anthony Blunt. At the time, Blunt was an art historian of international reputation and held the position of Surveyor of the Queen's Pictures. Evans' team had been keen to talk to him in connection with his time at Cambridge before the Second World War, where he had been a don at Trinity and had moved in the same social circles as a number of leftist undergraduates, including Guy Burgess. The newspaper's reporters held the distinguished academic in the highest regard and wanted to speak with him for no other reason than to get some juicy anecdotes about Burgess. What they did not know – what nobody outside of a handful of senior officials knew – was that Blunt was in fact the 'Fourth Man' in the Cambridge spy ring. Recruited in 1936, he had worked for the Russians first as a university 'talent-spotter' and then, after joining MI5 in 1940, directly as a spy.[205] In 1964, Blunt confessed to MI5; unlike Portland spies Harry Houghton and Ethel Gee, who in 1961 were sentenced to fifteen years in prison, the blue-blooded Blunt was granted immunity from prosecution and allowed to continue his privileged life at Buckingham Palace. Not until 1979 was his past made public and the government's complicity in a cover-up exposed.

Although Evans had nothing on Blunt, Whitehall could not afford to take any risks. Officials arranged for his solicitor to warn the newspaper that any further attempts to contact their client would be treated as harassment.[206] To make doubly sure that Blunt could not be got at, at the very least until the Philby storm had blown over, officials put him on a plane to Italy with instructions to lie low.[207] Thankfully for Whitehall, the Insight team made no further enquiries, and for the time being this particular can of worms remained firmly shut. In his 2009 memoir *My Paper Chase*, Evans conceded that one of his biggest regrets and mistakes was not to pursue Blunt. He was, sadly, the 'one that got away'.[208]

For Whitehall, this still left the problem of the Philby story. In late September, it was decided that a further high-level approach should be made to the newspaper, with responsibility this time being given to Greenhill. On 26 September, Greenhill duly met with Hamilton and reiterated that, if the newspaper went ahead, 'there would be drinks all round at KGB headquarters'.[209] Greenhill also explained that the proposed 'happy ending' would not be sufficiently strong to counterbalance the overall negative picture. Hamilton once again refused to acquiesce.

The next day, Greenhill reflected on recent events and one thing stuck in his mind. Hamilton had said, when pressed on the need to present a balanced picture, that this could be achieved if officials gave the newspaper some material to work with. Off the cuff, Hamilton suggested there were 'probably some codebreaking achievements' which could go on record.[210] At the time – with one eye on protecting the Ultra secret (see Chapter 7) – Greenhill had quickly and flatly disillusioned him of this. With more time to consider the idea, however, Greenhill came round to a different view. As things stood, the chances of the newspaper playing ball were slim, and HMG was certainly not prepared to use its enfeebled D-Notice system to force the issue. Backed into a corner, with damage limitation the only option left available, Greenhill decided to run with Hamilton's suggestion. Accordingly, on 28 September, he invited the Times Newspapers editor-in-chief to lunch and gave him a document entitled 'What the Public Needs to Know about the KGB'.[211] The document was unashamed propaganda. It stated that the aim of the KGB was 'to disrupt and control the activities of all Western official representation in the Soviet Union ... including attacks on business visitors, exchange students and tourists'. It underlined the 'ruthlessness of KGB methods', which included every kind of sexual entrapment; the corruption of agents by blackmail, and the crushing of opponents by kidnapping or murder. It pointed out the 'insidiousness of KGB manoeuvres in the political field', highlighting their exploitation of the mass media and their willingness to 'use every form of lie and distortion to discredit any attempt by the West to publish the truth about the Soviet Union and its policies'. It concluded by saying that the public should be sympathetic to the difficulties faced by British intelligence.[212] To help field questions from Hamilton, Greenhill brought along 'a friend' from SIS called 'Mr Lecky'.[213] In doing all of the above, Greenhill was on new ground. Handing journalists snippets of information and introducing them to intelligence officers was a bold departure from the time-honoured policy of stonewalling. Unfortunately, Hamilton recognised the tactic for what it was – a last-ditch attempt to save face – and refused to include the unflattering material.

On 1 October, the *Sunday Times* revealed its investigation to the world with a thundering article, 'The Spy Who Betrayed a Generation', accompanied by the dramatic picture of Philby in Red Square and the lead 'I Spied for Russia from 1933'. Publication caught Whitehall by surprise. The newspaper had planned to publish near Christmas. At 6 p.m. on Saturday 31 September, however, a copy of the *Observer* had landed on Evans's desk advertising the imminent serialisation of the Eleanor Philby memoir. Only a few days before, the *Observer* had discovered from the talkative John Philby that the *Sunday Times* had been following Kim's traces. Unsurprisingly, therefore, it had looked to steal a march on its rival. To blunt the *Observer*'s blow, Evans flew into action, calling in his team of super-sleuth reporters to work through the night to ensure that its first instalment hit the streets on Sunday morning.[214] Over the next five weeks, the two Sunday 'heavyweights' competed in one of the bloodiest journalistic battles in memory, each offering startling insights into the life and times of Russia's most important spy in the West. The *Washington Post* informed its readers that Britain was enjoying a 'Spy Spectacular from Fleet Street'.[215] With every passing week there was a further round of revelations. The *Observer* explained that it had hired Philby, against its better judgement, after receiving what proved to be erroneous assurances from the Foreign Office that he was out of the spy business. Inexplicably, someone from Whitehall had even pleaded with the newspaper's editor, David Astor, to be charitable and give Philby a job, claiming that he needed an income to support his children.[216] *The Times* revealed that Philby had been groomed to head SIS and, amazingly, had come within a hair's breadth of doing so before his luck ran out. The Insight team also gave examples of the damage that Philby had caused, such as the fact that, in 1950, he had forewarned the Soviets that some three hundred guerrillas were about to be parachuted by the CIA into communist-controlled Albania; with this, Moscow arranged a welcoming party, leading to the death or capture of nearly half of the rebel force. The rest of Fleet Street meanwhile struggled to compete and was required to fall back on more trivial revelations, such as telling readers that Philby's favourite drink was raki, a Turkish liqueur.[217] Even Pincher, for the first time in his professional career, was required to ride on the coat-tails of others.

As officials had feared, the heartbeat of the Philby story was not so much the evidence of grand betrayal but the broader attack on the efficiency and efficacy of the secret service in Britain. Well-born, charming, and instructed in the ways of the ruling elite at Westminster school, Cambridge and the Athenaeum (the foremost gentleman's club in London), Philby had got away with his crimes because SIS was a caricature of the Establishment and had refused to question the loyalty of anyone who wore the old school tie and had the right connections. Newspapers were incredulous. What sort of organisation accommodated someone who had shown marked leanings to the left while at university and whose first wife, Litzi Friedmann, was a Jewish communist? What sort of service ignored warnings from other departments, including MI5, about Philby's erratic behaviour, squalid private life and heavy drinking? Moreover, what sort of spy agency dismisses someone amidst strong suspicions that he had helped Burgess and Maclean decamp to Moscow, and then, several months later, decides to re-employ him as a field agent in the Middle East? The calls for reform were deafening. According to the *London Evening News*, 'These hair-raising reminiscences have shown British intelligence in a light which makes the Keystone Cops by comparison look like a deadly efficient force.'[218] The American press was similarly outraged. Several US papers suggested that Britain needed a Senator McCarthy.[219]

As the articles rolled out, Greenhill continued his informal contacts with Evans, albeit to no avail. Official government policy was to refrain from comment. On 2 October, amidst a spate of press enquiries, the Foreign Office instructed staff 'not to discuss the facts of the case at all'.[220] On a strictly unattributable basis, officials were permitted to state that Philby was 'an accomplice of the Stalin regime deserving of no sympathy', and that press interest suited the KGB, whose object was to discredit Western intelligence services.[221]

A number of intelligence veterans nevertheless felt moved to go on record in defence of the SIS. Stewart Menzies, a former head of SIS, gave an interview to the *Daily Sketch* in which he claimed that Philby had never been in the running to be SIS chief. Donald McLachlan, a former naval intelligence officer and editor of the *Sunday Telegraph*, criticised *The Times* for unleashing a 'wave of anti-gentleman, down-with-the-old-boy-ring, let's-expose-the-Establishment fervour'.[222] Calls to clean up SIS, he argued, displayed an ignorance of the practicalities of intelligence work and amounted to a terrible slur on the scores of men and women who worked in complete loyalty to their country. 'A secret body', he continued, 'must be a co-opted one; it cannot be chosen by competitive examination.'[223] McLachlan even proposed that the public should not discount the possibility that the Insight team's investigation had been facilitated by the Soviet Ministry of Information and that the life story was a plant: 'We should beware of falling for Communist propaganda.'[224] Unintentionally, the photograph in Red Square and the interview material collected by Kim's son had given some people the false impression that the series had been inspired by Philby or the KGB.

In early November, after five weeks of exposé after exposé, both the *Sunday Times* and the *Observer* wound down their respective investigations. Evans had planned to send a reporter to Moscow to interview Philby. Philby – betraying all the hallmarks of a champagne socialist – had contacted the newspaper stating that he would be prepared to talk about his life in return for a substantial fee. However, Evans was forced to backpedal after George Brown, in his own inimitable way, ripped into the Insight team at a dinner party hosted by Lord Thomson (the *Times* proprietor). In a departure from his prepared speech, the Foreign Secretary had turned to Thomson and accused him of being a traitor: 'It is about time you shut up ... and stopped giving the Russians half a start on what we are doing ... for God's sake, stop.'[225] Despite his reputation for being hands-off with editors, effectively giving them carte blanche, Thomson feared that he might be stripped of his peerage and immediately ordered Evans to turn down Philby's invitation. The next day, the newspaper managed to exact some measure of revenge against Brown when it headlined, 'Ebullient Brown Hits Out' – *ebullient* being a way of saying he was intoxicated without breaking libel laws.[226] In the days following, Brown was reprimanded by Wilson for yet another display of public drunkenness, while in Fleet Street there were calls for his resignation.

The combination of the cable vetting affair and the Philby investigations had ushered in a new age of espionage reporting. Greenhill observed that journalists were now taking an 'almost pornographic interest in intelligence matters'.[227] In mid to late October, keen to steal back some of the limelight, the *Daily Express* serialised *The Espionage Establishment* by American journalists David Wise and Thomas Ross. This serialisation was another landmark. The first instalment printed the names of the incumbent heads of MI5 and SIS, Martin Furnival Jones and Dick White; it also disclosed where they worked – Leconfield House and 21 Queen Anne's Gate – and provided telephone numbers. This information was given in open violation of D-Notice Number 10, 'British Intelligence Services'. The *Express* argued, in its defence, that since the information had been published in the United States, the D-Notice was meaningless. Whitehall agonised over whether to punish the newspaper. This was the first time in twenty years that a British newspaper had published the identity of a serving intelligence chief. (In 1946 MI5 had its fingers burnt with the public announcement of Percy Sillitoe as Director General; over the next few years, until his retirement in 1953, Sillitoe often could not go into a restaurant without people gaping at him, and he was forced to wear dark glasses at football matches.)[228] Sammy Lohan, now earning his crust as a political commentator for hire, summed up official attitudes when he stated on the current affairs programme *24 Hours* that operational efficiency would suffer if the intelligence services became 'like the Beatles – gaped at everywhere they go'.[229] Ultimately, however, officials concluded that they could not stomach another public row and ruled that the policy should be 'Heads Down' and 'No Comment'.[230]

In Whitehall, the events of 1967 concentrated minds on developing a long-term strategy of controlling the press. For Wilson, the key issue was to stop journalists from getting information via official channels. Accordingly, he ruled that leak enquiries should be activated whenever an unauthorised disclosure occurred. Trend had been against this. Most investigations, he lamented, were a 'waste of time and effort'; not once had an offender been brought to book.[231] Moreover, civil servants were left demoralised because, in most cases, it was clear that the leak had come from a minister. Trend was not alone in thinking that the leak procedure was – in the Cabinet Secretary's words – 'ghastly' and 'farcical'.[232] In February 1968, a Downing Street Committee on Security claimed that it attracted 'contempt' and 'cynical odium' from participants.[233] Wilson nevertheless stood firm. As he saw it, the purpose of the leak enquiry was not to identify wrongdoers, but to serve as a deterrent to those who might engage in loose talk. In April 1970, he made the procedure even more heavy-handed by sanctioning the use of professional interrogators, 'of a gentlemanly sort, of course'.[234]

Whereas Wilson was seemingly intent on finding more draconian ways to hinder the press, other voices in Whitehall could be heard advancing a more progressive strategy. On 26 October 1967, Greenhill circulated a think-piece, entitled 'Philby – The Aftermath', in which he argued that journalists would be less inclined to push the envelope of disclosure if the government of the day showed a greater willingness to take them into its confidence. One way of doing this, he suggested, would be to announce formally the name of Dick White's successor as 'C' and allow editors to meet him so that he could make a few uncontroversial remarks about how the Service was becoming an equal opportunities employer and no longer relying on old-boy-network recruitment. In the light of the *Express* revelations, Greenhill claimed that 'we cannot now put the clock back and work the previous system of denying the name of the Chief to the public'. [235] White, who was due to retire as 'C' in early 1968, saw merit in the idea: 'I should be in favour ... for I can testify from my own experience that to be smoked out by the press and to become the subject of their hysterical curiosity is a very great handicap to one's work.'[236] Despite White's support, most senior officials disapproved. Furnival Jones was not convinced that it would be impossible to revert to the time-honoured practice of total reticence about secret services. He declared that the priority remained to restore the D-Notice Committee to its former glory, even changing its name if the consensus was that it had acquired the wrong connotation.[237] Trend was equally sceptical about moving away from the old system of immunity from press comment, suggesting that officials should have a 'jolly good try' to maintain the current position before embarking down a new course.[238] While admitting that his opinions might be perceived by some younger folk as 'stuffy, square and old-fashioned', Trend was principally concerned about the constitutional implications of Greenhill's plan. It was still largely accepted in Britain that civil servants were anonymous and faceless beings, and that ministers stood between them and the public. Naming White's successor would represent a major departure which, in Trend's view, could lead to SIS becoming an independent power base, free of ministerial control and seeking to influence government policy in its own right. Trend's other fear was that the press would not, as Greenhill cheerily predicted, simply lay down its arms if C's name was disclosed: 'All experience shows that ... the appetite grows with the eating.'[239] In other words, if you give journalists an inch, they will take a mile.

The government shared these misgivings and Greenhill's plan was promptly abandoned. Ministers also doubted whether the press would again discover anything as explosive as the Philby story. The Insight team had benefited from unprecedented riches, bestowed by a newspaper making a handsome profit and a proprietor, in Thomson, who ensured that much of that money was 'recycled back onto the editorial floor'.[240] Accordingly, its reporters were able to follow up every lead and explore down every unbeaten track. They were also afforded eight months to conduct their investigation – unparalleled in the history of Fleet Street – during which time the journalists involved published little and were rarely seen in the newsroom. With some justification, ministers had serious reservations about whether newspapers, in future, would have either the resources or the time to delve so deeply into the secret state.

That said, they could not afford to take any chances. In their deliberations, people came round to the view that, sooner or later, they would have to take a stand with the press and fall back on the club of the Official Secrets Act. Wigg, in particular, called for a line to be drawn. If a journalist went beyond that line – by 'one millimetre' – he would find himself in court: 'Are we prepared to run the risk of a thousand cuts? I am not ... No death by a thousand cuts, or to put it another way, no tooth-paste approach of a gentle squeeze always producing a little more.'[241] Wigg's belief in the panacea of the law may have been fuelled in part by Kerby. Only a few months before, Kerby had sent Wigg a letter, claiming that 'the national press can be bludgeoned into submission overnight' with a successful prosecution. He went on: 'Two or three journalists will be sent to prison – and that will be that. All press sources will dry up overnight and all editors will be "in the net".'[242] In the 1970s, the government would put this theory to the test.

1 David Lloyd George bulldozed his way through the rules of official secrecy to produce his *War Memoirs*.

2 Albert James Sylvester worked tirelessly in support of Lloyd George's literary projects, even spending days and nights in secret Whitehall archives to locate primary materials.

3 As Cabinet Secretary, Maurice Hankey (left), pictured here with Sylvester, would establish the rules governing the publication of political memoirs. In retirement, he would be hamstrung by the very same rules as he sought to publish his own recollections.

4 Chapman Pincher, scoop-gatherer extraordinaire.

5 Socialising for secrets: Chapman Pincher at a party with former Labour politician Lord Shawcross (right).

6 Chapman Pincher with *Express* proprietor Lord Beaverbrook (right) at the latter's home, Cherkley Court in Surrey.

7 Press coverage of the mysterious disappearance of Lionel 'Buster' Crabb (middle), pictured here with Royal Navy divers in Haifa in 1947, would force the intelligence community into the spotlight like never before.

8 The globalisation of newsgathering: Chapman Pincher with two of his American contacts, former CIA officers Philip Agee (left) and Miles Copeland Jr (right).

9 Chapman Pincher with Conservative politician Duncan Sandys (right).
As Minister of Defence, Sandys resisted calls from his colleagues to have security
authorities 'watch Chapman Pincher's movements'.

10 'Harold's Rasputin': As Paymaster General in Harold Wilson's first Labour government, George Wigg was tasked with reducing leaks, but succeeded only in fuelling the prime minister's paranoia.

11 Harold Wilson (right) was obsessed with the problem of leaks. President Richard Nixon, himself no stranger to the subject, lends a sympathetic ear during a visit to Downing Street on 25 February 1969.

12 The D-Notice Affair saw key personalities intoxicated at critical stages. One of the worst offenders was the Foreign Secretary, George Brown (right), pictured here at a tea party, seemingly clear-headed.

13 President Richard Nixon was destroyed by muckraking reporters in the United States, but here enjoys a convivial moment with Britain's leading investigative journalist, Chapman Pincher (right).

14 As editor of the *Sunday Times*, Sir Harold Evans would publish groundbreaking stories about Kim Philby and play a crucial role in getting the *Crossman Diaries* into print.

15 The ABC Trial: radical journalists Duncan Campbell (left) and Crispin Aubrey (centre) appear with former sigint operator John Berry at Tottenham Magistrates' Court charged under the Official Secrets Act.

16 Sir Edward Bridges, the quintessential mandarin, strongly disapproved of civil servants writing memoirs.

17 US Secretary of State John Foster Dulles (left) with Anthony Eden on 18 September 1954. Eden would later cause consternation in Whitehall by attacking Dulles in his Suez apologia. Officials were concerned that criticism of Dulles would damage the Anglo-US special relationship.

18 Richard Crossman scored a major victory for openness with the posthumous publication of his *Diaries*.

19 Sir John Masterman. His 1972 book on the Double-Cross system paved the way for grander revelations, including that of the Ultra secret.

20 Author of the landmark publication *The Codebreakers* (1967), David Kahn was one of several writers who came tantalisingly close to discovering the Ultra secret, before its eventual public disclosure in 1974.

21 The Ultra secret was finally revealed by Group Captain Frederick Winterbotham (left), pictured here with SIS agent Baron de Ropp on the Baltic shore in East Prussia in 1936.

22 Sir Percy Sillitoe, a Director General of MI5,
shocked the Service by writing a memoir in retirement.

23 M. R. D. Foot, author of *SOE in France*.

24 Sir Burke Trend (left) greeting President Lyndon B. Johnson (alongside Harold Wilson) in Washington, DC. As Cabinet Secretary, Trend would campaign for an official history of British intelligence in the Second World War.

25 A puppet of Prime Minister Margaret Thatcher, used on the satirical television show *Spitting Image* in 1987. Thatcher's failed attempt to ban the publication of *Spycatcher* by Peter Wright brought ridicule upon official secrecy and would lead to a rethink of information control strategy.

5 PUBLISH AND BE DAMNED

Journalism is becoming a high-risk occupation in this country.
RON KNOWLES, NATIONAL UNION OF JOURNALISTS, 1977[1]

The most likely candidate to fall foul of the government's new tough stance was Pincher. Emboldened by his success, the journalist had continued to cover in loving detail the inner workings of government. However, by no longer seeking guidance from the D-Notice Secretary, and by relying therefore on his own judgement and ability to second-guess the reaction of officials, Pincher was playing with fire. Former D-Notice Secretaries Admiral Thomson and Colonel Lohan, despite all of the latter's failings, had always been on hand to advise him about potential infringements of the Official Secrets Act; in contrast, Denning, the new Secretary, was someone who he refused to talk to, believing him to be a poodle of the government machine. In a lecture on 'Press Freedom', delivered in the Harcourt Room at the House of Commons in autumn 1969, Pincher suggested mockingly that Denning's job involved taking orders from Denis Healey, the secretary of state for defence, and referring to Healey as 'Dad'.[2]

True to form, Pincher succeeded in skating over thin ice. The closest he came to being prosecuted was in November 1971, after he published verbatim passages from a confidential 'Haul-Down Report', written by Admiral Sir William O'Brien, the recently retired Commander-in-Chief of the Western Fleet.[3] The article triggered one of the largest leak enquiries in Whitehall's history, with over 300 officials being required to comment, either in questionnaire form or through witness testimony.[4] Senior civil servants were delighted with the results, and believed that there was enough evidence to begin to build a case, should the government wish to pursue the matter. A number of interviewees had flirted with self-immolation by foolishly admitting that they knew Pincher and had lunched with him in the past. 'One has to be permanently on one's guard because every piece of conversation is loaded,' suggested one regular lunch partner, Commander Montanaro.[5] Questionnaires had shown that the journalist had been spending a large amount of time in restaurants and bars around Whitehall, where there were good indications that naval officers had been talking shop.[6] It also came out in the investigation that John Coote, general manager of the *Express*, could well have been the source of the leak since he had recently been put up for the Army and Navy Club, nicknamed 'The Rag', and was known to consort with service personnel. With an unusually impressive amount of leads, mandarins put it to Edward Heath's Conservative government that follow-up enquiries had a good chance of producing the proof that was needed for an Official Secrets Act charge to stick. For political reasons, however, the government declined to take the matter further. The article, which exposed Wilson's failure as prime minister to equip the navy with new strike missiles and aircraft carriers, had led to criticism of the Labour Party. As a politician first and secret-keeper second, Heath let Pincher off the hook.

The newspaper that ultimately crossed the line was the *Sunday Telegraph*. On 11 January 1970, it published extracts from a confidential report on the Nigerian civil war, written by Colonel Robert E. Scott, defence adviser to the British High Commission in Lagos. The passages were embarrassing to the Labour government, since they revealed that Britain had been secretly helping federal Nigerian forces to crush the secessionist state of Biafra by sending arms supplies and equipment well in excess of what ministers had acknowledged in Parliament. The newspaper's editor, Brian Roberts, had been given a copy of the report by Jonathan Aitken, a successful journalist for the *London Evening Standard* and a rising star in the Conservative Party. A staunch supporter of Biafran self-determination, Aitken himself had acquired a copy of the report from Major General Henry Templer Alexander, a decorated army officer who, in 1968, had served as Senior

British Representative on the International Military Observer team to Nigeria. Alexander, who was the father of one of Aitken's girlfriends, had shown the aspiring politician the document at a dinner party after the latter had questioned his assertion, during a postprandial drinking session, that the war was nearing its end. Delighted to have in his possession evidence that government spokesmen had been misleading the public, Aitken made two copies of the report; one went to Roberts, who used it as the basis of an article, and the other went to Hugh Fraser, another pro-Biafra Tory MP.[7]

In one of his last major decisions before losing the election in June 1970, Wilson instructed the Attorney General, Sir Elwyn Jones, to initiate legal proceedings. Its secret part in the bloody civil war exposed, the shamefaced Labour government was essentially delivering on its promise to get tough on leaks in the hope that, if it made an example of the *Sunday Telegraph*, Fleet Street would in future think twice about publishing sensitive information. The Labour government had also come under diplomatic pressure from the Nigerian government, since certain passages from the report had alleged corruption in federal armed forces. The decision to prosecute attracted a wave of criticism. On the day the of leak, the Biafran effort collapsed, the civil war was over and the report was academic. The biggest furore concerned the Attorney General's selection of whom to prosecute. The defendants were Aitken, Roberts, the *Sunday Telegraph*, and Colonel Douglas Cairns, a retired soldier who, it had been established, had given Alexander the Scott Report in the first place. All were indicted with charges of 'communicating' or 'receiving' the document in contravention of Section 2. Controversially, HMG had not summoned either Fraser or Alexander, despite the fact that both men had admitted that they too had been given copies of the report. Despite his admission of guilt, Alexander had even been earmarked as the prosecution's star witness. The press lambasted the hypocrisy. What kind of law permits some receivers to be prosecuted, others not? Allegations surfaced that the government had corruptly excluded the two men on the grounds that they were persons of status, whereas Cairns et al. were lesser lights and thus more vulnerable.[8]

The trial began on 12 January 1971 and lasted for three and a half weeks. For Fleet Street, the sight of a journalist in the dock at Court Number 1 at the Old Bailey – the venue where committal proceedings had taken place against some of Britain's most notorious criminals, including, most recently, the Kray twins – was deeply unedifying and attested to the vulgarity of the legislation. In Aitken's words, the outcome of the trial 'made legal and political history'.[9] All four of the defendants were acquitted, with the prosecuting authorities being ordered to pay the costs of each defendant out of public funds.[10] In a historic summing-up speech, the judge, Mr Justice Caulfield, explained that neither Aitken nor his co-accused could be found guilty on the grounds that it was impossible to determine a chain of guilty mind, or *mens rea*, unless Alexander was tried too. He assailed the notion that once an official document was stamped 'secret', anyone handling that document was breaking the law. In the interests of freedom of speech, Caulfield concluded that the unruly Section 2, which was nearing its sixtieth birthday, had reached retirement age and should be 'pensioned off'. What was needed, he continued, was a 'section that will enable men like Colonel Cairns, Mr Aitken and Mr Roberts and other editors ... to determine without any great difficulty whether a communication is going to put them in peril of ... facing a criminal charge'.[11]

The failure to secure a conviction, coupled with Caulfield's scathing criticisms, made it inevitable that the government would be required to call an inquiry to review the Official Secrets Act. Among the higher civil service in particular, this unforeseen eventuality caused great alarm. In the two or three years leading up to the trial, mandarins had been doing everything in their power to make certain that ministers did not reform the Act. The issue had first surfaced with the publication of the Fulton Report in June 1968. Lord Fulton, then Vice-Chancellor of Sussex University, had been appointed by Wilson to examine and to report upon the structure, recruitment and management of the Home Civil Service. Whitehall had long been the butt of light-hearted banter; Sir Edward Bridges famously grouped senior civil servants with Wigan Pier and mothers-in-law as objects of ridicule. In the 1960s, however, the civil service had started to come in for strong criticism. As Kevin Theakston has argued, political failure over Suez, together with a growing awareness of the economic malaise caused by 'stop-go' policies, had led many people to ask 'what's wrong with Britain?'[12] In the search for scapegoats, the accepted wisdom of the day was that the public had been let down by the 'Whitehall Village',[13] with civil servants being too inbred, elitist and amateur to face the challenges of what Wilson had dubbed the 'white heat' of the technological revolution. As a moderniser with a well-publicised bee in his bonnet about class bias and social exclusivity, Wilson needed no encouragement to call on Fulton to investigate.

Fulton's report, published after two years of evidence-gathering, showed little sympathy for the old ways in Whitehall, criticising the prevailing 'cult of the amateur' and calling for professionalism and a move toward greater managerialism.[14] In furtherance of this, Fulton recommended 'getting rid of unnecessary secrecy'. There was, he observed, a growing apartheid between the rulers and ruled, which could only be broken down if officials exhibited a greater willingness to engage in a more transparent dialogue with the public. In a much-quoted passage, the report underlined: 'We think that the administrative process is surrounded by too much secrecy. The public interest would be better served if there were a greater amount of openness.'[15] Looking to the future, Fulton proposed a follow-up inquiry, charged with reforming the Official Secrets Act and modifying the convention of anonymity, so that civil servants could go further than at present in explaining what their departments were doing.[16] At first, Wilson saw 'some merit in an enquiry of the kind suggested by the Fulton Committee'.[17] The Official Secrets Act was hated by the press. Journalists abhorred the fact that newsgathering was punishable under the same statute as acts of treason and espionage; moreover, they deplored the Act's extreme breadth and were fearful that ambiguity attached to its interpretation could lead to wrongful prosecution. Wilson, who was anxious to put the D-Notice Affair behind him, saw an inquiry as an opportune way of earning Brownie points with Fleet Street.

Before the idea of an inquiry could gather political momentum, senior administrators raised a host of objections. The Head of the Home Civil Service, Sir William Armstrong, emphasised to the prime minister that it was 'by no means clear that an enquiry by a body of outsiders – the bulk of whom would probably be naturally biased against secrecy – would advance matters'.[18] Committed to defending the status quo, Trend reminded Wilson that the Official Secrets Act had a 'remarkably stabilising effect', not unlike the 'cane in the best type of orthodox school'.[19] American allies, he continued, were extremely envious of Section 2 for its inhibiting effect on the behaviour of journalists. Trend also warned that, if civil servants became known to the public and were eligible to receive praise or incur blame, the risk of embarrassment to ministers would be greatly increased. If a civil servant's neck was publicly on the line, his or her instinct would be to fight their own corner, rather than identify with or promote their minister's policies as a matter of course. Mandarin scare tactics had the desired effect; by November 1968, Wilson was reported to be 'not in any particular hurry' to call an inquiry.[20]

In January 1969, the possibility of an inquiry was raised again after Heath, looking to score political capital, announced in Parliament that the government had reneged on its promise to investigate Fulton's recommendations. The Opposition leader also raised the stakes by declaring that the Conservative Party's election manifesto would include a pledge to reduce secrecy. 'The whole question of the release of official information, including the Official Secrets Act, should now be under consideration,' decreed Wilson in a private letter.[21] This decision earned the prime minister few friends in Whitehall. 'To my mind,' protested Sir Anthony Part (Permanent Secretary at the Board of Trade), 'the whole character of civil service work would be changed for the worse if we were to go anything like as far as the Swedes in the way of open government. We should go to the stake to preserve secrecy.'[22] (Sweden had a long tradition of – and legislation for – freedom of information, the first Act on the subject having come into force in 1776.) In a bid to dissuade Wilson, mandarins provided him with a document abounding in dire warnings. It was put to him in the document that a more generous disclosure policy would require hundreds of new staff and necessitate a major injection of government money. In a classic piece of chicanery, it was emphasised that if public business was 'carried out in a kind of "goldfish bowl"', with civil servants more accountable and less 'faceless' to the public, they would be 'free to disclose in what respects their advice had not been accepted by ministers'.[23] In other words, whenever politicians messed up, officials would smugly say, 'I told you so.'

As mandarins had hoped, Wilson was so unnerved by the document that he immediately shelved plans for an inquiry. Predictably, both the press and the Tory Opposition took this as back-pedalling. To offset some of the damage done by not holding an inquiry, and crucially to ward off demands for legal reform, the government published a White Paper entitled *Information and the Public Interest*.[24] The result of an internal as opposed to external inquiry, the White Paper emphasised that the Labour government had made giant strides in the direction of greater openness. Since coming to power, it had multiplied the number of official press releases. In 1967, it had introduced the 'Green Paper', a preliminary report setting out major policy initiatives while they were still at the formative stage. Since then, Green Papers had been published on health service reorganisation, highways strategy and a proposed national minimum wage.[25] Also in 1967, the government had amended the Public Records Act, reducing the embargo placed on the opening of official records from fifty to thirty years. (Wilson's decision to introduce the thirty-year rule was in part politically motivated; in doing so, he cunningly ensured that, in January 1968, documents would be released relating to the Conservative government's disastrous policy of appeasement, culminating in the fateful Munich Agreement of 1938.) The White Paper concluded by reiterating that the Official Secrets Act 'affect[ed] only disclosures of official information made without authority'; as such, provided journalists behaved responsibly, like gentleman, they had nothing to worry about.[26]

An inquiry nevertheless became inevitable after the Scott Report Affair. The episode, which had strong hints of political censorship, had thrown into sharp perspective the dangers Section 2 posed for press freedom. On 21 April 1971, as the etiquette of public discourse demanded, the Home Secretary, Robert Carr, appointed a committee to 'review the operation of Section 2' and 'to make recommendations'.[27] Chairmanship of this historic inquiry was always going to be a humdinger of an appointment. Two years earlier, Wilson had suggested the former Labour minister Herbert Bowden, only to be told by his principal private secretary, Michael Halls, that Bowden 'might well come out with a far too liberally minded report – almost Swedish'.[28] Keen to minimise the risk of manipulation by the Whitehall machine, Heath opted for Oliver Franks, on the one hand an avatar of the British state (he had taken Mods and Greats at Oxford followed by diplomatic service and then a career in public administration), but on the other hand unfailingly fair-minded with a reputation for straight talking.[29] 'When it came to establishments, he was in them but not of them,' suggests Franks' biographer Alex Danchev.[30]

Franks invited a number of representative bodies, mainly in the fields of the media, government and the law, to make written or oral submissions to the Franks Committee. Permanent secretaries weighed in with cautionary tales. Trend, for example, lamented: 'Once you embark on the business of striptease of a government – where do you stop?'[31] Journalists, by contrast, demanded the total elimination of Section 2. 'Section 2 is an absurdity,' stated Maurice Green, editor of the *Daily Telegraph*. 'It was tolerable', he continued, 'only because it was never used. Since the *Telegraph* case ... the Act has ceased to be tolerable.'[32] Members of the press condemned Section 2's catch-all nature, which, in the words of David Astor, 'made every disclosure of every piece of information, however trivial, an offence'.[33] A common press complaint was that, because there was no precise definition of the categories of official documents requiring legislative protection (save the antiquated mantra of the still-unnameable Director General of MI5 that 'it is an official secret if it is in an official file'),[34] the line between authorised and illegal communication was imperceptible until it was transgressed. 'The net result' – protested the Press Council – 'is that both journalists and civil servants spend their lives walking through an ancient minefield. Most of the mines are now dud, but one may at any moment blow up in their faces.'[35] Embarrassingly, when asked by Franks to give a concrete example of a Section 2 offence, William Armstrong replied, 'I do find it very difficult to define that line.'[36]

Published on 29 September 1972, the Franks Report branded Section 2 a 'mess' and called for its repeal: 'People are not sure what it means, or how it operates in practice, or what kinds of actions involve real risk of prosecution under it.'[37] In its place, Franks proposed a more tightly drawn statute, called the Official Information Act, which would delimit precisely the classes of information which required legal protection against their illicit disclosure. Such classes would encompass: Cabinet documents; information entrusted to the government by private individuals; classified information relating to defence, national security, foreign relations and currency; and information likely to assist criminal activities or hinder law enforcement. As an additional safeguard to prevent the capricious application of the law for political motives, Franks underlined that the test of criminality would be whether an unauthorised disclosure had 'caused serious injury to the security of the nation or the safety of the people'. Unlike Section 2, the maximum penalty on conviction would be two years' imprisonment, or a fine.

With some justification, Franks expected Fleet Street to react favourably to the proposed new Act. Journalists were nevertheless lukewarm in their support. Some bemoaned that it was still the Attorney General who was empowered to institute legal proceedings.

As a member of the government, the Attorney General was seen as too politically committed to weigh up objectively the intrinsic worth of prosecuting a newspaper which might have embarrassed his party. Others were critical of the fact that, although press representatives would be invited to sit on an advisory committee to decide which type of documents counted as 'classified' under the Act, the risk of over-classification was still too great since Franks had left no provision for judicial review and ruled that ministers had the final word on certification.[38] A common feature of press criticism was that, in contrast to freedom of information laws in the US and Sweden, Franks had fallen short of conferring citizens a general right of access to documents held in public offices.

By pushing for something akin to freedom of information, Fleet Street took a calculated risk and it backfired. Privately, ministers were terrified by the prospect of Section 2's repeal and were looking to wriggle out of legal reform without being seen to be breaking their election pledges. Ministers feared that, by abolishing Section 2, they would lose an effective deterrent. Evidence given to Franks had supported the view that the law, as opposed to exhortations, threats and internal discipline, was still the most effective way of ensuring that tens of thousands of civil servants declined from making unauthorised disclosures to the press. The deterrent value of Section 2 was believed to be particularly important at the 'penumbra of the system',[39] among the temporary clerks, dockyard workers, and 'girls who get married, go off to have babies and then come back'.[40] Among these people, it was felt that the carrot of job security and promotion counted for little, but the stick of legal action was a significant restraint. Because senior officials valued their careers and pensions, and in some cases were looking for an OBE or knighthood on retirement, they were believed to be trustworthy, irrespective of Section 2. According to James Dunnett, 'If you cannot rely on them to have a reasonable measure of discretion as to how they deal with journalists, I think there is something lacking in them as under secretaries or deputy secretaries.'[41] In practice, of course, as we have seen, the top brass was just as likely to communicate with the outside world as their underlings.

The press's unwillingness to take the bird in the hand and instead fight for an all-embracing freedom of information Act was bold, but unwise, since it broadened the issue into something that could not be solved overnight and gave the government the perfect excuse for going back to the drawing board, without being criticised for not fulfilling its election pledge. On 8 March 1973, ministers met to discuss the Franks Report and observed gleefully that journalists showed no 'marked enthusiasm' for the Official Information Act as they were clinging to the notion that something better could be had.[42] In the words of the later-to-be Home Secretary Douglas Hurd, 'dickering and dispute' followed.[43] Much was said, but nothing was achieved. In opposition, the Labour Party criticised the deficiencies of Section 2 and championed the need to change the law; when re-elected in October 1974, its attitude soon changed and no repeal was forthcoming. Although a number of backbenchers kept the issue alive, by submitting what they saw as workable alternatives to Section 2, legal reform became much like Penelope's web – something endlessly woven by day, only to be unpicked again by night. For journalists, the flow of empty promises was tolerable only because the chance of change had not been completely ruled out. They also took comfort in the fact that, following the wholesale acquittal of Aitken et al. in 1971, there had been several occasions when the state might have used Section 2 but had favoured a less heavy-handed approach. In late 1972, the *Railway Gazette* had been caught red-handed in possession of a confidential document on rail policy when police had raided its offices. The government opted against laying charges. Similarly, in June 1976, no action was taken against the *New Statesman*, despite the clear leak of a Cabinet minute on child benefit.[44] However, if journalists thought the state had truly turned over a new leaf, they were mistaken.

* * *

'Deep Throats' do not exist for the most part: uncovering
secret Government deceptions, be they about the level of
phone tapping or the occurrence of nuclear accidents, depend
99 per cent on the exhaustive analysis of non-confidential
material.

Duncan Campbell, 1984[45]

In February 1977, charges under the Official Secrets Act were brought against three men accused of being 'subversive' and engaged in activities harmful to national security. The defendants – Crispin Aubrey, John Berry and Duncan Campbell – were initially prosecuted under Section 2 of the Act (Figure 15). When committal proceedings began at Tottenham Magistrates' Court in November, each defendant faced additional charges under Section 1. Designed for use against spies working at the behest of a foreign power, Section 1 carried a maximum sentence of fourteen years. However, at the discretion of the judge, it was possible for consecutive custodial sentences to be passed, as in the case of the Soviet spy George Blake, who in 1961 was given 42 years' imprisonment.

What was striking in this case was that none of the defendants were spies. Berry was an ex-soldier at the time employed as a social worker; Aubrey and Campbell were journalists. In authorising the prosecution, the Attorney General, Samuel Silkin, made legal history. This was the first occasion on which a Section 1 charge had been brought against a journalist, and it set in train what became known as the ABC Trial, after the surnames of the three accused. Lasting nearly two years and attracting extensive media coverage, the trial left its mark not only on the law but also on the fabric of official secrecy. For the state, what started out as an attempt to clip the wings of two journalists turned into a horror show and ended in farce. As the celebrated barrister Geoffrey Robertson QC contends, by the time the defendants stood outside the Old Bailey as free men and drinking champagne, 'Britain was a less secret country'.[46]

The origins of the case can be traced, in no small measure, to tumultuous events in the United States. In the mid 1970s, the CIA had been brought to its knees by influential senators and congressmen, such as Frank Church and Otis Pike, and by muckraking investigative journalists, such as *New York Times* reporter Seymour Hersh. Between them, they revealed that the CIA had conducted illegal domestic operations against opponents of the Vietnam War and other dissident groups, including mail opening, wiretapping, break-ins and surveillance. In 1975 – the so-called 'Year of Intelligence' – congressional committees combed through Agency files and discovered evidence of planned assassinations against foreign leaders, most notably the Cuban revolutionary Fidel Castro. The CIA was not the only secret service dealt a bloody nose. Before the Senate Intelligence Committee in 1975, NSA Director Lew Allen testified that the NSA, between 1967 and 1973, had run a highly illegal 'watch list' programme called Project Minaret, which involved the electronic monitoring of more than 1,000 domestic radicals. Although this disclosure was not meant for public airing, it did not take long for details to leak to the press. The ugly secrets unearthed by nosy reporters and congressional investigators caused

Whitehall great alarm. According to David Atlee Phillips, the CIA's chief of Western Hemisphere operations from 1973 until 1975, 'British intelligence officials were aghast at what they described as the "disembowelment by headline" of US intelligence'.[47] The fear was that something would come out on the British contribution to US–UK intelligence operations. In April 1976, in a bid to alleviate British concerns, new CIA Director George H. W. Bush flew to London to tell Harold Wilson in person that the Agency was going to great lengths to ensure that the various inquiries did not get their hands on every conceivable bit of information held in the vaults at Langley.[48] Records that discussed joint operations were, in some cases, destroyed. In 1995, when the Agency was required by an Executive Order to review the classification status of documents from the early Cold War, its declassification team found next to nothing on Operation Ajax, the SIS/CIA covert operation in 1953 that restored the exiled Shah of Iran to the throne.[49]

What most troubled British officials about the 'intelligence flap' in the United States was the impact it would have on Fleet Street. The frenzy of revelation had brought to light not only what American secret services had done in the past, but what some of them were doing in the present. For example, the disclosure of Minaret was followed up by a host of press articles on the NSA – once dubbed 'No Such Agency' – focusing on its new high-tech sigint collection systems.[50] Notwithstanding a few notable exceptions, such as the cable vetting affair, British journalists had seldom looked into current intelligence matters. As we have seen, the majority of disclosures related to traitors, such as Philby, who had been recruited in the 1930s and who had inflicted damage either during the Second World War or in the immediate postwar period. It stood to reason – so Whitehall feared – that when British reporters read stories in the American press about the NSA's latest satellite, computer or listening post, they would naturally seek to establish if there was a British dimension. This fear was realised when, in May 1976, the underground entertainment guide *Time Out* published a ground-breaking, double-page spread entitled 'The Eavesdroppers'.[51] Written for the most part by Duncan Campbell, with contributions from an American journalist based in London (Mark Hosenball), the article revealed the existence of GCHQ for the first time and gave a detailed description of what it did, including information about its methods and partnership with the NSA. The article's opening sentence read: 'Britain's largest spy network organisation is not MI5 or MI6 but an electronic intelligence network controlled from a country town [Cheltenham] in the Cotswolds.'[52]

'The Eavesdroppers' stands as one of the most sensational and gutsy press articles ever published. At the time, few people would have known that Britain had a peacetime intelligence service devoted to sigint. The public had only recently learned about codebreaking achievements at Bletchley Park, with the publication in 1974 of Frederick Winterbotham's memoir *The Ultra Secret* (see Chapter 7). By publishing the essay, Campbell and Hosenball had taken a big risk. The last individuals who had dared to write about peacetime sigint had ended up behind bars. In July 1958, two Oxford University undergraduates had been sentenced under Section 2 to three months' imprisonment after using information ascertained during their National Service to write an article in *Isis*, the student newspaper, which claimed that British monitoring stations along the Russian frontier were recording every 'squeak' that was made by Soviet transmitters.[53] Although that article had not mentioned GCHQ and had revealed nothing that had not already been disclosed in the American press, the state wanted to send a message that eavesdropping was a forbidden subject. The message could not have been made conveyed more clearly. Special Branch detectives interviewed tens of Oxford students. They also temporarily seized the *Isis* office to go through files.[54] Among the national press corps, there had been an expectation that, since the two men in question were well-to-do, bright young things destined for a golden future, the state would go easy on them. The article, moreover, had all the hallmarks of youthful folly. They were wrong. Where matters of sigint were concerned, the state was unwilling to show mercy.

GCHQ was not amused by 'The Eavesdroppers', and considered legal action against its principal author. The problem, however, was that Campbell had not broken any laws. Like Pincher, he was frighteningly gifted when it came to piecing together a story from open sources and interviews. With a library card, a telephone directory and a travel allowance, he was capable of discovering things that no mortal was meant to know. With a first-class degree in Physics and a postgraduate qualification in Operational Research, he was uniquely qualified, also just like Pincher, to investigate recondite subject matters.[55] In the case of 'The Eavesdroppers', he had simply used his talents to brilliant effect.

With no evidence to support a prosecution, GCHQ looked to exact retribution in other ways. Officials discovered that some of the information in the article had come from Perry Fellwock, a disgruntled former employee of the NSA, famous for baring his soul in 1972 to the leftist Californian magazine *Ramparts* under the colourful alias Winslow Peck.[56] For assisting Campbell, Fellwock was banned from ever again entering the UK by Merlyn Rees, the Home Secretary.[57] Even more drastic measures were taken against Hosenball. In November 1976, Rees declared him a threat to national security and ordered him out of the country. Deportation orders were also served against ex-CIA officer Philip Agee. Domiciled in England since 1972, Agee was already *persona non grata* in the Western intelligence community. CIA Director George H. W. Bush had said that he had 'nothing but contempt' for the man.[58] After leaving the Agency in 1970, Agee had converted to revolutionary socialism and made no secret of his desire to 'destabilise' his former employer. Controversially, he became the nominal head of a movement to name the agents working undercover around the world. Published in Britain to avoid censorship by the CIA, his whistle-blowing book *Inside the Company* contained the identities and locations of some 250 alleged CIA men and women. When Richard Welch, the CIA's station chief in Athens, was murdered in a terrorist attack outside his home in December 1975, the blame was immediately laid at Agee's door. Although Welch had not been named by Agee but by other publications, the renegade spy bore the brunt of public anger. When the CIA demanded that Agee be deported so that he could be tried for his crimes, HMG obliged. While residing in the UK, Agee had become professionally involved with a number of anti-Establishment newspapermen, including Hosenball and Philip Kelly, journalist for the revolutionary periodical *The Leveller*, famous for campaigning to expose SIS operations. Importantly, rumours were rife that Agee had played a part in 'The Eavesdroppers'.[59]

The deportation orders issued against Agee and Hosenball provoked left-wing protest, not least because the Home Secretary had refused to give detailed reasons for his decision. Rees strongly denied that the CIA had pressed for Agee's expulsion, stating that the former agent was a danger to UK security because he had contacts with foreign intelligence officers. In Hosenball's case, Rees was even more non-committal, suggesting that the journalist had 'sought information for publication which would be harmful to state security'.[60]

Both Agee and Hosenball challenged the ruling, and a Defence Committee formed round them, care of the National Council for Civil Liberties, which campaigned for their right to stay in the country. The committee was harassed by MI5 and the Special Branch, its members finding themselves on the receiving end of break-ins, physical surveillance, theft of documents and phone taps.[61] There was, however, to be no change in Hosenball or Agee's fortunes. In February 1977, a tribunal met at the Senior, a gentleman's club in Pall Mall, and upheld the Home Secretary's decision. Within weeks, both Hosenball and Agee had left the UK. Deprived of his American passport and refused entry to several countries at the request of the US, Agee went on to live a peripatetic life, dragging his family to and from places that offered him asylum. He died in Havana, Cuba, in January 2008.

Among the individuals who were angered by the government's treatment of Hosenball and Agee was John Berry, a social worker in north London who some years before had served as a corporal with 9 Signals Regiment at the British sigint base in Ayios Nikolaos in Cyprus. Berry's career as a sigint operator had ended in peculiar circumstances. In December 1969, during a 'drinking and drug-taking party' in Famagusta, he had made a hoax call to his commanding officer warning that there was a bomb in the sergeants' mess.[62] For the prank, he was court-martialled and reduced to the rank of Lance Corporal. Following his discharge from the army in August 1970, Berry became increasingly sympathetic to left-wing political views. The Agee–Hosenball case focused his attention on agitating for greater accountability of the intelligence agencies. Accordingly, he contacted the Defence Committee offering his services. The committee subsequently put him in touch with two of its members, Crispin Aubrey, a *Time Out* staffer, and Duncan Campbell. On 18 February, Aubrey and Campbell visited Berry at his flat in Muswell Hill. The men chatted for three hours, in which time Berry provided an extended curriculum vitae, describing the work he had done with army intelligence. Campbell taped the conversation, but was left feeling underwhelmed by the disclosures. Few details emerged that were not already known to him. The only sensitive item of the conversation related to the interception of Allied traffic and the monitoring of radio networks belonging to 'friendly countries'. For his part, Aubrey muttered only a few words, the technical subject matter being over his head.

Unbeknownst to the trio, MI5 knew all about the meeting. For his no-holds-barred investigative journalism, Campbell had made it onto a watch-list, his phones were tapped and his movements were followed. Accordingly, when he, Aubrey and Berry left the Muswell Hill property, they were arrested by Special Branch officers and taken to the local police station, where they were denied legal representation and kept in cells for two days. With the men held incommunicado, Special Branch carried out search-and-seizure operations. From Campbell's Brighton flat they removed a filing cabinet of documents, as well as a personal library of more than four hundred books.[63] The material was adjudged to be of such sensitivity that it warranted transfer to Scotland Yard by armoured transport. After forty-four hours in custody, the men were charged under Section 2 and moved to a top-security wing in Brixton prison. Aubrey and Campbell had to wait several days before their bail application was approved; Berry was not released until two weeks later.[64]

Seven weeks after the arrest, the defendants were hit with Section 1 charges, relating to their taped conversation. The argument behind this was that the men had communicated information calculated to be of value to an enemy of the state. Already facing serious jail time if convicted, Campbell alone was then made the subject of an additional Section 1 charge. In his dwellings, the police had found hundreds of pages of correspondence, maps and notes. The material displayed a major interest in defence establishments, war planning, sigint, electronic warfare developments, radio devices, and telephone interception. Some 350 slides and 2,000 negatives were discovered, mainly concerning prohibited locations in the area of defence communications.[65] The police also found a large card index of contacts including the names of GCHQ employees, both serving and retired, as well as the details of many people known to MI5 as subversives.[66]

The counter to the new charge was that everything seized from Campbell's flat was publicly available and had been legally acquired by a skilled journalist who wanted to know more about the layout and function of sigint in the UK, so that he could give the taxpayer an informed idea of where public money was being spent. The state, however, saw things differently. In the 'professional opinion' of Major-General Henry Sturge of the MoD, the material would be 'directly useful to an enemy'.[67] In effect, it did not matter how the information had been obtained, or for what use it was intended.

Campbell could argue until he was blue in the face that he had acted as a journalist and not as a spy. The charge hinged on the argument that, if his research were to be revealed, he would have prejudiced the safety of the state by doing the work of a hostile power for them.

If found guilty of all charges, Campbell would be incarcerated for 32 years; murderers, war criminals and terrorists had been locked away for less. Why any government would want to dish out such a horrific penalty was unclear. A tremendous sensitivity about signals intelligence gathering – regarded as the quickest and most reliable means of understanding an enemy's capabilities or intentions – unquestionably factored into the decision. One irony of the case, as we shall see, is that the trial drummed up more publicity for GCHQ than would have been the case had legal action not been pursued. Evidence seems to suggest, however, that the underlying reason for the prosecution was a desire to crack down on Campbell's reporting and to send a message to similar-minded individuals that reputation-making scoops on the secret state would not be tolerated. Campbell represented all of Whitehall's worst fears made flesh. As illustrated by 'The Eavesdroppers', he was, in the words of one official, an 'extremely clever and able journalist' from whom no secret seemed safe.[68] Instead of following the natural career path of a science graduate, he had chosen to use his skills to make news out of a specialised area of enquiry that few journalists could comprehend. Officials had evidence of him attending conferences, put on by scientists with links to the defence industry, and introducing himself not as a reporter but as a boffin, in order to extract unguarded comments from unsuspecting delegates.[69] Alarming to Whitehall was the fact that Campbell had, in their view, no regard for authority: he socialised with anarchists; considered D-Notices an anachronism; and investigated subjects that were meant to be off limits. According to one official, he possessed an 'anarchical bent'.[70] The last thing the state wanted was for Campbell to become a standard-bearer for what was possible to discover and publish.

The trial became a cause célèbre. From the outset, the prosecution was criticised for shrouding the trial in absurd levels of secrecy. On the second day of the committal proceedings, the Crown had planned to introduce its expert witness, someone who would give a damage assessment of the three-hour tape recording and testify to the seriousness of Berry's disclosures. The individual selected for this was Lieutenant-Colonel O'Connor, a member of the Intelligence Corps based at Cheltenham.[71] At the prosecution's insistence, O'Connor's identity was to be a secret: he would be transported to and from the court by giant horsebox; be referred to only as 'Colonel A'; and give evidence from behind a curtain. The defence considered this not only melodramatic, but unworkable. An effective cross-examination of the witness necessitated that they knew something about him.[72] As such, they suggested that his name be revealed to the magistrates and to the defence counsel. After several days' mulling over the proposal, the prosecution decided that it could not possibly allow Colonel A's identity to be revealed, even to a handful of selected lawyers, so sent in his place another letter in the military alphabet, 'Colonel B'. Although still required to arrive by horsebox, Colonel B was evidently not as sensitive as O'Connor, meaning that his real name could at least be relayed to the defence.

The introduction of the anonymous Colonel B would end up causing the state great embarrassment. Make no mistake, the prosecution emphasised, the identity of Colonel B was a closely guarded secret. Problematically, this was not true and the defence knew it. The individual in question was Colonel Hugh Johnstone, who had been Commander of 9 Signals Regiment at Ayios Nikolaos. Over the years, Johnstone's activities had been regularly reported in *The Wire*, the publicly available journal of the Royal Corps of Signals. In court, Johnstone was shown a copy of *The Wire* which contained details of his latest posting, his photograph and the statement 'don of the communications underworld'.[73] When the court clerk, aptly named Mr Pratt, unthinkingly asked Johnstone to state what edition of the journal he was looking at – 'December 1974 – January 1975' – everyone in the room was given the means by which to identify him. One of the individuals present was a journalist from *Peace News*, who went to the British Library and looked up the relevant edition of *The Wire*. In the days following, Colonel B was unmasked – his name was revealed not only in *Peace News* but in the *Leveller* and the *Journalist*, the official publication of the National Union of Journalists (NUJ). The *Leveller* headlined: 'Who are you trying to kid, Colonel H. A. Johnstone?'[74] Instead of accepting that Colonel B was not so secret after all, the Attorney General tried, unsuccessfully, to prosecute the three papers for contempt of court. More farcically, when it was discovered that delegates at the annual NUJ conference at Whitley Bay were muttering Johnstone's name in their conversations, two Special Branch officers were sent to lecture the union's General Secretary. Had they arrived before the tide came in, they would have seen the name in 10 foot high letters carved into the sand.[75]

Further embarrassment ensued for the state when the Attorney General was forced to admit that the jury had been secretly vetted by the security services, a practice not without precedent and performed on no fewer than 24 occasions since 1975.[76] Without notifying the defence, the names and addresses of all the jurors on the panel had been given to the prosecution, ostensibly so that they could be cleared to hear the tape recording of the interview in Berry's flat. Having only learned of this from an indiscreet court clerk, the defence counsel was understandably alarmed, especially when follow-up enquiries revealed that three members of the jury had signed the Official Secrets Act, including the foreman – a former SAS soldier who had previously worked in Cyprus on security detail. Concerned that this would not lead to a fair trial, the defence applied to have the jury discharged. The judge initially turned down the request and forbade the press from reporting the matter. To his disgust, Christopher Hitchens, a journalist with the *New Statesman*, ignored the ruling and spoke about the jury's composition on a chat show hosted by Russell Harty on London Weekend Television. The judge then had no option but to call a retrial. The government was not amused and consideration was given as to whether any action should be taken. On Monday morning, Special Branch raided LWT's headquarters and confiscated the video of the programme.[77] In the event, no action was forthcoming – Attorney General Silkin sensibly deciding that the government could not afford another courtroom clash, this time with a large television company.

The trial finally concluded in winter 1978. As if the embarrassments of the previous eighteen months were not bad enough, the state then failed to get the denouement it was hoping for. On 24 October, Mr Justice Mars-Jones stunned the courtroom by proclaiming that he was 'extremely unhappy' about the charges under Section 1, branding them 'oppressive'.[78] Section 1, he declared in a prepared speech, was designed to punish spies and saboteurs, not journalists whose job it is to inform the public in service of the democratic process. Campbell was, to coin the phrase used by Robertson during the trial, 'a ferret, not a skunk'.[79] Mars-Jones scoffed at the idea that Campbell had prejudiced the safety of the state by collecting and interpreting information that was freely available in the public domain – the unmistakable implication being that the so-called 'jigsaw puzzle' offence had been fashioned by the state to clamp down on hard-digging investigative reporting. The lead prosecutor, seeing the government's case unravel before his eyes, attempted to interject, only to find himself on the receiving end of a bruising counter: 'If the Attorney General can authorise the prosecution, then he can unauthorise it.'[80] With this, the prosecution consulted Silkin and, unsurprisingly, the Section 1 charges were dropped. Campbell and company were naturally overjoyed. Moreover, had the charges not been withdrawn, the ramifications for journalism in Britain would have been severe; theoretically, any bona fide reporter who used open sources would be at risk of prosecution.

The trial dragged on for several more weeks, with the defendants continuing to contest the Section 2 charges. By this stage, the government was desperate to wash its hands of the whole wretched business. The Foreign Secretary, David Owen, who had been a strong supporter of the prosecution, was now privately beseeching government lawyers to accept any sort of plea bargain. 'Almost any accommodation', he implored, 'is to be preferable.'[81] The defendants eventually received minor, non-custodial sentences, tantamount to an acquittal. Aubrey and Campbell were conditionally discharged, while Berry was given a six-month sentence, suspended for two years. During the final days of the trial, there had been a distinct possibility that the men would escape the charges altogether. In his summing-up, the judge had explained to the jurors that the strict letter of the law left them no alternative but to convict. As a former crown servant, Berry had no authority to communicate information to unauthorised persons, irrespective of whether that information was trivial, and regardless of whether there was a moral obligation to see it brought to public attention. 'We will not tolerate ... whistleblowers from our intelligence services who seek the assistance of the press or other media to publish secrets, whatever their motives,' the judge emphasised in court.[82] Despite a clear judicial direction to convict, the jury nevertheless spent three nights deliberating in a hotel before, reluctantly, reaching its verdict. Some of the jurors were so upset by their decision that they apologised to the defendants in full view of the court, explaining that the catch-all nature of Section 2 had given them no other option.[83]

For many reasons, the trial was an unmitigated disaster for the state and a milestone in the history of official secrecy in Britain. The government, which had set out on a political course to teach a lesson to misbehaving journalists who could not be controlled with D-Notices, had been lambasted for using the Official Secrets Act for a reason other than the protection of legitimate defence concerns. Its law officers had been required to admit to the practice of jury vetting and had been forced, by an august judge no less, into an ignominious withdrawal of the Section 1 charges. In the months following – such was the stink caused by the trial – the libertarian cause was stronger than it had ever been.[84] Ministers faced questions about jury tampering, whilst a Freedom of Information Bill, albeit far from the polished article, achieved a wholly uncontested second reading in the House of Commons. Longer term, the trial sensitised the civil liberties community to intelligence matters. Radical campaign groups sprung up with a mission to 'watch the watchers', the most famous of which was Statewatch, led by Tony Bunyan and funded by the Joseph Rowntree Foundation. As a result, as Campbell observed in an article for *The Socialist Register* in 1979, there was a 'clearly perceptible undermining of the national security myths which are the civil servants' and politicians' handy blank walls behind which illiberal activities can be screened'.[85]

Alarmingly for the state, the trial had shown that in security-sensitive cases, it could not rely on the judiciary as an ally. Critics had long argued the unsuitability of judges as defenders of human rights against the state, suggesting that the requirements of fairness and independence can be forgotten if the authorities are determined to secure a conviction.[86] Here, however, the judge refused to cave in to intense pressure. The spectacle of nameless witnesses arriving by pantechnicon had no effect on him. When witnesses began 'incanting the magic words "danger to national security"',[87] so long a tactic for impressing courtrooms and blinding them to the underlying matters at stake, he was incredulous. Mars-Jones realised that officials had an ulterior political motive in wanting to strike a blow to the heart of investigative journalism, and carpeted them for invoking Section 1 in pursuit of that goal. He was rightly lauded as a hero of civil liberties.

For Whitehall, one of the most damaging aspects of the trial was the unprecedented publicity given to GCHQ. Because of this, as JIC member Anthony Duff conceded, it would now be impossible 'to refuse to acknowledge that we undertake sigint in peacetime or that

GCHQ is involved'.[88] Although witnesses had not referred to the organisation by name, their appearance in open court was the first public admission that Britain practised sigint outside of war. During the hearing, the defence revealed a myriad of things that officials would have preferred not to come out, including bureaucratic bafflegab such as sigint, comint (communications intelligence) and elint (electronic intelligence).[89] In addition to briefings from Campbell, the defence received information, which it subsequently aired in court, from disaffected former GCHQ employee Jock Kane.[90] (Kane later wrote a memoir, entitled *GCHQ: The Negative Asset*, which was confiscated by Special Branch and remains to this day unpublished.)

Outside the courtroom, an ABC Defence Committee, set up in support of the defendants, had pursued an aggressive strategy of trying to shine as much light on GCHQ as it could. On the first day of the trial, more than two hundred members formed a picket at the entrance to the Old Bailey, in effect a corridor of shame for the lawmakers who entered the building. Here, they handed out badges and flyers, the majority of which had a picture of a 'secret' antenna or communications tower, accompanied by slogans such as 'This Building is an Official Secret' or 'Don't Look – Official Secret'. Other slogans included 'Who's Tapping YOUR Phone'; 'ABC Spells POLITICAL TRIAL'; and 'Official Secrets Act against YOU'.[91] Even more destructive publicity was to follow. On 27 May 1978, three hundred members marched through Cheltenham. Protestors assembled outside GCHQ buildings at Benhall to the east of the fashionable spa town, before making a five-mile walk west to the organisation's main site at Oakley. Along the way, thousands of leaflets were handed out and a black ball was left at the private club where Sir Leonard Hooper, a former GCHQ Director, was a member. Moreover, hundreds of balloons were released into the sky bearing the real names of colonels A and B. In the words of a committee newsletter, 'Cheltenham had not seen a demonstration quite like it.'[92]

After nearly two years in court spent clearing his name, it did not take long before Campbell was back doing what he did best, embarrassing Whitehall by discovering its secrets. Increasingly, he was working with other journalists in teams and had a network of contacts reaching into the third sector, Parliament and Europe. In late 1979 and early 1980, now working predominantly for the *New Statesman*, he published a series of revelatory articles on the intelligence services, the most explosive of which alleged that thousands of telephones were being tapped illegally without the consent of the Home Secretary, William Whitelaw. As a result, Whitelaw was besieged in Parliament by pleas for an inquiry.[93] Campbell's *New Statesman* articles were instrumental in sparking renewed hostility towards the D-Notice system, still struggling to reinvent itself as an honest broker between government and the media. Rear Admiral William Ash, D-Notice Secretary, had responded by issuing a memorandum reminding editors that two D-Notices – No. 10 ('British Intelligence Services') and No. 11 ('Cyphers and Communications') – were still 'in force', prohibiting the subjects recently discussed by the *New Statesman*.[94] The journal's editor, Bruce Page, reacted angrily at what he saw as a clear attempt to stop the press from entering into any debate about the nature and usefulness of intelligence work. In a strongly worded letter to Ash, he upbraided the D-Notice Committee for not having updated the twelve D-Notices since they had been promulgated in August 1971. In their present form, D-Notices 10 and 11 were inappropriate in the light of the revelations that had come out during the 1970s.[95]

Page's complaints prompted parliamentarians to set up a House of Commons Defence Committee Inquiry to examine the workings of the D-Notice system and to make recommendations. Published in October, the committee's report was not pleasant reading for officials, confirming that key players in Fleet Street had turned their back on the system. In his written evidence, Harold Evans labelled the system 'a massive irrelevance', one that was 'dying of senility'.[96] David Chipp from the Press Association suggested that recent legal actions taken against journalists had made it clear that the government viewed 'cosy press–official consultations' as a thing of the past.[97] Although officials were reluctant to make wholesale changes (Ash had warned against 'salami-slice' revision),[98] by 1982 the number of D-Notices had been reduced to eight, and redrafted to take into account what had been revealed in the public domain.

Campbell caused a further stir later in the decade when he was commissioned by BBC Scotland to make a six-part television series called *Secret Society*. In the summer of 1986, officials discovered that one of the programmes would be dedicated to the new sigint satellite Zircon, a highly secret defence project. The disclosure of Zircon's existence was not Whitehall's chief concern. As Sir Frank Cooper, a former Permanent Undersecretary at the MoD said, 'Everybody knows where everybody's satellite is and you can see lists which are published in defence journals of who's launched what, where and what its orbit is.'[99] The controversial issue in the film was that of accountability to Parliament. By speaking to Robert Sheldon, Chair of the House of Commons Public Accounts Committee (a powerful financial watchdog), Campbell had elicited the explosive detail that the cost of the project, estimated to be £500 million, had been hidden from Parliament. Disclosure of this point had the potential to unleash a constitutional crisis. Accordingly, officials appealed to the BBC's senior management in London. On 5 December, Peter Marychurch, head of GCHQ, met with Alasdair Milne, the corporation's director general, arguing that the programme needed to be shelved on security grounds. Under pressure from the BBC's governors, who questioned the logic of employing a 'radical' journalist like Campbell in the first place, Milne complied.

With this, an angry Campbell revealed the content of the film in an article for the *New Statesman*, ignoring an injunction placed on the story by the Attorney General.[100] The article, which identified as possible sources several defence officials, prompted the government to call an inquiry into a prima facie breach of the Official Secrets Act. Armed with search warrants, Special Branch raided the offices of the *New Statesman* and BBC Scotland in Glasgow, together with the homes of Campbell and a number of his researchers. Television cameras captured in real time the sight of police officers breaking down the door of Campbell's flat. Police seized every foot of film footage, as well as associated research materials. The BBC was appalled at the seizure of its property and made its feelings known to the government. In Parliament, the Secretary of State for Scotland, Malcolm Rifkind, faced a barrage of criticism: the spectacle of buildings being ransacked was like something from George Orwell's dystopian novel *Nineteen Eighty-Four*.[101] In retaliation, Campbell attempted to have the Zircon programme shown to MPs in Parliament. When the Attorney General forbade this by way of a further injunction, Campbell arranged a private screening in a nearby venue. A sanitised version of the Zircon episode was eventually broadcast two years later, the project by then having been cancelled on grounds of cost, and with police inquiries into a potential leak having run aground. A sour postscript was that the *Secret Society* series contributed to Milne losing his job. In January 1987, he was forced to resign by Marmaduke Hussey, who only months before had been appointed by Margaret Thatcher as Chair of the BBC Board of Governors. Among the BBC's old guard, Hussey was widely seen as a government stooge, charged with cleansing the corporation of its supposed left-wing bias.[102]

* * *

We were a handful. No doubt about that. I wouldn't have wanted to be in Whitehall's shoes.

Chapman Pincher, 2007[103]

On 29 March 1979, the day of his sixty-fifth birthday, Chapman Pincher retired from the *Express* to focus on a second career as a full-time espionage writer. As he left it, Fleet Street was a very different place to the one he had joined as a thrusting young reporter in 1945. In the intervening years, the press in Britain had developed into much more of a challenge to the secret state. Pincher's thirty-four years in the newsroom saw the emergence of a new species of journalist, one that he helped to shape and that he personified above all others. This new species was remarkably skilled at ascertaining sensitive information. In this period, journalists persuaded influential people to talk off the record like never before. Importantly, they built up vast networks of contacts within the government machine, taking advantage of the fact that many officials had private or departmental agendas to advance and thought nothing of using news-hungry reporters to promote these causes. One of the paradoxes of the British state is that, while officials advocate the importance of secrecy in the majority of cases, they happily countenance deliberate leakages when it suits them. With good reason, this double standard undermines public trust in the need for closed government more generally. Pincher, in particular, excelled at getting officials to talk. A bon viveur who delighted in building human relationships, he invested years getting to know, and be trusted by, the individuals with whom he dealt – taking them to lunch, socialising in their clubs, and indulging in their passion for traditional British field sports. Being a gentleman was an advantage: his contacts, mandarins to the man, trusted him because he was a social peer.

In the post-war period, journalists became increasingly adept at using open sources to reveal government secrets. With a scientific background and training, the likes of Pincher and Campbell spliced together esoteric details from otherwise safe technical publications to produce articles that horrified the authorities. Moreover, in testament to the growing perils of globalisation, reporters found material overseas that was unavailable on domestic shores and held to be inviolable.

For governments, damaging articles drawn from open sources were especially difficult to stop without embarrassment. When an attempt was made to do so, such as the ABC trial, officials were upbraided for defending secrets that were not really secrets at all. Another feature of the new species of journalist that plied its trade after the war was a diminished deference for government controls. By the late 1960s, the D-Notice system had fallen into desuetude as a respected forum, with eminent newspapermen such as Evans choosing to ignore the system after it became apparent that governments were exploiting D-Notices for political convenience rather than for genuine matters of security or defence. Lack of respect for D-Notices was a microcosm of a larger problem for the secret state: namely, that it was now infinitely harder to justify secrecy with the mantra of 'national security'. Where before, journalists would baulk at the thought of questioning this mantra, they now did as a matter of course.

Try as they might, governments proved largely unable to cope with the challenge posed by a transmogrified Fleet Street. Eventually, the gloves came off. Harold Wilson had no scruples when it came to controlling the media, even considering it appropriate to smear the name of a perceived troublemaker, in Colonel Lohan, in order to reduce press attacks against his government. In the 1970s, desperation led officials to reach twice for the ultimate Doomsday weapon, the Official Secrets Act, with disastrous consequences. One of the downsides of legal action is that governments invariably end up giving more publicity to a sensitive issue than it would have attracted had a less belligerent strategy been pursued. On the eve of Campbell's prosecution in 1977, Cheltenham was famous for its racecourse, its literary festivals, and its Regency heritage and architecture; only the readers of a trendy alternative magazine would know otherwise. Eighteen months of courtroom drama later, Cheltenham was recognised the world over as home to a vast, global eavesdropping centre. As chapters 8 and 9 will show, the pitfalls of using the law, coupled with the failings of the D-Notice system, would be instrumental in convincing governments of the need to embrace an 'offensive' strategy of information control, specifically official histories of intelligence, designed both to pre-empt and to drown out the revelations of an unfettered press.

Part III

Secrecy and political memoirs

6 CABINET CONFESSIONS: FROM CHURCHILL TO CROSSMAN

> I am firmly convinced that posterity has everything to gain
> and nothing to lose from the publication of the struggles, the
> failures and the successes of a lifetime devoted to the development
> of our system of Cabinet Government, whether for peace
> or war.
>
> SIR MAURICE HANKEY,
> *30 May 1957*[1]

In Chapter 2, we saw how the secret state, in the inter-war period, struggled to prevent the disclosure of sensitive information in the autobiographical writings of senior statesmen. More often than not, officials were rebuffed by authors who had a mind of their own about how the 'rules' should be applied, if at all, in their case. This chapter takes the story up to the seminal Crossman Affair in the mid 1970s, where the government made a controversial and ill-fated attempt to use the courts to block publication of the late Richard Crossman's diaries, to the delight of the chattering classes and advocates of open government. The thirty years or so following the end of the Second World War represented a particularly difficult time for secret-keepers charged with stopping politicians from doing too much damage in their reminiscences. Just as before, many of the individuals in question were loath to cooperate, believing themselves to be above common law and the common man. Former prime ministers expected and received the most preferential treatment, but this, in turn, only served to embolden those lower down the ladder to demand similar leeway.

The chief problem that surfaced in this period was that retiring ministers were less inclined to be dilatory in writing their memoirs, desiring to produce 'instant history'. Fewer politicians were leaving the political stage with their reputations intact – a reflection perhaps that politics itself was becoming more heartless and unforgiving. For failure-stained individuals like Anthony Eden, desperate to alter the trajectory of public opinion, there was no time like the present. Moreover, there was more money to be made out of immediate material, with publishers and newspapers keen to provide a news-hungry public with the 'inside' story on those who occupied positions of power. As Whitehall saw it, in leaving only a small distance between the publication date and the events and people described, authors posed a direct challenge to the Westminster system of government. The concern was that, if instant memoirs provided details of ministers and their policy deliberations, or if they commented on named civil servants and their advice, there would be a breakdown of trust which was seen as vital if public servants were to exchange opinions freely and frankly. Moreover, if instant accounts revealed the dissenting private views of individual ministers, or elaborated on the squabbling that took place around the confidential setting of the Cabinet table, this would threaten the doctrine of collective responsibility which dictated that, once the government reaches a decision, ministers must support it *in toto*. Problematically, of course, authors and their sponsors in the publishing world argued differently. As they saw it, authors had a right to record their actions, while the public had a right to know how they were governed. In the period covered by this chapter, the challenge for the secret state was to protect a public interest in confidentiality, without appearing to reject a public interest in accountability. This was to be a balancing act that it often failed to accomplish and for which it would attract widespread criticism.[2]

In the main, the favoured strategy of control was remarkably informal. With the exception of the Crossman Affair, legal action was generally regarded as being so incommensurate with the true measure of the offence as to render it wholly unrealistic to entertain the idea. In 1948, Sir Hartley Shawcross, then Attorney General, likened prosecution to using a 'Naismith hammer to crack a nut'.[3] Whenever a difficult case presented itself, therefore, the strategy would be for the Cabinet Secretary to consult and parley with authors in a de facto bid to find a solution that assuaged official concerns. In some cases, a solution would take many months to achieve and necessitate the exchange of hundreds of pages of correspondence. Occasionally, the Cabinet Secretary would resort to underhand tactics, such as inviting every department in Whitehall for its views in order to delay the date of publication. Ultimately, however, the success of the informal arrangement hinged on two overriding factors. First, as Burke Trend recognised, was the need for officials to 'bargain and to compromise'.[4] The moment when negotiated blue-pencilling of texts becomes enforced blue-pencilling is the moment when authors break off communication and threaten to 'publish and be damned'. The second key to success is the ability of authors to know where to draw the line. The quid quo pro of government not imposing more formal codification is the expectation that authors will behave like gentlemen and demonstrate goodwill like a gentleman should. This is very much an extension of what Peter Hennessy calls 'the good chaps theory of government'.[5] At the heart of this is the notion that the governing classes know what is expected of them and know not to push things too far. Accordingly, they will self-regulate for fear of being ostracised from the community and being labelled a 'bad chap'.

As will be shown, this remedy of self-regulation has proved remarkably enduring. Despite setbacks and failures, Whitehall has consistently managed to squeeze more lifeblood out of it, fortified it seems by a faith in the ability of British institutions, through trial and error, to persevere until something approaching an ideal system is reached. In consequence, the 'rulebook', if one can call it that, has steadily evolved. Like a palimpsest, new features have been constantly superimposed upon older contours. It is the memoirs and personalities that have defined this rulebook to which we now turn.

*   *   *

> It seems to me that the Prime Minister [Winston Churchill], when he writes, can take whatever material he wants, and say whatever he likes; but then I suppose he is in a class by himself!
>
> *publisher John Murray to Hankey, 30 June 1954*[6]

Nothing stimulates the proliferation of political memoirs more than controversy or war. Ministers want to produce them to set right their place in history, while the public is keen to get a ringside view of a genuinely significant episode in history. And so it was with the Second

World War. After the cessation of hostilities, those who had held public office during the conflict sought to reveal their experiences. With some justification, Whitehall was nervous, remembering the problems that had surfaced with the 'frocks' and 'brass hats' at the end of the Great War. Accordingly, in spring 1946 the Cabinet Secretary, Edward Bridges (Figure 16), drafted a memorandum setting out the principles and processes underlying publication. Bridges' document, which was given ministerial approval on 23 May, restated the conventions that had been pragmatically established by his predecessor, Hankey. Ministers were reminded that they were obligated to consult the government of the day before publication, and would only be allowed to quote from official documents that would not damage the confidentiality of government or Britain's relations in the international sphere. In an attempt to prevent the long, verbatim regurgitation of sources that had been such a hallmark of the Lloyd George memoirs, the memorandum ruled that extensive quotation of official documents 'should only be allowed in very exceptional cases'.[7]

It was not long before the guidelines were being bypassed by Churchill.[8] With a series of backdoor deals, the wartime premier secured permission to quote at length from a host of classified sources, and even managed to twist Bridges' arm into letting his research assistants 'devil' on his behalf in Whitehall archives. The true extent of Churchill's disclosures is masterfully revealed in David Reynolds's book *In Command of History* and will not be repeated here.[9] Suffice to say that he bulldozed his way through almost every restriction and, in doing so, made it difficult for Whitehall to prevent other members of the War Cabinet from doing the same in their writings. These included: Samuel Hoare (Lord Privy Seal); Viscount Halifax (Foreign Secretary); John Simon (Chancellor); Clement Attlee (Deputy Prime Minister); and Hugh Dalton (Board of Trade).[10] By the early 1960s, Whitehall had more or less accepted that ministers, in their memoirs, could say almost anything about either the First or the Second World War. Disclosures relating to wartime administration, when the world was divided between allies and enemies, and when rival politicians had come together as part of a coalition, were judged unlikely to damage diplomatic relations or cause party political embarrassment.[11]

While Churchill and his former ministerial cronies were given remarkable latitude to publish as they pleased, the same could not be said of civil servants who desired to go into print. Before the war, Hankey had laboured day and night on a large volume of reminiscences, only to be thwarted in his quest for publication by officials constantly moving the goalposts. In spring 1946, he tried again to break the deadlock, this time making his case to Attlee's government. Like Churchill before him, Attlee considered the memoir destructive to the confidential relationship between ministers and their advisers. Accordingly, Hankey was told to eliminate all extracts from his diary and delete every sentence that discussed his day-to-day dealings with ministers; even then, there was no guarantee of publication, since a further requirement was that the memoir had to be resubmitted in its revised form.[12] Hankey's initial reaction was to make the changes but, on reflection and taking advice from friends and former colleagues, he concluded that if he did so the book would be 'ruined'.[13] Field Marshal Jan Smuts had said to him: 'After all these changes in your book, does it remain first-class history?' 'Time', he emphasised, 'is of secondary importance, but do not publish anything that is not first-class history.'[14] To date, Hankey had made hundreds of excisions – unavailingly – in a bid to meet the 'timidity of the official censorship'.[15] The latest version already bore little resemblance to the original book, which had been met with the highest encomiums from several distinguished readers; to make a further round of cuts, therefore, would be plain silly. With this, Hankey had two options open to him: publish without official approval, or bide his time. He chose the latter, believing that the risk of 'gate-crashing' was too great for him, and predicting that someday Whitehall was bound to give way.[16] In a letter to Viscount Addison, he wrote positively: 'A strong feeling is growing up both inside and outside the Services about the Government's obscurantist attitude in recent years towards the publication of memoirs.'[17]

Hankey's optimism about there being, sooner rather than later, a new landscape of opportunity for memoirists drawn from the ranks of the civil service proved wide of the mark. Several years later, in 1953, when confronted with the autobiography of Dr Thomas Jones, Deputy Secretary to the Cabinet from December 1916 to 1930, officialdom gave no quarter. As discussed in Chapter 2, Jones had initially been baffled by the Cabinet Office's decision to block Hankey's memoir, considering it extraordinary that whereas Churchill and Lloyd George tore up the rule book to produce richly documented accounts, relatively poor retired civil servants were precluded from having their say. Having then actually read the manuscript, he changed his mind and believed it to be inappropriate for publication. Needless to say, by 1953, with his own literary career now at stake, Jones was again championing the rights of Whitehall retirees. His memoir, however, came up against the full force of the government machine. Norman Brook, the Cabinet Secretary, had two principal objections. First, the manuscript disclosed the extent to which Jones had helped ministers write their speeches, and on occasion, had taken policy decisions himself.[18] Jones was told this and was encouraged to delete the offending passages. Brook's second objection – not relayed to Jones – was of a more mischievous kind; namely, if publication was permitted, the Cabinet Office would soon have Hankey renewing his request to publish *The Supreme Command*. The quarrelsome Bridges, now Permanent Secretary to the Treasury and head of the Home Civil Service, had also read the draft and had drawn up his own list of objections. For Bridges, the worst thing about the book was that it said too much, especially in 'bad taste', about the private lives of politicians. A recurring theme was that ministers would hit the bottle as soon as the sun was over the yardarm. According to Jones, for example, 'the question of drink when staying with Lloyd George is a diverting one'.[19] Bonar Law was portrayed as relying on alcohol to unwind from his prime ministerial responsibilities. 'I do not think Law's drinking ought to be immortalised,' considered Bridges.[20] The memoir also included a number of off-the-cuff remarks made by ministers, which appeared wholly offensive. For example, upon learning in January 1918 that Herbert Samuel was to be the chairman of the National Salvage Board, Lloyd George reportedly muttered: 'The very man – a Jew to collect old clothes.'[21]

Having returned to Downing Street for his 'Indian Summer' premiership, Churchill, interestingly, was not on impulse against publication. Whereas in the past, he had regarded memoir writing by mandarins as abhorrent, he was now of the opinion that 'Time passages its sponge across the significance of all records.' 'Each case', he went on, 'must be dealt with on its merits and individual instances must be turning points of judgement.'[22] Recognising that no 'hard and fast rule' existed – and being a self-confessed 'expert in these matters' – he offered to inspect the manuscript with an open mind. Churchill, however, was incapable of being objective as soon as he started reading the text. In the memoir, rather foolishly perhaps, Jones had singled out a number of politicians for special criticism, the most notable of whom was none other than Churchill himself. 'Churchill had never known how to use experts,' claimed Jones in one passage. 'Nelson', he continued, 'would never have allowed the German fleet to escape at Jutland.'[23] Several swipes were taken at *The World Crisis*, with Jones accusing Churchill of bending and breaking the historical record to give the impression that he was uniquely skilled and pansophical. For example, using evidence from his own diary and quoting from official sources, Jones exposed the distortions underlying Churchill's recollection of his appointment as First Lord of the Admiralty in 1911: 'Winston's account of his appointment to the Admiralty, in *The World Crisis*, was not very close to the facts.'[24]

Churchill hit the roof. Jones had not only attacked his record as a statesmen and military strategist but, in the ultimate insult, had charged him with being unreliable as a historian. With his reputation to consider and book sales to protect, the last thing Churchill wanted was a respected figure like Jones revealing his mistakes and spin-doctoring techniques. 'Such extracts', he protested, 'show how utterly unsuitable and improper its publication would be. I consider that severe objection should be taken.'[25] With this, Brook was required to find a way of stopping the memoir, without, of course, making it apparent that the reason for doing so was to save Churchill's face. He rose to the challenge expertly, appealing to Jones' sense of corporate responsibility. It was put to the author that publication represented a betrayal of trust: 'By the nature of their job, [senior advisers] will receive many confidences which they will be expected to respect. This does not apply only to Cabinet discussions; it extends equally to the gossip they hear and the confidences they receive about policies and personalities.'[26] There were to be no references to the unguarded thoughts and personal foibles of ministers: 'It may be that no man is a hero to his valet; but a man who relaxes his self-control in his valet's presence usually assumes that his valet will not write memoirs.'[27] The manuscript would have to be expunged of any suggestion that civil servants had ghosted ministerial speeches. The tactic worked. Jones had second thoughts about whether it was appropriate for mandarins to publish autobiographies. Now in his eighties, he also doubted if he had the stamina to complete what amounted to a major rewrite. Accordingly, he turned his back and instead bequeathed his diary to Oxford University Press for posthumous publication. This appeared, in three volumes, between 1969 and 1971.[28]

As Jones discovered, the only option for civil servants with authorial aspirations was to designate literary executors and instruct them to arrange for the posthumous publication of works. Even this was not plain sailing, as illustrated by the struggle that broke out in 1956 between Whitehall and Henry Bunbury, editor of the diurnal scribblings of William Braithwaite, a mandarin who had been personal assistant to Lloyd George, then Chancellor, during the creation of the landmark National Insurance Act in 1911.

Braithwaite had been dead for nearly twenty years and his family were keen to cement his place in history as the architect of modern social welfare, a legacy distorted by the fact that Sir Robert Morant, Permanent Secretary to the Board of Education in 1911, had controversially been chosen ahead of Braithwaite to spearhead the Act after it had become law.[29] Submitted for clearance in October 1956, the memoir arrived first on the desk of Thomas Padmore, Second Secretary to the Treasury, before being passed to Bridges and Brook. Although the events described were some forty-five years old, Padmore's assessment was not favourable. The text was interlarded with snide comments about officials, which, taken together, implied that the civil service was beset with in-fighting and petty rivalries. Morant was labelled a 'treacherous hound'; others, such as Lister Stead, were described as being 'rather dense' and 'slow mentally'.[30] Sir Hubert Llewellyn Smith – a civil servant of some considerable stature – was mocked for his inability to put on a hat without the aid of a shoehorn. The memoir also contained unflattering remarks about ministers. Like Jones, Braithwaite had seemingly inhabited a world where dipsomania was widespread. The Liberal prime minister, Herbert Asquith, was said to be routinely 'drunk after dinner'; others passages suggested that he walked 'badly', looked 'blotchy' and enjoyed 'slouching out' when intoxicated.[31] Padmore considered these insults wholly inappropriate. He was also uncomfortable with the fact that the memoir had been based on a diary. Ministers, he feared, would not speak freely to their advisers if they were known to be 'chaps who [went] home after talking to them and scribbled it all down in a little book'.[32] Bridges shared Padmore's concerns: 'What we have to secure is that ministers are not discouraged from being frank with their civil servants and inviting them to confidential meetings, by seeing catty things about their predecessors published in memoirs by deceased officials.'[33] In the event, Bunbury was allowed to publish, but only after only making hundreds of deletions. The final publication, therefore, was largely unrecognisable from the original manuscript.[34]

By the late 1950s, Hankey was once again pressing the Cabinet Office to rescind the ban on his Great War memoir. Hankey had no intention of dazzling readers from beyond the grave, fearful of the potential for mutilation of the text by the Whitehall machine. The catalyst for his latest bid to secure approval was a letter of congratulations from the prime minister, Harold Macmillan, wishing him a happy eightieth birthday. In the letter, dated 31 March 1957, Macmillan praised Hankey for his 'notable contribution' to the development of the system of Cabinet government.[35] With this, the recently turned octogenarian wrote to the premier and pleaded his case on the grounds of 'three new factors'.[36] He highlighted that nearly forty years had elapsed since the last episode in the book, namely the Armistice of 1918. He stressed that the book's principal characters were now dead, with the sole exception of Churchill, who, in the period covered by the book, had yet to reach his 'full political stature'.[37] Hankey also pointed to several recent publications, such as Field Marshal Viscount Alanbrooke's *Turn of the Tide* (1957), which had been derived from startlingly detailed handwritten diaries. This, he contended, was a sign that 'a more tolerant attitude' was now being taken.[38]

Macmillan was no more sympathetic to Hankey's appeal than Churchill had been a decade earlier. The basic argument against the memoir remained the same: 'publication of the book, by laying bare the inner workings of the Central Government machine, would be likely to impair for the present and the future the relations between Ministers and their most intimate official advisers'.[39] Macmillan also reiterated the danger of Cabinet Secretaries maintaining a diary: 'I can only say that, if I thought that the present holder of this office was keeping a private diary, my official relations with him would be very different to what they are now.'[40] Hankey was enraged. Since 1918, he had witnessed an 'orgy of revelation' and yet, as far as he could tell, there had been no discernable deterioration in relations between ministers and their most intimate advisers.[41] Hankey felt doubly aggrieved since, during that time, he had lent his knowledge and expertise to countless memoirists, biographers and historians.[42] With officials obdurate, he began seriously to entertain the idea of publishing without approval, a staggering development for someone who had practically defined the foundations of Cabinet secrecy. Wary of infringing the Official Secrets Act, he sought legal advice from former Conservative Attorney General Sir Lionel Heald. The latter confirmed what many people knew already:

'The Act is a most unsatisfactory and indefinite statute, on which it is impossible to give an opinion with any confidence.'[43] Accordingly, he strongly warned against running the risk of unauthorised publication.

Hankey noted Heald's advice but, in a deliberate act of provocation, continued to make noises to the government that he was contemplating an illicit release. Well-connected friends, such as Lord Ismay, spread word around Whitehall that he was in a 'very truculent mood' and was refusing to be intimidated by the threat of prosecution.[44] In actual fact, unbeknownst to the Cabinet Office, Hankey did not even have a publisher. Reneging on earlier promises, Cassells had declined to contract the memoir on the grounds that the subject matter was old-hat, the public now being interested in the Second, not the First World War. Other publishers agreed. An anonymous peer-reviewer for Hutchinson claimed that the book was 'forty years too late'. In his report, he wrote: 'If it had been brought out at any time between 1918 and 1925 – or even 1918 to 1929 – it might well have had the success that Alanbrooke's memoirs had a short time ago. In 1958, however, 1914 is hardly more real to the average man than 1814. Between us and the First World War rises the Himalayan heights.'[45] Hankey was caught between a rock and hard place. Whereas publishers rejected the memoir because of its antiquated content, officials believed that the material therein was highly relevant and thus unfit for public consumption.

The manuscript suffered from other problems. Hankey was attempting to sell the book to trade publishers, yet it was written largely in the (to outsiders) universally non-understandable tongue known as 'Whitehallese' – pompous, abstract, polysyllabic, periphrastic and obfuscating. One of Hutchinson's reviewers struggled to 'keep track of all the Committees and Sub-Committees which were set up, discontinued, allowed to lapse, revised, [and] transformed'.[46] The mandarin in Hankey ensured that he seldom took sides, and rarely provided anything more than a simple character sketch of the book's personalities. One reviewer complained that the depiction of Churchill resembled an obituary column in *The Times*. The general reader, by contrast, would desire 'some shrewd judgement of his character, his weakness and his greatness, seen in the light of what we now know'.[47] Moreover, it was felt by publishers that Hankey had been 'too scrupulous to reveal one single secret, one tiny insignificant scandal'.[48] One reader's report likened the book to the opening of Mme Humbert's treasure chest: 'a terrible disappointment'.[49]

Hankey eventually found a publisher in the shape of Allen & Unwin, signing a contract on 6 July 1959. To give the manuscript some needed lifeblood, the journalist V. R. T. Clark was enlisted as a secret editor.[50] Of course, this still left the problem of official resistance to the project. Acting on Heald's advice, Hankey had earlier asked Macmillan to put the case before an arbitrator, perhaps Lord Salisbury, who had resigned from office in March 1957. This, however, came to nothing. Salisbury said that he was unable to read the book with an 'open mind', since personally he 'regard[ed] it as entirely wrong for anybody who has held the position of Secretary to the Cabinet to publish within his own lifetime'.[51] Remarkably, then, in early 1961, after nearly twenty years of government haggling, and to the shock of Hankey, Macmillan suddenly decided to turn a blind eye to publication. Released to favourable reviews in mid April, the book was accompanied by serialisation in the *Sunday Times*, with the newspaper paying £1,000 per article.[52] Despite modest sales, publication marked a truly momentous moment in the history of British secrecy, bringing to an end the time-honoured rule that civil servants do not publish works, in their lifetime, based on officially obtained information. Hankey duly delighted in sending a signed copy to Churchill, who wrote back with affection, 'I remember full well the commanding part you played in the events of those days. Thank you also for your inscription, which recalls for me agreeable thoughts of our long friendship.'[53] In the words of Hankey's biographer Stephen Roskill, 'Plainly all the hatchets of 1942–3 were buried and forgotten in the benevolent twilight of old age.'[54]

What prompted Macmillan's change of heart? As Roskill claims, in allowing publication he almost certainly went against the wishes of Bridges and Brook, neither of whom had shown any willingness to give way.[55] Historian John Naylor speculates that Macmillan had no choice but to back down after approving the Public Records Act in 1958, which gave a statutory, general public right of access to government records 50 years after their creation. With this, HMG accepted the recommendation of the Grigg Committee on Departmental Records (1954: Cmd 9163) that 50 years constituted a 'normal period in relation to the life of a man' and thus would guarantee the 'preservation of unself-consciousness in the writing of records'.[56] Crucially, the introduction of the Fifty Year Rule meant that, in 1964, official papers of the Great War would start appearing in the Public

Record Office. By 1968, researchers would have records from the entire conflict. Another factor which may have influenced Macmillan was that, in 1960, a political memoir came out that not only made all before it look passé, but shattered the rules of the game as far as autobiographical writing was concerned. That memoir was *Full Circle*.

* * *

> I have had a fierce but agreeable letter from Sir Norman Brook which in fact, under penalty of being sent to the Tower of London, will allow me to consult any papers at Cabinet Office that you might wish.
>
> *Alan Hodge (research assistant) to Anthony Eden,*
> *28 November 1957*[57]

Anthony Eden, first Earl of Avon, was passionate about his reputation and the verdict of history.[58] Before 1956 his legacy as a 'Great Briton' was largely taken as axiomatic. As a staunch opponent of appeasement, who in February 1938 famously resigned as Foreign Secretary to protest against Neville Chamberlain's de jure recognition of Italian policy in Abyssinia ('There are occasions when strong political convictions must override all other considerations'),[59] Eden was omitted from the cast list of Cato's 'Guilty Men', the celebrated indictment of the 'White Paper' generation. Eden's illustrious place in the history books – fortified during his third term as Foreign Secretary (1951–5) – was afforded the priceless endorsement of Churchill who, in *The Gathering Storm*, called him 'the most resolute and courageous figure in the [wartime] Administration'.[60] In 1954 he was knighted – an achievement treated with tremendous fanfare in the popular press – but 1955 marked his *annus mirabilis*; as a 'conviction' politician noted for his urbane realism, mastery of modern diplomacy and unrivalled political experience, his accession to the premiership was greeted with 'fulsome praise and without demur'.[61] 'By every conceivable test of history, politics and popularity,' wrote James Margach, 'Eden should have been one of Britain's truly great Prime Ministers.'[62] After Suez, however, his reputation was in tatters. Suez, which confirmed Britain's precipitous decline from world-power status to that of a second-class nation, heaped personal humiliation upon him and his *folie des grandeurs*. Critics had been given a sword and they stuck it in and twisted it with great gusto. As David Dutton argues, it was 'precisely because of the reputation which Eden enjoyed, and cultivated, that Suez proved so damaging to him'.[63] Indeed, despite their barefaced support for the campaign, character assassinations were not dealt out to either of the leading French players, Christian Pineau (foreign minister) and Guy Mollet (prime minister), or to Harold Macmillan, whose political currency actually flourished after the soap opera of Suez.

Eden's short and ill-starred premiership prompted an immediate full-scale literary inquisition. Paul Johnson's *The Suez War* (1957) portrayed a statesman with bloodstained hands, evangelising and practising a policy of violence in the Middle East.[64] Replete with petty asides and general haughtiness, Randolph Churchill's *The Rise and Fall of Sir Anthony Eden* (1959) speculated whether Eden would have been so successful had he not been blessed with good looks and brownnosed the right people.[65] Seen through the prism of Suez, and through the splenetics of his detractors, Eden was reconstituted as a second-rater, renowned as much for his fragile temperament and political opportunism as for his parliamentary adroitness. Such assessments, of course, relied heavily on retrospective hindsight – or what D. R. Thorpe refers to as an approach distorted by 'syllogistic inevitability' (that is, the tendency to write a career backwards).[66]

Eden became deeply concerned about how posterity would judge his political record. In retirement, therefore, recognising that his reputation required gilding, Eden fought relentlessly to vindicate his actions, most notably over Suez – the most controversial episode of his public life. Published in 1960, *Full Circle* set out to plead for justice before the bar of history: 'This book will expose wounds', prefaced the author; 'by doing so it could help to heal them.'[67] *Full Circle* covered the period from October 1951, when Eden became Foreign Secretary, to his resignation as prime minister in January 1957. Its title, taken from William Shakespeare's *King Lear* ('The wheel is come full circle: I am here'), attested to his obsession with rationalising the political vicissitudes of Suez and restoring balance to his career. *Full Circle* also confirmed Eden's faith in the utility of learning from the past; its central theme was 'the lessons of the Thirties and their application to the Fifties'.[68] Drawing analogies with Hitler and Mussolini, it forcefully put forward the argument that the Egyptian president Gamal Abdel Nasser had been a modern-day dictator incapable of responding positively to a policy of appeasement.

From the perspective of post-war secrecy, there are few political memoirs more significant than *Full Circle*. Published within four years of the Suez crisis, it was one of the first memoirs to fall into the category of 'instant history'. Hitherto, works had related either to the two world wars, periods regarded by the state as *sui generis*, or to subject matter dating back to the late nineteenth and early twentieth century. *Full Circle* changed this, and did so in eye-catching fashion, quoting extensively from material in the Whitehall archives about a contemporary event of enormous public interest. Exactly how Eden managed to secure official consent for such an enterprise will be considered in detail below, but for now it is sufficient to say that the advent of retired ministers writing 'instant history' presented a new and difficult challenge for the censor. 'Instant memoirs' drawn from officially acquired information increased the likelihood of a backlash from historians. As we shall see, with the Fifty Year Rule precluding public access to records of recent history, *Full Circle* became the 'thin end of the wedge', prompting furious reprisals from academics dismayed at the bias shown in favour of politicians. Problematically, the more recent the period which memoirs discussed, the more likely they were to deal with matters of current political importance. Unsurprisingly, the sorry tale of Suez had to be told with great care. Britain's position in the Middle East, and her relations with the United States above all else, hinged to a large extent on ensuring that Eden was kept on a tight leash. As we shall see, when vetting *Full Circle*, the question invariably asked by the Cabinet Secretary was not 'Is this damaging to national security?', but 'Is this likely to offend the Americans?' It has been said by historians such as Richard Lamb that 'there is no means of telling how much Eden toned down his memoirs for 1956 because of advice from [Selwyn] Lloyd, [Norman] Brook and the Foreign Office'.[69] This is not the case. Files at the National Archives, as well as documents from Eden's private papers at Birmingham University, are rich in evidence of the doctoring of the manuscript by the official machine.

Full Circle is doubly arresting for the student of official secrecy because it obscured, concealed and lied about vital elements of the Suez story. Without any prompting by government, Eden said nothing on the question of whether the British, French and Israelis were acting in concert when they invaded Egypt in 1956. Sidestepping allegations of collusion, he maintained that Britain had joined the conflict as an unscheduled peacekeeper, separating warring Egyptian and Israeli forces: 'We had intervened to divide and, above all, to contain the conflict ... Once the fighting had ceased, justification for further intervention ceased with it.'[70] This, of course, was entirely consistent with what he had said to Parliament at the time of the crisis: 'There was not foreknowledge that Israel would attack Egypt – there was not.'[71] With the benefit of several first-hand accounts, as well as the opening of pertinent government records (most importantly in January 1987 when documents from 1956 became available at the Public Record Office, now the National Archives), we now know that this was outright deception.[72] On 24 October 1956, a few days before the Israeli attack on Egypt, representatives of the British, French and Israeli governments met at Sèvres on the outskirts of Paris to sign a secret plot. The essence of the tripartite agreement – otherwise known as the Sèvres Protocol – was remarkably simple: Israel would attack the Egyptian army near the Suez Canal, thereby enabling Britain and France to express consternation over the safety of the waterway, and intervene forcibly as peacemakers.

What follows is the first in-depth examination of *Full Circle*. It examines – in terms of Stuart Hall's important schema – each of the three 'moments' of any cultural form: its production (encoding); the text itself; and its reception (decoding). Several key questions are addressed. What was the attitude of the Cabinet Office towards publication? What was removed from the text and on what grounds? A central argument will be that *Full Circle* did not, as is often claimed, 'shape interpretations that prevailed for a generation'.[73] Even by 1960, as reviewers sharpened their pencils, the rudiments of collusion were too well known for Eden's carefully packaged disguise to stick.

Eden left Downing Street on 9 January 1957 with a cheerless and uncertain future ahead of him. His political career was over; his medical prognosis was grim; and, with small private means and mounting medical bills, his financial situation was perilous.[74] 'With the heartlessness of politics,' wrote his official biographer Robert Rhodes James, 'it was generally assumed that he was finished.'[75] At the same time, however, Eden was a publisher's golden ticket. Having held ministerial office for a quarter of a century, he had been witness to Suez and Munich, the two most divisive political crises of the twentieth century. Unbeknownst to the erstwhile premier, his close friend Brendan Bracken had been making overtures to the General Manager of *The Times* (Mathew Wellsian), suggesting the idea of Eden writing a political life history and syndicating the world rights to the newspaper.[76] The sum tentatively mooted by Wellsian was £100,000. Wellsian underestimated

Eden's literary capital; the *Telegraph* had reportedly offered £150,000 whilst Lord Beaverbrook had enthralled several dinner parties with a proposal to bid £1 million. Bracken saw considerable merits to the venture. Publication would help to rebuild Eden's shattered reputation and thus influence history's judgement on his political record. The remunerative benefits, moreover, would allow Eden to purchase a new home – one where he could 'dig his hands deep into the English countryside'.[77]

Eden initially resisted the blandishments of the press. The permanence of ill health was certainly an issue; the fact that most newspapers, including *The Times*, had withdrawn their support for his policies in the Middle East also stuck in the craw. By the autumn, however, he had changed his mind. While lacking in hard evidence, let alone a smoking gun, rumours of collusion had failed to go away. Merry and Serge Bromberger's polemic *The Secrets of Suez* (1957), which accused Eden of lying to Parliament, demonstrated the pitfalls of leaving his reputation to 'history'.[78] In his own defence, therefore, he decided to write his memoirs and, on 5 October 1957, formed a literary trust that would arrange publication as well as the sale of serial rights to *The Times*.[79] His contract with the newspaper provided for an initial capital payment of £100,000; an annual income for each year of writing; and an equal share of the profits. As paymaster – 'insistent on having its Suez pound of flesh first'[80] – *The Times* postponed annual payments until Eden had delivered chapters relating to his premiership. This reflected a natural fear that he would not live long enough to finish the book and thus provided an incentive to finish quickly. Eden had no qualms about publishing out of chronological sequence; Suez was a millstone around his neck and, as his wife explained, there was no telling how long it would be until he 'falls down dead'.[81]

Eden assembled a stellar research team which included Alan Hodge (on the staff of *History Today*), Bryan Cartledge (St Antony's College, Oxford), David Dilks (St Antony's), Robert Blake (Christ Church, Oxford) and Robin Furneaux (Third Earl of Birkenhead).[82] The perquisites of being a research assistant were not insignificant. Furneaux received an annual salary of £750 and could claim expenses for his London flat.[83] With an expectation that he was entitled to the same facilities accorded to Churchill, Eden at once asked the Cabinet Office to allow his research assistants access to official records. This special dispensation was granted ostensibly on the grounds that

Eden's poor health precluded him from making regular trips to London, although other factors also influenced this decision, as will be considered later in this section. As a former private secretary at the Ministry of Information, Hodge, in particular, was permitted to inspect (and transcribe) a range of sensitive documents, from Foreign Office telegrams to the 'rough notes' that Hankey had written for the meetings of the Foreign Policy Committee in 1938.[84] It is probably fair to say that Hankey would have been chastened to know this, given his personal experience with Cabinet Office obstruction.

Eden began submitting chapters to Brook in May 1958. Immediately, Brook identified a major problem. The general presentation of Suez was an implied indictment of American policy, with the late US Secretary of State, John Foster Dulles, singled out for criticism (Figure 17). Mindful of President Eisenhower's hopes for re-election in November 1956, Dulles had publicly opposed the Anglo-French invasion of the Suez Canal, but, according to Eden, Britain had been driven to use force after Dulles had 'cynically' undercut Downing Street's efforts to undo by economic and diplomatic pressure Nasser's nationalisation of the waterway. Dulles, claimed Eden, 'had strung [Britain] along over many months of negotiation from pretext to pretext, from device to device and from contrivance to contrivance'.[85] The chapters also accused Dulles of being two-faced. Following the ceasefire, he had reportedly told the Foreign Secretary, Selwyn Lloyd, from his hospital bed, that he 'deplored that we [Britain] had not managed to bring Nasser down'. Schooled in the importance of the Special Relationship with the United States, Brook questioned the wisdom of such observations. Eden, however, was in no mood to make concessions for the sake of American sensibilities. In a letter to the Cabinet Secretary, he explained that he had been 'very restrained' in his treatment of the Americans and could have said 'much more' if he had desired.[86]

By July, Brook had parcelled out copies of the chapters to stakeholders in Whitehall. The feedback had a common theme; that Eden had said too much that might offend the Americans. Sir Philip de Zulueta, Harold Macmillan's private secretary, was horrified.[87] The draft showed that Macmillan, as Foreign Secretary in the early days of the crisis, had been a leading hawk in the Cabinet, constantly pressing Eden for military action irrespective of feelings in Washington. Now prime minister, Macmillan had since set great store by re-establishing relations of cordiality with the White House. 'The American administration', underlined de Zulueta, 'are more co-operative than they were in their more ignorant days.'[88] Evidence of this new rapport was the agreement at Bermuda in March 1957 for sixty Thor missiles to be based in Britain. De Zulueta also feared that Eden had been too candid in his descriptions of personalities from the Middle East. For example, although the Shah of Iran would not repudiate his hatred of Nasser, it was considered inappropriate that he should be quoted to this effect in a British political memoir.

Prefaced with the important rider 'to be shown to no-one except, at Brook's discretion, the Prime Minister', Selwyn Lloyd produced a list of several grievances.[89] Firstly, the draft had a strong anti-American bias throughout, including 'pretty outspoken criticism' of Dulles; publication of these passages, within a year of his death, would gravely endanger the Special Relationship – a relationship only recently renewed.[90] As Lloyd saw it, particular harm might be done in the area of intelligence liaison, since the deceased Secretary of State's younger brother was none other than CIA Director Allen Dulles. Secondly, Eden's partisanship of the Israelis against the Egyptians would impair British efforts to improve relations in the region; indeed, Eden's 'rather crude' belief that the 'Israeli–Egyptian explosion was advantageous to the free world' had the potential not only to strengthen suspicions that he had inspired the crisis, but to imply that there had been foreknowledge of the Israeli attack of 29 October.[91] Lloyd's third complaint was that 1960, the date set for publication, was simply too soon after the crisis. Many of those principally concerned were still active in politics and would be mortified by the disclosure of what they had entrusted to Eden in confidence. Lloyd concluded by saying that he had hoped for a 'broadminded, tolerant and statesmanlike' account – a work that would stand the test of history and befit Eden's reputation.[92] Instead, he had been left with the impression that Eden was motivated by personal malice.

While the Cabinet Office fretted over the manuscript's inclusions, Lord Avon's research assistants were more disturbed by what Eden had omitted. 'It is certain that the book will be very largely judged by the Suez chapters,' wrote Blake: 'It is absolutely vital to answer the questions still left in people's minds, and not to give any impression, however unwittingly, of evading problems or suppressing facts.'[93] Blake's concerns were threefold. Firstly, that the draft did not unpack the 'exact motive' for Anglo-French intervention. Eden, despite claiming that the object was to prevent war spreading all over the Middle East and to safeguard free passage through the canal, had revealed neither when the Cabinet arrived at the decision to intervene, nor where or when the concerting of a joint policy had been discussed with the French.[94] In view of all the allegations and counter-allegations, Blake called on Eden to deal with the charge of collusion 'quite specifically', otherwise public reaction was bound to be 'sceptical and incredulous'.[95] Blake – who admitted that he had 'heard something about our extreme secrecy'[96] – had clearly not been taken into Eden's confidence on the subject of collusion. His correspondences betray a total ignorance of the real events in late 1956. In one letter, he derided the Suez Group's (perfectly accurate!) claim that Eden had travelled to Paris where he 'concerted some allegedly mysterious and sinister plans with French Ministers'.[97]

Blake's second fear was that Eden had not properly explained the reasons for British withdrawal. The average reader, he opined, would find it difficult to believe the claim that Britain had pulled out merely because Egypt and Israel had stopped fighting. Although, in a sense, Britain had achieved its intention of 'separating the combatants', surely ministers had also hoped to obtain a settlement of the canal question and to deal a decisive blow to Nasser? According to Blake, unlike 'left-wing intellectual moralists', the 'ordinary man in the street does not care a damn whether there was collusion or not'; what he failed to understand was why 'we did not finish the job, occupy the whole canal, clear it with our own salvage fleet, and then negotiate a new settlement with Nasser'.[98] Blake's third critique was that Eden had given insufficient attention to the military side of Suez.[99] The manuscript said nothing on the alleged differences between British and French forces over how to stage the intervention. For Blake, it was widely held that the British had insisted upon a slow preliminary air bombardment, whereas the French had preferred a lightning action with forty-eight hours of bombing followed by parachute descents.

Blake was not the only person to express his concern over Eden's failure to come clean about certain events. Lord Chandos, former Conservative Secretary of State for the Colonies, advised that 'complete silence [with regard to collusion] may tend to provoke more controversy than if you were able to put something which headed them off'.[100] Eden, however, was his own man (arguably, worst enemy), and decided to say nothing explicit: 'As regards the other charge against us, after much reflection I thought a detached account of events without protestation was the best way to handle the business.'[101]

Judging by the assistance provided by Brook in the preparation of *Full Circle*, one might be forgiven for thinking that the Cabinet Secretary was a paid-up member of Eden's research team. An omnivorous bibliophile, well versed in the related historiography, Brook spent considerable time reading draft chapters and recommending substantive revisions in the service of accuracy, style and even argumentation. Brook moderated objectionable passages by shrewdly reconfiguring syntax, punctuation, style and idiom. A good example of this is the opening of Chapter 3. Eden had written: 'Dulles was not forthcoming. He sidestepped the point by telling us much that we already knew about the disadvantages of sailing round the Cape and the undesirability of petrol rationing.'[102] Brook's alteration, in contrast, was less scurrilous: 'Dulles was not forthcoming. He enlarged upon the disadvantages of sailing round the Cape and the undesirability of petrol rationing.'[103] Brook successfully convinced Eden to omit some of the manuscript's more blatant condemnations of the Eisenhower administration. For example, the following statement was deleted on the grounds that it would 'evoke strong protest' from Washington: 'Two of the more backward countries in the Middle East and in Africa, South Africa and Liberia, are two where American interests play a conspicuously large part.'[104] Under pressure from Macmillan, who feared that *Full Circle* would trigger calls for a Suez inquiry (calls which would be refused), Brook was instrumental in convincing Eden to defer publication until after the 1959 General Election. Eden had earlier argued that the book might actually help the Conservative cause in the polls, by stressing that the government had been right in thinking that Nasser's action, if left unchallenged, would lead to endless trouble in the Middle East.[105] Brook also made sure that nothing untoward was said about Churchill. The latter would later acknowledge that Lord Avon had been 'honourable to his name'.[106]

Why was Brook so helpful? To some extent he was making a virtue out of necessity.[107] Eden was publishing his memoirs whether HMG liked it or not: 'Our difficulty', Brook explained to ministers, 'arises from the fact that the control we can exercise over anyone in Sir Anthony's position cannot be more than persuasion.'[108] He may have felt sympathy for the former prime minister. Eden himself had said that he was more sinned against than sinning. Brook, who had been Cabinet Secretary in 1956, almost certainly had a vested interest in keeping Eden at close quarters. Retelling the Suez episode in his auto-biography, *The Course of My Life* (1998), Edward Heath divulged that Eden had ordered Brook to destroy all documents confirming collusion between Britain, France and Israel. In carrying out this thankless task, the Cabinet Secretary was said to have looked like 'an old samurai who had just been asked to fall on his own sword'.[109]

In assessing the Cabinet Secretary's role, it nevertheless tempting to follow David Reynolds' cue about the part played by Bridges and Brook in the production of Churchill's *The Second World War*.[110] In Reynolds' view, the two men considered the volumes as 'not merely inevitable but desirable' – a 'surrogate for an overview official history'.[111] With a tide of sensationalist and misleading histories of the war 'swelling across the Atlantic', the works were seen as the perfect antidote.[112] As a statesman and historian, Churchill had impeccable credentials. While there is no hard evidence, Brook arguably saw Eden's memoir in exactly the same way. 'Outsider' accounts, replete with wayward charges, were already hoving into view.[113] The proposed histories of Henry Azeau (*Le Piège de Suez*), Michel Bar-Zohar (*Suez Ultra Secret*) and Dwight D. Eisenhower (*The White House Years*), all of which Brook would have known about, were a forewarning that the French, Israelis and Americans would soon be publishing their own narratives.[114] The perfect counterblast would be a carefully con-trolled best-seller from Eden.

Was *Full Circle* an official history by proxy? The evidence for such a deduction is tantalisingly compelling. Macmillan admitted that 'Eden can (and anyway must) be treated as *sui generis*.'[115] Eden was given virtually open access to official records. It had long been government policy not to transmit secret material via normal postal channels,[116] but in Eden's case departments circumvented the ban by communicating documents in locked pouches. On occasion, the Cabinet Office even laid on a special courier service to deliver items 'by safe hand'.[117] His coadjutors were granted remarkable privileges. Hodge – 'under penalty of being sent to the Tower of London for indiscretion'[118] – was allowed to consult mountains of files, including sensitive intelligence reports. The Foreign Office even provided Hodge with an official car (with a boot big enough to be 'loaded with papers') so that he could fetch confidential material from London.[119] Brook, meanwhile, was like a doctor on call, on hand day and night to search the archive, offer editorial support and, on occasion, perform ghost-writing duties. On the eve of publication, fearing that historians would expect the same exceptional facilities afforded to Eden for the period after 1945, the government found it advantageous to classify *Full Circle* as a category unto itself – in effect an official history. In 1961, Macmillan released a communiqué stating that Eden's memoir was a departure from the normal rules applicable to peacetime government, and that in future a 'stricter standard' would be applied in dealing with applications relating to the post-war period.[120]

The problem for Brook et al. was that, while they seemed to regard *Full Circle* as a quasi-official history, and clearly made arrangements for that to be the case, Eden was still his own man. Much to the chagrin of the Cabinet Office, the proofs remained sharply critical of the Eisenhower administration and were suffused with personal attacks. Eden had refused to soften his criticism of Dulles – his bête noire. To Eden, Dulles was a 'preacher in a world of politics' who, as evidenced by his declaration in October 1956 that America must play an 'independent role' in areas affected by 'so-called colonialism', had 'little regard for the consequences of his words'.[121] Later in the text, while responding to the allegation that the crisis had been colonialism masquerading as international law enforcement, Eden added – touché – that 'if the United States had to defend their treaty rights in the Panama Canal, they would not regard such action as colonialism'.[122] Eden's disdain towards Dulles crystallised on page 484: '[his] cynicism towards Allies destroys true partnership. It leaves only the choice of parting or a master and vassal relationship in foreign policy.'[123] The Foreign Office, in pressing the point that Eisenhower was still in office, desperately tried to agree an eleventh-hour arrangement for changes. What made *Full Circle* in its present form even worse was its scheduled publication date – 1960. America's quadrennial elections would take place in the same year. The Republicans' presidential candidate, Richard Nixon, who had been Eisenhower's Vice-President in 1956, could ill afford to be humiliated by accusations of cold-shouldering British allies. Eden – who informed Brook that he had received 'a very pleasant message from the White House' – nevertheless stoutly refused to make further alterations to the text.[124] *Full Circle* was his apologia and the criticism of US policy was essential to it.

Macmillan sanctioned publication ('[there] is no alternative now but to put up with the book as it now stands'),[125] but remained acutely aware that it had the potential to cause controversy, both domestically and in the US. With serialisation set to start on 11 January

1960, he sent a 'Top Secret' telegram to Eisenhower informing him that suggestions had been made for softening the many unqualified verdicts on American personalities, and that responsibility for the opinions in the memoir lay solely with the author.[126] Macmillan paid tribute to the Bermuda conference where both countries had agreed to put recriminations about Suez behind them. The telegram ended with Macmillan making the case for banishing politicians from the house of history: 'My own feeling is that we should leave history to the historians. You and I have quite enough trouble with the present and the future without going back over the past.'[127] (It almost goes without saying that, years later, Macmillan would hold a different view, publishing six volumes of memoirs between 1966 and 1973.) The prime minister then invited Eden to Chequers for a private meeting. Here it was put to Eden that he should avoid being drawn, especially by the press, into giving further information or explanations about Suez. *Full Circle* was conceived as the final word and Eden was asked to take the line 'I have nothing to add to the account.'[128]

In early 1960, then, Eden broke new ground as the first senior minister to publish a memoir relating to the post-war period. *Full Circle* was an unqualified commercial success. By 14 October 1960 it had sold 77,000 copies at 35 shillings per copy.[129] According to Blake, the memoir's serialisation increased *The Times'* circulation by 15 per cent, a 'remarkable jump' for a newspaper whose sales were very rigid.[130] The corollary of spectacular sales was financial security. Eden's multilayered contract with *The Times*, coupled with book royalties, brought him an estimated £160,000 – a sum equal to £2.8 million in present-day terms: no other 1960s political memoirist would have it so good.[131] In America, impressive sales were matched by impressive reviews. Drew Middleton, foreign correspondent for the *New York Times*, described the book as 'one of the most important diplomatic records of our times – a compelling, informative and convincing personal account of [Eden's] stewardship'.[132] Middleton was left in no doubt that Eden had been 'an international negotiator of the very highest order'.[133] On 10 February, Downing Street received a telegram from the White House reporting that the reaction to publication had been 'mild', and that the volume of comment in the press had been 'relatively small'.[134] With few exceptions, American reviewers refused to revisit the rights and wrongs of the Suez invasion, arriving instead at a more refined assessment: it had been an ill-advised adventure. For the esteemed British scholar of international relations Martin Wight, Suez seemed in US consciousness 'less consequential internationally than the Mexican expedition of Napoleon III, less consequential domestically than the failure to relieve Gordon at Khartoum'.[135] The serenity of US public opinion probably reflected the fact that Suez had 'dropped further back in the national consciousness' than was the case in Britain.[136] Since 1956, in the harsh words of one commentator, Britain had become a 'butterfly content to flutter pathetically on the periphery of the world';[137] America, by contrast, had cemented her place as a superpower of unrivalled strength.

UK press reviews, both popular and patrician, were less positive. Martin Wight suggested that 'Eden's Memoirs have had a worse press than his premiership itself did.'[138] The style of *Full Circle*, complained reviewers, made few concessions to the general reader. For Randolph Churchill, writing for the *New Statesman*, the text was 'pedestrian', 'dull', and gave little sense that there was a private human being behind the public political life.[139] The Labour MP Francis Noel Baker accused Eden of using deep blacks and stark whites, and of only seeing events from his point of view. Baker also insinuated that Eden had treated certain documents with deliberate superficiality, thereby making a better case for his argument than a more rigorous and objective analysis could sustain.[140] Complaints on points of style were clearly influenced by political prejudice. In its language, tempo and cadences, *Full Circle* followed the much-revered formula employed by Winston Churchill. Eden used the same characteristic vocabulary ('disarray', 'sustain', 'crunch'); the same double verbs ('Communist power was thrusting and obtruding itself in many lands'), and the same indulgently dismissive climaxes ('all this did not matter very much').[141]

Eden's account of Suez provoked universally tart reviews. Paul Johnson, columnist for the *New Statesman*, rounded on Eden's failure to afford any new information on the crisis, despite the fact that he had been given the full run of the state archives: 'He can make no better case for his Suez adventure than such journalists as John Connell and T. E. Utley.'[142] *Full Circle*, protested Johnson, was an exercise not in commission but in omission, and regarding many issues on which his policy had been questioned Eden had not attempted to find an answer. The resignation of Anthony Nutting (Minister of State for Foreign Affairs) was not discussed, still less his remarkable self-abnegation in refusing to express public criticism of his former chief. Needless to say, lamented Johnson, the word 'collusion' was not allowed to sully Sir Anthony's pages; Israeli military operations were treated as wholly independent of Britain and France. Eden's attempts at self-justification were considered unconvincing and disingenuous. No one, declared Randolph Churchill, would believe Eden's argument that British intervention, though called off in less than two days, was essential because it prevented the outbreak of a major war in the Middle East and brought into being a UN police force in the region.[143] This was certainly a small and fugitive dividend to achieve at such an enormous cost. In other episodes, too, it was obvious that Eden had been less than frank. His claim that during the crisis 'Not a mouse moved in Arab lands' was pure dissimulation, not least because he had omitted any reference to Saudi Arabia breaking off diplomatic relations with Downing Street and Iraq proposing Britain's expulsion from the Baghdad Pact.[144] Hugh Gaitskell, plainly nettled by the author's statement that he regarded Gaitskell's rise to leadership as a 'national misfortune', said that his own view of Eden was now 'even stronger', and called *Full Circle*'s account of the Opposition's role during the crisis 'exceptionally misleading'.[145] Worst of all, protested Randolph Churchill, was that Eden still refused to admit to the cardinal blunders he had made. *Full Circle* was rather like the housemaid who, having broken the valuable chinaware, proceeded to claim, 'It came to pieces in my hand.'[146]

Since *Full Circle* was bursting with extracts from official documents, there was a great deal of anger directed at the Fifty Year Rule, which governed that the general public would not get to see the documentary material until 2006. A. J. P Taylor resented the fact that the former premier had been given privileges to write his history, whilst the academic community would have to wait until the twenty-first century to see how partisan, if at all, he had been. Tristan Jones, editor of the *Observer*, voiced a growing sentiment that there was 'one law of the high and mighty and another law for ordinary mortals'.[147] 'The high and mighty', he went on, 'are enabled to put out their versions of events and prevent other people, who may have other evidence, from challenging them.'[148] As a direct consequence of *Full Circle*, there emerged a vocal group of historians determined to bring about a change in the law. In the years following, the correspondence column of *The Times* became legendary for staging fiery exchanges between campaigning academics, such as Taylor, and crown servants defending the status quo.

Not oblivious to the double standard, Macmillan took swift steps to ensure that, in future, it would be much harder for authors to produce something as richly documented as *Full Circle*. In 1963, he created 'the Suez Embargo', stipulating that ministers and officials could not consult records relating to the crisis without the express permission of the prime minister. (To compound matters, as a prime minister had imposed the restriction, only one of his successors could revoke it.) Also in 1963, he re-established the rule that research assistants should not be allowed independent access to official papers.[149]

The first author duty-bound to work within the parameters of these revised constraints was the former Lord Chancellor, David Kilmuir. Submitted in November 1963, the draft of *Political Adventure* was, for the most part, 'unexceptionable'.[150] Its examination of Suez, commented the new prime minister, Alec Douglas-Home, revealed 'no more than all of us said in Parliament at the time'.[151] The job of vetting the manuscript fell to Burke Trend, Brook's successor as Cabinet Secretary. At first, Trend found the process somewhat daunting: 'I find it difficult to decide how far I am officially entitled to offer comment on the passages which trouble me.'[152] Nevertheless, he soon got to grips with his task. Indeed, it became apparent that he had an excellent eye for spotting objectionable items. The amateur observer might have passed over the comment 'The [Suez] cease-fire was ordered on November 6 purely because the United Nations had decided to intervene.' Trend recognised immediately, however, that this was not consistent with the fiction that Britain had been 'peacekeeping' in the Middle East. Accordingly, he changed the sentence to: 'The cease-fire was ordered on November 6 because, by that time, the U[nited] N[ations] was ready to take our place.'[153] Cognisant of the fact that ministerial committees were never to be mentioned in public by name, he replaced all references to the 'Suez Committee' with the phrase 'a meeting of ministers'.[154] Trend took a particularly active role in preparing the memoir for serialisation. His predecessors had tended to focus their energies exclusively on the book manuscript, but Trend astutely realised that this was a fatal oversight, since newspapers had a penchant to take things out of context and give prominence to the 'juiciest passages uppermost'.[155]

By the mid 1960s, as details of collusion were revealed, Eden's revisions of history were exposed. In May 1964, during a television interview promoting his new book *Dulles over Suez*, the political scientist

Herman Finer produced a letter he had received from Christian Pineau revealing that Selwyn Lloyd had travelled incognito to Paris and had, along with Pineau and the Israeli prime minister, Ben-Gurion, devised a joint plan of action against Nasser.[156] Two years later, in plain defiance of all the assurances that he had given at the time, Pineau himself spilt the beans. When interviewed by the BBC's Third Programme in July, he referred to 'an Anglo-French-Israeli Treaty' – a phrase that could not have been inadvertent because the BBC's technique was to break off the recording before each question and go over the ground in French to ensure it was correct. In November, with the tenth anniversary of Suez provoking renewed interest in the press, Pineau published an article in *Le Monde* in which he confirmed that a secret accord had been signed at Sèvres 'in the last ten days of October 1956'.[157] As Gaitskell had predicted years earlier, if there had been collusion, sooner or later the men who had been party to it were 'bound to start giving one another away'.[158]

In view of Pineau's startling revelation (qualified on the grounds that the operation was now 'old history'), some Labour MPs, including Michael Foot, called for an official inquiry – comparable to the Dardanelles Commission after the Great War – into the origin, inception and conduct of the Suez campaign.[159] The idea failed to take off. Senior civil servants put forward the strongest possible appeals, with Trend warning of the 'very violent international passions' that could result from the disclosure of the collusion story.[160] In Israel, for example, candour about foreign assistance would detract from the image of a dashing military success, and mar the appearance of military strength that its embattled politicians wanted to present to the Arab world.

It ultimately proved impossible to keep the truth about Suez hidden forever. 1967 was to be the decisive year, with the collusion jigsaw puzzle being pieced together by a spate of revealing works, including *The Suez Affair* by Hugh Thomas and *Suez: Ten Years On* by Peter Calvocoressi.[161] By far the most significant book on the subject was *No End of a Lesson*. The memoir of former minister of state Anthony Nutting, the book marked the first time that a British insider had admitted to the events surrounding the Sèvres Protocol. Nutting had been a protégé of Eden, to whom he was much indebted for his political advancement. In Churchill's final years as premier, he was widely seen as the heir presumptive to Eden.[162] Like his mentor, Nutting was one of the great 'casualties' of the Suez crisis. Privy to the secret plot to invade Egypt ('a sordid manoeuvre ... morally indefensible and politically suicidal'),[163] on 31 October 1956 he wrote Eden a letter of resignation, stating that he found it impossible to defend such a duplicitous policy in public. On 5 November, the day before British troops landed at Port Said, he resigned his seat in Parliament. Recognising that disclosure of the tripartite agreement might result in the fall of HMG, Nutting refrained from making a customary resignation speech in the Commons: 'As long as any of the chief protagonists of the Suez War still held high office,' he later explained, 'it would clearly have been a grave disservice to the nation ... to have told the whole story.'[164] Nutting's silence, while admirable, backfired. Feeling betrayed by a man whose career he had personally groomed, Eden spread rumour and innuendo around the lobbies of Westminster, suggesting that Nutting had used Suez as an excuse to dampen constituency trouble emanating from an imminent and distasteful divorce. Many Tory backbenchers regarded Nutting's resignation as malicious and, although he was proved correct in all his forebodings, the 'second golden boy' became *persona non grata* in the tribal world of Conservative politics. Eden never spoke to him again whilst Lloyd cynically brushed off his political estrangement as a case of 'Much Ado About Nutting'.[165] Nutting later spoke of being: 'Bereft of friends, a castaway adrift on a sea of anger and recrimination, an object of distrust, torn between loyalty to principle and loyalty to friends and associates.'[166]

Despite being driven out of politics at the tender age of thirty-six with his integrity impugned, for ten years Nutting did not regard it as within his prerogative to unmask the secrets of collusion. His silence was extraordinary when one considers that it came at the cost of a career that appeared preordained for the premiership. By early 1967, however, with so much being written, Nutting informed HMG that he had a right to tell his side of the story. 'None of those responsible hold office,' he informed Trend, '[whilst] Britain is now represented by a government which bears no responsibility for Suez.'[167] As the son of a wealthy landowner, Nutting was not swayed by thought of financial reward. His motive for publication was simple: to answer charges of betraying his leader and patron and to explain the stand that he had taken. Trend received a bound page proof of the book on 3 April to which Nutting had affixed a note explaining that, while he had had no resort to official documents, he was nevertheless happy to make amendments on points of security and Cabinet protocol.[168] With serialisation in *The Times* set for 29 April, thus precluding a lengthy deliberation, Trend sent copies forthwith to Eden, the Foreign Office and the sitting prime minister, Harold Wilson. What they received was a flesh-and-blood recapitulation of the events surrounding the Sèvres Protocol. It revealed, for example, how on 14 October 1956 General Maurice Challe (Chief of Staff of the French Air Force), accompanied by Albert Glazier (Acting Foreign Minister in Pineau's absence), had visited Chequers to present Eden with a plan to invade Egypt on the pretext of 'separating the combatants' and 'extinguishing a dangerous fire'.[169] According to Nutting, who was present at the meeting, this was the *casus belli* for which Eden had been looking. Such was his pathological hatred of Nasser, he 'could scarcely contain his glee' and instructed Guy Millard (the Duty Private Secretary) not to keep a record of what unfolded. With great alacrity, Eden then arranged two more meetings, one at the Palais Matignon, the official residence of the French prime minister, and the other at Sèvres, to ratify the secret treaty.

Nutting's revelations were a bombshell. No foreknowledge and no prior agreement: that was Eden's stance at the time, again in *Full Circle* and once more as evidence accumulated over the seven years since publication. 'How can he get away with this,' Eden protested in a private letter to Trend; the text was a 'gross breach' of collective responsibility.[170] Eden delineated more specific objections in correspondence with Brook (by then ennobled as Lord Normanbrook). Nutting's account, he complained, relied upon unsubstantiated reminiscence of conversations with colleagues: 'As to [these] reconstructed dialogues, I have no recollection of a single one of the exchanges here wished upon me – nor do they read like me.'[171] The reference to Eden's bile duct wound as being 'generally affected by nervous pressures' he considered 'erroneous', as was the allegation that he had a 'strangely bitter dislike of the Greeks'.[172] Eden was shocked at how Nutting 'harp[ed] continuously on' about the two men's alleged divergences of opinion: 'If these views were in fact his sentiments, I was not conscious of them.'[173] What really galled the former premier was the book's portrayal of him as a man 'eager for hostilities' with Egypt: 'The charge of dictatorship on my part can only be described as hysterical. No member of Cabinet would endorse it for an instant.'[174] In the event of the book's publication, however, Eden decided not to issue a statement. To do so, he confided in Brook, would necessitate revealing 'information which I am not prepared to make use of at the present time'.[175] Disclosing such information, he argued, would imperil the lives of several state functionaries who were currently active in the political arena.[176]

The Foreign Office shared Eden's abhorrence of the book. Confirmation of collusion could not but reflect adversely upon the methods by which officials might be thought to practise diplomacy and upon Britain's general probity in its relations with other countries.[177] Since the legality of the Sèvres Protocol was highly dubious, possibly even a breach of *jus cogens* (the fundamental and 'higher' norms of international law that concern the safeguarding of peace and the prohibition of force), its disclosure carried potentially serious constitutional implications. For Downing Street, there was the problem of precedence. Nutting had excused himself on the grounds of a self-devised ten-year rule: what was to stop 'someone even more unscrupulous', 'and [even] more speedy with his pen', from doing the same?[178] 'I am not hopeful', lamented the prime minister, Harold Wilson, 'that Nutting will prove to be a gentleman'; the cost to the publisher – and probably to himself – would be too great.[179] It is apposite to note Wilson's choice of words. As he saw it, the matter at hand was objectionable not because Nutting was proposing to break the law, but because his behaviour did not befit a 'gentleman'. Although in public proud of his working-class roots and committed to breaking down social barriers, Wilson, like his institutional ancestors, privately believed that government was a gentlemen's club, made up of individuals who could be trusted to respect the confidences of government. In short, by blowing the whistle on Sèvres, Nutting was abandoning an elite code.[180]

On 20 April, accompanied by Sir Paul Gore-Booth (Head of the Diplomatic Service), Trend met with Nutting to discuss possible alterations to the text. In testament to the gentlemanly way of doing business, the meeting was held not in the Cabinet Office but in a members-only private club in London's West End. Nutting, however, refused to play by the rules. He ridiculed Trend's suggestion that the manuscript represented a 'serious departure' from the convention of collective responsibility. He pointed to the precedent of *Full Circle* and underlined that Suez had been a 'departure of sorts' from every principle that had guided the conduct of British diplomacy throughout history. While agreeing not to mention the views of certain diplomats, such as Sir Humphrey Trevelyan (ambassador to Egypt in 1956),

Nutting steadfastly refused to omit his discussion of collusion. To delete the relevant chapter, 'Invitation by Conspiracy', would 'be to suppress the essential truth contained in [the] book'.[181]

On 27 April – following an almighty 'hoo-ha'[182] in Cabinet – it was decided not to prevent publication. Elwyn Jones, the Attorney General at the time, later wrote that Nutting had come within an 'agonising hair's breadth' of being struck off the roll of Privy Councillors and prosecuted.[183] This, of course, would have been the first occasion on which such an action had been taken against a former minister. According to *The Crossman Diaries*, 'Burke ... made it perfectly clear that he and he alone had taken the decision about Nutting's book because the Prime Minister, like any other Labour Minister, must be denied access to the minutes of the other side.'[184] This assessment is not reflected in the declassified documents. Trend had in fact made it clear that he did not want to be caught in the crossfire between the competing priorities of government and author. This implies, therefore, that the prime minister made the final call. For what precise reason is not delineated in government papers. One can surmise that, with memoirs of his own in the pipeline, Wilson did not want to establish a constraining precedent. In discussions, tellingly, he spoke of the 'inhibiting effect' non-publication would have on future writers.[185] One can also surmise that the Labour leader saw publication as an opportunity to make cheap political capital at the expense of the Tory opposition. The illicit manoeuvring over Suez was hardly the Conservative Party's finest hour and, with the shifting sands of public opinion turning against the Labour government following its handling of the D-Notice Affair, there seemed to be much to gain from sanctioning publication. Indeed, Wilson had already written to Trend on 10 April and stated that the book had 'important consequences in the field of Party politics, highly favourable to the government'.[186]

In the event, the impact of *No End of a Lesson* was negligible. As David Carlton has argued, the long delay on the author's part, however honourable and constitutionally correct, 'deprived him of his chance to shape history', for had 'his authoritative revelations come during the 1950s, the political consequences would have been incalculable'.[187] Publication coincided with the outbreak of the Third Arab–Israeli War, when even some of Eden's critics were prepared to entertain the possibility that contemporary events might have proved the former premier to have been right all along. Nutting's most piquant disclosure – from the vantage point of 1967 – was arguably not the full extent of collusion but Eden's opinion in 1956 that the incipient Common Market yielded no benefit for Britain.[188] Publication also failed to affect any further confessionals. Harold Macmillan's fourth volume of memoirs, *Riding the Storm 1956–1959* (1971), totally snubbed Nutting's revelations.[189] Published in 1978, Selwyn Lloyd's memoir, *Suez 1956*, nonsensically maintained that the Sèvres meetings foreclosed rather than approved a secret agreement – although he was goaded by the *Sunday Times* to come clean to the tune of £20,000.[190] Demands for an official history of the Suez–Sinai campaign never took wing, and, despite scores of requests, historians were repeatedly denied access to Suez papers. 'Once we breach the principle of a "closed" period for the benefit of one individual historian,' asserted Trend, 'we open a floodgate which we have thereafter no means of closing again. And on such a sensitive subject as Suez, the water will come through at a considerable rate.'[191] In private, Eden was 'more convinced than ever that the action taken by the Anglo-American forces in 1956 was inescapable', resolute in his personal conviction that military intervention averted an Arab–Israeli war in 'worse and much more dangerous conditions'.[192] In public, however, he refused to elaborate on what he had said in *Full Circle*. As Nutting had predicted, 'to reveal the truth now would involve an act of confession too mortifying for any man to volunteer'.[193]

* * *

> It really strips a veil away from the way we are governed. It tells the nature of civil service advice, the way it is given, and the way the press is manipulated.
>
> *Harold Evans, speaking on BBC1, 22 June 1975*[194]

In June 1975, Wilson's second Labour government made history when it moved for an injunction to bar publication of Volume I of *The Diaries of a Cabinet Minister*, the late Richard Crossman's account of his twenty-two months as Minister of Housing and Local Government between 1964 and 1966 (Figure 18). This marked the first time that a British government had sought judicial intervention to block the printing of a ministerial reminiscence. The Crossman Affair, as it became known, was a cause célèbre with important implications not only for political memoir writing, but for British secrecy in the round. As John Naylor has argued, 'Weighed in the balance were such concerns vital to a democracy as the need for secrecy in the highest reaches of government, on the one hand, and, on the other, the right of the citizenry to be informed witnesses and critics of the actions carried out in its name by the government.'[195] At Wilson's behest, the Cabinet Secretary, John Hunt, was even constitutionally dragooned to the High Court to represent Downing Street's case for a ban on publication. For Wilson to throw Hunt into the limelight, and then watch him have verbal fisticuffs with Crossman's lawyers on matters of government policy, was unprecedented. Anthony Howard, the celebrated former editor of the *New Statesman*, has compared Hunt's trundling off to court to the 'descent from Olympus to the forum' – a 'bad day for the mystique of a very special post'.[196] Hunt's predecessors had been scarcely known by the public, the only proof of their vocation being a truncated entry in *Who's Who*. What possessed HMG suddenly to turn to the law and abandon the gentlemanly strategy of wheeling and dealing with authors behind the scenes? To understand this, it is necessary to return to the fallout from *Full Circle*.

Eden's gold-plated Suez apologia moved the goalposts in terms of political memoir writing. Despite attempts by the state to categorise the book as *sui generis*, a flurry of authors were quick to demand similar privileges and pen similar-looking works, a development that caused considerable alarm in Whitehall. Suddenly, there was an expectation among politicians that memoirs could be published within a short space of leaving office. Allied to this was a realisation that the market was strongest for 'instant history', and that publishers and newspapers were prepared to offer larger sums for works that dealt with recent events. As a general principle, the longer the author waited, the more the value of the memoir would depreciate. With Trend at the helm, the state was confident that this breed of memoir could still be controlled by ad hoc means. 'We cannot hope to put this particular clock back,' he conceded in July 1970. He continued: 'We have to bend our efforts to ensuring, so far as we can, that it does not go too far forward.'[197] In short, so long as Trend was captaining the ship, legal action was unlikely.

Trend's capacity for dealing with 'instant' memoirs was sorely tested on several occasions. One of the most difficult cases involved the book *Decision in Government* by Dr Jeremy Bray, an econometrician who in 1967 became parliamentary secretary to Tony Benn in the newly created Ministry of Technology. Abounding with statistics, forecasts and tables, the book was less a memoir than a textbook on economic policy in the 'white heat' age. Contracted with Victor Gollancz for a diminutive advance of £500, it was not intended to net Bray a fortune.[198] When it was submitted for vetting in February 1969, it caused a stink. For Trend, the major issue was that Bray was still a minister. As Trend saw it, publication would represent a 'serious blow' to collective ministerial responsibility. In particular, he was concerned that, if one minister was allowed to go into print, the Cabinet Office hereafter would have no grounds on which to stop other serving members of government from doing the same: 'The net result would be "open" government with a vengeance.'[199] Wilson shared the concern that publication might lead to a '"war of the books" between Ministers'.[200] Wilson also had his own unique reservations – reservations influenced by party political interest. The main proposition of the book was that the government's present methods of regulating the economy were clumsy and ineffectual, and should be overhauled. Moreover, Wilson feared that, if Bray went ahead, the electorate would deduce that Labour ministers were not doing their job, preferring instead to write books at the taxpayer's expense.[201]

Wilson's ministerial colleagues had similar views. Peter Shore, the Secretary of State for Economic Affairs, had 'very strong words' to say about it. In a letter to Bray, he declared, 'Politically in a period before the general election it would be downright folly to publish such a work.'[202] One of the only ministers to dissent from this assessment was Tony Benn. As a campaigner for open government, he considered it a 'great pity if Ministers were, in office, absolutely precluded from commenting upon the developing situation with which the Government has to deal'.[203] Benn doubted whether there was much political mileage, or votes, to be gained by Tory Central Office from quoting passages from the book. To the contrary, it was his view that publication, by distilling the many challenges that lay ahead, would help the Labour government reconnect itself with 'opinion-formers' and 'thinking people' in industry, higher education and elsewhere.[204]

Benn's thinking was ignored. On 24 September, in a letter ghosted by Trend, Wilson wrote to Bray and explained that publication was forbidden: 'I have no alternative but to uphold the principles ... in relation to the collective responsibility of this Administration.' He went on (rather glibly): 'I know how keenly you feel, in particular about the methods of statistical analysis which should underline Government decision-making, but it was open to you to press these ideas from your position as a junior Minister.'[205] Bray was furious. Indeed, he immediately drafted himself an aide-memoire, which contained the outburst: 'I don't care a damn about statistical analysis.'[206] Like Benn, he did not believe the book to be damaging to the government, quite the opposite in fact. By developing new arguments on the management of the economy, it showed that HMG was open to change when necessary. Change – lest ministers forget – had been one of the slogans of Labour's successful election campaign in 1964. 'Just as we begin to reap the fruits of our efforts,' Bray argued, 'it is no time to lose the will to change.'[207] Speaking some years later, Benn recalls that, at this critical juncture, he spent half his time trying to persuade Wilson not to fire Bray if the latter decided to 'publish and be damned', and half his time attempting to convince Bray not to be stubborn and get sacked.[208] He 'failed on both counts'. By the close of play on 24 September, Bray had tendered his resignation, which was accepted, thus freeing him to publish under the auspices of a management scientist devoid of party political affiliation. The press had a field day.[209] Bray had been a poster boy for the technological revolution. His resignation, therefore, was a major blow to government credibility. Moreover, coming only a year after the Fulton Report, which had recommended that more information should be made available to the public, the premature end to his ministerial career was taken as evidence of the government's lack of commitment to reducing official secrecy. Vexing to Wilson, the book won many admirers. Bizarrely, there was even talk of it being turned into an ice show.[210]

Pre-Crossman, the other 'instant memoir' to cause Trend significant hassle was *The Labour Government 1964–1970: A Personal Record*, by none other than Harold Wilson. Wilson had lost the premiership in June 1970 and, with not a hint of self-consciousness, immediately signed a lucrative book deal to write about his years in power. Submitted in January 1971, the manuscript showed every evidence of hasty composition, suffering from grammatical errors and undisciplined ramblings. Trend's anxiety about the book went beyond the quality of the prose. Wilson, who had aspirations of returning to office at the next general election, had been critical of several statesmen with whom he had had dealings and who were still active in politics. For example, he had twice described Hastings Banda, President of Malawi, in 'rather unflattering terms'.[211]

The argument was put to Wilson that if he was re-elected and had to work with any of these statesmen again, would he not be embarrassed by such comments? Trend's other problem with the text – part policy primer, part stump speech – was that Wilson had, on occasion, used secret information in a deliberate attempt to queer the pitch of his Conservative successor. Controversially, the memoir included a documented breakdown of the so-called Soames Affair of 1969, when Wilson leaked General de Gaulle's private suggestion to Christopher Soames (British ambassador to France) that, before making a further application to join the European Economic Community, Britain should first cut a confidential deal with France about the sort of Europe both countries desired. At the time, the episode had provoked accusations by the French of bad faith, and it was Trend's view that Wilson was now using it as a peg to undermine Anglo-French relations at a time when Heath was negotiating Britain's way into the Common Market.[212] In effect, memoir writing had become a vehicle for electioneering by other means.

Trend tried in vain to persuade Wilson to self-censor. The former premier's lawyers scrutinised tens of memoirs to determine how the rules had been applied in the past, if at all. Ultimately, it was not hard to find examples of where ministers had done as they pleased. Accordingly, whenever Trend called for moderation, Wilson was able to defend his position with reference to a slew of precedents. Typically, his reply would be, 'This was certainly not true of Churchill.'[213] With Trend unable to dispute the history lesson, Wilson retained his discussion of the Soames Affair, as well as the references to foreign statesmen. He also angered the intelligence community by revealing how MI5 had provided him with evidence of communist infiltration of the National Union of Seamen.

Following Wilson's lead, it became commonplace for memoirists to have someone on their staff who was required to examine past publications and identify potential loopholes. This was certainly the case with Macmillan. When the former premier submitted *At the End of the Day* for vetting in early 1973, he did so armed with an encyclopaedic knowledge of what had gone before him, rendering Trend powerless. For example, in the interests of the Special Relationship (something that Macmillan, as Britain's first post-Suez prime minister, had sought to resurrect and then cultivate), Trend asked him not to quote from American sources, especially the transcripts of telephone conversations he had had with President Kennedy at the time of the Cuban Missile Crisis. In 1973, the Americans were still reeling from the leaking of the top-secret Pentagon Papers by former military analyst Daniel Ellsberg, which had brought to light a succession of lies and false pretences under which the US had invaded Vietnam. 'In the light of the Pentagon papers case,' explained Trend, 'we are rather concerned to keep our record clean in this respect.'[214] Macmillan was unsympathetic, and backed up his refusal to expunge the material on the grounds that Wilson's memoir had given the substance of the latter's acrimonious dealings with President Johnson, seemingly with no concern about the impact on present-day Anglo-US relations. Wigg was another memoirist to know his 'history' and thus be in a position to resist censorship. With supreme confidence, he declared, 'I do not consider myself bound to play cricket when others have abandoned the cricket bat, stumps and the ball for a shillelagh.'[215] Wigg's comment perfectly encapsulates the problem the state was now facing. Increasingly, memoir writing was not done by gentlemen according to gentlemanly behaviour. Authors had become unsportsmanlike. This left Whitehall with two options: either it could persevere with its current tactics and hope that the opposition started to play by the rules, or it could turn to the law. When Trend, the calming influence, retired in 1973, it was not long before it chose the latter.

Dictated on tape, the Crossman diaries covered the period from 1952 to the end of 1970. Every Saturday evening, Crossman would retire to his study for a few hours to consider the week's events and organise the bundles of papers sent down to him by his office. On Sunday, with his memory refreshed and with documentation readily to hand, he would go about recording a chronicle of his ministerial experiences. The contents of these tapes would eventually add up to some 1.5 million words.[216] His ambition had been to 'write a book which fulfilled for our generation the functions of Bagehot's *English Constitution* a hundred years ago, by disclosing the secret operations of government, which are concealed by the thick masses of foliage which we call the myth of democracy'.[217] Specifically, he wanted to expose the rise of 'Prime Ministerial Government', a post-war shift in the concentration of power away from the Cabinet into the hands of the premier. This, he argued, could only be done by someone who knew the government machine from the inside.

Crossman's desire to 'light up the secret places of British politics' was not out of character and certainly not without warning.

In life, he had been committed to breaking down secrecy, which he called the 'Real English disease' and a 'chronic ailment of the British government'.[218] He sneered at traditional arguments about the need for secrecy in the service of unencumbered decision-making. His basic attitude was that ministers should not put forward in Cabinet what they were not prepared to support in public. His 'open government' credentials were beyond dispute. Wilson called him a 'compulsive communicator'.[219] In her diary, Castle commented on the 'glorious candour' with which he handled the press.[220] He had wholeheartedly supported the reduction of the closure period for state documents from a fifty- to a thirty-year rule. When the matter was discussed in Cabinet, on 5 August 1966, he called it 'long overdue' and argued that:

> the present ban, quite apart from all its other drawbacks, was made intolerable by the permission which a Cabinet Minister, particularly a Prime Minister, can obtain to use official documents denied to academic and objective historians for writing his memoirs. If we are going to go on exercising the right to turn out memoirs which are often nothing but personal *plaidoyers*, there is a powerful case for letting the historians get at the documents as soon as possible.[221]

From very early on, it is clear that Whitehall was not only aware of his plans to publish, but looking for ways to stop him. In Cabinet on 26 January 1967, the prime minister, in a brief 'no doubt . . . prepared in Burke's office', treated colleagues to a speech on the hazards of signing book contracts intended to destroy effective Cabinet government. As Crossman remembered it, although Wilson refused to name names, 'by the end he'd managed to weave a web of hostility and surround me with it'.[222]

Whitehall's tactic eventually switched from scaremongering to outright obstruction. In 1971, concerned that his worsening health would prevent him from taking regular research trips to London, Crossman asked Trend if his right of access to Cabinet papers could be passed to Janet Morgan, the editor of the diaries. This was turned down, with no explanation, prompting him to write in protest: 'I find it difficult to believe that no trained academic helper on Churchill's or Lord Avon's staff was permitted access to any Cabinet paper.'[223] He then posed the rhetorical question: 'Does this mean that Churchill was compelled personally to sit in a room in the Cabinet Office?' With an extraordinary indifference to Crossman's own well-being, Trend responded that these were 'very exceptional cases', resulting from the particularly poor health of the men in question and the fact that they were working at a distance from London.[224] Trend added, moreover, that the conventions had invariably 'differentiated' in favour of prime ministers. Unimpressed, Crossman questioned how it was, then, that George Brown, as a 'mere' Foreign Secretary with no obvious debilitating illness, had been allowed to have Janet Elliot conduct research on his behalf in preparation of his 1971 memoir *In My Way*.[225] Once again, Trend gave as good as he got – explaining that Elliot, as Brown's former Assistant Private Secretary, had already seen the papers. Crossman decided not to press any more, recognising that no matter how many anomalies he identified, Trend would always have an answer. This particular battle had been lost, but the war was what counted.

Not long after this, Crossman was diagnosed with terminal cancer. With no time to lose, he devoted his energies entirely to the preparation of his reminiscences for publication. It had always been his intention for these recollections to take the form of a diary rather than a memoir. His opinion of Westminster memoirs was that they seldom captured the spirit of the moment and were invariably 'cooked': that is to say, they had no soul and were full of tunnel-vision judgements, doctored by hindsight and self-interest.[226] As he put it, 'Memory is a terrible improver ... And it is this which makes a politician's autobiography (even when he claims his rights and uses official Cabinet papers) so wildly unreliable.'[227] By choosing a different approach, he hoped to produce a more accurate window onto ministerial life. To this end, his diary was to be completely unexpurgated. Morgan was instructed to 'leave in EVERYTHING'.[228]

Crossman died on 5 April 1974. Honouring his instructions, his literary executors moved to get the diaries into print. His executors included Graham Greene (managing director of Jonathan Cape; Crossman's widow, Anne (herself no stranger to secrets having worked at Bletchley Park); and Michael Foot, a long-time companion and ally. Foot's involvement was particularly eye-catching since he was, at the time, a member of Wilson's Cabinet. Throughout, it is interesting to note that Foot's loyalty was to his friend, not to his party. According to Tam Dalyell, he 'fought all the way' to see the diaries published.[229]

By late spring, private negotiations between the executors and Whitehall had ground to a halt. Although they had been warned by Crossman not to expect an easy ride, nothing could have prepared them for the struggle that would ensue. In May, allegations surfaced that transcripts had mysteriously been erased after their arrival at the publishers.[230] On 21 June, worse followed as the new Cabinet Secretary, John Hunt, laid down that the diaries could not be published for thirty years, arguing that publication would destroy the mutual trust that should exist between ministers, their colleagues and their advisers.[231] In coming to this decision, Hunt had consulted a host of mandarins, who were sent drafts. The book's representation of the civil service caused them the most alarm. From the outset the image of the civil service was that of a fifth estate – 'at times an *imperium in imperio*' (to quote C. J. Child of the Cabinet Office) – obstructive towards ministers but opportunistically slavish towards the Treasury, whose top brass determine, in the final analysis, all promotions to the higher echelons.[232] Far from being a sleekly purring Rolls-Royce, the civil service was shown to be a body of men consumed by incompetence. A number of senior civil servants were singled out for special criticism. Ian Bancroft, then Second Permanent Secretary at the Civil Service Department, was appalled:

> It seems to me to be importing a new element into our affairs for a Minister to take advantage of a quite special relationship which exists between him and his civil servants to publish subjective opinions about their inability, appearance and manner as if he were a buttonholing novelist and they were fictional characters. They exist in real life with families, colleagues and a degree of self esteem to live with. Some of the civil servants may want to publish their own experiences of Ministers. Some have a long memory, a ready pen, and the ability to wound in return. I believe that a Civil Service which is fraying at the edges would regard the publication of the diary as a huge, perhaps irreparable breach in the compact which governs relations between Ministers and their officials. Nothing would be the same again.[233]

Hunt, who cared passionately about the timeless verities and reputation of the civil service, wholeheartedly agreed with his colleagues. Every effort should be made to stop publication.

With this, the executors sought the help of Lord Goodman, an Establishment mediator and fixer, famous for hammering out settlements between warring parties from government and the outside. He also had the ear of Number 10. This seemed to work, as Hunt gave his consent to an edited version of the diaries. However, when the finer details of this apparent concession were discussed, deadlock again resulted. Hunt required all passages that mentioned Cabinet meetings, or advice by civil servants, to be removed. To the executors, this was clearly unacceptable and Goodman was sent to reconcile the quarrellers once more. This led to a farcical exchange where Goodman asked Hunt, 'What *can* we say? Can we say that Crossman sat at his Cabinet table and looked at St James's Park?' Hunt paused, before replying: 'Yes, provided you don't indicate who else was sitting with him.'[234]

The *Sunday Times*, which had paid a five-figure sum to serialise the diaries, was exasperated by the impasse. Hunt's refusal to budge was very much at odds with Trend's evidence to the Franks Committee in 1972, where he had claimed that the Cabinet's Secretary's role in 'vetting' memoirs amounted to nothing more than polite persuasion.[235] There was nothing polite about Hunt's 'ruling'. In a bold move, the newspaper's editor, Harold Evans, decided to serialise the diaries in any case. Since breaking the Philby story in 1967, Evans had gone on to reach the summit of British journalism, a remarkable rise for the son of a working-class train driver from Manchester in what was still largely an elitist and Oxbridge-educated profession. With a reputation as a brazen Northern interloper, even with his own trade, he was the ideal person to challenge the Establishment. As Evans saw it, the key was to take the government by surprise by releasing the first extracts before an expected injunction could be issued. This was not going to be easy. Evans feared, needlessly as it turned out, that Foot might feel compelled to tell his colleagues in government. It was decided, therefore, to keep Foot out of the loop. The critical decisions were taken on the night of Saturday 25 January 1975. With only a handful of newspapermen and lawyers in attendance – among them Denis Hamilton (editor-in-chief) – Evans argued that, while the paper could find itself in hot water, publication was a risk worth taking. In the event of a future trial being brought by the Crown to prevent the release of the full diaries, the appearance of one extract would carry great weight in terms of precedent. To minimise the likelihood of the government seeking legal retribution, Evans suggested that the first extract should be fairly anodyne in nature, omitting the kind of scurrilous material likely to set pulses racing in Whitehall. The picture would be that of a minister softly shepherded by his civil servants. Hamilton agreed and, with this, the presses started rolling.[236]

As hoped, the sudden serialisation caught Whitehall unawares. The Cabinet Secretary was not even in the country. With one of the most significant leaks in the history of British secrecy taking place, he was in Washington, DC, on official business. Only thirty-six hours earlier, before departing, he had written a memo to Wilson explaining that he had briefed his deputy on how to secure a last-minute injunction if Evans telephoned to say that the newspaper was publishing without permission. Of course, there was no call. At the top of the memo, obviously written after the event, the prime minister scribbled: 'We were overtaken.'[237] Upon his return from the US, Hunt implored Wilson to move for an injunction to halt the second wave of extracts. The recent revelations, he argued, represented only the 'tip of the iceberg'.[238] Sooner or later, the extracts were bound to get to the 'meat' of the book, which dealt with Crossman's struggles to formulate and enact policy against the 'will' of the civil service, the impression being that the latter was an alternative power bloc to the government. Much of the drama of Volume I consisted of Crossman's frosty relationship with the formidable Dame Evelyn Sharp, Permanent Secretary at the Ministry of Housing.[239] Sharp was portrayed as a master of obfuscation and manipulation, the personification of a machine that possessed no gears, only brakes. To Crossman's frustration, the biggest challenge in government was to carry out policy *per media* the 'Dame', as she was known: 'I've had difficulties with Dame Evelyn: she's a magnificent woman but she wants her Ministry run in her own way and there is a constant struggle between us.'[240] Sir Humphrey Appleby, the brilliant yet two-faced and scheming mandarin in the BBC series *Yes Minister*, is said to have been largely modelled on Crossman's bureaucratic nemesis.

Wilson faced a serious dilemma. On the one hand, he agreed with Hunt's assessment that this material would threaten the confidential relationship between ministers and civil servants. He was also nervous about evidence surfacing in the extracts which suggested that his style of leadership circumvented Cabinet, and was tantamount to a de facto

'British Presidency'.[241] As C. J. Child had noted, the diaries depicted him as 'erring in the direction of too much dependence on his close contacts and advisers'.[242] On the other hand, Wilson was committed to making the processes of decision making more open; indeed, this, along with the related issue of Official Secrets Act reform, had been one of his party's key pledges in its 1974 election manifesto. Gagging the newspaper, therefore, would represent a cynical betrayal of this programme.

To complicate matters, the Conservative Party, while in power under Heath, had taken big strides in the area of open government. Following the Franks Report, Heath had called for a 'radical change' in the 'art and science' of presenting information about government projects.[243] He advocated the publication of working papers and other consultative documents designed to highlight the facts and, where possible, the assumptions on which the government based its policies. This proposal had been met with strong resistance from advisers. Robert Armstrong, then Principal Private Secretary to the prime minister, called it 'too extreme and not workable'.[244] In a classic mandarin trick, befitting Sir Humphrey, Armstrong tried to dissuade Heath by explaining that open government, like so many administrative improvements, came at a price. In each case, he underlined, the value of more information would have to be weighed against the cost of 'getting it, processing it and publishing it'.[245] Heath nevertheless refused to succumb to mandarin chicanery. Between 1972 and 1974, he raised the open government stakes with a string of progressive measures. He ruled that Green Papers should accompany every major policy initiative, and that an annual White Paper should be published adumbrating the government's expenditure strategy. He tasked the Central Office of Information with producing a weekly bulletin of government announcements and news. He set up weekly press conferences for ministers to respond to questions of 'current interest'. He required ministers to participate more regularly on current affairs programmes, including 'talk-in' broadcasts. (Departments soon became concerned that ministers were being drawn into unrehearsed debate by members of the public; thus, they arranged for 'our people' to phone in with pre-approved enquiries.)[246] Heath also did much to break down the facelessness of the civil service, encouraging officials to contribute specialist articles to journals and getting them to speak on radio programmes such as the BBC Radio 4 series *No, Minister*.

Not wanting to score a political own goal, Wilson initially resisted mandarin pressure to seek an injunction, opting instead to breathe life into the strategy of ad hoc censorship by requiring the Cabinet Secretary to negotiate with Evans and shepherd the extracts through publication with the minimum of damage. For nine weeks of serialisation, Hunt 'played cat and mouse' with the newspaper, successfully enforcing some deletions, but not others.[247] By the end, some 100,000 words of the diaries had entered the public domain and the path seemed clear for the complete work to be published.

In June, however, when it was announced that Volume I was ready for printing, the Attorney General, Sam Silkin, applied to the Queen's Bench Division to bar publication. There was genuine shock at this decision, which smacked of closing the stable door after the horse had bolted. Angry that the executors had been singled out in this way, Evans retaliated by publishing, without official clearance, a series of new, unexpurgated extracts.[248] For this act of defiance, he too was served with a court order. Wilson bore the brunt of public criticism, but, as declassified files confirm, responsibility rested largely with the higher civil service. For weeks following the first extract, he had been harassed constantly by his most senior advisers to take a stand. Hunt led the pack: 'There will inevitably be problems since the diary contains a blow by blow account of many Cabinet discussions, and it could therefore mark something of a watershed.'[249] Sir William Armstrong, Head of the Civil Service, was even more melodramatic: 'Mr Crossman breaks a tradition of mutual trust and for that matter, of good manners.' With publication, he warned, 'nothing would be the same again'.[250] Had Crossman been alive, it is tempting to suggest that he would have found this amusing. Wilson's susceptibility to mandarin charms was the perfect validation of Crossman's thesis that bureaucrats, and not elected politicians, were the ones that held the power.

The case was heard before Chief Justice John Widgery. Surprisingly, Silkin did not proceed with an Official Secrets Act charge, opting instead to invoke the arcane law of confidentiality and to make the case that the content of Cabinet meetings should be covered under its aegis. This delighted Crossman's executors. Prosecution under the catch-all provision of Section 2 would have meant a criminal trial with a jury. It had also been the opinion of Lord Goodman, now legal representative for the executors of Crossman's estate, that an action under Section 2 would succeed.[251] Interestingly, government lawyers had taken a different view. As they saw it, the requisite of success was the ability to demonstrate the link between Crossman, the person who disclosed the information, and the publisher, the recipient of that information; his death, however, made this necessary link difficult to establish. Privately, moreover, the government had lacked the nerve to use the Official Secrets Act. At the time, as public opinion demanded, ministers were still making noises about reviewing it. In a recent interview on Granada Television, the Home Secretary had promised 'sweeping changes'.[252] The law of confidence, therefore, offered a politically less contentious alternative.

Delivered on 1 October 1975, Widgery's judgment has been described as a 'constitutional lawyer's dream', packed with explanations of murky conventions, and containing ruminations on the difference between moral and legal obligations.[253] It even introduced a new word into the constitutional dictionary – 'parameters' – although the Lord Chief Justice was quick to point out that this was a word 'much abused' in the course of the case. Widgery's decision divided opinion on who had actually 'won' the trial. The government had reason to be pleased. His Lordship stressed the importance of collective responsibility, and recognised an obligation on the part of ministers to respect that doctrine. Crucially, he supported Silkin's contention that the law of confidentiality *should* extend to Cabinet proceedings and was not, as Crossman's legal team had argued, only applicable to marriage and industrial secrets. Judicial recognition on this point of principle was a major coup for the prosecution. However, the victory was of a pyrrhic kind. Thankfully for the defence, Widgery was sensitive not only to the issue of substance (what subjects warrant secrecy?) but also to the question of timing (how long should secrecy last?).[254] His attitude was that there had to be a time limit on how long confidential information remained secret. In Crossman's case, he felt that such a limit had lapsed, and that there was no danger therefore of inhibiting free discussion in the Cabinet of today. Many of the events described in Volume I were up to ten years old, in which time there had been three general elections and a spate of works covering similar ground. Accordingly, he ruled in favour of immediate publication. 'A surprise, but splendid decision,' hailed Crossman's widow, clearly delighted to have honoured her husband's dying instruction.[255] The publicity that accompanied the trial guaranteed that the book was a best-seller. Indeed, Jonathan Cape marketed it as 'the book they tried to ban'.

Publication delighted supporters of open government. The appearance of Volume I, swiftly accompanied without incident by Volumes II and III in 1976 and 1978 respectively, was heralded as a breakthrough in the battle against excessive official secrecy. It was the view of most observers that governments would now find it much harder to suppress information, especially of material contained in ministerial accounts. Although Widgery had made it clear that the publication of each future memoir or diary would be decided on its own merits, suddenly the contents of civil service advice had a shelf life, whereas before the time limit was of infinite duration.[256] According to the controversial journalist Bernard Levin, Crossman's lasting memorial would be 'to help ensure that the doors of secrecy, so firmly shut and so zealously guarded, were forced open'.[257] Certainly, there was no shortage of diarists waiting in the wings, looking to exploit the precedent. There followed diaries from Crossman's Cabinet colleagues Barbara Castle and Tony Benn, and, much later, from the Conservative Party, Alan Clark.

It would be inaccurate, however, to suggest that everything was plain sailing post-Crossman. The total cost to the defence of fighting the injunction was a whopping £70,000, a figure the executors could never have afforded had the *Sunday Times* not footed the bill. 'I'll always be grateful to Evans,' said Crossman's widow in a 2005 interview. 'Without him, there would have been no hearing and the government would have got its way.'[258] In effect, the trial had introduced a potentially prohibitive economic sanction. In cases where authors and publishers did not have deep pockets, the Cabinet Office could dangle the threat of a costly legal battle and censorship would be achieved by proxy.[259]

Menacingly for the next generation of memoir writers, the gatekeepers of official secrecy took the tumult of the Crossman Affair as a sign that they needed to strengthen the floundering internal mechanisms that regulated the publication of works. In April 1975, two months before the writ had been filed, a committee of privy councillors was set up to conduct an inquiry. Chaired by Lord Radcliffe – the usual lifeboat to whom governments turned in stormy seas – the committee worked quickly and quietly. Its report was completed in December and immediately endorsed by the government as an Annex to the Ministerial Code, an indication perhaps that there had been some measure of supervision by the official machine.[260]

The recommendations amounted to backsliding and a clear attempt to repair the damage of the Crossman diaries. For the sake of confidence within government, Radcliffe stipulated that a closed season of fifteen years would have to pass before ministers were free to publish. While this time restriction was much better than the embargo placed on historians (who were required to work with documents at the remove of thirty years), it was still a half-decade longer than the ten-year period deemed appropriate by Widgery in Crossman's case. Radcliffe went on to underline that – even at a distance of fifteen years ('enough to cover the life span of three successive Parliaments') – authors would still be required not to reveal any advice given to them in confidence by civil servants.[261] Moreover, where matters of national security or international relations were at stake, the requirement for non-publication could be extended beyond fifteen years. Radcliffe also recommended that every minister, on taking and leaving office, sign a declaration of loyalty, akin to the document signed with reference to the Official Secrets Act, pledging that he or she is aware of the 'parameters' against which the acceptability of manuscripts will be judged.

The Radcliffe guidelines typified the secret state's preferred method of dealing with the problem of political memoirs. After showing its teeth in the Crossman case, Whitehall was now prepared to return to non-legal mechanisms of control, which, despite being far from perfect, kept governments out of messy court battles and did at least have some measure of success, save perhaps when obstinate former prime ministers were involved. Radcliffe even conceded that the system could survive an 'occasional rebel' or an 'occasional breach'. In the report, he and his coadjutors laid down: 'But so long as there remains a general recognition of the practical necessity of some rules and the importance of observing them, we do not think that such transgressions, even though made the subject of sensational publicity, should be taken as having shattered the fabric of a sensible system.'[262] Just as in Hankey's day, the fabric was one that relied on ministers being gently persuaded to self-censor by the Cabinet Secretary. According to Radcliffe, it was the Cabinet Secretary's job to scrutinise texts, balance competing facets of the public interest, and then remind authors that they had a moral duty to do the right thing. 'There is no one else', he claimed, 'to whom Ministers, past and present, can look with the same confidence on what is essentially a question of Ministerial conduct.'[263] For all the shortcomings of this arrangement, it is one that seems to suit authors. As Wilson said at the time, doubtless anticipating another volume of his own memoirs, 'Compliance should be allowed to rest in the free acceptance by the individuals concerned of an obligation of honour.'[264] Despite a number of subsequent inquiries, no suitable practical alternative has been found and the governing principles of Radcliffe remain to this day. In short, the gentlemanly way of censorship is alive and well.

Part IV

Intelligence secrets, spy memoirs and official histories

7 KEEPING THE SECRETS OF WARTIME DECEPTION: ULTRA AND DOUBLE-CROSS

> The Ultra Secret was kept not merely during the war but for thirty years afterwards – a phenomenon that may well be unparalleled in history.
>
> PETER CALVOCORESSI, HISTORIAN AND BLETCHLEY PARK
> VETERAN, 1980[1]

The Second World War gave British intelligence its fair share of successes. Chief among them was the work of codebreakers at Bletchley Park. From 1940, under conditions of absolute secrecy, a silent army of cryptographers started to intercept and decrypt the supposedly impenetrable German machine ciphers (Enigma); the resulting Special Intelligence – otherwise known under the collective cover name of Ultra – provided 'information of the greatest importance and reliability concerning the activities and intentions of the enemy'.[2] Although some revisionists, such as Ralph Bennett, have since questioned its place as a primary element – 'deception is nothing but the handmaid of operations with no independent life of [its] own'[3] – conventional wisdom has it that Ultra played a decisive role in the Allied victory. General Dwight D. Eisenhower, Supreme Commander of the Allied Expeditionary Force, believed that Bletchley Park cryptography 'saved thousands of British and Americans lives and, in no small way, contributed to the speed with which the enemy was routed and eventually forced to surrender'.[4] Sir Harry Hinsley, official historian of British intelligence in the Second World War, proposed that Ultra shortened the conflict by 'not less than two years' and probably by four.[5]

In the twenty-first century, the story of Bletchley Park's penetration into Hitler's communications empire is well known. Its success has become a common touchstone for popular culture – celebrated both on the printed page and on the silver screen. Its gifted practitioners became a shorthand term for community, triumph over adversity, even the idea of Britishness itself. It is easy to forget, however, such is the importance of Bletchley Park to our national heritage, that the Ultra secret was not revealed to the public until the mid 1970s, some three decades after the end of the Second World War. Published after 1945, the official histories of the conflict contained no references to, or mention of Bletchley Park. The ordinarily garrulous Winston Churchill, who by common consent masterminded cryptography's revival in 1940, was silent on the subject in his best-selling multi-volume *History of the Second World War*. According to Michael Howard, esteemed official historian of the Grand Strategy series, the absence of Ultra from the first generation of war histories was comparable to Shakespeare 'writing *Hamlet* without the ghost'.[6] Only in 1974, with the publication of *The Ultra Secret* by Group Captain Frederick Winterbotham, did 'the greatest secret in warfare' finally emerge, catching the public and the majority of professional historians alike by complete surprise.[7] Such a degree of secrecy, as Peter Calvocoressi has argued, was a 'phenomenon that may be unparalleled in history'.[8]

It is self-evident why Bletchley Park cryptography was kept walled off from public view during the war; its disclosure, or even the suspicion of it, would have had fatal consequences. It is nevertheless a matter of enormous conjecture why it remained secret for nearly thirty years thereafter. With some justification, one might think that such a blackout was counterintuitive. The fact that the British had broken German codes, and then used them to outwit Hitler, was a truly remarkable feat: why not celebrate this achievement as loudly as possible? In an article for the *New York Times*, published in 1974, David Kahn suggested that the British kept the secret to hide the fact that, after the Second World War, they had sold 'pre-owned' Enigma machines to Third World countries and had surreptitiously continued to read the messages of the machines' new owners.[9] More recently, Richard J. Aldrich has shown that, in summer 1945, defence planners were concerned that public knowledge of Ultra would threaten post-war rapprochement with Germany, whose leaders would claim that they had been 'stabbed in the back' by sleight of hand.[10] However, while both explanations are perfectly valid for the years immediately after the Second World War, neither satisfactorily explains the logic behind keeping the secret as late as 1974. It will be argued in this chapter that, by the 1960s, the key reason for maintaining the blanket of secrecy was to protect the anonymity of GCHQ, the agency responsible for covert peacetime signals intelligence (sigint). Since GCHQ was not openly avowed until 1983 (when the trial of Geoffrey Prime, a former employee turned KGB spy, made its existence undeniable), it was feared that Ultra's disclosure would lead to a host of sticky questions about whether or not Britain had continued its cryptography beyond VJ Day.

Just as interesting as why the British protected the Ultra secret for so long, is the issue of how exactly they went about it. One might think that keeping it from public disclosure was a relatively painless task. As well as being gagged by the Official Secrets Act, the twelve thousand men and women who worked at Bletchley Park were trained to be inveterate 'hiders of things'; indeed, during a visit to Bletchley Park on 6 September 1941, Winston Churchill famously described them as 'the geese that never cackle'. It will be shown in this chapter that concealing Ultra was extremely difficult, and attracted a good deal of resentment from both within and outside Whitehall. Memoir writers, eager to leave a chronicle of their wartime experience and achievements, repeatedly asked for the ban to be lifted. Because they were often men of status, safe in the knowledge that no government was realistically going to frogmarch them off to court, such individuals presented a huge problem. Foremost among them was Churchill himself, a man notoriously wanting in restraint and fickle in his loyalties to the rules of censorship. Having learned of the secret through their own ingenuity and detective work, well-informed historians presented a problem of a different kind, since no legal hold technically applied. Official attempts to suppress the writings of both 'insiders' and 'outsiders' invariably rested on little more than the ability of the Cabinet Office and the D-Notice Committee to wheedle and coax authors into self-censoring. The Cabinet Secretary, in particular, was the proverbial man in the middle. His job was to protect the secret at all costs, and yet he had to contend with intense pressure from authors. By the late 1960s, with a myriad of writers threatening to reveal the secret for the first time, this became a high-wire act from which he would sooner or later tumble. The traditional explanation of why the government allowed the publication of Winterbotham's history in 1974 is that, by the 1970s, the advent of computer-based cipher machines had greatly reduced the usefulness of Enigma technology. It will be offered here, by contrast, that the primary reason for Ultra's officially sanctioned disclosure was the powerlessness of officials to stop the secret from leaking out via 'unofficial' channels.

* * *

> The time limit for reticence about Special Intelligence never expires and although from time to time reports of alleged activities in connection with Special Intelligence may be broadcast or published, it is of the utmost importance that complete and absolute silence on such matters should be maintained.
>
> *Joint Intelligence Committee, 20 July 1945*[11]

Ultra was one of the most closely guarded secrets of the Second World War. The London Controlling Section, Britain's foremost strategic military deception coordinator, ruled that all information regarding the use of sigint as an organised weapon of war should be classified Top Secret. In Whitehall, receipt of Ultra material and knowledge of its existence was confined to approximately thirty war-related staff, and included only half a dozen of Churchill's thirty-five ministers.[12] The armed services worked on a strictly 'need to know' basis; only small cells of officers – usually theatre commanders – handled Ultra material in operational zones and they were directed to explain its origin to subordinates by reference to an apocryphal agent buried within enemy headquarters. In April 1944, with the invasion of France imminent, a Combined Intelligence Priorities Committee was established to oversee the removal of all Ultra-related documents found in the archives of liberated Europe. By August, with German records exposed like rabbit droppings in the bedlam of the Axis retreat, it was agreed that a Foreign Office archivist, with 'commonsense and training in interrogation', would accompany parties of troops with the task of safeguarding special intelligence records.[13] At Bletchley Park, the nerve centre of wartime cryptography, secrecy was paramount. A barbed-wire boundary fence surrounded the site; armed sentries were posted at the front gate; huts (where the decrypt teams worked) had wooden table-flaps across the door with bells on them; and a system of passwords, changed at 8.00 a.m. each day, was introduced to enable authorised personnel to circulate in the grounds after dark.[14]

In spring 1945, with the war in Europe drawing to a close, the London Signals Intelligence Board – Britain's premier sigint authority – became concerned that the secret might get out. In 1942, the War Office had begun writing history long before history itself had been played out, with the Chairman of the Committee for the Control of Official Histories, Rab Butler, commissioning a broad range of studies of the war.[15] Encompassing civilian as well as military topics, the histories were to be beefed up with sensitive material, since Great War volumes were believed to '[omit] the essence of human nature' and be 'so dull that they have no public'.[16] In February 1942, Sir Keith Hancock, editor of the UK Civil Series, reported that: 'Ministries have without exception shown themselves eager to co-operate. They [have] a natural zeal to carry out government policy; a realisation that experience ought to be funded for the sake of the future; and a conviction that the work will have a practical value during the transition from war to peace.'[17] The London Signals Intelligence Board now feared that when official historians put captured German records alongside relevant British documents, it would be revealed to them that the Allies had been in possession of event-influencing information, which could not have been obtained from agents or other means slower than Ultra.[18] The telltale sign would be the speed with which the Allies responded to Axis moves: the immediate rerouting of convoys to avoid U-boat attacks; the redeployment of field forces in the face of German dispositions; the counter-measures to negate the purposes of Luftwaffe raids.[19]

In July 1945, the matter was passed to the JIC. Its report emphasised that most aspects of wartime deception should remain permanently hidden. These aspects included:

1. That Ultra formed the basis upon which Britain gauged the plausibility and the effect of strategic plans;
2. That deception was coordinated in every theatre of war;
3. That double agents were employed for misinforming the enemy.[20]

For GCHQ, the peacetime successor to Bletchley Park, the JIC foresaw that disclosure of the story of Ultra, and the intelligence it yielded, would present a particular set of issues. Firstly, 'enemies may arise in the future'; were the Soviet Union, in particular, to know what successes were achieved in the war as a result of Ultra, they could ensure that this source was not available again.[21] (The irony is, of course, that GCHQ had no idea that Soviet spies such as Kim Philby and Anthony Blunt had long since betrayed the secrets of Britain's wartime deception apparatuses.) Secondly, 'no possible excuse must be given to the Germans [or Japanese] to explain away their complete defeat by force of arms'. If it became known that the plans of the Axis powers had been available to the Allies, the Germans could again claim that they were not 'well and fairly beaten' à la 1918.[22] Fascist revanchism and 'defeat by betrayal' discourses would be rife, as would the myth of an infallible Hitler, a genius robbed of victory by perfidious Albion. The beneficiaries of Ultra had long conceded its possible 'stab-in-the-back' quality. In July 1944, having just received a particularly 'good morsel', the US 7th Army Intelligence Officer had quipped: 'You know, this just isn't cricket.'[23]

Disclosure of the Ultra story also had the potential to disrupt Western intelligence cooperation. During the war, despite official lip service to full collaboration, Britain had taken considerable umbrage at Allied security negligence and secretly withheld many decrypts from co-belligerents. Declassified Bletchley Park files demonstrate the degree of concealment. In November 1943 – 'dictated not by any lack of confidence in French personnel but because we have every reason to be distrustful of their Signals security' – French circulation was restricted to low-grade ciphers.[24] British fears were initially aroused by a captured enemy cryptanalyst who suggested that French codes in Syria had given the Germans 'a full picture' of the strength and organisation of Gaullist forces, as well as valuable details of British troop movements. Britain also regulated its cipher exchanges with the Americans. In 1942–3, US mistakes (excessive devotion to plain language, and persistent use of the 'compromised' Hapelin machine) had supplied 'a continuous stream of information to the German Intelligence Service'.[25] Thereafter Britain was very careful about what it supplied to the US. What could be more damaging to Anglo-American cooperation in the sigint field – let alone to the broader 'special relationship' – than the revelation that Britain had surreptitiously held back decrypts in direct contravention of the landmark BRUSA (Britain/USA) sigint exchange agreement of May 1943?

The JIC was fairly certain that Ultra would not be revealed by Bletchley Park staff.[26] Everyone who had worked at the Park had signed the Official Secrets Act and had been sworn to silence. Moreover, Bletchley's conditions of utmost secrecy were believed to have imbued staff with a powerful psychological inhibition against disclosure. Similarly, the JIC had no concerns about ministers, senior civil servants and military commanders. Generals and admirals, it was even believed, would welcome Ultra's non-disclosure since it would enable them to attribute their successes to an uncanny gift for reading the battle-space and second-guessing the enemy's intentions. The problem was what to do with official historians. Denying them access to records was impractical; cancelling the histories would anger the public.[27] The JIC settled on a plan whereby official historians would be told the Ultra secret and then 'indoctrinated': that is, sworn not to reveal it in their writings. In late July 1945, Historical Sections were issued with a General Directive, which emphasised: 'It is imperative that the fact that such intelligence was available should NEVER be disclosed.'[28] The directive underlined that official historians would be denied access to sigint material; would be required 'not to probe too deeply' into the reasons for apparently unaccountable operational orders; and would be expected to sign a declaration prohibiting them from mentioning Ultra in their work.[29] Such a praetorian approach was mirrored in Washington. On 7 September 1945, in a memorandum to the London Controlling Section, the US Joint Chiefs wrote: 'It is desirable and necessary to take appropriate action to ensure the protection of sources of signals intelligence in connection with the preparation of official histories.'[30] Contrary to expectations, no one objected. As Richard J. Aldrich argues, 'The official history programme [had] become the last deception operation of the Second World War.'[31]

The first lifting of the sigint veil came from outside the UK. In autumn 1945, the Australian Defence Minister, Jack Beasley, spoke publicly about American naval intelligence success during the Battle of the Coral Sea. The *Washington Post* headlined: 'Hush Hush. Intelligence Officers "cracked" the naval code. Now it can be told'.[32] Held from November 1945 to July 1946, the Congressional Inquiry into Pearl Harbor publicly revealed the accomplishments of 'Magic', the cryptonym for American efforts to break Japanese military and diplomatic communications during the Second World War. In America, wartime deception became a 'hot topic' for memoirists. In *My Three Years with Eisenhower*, Captain Harry C. Butcher, Eisenhower's former naval aide, discussed the ruses used in advance of the North African invasion, as well as mentioning such unmentionables as the technique of encryption known as 'one-time pads'. In *The Strange Alliance*, Major-General John Deane, Chief of the US Military Mission in Moscow, gave a detailed account of Operation Bodyguard, the 'brilliant and successful deception to shield the Second Front'.[33] The American government – 'though doing its best' – was unable to block publication. As Brigadier Cornwall-Jones, Head of the Joint Staff Mission (JSM) in Washington, lamented, without an Official Secrets Act with which to threaten whistle-blowers, the most that could be done was to identify objectionable passages and 'tone them down'.[34] Given the almost universal awareness of American cryptographic success against Japan, officials in London became convinced that it was only a matter of time before scholars realised that the British had enjoyed similar sigint success against Germany. The clues, it was assumed, were too obvious to miss. In the words of one official: 'We must now accept certain facts; and having, like a good bridge player, counted our winners and losers, only then decide how to play the hand.'[35]

The individual who emerged as most likely to spill the beans at this time was Churchill, who was engaged in writing his six-volume history of the Second World War. Churchill had long been fascinated by the stratagems, to employ the military lexicon, of 'special means'. Bletchley Park, in particular, had a special resonance to him. By May 1940, to the dismay of his Chiefs of Staff, he had insisted on receiving a personal and daily supply of raw intercepts from his Bletchley Park 'hens'. Ronald Lewin has suggested that the magic and mystery of cryptography had 'an irresistible appeal for the schoolboy working inside a great man'.[36] Historiographical orthodoxy dictates that 'Churchill needed no guidance on the need to avoid mentioning Ultra in his memoirs'.[37] According to scholars, he approached the subject with great restraint, painfully aware from past experience of the hazards of discussing cryptography. Churchill's self-discipline, we are told, stemmed from witnessing the knock-on effect of Stanley Baldwin's decision, as prime minister, to read aloud in Parliament in May 1927 a deciphered Soviet telegram. Baldwin's disclosure prompted Moscow to change its cipher, thus denying Britain its best source of intelligence on the Soviet Union. Recently declassified material, however, suggests that Churchill had forgotten all about Baldwin's carelessness. The galley proofs of Volume I of Churchill's history, *The Gathering Storm*, contained manifold references to 'Boniface', his much-loved euphemism for Ultra. The proofs also mentioned 'Most Secret Source' and 'Very Special Intelligence' – both synonyms for wartime sigint.

As a result, on 27 January 1948 the Cabinet Secretary, Norman Brook, met with Churchill to discuss the author's sigint indiscretions. Despite promising Brook that he would not reveal the extent of Ultra's success, Churchill was not dazzled by the cry of national security and insisted that he would 'find it difficult to complete his book without including at some point statements which implied that we were able to break the codes and cyphers of enemy powers'.[38] E. G. Hastings of the London Signals Intelligence Committee was horrified at Churchill's nonchalant attitude. Because Churchill's history would 'be regarded as an authentic statement of the facts of the war', and would 'be more widely read than any other book of modern times', disclosures of this nature would cause 'irreparable harm'.[39] The temptation for the many thousands 'in the know' to be less guarded – or to appear wise among friends and colleagues – would be irresistible once sigint matters had been disclosed by no less a person than Churchill. The floodgates would be open.[40] Churchill eventually succumbed to the 'strongest possible appeals'; Ultra was completely removed from Volume I.[41]

In a draft of Volume II, *Their Finest Hour*, Brook was shocked to find a reference to the speedy receipt of enemy signals. In depicting General Wavell's counter-offensive against the Italians in Egypt on 9 December 1940, Churchill had written: 'At home in Downing Street they brought me from hour to hour intercepted signals from the battle-field.'[42] Brook demanded its excision: 'You should say nothing which would encourage those who worked in this organisation to think that they are now at liberty to speak more freely about their work.'[43] The word 'intercepted' was duly deleted. Despite his reputation as something of a loose cannon, less bound by the mortal requirement of being discreet, Churchill proved to be remarkably restrained in each of his six volumes.[44] In the text, sigint was skilfully repackaged as information derived from either 'two-legged sources' (humint) or captured enemy documents. Operation Fortitude – in which Ultra had been used to fabricate the ruse that the Allied invasion force would land at the Pas de Calais – was completely omitted.[45] Even oblique references – such as, 'although London was still referred to *in their orders* [emphasis added] as the principal target' – were expurgated for 'skating pretty near the wind'.[46] Behind closed doors, officials admitted that the Australian official historian, Chester Wilmot, had been far more indiscreet in his 1952 publication *The Struggle for Europe*. According to John Drew of the Directorate of Forward Plans (the body responsible for Cold War deception planning), the fullness of Wilmot's account, on Fortitude, had made Churchill's references to the same matter 'look rather jejeune'.[47] As David Reynolds argues, for such a great aficionado of sigint, Churchill had made a 'considerable sacrifice', a point not lost on Bletchley Park veterans who, should their wartime prime minister have spilt the beans, might have followed suit.[48]

* * *

I have just finished your magnum opus. I would like to congratulate you on a first class piece of work. As a hardened reader of thrillers, I think your latest work is one of the best ever! How sad that its circulation has to be so restricted!
David Petrie, DG (MI5), to John Masterman, 11 December 1945[49]

In summer 1945, Sir David Petrie, head of MI5, commissioned a 'Top Secret' report on the Double-Cross System, the Security Service's ingenious scheme of 'turning' German agents in the Second World War. The task was given to John Masterman (Figure 19), the former Chairman of the Twenty (XX) Committee, set up in January 1941 to funnel the flow of information through double agents to the enemy. Written with no thought of publication, the report was densely packed, beginning with a discussion of the origins of the system, when the chief concern was security against German espionage, and taking the story through to the implementation of deception plans for the D-Day landings. On Petrie's insistence, only 100 copies of the highly sensitive report were printed.[50] Of these 100, some were given to intelligence staff, others to senior civil servants, including Sir Edward Bridges, the Cabinet Secretary. All but a few of these copies were subsequently destroyed by fire. Unbeknownst to Petrie, when Masterman was elected provost of Worcester College, Oxford, the following year, he illicitly took a bound copy of the report with him and placed it on his bookshelf. He called it his 'precious (though illegal) possession'.[51] For Masterman to have retained a copy is remarkable. As head of the double agent programme, his life had revolved around secrecy, with document security being of paramount importance. More remarkable still, he would eventually call for the report's publication.

In December 1954, Masterman stunned Dick White, Director General of MI5, when he revealed to him that he owned a copy of the report and hoped to see it published.[52] White balked at the request. Although Masterman had removed all mention of Ultra, a close reading of the text would have made it obvious that the Double-Cross system could not have been so successful, or have lasted for so long, had it not been for sigint providing reliable means of verification.[53] White also feared that, if one person was allowed to publish with impunity, it would be infinitely harder to prevent others from doing the same. Appealing to Masterman's standing as the 'quintessential Establishment figure',[54] White suggested that Whitehall could ill afford another major disclosure after failing, in 1953, to prevent the publication of *The Man Who Never Was* by former Naval Intelligence officer Ewen Montagu: 'My legal adviser, who is fighting the battle with the Ewen Montagus of this world, is dead against my sponsoring such a project.'[55] Montagu's memoir had described the planning and execution of the now legendary deception story Operation Mincemeat, in which a corpse – the apocryphal Major William Martin – was dropped off the Spanish coast, carrying false plans for an Allied invasion of southern Greece.[56] The authorities had tried desperately to suppress the memoir. On the eve of the book's publication, Petrie had even called for legal action: 'The Government should stamp firmly on anything done that would tend to lower the sanctity ... which should be afforded by all intelligence staff to information coming into their hands.'[57] He continued: 'If this cardinal principle of a feeling of trust among those so employed is allowed to crumble away, I would regard it as a matter both grave and dangerous.'[58] Petrie ended up disappointed. HMG could not realistically prosecute Montagu, having failed in 1951 to prosecute Duff Cooper, a prominent Conservative politician, for a semi-fictionalised and alarmingly accurate account of the same wartime bluff.[59] Against this background, Masterman decided to sit on his report until a more appropriate time.

While Masterman held back from giving Whitehall a bloody nose, others who had been involved in Double-Cross were less forgiving. Chief among them was Eddie Chapman. A professional criminal before the war, specialising in smash-and-grab burglaries and safebreaking, Chapman had been a German spy before being 'turned' by MI5 in 1942 to work as a double agent. Codenamed Zig-Zag, he pulled off some of the most extraordinary deception operations of the war.

In January 1943, under the supervision of MI5, he informed his German controller that he was preparing to sabotage the De Havilland aircraft factory in Hatfield, Hertfordshire. The Germans were delighted since the factory was producing the new and much-feared Mosquito bomber. With the aid of Jasper Maskelyne, a stage illusionist and expert in camouflage, he made it appear to German reconnaissance aircraft that a major explosion had taken place inside the factory's power plant. Separately, MI5 planted a fake story in the *Daily Express* reporting that the factory had been demolished by enemy sabotage. The ruse was an enormous success. Upon his return to Germany, Chapman was given a hero's welcome, even receiving the Iron Cross in recognition of his work for the Abwehr. He was, and remains, the only British national to have ever been awarded this medal. Chapman's biggest contribution to the Allied war effort arguably came after D-Day when, with the tide of the war turning against Germany, he reported to his controller grossly inflated figures about deaths from V1 rockets and, wherever possible, convinced him to redirect attacks to sparsely populated areas.[60]

Despite his invaluable wartime service, Chapman was never fully trusted by MI5. As a working-class boy from Newcastle who enjoyed living the life of a wealthy playboy in Soho, he did not conform to the traditionally narrow social base of the Service and had little affinity with its values and customs. When the war ended, Chapman proved that he had no regard for the sanctity of Whitehall secrecy by returning to his old haunts in the West End and holding drinkers spellbound with his own distinctly colourful tales of derring-do. Soon short of money, and fully alert to the commercial possibilities of publicising his life story, in December 1945 he sold extracts from a memoir he had secretly written to a Paris newspaper. For this indiscretion, he was prosecuted – in camera – and fined £50.[61] Desperate to impound the manuscript on which the serialisation was based, MI5 officers raided his flat in Queen's Gate. The manuscript was found and confiscated.[62] A few years later, Chapman resurrected his memoir project by enlisting the help of Frank Owen, former editor of the *Daily Mail* and a member of Mountbatten's staff in wartime Burma. Although Owen was brought on board principally to ghost-write the memoir, as someone with friends in high places, Chapman also hoped that he would help to steer the book past the censor.[63] In spring 1953, with the manuscript written, Owen sold the serial rights to the *News of the World* for a 'large figure'.[64] Frantic discussions followed in Whitehall. 'In no circumstances can consent be given to the publication of the part of the story which deals with the time when Chapman was employed by us,' underlined White.[65] At the eleventh hour, Rear Admiral Thomson, D-Notice Secretary, convinced Hugh Cudlipp, editor of the newspaper, to delete all references to Chapman's time in MI5.

Chapman was nevertheless determined to see his memoir published. For MI5, the problem was precedent; should permission be given to Chapman, it would be difficult to deny the same privilege to others. For John Drew, there was a further problem since the memoir revealed how the War Cabinet had allowed Lambeth and Southwark 'to take the brunt of the [V1 rocket] attack' when it could have been laid off to a more lightly populated district.[66] Both departments, therefore, sent several strongly worded letters to Chapman, making it clear that any reference to his employment as a double agent would lead to prosecution under the Official Secrets Act. In the opinion of Bernard Hill, MI5's legal adviser, the book would still be 'exciting enough for anybody'.[67] When the revised version was published, however, officials realised that they had made a major miscalculation. Because all references to Chapman's time with MI5 had been cut, it appeared as though he had never left the service of the Germans! Readers would be entitled to ask why he had never been hanged for treason. Well-informed reviewers, such as Maurice Richardson from the *Observer*, castigated the government's 'gratuitous' censorship of the book.[68] 'Woefully castrated and lopsided', was his assessment. Recognising that officials had been overly keen to threaten Chapman with the Official Secrets Act ('in future we ought not to be too legalistic about these matters'), Drew wrote a memorandum to all senior officials, suggesting that, in future, every attempt should be made to 'negotiate' with the author in question. The best policy, he claimed, was to 'get close to a kicking horse'.[69]

In the late 1960s, as Chapter 4 demonstrated, the British press feasted on the exploits of Kim Philby, the Cantabrigian communist who had penetrated the highest levels of British intelligence during his thirty-year career as a Soviet agent. His story made a mockery of the intelligence services, making them appear bumbling idiots, who were so blinded by class prejudice that they refused to entertain the possibility that someone from the right background could betray his blue-blood legacy. Against this background, Masterman sensed an opportunity. In a letter to White, now head of the SIS, on 3 October 1967, he emphasised that the 'Philby stuff' had shattered the confidence of both MI5 and the SIS, and suggested that the public image of both services 'badly need[ed] a shot in the arm'.[70] That shot, he continued, could be provided by his Double-Cross book – a tale of unalloyed intelligence success. White agreed that the Philby saga had been 'very tiresome' for the intelligence community and, being sympathetic to Masterman's proposal, forwarded a copy of his letter to Martin Furnival Jones, the new head of MI5.[71] Furnival Jones did not share White's enthusiasm, explaining that the memoir would provide a future enemy with a valuable primer on Britain's aptitude and skill in the field of Double-Cross. A further concern was the effect that publication might have on the D-Notice system, presently 'on its knees' in the wake of the cable vetting scandal.[72] Should the government release, at this juncture, a work containing so much secret information, the D-Notice Committee would likely be inundated with requests from veterans to publish their life stories. Journalists, moreover, would be inclined to take the view that it was now fair game to investigate wartime intelligence. In addition, Furnival Jones saw no value to telling the Double-Cross story without relating it to other aspects of deception. Since such an account would inevitably discuss Ultra, and thus potentially bring the spotlight onto GCHQ, there was no chance of it being sanctioned.

Masterman refused to let the matter rest. In his view, Furnival Jones's argument about the D-Notice system ignored the fact that, were journalists to 'ferret about in the rabbit warren' of wartime intelligence, they would find considerable achievements.[73] For Masterman, the old tradition that it is better for secret services to remain in the shadows and not invite publicity, either good or bad, was unsuitable to modern times. 'Whether we like it or not,' he opined in a letter to Furnival Jones, 'people are influenced by what they read and see on the television; they read much of the failures though never hear of the successes'.[74] The Double-Cross book, he continued, was a 'heaven-sent opportunity' to reveal something which redounded greatly to the credit of MI5.[75] Many of his former colleagues and friends concurred. 'Publication ... would do much to counter the ill effects of the Philby affair,' was the opinion of Herbert Hart, a one-time MI5 officer and incumbent Professor of Jurisprudence at Oxford University.[76] Jim Butler, editor of the Official Military Histories of the Second World War, was of a similar mind: 'I agree entirely with what you say about the desirability of bringing out a counterblast to the Philby literature as soon as possible.'[77] For Tommy 'Tar' Robertson, the head of MI5's double-agent section during the war, there was nothing in the memoir that was damaging from a security point of view: 'I can see no reason why the book should not be published as it does not divulge any secrets or techniques which are not by now fairly common knowledge.'[78] In April 1970, over two years after Masterman first approached White with the idea, ministers finally met to discuss the case. Under considerable pressure from Furnival Jones, the answer from Downing Street was once again in the negative.[79]

Masterman was enraged. As a symbol of his determination to see the book published, he included it in his 1971 *Who's Who* list of publications. In a bid to cut the red tape, he began to pitch the book to publishers in the United States, where the Official Secrets Act could not stifle it. He called this Plan Diabolo. In Whitehall, word of Masterman's threat to publish in America spread like wildfire. Peter Fleming, a lifelong friend and former head of strategic deception in South East Asia Command, made it known to both MI5 and SIS that Masterman was deadly serious: 'I revealed your diabolical plan and [emphasised] that there was no telling what you might do if thwarted.'[80]

In addition to Diabolo, and even more mischievously, Masterman began to talk candidly about Double-Cross to outside authors. The author with whom Masterman developed the closest relationship was Ladislas Farago who was writing *The Game of the Foxes*, a history of German espionage in Great Britain and America during the war. A part-time journalist with a penchant for the sensational, Farago was definitely not the sort of person the authorities wanted cosying up to Masterman. In 1963, angered by the fact that Farago's US-published *Burn after Reading* had been critical of SIS and had spelled out the name of 'C', White had successfully forestalled an English edition by getting his brother, who was a director for the UK publisher interested in the book, to claim that it was marred by factual inaccuracies.[81] Farago met Masterman in Oxford in June 1971. Conversation, as Farago recalled it, was confined to 'general discussions' about the Double-Cross system.[82] The upshot of the meeting was that Farago would help Masterman initiate Plan Diabolo. Over twenty US publishers had in fact turned down the history. Some thought it too much of a 'source book'; others felt it 'too British' for the American market.[83]

Most turned it down for fear of official reprisals. Curtis Brown, for example, reported: 'I find your proposed course of action exceedingly disturbing.'[84] Thanks to Farago, who made the case to publishers that no legal action would be possible after *The Game of the Foxes* had been published, Yale University Press gave Masterman a contract.[85] They also coughed up a $5,000 advance.[86] Masterman was delighted – so delighted in fact that he offered to show Farago a copy of his book. However, Yale University Press forbade this gesture in order to ensure that Farago's account in no way scooped Masterman's history.[87]

As Masterman had hoped, his involvement with Farago, a lurid hack with a reputation for revealing the seamier side of espionage, did not go unnoticed by officials. In early August 1971, he was summoned to a conference with the Home Secretary, Reginald Malding, and the Foreign Secretary, Alec Douglas-Home, where the question was put to him: 'How much of this has Farago?'[88] In a bid to force the hand of the authorities into sanctioning the publication of his own book, Masterman reported, untruthfully, that Farago 'had it all'.[89] Masterman subsequently wrote a letter to his new friend insisting that, should the authorities inquire about how much he *really* knew about Double-Cross, he should at all times 'keep the fiction'.[90] The subterfuge worked; in the months that followed, MI5 and SIS held a series of panicked meetings dedicated to the problem of Farago's book. Their fears were heightened when, in mid August, Robin Denniston, editorial chief of Farago's publisher Hodder & Stoughton, passed to them one of the book's draft chapters, which included, in the footnotes, a reference to the 1945 XX report.[91] Denniston, whose father Alastair had been Director of Bletchley Park, was thought to have been disappointed that, for reasons of secrecy, his father's death in 1961 had been marked by not a single obituary and thus his achievements had not received public recognition. Possession of the chapter would have alerted the authorities to the fact that the Ultra secret could not be kept forever, and that outsiders like Farago were getting ever closer to the truth.

The fear that a troublemaker like Farago was about to blow open the secrets of wartime deception grew among officials. In summer 1971, as a pre-emptive strike, MI5 sanctioned the publication of *The Counterfeit Spy*. Written by Sefton Delmer, a *Daily Express* journalist who had worked for the Political Warfare Executive (PWE) during the Second World War, *The Counterfeit Spy* focused on double agents – particularly the D-Day infiltrator GARBO – in support of field operations in the Western Desert in North Africa, and in Europe. Delmer had cleverly pitched his memoir to the authorities as a counterblast to Farago's forthcoming history of deception. *The Game of the Foxes*, he argued, would be an 'erroneous and garbled version of events'; by contrast, *The Counterfeit Spy* would be an 'authentic history'.[92] At first, officials were lukewarm about the idea. GCHQ was nervous on account of the fact that the first draft of the memoir had proposed that the British had no difficulty in cracking German U-boat ciphers.[93] SIS had taken considerable umbrage at Delmer's decision to identify certain agents. A further problem was that Delmer had heavily plagiarised Roger Hesketh's in-house history of Operation Fortitude. Hesketh had threatened to sue Delmer for what he regarded as a 'pirated and vulgar edition of his work'.[94] The JIC had the final say on publication and agreed with the view of Admiral Norman Denning, Secretary of the D-Notice Committee, that: 'If Farago's book is likely to create a false impression of our activities, then it might be as well to let Delmer go ahead and pre-empt it with a book whose contents we control.'[95] Hesketh was rewarded with a lucrative out-of-court settlement, and sensitive parts of Delmer's text were either deleted or fictionalised. GARBO, for example, was given the spurious code name Cato.

In September 1971, ministers finally bowed and the Masterman history was approved, subject to a number of changes. Several factors lay behind this decision. Ministers recognised that *The Game of the Foxes* had to be counterbalanced with a more sober and accurate version of events. Farago encapsulated this nicely when he suggested that officials saw his book as a 'medley hotch-potch of mixed fodder'.[96] Plan Diabolo had to a large extent made publication inevitable; sanctioning the history was the lesser of two evils when the alternative was taking Masterman to court and getting into a 'very public scrap' with Yale University Press.[97] A further factor was that Masterman was on excellent personal terms with the individuals who ultimately had the authority to sanction his book. Many members of the new Conservative government had a great respect for him. Masterman had been a man of distinction in many walks of life; a scholar-sportsman almost without compare, he had played lawn tennis at Wimbledon, competed at hockey for England, and toured with the Marylebone Cricket Club. As a History don at Christ Church, he had taught many of the 'elite', including the then Foreign Secretary, Alec Douglas-Home, and the prime minister, Edward Heath. Astonishingly, both felt indebted to their former tutor. Douglas-Home later claimed that, despite the best efforts of MI5's top brass, there was never any chance of him 'lock[ing] up the best amateur spin bowler in England'.[98] Predictably, Furnival Jones was none too pleased with the government's decision. In a letter to the Foreign Secretary, he protested: 'I do not understand this argument that he is morally obliged to publish.'[99] Furnival Jones reserved most of his venom for Masterman himself, calling the octogenarian spymaster 'disgraceful'.[100] 'When you left the Service after the war,' he ranted in a private correspondence, 'you signed an undertaking not to do precisely what you are now proposing to do.'[101] Furnival Jones was by no means alone in this opinion. Some of Masterman's wartime colleagues, including John Marriot (Robertson's deputy), were horrified and never spoke to him again.

Yale University Press had planned to make a formal announcement of the government's decision in early 1972. When, in October 1971, Farago leaked the news to the press and began releasing extracts of his book to the *Daily Express* which described Masterman's involvement with Double-Cross, they were scandalised. Some of the serialisations had even attributed quotations to the retired spy. Yale University Press's Director, Chester Kerr, wrote to Farago in protest: 'Surely a man of your experience is entirely aware that to leak such a story in advance is to reduce the impact of the final announcement ... You may consider any cooperation between us at an end.'[102] As Kerr saw it, Farago's premature disclosures were motivated by self-interest, designed to promote *The Game of the Foxes*. Name-calling and bitter recriminations ensued. Farago labelled Kerr 'out of his mind'; Kerr hit back by claiming that Farago was 'as contentious' as he was 'unreliable'.[103] Yale University Press's disdain for Farago intensified with the publication of *The Game of the Foxes*. Large parts of the book were remarkably similar to Masterman's as yet unpublished account. A total of 150 unacknowledged sentences had been taken verbatim from the 1945 report.[104] Spotting the same parallels, officials in Whitehall scratched their heads as to how Farago had seemingly seen the secret history. Had Masterman been a naughty boy and provided him with a copy? Farago was incredulous, suggesting that the allegation of plagiarism was part of a 'vicious smear campaign', manufactured by a 'Yale clique' to discredit *The Game of the Foxes*.[105] Protesting his innocence, Farago maintained that he had assembled his history through five years of painstaking, diligent and costly independent research, learning the basic facts from Abwehr documents and interviews with surviving eyewitnesses.[106] After a further round of insults and accusations, it dawned on both Yale and Whitehall that Farago had, in all likelihood, received a copy of Masterman's history from his own publisher, David McKay. In early 1970, before the Yale contract had been struck, Masterman's literary agent had sent out copies of the Double-Cross report to most American publishing houses, including McKay. Rather than keep it to itself, it was likely that McKay had forwarded it to Farago. Of course, there was no way of proving this.

The Double Cross System in the War of 1939 to 1945 was published in spring 1972, twenty-seven years after it had been penned. The published version contained no reference to Ultra and preserved the anonymity of Masterman's wartime colleagues by referring to them as 'Senior Officers'. Sales were better than expected, especially in North America, where 38,000 copies were sold by 1 June 1972.[107] As John Campbell has argued, high sales in the US reflected the fact that the book's main themes, namely penetration and deception, resonated with the 'ethos of the Cold War'.[108] Disappointingly, the book's success paled in comparison to *The Game of the Foxes*. Hard-cover sales of Farago's history soared beyond 100,000 copies; in March 1972 it topped the *New York Times* list of best-selling non-fiction titles.[109] Farago, nearly twenty years Masterman's junior and possessing a truly electric personality, had the added advantage of taking a grand promotional tour.[110] There was no doubting, however, that Masterman's history was the more significant. In the opinion of Ronald Mansbridge at Yale University Press, for the state to relent on its long-standing policy of non-disclosure with respect to MI5, made the book just as important as the Kinsey Report of 1948 which had famously lifted the lid on human sexual behaviour.[111] Officials were under no illusion that, in allowing the history, it was only a matter of time before Ultra was revealed. Double-Cross and signals intelligence were interwoven.

* * *

> What a dreadful book *The Ultra Secret* was, but it was a breakthrough of the security ban.
>
> > *Patrick Beesly, 3 November 1975*[112]

By the late 1960s, the hermetic seal surrounding strategic deception was starting to break. Several authors – some inadvertently, others mischievously – alluded to the Ultra secret in their writings. David

Kahn, in *The Codebreakers* (1967), revealed that Abwehr signals were read on 'machines that filled several buildings' (Figure 20); Władysław Kozaczuk, in *Bitwa o Tajemnice* (1967), claimed that Polish crypt-analysts had cracked the Enigma before 1939; and Kim Philby, in *My Silent War* (1968), concluded that codebreaking was far more important than human intelligence.[113] In his history of Britain's wartime Naval Intelligence Division, Donald McLachlan referred to 'Station X', the code name for Bletchley Park.[114] His account, moreover, discussed several episodes in which the British had successfully captured German cryptographic material, including the seizure from U-boat 110 in May 1941. Behind the scenes, officials were amazed that these revelations had not made a bigger splash. To their surprise, McLachlan et al. had been snobbishly dismissed by the academic community as charlatans, not to be trusted on account of their lack of scholarly rigor. The journal *Military Affairs*, for example, suggested that McLachlan's major revela-tions had no credibility such was the 'weak index, inept footnoting and inadequate documentation'.[115]

In winter 1968, the viability of keeping the Ultra secret became a hot topic in Whitehall following the government's announcement that, on 1 January 1972, it would open up the 'cream' of its Second World War archive for public inspection. To aid researchers wanting to examine the war period as a whole, the prime minister, Harold Wilson, agreed to release documents 'en bloc' rather than parcelling them out in annual batches under the Thirty Year Rule. There was, of course, no legal requirement for Ultra material to be included in the release. Section 3 (4) of the Public Records Act, otherwise known as the 'blanket' exemption, gave the Lord Chancellor discretionary powers to withhold all records related to intelligence. The JIC nevertheless thought it only right to give the matter proper due care and attention. On 13 November 1968, it provided ministers with a detailed report considering the pros and cons of releasing wartime sigint records.[116] It identified several good reasons for coming clean about Ultra. Firstly, through memoirs and outsider histories, much was now known about the stratagems employed to hoodwink the Nazis. Although Ultra was not yet known to the public as one of them, such was the interest in wartime deception it was clear that officials were fighting a losing battle to keep it that way. Secondly, both the D-Notice Committee and the Cabinet Secretary had become increasingly ineffective as means to protect the secret. The Masterman case had confirmed that, if veterans were undeterred by the bumble of bureaucracy and elected to publish and be damned, there was nothing that could be done, short of reaching for the Official Secrets Act. A final reason in favour of release was the fact that the Soviet Union – 'largely through the disclosures of defectors' – knew all about British cryptography.[117] As mentioned above, one of the main reasons for keeping the secret in 1945 and throughout the early Cold War was the fear that, if disclosed, it might provide hints to the Russians about the activities of GCHQ. It was now obvious to everyone that this game had long since been given away by the Cambridge spies.

Yet a policy of releasing the records was still fraught with considerable danger. Any discharge of Ultra documentation, the report underlined, would 'focus attention on [sigint] as a whole' and thus make it infinitely more difficult to maintain reticence about GCHQ.[118] In their official pronouncements and answers to parliamentary questions, ministers were able to 'check the curiosity of the uninformed' by claiming that sigint was not avowed government policy.[119] Releasing papers, even from the Second World War, would invalidate this cover story and encourage a wider circle of people to start guessing about the peacetime activities of GCHQ. It was also feared that, were successes in the war revealed, communications security in other countries would be increased.

The JIC made several recommendations. Firstly, Great War sigint records (the 40 O.B. archives) should be released as soon as practicable. Disclosure would not cause 'embarrassment, resentment or misapprehensions' as to the reasons for Allied victory; neither would it risk current operations.[120] Secondly, departmental and Cabinet Office papers relevant to Ultra should be released, albeit with redactions and done by 'creeping barrage', spread over many years 'so as to generate the minimum public interest'.[121] Thirdly, all sigint records relating to the inter-war years and the period after 1945 should be withheld under the Lord Chancellor's special dispensation. Fourthly, all Ultra material from the war held by GCHQ should not be released. And fifthly, under no circumstances should permission be given to any individual seeking access to sigint records. Any departure from this rule, even for serious academics or official biographers, would lead to a 'slippery slope' of disclosure.

The government accepted these recommendations in late 1969. This was a bold move. By sanctioning the slow release of departmental records containing evidence of wartime sigint, ministers made it inevitable that the Ultra secret would one day become public knowledge. However, as the Cabinet Secretary, Burke Trend, recognised, it could take historians years, even decades, before they realised the significance of fleeting references to 'Boniface' and 'Most Secret Source'. On 9 November 1970, he wrote to the prime minister, now Edward Heath, stating that it was both 'anomalous' and 'conspicuous' to treat Ultra records held by GCHQ as a separate category, and urged that they should be released simultaneously with the Second World War 'cream'.[122] If ministers did not countenance an authoritative release on Ultra, counselled Trend, they would find other people – 'over whom [they] had no control' – doing the job for them. David Kahn, whose book *The Codebreakers* was being readied for a television programme, was seemingly on the verge of disclosing the secret; so was the author David Seale, who was writing a book on intelligence in the 1940s and was known to have acquired a copy of a secret report written by a former GCHQ officer outlining GCHQ's origin and development in the post-war years.[123] In Trend's view, a controlled release of Ultra materials would discourage 'the wilder types of irresponsible writing' on the subject, not to mention help to demonstrate to the public that the government was prepared to be as frank as circumstances permitted.[124] Trend also played down the fear that American and Commonwealth allies would kick up a fuss; prior consultation with Richard Helms, the Director of the CIA, as well as Australian, Canadian and New Zealand authorities, had confirmed that all parties 'officially endorsed and welcomed' proposals. Heath nevertheless dismissed Trend's advice.

Government attitudes finally started to change in 1973. As Trend had predicted, there had been no slackening in the number of books dedicated to wartime deception, with many giving tantalising references to Ultra. In *The Game of the Foxes*, Farago had disclosed that the British had obtained a working model of the Enigma machine from a Polish–Swedish spy ring in 1941.[125] In his memoir, Gustave Bertrand, the former Deputy Director of the French intelligence agency Service de Documentation Extérieure et de Contre-Espionnage, had claimed to be 'le véritable et seul artisan de cette Enigme' and ascribed 'all the credit and all the glory' for breaking the machine to a Franco-Polish collaboration.[126] Masterman's history, moreover, had described the work of the London Controlling Section, the organisation responsible for global deception policy. By 1973, it had also become known to Whitehall that the journalist Anthony Cave Brown was preparing a comprehensive history of Allied deception in the Second World War, entitled *Bodyguard of Lies*. Like Farago, Cave Brown had a reputation for racy narratives. He had first come to the attention of the authorities in March 1963 when a UK Chiefs of Staff paper, illicitly loaned to him by General Freddie Morgan, was put up for auction at Parke-Bernet Galleries, New York.[127] Consular staff at the British embassy discovered that Cave Brown had been living well beyond his means and had attempted to sell the secret document to support his lavish lifestyle.[128] In the years that followed, unperturbed by the antediluvian attitude of officials towards secret service records, Cave Brown perfected the art of 'archival intelligence hacking'.[129] As well as interviewing veterans and practitioners, he was notorious for prising things out of the libraries and archives of foreign countries, especially those with a more liberal approach to declassification. From the mid 1960s, he regularly visited America to take advantage of the landmark Freedom of Information Act, signed into law by President Lyndon B. Johnson on 4 July 1966. For Cave Brown, America was an Aladdin's cave – or 'wonderland' – where all sorts of jewels and nuggets could be found.[130] Cave Brown's globe-trotting antics did not go unnoticed in Whitehall. In November 1966, William McIndoe of the Cabinet Office Historical Section warned the D-Notice Committee that he 'needs to be watched like a hawk'.[131] A splendid irony was that unbeknownst to the British, retired CIA Director Allen Dulles was at the same time *encouraging* Cave Brown to write a history of wartime deception and had even put in a good word for him with Harper & Row publishers.[132]

Word of the 'Bodyguard of Lies' manuscript first reached Whitehall in late 1971 when Brown's American publisher, Harper & Row, started an auction for the British book rights. In its sales pitch, the publishing house underlined that the book contained a number of revelations, one of which, namely Ultra, was 'so explosive that it is considered the biggest secret of the war'.[133] (Because of this, interested parties were asked to submit bids of no less than $100,000.) Whitehall's response was to summon Cave Brown before Admiral Denning. This failed; Cave Brown emphasised that he had learned of the Ultra secret by interviewing several high-ranking Americans, long since deceased, and that he had no intention, therefore, of letting Whitehall pulp his manuscript. To ensure that he was free from British interference,

Cave Brown relocated to America, bringing all his files with him. Harper & Row even gave him an office in their New York headquarters.[134] With Cave Brown refusing to communicate with the D-Notice Committee, deliberations went up to Cabinet level. Realising that he could not be stopped, ministers decided that Ultra had to be 'officially' disclosed in advance of the publication of *Bodyguard of Lies* in 1975. Since the idea of releasing Ultra records held by GCHQ still attracted hostility from security chiefs, ministers agreed that the best option open to them was to reveal the secret in an authorised memoir. In 1974, therefore, an old Bletchley Park hand, Group Captain Frederick Winterbotham (Figure 21), was allowed to publish the first English-language work dedicated to the Ultra secret and the influence of Enigma decryption on the course of the war. Winterbotham was an interesting choice of author. He knew nothing about the technicalities of cryptanalysis; his job had been to supervise the security of the intelligence material, a far less important task than those of the people who solved the intercepts or who evaluated the results. In order to scoop Cave Brown, he had to write in some haste. With no access to official documentation, he was required to work entirely from memory. Weidenfeld & Nicolson gleefully rushed the book into print. The publisher's newly appointed Deputy Chairman, none other than Robin Denniston, was presumably delighted at the long-overdue recognition of his father's accomplishments.

Although the book contained many inaccuracies (understandable perhaps, given the time pressures involved and given the fact that Winterbotham was not an expert in the art of cryptography), reviewers rightly considered it a momentous publication. Newspapers around the world were emblazoned with eye-catching headlines such as 'British Ear at the German Keyhole'.[135] Press reviews forecasted wholesale revision of the history of the Second World War, with some journalists excitedly proposing that Ultra alone had won it. For many military historians, previously enamoured with this general or that admiral, Winterbotham's bombshell would inspire a completely new way of looking at the conflict. The fact that the Allies had known almost every strategic decision and operational order of the German High Command suggested shocking delinquencies and incompetence on the part of military planners. Allegations abounded that certain calamities could have been avoided had officials taken full and proper advantage of the Ultra information at their disposal. The most serious allegation, eventually put forward by Cave Brown's

Bodyguard of Lies, was that they had foreseen the bombing of Coventry in November 1940, but decided to let it occur so as not to arouse German suspicions about the security of their communications. As GCHQ had warned in 1945, a further consequence of Ultra's disclosure was grudging sympathy for Germany. 'I never thought a book would make me sympathise with Hitler,' commented the *New Republic*.[136] Winterbotham had shown that many of Hitler's military decisions, far from being madcap or deluded, were remarkably clever and might well have succeeded, had it not been for Ultra betraying his every move.

Once the initial furore over Winterbotham's book had settled down, a more nuanced appraisal about the value of Ultra to the Allies began to take shape, documenting the links between Enigma-derived information and particular events. With the 'Top Secret' lid taken off the story, other 'old boys' decided to publish accounts, including Ewen Montagu, the naval liaison officer who had masterminded Operation Mincemeat, and Patrick Beesly, who had worked in the Admiralty's Operational Intelligence Centre, where German naval signals had been assessed for operational significance and then disseminated to the fleet as required.[137] Drawing on his own personal experience as an army duty officer in Hut 3, as well as the first batch of Ultra summaries released to the Public Record Office in October 1977, Ralph Bennett wrote *Ultra in the West* (1979) with the explicit intention of correcting 'the fictions of Cave Brown' and other such sensationalists, of whom he vehemently disapproved.[138] Taken together, the works of Montagu, Beesly and Bennett established the historiographical consensus that, while Ultra shortened the war by many months, perhaps years, it did not automatically bestow victory upon the Allies; men and machines still had to clash. It should be said that not everyone approved of these publications. Guy Hughes, a Bletchley Park veteran, hated 'Winterbotham's awful effort' and was deeply saddened that the seal of secrecy had been broken.[139] Clive Loehnis, a Bletchley Park codebreaker who went on to become Director of GCHQ, confessed to being 'maddened' by the revelations. 'Words failed me when I read the Winterbotham saga,' he wrote in a private correspondence.[140] He went on: 'I was indeed surprised that publication had been allowed and not totally convinced by those arguments in support of publication that were advanced.'[141]

Even allowing for the benefit of hindsight, that no historian discovered the Ultra secret before 1974 is remarkable. The clues to its existence were surely too obvious to have been missed. It was widely known that British cryptographers had cracked German codes during the Great War; indeed, Room 40's successful interception of the Zimmerman telegram, which accelerated the United States' entry into the war, had achieved extensive notoriety and fanfare in the press. In 1946, following the Congressional Inquiry into Pearl Harbor and the public disclosure of 'Magic', it is bizarre that no one considered the possibility that the British had enjoyed similar success against Hitler's ciphers. Just as baffling is the fact that, when a handful of references to Ultra trickled into the public consciousness in the late 1960s, historians failed to give them proper attention. The historian Christopher Andrew has argued that the absence of wartime sigint from thirty years of historical writing reflected widespread 'cognitive dissonance' within the discipline: that is, an innate reluctance among scholars to embrace a subject that threatened to overturn fundamental ideas about the Second World War.[142] Traditional military and diplomatic historians, guided by a misplaced notion that 'great men' have and always will influence the course of history, were arguably the least inclined to subject their research to complete reassessment. A further reason for Ultra's neglect was that historians (and their publishers) were swayed by market forces and thus preoccupied with 'sexier' aspects of the intelligence war against the Axis powers. The fast-paced world of secret agents, epitomised by the Special Operations Executive (SOE), was far more arresting than the mundane setting of moth-eaten desk men combing transcripts of radio messages and burrowing in mountains of diplomatic correspondence. The day-to-day life of a Bletchley Park mathematician was diligent but pedestrian, especially when compared to the James Bond-style exploits of humint-centred secret services. Publications dealing with secret agency were plentiful, and form the basis of the next chapter.

8 SOE IN FRANCE

Secrecy may be essential but confidence must be restored.

HUGH GAITSKELL,
May 1961[1]

The publication in 1966 of M. R. D. Foot's *SOE in France* stands as a significant milestone in the history of British secrecy. The book, which details the exploits in France of the Special Operations Executive (SOE), the organisation set up by Churchill in July 1940 to 'set Europe ablaze' by conducting sabotage and subversion throughout German-occupied territory, was the first history of any secret service officially published by HMG. As such, it went against the grain of the long-established convention that Britain never 'did' intelligence and that its activities should never be mentioned, save in the highest circles. What prompted HMG to endorse such an unprecedented work? In the book's preface, Foot offered a short explanation, suggesting that the history had derived from mounting pressure, primarily from Parliament, for an 'accurate and dispassionate' account of SOE's role in the war.[2] Foot's failure to elaborate on the genesis of the project vexed Dame Irene Ward, Conservative MP for Tynemouth. In the months following the book's publication, and with a serious bee in her bonnet, Ward took to telling all and sundry that *she* had been the driving force and, accordingly, was deserving of some acknowledgement. Her case, which she made in a succession of angry letters to the press, hinged on the fact that, during the late 1950s, she had lobbied intensively in the House of Commons for an official investigation into charges of incompetence and callousness in the administration of SOE.[3] A woman renowned for charging into parliamentary battle, if at times impetuously, Ward had been particularly anxious to clear up allegations that female resistance fighters had lost their lives on account of incompetent SOE leadership.

For a long time, it was the established historiography that Ward's lobbying had been the decisive factor, forcing the authorities to answer their critics by sponsoring an official history. 'There was one useful outcome of the parliamentary exchange initiated by Dame Irene Ward,' wrote SOE alumnus Patrick Howarth in 1980: 'This was an undertaking by Harold Macmillan as Prime Minister that an official history of SOE in France would be published.'[4] More recently, this view has been challenged. In an important article for the *Historical Journal*, published in 2003, Christopher Murphy demonstrated that Ward's role in facilitating the book was not as great as she herself believed.[5] The Foreign Office, Murphy showed, had been considering an official history long before Ward's vocal campaign. By the early 1960s, communist scholars had effectively rewritten the history of the Second World War, claiming erroneously that British forces had played little or no part in fermenting European resistance. Leading French scholars, such as Henri Michel, had displayed a similar lack of attention to British efforts, whilst a spate of memoirs in the 1950s on the Office of Strategic Services (OSS), the American wartime counterpart of SOE and forerunner of the CIA, had also queered Britain's pitch. In Whitehall, Murphy argued, officials were disturbed that the SOE had been overshadowed, and they commissioned Foot's history to highlight Britain's sizeable contribution to wartime resistance.

This chapter will take a fresh look at how *SOE in France* came to be written, adding new evidence to support the general conclusion that Ward was 'pushing at an already open door' and that other considerations were behind the origins of the book.[6] I will show that Foot's history stemmed primarily from growing resentment in official circles about the depreciation of the British war effort: American bluster about the pivotal role of the OSS in hastening the end of war, coupled with concerted efforts by Russian historians to tell the history of resistance in terms of communist dogma, was instrumental in alerting Whitehall to the dangers of not being open about its own exertions in the field of special operations. Accordingly, this chapter builds on one of the central arguments of this book, namely, that when defensive strategies of information management fail, the secret state is only too happy to go on the offensive with its own releases of information. At the same time, this chapter will add some new insights. Murphy's article does not go beyond late 1960, and thus does not map how the book developed in the years leading up to its publication. Existing historiographies of the book's genesis have tended to assume that, once the arguments were made in favour of the history, everyone in Whitehall was behind the project and publication went ahead without controversy. This was not the case. Foot was authorised on 9 November 1960 to write the history on the strict proviso that it was a 'pilot project' or 'trial run'.[7] HMG gave no commitment to its eventual publication. When the draft was submitted in spring 1963 and subsequently sent out by the Cabinet Secretary for vetting by departments, the response was extremely hostile, a reaction which jeopardised the whole enterprise. Complaints varied: some suggested that the book reflected unfavourably on individuals and foreign governments, while others claimed that a secret history, on principle, should never be published. Certain SOE veterans, including Lieutenant Colonel Maurice Buckmaster and Douglas Dodds-Parker (by then a prominent Conservative MP), lodged their objections with the prime minister himself. Against this background, publication was far from the fait accompli that has hitherto been suggested.

* * *

> Widespread publicity has been given to the exploits of OSS and there may be some danger of opinion on the continent as well as in the United States forgetting the extent of British help.[8]
>
> *Sir Alexander Cadogan, Permanent Undersecretary at the*
> *Foreign Office 13 November 1945*

Unlike Ultra and XX, the existence of SOE was not a closely guarded secret at the end of the Second World War. Its responsibilities (sabotage, guerrilla actions, black propaganda, etc.) had been readily reported in Fleet Street and fitted the popular swashbuckling impression of British intelligence. With just fewer than 10,000 men and 3,200 women, as the historian Mark Seaman states, SOE was the 'least secret of Britain's secret services'.[9] That said, officials were still determined to keep certain things out of the public domain. 'As individuals we may hope that the last war has been fought,' declared Colin Gubbins, SOE's third and final executive head, in August 1945. '[However], as a department of state we must recognise that there might be another and we must prevent the release of secret matters detrimental to the security of the Empire.'[10] At a meeting held to discuss 'SOE Publicity' on 19 September 1945, senior intelligence staff underlined that many parts of the SOE story should 'NEVER be published', a no-nonsense verdict that could be heard in many of Whitehall's corridors at that time.[11] In terms of the risk of fuelling tension and distrust between nations, the most sensitive aspects were activities that had involved breaches of neutrality, or those which had been carried out contrary to the rules of war. (By 'breaches of neutrality', intelligence staff were almost certainly referring to the fact that SOE had set up stations in a range of neutral countries, including Thailand, Turkey, Switzerland and Spain. By actions that had been conducted 'contrary to the rules of war', they may have been thinking about 'currency operations', most notably Operation Remorse – a scam to fund relief and repatriation of Allied prisoners of war by playing the money markets in China.)[12] Also for non-disclosure were materials that could undermine the work of Britain's peacetime intelligence services. These included: SOE-devised methods and devices; locations of headquarters and training schools; and techniques of sabotage. Gubbins, moreover, was clear that no publicity should be given to any officer who did not want his or her name revealed. To do so would fundamentally breach the trust placed in SOE by its agents, not to mention run the risk of inviting reprisals from vengeful groups. 'In Eastern Europe', Gubbins emphasised, 'an admission that a person had been a British agent during the war would be most harmful to his [or her] interests.'[13] Everyone, he continued, should 'respect their silence'.[14]

Having the will to protect SOE secrets was one thing; having the means to do so was another thing altogether. When SOE was officially liquidated on 15 January 1946, 280 of its agents were brought into SIS, initially under the auspices of what was called the Special Operations Branch. SIS also acquired a number of SOE's training and research staff.[15] As serving officers, all of SIS's new recruits were severely restricted in what they could reveal about their wartime employment. This, however, left nearly 13,000 individuals who left SOE to return to their peacetime occupations. As civilians, Gubbins feared, they might soon forget the importance of secrecy. Those who had never been Whitehall 'careerists' but had been recruited pragmatically on account of their technical expertise or willingness to work behind enemy lines were viewed as particularly problematic. Although the Official Secrets Act could be activated *after* an indiscretion had been made, in practice, lamented Gubbins, all that prevented such individuals from speaking to the press or writing memoirs was 'good sense and good taste'.[16]

By mid October, scarcely a month after officials had so dogmatically ruled that SOE publicity was a bad idea, certain individuals in Whitehall suddenly started to reconsider this position. The catalyst for a rethink was an alarming development in the United States. On 20 September 1945, President Harry Truman passed an Executive Order disbanding OSS ten days hence. In the weeks that preceded this decision, a bitter public quarrel had taken place between the celebrated OSS director Major General William J. Donovan and his enemies, who included FBI director J. Edgar Hoover, who saw the OSS as competition to his plan of expanding the FBI's operations internationally. In a futile bid to prolong the OSS's existence, and to the horror of some senior figures in London, Donovan embarked on a semi-official crusade to publicise its achievements. By early October, American newspapers and popular magazines were awash with the recollections of former agents, rhapsodising about how the OSS had excelled in the field of 'irregular warfare'. Donovan was also in the process of co-opting Hollywood studios and directors to dramatise the exploits of the OSS on the silver screen.[17] The scripts made no reference to SOE's work with the European resistance, focusing solely on American successes and heroic deeds. Take for example, the screen treatment for *Cloak and Dagger* (1946), submitted to Warner Bros on 1 October 1945: 'This is a picture of America's race to win the desperate battle of espionage, our secret war behind the headlines, the war nobody knows.'[18] The reluctance to acknowledge Britain's contribution is particularly apparent in the following declaration: 'The OSS story – the story of average everyday Americans who outmanoeuvred and outwitted the centuries old spy rings of Europe and Asia – is one of the war's great epics.'[19]

SOE's second in command, H. N. Sporborg, was dismayed by Donovan's shameless self-promotion and wrote to the Foreign Office with the idea that the BBC should broadcast a programme on SOE. The programme, which would be allotted a 'peak listening hour' and include only 'en passant' references to sensitive areas such as training and planning, would be accompanied by an SOE press conference highlighting Britain's support of resistance movements in occupied countries.[20] The Foreign Office saw merit in Sporborg's proposal: 'We are very glad to hear that something is being done about this because it is getting more urgent both from the point of view of the American public, who have recently been told all about the exploits of the OSS, and from the viewpoint of continental opinion, which is rapidly forgetting what we have done to help the Resistance.'[21] Sir Alexander Cadogan, Permanent Undersecretary, put his considerable weight behind the scheme: 'Widespread publicity has been given to the exploits of OSS and there may be some danger of opinion on the continent as well as in the United States forgetting the extent of British help.'[22] So did Harold Caccia, minister at the Athens embassy: 'The spate of publicity in America renders the question of giving publicity here more importance.'[23] In November, the matter was put before the JIC, which ruled that there was insufficient demand, both at home and abroad, for an authoritative disclosure of SOE activities.[24]

By late 1946, the wisdom of a continued British policy of silence had again been thrown into doubt. Resigned to the extinction of the OSS at the hands of his federal enemies, but now determined to strengthen support for a peacetime foreign intelligence service (the CIA), Donovan and his publicity machine had continued to flood the media with stories showcasing the invaluable work of American agents during the war.[25] As Donovan had hoped, Hollywood touted the accomplishments of OSS: three films dealing specifically with the organisation were released in 1946. The first – simply titled OSS – starred Alan Ladd, Paramount Studios' resident 'fists-a-flying' tough guy, as an agent parachuted into Nazi-held France before D-Day. The opening credit sequence, which featured a signed statement by Donovan praising American secret service men and women, boasted of the full cooperation of the OSS in the making of the film. Fritz Lang's *Cloak and Dagger*, which starred Gary Cooper as a scientist sent behind enemy lines to investigate the status of Nazi A-bomb experimentation, had benefited from massive OSS support. During the film's production, scores of decorated veterans had lent their assistance, including Andreis Deinum, an expert in cryptography, and Michael Burke, a Silver Star recipient who many years later became President of the New York Yankees. So delighted was Warner Brothers movie executive George Skouras with the quality of assistance from the OSS, that he invited all of the film's technical advisors to a grand banquet at Perino's Restaurant, Los Angeles. 'Champagne flowed and toasts resounded,' recollected studio chiefs.[26]

The third epic, *13 Rue Madeleine*, starred the inimitable James Cagney as an instructor of would-be spies who was charged with feeding false information to one of his students suspected of being a German mole. Old hands from the OSS, including Donovan, were at first heavily involved in the film's production. According to Harry Brand, then Director of Publicity for Twentieth Century Fox, the source material for the film had been culled from the 'vaults' of the OSS, an admission which seems to confirm the belief of film scholars James Parish and Michael Pitts that 'for a three week period, the OSS opened their closed case journals to several moviemakers'.[27] (James Deutsch, in a more recent article for *Intelligence and National Security*, had doubted whether this had in fact been the case.)[28] Halfway through filming of *13 Rue Madeleine*, it is interesting to note that Donovan withdrew his support for the picture and ordered all references to the OSS to be deleted – a ruling that forced the producer, Louis de Rochement, to rename Cagney's organisation 'The Army of Secret Intelligence'. 'The picture is a phony,' Donovan declared in a private letter to de Rochement. 'With all the excellent authentic material which we have sought to make available to you it seems absurd that your company would persist in making a picture that not only lacks reality but plausibility.'[29] Colonel J. Russell Forgan, a former OSS officer who headed an informal committee set up by Donovan to assist filmmakers, called the plot 'completely and utterly ridiculous'.[30] Amongst his many complaints, Forgan was concerned that the film would upset British sensibilities. As it stood, the script suggested that the SOE had failed to reconnoitre sabotage targets before D-Day, an oversight that could only be rectified by sending Cagney on an eleventh-hour mission behind enemy lines. It is also posited that Cagney, at the last moment, had to reorganise the French Resistance on account of Britain's failure to whip it into shape. 'Ridiculous in the extreme,' was Forgan's damning verdict.[31] Neither Forgan nor Donovan, however, could convince the filmmakers to make the movie more realistic. 'This is Hollywood,' asserted the studio, 'and, in obeisance to local tradition, our picture will not avoid entirely a certain creative license.'[32]

The trio of OSS films offered a remorselessly one-sided version of events, emphasising that the outcome of the war could very well have resulted in an interminable stalemate had it not been for the undercover operations of American agents. Such blatant propaganda angered British officials. Believing that something had to be done to correct misconceptions, in 1947 HMG authorised the release of *School for Danger*, a feature-length documentary depicting how SOE had provided trained personnel, arms and other assistance to the European Resistance. Produced as a restricted film for the armed forces in 1944, *School for Danger* starred two actual British agents, Captain Harry Rée and Jacqueline Nearne. Whitehall also relented on its position with regard to memoirs, permitting a series of hyper-patriotic accounts.[33] Aptly described by Mark Seaman as 'Good Thrillers, But Bad History', these works left a clear message; resistance movements did not stand alone against the Nazi invader, but were supported unerringly by SOE, a foe to be feared by those foolish enough to arouse her fury.[34]

In May 1947, enraged by the way public discourse over American intelligence had relegated the work of SOE to a mere footnote in the larger history of the Second World War, the Cabinet Secretary, Norman Brook, called on intelligence chiefs to endorse a single-volume history of Britain's wartime secret organisations. 'If official historians [are] kept silent, there is a real danger that the credit due to the man who took part will go elsewhere.'[35] Brook's proposal was not out of character. At the time assisting Churchill with his memoirs, Brook was increasingly subscribing to the wartime premier's whiggish view that Britain should not only make history but write it. The Director General of MI5, Dick White, was impressed by Brook's idea. A wide-ranging history, divided into four sections (counter-espionage, resistance work, political warfare and special operations), could show to the world some terrific tales of derring-do. These included:

1. The account of 'JOE K' – an espionage network brought to light entirely through the work of Imperial Censorship in Bermuda.
2. The exploits of the Norwegian patriot Odd Starheim in capturing the German ship *Gal tesund* on the high seas.
3. The story of Sybarill, the Breton boatbuilder who, entirely unaided, arranged the escape of over a hundred persons from France.
4. The sabotaging of the heavy water plant at Vemork in Norway, including a sensational race on skis.
5. The appalling incident in which one SOE operative found himself lying wounded in a hotel otherwise occupied by the Nazi Governor of Norway and his entire defence staff.[36]

White shared Brook's assessment that such an account could serve as useful propaganda, suggesting that a chapter on the Yugoslav missions of Hudson and Deakin – why the agents were sent and how they made contact with Tito – would provide a 'mild corrective' to the Soviet allegation that Britain did nothing to assist the revolutionary until he had become the dominant figure in Yugoslavia. To the disappointment of Brook and White, departments forbade the project. SIS put forward an 'unreasoned veto', a stance that was echoed by the War Office and Foreign Office.[37] The only department to offer quantitative objections was the Admiralty. According to Sir Richmond Walton, 'there [was] a serious danger that the information [concerning] methods and ruses will, on future occasions, imperil those who are charged with similar enterprises'.[38] It was also feared that an unchecked history would endanger Allied confidants who were now leading normal lives. Although Brook believed that such risks could be mitigated, if not altogether obviated by the suppression of names, this was the point at which the venture stalled.[39]

* * *

> I do not know whether the idea of using you as an
> instrument for combating the Cold War after your retirement
> would commend itself to [Edward] Bridges and Norman
> Brook.
>> *Sir Frank Newsam to Sir Percy Sillitoe, August 1952*[40]

During the early to mid 1950s, more and more former SOE officers went into print.[41] While none of these authors was ever going to win literary prizes, their accounts were unashamedly partisan, giving officials no problem when it came to sanctioning their publication. This is not to say, however, that Whitehall would not resort to stonewalling when it needed to. The latitude given to members of SOE was the exception rather the rule. Indeed, as the previous chapter revealed, Whitehall created formidable hurdles in the 1950s for the likes of Eddie Chapman and John Masterman. In official circles, the stance with regard to memoirs that dealt with MI5 and SIS was as rigid as it had ever been. Under no circumstances should such works be published. Imagine the horror, then, when in August 1952 none other than Sir Percy Sillitoe (Figure 22), the serving Director General of MI5, submitted a précis for an autobiography. Although dealing largely with Sillitoe's gang-busting days as Chief Constable of Glasgow, the memoir would also discuss his time as MI5 head. 'My position as head is fairly well known and it would create an anti-climax if I were to say nothing

about it', he emphasised.[42] To improve his chances of obtaining permission, Sillitoe suggested that the book might be used to present
'educational matter' on the Cold War, revealing, for example, the
merits of positive vetting, the need for collaboration with allies and
the tactics employed by communists to subvert trade unions.[43] This
would not be the only occasion when Sillitoe promoted the value of
propaganda masquerading as public interest story. In 1957, he commissioned Ian Fleming, author of the James Bond novels, to write an
account of the International Diamond Security Organisation, founded
in 1954 to combat the illicit trafficking of diamonds from Africa.[44]

The odds were stacked against Sillitoe from the outset. His
relationship with his underlings in MI5 had been prickly at best. Many
within the Service had objected to his appointment as director general
in 1946. Sillitoe had been invited to apply for the post by the Home
Secretary, Herbert Morrison, even though Guy Liddell, MI5's leading
expert on subversive Bolshevik activities in Britain, was the favoured
candidate among intelligence staff. As a mere 'plod' from humble
beginnings, Sillitoe lacked the Establishment background of his peers
and was viewed as an 'outsider'. In the high season of Russian espionage, MI5's old guard believed, the last thing the Service needed was
someone who had earned his spurs cracking down on Glasgow's gang
culture. During his time as director general, moreover, Sillitoe had
hardly endeared himself to MI5's cynical clique, being often heard
complaining about the Service's 'book-learned intellectuals'.[45] Senior
mandarins instinctively opposed Sillitoe's memoir. Sir Edward Bridges,
Permanent Secretary to the Treasury and archetypal mandarin, and
Sir Frank Newsam, Permanent Secretary to the Home Office, each
drew up a comprehensive list of objections.[46] Submitted to ministers
in November 1952, the list emphasised that any discussion of MI5, as
well as raising a host of undesirable questions about objects, methods
and procedures, would represent an unparalleled departure from the
rule that officers in MI5 and comparable organisations should remain
both anonymous and entirely silent in public. Newsam explained that
he had been brought up to deny the existence of MI5 and for a long
time had never known its address or entered its sacred portals.[47]
Bridges and Newsam also questioned the desirability of a director
general publicly embarking upon an anti-communist crusade: 'It is no
business of Sillitoe to set up as one who can expound on these topics
with authority.'[48]

Fortunately for Sillitoe, ministers did not share Whitehall's antipathy to the project. The Conservative Home Secretary, David Maxwell Fyfe, considered Bridges and Newsam to be unnecessarily bloody-minded in their unwavering devotion to total secrecy. Fyfe was also attracted by the idea of showing off – 'in broad outline' – MI5's recent achievements. In consequence, he instructed Bridges to give Sillitoe unprecedented freedom to 'round off his book'.[49] Moreover, the soon-to-be-retired Director General was permitted to visit Britain's leading public schools, where he would lecture high-fliers about the treachery of Burgess and Maclean and about the dangers of 'getting muddled up with silly Communist societies at University'.[50]

After stepping down as Director General in 1953, Sillitoe spent the remainder of the year writing, before submitting the whole work that winter. As the manuscript was circulated between departments, on 22 November the *Sunday Times* suddenly began serialising extracts.[51] Sillitoe's successor, Sir Dick White, was appalled. White had never liked Sillitoe, considering him an 'empty-headed character' who 'loved playing to the gallery'.[52] The premature disclosure confirmed this opinion. The contents of the extracts did nothing to lift White's spirits. Contrary to Sillitoe's earlier guarantee of using the memoir as a vehicle for MI5 propaganda, the material in *The Times* had focused solely on failures. 'An unjustified slur,' was White's assessment of Sillitoe's claim that 'MI5 had been badly taken in over Klaus Fuchs,' ignoring compelling evidence of the scientist's communist sympathies as far back as 1942.[53] Sillitoe, protested White, had no relation to MI5 at that time. In Parliament, moreover, on 6 March 1950 the prime minister, Clement Attlee, had publicly defended MI5 against charges of slackness, pointing out that scientists of the highest quality had been in short supply and a decision had been taken to overlook Fuchs's character flaws for the sake of the atom bomb. White was also angry at Sillitoe's apparent contempt for his former employer. The first serialisation underlined that Sillitoe did not see his appointment as Director-General as fulfilling a lifetime ambition. It explained that he had become so disenchanted with the organisation that he could not wait to leave. There were, he felt, too many dubious customs for any normal person's liking, not least 'excessive secrecy' and the inclination of staff to work in 'withdrawn isolation'. For a dyed-in-the-wool intelligence man like White, such statements were simply in bad taste.

The revelations in *The Times* prompted White to oversee personally the book's vetting. His chief concern was to delete, in its entirety, Chapter 18 – 'The Case of Dr Klaus Fuchs'.[54] Many passages were difficult to square with Attlee's parliamentary denial of MI5 incompetence. Chapter 18's most troublesome statement was: 'I would not dream of denying that MI5 were mistaken about Fuchs, and that it would have been much more laudable had the Department been able to establish – or even to suspect – in 1942 instead of in 1949 that Fuchs was passing information to the Russians.'[55] Was it really in the public interest to have MI5 hauled over the coals? Chapter 18 also had the potential to 'reopen old controversies' with the FBI – 'relations with whom', to quote White, '[were] difficult enough to conduct in normal circumstances'.[56] Sillitoe had described how the FBI had derided British officials for declining to extradite Fuchs to the US. He also revealed how the FBI Director, J. Edgar Hoover (known for his 'extraordinary sensitivity to criticism'),[57] had bullishly sought permission to interrogate Fuchs before the physicist's trial, a practice forbidden by British law.[58] Sillitoe had no time for White's complaints. Come hell or high water Chapter 18 would not be deleted: 'I do not see any reason based on national security or the public interest why I should be muzzled in these matters.'[59] Pinning his argument on past precedents, Sillitoe found it deplorable that while his 'poor and humble efforts' were seen as seditious, Winston Churchill in his memoirs had seemingly been given the freedom to do as he pleased.[60]

Officials were shocked by Sillitoe's decision to play hardball. The chief concern was that the memoir would set a new benchmark for what might be discussed in the public domain. According to Bridges, 'its publication will make it infinitely harder to deal with others in the public service who may wish to embark on undesirable publicity'.[61] By the mid 1950s, the pace of erosion of secrecy had quickened beyond Whitehall's control. As discussed, the colourful life story of Eddie Chapman had been published, much to the chagrin of the authorities and in spite of what one member of the government described as a 'Roman Circus' of official attempts to suppress it.[62] More recently, Richard Pape, a former RAF navigator, had elicited sulphurous ruminations from the JIC by publishing *Boldness Be My Friend* (1953).[63] Detailing the activities of MI9, Britain's wartime Evasion and Escape Organisation, Pape's memoir had made several damaging disclosures. According to the JIC, Pape's disclosure that MI9 had communicated with prisoners by means of parcels containing private codes not only diminished the likelihood of using such methods again, but might cause a future detaining power to refuse the repatriation of the sick and wounded.[64] The revelation that certain humanitarian bodies, such as the Red Cross, had assisted prisoner escapes could prevent visits in a future war.

The big fear in Whitehall was the detrimental impact that Sillitoe's memoir would have on the state's ability to control SOE publications. A new breed of SOE book was starting to appear on the horizon, turning its attention to the organisation's French (F) Section and accusations about penetration of networks by the Germans. In the Cabinet Secretary's in-tray sat the drafts of Jean Overton Fuller's *Born for Sacrifice*, R. J. Minney's *Carve Her Name with Pride* and Elizabeth Nicholas's *Death Be Not Proud*. All of these were likely to give the intelligence community a bloody nose. At the centre of these accounts was the controversial tale of the collapse of the Paris-based PROSPER network. In June 1943, several members of PROSPER had been parachuted into France and arrested by the Sicherheitsdienst (SD); they would later be tortured and executed by the Germans. For Fuller et al., the network had to have been compromised by an SOE double agent, the most likely offender being Henri Déricourt, a former pilot whose job had been to find landing grounds and to arrange receptions for SOE agents arriving by air. (To this day, doubt remains as to whether Déricourt was a traitor, or whether in fact he was working under MI6/SOE instructions, tasked to sacrifice agents to distract German attention from Allied D-Day plans.)[65] In Whitehall, it became axiomatic that, to have any hope of preventing the PROSPER story from breaking, Sillitoe had to be stopped from making too much fanfare about his time in MI5.

Throughout 1954, Sillitoe continued to rile officials by releasing extracts to the press. Articles were replete with matters not for public airing, including the claim that in 1952 the police had arrested the KGB spy Pavel Kuznetsov despite 'knowing perfectly well' that he was the incumbent Second Secretary at the Soviet embassy and therefore entitled to diplomatic immunity.[66] By early 1955, it had become obvious that the memoir could not be stopped. Despite being a pariah in the intelligence world, Sillitoe still had friends in high places and, like Churchill, was convinced that his standing as an eminent crown servant would scare off the state prosecutor and thus force a crossing of the

Rubicon into print. The fact that Attlee had publicly declared his support of the book, to be published under the name *Cloak without Dagger*, even writing a foreword, meant that officials had little choice but to approve its publication. The last thing anyone in Whitehall wanted was a very public scrap with a former prime minister.

In spring 1955, therefore, Sillitoe broke new ground by becoming the first intelligence chief to publish a memoir. He did this knowing full well that it would leave him bereft of friends in MI5. In certain respects, Whitehall had the last laugh. Many years later Sillitoe, by then a sweetshop proprietor in Eastbourne, revealed that MI5 had secretly emasculated the work *after* he had sent the 'final' version to the printer. '[They] tore the guts out of the book,' he lamented.[67] While this may or may not have been the case (regrettably the version to which Sillitoe refers has not been declassified), one cannot underestimate the significance of the text. It is easy to forget – such is the evanescence of novelty – that publication of Sillitoe's memoir was a sensation. In 1945, few could have foreseen a czar of MI5 spilling the beans. Indeed, few people outside government would have even known the director general's name. Although Sillitoe clearly felt aggrieved that MI5 had mischievously deleted things when his back was turned, *Cloak without Dagger* still had entire chapters dedicated to secret service work. The accusation that 'MI5 was mistaken about Fuchs' was not removed. The FBI's desire to pump Fuchs for information is clearly documented, as is the implication that Scotland Yard had knowingly arrested Kuznetsov contrary to the rules of diplomatic privilege. Such revelations were duly noted by other authors, setting in motion a chain of events that would lead to *SOE in France*.

*   *   *

> I must say the more I see of Foot, the more I think he was a very good choice: he has not let his historical zeal obscure the political difficulties of publishing a work of this sort.
> *Peter Wilkinson, Permanent Undersecretary's Department at the Foreign Office, 24 January 1962*[68]

In the wake of *Cloak without Dagger*, it became impossible to stop books about PROSPER from being published. All that could be done, lamented the Cabinet Secretary, Norman Brook, was to present the author in question with 'faintly discouraging remarks'.[69] The revelation that certain female agents had been betrayed gripped Parliament.

The cause of these women was picked up principally by the MP Irene Ward. A lifelong campaigner for women's rights, notorious for wearing loud jewellery and large hats which mirrored her bulldog personality, Ward had befriended many people in SOE. On 22 February 1956, she announced in the House that the time had come for the government to authorise an official history of the organisation.[70] By late 1958, she was regularly writing to senior ministers such as Selwyn Lloyd (Foreign Secretary), calling on them to answer what she viewed as 'an outstanding question' concerning the purported duplicity of Déricourt.[71] Her lobbying intensified following the publication of Buckmaster's *They Fought Alone* (1958), which claimed that many agents in Holland had been picked up and executed because the Dutch Réseaux had been successfully penetrated. Buckmaster had also hinted that the circumstances surrounding the deaths of some agents had been deliberately kept from their next of kin.[72] Incensed by Buckmaster's book – 'it just got my goat' – and determined to do justice to those who had been sacrificed, in October Ward tabled a parliamentary motion for a 'full and frank' investigation.[73] Ministers were slightly bemused by Ward's actions – a sign that they too perhaps did not know the full truth about PROSPER. 'She thinks that there is some sort of conspiracy of silence among officials,' reported Selwyn Lloyd, 'a desire to hush-up SOE's mistakes while publicising its successes.'[74]

During November and December, Ward and Buckmaster had a slanging match in the press.[75] The prime minister, Harold Macmillan, who adhered to the school of thought that believed to talk about intelligence was bad form, was appalled. Mindful of what the protagonists would do next (Ward had written to Lloyd asserting, 'unless somebody is going to play straight with me, I have every intention of raising the question of the Secret Service in the House'),[76] Macmillan grudgingly formed an inquiry. The conclusion of that inquiry was that 'striking successes [had been] balanced with disastrous failures', although none of those failings had come about as a result of wilful negligence by senior SOE personnel.[77] 'Wars are invariably full of muddle, confusion and human fallibility,' was the overriding message of the ensuing report.[78] Crucially, the inquiry felt that the possibility of an official history should, at the very least, be examined. On 17 March 1959, therefore, John Profumo, the Parliamentary Undersecretary of State at the Foreign Office, endorsed the creation of a working party to consider the matter.

Burke Trend, who handled secret service accounts for the Treasury in the 1950s, was deputed to chair the working party. SOE was represented by some of its most prominent members, including Gubbins and Brigadier Robin Brook, who had directed operations in France and the Low Countries. At the first meeting it was emphasised that the lobbying of Ward should have no bearing whatsoever on the final decision. 'If it were only a question of her, we could probably turn the proposal for an SOE history down flat and ride out [the] trouble,' explained Patrick Dean, Deputy Undersecretary at the Foreign Office.[79] Nor was the decision to be overly influenced by the insults and accusations currently circulating in public discourse.[80] According to the working party, the merits of an official history were threefold. First, it would meet the pressure in 'responsible academic circles' for an authentic account. Second, it would place SOE's contribution in 'its proper place and perspective' against the general background of the war. And, third, it would remind Britain's allies of the indispensible support which the country had given to indigenous resistance movements.[81] In the 1950s, thanks to blockbusters such as *Captain Carey USA* and bestselling memoirs like *The OSS and I* by William J. Morgan, the Americans had continued to appropriate wartime special operations and thus fashion a very one-sided view of Allied support to the Resistance. It was now also clear that the communists were doing the same. In their writings, Soviet and Satellite historians had been spreading the view that successes in the field had been the result of either national efforts or communist initiatives. Against this background, it was agreed that an official history was 'desirable'.

But was it feasible? A big sticking point was the question of which department would fund the enterprise. The Cabinet Office, which was bankrolling the mainstream official war history programme, the costs of which were spiralling out of control, wanted the financial burden to be borne by the Foreign Office. Edward Hale, Cabinet Office Historical Section, underlined that the 'pressure to write this history comes from the Foreign Office'; as such he felt that it was wrong for any other department to defray the cost.[82] Equally delicate was the issue of how the history would pass over certain subjects without arousing the suspicion or contempt of 'informed' readers. As far as violations of neutrality and actions performed 'contrary to the rules of war' were concerned, the expectation was the same as it had been in September 1945; such things should 'NEVER be published'. Any history, it was feared, was bound to associate certain failures with certain individuals, 'in particular the breakdown and penetration by the enemy of resistance organisations through treachery or weakness under interrogation'.[83] In the view of F. A. Bishop, Deputy Secretary to the Cabinet, there was a strong possibility that the work would stimulate, rather than dispose of, the bitter public debate about PROSPER.[84] A further problem was deciding on the structure of the history, and another was to settle on a possible author. One option was to resurrect the existing in-house SOE history, written in 1945 by Professor William Mackenzie (the wartime head of the Air Council Secretariat), and make it fit for public consumption. Mackenzie did not – as some scholars have claimed – 'argue vigorously for this'.[85] When invited by the working party to give his opinion on the subject, Mackenzie said that removing high-level source material would be a painstaking task, and would render the narrative unreadable.[86] Another option was to start from scratch by authorising a 'pilot project' addressing a single region of SOE activity. France was believed to be the most sensible choice, because 'it posed the most acute problems of treatment, both on account of the complexity of the operations involved and the delicacy of the political background'.[87]

In May 1960, the Foreign Office approved the French option, albeit without giving any guarantee of its publication.[88] 'The more we think about it,' Dean wrote, 'the more we are forced to the conclusion that the only way to discover whether one can be written is to try and write it.'[89] Edward Heath, Lord Privy Seal, duly informed Ward that a 'trial run' was now in hand. As a quid pro quo for keeping her abreast of the history's progress, Heath asked Ward if she 'could forbear from prodding us about it in public'.[90] He concluded his letter to her with the rider: 'For your information – nobody outside this Office, the Cabinet Office and the Treasury is being told of this.'[91] To avoid accusations of bias, the task was not given to a serving member of government, but to an independent historian from Oxford, M. R. D. Foot (Figure 23), for the fee of £1,800 per year plus a £300 completion bonus.[92] As a former intelligence officer with the Special Air Service, and having worked closely with the French Resistance after D-Day, Foot had a good grounding in the subject. Moreover, his ideas and beliefs were traditional – something that made him *persona grata* with potentially nervous government departments.[93] Foot was provided with an office in government premises in London. He was given access to SOE files, chronologies and Section Histories, including Mackenzie's secret narrative (though he was required to read secret documents in a telephoneless locked room in a basement).[94] Permission to interview all but a few participants was denied. Those with strong partisan views, such as Buckmaster and other senior members of F Section, were 'off-limits' on the grounds that, were Foot to consult such figures, it would lay the government open to the charge that it had sponsored a one-sided version of events.[95] Foot was also refused permission to visit French archives, a decision the author found baffling, since access to French sources would have done much to allay local suspicion.[96] The history, moreover, would be written on the 'understanding that there had never been such a body as SIS'.

While Foot turned to the job at hand, Whitehall had to deal with yet more troublesome exposé merchants. Generally, officials had greater success suppressing the works of 'outsiders' than of 'insiders', mainly because the former felt more vulnerable to the threat of prosecution. For example, between early 1961 and late 1962 an independent filmmaker, Fred Feldcamp, repeatedly sought approval for a UK-funded film based on the exploits of Eddie Chapman. Richard Burton, one of Britain's great actors, had been provisionally cast for the title role. Feldcamp had the backing of Dame Patricia Hornsby-Smith, MP for Chislehurst. From 1941 to 1945, Hornsby-Smith had served in the Ministry of Economic Warfare, the department with overall responsibility for SOE. After the war, she had maintained her affiliation with SOE by joining the Special Forces Club.[97] As she saw it, the film would reflect favourably upon the skill of British intelligence; to ban it, moreover, would run the risk of Hollywood gazumping Feldcamp with an 'exaggerated Americanised version over which the War Office will have no control'.[98] Rumour had it that Twentieth Century Fox and Paramount Pictures were battling it out to secure the screen rights and make the Chapman story using American actors and an all-American lead.[99] Although officials were not in principle against the idea of showcasing British wartime efforts, the timing of the film made them nervous. For much of 1961 and 1962, the prime minister had forbidden Fleet Street from reporting the George Blake scandal, despite front-page treatment in the foreign press. Should ministers acquiesce to the film, journalists would condemn the hypocrisy. In consequence, the D-Notice Secretary, George Thomson, threatened Feldcamp with the 'full armoury of the Official Secrets Act' and informed him that if he persisted in making the film, he would do so at his 'peril'.[100] The filmmaker was even told by a legal spokesman for MI5 that the movie would be made 'over my dead body'.[101] With this, Feldcamp conceded defeat.

When it came to 'insiders', however, Whitehall was increasingly powerless to do anything. Perhaps the best illustration of this was the publication of Montgomery Hyde's *The Quiet Canadian* (1962).[102] During the war, Hyde had been involved in counter-espionage work in the United States under Sir William Stephenson, the Canadian controller of the British Security Co-ordination (BSC). With its headquarters in the Rockefeller Center in New York, the BSC was an umbrella organisation tasked with representing the interests of British secret services throughout North and South America. Hyde, colloquially known as 'Little Bill', had refused to submit the manuscript for security clearance. His book was about a Canadian, not a Briton, and had been written with the aid of non-official sources.[103] On the eve of its publication, a panicked meeting was held in Whitehall, with attendance from the Chairman of the JIC and the Head of SIS. As they saw it, the book's damage spread in three directions. First, it referred to SIS as an existing organisation and, contrary to custom, named its wartime head, Major-General Sir Stewart Menzies. Second, it exposed the late Admiral Lais as the Italian naval attaché in Washington whom a female agent had seduced into parting with his government's naval code. And third, it left a general, but misleading, impression that the British state had relaxed rules about intelligence disclosures.[104] Despite these concerns, it was agreed *not* to initiate legal action. Part of the reason for this was the fact that Hyde had received help from at least one former SIS officer. Were Hyde taken to court, government lawyers believed, a judge might well interpret his relationship with the officer as SIS giving its blessing. A further problem was that Stephenson had never been remunerated by SIS for his time as BSC head. In consequence, his relationship with HMG was 'tenuous and difficult to define'.[105] Moreover, Hyde's dealings with Stephenson had all been conducted in America, and thus outside the jurisdiction of English law.

The Quiet Canadian warranted massive media interest, principally because it was one of the first books to discuss SIS. The *New York Times* book review asserted that the biography was 'to the literature of espionage what Lady Chatterley's Lover was to belles-lettres'.[106] Ian Fleming, reviewing the book for the *Sunday Times*, astutely commented that it would 'cause a shudder to run down the spines of many members of the clubs and local hunts'.[107] As officials had feared, those with a beef against the injustice of the state censor found it baffling that Hyde had escaped prosecution for what was a major breach of the rules. On 8 November 1962, Ward went to the House declaring double standards: 'Why do some people feel that they must adhere to the Official Secrets Act and others that they need not do so? It is a most terrible muddle.'[108] In a bid to prevent further embarrassing outbursts by Ward, Macmillan invited her to Downing Street. There, he passed off the episode as the result of a 'regrettable misunderstanding', the consequence of Hyde believing he had clearance, when in fact he did not.[109] Common sense told Ward that Macmillan was being untruthful. Hyde, she replied, 'was never under misapprehension and knew exactly what he was doing'.[110] Fortunately for the government, Ward eventually cooled off – comforted by the fact that Foot's history was at least under way.

The importance of staking SOE's claim to ownership of resistance was brought into renewed focus in early 1961. Interest in resistance history was such that academic conferences on the subject were now being held. The most prestigious of these was held in Milan in March. In advance of the conference, fearing that communist historians would use the occasion to disseminate propaganda, the Foreign Office asked William Deakin, Warden of St Antony's College, Oxford, if he would give a paper advancing the 'official' British perspective. Deakin was a natural choice; he had enjoyed a highly meritorious war career with SOE and, as Churchill's principal research assistant in the writing of his memoirs, was well accustomed to using 'history' to trumpet the British point of view. Deakin was only too happy to assume the role of literary cold warrior and, for this purpose, was given access to official records.[111] Brigadier Barry, a former SOE officer, was allowed to do the same for the Liège symposium in 1959.

The Milan conference did not go well. Western scholars were outnumbered by Soviet and Satellite historians, most of whom had been 'exceptionally well briefed'.[112] Many had 'come armed with detailed material' about SOE mistakes. Presentations by the Eastern Bloc argued that the Resistance was a communist-led 'social movement' which ensured that 'anti-popular and reactionary' regimes did not return after liberation to exploit the workers. According to communist scholars, Anglo-American support for the Resistance was strictly self-serving: its principal purpose was not to help in the defeat of the Axis forces – for this was already being realised in any event by the military might of the advancing Red Armies – but to establish Western economic and political hegemony in a post-war Europe. Eastern Bloc speakers also alleged that the 'phoney war' of 1939–40 was a deliberate British continuation of the 'spirit of Munich', designed to channel German aggression against the USSR and thus lessen the chance of an invasion of Britain.[113] 'Double-think' delivered in 'newspeak' was the Western delegation's assessment of the communist presentations.[114] In his report to the Foreign Office, Deakin wrote: 'The [conference] made it clear ... that a deliberate and coordinated attempt is being made on the Soviet and Satellite side to denigrate and distort the British position in relation to occupied Europe during the Second World War, and that the intrinsic purpose of this operation is to capture exclusively for the Russians the myth of European Resistance.'[115] The Americans were similarly appalled by events in Milan. Sherman Kent, head of the CIA's Office of National Estimates, lamented that it was 'just a sample of what they [the Russians] were spewing out in their official histories and papers and books'.[116] For Kent, Soviet historiography had to be countered: 'The West cannot leave the history of the war and the Resistance to the Communists. A true historical picture must be drawn, and it must get circulation behind the Iron Curtain and in the uncommitted nations of the world. From the standpoint of the Milan Conference, this is the unfinished business of the West.'[117]

Thankfully, Foot's history was not far off completion. By spring 1963, the Cabinet Secretary had started to send out individual draft chapters for vetting. By late 1964, the entire work was doing the rounds in Whitehall. Officials had not anticipated any major problems. Peter Wilkinson, a former SOE officer who went on to work with the Permanent Undersecretary's Department in the Foreign Office, had earlier remarked: 'I must say the more I see of Foot, the more I think he was a very good choice. He has not let his historical zeal obscure the political difficulties of publishing a work of this sort.'[118] The first person to offer his views on the draft was Captain Norman Mott, 'a much liked, laconic pipe-smoker' who during the war had overseen the security arrangements for SOE Headquarters in London.[119] Mott suggested that Foot had done a 'remarkably good job', putting SOE's activities into proper perspective and correcting the patchy, unbalanced and in part fictionally embellished picture that had emerged from unofficial writings over the previous decade or so.[120] Foot, he continued, had stated only the 'incontrovertible and established facts' and had neither 'trod unnecessarily hard on French toes' nor said anything about the *amour propre* of the fighting French that had not been said before.[121] Professor James Butler, editor of the UK Military Series of the *History of the Second World War*, considered it a 'brilliant piece of work'.[122]

Yet positive feedback was in short supply. Lieutenant-Colonel Eddie Boxshall, whose job as SOE Adviser was to assist on matters connected with the disclosure of information, felt that there were far too many comments belittling the French Resistance. Foot had stated that 'Gaullists seemed unable to understand what security meant' and referred to the 'notorious French carelessness of security'.[123] At one point in the text, he had claimed that 'the British never passed a secret to the French except in dire necessity'.[124] Gubbins, with one eye on anything that could result in libel or injurious falsehood actions, was more alarmed by the gratuitous statements about individuals. Criticism of the 'Réseaux Buck' (Buck networks) was deemed far too personal. Describing the moment when officials decided that executed agent Jack Agazarian would not receive any decorations, Foot had painted the picture of George Starr, head of the Wheelwright network in southern France, sitting back contentedly 'stroking his silky moustache'.[125] Wilkinson too – despite his earlier assessment that Foot was a safe pair of hands – was shocked by some of the draft's contents. There were, he complained, many 'objectionable passages' detailing the rivalry between SOE, SIS and the Foreign Office. Such passages were deeply unedifying and would definitely be 'picked up by the sensational press'.[126]

Foot's history was thrown into further doubt with the reaction of Maurice Buckmaster. Buckmaster abhorred the draft's 'flippant tone', especially its description of 'events of life and death importance' to individuals.[127] Glib remarks about some of the personalities involved were deeply troubling to him. Was it not 'monstrous', he protested, that Foot labelled Arnaud – 'one of our most able wireless operators and a person of great gentleness and charm' – with the epithet 'foul-mouthed'?[128] Would this not cause unnecessary and irreparable hurt to his widowed mother? Just as upsetting to Buckmaster was the demeaning description of Denise – the first woman dropped into Occupied France – as 'sultry and attractive'.[129] Was it not deplorable, he declared, that the author had chosen not to highlight her more important qualities? The book's treatment of PROSPER caused Buckmaster great distress. Foot had attributed the collapse of the network to agent incompetence and lack of security, a verdict which in turn reflected badly on F Section recruitment, training and control.[130] Especially damaging was the allegation that one officer, Major Nicholas Bodlington, had been 'bold to the point of foolhardiness' – a state of mind which had led him to send Agazarian to his capture and death. By 1943, contended Foot, PROSPER had become too large for its bungling controllers and contained too many untrained, locally recruited agents. Heavy criticism was also dished out to agents who, after arrest and under pressure, had betrayed Resistance members or cut deals with their Nazi captors. Nothing could possibly be gained, admonished Buckmaster, from throwing the tag of 'cowardice' at the dedicated men and women who had loyally served their country. Were such opinions aired in public, there was a risk that people would refuse to sign up for intelligence work.

Buckmaster's protestations did not stop there. The draft discussed his alleged failure to write to the next of kin of agents, informing them that the person in question was known to be dead or captured. Even more sensational was the accusation that Buckmaster had sent letters to relatives saying that their loved ones were alive and well when, in fact, F Section had every reason to suspect the contrary. In his defence, Buckmaster explained that he had sent many letters to family and friends, which, on account of being handwritten, were never copied and put into SOE files.[131] Buckmaster's biggest complaint was that he, above all others, had been made out to be the bad guy: 'The book is full of cynical innuendoes, and tendentious conclusions based on a haphazard and arbitrary assessment of motives. I am made to appear irresponsible, callous, partial, inefficient, "crassly" insensitive in my optimism, and frequently mistaken in my judgment.'[132] Buckmaster was joined by Douglas Dodds-Parker in calling for Foot's account to be scrapped. A prominent Conservative backbencher with the ear of the prime minister, Dodds-Parker had written several letters arguing that the history 'MUST NOT be published'.[133] His first letter suggested that it would 'stir up a good deal of mud best left undisturbed'.[134] In particular, it might allow the non-Free French section in SOE to claim undue credit for the gallantry of their field personnel. His second letter, as well as claiming that 'every sensitive French nerve would be set on edge by the general tone', stressed the point of principle that SOE had recruited its officers on the understanding their activities would 'NEVER' be disclosed: 'When we all became involved ... we believed that our activities were covered by the Official Secrets Act, and that this was a two-way obligation.'[135]

The negative feedback received about the book greatly diminished the likelihood of it ever being published. Ministers required a sure-fire guarantee that its publication would not come back to haunt them. As it stood, the draft contained too many passages that could constitute grounds for libel actions. Government lawyers were particularly concerned about individuals exploiting a loophole in French law. In the French legal system, 'truthfulness' was not a defence when the facts to which defamation related were more than ten years old. It was essential, therefore, that changes were made to the text. Foot was initially reluctant to do this. In his eyes, he was writing an official history, yes, but not a history with an official muzzle. Moreover, personal details and the occasional anecdote added 'life-blood' to what was, at its core, a history of an organisation. His attitude was summed up in a letter to Boxshall: 'my job was to write history, on such evidence as I could get, not to inflate or deflate personalities'.[136] Buckmaster, he continued, had to be criticised for some things and was only angry because the book did 'not fit in with his own press image'.[137] Eventually, however, with the whole project hanging in the balance, Foot accepted that some revisions were necessary. He went about this in two ways: firstly, by deleting overly 'Harsh things said about SOE officers'[138] and, secondly, by building up a more benign picture of F Section that focused less on the cold unvarnished truth, and more on the successes that it had achieved in the face of extreme adversity. The end product was much more to everyone's liking. Buckmaster welcomed the inclusion of a 'firm statement' emphasising that incorrect decisions had never been the consequence of deliberate Machiavellianism, but of genuine, if occasionally misplaced, enthusiasm. He was also 'delighted' by the indisputable conclusion to which the history now led that F Section, despite all its errors, was instrumental in achieving results far beyond those which its originators could have wished for.[139]

On 6 April 1964, subject to Foot completing the revisions discussed, *SOE in France* was given ministerial approval.[140] A week later, this decision was announced in Parliament by Peter Thomas, Minister of State for Foreign Affairs. As the prime minister saw it, the arguments in favour of publication were threefold. Firstly, it would enable justice to be done to the many agents, alive and dead, who had secretly played their part in the final Allied victory. This was the argument that the government emphasised publicly. Secondly, it would help deflect public interest away from salacious 'penny packet' publications, which, to the dismay of officials, showed no signs of halting. Around this time, the Foreign Office was worried about a forthcoming history of SOE by E. H. Cookridge. His previous book, *Secrets of the British Secret Service*, had manufactured the cock-and-bull story that he had been a confidant of George Blake for eighteen years.[141] His publisher had also refused to replace the forbidden expression 'British Secret Service' with the more nebulous phrase 'British Intelligence authorities'.[142] The final reason to publish *SOE in France* was that it would counter the 'determined attempt by some countries to demonstrate that successes in the [Resistance] field . . . owed little to British help'.[143]

Ward was 'thrilled to bits' – delighted that recognition would finally be given to SOE's unsung heroes and heroines.[144] So secret had Foot's history been, it came as a total surprise to many of the Oxford don's colleagues and friends. In his academic activities (teaching, conferences etc.), he had not told a soul of his 'official' employment, always maintaining that SOE was of purely personal interest to him on account of his wartime experiences. Behind the scenes, officials had been concerned that Foot might let something slip or that one of his co-workers would raise questions about his extended stays in London, not to mention his apparent lack of research activity over a three-year period.[145] The magnitude of the government's decision to reverse its policy of secrecy with respect to SOE was not lost on the press. Headlines such as 'Frozen Secrets Start to Thaw' were accompanied by excited commentaries on how the book would represent a landmark moment in the breaking down of government secrecy.[146] After its publication, journalists stressed gleefully, it would be open season for researching and writing about British intelligence. However, officials had different ideas.

* * *

I am afraid there will be a lot of red faces when it comes out though mine will probably be the reddest.

M. R. D. Foot, 17 April 1964[147]

Every once in a while a book comes along that assumes classic status almost from the day of publication, receiving generally positive reviews, impressive if not spectacular sales, and an ever-widening circle of appreciation for its considerable merits. Published by HMSO in 1966, *SOE in France* was that kind of book. Historians greeted Foot's history with hosannas of praise. Stephen Ambrose, the esteemed official biographer of Dwight D. Eisenhower, called it 'the best-written and best-organized book that I have read in a decade'.[148] The press lauded the history as being fair and just, dismissing any notion that Foot had sacrificed historical accuracy for the sake of government sensibilities. Reviewers were astonished that Foot had done such a good job given that he had been largely unable to double-check his facts with SOE personnel. As an attempt to reclaim for Britain some of the credit for the support of the Resistance, *SOE in France* was an unqualified success. From reading the book, Ambrose drew the conclusion: 'It remains to say that America's OSS was nowhere near as good as SOE.'[149] Reviewing the book for the CIA's classified journal *Studies in Intelligence*, John Bross felt compelled to ask, 'where were the Yanks?'[150] Foot had suggested that the OSS – poorly trained, inadequately equipped and lacking experience – had had only a 'small' influence until the summer of 1944. Bross rejected this as British propaganda. Between 1 January and 1 October 1944, he protested, 524 Americans had served in France behind enemy lines, while American aircraft assigned to joint OSS/SOE operations had flown 2,717 sorties. Moreover, in the first nine months of 1944, some 5,000 tons of American-packed equipment had been sent to the field – nearly twice as much as that dispatched by Britain.[151]

Ostensibly, therefore, Foot's history had achieved what it set out to do. It provided an authoritative account of the support which Britain had given to the French Resistance and, most important, countered glaringly lopsided interpretations propagated by American and Soviet historiographies. Accordingly, it vindicated Whitehall's decision to relent on its long-standing policy of secrecy with respect to intelligence. However, as officials had cautioned as far back as autumn 1945, to bring SOE out of the shadows was a big step into the unknown. The decision to reveal the identity of individuals was, in hindsight, a big mistake. Major-General Laurence Grand, former Head of Section D of SIS (formed in 1938 to coordinate sabotage and subversion behind enemy lines in the event of war but amalgamated in 1940 into SOE), was scandalised by the failure to use pseudonyms: 'He [Foot] has gone beyond the proper role of a historian.'[152] As the director of an international engineering firm, Grand was concerned that disclosure of his wartime duties would hinder his peacetime occupation: 'No one [will] believe that I have long since been clear from such activities; this may cost several millions of exports.'[153] Amazingly, despite fastidious prior inspection by officials, Foot's history retained some rather caustic comments about individuals. French reviewers, such as *Nouvel Observateur*, were not amused by the painting of certain French Resistance fighters as gossipers. Foot's assertion that all new recruits had drummed into them a golden rule – never entrust a secret to the French except in dire necessity – generated fevered comment in the Gallic press.[154] Foot's taste for underhand remarks brought a string of libel suits from former SOE officers – luckily for him, paid for by the state. Odette Sansom was outraged by the book's suggestion that she had lived a life of luxury on SOE funds. Foot's retelling of her interrogation at the hands of the Gestapo was vastly different from how she remembered it. Foot had scoffed at the idea that her interrogators had removed her toenails, proposing that the episode was most likely a figment of her imagination. He had also sensationally suggested that she had returned from France 'non-composmentis' in a 'state of nervous tension so severe that she had considerable trouble in distinguishing fantasy and reality'.[155] 'The book leaves not a shadow of a doubt that its author and sponsors regard her as unworthy of the George Cross,' charged Odette's solicitors. Peter Churchill initiated legal action for what he considered a litany of slanderous comments. The book, for example, had claimed that 'neither patience nor diplomacy was his long suit' and alleged that he had a 'careless habit of keeping old [deciphered] messages'.[156] A third person to take legal action was Rubeigh Minney, author of *Carve Her Name with Pride*, a biography of SOE heroine Violette Szabo. Foot had labelled Minney a 'sensationmonger' and proposed that he had used his 'prurient imagination', especially with regard to Szabo's purported torture, to boost book sales.[157] Shamefaced, HMSO was required to arrange expensive out-of-court settlements. Churchill and Minney each received £5,000 in damages. Foot made a full apology to Odette in the press, and promised to remove the offending passages from any future editions.[158]

From the outset, *SOE in France* had been regarded as a 'pilot project', potentially paving the way for further histories dealing with other countries. The fallout from Foot's history, however, gave departments cold feet. In May 1967, representatives from the Foreign Office,

Cabinet Office and SIS ruled out the possibility of additional volumes, claiming that, while *SOE in France* had been 'profitable historically', it had proved 'embarrassing politically'.[159] Moreover, although the book had been a best-seller, legal action and other costs had resulted in a net loss of £42,885.[160] Whitehall's reluctance to see any more of the SOE story revealed was underlined by the decision, in January 1967, to refuse Greek official historians access to SOE files. This decision was also influenced by the fear that Greek scholars would discover details of Britain's controversial buttressing of right-wing resistance organisations, such as the National Republican Greek League (EDES), against communist forces.[161]

By early 1968, the mood in Whitehall had changed again, this time *in favour* of further SOE accounts. The catalyst for a rethink was the explosion of press interest in Kim Philby. As discussed in previous chapters, in November 1967 the *Sunday Times* ran a series of articles showing how British intelligence had been nullified in the years after 1945 by traitors in its entrails. By propagating the view that the Secret Service was either dud or distasteful, press reports set new standards for what might be revealed publicly and convinced many officials, including old hands like John Masterman, that something had to be done to combat this negative publicity. In Parliament, moreover, a number of backbenchers could be heard asking how it was that further SOE histories were forbidden, when so much was now known about SIS in the early Cold War. Against this background, Trend asked Dame Barbara Salt – a former SOE Head in Tangier – to produce a detailed report outlining the pros and cons of further volumes. Her report, completed in July 1969, started off by looking at the question of authorship. One option the report mulled over was to give 'a few handpicked historians' access to the archives – albeit with 'strict safeguards' – and encourage them to publish through commercial channels.[162] Advantageously, this would reduce the cost to HMG and remove the likelihood of legal comeback. Salt nevertheless considered this unworkable. Allegations of favouritism would be impossible to refute; the state would find itself in what she described as a 'historical beargarden'.[163]

According to Salt, a single history, as with Foot, focusing on one region of SOE activity involved far less risk of legal action than a series of volumes. Moreover, a single volume would be significantly cheaper. So what subjects were considered? A history of SOE's operations in the Netherlands had the advantage of being the least likely to cause controversy. After the war, a Dutch Parliamentary Commission had published a lot of evidence on the so-called Nordpol Affair, the penetration of SOE in Holland by the Abwehr. A volume on Italy was possible because Italian operations represented an 'undoubted success story'.[164] They reduced Allied casualties in the final offensive of April 1945 to almost negligible proportions; they safeguarded economic patrimony concentrated in the Po basin and Alpine Valley; and they paved the way for the Allied policy of counter-scorch. Salt also believed that a study of Italy would incorporate the most entertaining material. There was SOE's role in Operation Monkey, the negotiations for the Italian Armistice in September 1943. The success of Monkey had depended, in large part, on the wireless communications of radio operator Lieutenant Mallaby, who only months earlier had been parachuted accidentally into a lake near Milan, been taken captive and then released at British request. Had it not been for Mallaby establishing a secret radio link between Eisenhower and Marshall Badoglio (Mussolini's heir apparent), the armistice might not have happened, or would have been delayed. As well as rectifying the strange absence of the Asiatic arena from the existing literature on SOE, a volume on the Far East would do much to spread what Lord Mountbatten called the 'new spirit of Empire'. SOE had fought with indigenous populations as 'brothers', recognising that one day they would achieve independence from the colonial oppressor.[165]

Generally speaking, however, Salt's report was against the idea of further histories. One of the key reasons for sponsoring *SOE in France* had been to arrogate for Britain some of the credit for partisan activities in Europe. As she saw it, this particular East–West political battle had now been won. Salt doubted whether in fact a demand for further volumes existed. Notwithstanding an innate professional preference for 'more history rather than less', historians consulted were of the opinion that a saturation point had been reached for SOE books.[166] Although there was still a vogue for spy stories – especially among 'would-be Ian Flemings' – the recent publicity afforded to Philby had arguably diverted public interest into more 'up-to-date channels'.[167] By the time a second SOE history could be published, lamented Salt, Whitehall might well have missed the boat. Writers like Cookridge were already 'scooping the market'; M. R. D. Foot had even signed a contract with Macmillan Publishers to produce a general history of SOE's war. Finding a historian of proven calibre, rather than an 'up-and-coming man' or someone nearing retirement, presented a big problem. In Salt's eyes, there was no obvious successor to Foot. A further complication was the depressing state of the SOE archive. SOE's liquidation after the war had been accompanied by the wholesale and indiscriminate destruction of records, carried out by a motley crew of happy-go-lucky clerks 'not adequately briefed for task'.[168] In 1946, a mysterious fire at the organisation's London HQ in Baker Street had destroyed many administrative and financial records. 'The surviving material is, to put it mildly, patchy,' was Foot's assessment.[169] Before any further histories could be commissioned, some poor soul would need to spend a considerable amount of time sorting and cataloguing the material. Such a task was complicated by the fact that many records had become muddled up with 'current secret intelligence files from which they could not be separated'.[170] There were, moreover, certain things that could still not be disclosed. Most sensitive were the Pickaxe operations. Pickaxe involved dropping more than twenty communist secret police (NKVD) agents behind enemy lines and has since been treated by historians as an example of SOE 'dealing with the devil'.[171]

Salt's report was considered at a meeting of senior intelligence staff on 12 September 1969. Here the decision was taken to postpone plans for further SOE histories. The legal debacle resulting from Foot's account had made this verdict inevitable. Indeed, the minutes of the meeting contained the damning statement, 'Never again should there be an official publication on the model of *SOE in France*, where trouble and expense had arisen over personalities.'[172] Perhaps more decisively, Trend – the most active campaigner for publicising secret history – was by then proposing something far more ambitious: a multi-volume official history of wartime intelligence.[173]

9 COUNTERBLAST: OFFICIAL HISTORY OF BRITISH INTELLIGENCE IN THE SECOND WORLD WAR

> There is a big difference between secrets reaching the public through journalistic or other revelations and their being presented with the authority of Her Majesty's Government.
>
> T. M. P. STEVENS, DEFENCE SECRETARIAT,
> *18 August 1972*[1]

As we have seen, the late 1960s were a traumatic time for Britain's secret keepers. In 1967, a year after attempting to establish a measure of control over journalists and private authors with *SOE in France*, officials tried but failed to stop a succession of damaging disclosures. Chapman Pincher led the way by carrying a story on clandestine government interception of international telegram traffic. The *Sunday Times* then brought revelations about Philby's thirty-year devotion to the Russian cause, before the *Daily Express* defied tradition by telling its readers the identities of the men who headed MI5 and SIS. In 1968, the exiled Philby delivered a devastating blow to his erstwhile secret bosses by publishing an intentionally misleading memoir, entitled *My Silent War*.[2] Sponsored by the KGB and published by Grove Press in New York, the book was a brutal indictment of Western intelligence operations against the Soviet Union, revealing how British and American secret services had been dogged by petty rivalries, lack of discipline and bad planning. *My Silent War*, which described SIS procedures and personnel in rich detail, contained not a spark of regret. Its author, appallingly, was pitiless in writing of those he had sent to their deaths. Philby had offered to withdraw the book if the British government agreed to release Peter and Helen Kruger, two convicted Soviet spies serving twenty-year terms in Wormwood Scrubs prison; his proposal was turned down.[3]

The state was deeply chagrined by the outpouring of sensitive material, and considerable time was spent thinking about the best future strategy for dealing with those who wanted to reveal ugly secrets. In one camp were people like George Wigg who argued that a line had to be drawn and that the government should not be afraid to use the Official Secrets Act to police that line. This crude and unsophisticated approach was famously put into effect in the 1970s when legal action was initiated firstly against *The Sunday Telegraph* and secondly against Duncan Campbell and his coadjutors. In another camp, there was a cluster of officials who believed that no matter how hard the state tried to stop the leaks, it could not stop them all. For this camp, the watchword was 'counterblast'. Instead of focusing its energies on trying to crack down on each and every irritant author or troublesome journalist, the state should devise ways of putting information of its own choosing into the public domain in order to drown out negative accounts. Put another way, these officials were of the opinion 'If you can't beat them, join them.'

The figurehead of the counterblast camp was Vice Admiral Sir Norman Denning. Denning had first made his mark as founder of the Admiralty's Operational Intelligence Centre (OIC), the hugely successful hub of British naval operations during the Second World War. After the cable vetting affair in 1967, as discussed in Chapter 4, he was appointed D-Notice Secretary, a job he held until 1972. As far back as the early 1960s, Denning had become fascinated with the idea of Whitehall becoming more proactive in managing the public profile of its secret services. As someone who had seen British intelligence at its brilliant best during the war, he was mortified by the proliferation of scandals, exposés and racy accounts. To correct public misconceptions, he championed the policy of giving discreet official assistance to trustworthy authors. Writers would be selected for their willingness to portray things in a positive light. His colleagues referred to this as the 'Denning Formula'.[4] The first author to be approached by Denning was Robert Harling. Then typographic consultant to *The Sunday Times*, Harling, had had a colourful and action-packed war. In May 1940, he was part of the flotilla that rescued British troops from Dunkirk. A year later, he was recruited by Ian Fleming, Assistant to the Director of

Naval Intelligence. Under Fleming's wing, he was part of the 30 Assault Unit, known colloquially as the 'Red Indians', an elite team of commandos that specialised in going behind enemy lines in advance of Allied troops to gather enemy documentation and equipment before it was destroyed.[5] In January 1961, Denning presented Harling with a remarkable opportunity, asking him if he would write a semi-fictional account of the unit's adventures with the aid of Admiralty records.[6] Days earlier, Fleming had vouched for his companion as an 'entirely reliable man'.[7] Sadly, Harling's workload precluded him from accepting the offer.

Undeterred, Denning bided his time until an alternative project presented itself. This arrived in 1964 when the *Sunday Times* commissioned John Pearson to write a biography of Ian Fleming, who had passed away in August of that year. Pearson knew the novelist well; in the late 1950s, he had been Fleming's assistant at the newspaper when the latter was writing the prestigious Atticus column. Denning was immediately attracted to the Fleming biography. A national treasure, Fleming was the anti- Philby, possessing many of the qualities expected of someone who worked for British intelligence. He had been patriotic, loyal, daring, and suave, and had believed fiercely in doing what was right. His career in naval intelligence had involved some memorable success stories and was a far cry from those revelations that made the secret services look like bumbling fools. Opportunistically, Denning arranged a lunch meeting with Pearson at which he proceeded to tempt the author with the carrot of semi-official support for the book. Denning's plan would involve retired intelligence officers talking to Pearson and providing him with information, in some cases on a strictly unattributable basis, which was thought to be beneficial both to Fleming's legacy and to the image of British intelligence. It was explained to Pearson that 'what must never be revealed [are] sources of intelligence, co-operation with other intelligence agencies and anything of a nature which could lead to political embarrassment'.[8]

Over the following months, Denning put Pearson in touch with a host of veterans, including Sefton Delmer, a 'black' propagandist for the PWE, and Peter Smithers, a former assistant naval attaché at the British embassy in Washington, responsible for intelligence liaison with the US Navy Department.[9] (Smithers, who knew Fleming from the war, is considered by some to be the model for the character of James Bond; indeed, when in 1957 the *Daily Express* adapted the novels as cartoon strips, Fleming advised the cartoonist to mould Bond's appearance on

Smithers.) By far the most important of Pearson's contacts was Rear Admiral John Godfrey, Fleming's demanding and quick-tempered boss as Director of Naval Intelligence. Godfrey, who is often cited as being the inspiration for 007's fictional chief 'M', was of the same mind as Denning. The intelligence community should not allow either the media or mischievous private authors to enjoy a monopoly on writing its history: 'Discriminating publicity, combined with broadminded censorship, appeal to me strongly.'[10] Pearson met Godfrey in person at the Cavendish Hotel in Eastbourne in early 1965. Here Godfrey – 'a large, pink-faced man in his early seventies' – talked in detail about the vital work of the Naval Intelligence Division (NID), also known as 'Room 39' after its room number at the Admiralty.[11] As Denning had hoped, Pearson was treated to tales of derring-do and general adventurism. Godfrey opened up about 30 Assault Unit, describing how, in advance of the Allied invasion of North Africa (Operation Torch), the commando force had ransacked the Italian headquarters in Algiers, capturing code books and enemy orders of battle. He dropped into conversation the priceless detail, subsequently disputed by scholars, that Fleming, at the request of OSS Director William Donovan, had written the charter for the formation of the CIA. According to Godfrey, Donovan was so pleased that he gave the Briton a .38 Colt revolver, inscribed with the words 'For Special Services'.[12] Pearson was not naïve enough to think that the veterans had spoken to him purely out of the goodness of their hearts. 'Everyone', he recorded in a private note, 'has too much at stake in maintaining that the Bond-world did exist at the Admiralty.'[13] Godfrey freely admitted that he wanted 'to see the department ... getting the praise it deserves'.[14] Yet Pearson could not afford to discard the material. The originality of the narrative necessitated the revelations volunteered by his secret sources. The end result – *The Life of Ian Fleming* – was a brilliantly written book, packed from stem to stern with new insights about Britain's best-loved spy writer.[15] More important, it showcased the work of Room 39, dubbed 'something of legend' by Pearson.[16]

The breaking of the Philby story gave an added edge and momentum to the idea that the secret state needed to retaliate in order to restore the reputation of the intelligence services. By early 1969, the ever-widening circle of people who favoured this approach included Burke Trend (Figure 24), the Cabinet Secretary, and Dick White, Britain's first Cabinet Office Intelligence Co-ordinator. Trend's support for 'counter-blasting' was not altogether unexpected. He had championed the case for *SOE in France*, seeing the history as an important counter to American and Soviet histories of wartime resistance. In 1963, he had argued in vain for reducing the closure period for public records from fifty to thirty years, on the grounds that the existing rule precluded British scholars from systematically addressing the history of decolonisation. 'So long as we resist,' he stated, 'the general public will base their judgements on episodes such as the transfer of power in India, the Malayan Emergency and African independence partly on memoirs, partly on histories derived from incomplete and biased material and on official histories from other countries.'[17] Dick White's conversion to counter-blaster was also not entirely surprising. In 1963, he had been hugely impressed by the CIA's decision to let its fabled director Allen Dulles publish a memoir, entitled *The Craft of Intelligence*, primarily to rehabilitate the CIA's standing in the wake of the Bay of Pigs debacle of 1961. The book, which in reality was ghost-written by a team of CIA veterans led by Howard Roman, was an authoritatively documented primer on the art and profession of intelligence, and involved earnest salesmanship on behalf of the CIA as an indispensable arm of government. White informed Dulles that the book was now 'required reading' for his subordinates. Moreover, he hoped that one day he too would be allowed to embark on a similar public discussion of the challenges of intelligence and security in a free society.[18]

As Trend and White saw it, the 'Denning Formula' of colluding with private authors was useful, but only up to a point. If British intelligence fully desired to rebuild its reputation, not to mention restore morale among staff, then it needed to be bolder in its approach to public engagement. On 26 February 1969, they decided to put this idea to the test by calling a meeting, held in Trend's room, with attendance from nearly all of Whitehall's premier secret-keepers, including Joe Hooper (Director of GCHQ), Sir John Rennie (White's successor as 'C') and Martin Furnival Jones (Director General of MI5). The Cabinet Secretary kicked off by outlining the predicament facing the secret services: 'A choice must be made between continuing to deal individually with each new "outside" book as it appeared (in which case the picture in the public mind was built up piecemeal, often inaccurately, and often bringing unjustifiable credit upon those who were involved at the time); and, on the other hand, sponsoring an official history which would be based on unpublished records.'[19] Trend argued that an official history would be a 'useful counter-balance to the distorted picture' that had been painted by outsider histories and the media. He also elaborated on the positive contribution to knowledge that such an account would make, reminding everyone that the existing official war histories were 'misleading' since they did not systematically address the part played by intelligence work. Trend's plan got a favourable reaction. The Philby revelations, in particular, had cast a long shadow over the psychology of all those in the room, and there was a grudging acknowledgement that the landscape had changed as a result. Moreover, everyone agreed that there had been far too many 'bunk books' inaccurately discussing intelligence. Accordingly, a decision was taken for White to write a report, which could be put to ministers, unpacking the pros and cons of the project.

Over the next few months, White canvassed the opinions of the intelligence community at large, giving representatives from each service the opportunity to submit to him any thoughts they might have. Frustratingly, there were no ringing endorsements, only concerns. GCHQ's anxieties were twofold. Firstly, that publication would make the public hungry for yet more disclosures and generate pressure for official histories on a range of sensitive subjects, including, most controversially, Suez. Even Trend had this concern. Throughout 1966, the tenth anniversary of the campaign, he had fought tooth and nail to ensure that Suez was not included in the Cabinet Office's new peacetime official histories series. Fearing that such a study would reignite calls for an official inquiry, and recognising that the episode was definitely not counterblast material, he had sent a spate of letters underlining that 'Nobody should write anything about Suez.'[20] GCHQ's second concern was that a history would not sit well with the Americans. *SOE in France* had not exactly won British officials any friends in Langley, and there was a general feeling that the CIA did not like official histories, full stop. During the time of Allen Dulles, the Agency had entrusted Whitney Shepardson to write an officially sponsored history of the OSS. Shepardson, who from 1943 had headed the Secret Intelligence Branch of the OSS, spent several years researching the book, travelling extensively to collect evidence and personal testimonies, before the Agency pulled the plug, citing 'insurmountable difficulties'.[21] Experience had shown that the NSA deplored publicity. When discussions were held in 1968 on the subject of releasing wartime sigint records, it had put up stern resistance, claiming that disclosures of any kind would result in 'target countries' becoming more security-conscious to the detriment of present operations. Any history, GCHQ went on, however tactfully handled, was bound to grate on Capitol Hill for it would unavoidably cast the OSS in the role of 'junior partner' in the wartime alliance.[22] There was also the danger that publication would expose the Americans to a corresponding pressure to write official histories, in relation not only to the Second World War, but also to more recent conflicts such as Korea and, heaven forbid, Vietnam.

MI5 and SIS were no more excited than GCHQ. For them, the key issue was whether the history could be written without naming names, something that had not happened in the case of *SOE in France*. The disclosure of names ran the risk of ending the careers or lives of long-term agents. A number of wartime personnel were still active and, as such, were the target of hostile services. Preserving the anonymity of employees from the past was believed to be an essential part of retaining the morale and confidence of existing agents. Experience had shown that many individuals only worked for these services on the assurance that their activities and their membership be kept absolutely secret, in perpetuity. 'Above all', SIS underlined, 'the element of trust with agents must be cherished.'[23] MI5 and SIS lawyers also emphasised that agent identification brought with it the danger of libel actions. Foot's provocative comments about named individuals in *SOE in France* had sparked a public outcry, and resulted in substantial damages being paid in compensation. All three services, MI5, SIS and GCHQ, warned of the many and varied political implications of publication. Any history would unavoidably revive the image of Germany as an enemy power, and one that was roundly beaten in the context of intelligence, sabotage and subversion. At a time when the government was looking to promote a united Europe, was it prudent to be publicising wartime successes that had been achieved at Germany's expense? A further problem was whether the book would discuss occasions where policymakers or commanders had failed to take account of accurate intelligence reports. If the core proposition was that British intelligence had been spectacularly successful, people might ask why the war had not been won sooner; a whole mythology might grow up about how politicians were hopeless users of intelligence.[24]

White's report, which stretched to over thirty pages, was completed on 4 July 1969. Despite the reservations, the tone of the document was heavily biased in favour of publication. There is little evidence of the civil servant's code – namely, the separation of facts from opinion. From the outset, White puts his cards on the table, highlighting two overriding reasons for the history. Firstly, it would 'help de-sensationalise the current concept of intelligence and might have the useful prophylactic effect of pre-empting or at least correcting distorted and damaging private histories'.[25] And secondly, it would allow the government to 'meet the claims of history by filling in the present gaps in the history of the Second World War, a period when intelligence played an unprecedented and crucial role in events'.[26] Although White was careful not to use words like 'propaganda', his belief that publication would boost morale and give the intelligence community some desperately needed good publicity was plain for all to see. At one point, he stated:

> Intelligence had a greater part to play in the conduct of the Second World War than in any previous conflict in history. There can have been few major land, sea or air battles fought by the Western Allies, whose outcome did not to some extent depend on an intelligence contribution. On the side of the Western Allies, the British intelligence contribution was paramount. The British developed their intelligence work on a great and complex scale and so fully demonstrated the value of intelligence to modern warfare that the Americans could do little else but follow and adapt themselves to British concepts and often enough to British leadership. The fact that the Americans today possess a great intelligence complex, which in many respects runs counter to their national philosophy of an open society, is due to the experience they gained of the value of intelligence in World War II.

The report delivered a clear warning to anyone who still believed in the policy of preserving silence about intelligence: 'Unless plans are laid for the sponsorship of an official history, the waters are likely to become increasingly muddy, to the general detriment not only of the reputation of British intelligence but also of security.'[27] In tandem with White's report, Trend also spoke privately with ministers, informing them of the urgent need to seize the initiative for the benefit of reputations. In a confidential letter, he put it to the prime minister, Harold Wilson: 'Are we really doing justice to ourselves by maintaining a total embargo on any official account of our intelligence record in the war?'²⁸

Despite strong backing from no less a double act than White and Trend, by late July no firm decision had been made. Old hands in the intelligence community continued to raise weighty objections to the history, with great emphasis put on the risks to sources and methods, as well as the potential alienation of allies in Washington. The only idea to find general acceptance among the secret services was that of a classified account, purely for the readership of officials. White was deeply frustrated. Those who favoured a secret history had clearly missed the point of the project, for such a work 'cannot play any part in the correcting of misconceptions or distortions caused by . . . the inaccuracies and special pleading of private publications'.²⁹ Moreover, as White saw it, there already existed a sizeable portfolio of in-house histories; in the case of GCHQ, for example, they ran to sixty volumes. 'It is difficult', he stated, 'to claim that there is a real need to provide further detailed histories of the intelligence organisations.'³⁰ With discussions stalemated, Trend suggested a compromise proposal. In his view, the chief sticking point was whether or not a history could be written in such a way as to guarantee that agents and methods were protected, and channels of information did not dry up. To overcome this, he called for a 'limited history'.³¹ In contrast to the 'full-scale history' envisaged, where the emphasis would be on *how* intelligence is collected, a limited history would focus on the consumers of intelligence and restrict itself to questions of *what* intelligence is used for. In other words, there would be practically no discussion of sources and methods.

The intelligence community warmed to Trend's plan and it was decided to put the matter formally to ministers. To lessen the likelihood of resistance, Trend made certain that the prime minister was fully briefed on the 'political' advantages of publication. In a private communication, dated 29 July, the Cabinet Secretary argued that the history would help to obviate accusations that the government was adopting an unnecessarily restrictive and obscurantist attitude towards the writing of intelligence history. In short, publication would enable ministers to demonstrate that, although they were denying historians access to intelligence records, they were at least doing their best to reveal the contribution of secret services to Allied victory in the Second World War. Trend also dredged up the problem of D-Notices, a particular sore spot for Harold Wilson. If HMG continued to stonewall those who desired to see more published about intelligence, it would need to call time and time again on the D-Notice Committee, with the associated danger that ministers might be drawn into a public spat à la cable vetting. 'Spare the D-Notice system the strain,' advocated Trend.[32] Trend's arguments clearly rubbed off. Within hours, Wilson had written back to him, stating 'I think I am prepared to agree to the proposals.'[33]

Despite Wilson's blessing, the project still had to get around some major stumbling blocks. Opposition parties as well as American allies had to be consulted before final approval was granted. When asked for his opinion, Edward Heath, Leader of the Opposition, was sceptical that any history could realistically avoid discussing the techniques of intelligence gathering. This concern was shared by former Conservative prime ministers Anthony Eden and Harold Macmillan; all three statesmen called for greater consideration on this matter.[34] Interestingly, the only person to give his unqualified and immediate backing was Richard M. Helms, Director of the CIA. No one in Whitehall had expected this. A notoriously discreet and close-mouthed public servant – aptly described by the Pulitzer Prize-winning journalist Thomas Powers as 'The Man Who Kept the Secrets' – Helms loathed openness in all its forms.[35] '"Wild blue yonder" thinking,' he called it.[36] As Deputy Director of the CIA, Helms had played a key role in convincing his boss, John McCone, to cancel the Shepardson official history of OSS; as Director, he had repeatedly turned down requests from the heirs and partners of General William Donovan, the fabled wartime head of OSS, for the history to be resurrected and written by Cornelius Ryan, author of *The Longest Day*.[37] Yet, Helms was only too happy to endorse the proposed British history. To Whitehall's surprise, he also agreed to allow the eventual author of the work near unrestricted access to the classified OSS archive. Unbeknownst to British officials, however, he simultaneously gave instructions to CIA officer Edward Proctor to weed the papers of material which might offend allies in London.[38]

Months passed without a firm decision being made. Peter Fleming, who had friends in Whitehall secretly telling him that he was being considered to write one of the volumes, complained of a 'Cabinet go-slow movement'.[39] By early 1971, the last remaining hurdle was Heath, who in June of the previous year had replaced Wilson as prime minister. Trend worked tirelessly in an effort to secure

Heath's consent for the project.[40] Like his predecessor, Heath was made acutely aware of the political implications of not sponsoring the history. The government, counselled Trend, was not doing itself any favours by maintaining an embargo on intelligence history. Authors were increasingly prone to air their grievances in public. Certain writers had become so frustrated that their attitude was one of 'publish and be damned'. As discussed earlier in this book, this was the moment when Masterman was cosying up to Farago and threatening to publish his Double-Cross history in the United States. In a bid to allay Heath's concerns about sources and methods, Trend explained that security staff had devised a 'special set of partially anonymous references', capable of disguising the most secret of details. Trend also made the crucial argument that a history could be commissioned *without* the promise of publication. When the history was written, ministers could see if they liked it and then make a decision. The 'proof of the pudding is in the eating', he emphasised.[41]

On 19 February 1971, Heath withdrew his objections and the history was at last under way. A steering committee was set up to exercise control over the writing. The committee, which was chaired by James Butler (editor of the United Kingdom Military Series of the *History of the Second World War*), consisted of representatives from each of the secret services, as well as the Intelligence Co-ordinator and a number of academics, selected on the basis of their 'personal experience of intelligence or special knowledge of the war period'.[42] (There is no record identifying which academics were chosen, although Trend had earlier suggested Hugh Trevor Roper, F. W. Deakin or Michael Howard.) As envisaged, the history would be a multi-volume work, divided into four parts: strategic intelligence, operational intelligence, counter-intelligence, and strategic deception. The plan was for the history to be a plural, multi-skilled effort, spearheaded by a general editor. It was thought that a panel of historians would 'reduce the danger of personal rivalry and public dispute'.[43] Single-authored official histories had, in the past, provoked fierce criticism from independent scholars. In 1951, the acid of envy had led the historian Hebert Butterfield, perhaps best remembered for his polemic *The Whig Interpretation of History*, to launch a stinging attack: 'I do not believe that there is a government in Europe which wants the public to know the truth.'[44] Butterfield, who moved in well-informed circles, almost certainly knew about the airbrushing of Ultra from the historical record.

His outburst included the telltale line: 'governments try to press upon the historian the key to all the drawers but one, and are very anxious to spread the belief that this single one contains no secret at all'.[45] To lessen the chance of academic jealousy, therefore, it was decided that a team undertaking was the way to go.

A decision on who should be appointed as editor-in-chief was made fairly quickly. Trend had earlier written that, while the individual needed to be 'professionally qualified' as a historian, the most important consideration was that he or she was 'reliable and trustworthy'.[46] In other words, Whitehall wanted a safe pair of hands, someone mature enough to stick to the brief and who could be trusted to act in general accord with its will. From the earliest discussions on the subject, there was a clear front-runner – Sir Francis Harry Hinsley. Hinsley was the natural choice. Since 1945, he had enjoyed a career that most historians can only regard with wistful admiration. Based at St John's College, Cambridge, he had climbed the escarpments to become Professor of International Relations, and was credited with writing a number of significant contributions in this area. His knowledge of wartime intelligence was unrivalled. In 1939, he had been recruited to the naval section of the Government Code and Cipher School at Bletchley Park, where he became the leading authority on the decryption and analysis of German naval wireless traffic.[47] As the steering committee saw it, moreover, he possessed an intuitive feel for what could reasonably be disclosed in the history. For years, he had spoken not a word about Ultra, except to his wife Hilary Brett-Smith, herself a Bletchley Park veteran.

It took Hinsley several years before he completed Volume I, in which time there was a fair amount of bickering with the secret services about access to records and the clearance process. According to Richard Langhorne, who became a Fellow of St John's in 1975 and knew Hinsley from his time there, the Cambridge don 'wrestled with every kind of sensitivity during its writing – internal and those of foreign governments, occasionally to the point of threatening to give up the whole project'.[48] For there to be friction was hardly surprising; the history, after all, was a giant step for a community whose maxim, only a quarter of century before was, 'Never to Be Disclosed'. When Dick White had canvassed the opinion of intelligence staff in 1969, all three services had promised him that they would be prepared to allow a historian, provided he or she was positively vetted, 'loose in the archives'.[49] Although MI5 and GCHQ were as good as their word, SIS declined to turn over its papers. SIS, in particular, proved to be a major obstacle. On 28 May 1976, Hinsley privately informed Patrick Beesly, at the time engaged in writing *Very Special Intelligence* and receiving discreet assistance from the don, that 'The MOD and the FO were in favour of publication but the SIS were the niggers in the wood-pile.'[50] Frustratingly, SIS gave no latitude when it came to discussing individuals, leaving Hinsley concerned that the narrative was heavy-going, dry and, dare he say it, lacklustre. SIS hostility to the history became so strong that the Cabinet Office offered Hinsley an early knighthood to walk away from the enterprise – a proposal that he turned down.[51]

By May 1978, every paragraph of Volume I had been trawled through and screened by a platoon of government weeders, as well as by American and Commonwealth authorities. With this, the prime minister, James Callaghan, was required to make a decision about publication.[52] Since the book covered a period of coalition government and had been commissioned by a Conservative prime minister, Callaghan invited the opinion of Margaret Thatcher, leader of the Opposition. Thatcher – who in the 1980s would oversee what has been described as a 'legendary period of Whitehall secrecy'[53] – was firmly against publication. 'I must confess to some disquiet at the prospect,' she wrote.[54] Despite meticulous 'sanitisation' of the text, Thatcher was unconvinced that the work would not endanger national security: 'Do we really have to lay bare to those who could profit from it, not only what intelligence we had, but how we interpreted it?'[55] She questioned the value of the CIA's endorsement of the project, implying that no one in Whitehall should give credence to the opinion of an organisation whose recent history had been blighted, firstly by the failure to stop disclosures by journalists and by disgruntled former employees, and secondly by the decision to allow congressional investigators to inspect and publicise its records. 'In view of the treatment meted out to their own intelligence service', she argued, 'I have little confidence in their judgement on publication matters.'[56] Her response was ultimately indicative of someone who adhered to the age-old view that the words *intelligence* and *openness* should never be used in the same sentence. No clearer is this illustrated than in her concluding statement: 'I was taught a very good rule by my two Masters at Law, both of whom are now judges: never admit anything unless you have to; and then only for specific reasons and within defined limits. It is a rule that has stood me in very good stead in many a complicated matter, and in the absence of further advice I should be inclined to stick to it now.'[57]

Thatcher's negativity failed to influence Callaghan. As he saw it, the history was 'scholarly, comprehensive and dispassionate', and represented an 'important and valuable supplement to the other official war histories', a view that was shared by his Cabinet Secretary, John Hunt.[58] 'I do not think that Mrs Thatcher's doubts are well-founded,' claimed Hunt.[59] With this, Volume I went to the printers, eventually being published in 1979. A class apart from so many other books on intelligence, Hinsley's history garnered laudatory press reviews and won wide-ranging praise from some of academia's most knowledgeable and discerning commentators. The US intelligence-officer-turned-scholar Walter Pforzheimer called it 'the single greatest work on intelligence ever produced', setting the benchmark by which all other works on the subject now had to be judged.[60] Critics were generally of the opinion that the book went a considerable way to improving public understanding of the Second World War. 'An indispensable source,' claimed one commentator.[61] Hostile reviews were in short supply, and tended to focus on the failure to name individuals. Sir Maurice Oldfield, a former head of SIS, was reported to have said: 'You get the impression that the intelligence war was won by committees in Whitehall rather than by people. This is a book written by a committee, about committees, for committees.'[62] A number of reviews also lamented the absence of any new revelations, especially with respect to the Cambridge spies, conspicuous by their absence. 'Alas for the sensation monger,' claimed the *Economist*, 'they [HMG] have lifted only a corner of the veil.'[63] These minor criticisms aside, the history was rightly applauded as an outstanding piece of scholarship, raising the bar for future histories and firmly elevating the field of intelligence studies beyond the realm of sensationalist accounts.

The tragedy for the state was that much of the good publicity generated by Hinsley's history, and by the spate of publications about Ultra's triumph, was soon negated by the dramatic exposure of Anthony Blunt as a Soviet agent in November 1979. The Cambridge spy ring had largely slipped off the radar since the publication of Kim Philby's memoir in 1968. Speculative pieces about the likelihood of a so-called 'Fourth Man' had occasionally surfaced in the Sunday newspapers, typically when there was nothing better to run. In November 1979, however, just as the public was warming again to the view that British intelligence was a first-class outfit, the Blunt secret reared its ugly head. The catalyst for the unmasking was a book by Andrew Boyle, founding father of the BBC Radio 4 programme *The World at One*. Published on 5 November, *The Climate of Treason* pointed the finger squarely at Blunt, albeit without explicitly identifying him as the Fourth Man. To comply with Britain's strict libel laws, Boyle codenamed the subject of his book 'Maurice', after a homosexual character in an E. M. Forster novel. It was not hard for readers to catch on. Blunt, whose name was mentioned throughout the book, had been a known associate of the flamboyantly homosexual Guy Burgess. Eleven days later, Thatcher, now prime minister, revealed the truth in Parliament, thus ending a fifteen-year cover-up. The fallout was immediate, vitriolic and damning. Newspapers that only months before had been carrying stories about the assemblage of Cambridge genius at Bletchley Park were scandalised. Blunt had confessed to his crimes in 1964, but instead of going to jail he was permitted to continue as an honoured courtier at the Royal Household and was even knighted for his services. Caught in a flareback of history, Thatcher responded by suspending the publication of any further volumes in Hinsley's series; Michael Howard's volume on strategic deception, completed in 1980, would not be published until 1990. Time was even called on Bletchley Park memoirs. In 1982, Gordon Welchman, who had been head of Hut 6, was required to publish his book in the United States to escape Thatcher's ruling.[64]

Thatcher's aversion to official histories of intelligence was personal and not reflective of broader attitudes in Whitehall, meaning that such works soon came back into fashion after the Iron Lady and her followers had left the stage. With Thatcher gone, further SOE official histories on the Low Countries and clandestine seaborne missions were published.[65] Becalmed in government offices for over fifty years, read only by the inner sanctum, William Mackenzie's in-house narrative *The Secret History of SOE* was declassified and published by St Ermin's Press in 2000.[66] The previous year had seen the publication of *The Security Service 1908–45*, a 'Top Secret' in-house history written after the Second World War by John Curry.[67] Detractors argued that all the declassified in-house narratives gave a distorted picture of intelligence work, since they focused on efforts to combat the evolving menace of Germany, an acknowledged enemy, and said nothing about the monitoring of potential threats from citizens, neutrals and allies.[68] Criticism along these lines faded when, on 18 December 2002, MI5 announced the appointment of Professor Christopher Andrew to write a sweeping authorised history of the Service from 1909 to 2009, to be published on its centenary. Following in the footsteps of its sister service, SIS subsequently commissioned Professor Keith Jeffery to pen a volume for its centenary, covering the years 1909 to 1949.

Unthinkable in 1945, official history has become a key part of the secret state's strategy of information management. Sitting conveniently at the nexus between secrecy and disclosure, it is appealing to officials of different hues and different beliefs. Hardliners – that is, those who would rather see nothing released at all – can take comfort from the fact that official historians work under the Official Secrets Act and that manuscripts are subject to forensic vetting; he who is commissioned is otherwise restrained. The regimental silver will not be given away and secrecy, albeit to a lesser extent, is still maintained. For the intelligence community, this is particularly important. Just as independent historians do not exist to serve secret services, secret services do not exist to serve independent historians. In short, they need to keep hidden a great deal of what they do. If they do not uphold some measure of secrecy, they will struggle to recruit future agents. Agents need to know that intelligence agencies can keep a secret, both for their own morale and effectiveness and for the sake of their families. Indeed, it is not always the case that the passage of time lessens the risks of disclosure, since the danger of retribution against a spy is not necessarily restricted to a single generation, especially in 'countries where memories are long' and where genealogy can be traced over many decades.[69]

Official history gives the secret state a voice in a crowded marketplace of press accounts, populist histories and memoirs. As Denning, Trend and White learned from bitter experience, it is too dangerous to leave secret history solely to private hands. Journalists, exposé merchants and memoirists: some are fair-minded and sophisticated in their analysis; others fall foul of sensationalism and focus exclusively on the negatives. In the dock, it is only right that the state has the means to defend itself and, in certain cases, pour cold water on colourful inaccuracies. The need for such a mechanism is particularly important in the area of intelligence history, where 'shock reporting' is common and where epistemic blindspots are often filled with conspiracy theory. 'Intelligence', retired CIA Director Allen Dulles considered in 1963, 'is probably the least understood and most misrepresented of the professions.'[70] From the state's perspective, official history also helps to keep the more difficult issue of declassification off the public agenda. The archive is the Holy Grail for researchers, but, to extend the metaphor, many will happily take a lesser vessel if the alternative is nothing at all. In short, the secret state can claim to be 'open' and reap the benefits of that, while at the same time wall off what needs to be walled off.

Within the academic fraternity, official history will always attract a certain degree of cynicism, although one suspects that some of this cynicism might be drawn from the acid of envy. Detractors claim that official historians are compromising their profession by agreeing to operate under restraints placed upon them by the state. Where they should be independent spirits, free to comment on the world outside from the 'sanctuary . . . of the Ivory Tower', they are instead prisoners in a gilded cage, their reputations as credible academics exploited in the service of government public relations.[71] 'Official but not history,' in the words of Basil Liddell Hart.[72] Suspicion about accuracy is exaggerated by the fact that 'outsiders' cannot follow the official historian's paper trail, since authorised works rarely identify, either in the footnotes or in a bibliography, the primary source material consulted. In the case of the recently published histories of MI5 and SIS, specific file references were in part omitted for fear of inquisitive researchers using the Freedom of Information Act to prise the documents out of secret archives.[73] Some academics see this as wrong. Its importance drummed into every undergraduate student of history, the footnote is held as being essential to the scientific nature of historical writing, conferring 'proof' that the historian has been to the archive and that his or her assertions rest on solid ground. As Anthony Grafton claims, the footnote is what distinguishes the professional from the amateur.[74] Is it also not profoundly unfair, critics argue, that official historians can feast their eyes on materials denied to the rest of the profession? This grievance is particularly acute when it comes to secret history, since the normal thirty-year rule is suspended for intelligence and security records, meaning that independent historians may never get the opportunity to inspect and dispute the same evidence. By virtue of their privileged access to records, it is feared that official historians will enjoy too much of a stranglehold on historiography, to the extent that it could be many generations before revisionism emerges.

This concern is overstated. One of the pleasing consequences of intelligence history produced under official auspices is that it has encouraged a growing interest in the subject on the part of serious academics. Written by experts and grounded in years of research, official histories contest the para-historian's attempt to annex intelligence to the domain of airport bookstall literature, replete with wayward charges, dubious sourcing and a general tenor of sensationalism. Since the publication of Hinsley's history in 1979, scholars in diplomatic history and kindred disciplines have been less inclined to scoff than once they were, seeing intelligence as a respectable field of enquiry. Intelligence is now a magnet for postgraduate and postdoctoral researchers around the world, so much so that a number of dedicated research and teaching centres have even been established to meet the demand. With a penchant for lateral thinking, academics toiling in this area have found creative solutions to circumvent the problem of access to classified material, recording witness testimony, for example, as well as using techniques from the social sciences. They also benefit from representation on a Cabinet Office Advisory Group on Security and Intelligence Records. Established in 2004, the group provides academics with an opportunity, once a year, to sit down and discuss declassification policy with key officials from major government departments. In short, it would be difficult for an official history to pull the wool over anyone's eyes. Moreover, given the large and variegated volume of research that is now being done, it would be hard for that official work to dominate historiography for any lengthy period of time. Official history, as Robin Higham once noted, should be viewed as the first, not final word.[75]

EPILOGUE: FROM WRIGHT TO WIKILEAKS

Being more open is a risk that has to be taken in the 21st century, if
the support and understanding of the public are to be obtained.

RETIRED MI5 DIRECTOR GENERAL STELLA RIMINGTON,
2002[1]

In today's open society, no government institution is given the benefit
of the doubt all the time.

SIS CHIEF SIR JOHN SAWERS,
28 October 2010[2]

Ostensibly, the past twenty years or so has seen a retreat from
secrecy on a scale that would have been unthinkable to many of the
personalities studied in this book. In 1989, the centenary of Britain's
inaugural secrecy legislation, the Official Secrets Act was amended at long
last, repealing and replacing the catch-all Section 2, and providing greater
specificity on what categories of information fell within the purview
of criminal law. On 1 January 2005, Britain finally joined a number of
other democratic countries in bringing into effect a Freedom of Information Act, codifying a right of access to information held by most public
authorities. Thirty years before, mandarins had run Machiavellian
rings around their ministerial masters to prevent anything even remotely
resembling a legally inscribed public right to know. The new Act turned
on its head the natural order that had prevailed for centuries in Britain;
namely, the preconception that information belonged to the state rather
than to the citizen. Now, information was public property and the state

had to justify withholding it. As a line of defence against government non-compliance, an Information Commissioner, wholly independent of Whitehall, was given powers to serve an enforcement notice and levy fines if he was satisfied that requests were being unjustly blocked or processed tardily.

Since 1989, there has been, on the face of it, a major reduction of secrecy within the intelligence community. In 1989, MI5 was placed, for the first time, on a legislative footing. In the eighteen months following her appointment as MI5 Director General in December 1991, Stella Rimington became the first serving spy chief to be publicly named officially and the first to pose openly for cameras. In 1993, MI5 lifted the veil further still, publishing a glossy booklet entitled *MI5: The Security Service*, which explained the role of the Service and even included a foreword by its much-talked-about female head.[3] A year later, on 12 June 1994, Rimington gave the Richard Dimbleby Memorial Lecture, televised on the BBC. In 2001, she became the first intelligence chief since Sir Percy Sillitoe to publish a memoir, entitled *Open Secret*. Lagging only slightly behind in the transparency stakes, SIS and GCHQ got full statutory underpinning in 1994, with the passing of the Intelligence Services Act, which also established the parliamentary Intelligence and Security Committee, or ISC, to oversee the policy, administration and expenditure of the three agencies. When the Act was debated in the Commons, on 22 February, the Foreign Secretary, Douglas Hurd, declared proudly that it was emblematic of the government's commitment to 'greater openness'.[4] Perhaps most surprising, on 7 May 1992, prime minister John Major acknowledged, in Parliament, that Sir Colin McColl was the incumbent head of SIS.[5] The identity of a serving SIS chief had long been a closely guarded secret. Most officials, even with in the higher echelons of government, knew him only as 'C', the fabled code name that originated with Captain Sir Mansfield Cumming, the first director of the Service.

As a sign of how far the secret services have seemingly opened up, in recent years there has been a startling transformation of policy towards the declassification of historical materials bearing on national security. In 1981, a Committee on Public Records, chaired by Sir Duncan Wilson, hoped that one day the word 'never' would 'never again' be used in connection with any public records.[6] Today, that forlorn optimism is starting to become reality. Pursuant to the promises of John Major's Open Government Initiative, in 1993 SIS facilitated the release of surviving SOE records, of which it had been custodian, as well as a number of its own pre-1909 files. In 1997, MI5 began transferring records to Kew; to date, it has declassified approximately 4,000 'pieces' of 'historically significant information' (in official usage, a piece may represent a whole file or a particular portion of it), including wartime material on German spies and double agents, early Cold War files on Soviet intelligence operations, and photographs of all its heads.[7] In 2004, GCHQ completed a decade-long undertaking to review and release the majority of records generated by the Government Code and Cipher School, spanning the period from 1919 up to VJ Day on 16 August 1945. Complementing a release made by the National Security Agency, its counterpart in Fort Meade, Maryland, GCHQ has also made available files relating to VENONA, the Anglo-US cryptographic project that succeeded in decoding top-secret messages passed among Soviet agents between 1940 and 1949. As a result of declassification, the discipline of intelligence studies in the UK has gone from strength to strength.

In a further apparent testament to the crumbling of secrecy, secret services have assisted in the production of a number of intelligence histories. The so-called Denning Formula of giving ad hoc support to selected authors was resurrected in the late 1990s, the most well-known beneficiaries being Gordon Brook-Shepherd and Alan Judd. Brook-Shepherd's semi-official account of Western intelligence manoeuvres against the Bolsheviks in Russia from 1917 was aided in no small measure by privileged access to SIS's dossier on its legendary agent Sidney Reilly, the 'Ace of Spies'.[8] For his biography of Cumming, Judd was allowed to inspect the fabled spymaster's diary.[9] The intelligence services have twice permitted Christopher Andrew to pen histories of the KGB in collaboration with Russian defectors. The first of these works, *KGB: The Inside Story* (1990), was written in consultation with Oleg Gordievsky, a former KGB colonel who had worked for SIS as a 'defector-in-place' for over a decade.[10] In 1999, Andrew published account of KGB operations in Europe based on copies of Soviet intelligence files made by Vasili Mitrokhin, a disillusioned Soviet archivist, and smuggled out of the USSR by SIS.[11] A second volume resulting from the Mitrokhin collaboration, looking at KGB operations globally, was published in 2005.[12] Recently, both MI5 and SIS marked their centenaries by turning over their files to Christopher Andrew and Keith Jeffery respectively, to write enormous official histories, totalling over 1,800 pages between them. In Andrew's case, this gave him access to some 400,000 files. A month after Jeffery's history was published, on 29 October 2010, Sir John Sawers delivered the first public speech by a head of SIS.

The key question to be asked from all of this is 'why': why has the British state, perhaps the most secretive of all Western democracies, pulled up the curtain in recent years? Unlike in the US in the mid 1970s, when congressional inquiries exposing White House 'horrors' and CIA dirty tricks demanded the setting up of review bodies and greater openness, the path of disclosure in the UK has not been visibly forced. Alas, the important drivers have never been clearly delineated by officials, although naturally there has been much political bluster hailing the changes that have occurred. When the Lord Chancellor made the case for the 1994 Intelligence Services Act in the Lords, his general justification for it was that 'Things have moved on.'[13] Accordingly, it has been left largely to academics to tease out the motives for reform.

The transformation is commonly attributed to the end of the Cold War, the argument being that the 'new world order' did not warrant the same heightened anxiety about global security and conflict. Ken Robertson, looking specifically at the passing of intelligence legislation, has argued that the changes were the result of 'risk management' rather than 'democratisation'.[14] According to Robertson, as the work of intelligence services transmogrified from making approximations of Soviet nuclear stocks to monitoring and interdicting drug smugglers, human traffickers, terrorists and organised crime, it became imperative that they had a statutory status – the logic being that it would be impossible to bring private individuals before a court of law and build cases against them using intelligence product, if the agencies themselves were still 'deniable'. Robertson also suggested that the new forms of accountability might be viewed as an attempt to prevent anything more sweeping being imposed by a ruling of the European Court of Human Rights. In 1985, MI5 had been criticised by the court for a lack of oversight when a former officer, Cathy Massiter, provided evidence that the Service had been illegally bugging the telephones of pressure groups, such as the Campaign for Nuclear Disarmament, as well as political 'high-fliers', including Patricia Hewitt and Harriet Harman, then leading members of the National Council for Civil Liberties. Around this time, the Swedish Security Service too was reproached for not having a legal identity. With this, Robertson claims, there was a pre-emptive rush towards regulation not just in Britain, but right across Europe.

Building on Peter Gill's research in this area, it is the contention of this epilogue that the relaxation of attitudes towards secrecy over the past twenty years should be seen as an expansion of the offensive strategy of information control that was born in the 1960s and 1970s.[15] This is not to say pejoratively that the changes have been fig leafs or mere token gestures to openness; it is arguing rather that the state has realised that it cannot afford simply to hide in the shadows and has come to appreciate that openness – selective, measured and not without limitations – has its benefits, not least in helping to shape public perceptions. When the state 'opened up' by sponsoring M. R. D. Foot's *SOE in France*, it did so very much with public relations in mind, hoping that the book would help to prevent both the Americans and the communists from claiming the lion's share of credit for resistance work in Axis-occupied Europe. The subsequent decision to embark on the Harry Hinsley official history of British intelligence in the Second World War was taken largely for a specific presentational purpose: namely, to place the story of successful wartime intelligence into the public domain as a counterblast to damaging revelations about Kim Philby, carried first in the *Sunday Times* in October 1967 and then in his memoir of the following year. Opinion-forming was at the heart of the decision to reveal the Ultra secret, with the state fearing that, unless it made an authorised release, its greatest wartime achievement would be disclosed instead by sensationalised 'outsider' publications. The remarkable latitude granted to Anthony Eden for his *Full Circle* memoir was a clear case of perception management, with the Cabinet Office concerned that the British side to the Suez crisis was being ignored. In none of these examples was the government of the day required by some enforceable obligation or legislative ruling to pursue the policy taken. In short, whenever the state has 'opened up' in the past, there has been a public relations agenda for doing so. It is natural to think, therefore, that recent displays of openness might have been motivated by similar thinking.

If, as is suggested, the changes since 1989 have been tantamount to an accelerated offensive strategy of information control by a more sophisticated and image-conscious secret state, then the origins of this acceleration can be traced to a seismic event: the *Spycatcher* Affair. In the history of British secrecy cases, the Thatcher government's misjudged attempt to suppress the memoirs of Peter Wright, an embittered former Assistant Director of MI5, is rivalled only by the cable vetting storm for its drama and lasting impact. The affair was a public relations disaster – for the government, for the intelligence services, for the civil service, and for the practice of official secrecy in-the-round (Figure 25). By the time it was over, there was a strong conviction in all corners of government that change was needed, that the return to absolute secrecy under Thatcher was irrational. Efforts in the realm of public relations became a high priority once more, valuable not only to regain the initiative and establish some overall control over rogue writers like Wright, but also to restore confidence in departments, especially MI5, and their claims to secrecy.

Since entire books have been written about the affair, including eye-witness accounts by some of the protagonists, all that is needed here is to provide the main contours of what happened.[16] When Wright left MI5 in 1976, he did so with two grievances against his former employer. First, that the Service was failing to take seriously his belief that British intelligence was awash with Soviet agents and that one of MI5's former directors general, the late Sir Roger Hollis, had in fact been a super-mole working for the Russians. Wright was regarded as something of a loose cannon, and his final days in MI5 had seen him become cut off and alienated, with many of his colleagues demoralised by his obsessive manhunt for traitors and fearful that this was distracting the Service from its core duties. Second, Wright felt a huge injustice over the fact that pernickety bureaucratic protocol had denied him a considerable portion of his retirement annuity, leaving him teetering on the brink of financial ruin.

In desperation, Wright emigrated to Tasmania, Australia, where he hoped to make ends meet by raising horses. When the stud farm failed, he sounded out his friend the wartime MI5 officer and millionaire banker Lord Victor Rothschild about writing a memoir about his career and suspicions in order to raise capital. Espionage books, especially those with revelations, were proven money-spinners, as evidenced by Andrew Boyle's best-selling book about the Blunt case. Poverty-stricken, Wright wanted a piece of this vast publishing pie. Rothschild supported the plan, although for what precise reason is hard to say, the most likely explanation being that he wanted Wright to put on record that he, Rothschild, contrary to malicious rumours circulating in Whitehall, was not and never had been a Russian spy. By summer

1980, Wright had produced 10,000 words of a book tentatively entitled 'The Cancer in Our Midst', aided by bundles of documents he had seized illicitly from MI5.[17] However, the quality of the writing was poor and, with his health deteriorating, there were concerns that he might not live to see it finished. To hasten his story into print, he and Rothschild decided that it should be written for him by a more experienced hand, ideally someone used to working to tight deadlines. Under the arrangement, Wright would communicate his information about Soviet penetration to the author in return for an equal share of the profits and on the proviso that his identity remain secret, thus alleviating another of his concerns – namely, that he would be hauled over the coals for breaking his secrecy agreement. The person chosen for this task was none other than Chapman Pincher.

The famous scoop-gatherer worked quickly. A nine-day trip to Tasmania in October to interview Wright, followed by two months of intensive writing, ensured that an important work, *Their Trade Is Treachery*, hit bookshops in March 1981. The charges levelled against Hollis forced Thatcher to make a statement to a hushed House of Commons confirming that the former director general had been suspected of being a mole, but that an investigation had revealed no evidence to support the charges. This, of course, was not the first time that Thatcher had been required to breach the traditional parliamentary taboo about intelligence and admit that a matter of public interest had been covered up. In 1979, she had confirmed Blunt as the 'Fourth Man'. However, if she thought that declaring Hollis innocent would be the end of it, she was wrong.

Out of sight in the fastness of his Tasmanian stud farm, Wright was infuriated that Hollis had been cleared and turned his mind, once again, to producing his own account. *Spycatcher*, as it was renamed, was completed by a ghostwriter, Paul Greengrass, now famous for directing the Jason Bourne spy films, but then a young filmmaker for Granada Television's tough investigative series *World in Action*. Wright's intention to publish became obvious when, on 16 July 1984, he appeared on an hour-long *World in Action* documentary entitled 'The Spy Who Never Was'. Recorded in Tasmania some months before, the programme contained a clip of Wright stating that he was 99 per cent certain that Hollis was a Soviet spy. In the wake of the broadcast, as Christopher Andrew's authorised history of MI5 shows, there was frantic discussion in Whitehall about how to stop Wright from going into print.[18] His television appearance and proposed memoir were flagrant violations of the Official Secrets Act, but since British statutes did not stretch extraterritorially, no criminal action could be brought against him so long as he resided in Australia. Officials considered stripping him of his OBE, awarded in 1972, but concluded that this would only encourage Wright to present himself as a martyr, a patriot who had done his job only to be victimised for his beliefs.[19]

Government pressure left potential publishers in no doubt that they would contract *Spycatcher* at their peril, but the book was eventually picked up by Heinemann, which astutely decided to launch it through its Australian subsidiary.[20] With this, in September 1985, Thatcher instructed the Attorney General to initiate a civil suit for an injunction, the grounds being that Wright was breaking an obligation of confidence to which he had solemnly given his word and signed a contract. The decision to initiate a civil suit for an injunction provoked immediate hostility, with the media interpreting it as yet another example of a repressive machine trying to conceal unfavourable truths for political purposes. In 1983, Sarah Tisdall, a young Foreign Office clerk, had been given a six-month prison sentence for leaking to the *Guardian* a document revealing that official policy, as directed by Thatcher and her Secretary of State for Defence, Michael Heseltine, was to misinform Parliament about the timing of the arrival of US cruise missiles carrying nuclear warheads at Greenham Common in Berkshire. Since the disclosure had not damaged national security, the government was criticised for trying to make an example out of a principled individual, acting out of a 'problem of conscience' but sadly too weak to fight back. Further recriminations had followed early in 1985 when Clive Ponting, a civil servant in the MoD, was charged under Section 2 of the Official Secrets Act for leaking documents about the sinking of the *General Belgrano*, the Argentinean cruiser destroyed by a British submarine during the 1982 Falklands War. Controversially, the documents undermined the government's line that the warship was threatening British lives when it was attacked, showing instead that it was sailing away from the Royal Navy taskforce and was outside the exclusion zone. However, in what was hailed as a landmark victory for the jury system, Ponting was acquitted on the grounds that there was a strong public interest behind the disclosure.[21] Once again, the government was savaged for its vengeful pursuit of someone who had dared to embarrass it.

Against this background, the *Spycatcher* trial opened in the Supreme Court of New South Wales in November 1986, generating 'a level of global publicity unequalled by any other book since the British government's equally ill-fated attempt to ban the publication of *Lady Chatterley's Lover* on the grounds of obscenity a quarter of a century earlier'.[22] The Crown's case fell apart with alarming speed. The defence made a mockery of the claim that the information contained in the book warranted the protection of confidentiality. Many of Wright's 'revelations' – from the charge about Hollis to the allegation that MI5 had plotted against, snooped on and defamed Harold Wilson – had been made elsewhere, in publications that the state had taken no action against. A great deal of the narrative concerned events at least a quarter of a century old, the disclosure of which was unlikely to impact upon current operations. Devastatingly for the government's position, it came to light during the trial not only that Wright had been the source of Pincher's allegations in *Their Trade Is Treachery*, but that a number of officials had known this fact, having stolen a pre-publication copy of the book from the publishers. Ergo, Pincher could have been stopped but, in effect, was allowed to publish with 'implicit government approval'.[23]

In a bizarre and desperate move that backfired spectacularly, Thatcher dispatched the Cabinet Secretary, Sir Robert Armstrong, to the Australian courtroom to make the government's case. This decision raised an important constitutional issue. Civil servants were supposed to be anonymous and, by convention, were not required to answer for the actions of their political masters.[24] Yet, by spending nine long days in the witness box, Armstrong became a 'household name' and synonymous with the views of his ministerial superiors.[25] Accusations of improper loyalty and politicisation of Whitehall could be heard from both the left and the right. David Steel, the leader of the Liberal Party, described the Cabinet Secretary as 'damaged goods', hijacked by the government to act as a 'garbage operator' for what was, at its core, a political trial. According to Colin Pilkington, anatomist of Whitehall, 'In making such a public spectacle of her most senior civil servant ... Margaret Thatcher had destroyed what was left of even the appearance of "anonymity" and "neutrality" in the Civil Service.'[26] A reluctant witness, not particularly knowledgeable about the operational history of the intelligence services, Armstrong was an easy target for Wright's counsel, Malcolm Turnbull, a brash and ambitious young Sydney advocate. During his time in the spotlight, the hapless Armstrong did enormous damage to his reputation and brought into ridicule the absurd levels of secrecy that plagued the British state. In accordance with the traditional line, he refused to admit the existence of SIS, a nonsensical position in the light of the books and press articles that had been written on the subject. When, in a moment of carelessness under pressure, he stated that Sir Dick White had been head of SIS, Turnbull opportunistically pounced on the slip, to which Armstrong replied, farcically, that SIS had only existed for the duration of White's leadership.[27] Worse followed. Caught off-guard under cross-examination, he admitted that, when he wrote a letter to Pincher's publisher asking for a copy of *Their Trade is Treachery*, he neglected to mention that he already had a copy. Harangued by Turnbull for telling lies, he conceded, in a priceless admission, that it was sometimes necessary for a person in his position to be 'economical with the truth' – a much-quoted locution that came to symbolise the depth of deceitfulness in the British state.

The judge, Justice Michael Kirby, said of Armstrong's testimony that it must be approached with 'considerable reserve', and it was no surprise when he eventually ruled that the government's claim should fail. As he saw it, *Spycatcher* was 'One rather cantankerous old man's perspective of technology long out-dated, people long since dead and controversies tirelessly worked over by numberless writers.'[28] In dismissing the government's case, Kirby laid waste the government's general proposition that all information acquired by intelligence officers warranted protection in perpetuity. Thatcher's ill-fated crusade to ban the book ensured that it became a global publishing phenomenon. The first print run for the US hardcover had been 50,000 copies; after the excitement of the circus trial in Sydney, 760,000 copies were rushed out to meet the demand.[29] Truly, there is nothing like controversy to fuel popularity. Skyrocketing sales made Wright a millionaire, whilst HMG was left to pick up an estimated £3 million bill in worldwide legal fees.[30] The irony was summed up by a newspaper cartoon showing a handful of bewigged barristers asking the Attorney General, tongue-in-cheek, whether it would have been cheaper simply to give Wright his full pension in the first place. Remarkably, Thatcher nevertheless still refused to accept defeat. In a ludicrous postscript, generating even more disdain of official attitudes towards disclosure, the government tried for over a year to enforce gagging orders on British newspapers preventing them from carrying excepts from Wright's book. To do so was illogical. The book ranked first on the *New York Times* bestseller list; thousands of copies had crossed the Atlantic and were washing up in second-hand bookstores. Claiming the right to free speech, Fleet Street was incensed. In a defiant gesture, Tony Benn read aloud from the memoir before a crowd of listeners at Hyde Park's Speaker's Corner. The book was finally cleared for legitimate serialisation and sale on 13 October 1988, when the Law Lords ruled that overseas publication had rendered secrecy a moot point. The European Court of Human Rights later said that, in delaying publication in the British Isles, the government had violated the Human Rights Convention.[31]

For the secret state, the *Spycatcher* Affair served as a wakeup call. In trying to defend an absolute right to secrecy, it succeeded only in making the situation worse. Reputations had been ruined. For Armstrong, a respected Establishment figure who before the saga was seen as a shoo-in to become Provost of Eton College upon his retirement, the affair proved disastrous; the prestigious sinecure from Eton never materialised, and his public image would forever be that of a 'supercilious "Pom" trussed up and barbecued by a sneering Malcolm Turnbull'.[32] For MI5, the highly publicised efforts to silence Wright ensured that an extremely embarrassing book, which under normal circumstances the reading public might not have given a second glance, became a runaway best-seller. Millions of people were introduced to the Service's alleged failures and misdeeds, which did great harm to its standing in the public eye. In addition to the sensitive details about Hollis and the plotting against Wilson, Wright had described how MI5 had 'bugged and burgled' its way across London and the world, including eavesdropping on Commonwealth Conferences. Unsurprisingly, critics took the bugging as evidence of the need for supervision of secret services by an elected body. Left licking his wounds, Sir Antony Duff, Director General of MI5, lamented: 'In the face of the sustained criticism and vilification of the last year, arising chiefly from the ramifications of the Peter Wright case, the Service has kept up its spirits pretty well. But these unremitting attacks do have their effect and my fear is that in the longer term the Service will be damaged in a number of ways.'[33] More generally, public confidence in the necessity for closed government had hit rock bottom as a result of *Spycatcher*. Importantly, the affair highlighted that there was a great deal of unnecessary secrecy at the heart of the British state.

Clearly, change was needed. The heavy-handed strategy of information control pursued against Wright was a disaster, leaving the state, and the intelligence community in particular, submerged in a public relations quagmire that it now had to pull its way out of. Interestingly, one of the biggest critics of the government's misguided handling of the book had been Sir Dick White, who had said: 'Had it been left to me, I'm sure that book would have sunk without a trace. Secrecy can be a two-edged weapon.'[34] White, of course, as Cabinet Office Intelligence Co-ordinator in the 1970s, had played a key role in convincing officials that sometimes secrecy was counterproductive and that public relations was as important to the secret state as it was for the business world. Thanks to his campaigning, Hinsley's history was put into production, the justification being that it would stave off the more awkward declassification issue and help to champion and legitimate the work of intelligence services in the wake of ugly revelations. White's foresight, sadly unheeded by Thatcher, was in realising that governments could be open in a measured way to win public trust and understanding, yet still maintain secrecy. After *Spycatcher*, the idea of having an information control strategy that combined both public relations and secrecy found a host of admirers in Whitehall. Accordingly, it is in these terms that we should see the glasnost of the last twenty years.

To build on the argument that the state has not so much moved in a linear direction from secrecy to openness, but rather has resurrected the more flexible formula of blending secrecy with public relations, it is worth probing some of the changes presented by the state as liberalising. The new Official Secrets Act, despite being less broadly drawn than its predecessor and protecting more limited classes of official information, contained two elements which to a large extent made it a more fearsome weapon of control. First, it excluded the 'public interest' defence that had cleared Ponting. As a result, it was no longer possible for a heroic whistle-blower or brave newspaper to save themselves by arguing that disclosure was excusable because it exposed malfeasance of office. Second, it introduced the new offence of 'unauthorised publication', which stipulated that a journalist could be prosecuted for publishing a story derived from secret information irrespective of whether or not there was any evidence of a classified document changing hands. In short, the mere act of publication warranted prosecution.[35]

The state has certainly not been shy in using the Act when informal mechanisms of censorship have failed. One of the more famous cases involved Richard Tomlinson, a former SIS officer, who in 1997 became the first SIS employee to be prosecuted under the Act since the traitor George Blake, in 1961. Tomlinson had been dismissed from SIS in 1995 – he claimed unfairly and without explanation. Stung by the further injustice of being denied the chance to take SIS before an industrial tribunal, he left the UK and pursued his grievance against the Service publicly, by giving interviews to the international press and by starting work on a memoir. SIS initially tried to neutralise the problem by buying Tomlinson's silence; George Temple, aide-de-camp to the Head of SIS, negotiated a bank loan of £15,000 to help the former agent clear his debts and even landed him a rather attractive job with Jackie Stewart's Formula One racing team.[36] Tomlinson went along with the deal, but later he changed his mind, sending a four-page synopsis to a publisher in Sydney. With this, he was arrested and went to jail for breaching the Act. In 2001, now living in exile, he published *The Big Breach* in Russia. The memoir was subsequently made available in the UK, but the royalties were frozen by a High Court Order. In May 2009, SIS finally agreed to bury the hatchet, releasing the proceeds from publication and conceding that legal action had been disproportionate to the offence.[37]

The Freedom of Information Act was proudly presented by the government of Tony Blair as an indication of its commitment to modernising politics, sweeping away unnecessary secrecy and building a partnership between citizens and officials. Shortly before he became prime minister in 1997, Blair declared that the Act would 'signal a new relationship between government and people: a relationship which sees the public as legitimate stakeholders in the running of the country and sees election to serve the public as being given on trust'.[38] Blair's message of a new dawn rising seemed to resonate. Maurice Frankel, long-standing Director of the Campaign for Freedom of Information, called the Government's White Paper on the Act 'stunning' and suggested that Blair had gone 'further' than anyone could have expected.[39] With similar legislation coming into force across Europe, from the Republic of Ireland to Turkey, the esteemed sociologist Anthony Giddens suggested that the world was experiencing a 'second wave of democratisation' and that 'secrecy was in retreat'.[40] However, with the Act now approaching its ten-year anniversary, it is arguable that reality has not matched the rhetoric. The implementation of the Act was delayed by four years, a sure sign that Blair's mindset had changed once he sat on the other side of the fence in government. Indeed, the former prime minister has since admitted, in his 2010 autobiography *A Journey*, that the Act stands as one of his biggest regrets: 'You idiot. You naive, foolish, irresponsible nincompoop. There really is no description of stupidity, no matter how trivial, that is adequate: I quake at the imbecility of it all.'[41]

When the Act finally arrived in 2005, it did so full of exemptions. The intelligence services were covered by an 'absolute exemption', meaning that they could turn down any request without having to make a judgement on whether it was in the public interest to do so. The Act included a loosely defined ban on the release of 'information relating to the formation of government policy', a convenient get-out clause that could be used to refer to every document in Whitehall. As Alasdair Roberts has expertly shown, there are a host of other loopholes, while officials have shrewdly refined bureaucratic procedures to ensure that the Act does not weaken their control of information.[42] Government departments can refuse requests if the cost of finding, sorting and editing information exceeds £600. They can also withhold documents if the time taken to locate and extract them surpasses 24 hours. At present, there is no statutory time limit for public authorities to decide whether the information is exempt from release, thus allowing for calculated foot-dragging to delay genuine inquiries. Frustratingly, departments have resisted calls to set up publicly accessible catalogues or registers of the information they hold, to help the public know what is available and to avoid large-scale 'fishing expeditions' with high cost and no return. In short, as Roberts argues, there is a 'hidden law', buried in administrative practice and thus difficult to combat, that undercuts the grandiose claim of a greatly advanced public right to know.[43]

The intelligence community has made great fanfare about how it has entered a new open chapter in its history, yet many of the monuments to greater candour either contain considerable limitations justified on the grounds of protecting sources and operational efficiency, or come with what appears to be a public relations agenda. Rimington's Dimbleby Lecture possessed little that would excite the open government campaigner, and was filled instead with reassuring statements about how MI5 was a 'modern, efficient, and law-abiding service', whose remit was 'compatible with personal liberty'.[44] Coming so soon after the *Spycatcher* debacle, it is hard not to see this as a measured display of openness, designed to restore public confidence. The same argument might be made of her memoir, *Open Secret*. Written without recourse to letters, diaries or official documents, the book contained a striking lack of revelations. The book was essentially censored twice: first, by Rimington herself, who acknowledged in the Preface that she was no whistle-blower; and second, by a band of obtuse weeders who made certain that there was no whistle to blow.[45] Important episodes in her twenty-seven-year career were either summarised with no new details or not discussed at all. Reviewing the book for the *Guardian*, Chris Mullin, then Chairman of the Home Affairs Select Committee, was disappointed that she had offered nothing new on MI5 activities during the 1984 miners' strike beyond assurances that everything was 'perfectly above board'.[46] The journalist David Rose found it curious that there was no mention of Mitrokhin's defection to Britain in 1992 – 'unquestionably the most important event in counter-espionage in the period Rimington was DG'.[47] One possible reason for the omission was that Rimington and MI5 had wanted to prevent more awkward questions about the failure to spot the 'granny spy', Melita Norwood, who was exposed as a long-time KGB intelligence source in 1999 following Andrew's *The Mitrokhin Archive* – a tardy seven years after Mitrokhin had brought his trunkloads of telltale files to Britain. Conveniently perhaps, while Rimington is quiet on these episodes, she is more forthcoming in her treatment of Peter Wright, who she calls 'strange' and 'paranoid' and whose allegations she roundly trounces.

The centenary celebrations of MI5 and SIS have involved several gestures towards greater transparency, but again such gestures are not without restraint or an underlying attempt to influence public perceptions. In the case of the two state-sponsored histories, reviewers have noted that both works are largely bereft of disclosures. The historian Philip Murphy suggested that what Andrew's authorised history 'does, above all, is to remind us of how much we already knew'.[48] Tellingly, the cut-off date for Jeffery's account is 1949, meaning that there is no opportunity to discuss SIS reaction to, and crucially damage assessment of, Philby's treachery. This is no criticism of the authors, who have used their vast knowledge of the subject to produce highly readable and informative accounts. Understandably, their employers have been careful not to give their opponents a stick to hit them with. Taken together, the two histories robustly challenge the proposition that success in intelligence remains secret while failure becomes public, casting a spotlight on countless achievements. Moreover, underscoring both works are clear messages for a sceptical public: intelligence professionals speak truth unto power; they are disinterested in politics; they work in strict accordance with the rule of law; they respect individual rights and privacy; they are accountable for their actions; and they are courageous, dedicated and do everything within their power to keep the nation safe. Recent public appearances by intelligence chiefs have seen the airing of the same arguments, as well as other positive messages including how the intelligence community has become an equal opportunities employer, no longer reliant on the tarnished 'old-boy net' method of discreet chats with white, male candidates in the junior common rooms of Oxbridge colleges. For example, when MI5 Director Jonathan Evans met selected journalists at his office in London on 6 January 2009, he claimed that more than 40 per cent of his staff were female, with many being recruited via the Internet.

The histories of MI5 and SIS, coupled with public briefings by their chiefs, serve a public relations role at a time when those organisations badly need it. While *Spycatcher* provided the catalyst for the intelligence community's mission to inform, the 'War on Terror' and related world events have unquestionably ensured its continuation. During the Cold War, the secret services fought threats that were remote from people's lives. The terrorist attacks of 9/11, Madrid and London, which in a world of media plenty were amplified by real-time coverage, have brought the threat of international terrorism, Al-Qaeda and its associates close to home. Accordingly, public expectations of intelligence services have never been greater, with the public demanding to know that the threat is being combated not only effectively, but legally. For MI5, in particular, it is essential that the public know that everything is being done to prevent future attacks on British soil. In 2006, the Service came under fire when it emerged that Mohammed Sidique Khan, ringleader of the 7/7 bombings, was in MI5's sights more than a year before the atrocity. Critics took the missed opportunity as damning evidence of intelligence failure, when in fact the reality, as proved by a subsequent inquiry, was that MI5 was trailing Khan not as a possible extremist but as a petty fraudster, and at the time had neither the proof nor or the resources to justify making him an 'essential target' for surveillance. 'Selling' MI5 as the first line of defence against terrorism was a key part of Evans's briefing in 2009. Choosing his words wisely, he explained that 2,000 terrorist suspects were the subject of constant surveillance in the UK, and he revealed that MI5 staff would rise to 4,100 by 2011, more than double the number at the time of the 9/11 attacks. Such disclosures are designed to be reassuring, but they also help to make MI5's case for funding at a time of budget cuts. The subtext of Evans's speech was that, with more resources, the likes of Khan will not be missed.

One of the messages that comes through particularly strongly in the state-sponsored histories is that MI5 and SIS are unswayed by politics and have no interest other than that of intelligence. This message could not have been more timely. Public trust in the intelligence community as being free from politicisation has perhaps never been lower, largely as a result of the unprecedented use of intelligence by the Blair government in the run-up to the enormously controversial invasion of Iraq in March 2003. To make the case for war, the government published two dossiers: the first claimed that Iraq had reconstituted its nuclear weapons programme and could 'deploy [chemical and biological] weapons within 45 minutes of a decision to do so'; the second focused on Saddam Hussein's security agencies, the persecution of Iraqi people and the obstruction of United Nations weapons inspectors.[49] What made the two documents especially eye-catching was that they were drawn from intelligence material, discussed and evaluated for all to see, including both humint gathered by SIS and JIC assessments. For Blair to deploy secret intelligence in an attempt to win the hearts and minds of a hesitant Parliament and a sceptical electorate was a watershed in British politics. Intelligence product was long regarded as the holiest of holies, and there had been no prior occasion in the UK when it had been used as a resource for public policy and education. Anthony Glees and Philip Davies have convincingly argued that Blair's political desire to publish intelligence would have been inconceivable in earlier times, and was only made possible by the gradual 'opening up' of the state since 1989.[50] In effect, Blair did what he did comforted by the fact that openness was no longer anathema.

His actions backfired and the intelligence community ended up being criticised in full public view. After Saddam was successfully toppled, months passed without any sign of the weapons about which Blair had ominously warned. By May 2003, the inability of coalition forces to find weapons of mass destruction (WMD) – the main justification for going to war – had provoked the biggest political storm about military action by a British government since Suez. Political discourse became consumed by the question of whether intelligence had been twisted in its representation to the public – or 'spun' – to sell the war on a false premise; and, if so, who had done the spinning? Based on information from a secret source (later revealed to be the country's leading weapons specialist Dr David Kelly), the BBC journalist Andrew Gilligan famously accused members of Blair's government, in particular Downing Street's Director of Communications and Strategy Alastair Campbell, of deliberately 'sexing up' intelligence in order to present an exaggerated case for military intervention. Over 12 months, between July 2003 and July 2004, no fewer than four inquiries were held to examine the intelligence dimensions of 'missing' WMD.[51] The third investigation, chaired by Lord Hutton, brought intelligence processes and product before the public eye like never before. Top-secret documents, written only weeks earlier, were posted on the Internet for worldwide consumption; scores of anonymous intelligence officers gave public testimony. By the end of Britain's 'season of inquiry' there were no winners, only losers. The government was shown to have been deceitful, there being no evidence that Iraq had been actively engaged in WMD production. The intelligence agencies were upbraided for succumbing to 'undue' or 'improper' political influence, and for falling victim to 'groupthink', in which the desire for unanimity with international intelligence allies had led them to give policymakers overblown or inaccurate estimates rather than appraise alternatives. In this context, it is easy to see why the state's strategy of information control was to go on the offensive with public relations. Trust in intelligence services had to be regained, and this could not be done by walking the path of non-disclosure.

The British state has fought many battles over secrecy on many different fronts. Individual threats to the state's grip on information have come in many different guises, from enterprising and well-connected investigative journalists to the highest politicians and officials in the land. Informal mechanisms, most notably D-Notices and the wily ways of the Cabinet Secretary, have historically been the preferred method of control, although there have been occasions when bolder governments, often in desperation, have turned to the law with disastrous consequences. By the second decade of the new millennium, there is good evidence to suggest that a steep learning curve has convinced the state to embrace a public relations-infused approach to information control, building on the experiments with opinion-forming that occurred under the thoughtful watch of figures like Trend and White. Measured disclosures by the state, at a time of the state's choosing, help to convey an important appearance of openness, while providing an opportunity to challenge unwelcome revelations and influence public perceptions.

In the coming years, it will be fascinating to see whether this offensive strategy of information control will survive what future scholars of secrecy will probably call the 'Age of WikiLeaks'. Today, the biggest challenge to secret-keepers, not just in Britain but across the world, is technological progress. There are, of course, arguments to suggest that advances in technology might actually help governments to protect classified information. Satellites and digital advances have hastened the arrival of a twenty-four-hour news cycle that discourages long-term, time-consuming investigations by journalists. Sir Harold Evans was able to break the Philby story with the aid of a large research team working for many months, with no distractions. Today, such a probing enquiry would be impossible, with a higher premium being placed on news that can be ascertained quickly to fill the manifold spaces created by technological development. Under competitive pressure to deliver, there is a tendency for the media either to produce 'journalism of assertion', based on claims not facts, or to rush out stories fed to them by government public affairs advisers.[52] Seasoned reporters, such as Duncan Campbell (of ABC fame), have argued that technological progress, particularly the rise of the surveillance state, has the potential to make investigative journalists – and their sources – an endangered species.[53] In recent years, new regulations have come into force requiring Internet and telephone providers to keep logs of what websites people visit and what numbers are called. Although this data cannot be accessed without clearance from a judge, the potential is there for governments to keep much closer tabs on reporters and their contacts. Campbell also fears a future in which governments will be able to exploit automatic vehicle number-plate recognition (ANPR) – already used by the police to track criminals and tax evaders – to monitor the physical movements of journalists and whistle-blowers. Technology has not yet advanced to the point where this can be done on a real-time basis, but when that moment comes, the likelihood of sources agreeing to meet reporters in underground car parks, à la Deep Throat, is slim.

On balance, however, technology presents more problems than solutions for the secret state. New technologies have caused the stock-pile of classified information to grow enormously in recent years. Government business is now typically documented in digital rather than paper form and communicated through email. The Internet, allied to better computers and innovative gadgets such as Blackberrys, has ensured that the flow of person-to-person communication of this material has grown exponentially. The Hutton Inquiry will be remembered for many reasons, but one of the most remarkable things was the mass of sensitive internal emails between civil servants that it released into the public domain. As a result of advances in office technology, the mechanics of illicit communication have been made much easier. The leaker of yesteryear would not have been able to pull off the industrial-scale 'document dump' achieved by WikiLeaks. He or she would have needed near round-the-clock access to a gigantic photo-copier, not to mention boxes of paper and a fleet of trucks to deliver the leaked information to its intended recipient. Bradley Manning, the US Army intelligence analyst who allegedly supplied Julian Assange with thousands of confidential diplomatic cables, simply started his computer, compressed the secret data onto CDs, and later uploaded it onto a commercial network computer. The Internet then provided the means to broadcast this material to a global audience. Once posted on the Internet and recycled onto tens of thousands of websites, it proved impossible to remove.

Although the British state has not yet experienced the full fury of Assange's website, whose target to date has been the US government, the fear of being WikiLeaked is a critical issue in Whitehall and solu-tions are no doubt being devised as this book goes to press. For sure, there will be a review of how electronic data is safeguarded. The US State Department is stripping computers of CD/DVD drive recorders, and software is being installed to detect downloads of unusually large amounts of information; one would expect something similar to happen in the UK. A more alarming solution would be for officials to stop writing things down, relying instead on word of mouth. If governments take one lesson from WikiLeaks it will probably be that everything that is word-processed should be presumed to be disclosable. As a result, we could see an intensification of the 'sofa' style of government that accompanied the premiership of Tony Blair, where informal chats involving a coterie of ministers and advisers were preferred to the rigour of briefing papers and minutes. This would have a chilling effect not only for historians, who down the line will find archives strangely empty, but for the efficient running of government. If this turns out to be the response, then society will have paid a very high price indeed for Assange's crusade.

NOTES

Introduction

1 For a detailed account of the WikiLeaks disclosures and the man responsible see D. Leigh and L. Harding, *Wikileaks: Inside Julian Assange's War on Secrecy* (London: Guardian Books, 2011).

2 F. Furedi, 'Wikileaks: This Isn't Journalism – It's Voyeurism', www.spiked-online.com.

3 R. W. Wilsnack, 'Information Control: A Conceptual Framework for Sociological Analysis', *Urban Life*, 8:4 (January 1980), 468.

4 Digital whistle-blowers are afforded additional protection by the fact that the site is hosted in Sweden, where anonymity is upheld by stringent legislation.

5 'Secrecy of Cabinet Proceedings', Note by the Prime Minister, CP (45) 282, 9 November 1945, The National Archives (hereafter TNA) PREM 8/436.

6 R. J. Aldrich, 'Policing the Past: Official History, Secrecy and British Intelligence since 1945', *English Historical Review*, 119, 483 (September 2004), 922–53.

7 'Secrecy of Cabinet Proceedings', TNA PREM 8/436.

8 D. Irving, 'The Scoop', www.fpp.co.uk/online/08/03/Enigma_memoirs.html.

9 D. Vincent, *The Culture of Secrecy: Britain 1832–1998* (Oxford University Press, 1997), p. 262.

10 P. Gill, 'Reasserting Control: Recent Changes in the Oversight of the UK Intelligence Community', *Intelligence and National Security*, 11:2 (1996), 313–31.

11 See A. Rogers, *Secrecy and Power in the British State: A History of the Official Secrets Act* (London: Pluto Press, 1997); E. Shils, *The Torment of Secrecy: The Background and Consequences of American Security Policies* (London: Heinemann, 1956).

12 *Third Report from the Defence Committee, Session 1979–80, The D-Notice System*, HC 773 (August 1980).

13 A. Sampson, *The New Anatomy of Modern Britain* (London: Hodder & Stoughton, 1971), p. 379.

14 M. Weber, 'Bureaucracy', in *From Max Weber: Essays in Sociology*, translated and edited by H. H. Gerth and C.W. Mills (London: Routledge, 1991), pp. 233–4.

15 Ibid.

16 P. Kellner and Lord Crowther-Hunt, *The Civil Servants: An Inquiry into Britain's Ruling Class* (London: Macdonald, 1980), p. 275.

17 P. Hennessy, *Whitehall* (London: Secker & Warburg, 1989), p. 346.

18 T. Bunyan, *Political Police in Britain* (London: Quartet Books, 1976); D. C. Rowat (ed.), *Administrative Secrecy in Developed Countries* (New York: Columbia University Press, 1979); D. Leigh, *The Frontiers of Secrecy* (London: Junction Books, 1980); D. Hooper, *Official Secrets: The Use and Abuse of the Act* (London: Secker & Warburg, 1987); R. M. Thomas, *Espionage and Secrecy: The Official Secrets Act 1911–1989 of the United Kingdom* (London: Routledge, 1991); R. Thurlow, *The Secret State: British Internal Security in the Twentieth Century* (Oxford: Wiley-Blackwell, 1994).

19 *Departmental Committee on Section 2 of the Official Secrets Act 1911* (London: HMSO, September 1972), Cmnd. 5104, Volume I, pp. 17, 116–18.

20 Leigh, *Frontiers of Secrecy*, p. 52.

21 *Departmental Committee on Section 2 of the Official Secrets Act*, Volume III, p. 320.

22 In court, conviction did not depend upon proof that the accused knew of, or had had his attention called to, the provisions of the Act.

23 Kellner and Crowther-Hunt, *Civil Servants*, p. 265.

24 'Signing of the Official Secrets Act Declarations by Government Employees', C2 to MI11, November 1944, TNA WO 32/19030.

25 Woolwich Arsenal Memorandum, 16 May 1923, TNA WO 32/17602.

26 G. Mitchell to R. Hewison, 18 September 1952, TNA CAB 21/4522; 'Record of Meeting at Treasury', 10 November 1952, TNA CAB 21/4522.

27 Ibid.

28 Poster located in TNA CAB 21/4522.

29 G. Drewry and T. Butcher, *The Civil Service Today* (Oxford: Wiley-Blackwell, 1988), p. 175.

30 C. Ponting, *Secrecy in Britain* (Oxford: Wiley-Blackwell, 1990), p. 1.

31 H. Heclo and A. Wildavsky, *The Private Government of Public Money* (Basingstoke: Palgrave, 1981).

32 *Departmental Committee on Section 2 of the Official Secrets Act*, Volume I, para 58.

33 Vincent, *Culture of Secrecy*.

34 Hennessy, *Whitehall*, p. 347.

35 P. Mandler, 'Reviewed Work: *The Culture of Secrecy: Britain 1832–1998* by D. Vincent', *American Historical Review*, 105:3 (June 2000), 1,013–14.

36 Vincent, *Culture of Secrecy*, pp. viii, 16.

37 See M. Rubin, 'What Is Cultural History Now?' in D. Cannadine (ed.), *What Is History Now?* (London: Palgrave, 2002), pp. 80–94; F. Inglis, *Culture* (London: Polity Press, 2004); P. Burke, *What Is Cultural History* (London: Polity Press, 2004).

38 E. P. Thompson, *Customs in Common* (New York: New Press, 1993), p. 13. D. Marsh, D. Richards and M. J. Smith, *Changing Patterns of Governance in the United Kingdom: Reinventing Whitehall?* (London: Palgrave, 2001), p. 15.

39 D. Reynolds, *In Command of History: Churchill Writing and Fighting the Second World War* (London: Penguin, 2005); A. Suttie, *Rewriting the First World War: Lloyd George, Politics and Strategy* (Basingstoke: Palgrave Macmillan, 2005).

40 J. Naylor, *A Man and an Institution: Sir Maurice Hankey and the Cabinet Secretariat* (Cambridge University Press, 1984).

41 N. Wilkinson, *Secrecy and the Media: The Official History of the D-Notice System* (London: Routledge, 2009).

42 *Departmental Committee on Section 2 of the Official Secrets Act*, Volume 1, p. 17.

43 Marshall, cited in D. G. T. Williams, 'Official Secrecy in England', *Federal Law Review*, 3 (1968–9), 23.

44 See D. P. Moynihan, *Secrecy: The American Experience* (New Haven: Yale University Press, 1999).

45 R. Crossman, 'The Real English Disease', *New Statesman*, 24 September 1971, p. 1.

46 B. Liddell Hart to J. Amery, KCLMA Amery, GB 099 Papers, Liddell Hart Centre for Military Archives, King's College London.

47 W. F. Kimball, 'Openness and the CIA', *Studies in Intelligence*, 44:2 (2000), 63–7.

48 Crossman, 'Real English Disease', p. 1.

49 'Transcript of Oral Evidence Given on 14 December 1971 by Mr Chapman Pincher', TNA HO 292/22.

50 Cited in K. Theakston, *The Labour Party and Whitehall* (London: Routledge, 1992), p. 159.

51 Bagehot, is cited in B. Emmott, 'Foreword', in B. Emmott (ed.), *Changing Times: Leading Perspectives on the Civil Service in the 21st Century and Its Enduring Values* (London: Palgrave, 1999).

52 W. Wark, 'In Never-Never Land? The British Archives on Intelligence', *Historical Journal*, 35:1 (March 1992), 195–203. See also R. J. Aldrich,

'Never-Never Land and Wonderland? British and American Policy on Intelligence Archive', *Contemporary Record*, 8:1 (Summer 1994), 132–50.

53 Wark, 'In Never-Never Land?'

54 *Report of the Committee of Privy Councillors on Ministerial Memoirs*, Cmnd. 6386 (London: HMSO, December 1975), p. 31.

55 'CIA and Openness: Speech by Dr Robert M. Gates: Director of the CIA, Oklahoma Press Association, 21 Feb 1992', Norman Mailer Papers, 706.2, Harry Ransom Center, Austin, Texas.

56 N. Cullather, *Secret History: The CIA's Classified Account of Its Operations in Guatemala, 1952–54* (Stanford University Press, 1999), p. vii.

57 P. Lashmar, 'Mr Waldegrave's Need to Know', *History Today*, 44 (August 1994).

58 P. Hennessy, *The Secret State: Whitehall and the Cold War* (London: Penguin, 2003).

59 Cited in G. Warber, '"Collusion" and the Suez Crisis of 1956', *International Affairs* (April 1979), 226.

60 R. J. Aldrich, *The Hidden Hand: Britain, America and Cold War Secret Intelligence* (London: Overlook Press, 2002).

61 This phrase was coined by M. Spufford, *Contrasting Communities: English Villagers in the Sixteenth and Seventeenth Centuries* (Cambridge University Press, 1974), p. xxiii.

1 Laying the foundations of control

1 *Departmental Committee on Section 2 of the Official Secrets Act 1911*, Cmnd. 5104, Volume I, p. 25.

2 A. Friendly, 'British Legal Monstrosity is Stirring New Controversy', *Washington Post*, 21 March 1970.

3 'Cabinet Committee on the Official Secrets Act', Attorney General to Law Officer's Department, November 1938, TNA CAB 21/4705.

4 D. Stafford, *Churchill and Secret Service* (London: Abacus, 1997), p. 41.

5 *Departmental Committee on Section 2 of the Official Secrets Act*, Volume I, p. 14.

6 Cited in D. Wilson, 'Information Is Power: The Causes of Secrecy', in D. Wilson (ed.), *Secrets File: The Case for Freedom of Information in Britain Today* (London: Heinemann, 1984), p. 13.

7 J. Anderson to R. H. Brade, 12 September 1911, TNA WO 32/13732.

8 Hennessy, *Whitehall*, p. 352.

9 K. G. Robertson, *Public Secrets: A Study in the Development of Government Secrecy* (London: Macmillan, 1982), p. 58. Also see Bunyan, *Political Police in Britain*.

10 Vincent, *Culture of Secrecy*, p. 91. See also D. Vincent, 'The Origins of Public Secrecy in Britain', *Transactions of the Royal Historical Society*, 6th series, 1 (1991), 229–48.

11 Wilkinson, *Secrecy and the Media*.

12 Stafford, *Churchill and Secret Service*, p. 41.

13 G. Egerton, 'The Lloyd George "War Memoirs": A Study in the Politics of Memory', *Journal of Modern History*, 60:1 (March 1988), 67.

14 'The Ionian Mystery is Solved', *The Times*, 29 November 1858.

15 Jeremy Bentham, cited in Vincent, *Culture of Secrecy*, p. 3.

16 Ibid.

17 'Extract from a Guide for Departmental Record Officers: Note by the Keeper of Public Records', 29 April 1963, TNA CAB 21/5230.

18 Wilkinson, *Secrecy and the Media*, p. 6.

19 W. Bagehot, *The English Constitution* (3rd edn, London, 1882), p. 92.

20 'Transcript of The Oath of the Privy Councillor', 1250, TNA CAB 21/2678.

21 Interview with Mrs Anne Crossman, 19 December 2005.

22 T. Benn, 'Labour's Oaths of Loyalty: Extracts from the Political Diaries of Tony Benn, 1963–72', *Guardian*, 10 April 2001.

23 R. Hattersley, 'The Republic: Let's Abolish This Absurdity', *Guardian*, 14 December 2000.

24 Hennessy, *Whitehall*, p. 349.

25 P. Hennessy, *The Hidden Wiring: Unearthing the British Constitution* (London: Weidenfeld & Nicolson, 1995).

26 Drewry and Butcher, *Civil Service Today*, p. 151.

27 Sir James Stephen, cited in Vincent, *Culture of Secrecy*, p. 44.

28 Ibid.

29 K. Robbins, *Politicians, Diplomacy and War in Modern British History* (London: Hambledon Continuum, 1994), p. 88; M. Conboy, *The Press and Popular Culture* (Gateshead: Sage, 2001), pp. 89, 136.

30 Robbins, *Politicians, Diplomacy and War*, p. 98.

31 Lord Lyndhurst, cited in G. A. Cranfield, *The Press and Society: From Caxton to Northcliffe* (London: Longman, 1978), p. 225.

32 R. Boston, 'From Inkwells to Computers', *British Journalism Review*, 5:63 (1994), 63–5.

33 *The Times*, 6 February 1852, p. 4.

34 Ibid.

35 *Departmental Committee on Section 2*, Volume 1, p. 120.

36 Cited in Vincent, *Culture of Secrecy*, p. 65.

37 *The Times*, 6 February 1852, p. 4.

38 John Stuart Mill, cited in Vincent, *Culture of Secrecy*, p. 30.

39 N. Chester, *The Administrative System 1780–1870* (Oxford University Press, 1981), p. 282.

40 *The Northcote–Trevelyan Report*, Parliamentary Papers, 27 (1854), cited in *The Civil Service, Report of the Committee 1966–68*, Cmnd. 3638 (London, 1968), Volume 1, Appendix B.

41 H. Roseveare, *The Treasury: The Evolution of a British Institution* (London: Allen Lane, 1969), p. 179.

42 'The Civil Servant and His Profession: Series of Lectures Delivered to the Society of Civil Servants', March 1920, The Modern Records Centre (hereafter MRC) MSS 232/scs/4/2/4.

43 Lord Romilly, cited in J. Morley, *The Life of Gladstone* (London: Macmillan, 1908), p. 380.

44 Lewis, cited in Vincent, *Culture of Secrecy*, p. 34.

45 Hennessy, *Whitehall*, p. 43.

46 'A History of Unauthorised Communications to the Press. Forthcoming Deputation by the Newspapers Proprietors Association', 13 June 1930, TNA HO 144/20992.

47 'Press Censorship Manual', October 1953, TNA CAB 134/1139.

48 Ibid.

49 Copy of Despatch from J. Young to E. B. Lyton, 14 July 1858, TNA CO 883/1/8; Copy of Despatch from J. Young to H. Du Pré Labouchère, 10 June 1857, TNA CO 883/1/8.

50 J. Young to E. B. Lyton, 19 August 1858, TNA CO 883/1/8.

51 'Central Criminal Court', *The Times*, 16 December 1858, p. 9.

52 *Departmental Committee on Section 2 of the Official Secrets Act*, Volume 1, p. 120.

53 'Case: Globe Statement', S. Hulhart, 15 June 1878, TNA CAB 41/11/14.

54 Cited in Naylor, *A Man and an Institution*, p. 41.

55 'Charge of Stealing Documents', *The Times*, 28 June 1878, p. 11.

56 Tenterden, cited in Vincent, *Culture of Secrecy*, p. 81.

57 C. Marvin, *Our Public Offices* (2nd edn, London, 1880), p. 248.

58 Ibid, p. 212.

59 'Dismissal of Dockyard Draughtsman for Breach of Trust', *The Times*, 9 March 1887, p. 7; 'Parliamentary Notices', *The Times*, 10 March 1887, p. 7; 'Parliamentary Intelligence', *The Times*, 6 April 1887, p. 5.

60 *Hansard*, 3rd Series, 10 March 1887, col. 1,745.

61 Ibid.

62 Rogers, *Secrecy and Power*, p. 18.

63 *Hansard*, 3rd Series, 338, 20 June 1889, cols. 52–3.

64 *Hansard*, 3rd Series, 325, 28 March 1889, col. 110.

65 See I. F. Clarke, *Voices Prophesying War* (Oxford University Press, 1966); David Seed, 'Erskine Childers and the German Peril', *German Life and Letters*, 45:1 (January 1992), 66–73.

66 Seed, 'Erskine Childers', 66.

67 'Official Secrets', *The Times*, 7 May 1908.

68 *Hansard*, 3rd Series, 338, 20 June 1889, cols. 52–3.

69 Parliamentary Counsel to War Office, 8 March 1895, TNA WO 32/6347.

70 'Memorandum: The Official Secrets Bill', 13 November 1895, TNA WO 32/13727.

71 Wilkinson, *Secrecy and the Media*, p. 14.

72 Ibid., p. 16.

73 Ibid., p. 20.

74 J. Baylen, 'Stead, William Thomas (1849–1912)', *Oxford Dictionary of National Biography*, Oxford University Press, September 2004; online edn, May 2008 (www.oxforddnb.com/view/article/36258, accessed 7 April 2010).

75 W. T. Stead, 'Government by Journalism', *Contemporary Review* (1886), p. 661.

76 J. Baylen, 'George Moore, W. T. Stead, and the Boer War', *Studies in English*, 3 (1962), 49–60.

77 J. Brien, 'Sir Arthur Conan Doyle and W. T. Stead: The Novelist and the Journalist', *Albion: A Quarterly Journal Concerned with British Studies*, 2:1 (1970), 11.

78 See A. Paget, 'Some Experiences of a Commandant: Prisoners of War at Deadwood Camp', *Longmans' Magazine*, October 1901; W. Churchill, *Ian Hamilton's March* (New York: Longmans, Green and Co., 1900); B. F. S. Baden-Powell, *War in Practice: Some Tactical and Other Lessons of the Campaign in South Africa 1899–1902* (New York: Kessinger Publishing, 1903, reprinted 2007); J. Barnes, *The Great War Trek: With the British Army on the Veldt* (New York: D. Appleton, 1901).

79 J. Harlow, 'Boer War Letter Reveals Churchill the Bounder', *Sunday Times*, 27 April 1997.

80 Ibid.

81 D. Stafford, *The Silent Game: The Real World of Imaginary Spies* (Athens: University of Georgia Press, 1989), p. 6.

82 Cited in L. Piper, *The Tragedy of Erskine Childers: Dangerous Waters* (London: Hambledon and London, 2003), p. 76.

83 K. Ward to E. Childers, 27 December 1910, Erskine Childers MSS, Trinity College, Cambridge, Box 2: 143.

84 R. Smith to E. Childers, 27 January 1903, Erskine Childers MSS, Trinity College, Cambridge, Box 2: 140.

85 Piper, *Erskine Childers*, p. 71.

86 'Special Military Resources of the German Empire'. Prepared by the General Staff, February 1912, p. 52, TNA WO 33/579.

87 E. Gleichen, *A Guardsman's Memories* (London: William Blackwood, 1932), p. 344.

88 Cited in Stafford, *Silent Game*, p. 30.

89 C. Andrew, *Secret Service: The Making of the British Intelligence Community* (London: Heinemann, 1985), pp. 37–8.

90 W. Le Queux, *Things I Know about Kings, Celebrities and Crooks* (London: Eveleigh Nash and Grayson, 1923).

91 Ibid., p. 238.

92 Ibid.

93 'Defenceless Dover', *Morning Post*, 21 March 1908, TNA ADM 116/4082.

94 F. Glover, 'To the Editor of *The Times*', *The Times*, 9 May 1908, p. 7.

95 *Hansard*, 4th Series, 178, 11 May 1908, col. 674.

96 'The Official Secrets Bill', *The Times*, 11 May 1908, p. 6; 'The Newspaper Society', *The Times*, 14 May 1908, p. 12; *The Times*, 7 May 1908, p. 11.

97 See W. Michael Ryan, 'The Invasion Controversy of 1906–08: Lieutenant-Colonel Charles à Court Repington and British Perceptions of the German Menace', *Military Affairs*, 44:1 (February 1980), 8–12.

98 D. French, 'Spy Fever in Britain, 1900–1915', *Historical Journal*, 21:2 (June 1978), 355–70; D. Trotter, 'The Politics of Adventure in the Early British Spy Novel', *Intelligence and National Security*, 5:4 (October 1990), 30–54; N. Hiley, 'Decoding German Spies: British Spy Fiction 1908–18', *Intelligence and National Security*, 5:4 (October 1990), 55–79.

99 W. Le Queux, *Spies of the Kaiser* (Abingdon: Routledge, new edn 1996), Introduction.

100 'Report and Proceedings: Sub-Committee of Imperial Defence: The Question of Foreign Espionage in the United Kingdom', 24 July 1909, TNA CAB 16/8.

101 Ibid.

102 'Intelligence Methods', S. Ewart, 1909, TNA KV 1/4.

103 'Report and Proceedings: Sub-Committee of Imperial Defence: The Question of Foreign Espionage in the United Kingdom', 24 July 1909, TNA CAB 16/8.

104 'Intelligence Methods', S. Ewart, 1909, TNA KV 1/4.

105 'Report and Proceedings', TNA CAB 16/8.

106 Ibid.

107 'Memorandum for the Law Officers', E. Trough to R. Isaacs, 4 May 1910, TNA LO 3/301. Also see Stafford, *Churchill and Secret Service*, pp. 36–9.

108 'Opinion', R. Isaacs, 20 April 1910, TNA LO 3/301.

109 'Memorandum for the Law Officers', E. Trough to R. Isaacs, 4 May 1910, TNA LO 3/301.

110 Stafford, *Churchill and Secret Service*, p. 38.

111 Ibid., p. 39.

112 *Hansard*, 5th Series, 29, 18 August 1911, col. 2,252.

113 Vincent, 'Origins of Public Secrecy', 246.

114 'Cabinet Committee on the Official Secrets Act', Attorney General to Law Officer's Department, November 1938, TNA CAB 21/4705.

115 Ibid., p. 14.

116 Cited in A. Palmer, 'The History of the D-Notice Committee', in C. Andrew and D. Dilks (eds.), *The Missing Dimension: Governments and Intelligence Communities in the Twentieth Century* (London: Palgrave Macmillan, 1984), p. 231.

2 Bending the rules: ministers and their memoirs, 1920–1945

1 E. Bridges, 5 November 1943, TNA CAB 104/229.

2 'Official Secrets', *The Times*, 13 January 1933.

3 T. Travers, 'The Relativity of War: British Military Memoirs from the Campaigns of Marlborough to the First World War', in G. Egerton (ed.), *Political Memoir: Essays on the Politics of Memory* (London: Frank Cass, 1994), p. 152.

4 'Publication of Cabinet Documents', R. Howorth, 21 January 1935, TNA CAB 104/142; R. K. Middlemas, 'Cabinet Secrecy and the Crossman Diaries', *Political Quarterly*, 47:1 (January 1976), 40.

5 Cited in *New York Times*, 22 October 1922.

6 Naylor, *A Man and an Institution*, p. 42.

7 Ibid.

8 Reynolds, *Command of History*, p. 23.

9 Cabinet 1 (19) 3, 4 November 1919, TNA CAB 23/18; Reynolds, *Command of History*, p. 24.

10 A. J. Sylvester, 'How I Helped Lloyd George Write His War Memoirs', National Library of Wales (hereafter NLW) E7.

11 Naylor, *A Man and an Institution*, p. 42.

12 F. Stevenson, *The Years That Are Past* (London: Hutchinson, 1967), p. 191. On relinquishing office, Leo Amery was believed to have kept, on principle, a copy of every paper circulated over his initials from 1924 to 1929 (E. B. Boyd to R. Howorth, 9 May 1934, TNA CAB 21/2824).

13 M. Hankey, 'Cabinet Papers', September 1934, TNA CAB 21/2824.

14 Ian F. W. Beckett, 'French, John Denton Pinkstone, first earl of Ypres (1852–1925)', *Oxford Dictionary of National Biography*, Oxford University Press, 2004; online edn, May 2009 (www.oxforddnb.com/view/article/33272).

15 'Note: Sir John Jellicoe, *The Gland Fleet*', TNA HW 3/13.

16 B. Bond, *The Unquiet Western Front: Britain's Role in Literature and History* (Cambridge University Press, 2002), p. 43.

17 P. Fraser, 'Cabinet Secrecy and War Memoirs', *History*, 70:230 (1985), 401.

18 W. S. Blunt, *My Diaries: Being a Personal Narrative of Events 1888–1914 Part Two* (New York: Alfred A. Knopf, 1921), p. 398.

19 Reynolds, *Command of History*, pp. 24–5.

20 Ibid., p. 25.

21 Naylor, *A Man and an Institution*, p. 118.

22 'Committee on the Use of Official Material in Publications: Composition and Terms of Reference', 24 February 1923, TNA CAB 27/213.

23 Cited in S. Roskill, *Hankey: Man of Secrets*, 3 vols. (London: Collins, 1970–74), Volume III: *1931–1963*, p. 365.

24 Reynolds, *Command of History*, p. 26.

25 Ibid.

26 Egerton, 'Lloyd George "War Memoirs"', 58–9.

27 Ibid., p. 57.

28 'Lloyd George Book to Bring $400,000', *New York Times*, 13 August 1922, p. 1. The figure of £90,000 was arrived at in the following way: US serial rights £40,000; US book rights £20,000; British book rights £15,000; British Empire serial rights £15,000.

29 Cited in *New York Times*, 13 August 1922, p. 1.

30 M. Lloyd George to D. Lloyd George, House of Lords Records Office (hereafter HLRO), Lloyd George Papers, LG/G/1/2/44, 1922.

31 'Lloyd George to Devote to War Charities All Profits of his Forthcoming Memoir', *New York Times*, 27 August 1922, p. 1.

32 United Press Association to F. Stevenson, 28 May 1923, HLRO LG/G/205/4.

33 Egerton, 'Lloyd George "War Memoirs"', 61.

34 Messrs Lewis and Lewis, 7 December 1922, HLRO LG/G/205/4.

35 A. J. Sylvester Papers, NLW; Suttie, *Rewriting the First World War*, p. 13. The typescript versions of Sylvester's diary entries can be found in Class A. These entries have also been inspected by Dr Andrew Suttie, albeit before they were catalogued.

36 Ibid.

37 Swinton to L. George, January 1924, HLRO, LG/G/216.

38 Suttie, *Rewriting the First World War*, p. 14.

39 Sylvester, 'How I Helped Lloyd George Write His War Memoirs', NLW E7.

40 J. D. Clare, 'Interpretation of Haig', www.johndclare.net/ wwi3_HaigHistoriography.htm. Clare's article provides a first-class overview of the 'Great Haig Debate'.

41 Ibid. This contrasts with the earlier assessment of David French, who argued that Haig was 'content to let history take care of his reputation'. D. French, 'Sir Douglas Haig's Reputation, 1918–1928: A Note', *Historical Journal*, 28:4 (1985), 953–60.

42 G. Jones, 'The Lloyd George War Memoirs', *Transactions of the Honourable Society of Cymmrodorion*, 14 (2008), 131.

43 L. George to M. Hankey, 10 April 1934, HLRO, LG/G/212/4.

44 'Room 40', H. Sinclair, September 1919, TNA HW 3/13.

45 'Sir Alfred Ewing's Lectures', O. Murray, 12 January 1932, TNA HW 3/13; R. V. Jones, 'Alfred Ewing and Room 40', *Notes and Records of the Royal Society of London*, 34:1 (1979), 65–90. During his talk, Ewing not only discussed the genesis and development of naval intelligence but used the phrase 'The Ultra Secret', not then carrying the implication it has today, referring rather to the old Admiral's code at the battle of Trafalgar.

46 Miscellaneous Note, TNA HW 3/13.

47 C. Usborne, 11 May 1932, TNA HW 3/13; H. Hoy, *40 OB: Or How the War Was Won* (London: Hutchinson, 1932).

48 W. Clarke, 1 February 1930, TNA HW 3/13.

49 A. J. Sylvester, 'Examples of My Work on This Book', NLW E5.

50 Egerton, 'Lloyd George "War Memoirs"', 66.

51 D. Lloyd George to M. Hankey, 10 April 1933, HLRO LG/G/212/3.

52 See C. Mowat, *Britain Between the Wars 1918–1940* (London: Methuen, 1955).

53 A. J. P. Taylor, *English History, 1914–1945* (Oxford University Press, 1965), p. 74.

54 Vincent, *Culture of Secrecy*, p. 170.

55 Hooper, *Official Secrets*, p. 45.

56 'Scots Author's Book of War Stories Withdrawn', *Scottish Daily Express*; 28 October 1932; 'Compton Mackenzie Summons', *Manchester Dispatch*, 5 November 1932; 'Summons Against Author of Sequel to a Banned Book', *Daily Mirror*, 5 November 1932; 'Novelist on Official Secrets Act Charge', *Daily Express*, 16 November 1932.

57 Andrew, *Secret Service*, p. 351.

58 Cited in Hooper, *Official Secrets*, p. 47.

59 C. Mackenzie, *My Life and Times: Octave Seven, 1931–8* (London: Chatto & Windus, 1968), p. 84.

60 Major M. Frost, 3 June 1942, TNA KV 2/1272.

61 'Need for Discretion', *News Chronicle*, 12 January 1933.

62 Ibid.

63 'Greek Memories by Compton Mackenzie', TNA KV 2/1271. Details of SIS objections can also be found in K. Jeffery, *MI6: The History of the Secret Intelligence Service* (London: Bloomsbury, 2010), pp. 239–41.

64 'Greek Memories by Compton Mackenzie', TNA KV 2/1271.

65 Jeffery, *MI6*, pp. 42–5.

66 Liddell Hart, Diary, 'Talk with Compton Mackenzie', 29 November 1932, King's College London Liddell Hart Centre for Military Archives (hereafter KCL), Liddell Hart Papers, LH/1932/47. See also Andrew, *Secret Service*, p. 351.

67 Cited in Jeffery, *MI6*, p. 241.

68 *Statesman and Nation*, 100, 21 January 1933.

69 *Sphere*, 21 January 1933.

70 Liddell Hart, Diary, 12 January 1933, KCL LH 11/1933/4.

71 Mackenzie, *My Life and Times*, p. 84.

72 M. Hankey, *The Supreme Command*, 2 vols., Volume II (London: George Allen, 1961), p. 591.

73 Sylvester Papers, NLW.

74 Sylvester, Diary, 28 September 1933, NLW Sylvester Papers A20.

75 Ibid. 21 October 1933.

76 Sylvester, 'How I Helped Lloyd George Write His War Memoirs', NLW E7.

77 Ibid.

78 Ibid.

79 Sylvester, 'Examples of My Work on this Book', NLW E5.

80 Hankey to Lloyd George, 2 December 1930, HLRO LG/8/8/18.

81 Ibid.

82 Ibid.

83 Ibid.

84 Ibid.

85 Sylvester, Diary, 29 March 1933, NLW Sylvester Papers A20.

86 Sylvester, 'How I Helped Lloyd George Write His War Memoirs', NLW E7.

87 Naylor, *A Man and an Institution*, p. 206.

88 Suttie, *Rewriting the First World War*, p. 25.

89 J. Edmonds to Sylvester, 19 September 1933, HLRO LG/G/235.

90 Naylor, *A Man and an Institution*, p. 208.

91 Hankey to D. Lloyd George, 11 April 1933, HLRO LG/G/212/3.

92 R. Lewin, 'Sir Basil Liddell Hart: The Captain Who Taught the Generals', *International Affairs*, 47:1 (January 1971), 79.

93 B. Liddell Hart to D. Lloyd George, 11 April 1933, HLRO LG/G/212/3.

94 B. Liddell Hart to D. Lloyd George, 'Notes on Mr Lloyd George's Memoirs', HLRO LG/G/212/3.

95 Hankey to Liddell-Hart, 15 February 1934, TNA CAB 104/141.

96 Sylvester, 'Examples of My Work on This Book', NLW E5.

97 Suttie, *Rewriting the First World War*, p. 20.

98 D. Lloyd George to M. Hankey, 18 April 1934, TNA CAB 104/141.

99 Sylvester, Diary, 29 March 1933, NLW Sylvester Papers A21.

100 Hankey to Lloyd George, 27 April 1934, HLRO LG/G/212/3.

101 Hankey to Lloyd George, 16 April 1934, HLRO LG/G/212/4.

102 P. Hart and N. Steel, *Passchendaele: The Sacrificial Ground* (London: Cassell, 2001), pp. 211–12.

103 Lloyd George, cited in Suttie, *Rewriting the First World War*, p. 12.

104 Sylvester, cited ibid., p. 17.

105 Ibid.

106 D. Lloyd George, *War Memories*, 6 vols. (London: Odhams, 1938), Volume I, p. 322.

107 Lloyd George, *War Memories*, Volume II, p. 1,243.

108 Ibid., p. 2,014.

109 Ibid.

110 Ibid., p. 1,409.

111 Egerton, 'Lloyd George "War Memoirs"', 77.

112 Lloyd George, *War Memories*, Volume II, p. 1,296.

113 Ibid., p. 1,312.

114 Ibid., p. 1,657.
115 Sylvester to Lloyd George, 10 April 1934, LG/G/212/3.
116 Ibid.
117 Ibid.
118 'Hankey Notes: Passchendaele', LG/G/212/4.
119 Lloyd George, *War Memoirs*, Volume II, p. 2,017.
120 Ibid.
121 Suttie, *Rewriting the First World War*, p. 4.
122 Hankey to C. Wigram, 28 May 1934, TNA CAB 104/142.
123 'Hankey Notes: Volume III, Chapter 1', HLRO LG/G/212/4.
124 Ibid.
125 Ibid.
126 M. Hankey to Lloyd George, 11 April 1933, HLRO LG/G/212/3.
127 Sylvester, 'Examples of My Work on This Book', NLW E5.
128 M. Hankey to Lloyd George, LG/G/212/4.
129 Sylvester, 'Examples of My Work on this Book', NLW E5.
130 Ibid.
131 Ibid.
132 Suttie, *Rewriting the First World War*, p. 23.
133 Sylvester, 'Examples of My Work on This Book', NLW E5.
134 Ibid., p. 24.
135 R. MacDonald to M. Hankey, 19 April 1934, HLRO, LG/G/212/3.
136 Suttie, *Rewriting the First World War*, p. 10.
137 Ibid.
138 Egerton, 'Lloyd George "War Memoirs"', 65.
139 Sylvester, 'Examples of My Work on This Book', NLW E5.
140 Suttie, *Rewriting the First World War*, p. 195.
141 Cited in Jones, 'Lloyd George "War Memoirs"', 138.
142 Cited in Suttie, *Rewriting the First World War*, p. 195.
143 See Naylor, *A Man and an Institution*, pp. 208–9.
144 Ibid., p. 208.
145 Ibid., pp. 208–9.
146 Ibid., pp. 223–4. Also: 'Additional Notes on the Establishment of the Conventions', 14 October 1975, TNA CAB 164/1297.
147 C 35 (34) 4, 17 October 1934, TNA CAB 23/80.
148 *Report of the Committee of Privy Councillors on Ministerial Memoirs* (London, 16 December 1975), Cmnd. 6386, TNA PREM 16/904; 'Publication of Cabinet Documents', R. Howorth, 21 January 1935, TNA CAB 104/142; 'Introductory Historical Note: The Use of Official Material in Ministerial and Other Memoirs', R. Howorth, 18 July 1941, TNA CAB 21/2165.
149 Sylvester, 'Examples of My Work on This Book', NLW E5.

150 'Last Labour Cabinet Papers Disclosed', *Manchester Guardian*, 6 March 1934.

151 *Report of the Committee of Privy Councillors on Ministerial Memoirs* (London, 16 December 1975), TNA PREM 16/904; 'The Lansbury Case', R. Howorth, 20 March 1934, TNA CAB 21/391.

152 Hooper, *Official Secrets*, pp. 54–6.

153 CII (34) 5, 21 March 1934, TNA CAB 23/78.

154 Cited in Naylor, *A Man and an Institution*, p. 214.

155 See D. Reynolds, 'Official History: How Churchill and the Cabinet Office Wrote *The Second World War*', *Historical Research*, 78:201, 400–22.

156 CP 218 (35), 'Cabinet Procedure: Recovery of Cabinet Papers', 29 November 1935, TNA CAB 24/257.

157 C. Addison to Lloyd George, 29 September 1934, HLRO LG/G1/4/3.

158 Reynolds, *Command of History*, p. 27.

159 Ibid.

160 Lloyd George to C. Addison, 3 October 1934, HLRO LG/G/1/4/4.

161 Naylor, *A Man and an Institution*, p. 221.

162 M. Hankey, 'The Supreme Command 1914–1918', Memorandum, 29 March 1945, Maurice Hankey Papers, Churchill College, Cambridge (hereafter CCC), HNKY 25/1.

163 'Notes on Volume 5', TNA CAB 21/2165.

164 S. Gaselee to Lord Chatfield, 11 September 1941, TNA FO 370/660; Lord Chatfield to S. Gaselee, 17 September 1941, TNA FO 370/660; S. Gaselee to Lord Chatfield, 18 September 1941, TNA FO 370/660.

165 'Lord Chatfield's Memoirs', TNA CAB 21/2165.

166 'Conclusions of a Meeting held at the War Cabinet', 21 November 1941, TNA ADM 116/447.

167 Churchill to Bridges, 23 November 1941, TNA CAB 21/2165.

168 Reynolds, *Command of History*, p. 30.

169 Hankey to Bridges, 22 September 1943, TNA CAB 104/229. Duplicated in CCC HNKY 25/1.

170 Ibid.

171 Hankey to Bridges, 27 October 1944, CCC HNKY 25/1.

172 H. Aubrey Gentry to Miss Pearn, 18 October 1944, CCC HNKY 25/2.

173 Newman Flower to M. Hankey, 13 November 1944, CCC HNKY 25/2.

174 Bridges to Hankey, 30 November 1944, CCC HNKY 25/1.

175 Ibid.

176 Ibid.

177 Hankey to Bridges, 3 December 1944, CCC HNKY 25/1.

178 Naylor, *A Man and an Institution*, p. 44; M. Hankey, 'The Supreme Command 1914–1918', Memorandum, 29 March 1945, CCC HNKY 25/1.

179 M. Hankey to D. Lloyd George, 7 December 1944, CCC HNKY 25/2.

180 M. Hankey to W. Churchill, 8 December 1944, CCC HNKY 25/1; Reynolds, *Command of History*, p. 31.

181 E. Bridges to M. Hankey, 23 February 1945, CCC HNKY 25/1.

182 M. Hankey to T. Jones, 28 February 1945, CCC HNKY 25/2.

183 Ibid.

184 T. Jones to M. Hankey, 1 March 1945, CCC HNKY 25/2.

185 Ibid.

186 T. Jones to M. Hankey, 19 April 1945, CCC HNKY 25/2.

187 Ibid.

188 M. Hankey to T. Jones, 24 April 1945, CCC HNKY 25/2.

189 M. Hankey, 'The Supreme Command 1914–1918', Memorandum, 29 March 1945, CCC HNKY 25/1.

190 Ibid.

191 Ibid.

192 Ibid.

193 Reynolds, *Command of History*, p. 28.

194 Ibid.

195 'Additional Notes on the Establishment of the Conventions', 14 October 1975, TNA CAB 164/1297; 'Wings of Destiny', 2 December 1942, TNA CAB 21/2677.

196 'Disclosure of Cabinet Proceedings and Papers', 9 February 1953, TNA CAB 21/3766.

197 Reynolds, *Command of History*, pp. 28–9.

198 Ibid., p. 29.

3 Chapman Pincher: sleuthing the secret state

1 Secret and Personal, Est 4 Security to A. J. D. Gordes (Ministry of Supply Storage Depot), Ruddington, TNA AVIA 65/2340.

2 C. Meyer, *Facing Reality: From World Federalism to the CIA* (New York: Harper & Row, 1980), p. 84.

3 See C. Bernstein and B. Woodward, *All the President's Men* (New York: Simon & Schuster, 1974).

4 Rogers, *Secrecy and Power*, p. 63.

5 Shils, *Torment of Secrecy*, p. 51.

6 E. P. Thompson, 'The Secret State', *Race and Class*, 20 (1979), 222.

7 Rogers, *Secrecy and Power*, p. 68.

8 R. Crossman, 'Real English Disease', p. 1.

9 J. Jenks, *British Propaganda and News Media in the Cold War* (Edinburgh University Press, 2006).

10 C. Brown, 'Annie's Bar, Scene of Political Plots, to Close', *Independent*, 18 February 2006.

11 P. Kellner, 'The Lobby, Official Secrets and Good Government', *Parliamentary Affairs*, 36:1 (1983), 277.

12 P. Hennessy, 'Accelerated History? Whitehall and the Press since 1945', James Cameron Lecture 2000; P. Hennessy, 'Government vs the Press', *The Times*, 21 June 1984, p. 9.

13 P. Hennessy, 'Modest Little Central Cell Keeps a Lookout for Hurricanes', *The Times*, 3 October 1978, p. 4.

14 Interview with Chapman Pincher.

15 Ibid.

16 Ibid.

17 E. P. Thompson, 'A State of Blackmail', in E. P. Thompson, *Writing by Candlelight* (London: Merlin Press, 1980), p. 115.

18 Ibid., p. 116.

19 'Enquiry into Report by Chapman Pincher', D/Sy (PE), September 1976, TNA DEFE 68/223.

20 Jenks, *British Propaganda*, p. 1.

21 C. Pincher, '75.lb, Safe + 75.lb, Safe = Atom', *Daily Express*, 28 September 1945, p. 1.

22 H. Smyth, *Atomic Energy for Military Purposes: The Official Report on the Development of the Atomic Bomb under the United States Government, 1940–1945* (Princeton, 1945).

23 Cpt. Clarke to J. F. Jackson, 9 November 1945, TNA CAB 126/302.

24 Interview with Chapman Pincher.

25 Ibid.

26 C. Pincher, 'Atom Secrets Out: America Has 96', *Daily Express*, 2 November 1946.

27 Interview with Chapman Pincher.

28 Wilkinson, *Secrecy and the Media*, p. 211.

29 Interview with Chapman Pincher.

30 Joint Services Mission (Washington) to Cabinet Office, 2 November 1946, TNA CAB 126/302.

31 Cabinet Office to Joint Services Mission (Washington), 19 March 1947, TNA CAB 126/302.

32 Ibid.

33 R. T. Read, 4 November 1946, TNA KV 4/356.

34 'Articles by Rear Admiral G. P. Thomson in the *Sunday Dispatch*', E. J. P. Cussen, 4 October 1946, TNA KV 4/355.

35 Cabinet Office to Joint Services Mission (Washington), 8 November 1946, TNA CAB 126/302.

36 Interview with Chapman Pincher.

37 Ibid.

38 Ibid.

39 C. Pincher, 'Faster than Sound Flight Fails', *Daily Express*, 17 October 1947.

40 'Leakage of Information: Supersonic Model Trials', C. B. Peel, 17 October 1947, TNA AVIA 65/2340.

41 L. P. Keen to Air Officer Commanding-in-Chief, 31 July 1947, TNA AVIA 65/2340.

42 'Leakage of Information: Supersonic Model Trials', C. B. Peel, 17 October 1947, TNA AVIA 65/2340.

43 Interview with Chapman Pincher.

44 C. Pincher, 'The Super-Speed Plan is Running Pretty Slow', *Daily Express*, 11 August 1948.

45 'Leakage of Information: Investigation by Air Ministry Constabulary', 18 August 1948, TNA AVIA 65/2340.

46 'Stop Press on Star – Penny on Beer', *Star*, 12 November 1947.

47 *Report from the Select Committee on the Budget Disclosure* (London, 11 December 1947), TNA PREM 8/435.

48 S. S. Cherry to W. R. C. Penny, 8 December 1948, TNA AVIA 65/2340.

49 W. R. C. Penny to W. D. Wilkinson, 15 October 1948, TNA AVIA 65/2340.

50 Est 4 (Sec) to A. J. D. Gerdes, 1 April 1949, TNA AVIA 65/2340.

51 'Report over MI5 Prevention of Leaks in the Light of *Daily Express* Exposé', 31 May 1949, TNA AVIA 65/2340.

52 C. Pincher, 'Now Who Left the Secret Plans on View?', *Daily Express*, 2 August 1949; R. F. Fenn to Est 4 (Sec), 2 August 1949, TNA AVIA 65/2340.

53 C. Pincher, 'Here is £1,000,000 Worth of Top Secret Exposed', *Daily Express*, 22 September 1949.

54 J. A. Jaggers to D. A. Shirlaw, 22 September 1949, TNA AVIA 65/2340.

55 Ibid.; Ministry of Supply (Atomic Division) to J. A. Jaggers, 10 October 1949, TNA AVIA 65/2340.

56 Interview with Chapman Pincher.

57 'D-Notices and Press Freedom: Lecture Given by Chapman Pincher in the Harcourt Room, House of Commons, 21 July 1969', *Freedom First*, Autumn 1969, Papers of George Wigg, London School of Economics (hereafter LSE), WIGG 4/159.

58 Wilkinson, *Secrecy and the Media*, p. 231.

59 Obituary, 'In the National Interest' (obituary of Rear Admiral George Thomson), *Sunday Times*, 14 May 1961.

60 Ibid.

61 Ibid.

62 Wilkinson, *Secrecy and the Media*, pp. 227–8.

63 Interview with Chapman Pincher.

64 Ibid.

65 K. de Courcy to Lord Salisbury, 14 June 1951. Kenneth de Courcy Papers, Hoover Institution, Stanford University. Reel 2, Box 2, Folder 5.

66 Aldrich, *Hidden Hand*, pp. 607–8.

67 *Hansard*, 5th Series, 150, 15 December 1924, col. 674.

68 M. Howard, 'Cowboys, Playboys and Other Spies', *New York Times*, 16 February 1986, p. 6.

69 D. Campbell, 'The Man in the Mac: A Life in Crime Reporting', *Guardian*, 5 September 2009.

70 Major D. I. Vesey, 17 January 1946, TNA KV 4/254.

71 Ibid.

72 Ibid.

73 'Observations by the War Office', E. J. P. Cussen, 8 May 1946, TNA KV 4/354.

74 Ibid.

75 Lord Rothschild, 31 January 1946, TNA KV 4/354.

76 S. Firmin, *Crime Man: Experiences as a Crime Reporter* (London: Hutchinson, 1950).

77 G. Thomson to E. J. P. Cussen, 29 April 1946, TNA KV 4/355.

78 Ibid.

79 B. A. Hill, 9.5.47, TNA KV 4/354. See also 'Liberal Minded Censor', *Daily Telegraph*, 3 May 1947; 'Chief Censor Helps Journalist Get Stories Passed!', *World Press News*, 12 December 1946.

80 C. Pincher, 'Fuchs Gave the Bomb to Russia', *Daily Express*, 2 March 1950.

81 M. S. Goodman and C. Pincher, 'Research Note: Clement Attlee, Percy Sillitoe and the Security Aspects of the Fuchs Case', *Contemporary British History*, 19:1 (2005), pp. 67–77.

82 Ibid., p. 72.

83 Ibid.

84 B. A. Hill to SIS, 28 August 1950, TNA KV 4/356.

85 Ibid.

86 See TNA KV 4/358.

87 Note, 26 January 1951, TNA KV 3/357.

88 C. Pincher, *Treachery: Betrayals, Blunders and Cover-ups: Six Decades of Espionage Against America and Great Britain* (New York: Random House, 2009), p. 388.

89 C. Pincher, 'Yard Hunts Two Britons', *Daily Express*, 7 June 1951.

90 Letters to the Editor, 'Ethics of Journalism', *The Times*, 21 July 1952, p. 5.

91 Ibid.

92 A. Pelling, 4 July 1951, TNA KV 4/357.

93 Confidential Note, 4 July 1951, TNA KV 4/3357.

94 R. J. Aldrich, *GCHQ: The Uncensored Story of Britain's Most Secret Intelligence Agency* (London: Harper Press, 2010), p. 1.

95 N. Ferguson, *Virtual History: Alternatives and Counterfactuals* (New York: Basic Books, 1998).

96 Confidential Note, 4 July 1951, TNA KV 4/3357.

97 C. Wilson, 'Revealed: the Duke and Duchess of Windsor's Secret Plot to Deny the Queen the Throne', *Daily Telegraph*, 22 November 2009.

98 'Interview Questions Submitted to Kenneth de Courcy by the Hoover Institution', 1983. Kenneth de Courcy Papers, Reel 6, Box 5, Folder 10.

99 N. West (ed.), *The Guy Liddell Diaries* Volume II: *1942–45* (London: Routledge, 2005), p. 28.

100 K. de Courcy to Lord Salisbury, 28 October 1952. Kenneth de Courcy Papers, Reel 2, Box 2, Folder 4.

101 K. de Courcy to Lord Salisbury, 4 August 1952. Ibid.

102 Handwritten comments by K. de Courcy. Penned at the bottom of a letter from Lord Salisbury. See Lord Salisbury to K. de Courcy, 27 October 1952. Ibid.

103 Handwritten comments by K. de Courcy. Penned on the back of a letter from Lord Vansittart. Lord Vansittart to K. de Courcy, 7 November 1951. Kenneth de Courcy Papers, Reel 2, Box 2, Folder 5.

104 Handwritten comments by K. de Courcy. Penned at the bottom of a letter from Lord Salisbury. See Lord Salisbury to K. de Courcy, 27 October 1952. Kenneth de Courcy Papers, Reel 2, Box 2, Folder 4.

105 C. Andrew, *The Defence of the Realm: The Authorised History of MI5* (London: Allen Lane, 2009).

106 K. de Courcy to War Office, 7 June 1951. Kenneth de Courcy Papers, Reel 2, Box 2, Folder 8.

107 Ibid.

108 Pincher, *Treachery*, p. 409.

109 C. Pincher, *Inside Story: A Documentary of the Pursuit of Power* (London: Sidgwick & Jackson, 1978), p. 177.

110 'JIC: Minutes of the One Hundred and First Meeting of the Committee', 18 September 1953, TNA CAB 159/14.

111 Det. Superintendent, A. Hoare, Crime Office, Chichester, 14 May 1956, West Sussex Record Office, Chichester, POL w/c6/2.

112 Aldrich, *GCHQ*, p. 141.

113 E. Bridges, 'The Report of an Enquiry on an Intelligence Operation against Russian Warships', 18 May 1956. www.cabinetoffice.gov.uk/media/cabinetoffice/.../bridges_rpt.pdf

114 Aldrich, *GCHQ*, p. 141.

115 Bridges, 'Report of an Enquiry'.

116 Ibid.

117 Ibid.

118 'On This Day: 9 May 1956: Mystery of Missing Frogman Deepens', BBC News, news.bbc.co.uk/onthisday.

119 Ibid.

120 Ibid.

121 Ibid.

122 Ibid.

123 R. Gleadowe to L. Crabb, 31 January 1944, TNA ADM 1/14531.

124 'Top Frogman Dies in Secret Test', *News Chronicle*, 30 April 1956.

125 'Red Sailor: I Saw Frogman', *Daily Mail*, 5 May 1956; 'We Saw a Frogman Say Russians', *Daily Express*, 5 May 1956.

126 Cited in N. Mews, 'Crabb's Last Dive', *Sunday Times Magazine*, 23 November 1969.

127 W. Crumley, 'Six Amazing Stories', *Daily Express*, 4 May 1956.

128 Ibid.

129 F. Dean, 'Alternative Answers to Parliamentary Questions about Commander Crabb', 7 May 1956. www.cabinetoffice.gov.uk.

130 *Hansard*, 5th Series, 150, 9 May 1956, cols. 1,225–30.

131 Ibid.

132 Ibid.

133 J. Cameron, 'The Cloak and Dagger Boys Have Dropped a Clanger', *News Chronicle*, 11 May 1956.

134 A. Brittenden, 'Cabinet Frogman Row', *Sunday Express*, 6 May 1956.

135 'No Authority for Dive by Commander Crabb', *The Times*, 10 May 1956; N. Monks, 'Just How Secret Is the Secret Service?', *Daily Mail*, 11 May 1956.

136 'Secret Service Blunders: Inquiry Demanded', *Sunday Dispatch*, 13 May 1956.

137 Cameron, 'The Cloak and Dagger Boys have Dropped a Clanger'.

138 'No Authority for Dive by Commander Crabb'.

139 D. R. Thorpe, *Eden: The Life and Times of Anthony Eden* (London: Random House, 2003), p. 444.

140 D. McLachlan, 'The Firm Smack of Government', *Daily Telegraph*, 3 January 1956.

141 *Hansard*, 5th Series, 153, 14 May 1956, col. 1,764.

142 Ibid., col. 1,760.

143 Ibid., col. 1,772.

144 'Sir James Hutchison' (obituary), *The Times*, 19 November 1979, p. 26.

145 *Hansard*, 5th series, 153, 14 May 1956, col. 1,783.

146 Ibid. col. 1,785.

147 C. Pincher, 'Eden Calls Frogman Talks: Secret Service Chiefs Face Three Demands', *Daily Express*, 14 May 1956.

148 Bridges, 'Report of an Enquiry'.

149 Ibid.

150 W. Clark, *From Three Worlds: Memoirs* (London: Sidgwick & Jackson, 1986), pp. 169–70.

151 'Transcript of Interview with Sir William Hayter Conducted by Anthony Gorst and W. Scott Lucas', King's College London Liddell Hart Centre for Military Archives, Suez Oral History Project 7.

152 J. Thomas, 'The Crabb Case', 25 June 1956, www.cabinetoffice.gov.uk; N. Brook, 'Note of the Discussion Held about the Action to be Taken on the Report of Sir Edward Bridges into the Frogman Incident', 26 June 1956, www.cabinetoffice.gov.uk.

153 P. Craddock, *Know Your Enemy: How the Joint Intelligence Committee Saw the World* (London: John Murray, 2002), p. 266.

154 H. Macmillan, Prime Minister's Personal Minute, 4 May 1959, TNA PREM 11/2800.

155 'JIC: Minutes of the One Hundred and First Meeting of the Committee', 18 September 1953, TNA CAB 159/14.

156 C. Pincher, 'New Nuclear Row Blows Up', *Daily Express*, 3 November 1958.

157 G. R. Ward to D. Sandys, 4 November 1958, TNA DEFE 13/169.

158 D. Sandys to G. R. Ward, 1 December 1958, TNA DEFE 13/169.

159 C. Pincher, 'Britain Does a Space Age Deal with the US: Now Rent-a-Rocket', *Daily Express*, 4 May 1959.

160 H. Macmillan, Prime Minister's Personal Minute, 4 May 1959, TNA PREM 11/2800.

161 N. Brook to H. Macmillan, 4 May 1959, TNA PREM 11/2800.

162 Ibid.

163 Thomson to Editors, 1 May 1961, TNA CAB 21/5163.

164 Wilkinson, *Secrecy and the Media*, p. 253.

165 Pincher, *Treachery*, p. 447.

166 B. Trend to N. Brook, 18 May 1961, TNA CAB 21/5153.

167 *Security Procedures in the Public Service*, Cmnd. 1681 (London, April 1962).

168 Ibid.

169 Ibid.

170 Ibid.

171 'In the National Interest', *Sunday Times*, 14 May 1961.

172 Wilkinson, *Secrecy and the Media*, p. 259.

173 Ibid.

174 S. H. Evans, 15 July 1963, TNA PREM 11/5090.

175 'Note for the Record', T. J. Bligh, July 1963, TNA CAB 21/6077.

176 L. G. Lohan to B. Trend 17 July 1963, TNA PREM 11/5090.

177 Ibid.

178 W. J. Haley to P. Thornycroft MP, 15 July 1963, TNA CAB 21/5163.

179 Ibid.

180 *Hansard*, 18 July 1963, cols. 722–3.

181 'Note for the Record', T. J. Bligh, July 1963, TNA CAB 21/6077; B. Trend to H. Macmillan, 26 July 1963, TNA CAB 21/5163.

182 R. Way to B. Trend, 8 August 1963, TNACAB 21/6077.

183 Ibid.

184 L. G. Lohan, 19 August 1963, TNA CAB 21/6077.

185 'D-Notices: Note of Meeting in Sir Burke Trend's Office at 2:40pm on 15 August', W. McIndoe, 16 August 1963, TNA CAB 21/6077.

186 L. G. Lohan to M. Cary, 17 September 1963, TNA CAB 21/6077.

187 Ibid.

4 Britain's Watergate: the D-Notice Affair and consequences

1 D. McLachlan, 'Intimate Enemies', *Listener*, 26 September 1968.

2 M. Williams, *Inside Number 10* (London: Weidenfeld & Nicolson, 1972), pp. 185, 195–6.

3 H. Wilson, *The Labour Government 1964–70: A Personal Record* (London: Weidenfeld & Nicolson, 1971), pp. 374–5, 478.

4 *Hansard*, 5th Series, 741, 21 February 1967, cols. 1,432–3.

5 C. King, *The Cecil King Diaries 1965–70* (London: Jonathan Cape, 1972), p. 128.

6 B. Castle, *The Castle Diaries 1964–70* (London: Macmillan, 1984), p. 268.

7 Interview with Chapman Pincher.

8 See M. Creevy, 'A Critical Review of the Wilson Government's Handling of the D-Notice Affair 1967', *Intelligence and National Security*, 14:3 (Autumn 1999), 209–27; Wilkinson, *Secrecy and the Media*, pp. 285–342; L. Baston, 'The D-Notice Affair', *Labour History*, 1 (Autumn 2003), 21–2.

9 R. Crossman, *The Diaries of a Cabinet Minister*, 3 vols., Volume II: *Lord President of the Council and Leader of the House of Commons* (London: Hamish Hamilton, 1976), p. 120.

10 Pincher, *Inside Story*, p. 226.

11 Castle, *Diaries*, p. 268.

12 C. Pincher, 'Healey's Plan to Save £800m', *Daily Express*, 13 January 1965.

13 H. Hardman, 15 January 1965, TNA PREM 13/576.

14 Ibid.

15 P. Hedley and C. Aynsley, *The D-Notice Affair* (London: Michael Joseph, 1967), p. 52.

16 Interview with Chapman Pincher.

17 R. Crossman, *The Diaries of a Cabinet Minister*, 3 vols., Volume 1: *Minister of Housing* (London: Jonathan Cape, 1975), p. 217.

18 Interview with Chapman Pincher.

19 Private information.

20 G. Wigg to C. Pincher, 20 June 1966, LSE WIGG 4/71.

21 C. Pincher to G. Wigg, 15 June 1966. Ibid.

22 Castle, *Diaries*, p. 189.

23 'Cabinet Procedure: Precautions against Unauthorised Disclosure of Information', Note by the Prime Minister, February 1966, TNA PREM 13/1182.

24 B. Trend to H. Wilson, 8 June 1966, TNA PREM 13/3072.

25 Private information.

26 A. Howard, 'The Lobby Correspondent', *Listener*, 21 January 1965.

27 Castle, *Diaries*, p. 15; 'Note for the Record', 21 January 1965, TNA PREM 13/501.

28 L. Helsby to H. Wilson, 26 July 1965, TNA PREM 13/503.

29 D. Mitchell to H. Wilson, 22 January 1965, TNA PREM 13/501; 'Relations with the Press', L. Helsby, 25 February 1965, TNA PREM 13/501.

30 Cited in J. Margach, *The Abuse of Power: The War between Downing Street and the Media from Lloyd George to Callaghan* (London: W. H. Allen, 1978), p. 154.

31 Wilkinson, *Secrecy and the Media*, p. 280.

32 Ibid.

33 L. Helsby to H. Wilson, 16 June 1967, TNA PREM 13/1814; interview with Rear-Admiral Nick Wilkinson, former D-Notice Secretary, 21 November 2007.

34 L. Helsby to H. Wilson, 16 June 1967, TNA PREM 13/1820.

35 Ibid.

36 Interview with Chapman Pincher.

37 'Press Disclosures', C. Morris to G. Wigg, TNA PREM 13/1816.

38 Interview with Chapman Pincher.

39 H. Kerby to G. Wigg, 7 June 1967. *SECRET*, LSE WIGG 4/119.

40 Wilson, *Labour Government*, p. 374.

41 Aldrich, *GCHQ*, p. 240.

42 *Final Report of the Senate Select Committee to Study Government Operations with Respect to Intelligence Activities, United States Senate: Together with Additional, Supplemental, and Separate Views*, 6 vols. (Washington: GPO, 1976).

43 Wilkinson, *Secrecy and the Media*, pp. 280, 285; 'Note of a Meeting between the Prime Minister and Lord Radcliffe', 16 May 1967, p. 6, TNA PREM 13/1817.

44 'Minute: Lohan', 22 February 1967, TNA PREM 13/1816.

45 J. Thompson, *Spectator*, 23 June 1967.

46 Interview with Chapman Pincher.

47 C. Pincher, 'Bugs in the Banquette', *Spectator*, 22 August 1998.

48 'Security D-Notices', Lohan to J. Dunnett, 22 February 1967, TNA PREM 13/1816.

49 Interview with Chapman Pincher.

50 Pincher, *Inside Story*, p. 232.

51 Wilkinson, *Secrecy and the Media*, p. 288.

52 Ibid., p. 289.

53 Ibid., pp. 289–90.

54 Aldrich, *GCHQ*, p. 238.

55 C. Pincher, 'Cable Vetting Sensation', *Daily Express*, 21 February 1967.

56 C. J. H. Keith to Joint Information Policy and Guidance Department, 21 June 1967, TNA FCO 26/122.

57 Cited in 'Unofficial Attempts to Gag Press Fail Narrowly', *Sennet*, 28 February 1967, TNA PREM 13/1816.

58 Pincher, *Inside Story*, p. 233.

59 *Hansard*, 5th Series, 741, 21 February 1967, cols. 1432–3.

60 C. Pincher, 'A Charge Refuted', *Daily Express*, 22 February 1967.

61 Wilkinson, *Secrecy and the Media*, p. 292.

62 S. Lohan to J. Dunnett, 22 February 1967, TNA PREM 13/1816.

63 'Statement by the Prime Minister', 23 February 1967, TNA PREM 13/1816.

64 Interview with Chapman Pincher.

65 L. Howard to S. Lohan, 24 February 1967, TNA PREM 13/1816.

66 D. McLachlan, 'One D'd Thing after Another', *Spectator*, 3 March 1967.

67 Robert Armstrong, 'Radcliffe, Cyril John, Viscount Radcliffe (1899–1977)', *Oxford Dictionary of National Biography*, Oxford University Press, 2004 (www.oxforddnb.com/view/article/31576, accessed 23 July 2010).

68 H. Wilson to E. Shinwell, 27 February 1967, TNA PREM 13/1816.

69 Williams, *Inside Number 10*, p. 195.

70 Wilkinson, *Secrecy and the Media*, p. 300.

71 E. Pickering to C. H. King, 15 March 1967, Howard Gotlieb Archival Research Center, Cecil H. King Papers, 607, Box 41.

72 Ibid.

73 Ibid.

74 Ibid.

75 Ibid.

76 Ibid.

77 Ibid.

78 H. Wilson to Lord Radcliffe, 28 March 1967, TNA PREM 13/1816; Creevy, 'D-Notice Affair', 216–17.

79 'Note of a Meeting between the Prime Minister and Lord Radcliffe, Held at Chequers on 16 May 1967', TNA PREM 13/1817.

80 Ibid.

81 Ibid.

82 Ibid.

83 Ibid.

84 Ibid.

85 Williams, *Inside Number 10*, p. 185.

86 'Note of a Meeting Held in the Cabinet Room at 3.00pm on 24 May 1967', TNA PREM 13/1817.

87 Williams, *Inside Number 10*, p. 185.

88 Ibid.

89 'Note for the Record', J. Drew, 12 June 1967, TNA PREM 13/1814.

90 Creevy, 'D-Notice Affair', 217.

91 G. Wigg to H. Wilson, 22 May 1967, TNA PREM 13/1817.

92 Wilkinson, *Secrecy and the Media*, p. 302.

93 Ibid.

94 Cited in D. Healey to B. Trend, 30 May 1967, TNA PREM 13/13/1 818; Creevy, 'D-Notice Affair', 217–18.

95 D. J. Trevelyan to G. Wigg, 30 May 1967, LSE WIGG 4/134.

96 Ibid.

97 B. Trend to N. Dunnett, 27 May 1967, TNA PREM 13/1820.

98 'Note of a Telephone Conversation between H. Wilson and B. Trend, 28 May 1967', TNA PREM 13/1819; Wilkinson, *Secrecy and the Media*, pp. 306–8; Creevy, 'D-Notice Affair', 217.

99 See note 98.

100 'Prime Minister's Personal Minute', H. Wilson to B. Trend, 29 May 1967, TNA PREM 13/1818.

101 Ibid.

102 Ibid.

103 Ibid.

104 Creevy, 'D-Notice Affair', 218.

105 'Prime Minister's Personal Minute', H. Wilson to B. Trend, 29 May 1967, TNA PREM 13/1818.

106 Creevy, 'D-Notice Affair', 218.

107 H. Kerby to G. Wigg, 21 December 1966, LSE WIGG 4/119.

108 Ibid.

109 Ibid.

110 Ibid.

111 H. Kerby to G. Wigg, 26 January 1967, LSE WIGG 4/119.

112 Ibid.

113 Ibid.

114 Ibid.

115 H. Kerby to G. Wigg, 21 February 1967, LSE WIGG 4/119.

116 Ibid.

117 Interview with Chapman Pincher.

118 *White Paper on the D-Notice System*, Cmnd. 3312.

119 Ibid.

120 'Note of a Meeting between H. Wilson, G. Wigg and B. Trend, held on 30 May 1967', TNA PREM 13/1818.

121 H. Kerby to G. Wigg, 7 June 1967, LSE WIGG 4/119.

122 H. Wilson to B. Trend, 29 May 1967, TNA PREM 13/1818.

123 G. Wigg to H. Wilson, 6 June 1967, TNA PREM 13/1819.

124 Crossman, *Diaries*, Volume II, p. 380.

125 Ibid., pp. 380–1.

126 Ibid.

127 Creevy, 'D-Notice Affair', 219.

128 Crossman, *Diaries*, Volume II, p. 380.

129 Ibid., p. 382.

130 Interview with Chapman Pincher.

131 J. Junor to C. Pincher, 14 June 1967. Private Papers of Chapman Pincher. Yet to be opened to the public.

132 Interview with Chapman Pincher.

133 'Note of a Telephone Conversation between H. Wilson and H. Cudlipp, 9 June 1967', TNA PREM 13/1819.

134 P. Hennessy, *The Prime Minister: The Office and Its Holders Since 1945* (London: Penguin, 2000), p. 313.

135 Crossman, *Diaries*, Volume II, p. 382.

136 Wilkinson, *Secrecy and the Media*, p. 318.

137 *New Statesman*, 16 June 1967, p. 1.

138 See, in particular, 'Brown in Trouble as Wilson Slithers Out', *Observer*, 25 June 1967; 'George Brown "In a Great Rage" Takes a Hand in Late-Night Phone Drama', *Daily Sketch*, 14 June 1967.

139 'What a Filthy Smear This Was', *News of the World*, 26 June 1967.

140 Crossman, *Diaries*, Volume II, p. 382.

141 Ibid., p. 398.

142 'Note of a Meeting at the Newspaper Proprietors Association offices on 16 June 1967', H. James, LSE WIGG 4/156.

143 Lord Chalfont to G. Wigg, 20 June 1967, LSE WIGG 4/156.

144 'Blue Pencil and Red Dagger: The New Threat Aimed at the Heart of Britain', *Privateer*, 1:5 (1967), 1–2.

145 Castle, *Diaries*, p. 268.

146 H. Kerby to G. Wigg, 16 June 1967, LSE WIGG 4/119.

147 Pincher, *Inside Story*, p. 239; Crossman, *Diaries*, Volume II, p. 394.

148 C. Andrew and V. Mitrokhin, *The Mitrokhin Archive: The KGB in Europe and the West* (London: Allen Lane, 1999).

149 *Hansard, HC Debate*, 22 June 1967, 478, cols. 1,972–2,100.

150 Ibid.

151 Ibid.

152 Ibid.

153 Ibid.

154 L. Helsby to H. Wilson, 16 June 1967, TNA PREM 13/1814.

155 H. Wilson to L. Helsby, 22 June 1967, TNA PREM 13/1820.

156 *The Times*, 23 June 1967.

157 Ibid.

158 Crossman, *Diaries*, Volume II, p. 402.

159 C. Pincher, 'The Love of Two Colonels', *Daily Express*, 24 June 1967.

160 G. Wigg to A. W. J. Lewis, 5 September 1967, LSE WIGG 4/110. By early September, Wilson had at least developed a sense of humour about the D-Notice Affair. In a private note to Wigg, he asked, 'Does the Paymaster General like to have his salmon positively vetted?' (H. Wilson to G. Wigg, 3 September 1967, LSE WIGG 4/110.)

161 'D-Notices White Paper Savaged: Scathing Attack by Lord Radcliffe', *The Times*, 7 July 1967, p. 1.

162 *Hansard*, 5th Series, 6 July 1967, 284, col. 778.

163 Ibid., col. 781.

164 Crossman, *Diaries*, Volume II, pp. 413, 414.

165 Cited in L. Baston, 'D-Notice Affair', 22.

166 Williams, *Inside Number 10*, p. 196.

167 L. G. Lohan, 'Slandered out of Business', *Spectator*, 30 June 1967.

168 'Civil Service Tribunal Investigating Complaints by Colonel Lohan', 8 August 1967, TNA PREM 13/1815.

169 Interview with Chapman Pincher.

170 L. Helsby to H. Wilson, 16 June 1967, TNA PREM 13/1814.

171 L. G. Lohan to H. Kerby, 8 February 1967, LSE WIGG 4/119.

172 *Weekly News*, 24 June 1967.

173 'Record of a Meeting at No. 10', 7 September 1967, TNA PREM 13/1813.

174 G. Wigg to B. Trend, 18 October 1967, LSE WIGG 4/157.

175 C. Pincher, *Not With a Bang* (London: Four Square, 1965); C. Pincher, *The Giant Killer* (London: Weidenfeld & Nicolson, 1967).

176 Interview with Chapman Pincher.

177 C. Pincher, 'French Say: We Can't Afford Swing Wing', *Daily Express*, 24 June 1967.

178 13 July 1967, TNA PREM 13/1790.

179 'Men of the Year', *Country Fair*, December 1967, LSE WIGG 4/119.

180 'Record of a Meeting Held in B. Trend's Room, 8 August 1967', LSE WIGG 4/153.

181 G. Wigg to B. Trend, 3 November 1967, LSE WIGG 4/154.

182 H. Kerby to G. Wigg, 20 September 1967, Confidential, LSE WIGG 4/11.

183 M. Bragg, 'Review', *Daily Telegraph*, 25 September 2009.

184 H. Evans, *My Paper Chase* (London: Abacus, 2009), p. 296. See also H. Evans, 'The Sunday Times and Kim Philby', *Sunday Times*, 20 September 2009.

185 Evans, *My Paper Chase*, p. 297.

186 Ibid.

187 *British Agent* has since been reissued in Frank Cass's Classics of Espionage series with a superb introduction by intelligence historian Wesley K. Wark. J. Whitwell, *British Agent* (London: Frank Cass, 1996). See also W. K. Wark, '"Our Man in Riga": Reflections on the SIS Career and Writings of Leslie Nicholson', *Intelligence and National Security*, 11:4 (October 1996), 625–44.

188 Evans, *My Paper Chase*, p. 302.

189 Ibid.

190 Ibid.

191 N. West (ed.), *Faber Book of Espionage* (London: Faber & Faber, 1993), p. 297.

192 D. Greenhill to Secretary of State, 8 August 1967, LSE WIGG 4/153.

193 Evans, *My Paper Chase*, p. 304.

194 'Philby', Col. R. A. Rubens, 9 October 1967, LSE WIGG 4/152.

195 'Record of a Meeting Held in B. Trend's Room, 8 August 1967', WIGG 4/152; Evans, *My Paper Chase*, pp. 299–301.

196 'Philby', Colonel R. A. Rubens, 9 October 1967, LSE WIGG 4/152.

197 D. Greenhill to Secretary of State, 8 August 1967, LSE WIGG 4/153.

198 D. Greenhill to B. Trend, 3 October 1967, LSE WIGG 4/153.

199 'Philby', Colonel R. A. Rubens, 9 October 1967, LSE WIGG 4/152.

200 B. Trend to H. Wilson, 11 August 1967, LSE WIGG 4/153.

201 Ibid.

202 H. Wilson, 14 August 1967, LSE WIGG 4/153.

203 'Philby', Colonel R. A. Rubens, 9 Oct 1967, LSE WIGG 4/152; 'Note of a Meeting Held on Friday 1 September 1967', LSE WIGG 4/153.

204 H. Kerby to G. Wigg, 20 September 1967, LSE WIGG 4/119.

205 'Note for the Prime Minister: Anthony Frederick Blunt', 18 October 1967, LSE WIGG 4/153.

206 Evans, *My Paper Chase*, p. 302.

207 'Note for the Prime Minister: Anthony Frederick Blunt', 18 October 1967, LSE WIGG 4/153.

208 Evans, *My Paper Chase*, p. 302.

209 D. Greenhill to G. Wigg, 26 September 1967, LSE WIGG 4/153.

210 Ibid.

211 Ibid.

212 D. Greenhill to Lord Chalfont, LSE WIGG 4/153.

213 D. Greenhill to G. Wigg, 29 September 1967, LSE WIGG 4/153.

214 Evans, *My Paper Chase*, p. 308.

215 R. L. Mott, 'A Spy Spectacular from Fleet Street', *Washington Post*, 8 October 1967.

216 M. McConville, 'The Spy We Took in from the Cold', *Observer*, 8 October 1967.

217 'Spies Every Sunday', *Time*, 10 November 1967.

218 Cited in 'Espionage: Not-So-Secret Service', *Newsweek*, 30 October 1967.

219 For American press reaction, see: 'London Papers Trace Philby's Rise in British Intelligence as Soviet Spy', *Washington Post*, 1 October 1967; 'How Philby Stabbed into the Heart of British Security', *Washington Post*, 8 October 1967; 'Philby a Double Agent for 30 Years', *Denver Post*, 2 October 1967; 'Stranger than Fiction', *US News and World Report*, 16 October 1967; 'On Display', *Time*, 29 December 1967; 'Hello Comrade Philby', *Newsweek*, 1 January 1968.

220 Memo, FCO to Missions and Dependent Territories, 2 October 1967, LSE WIGG 4/151.

221 Ibid.

222 D. McLachlan, 'In Defence of Our Secret Service', *Sunday Telegraph*, 8 October 1967.

223 Ibid.

224 Ibid.

225 Cited in 'Spies Every Sunday', *Time*, 10 November 1967.

226 Evans, *My Paper Chase*, p. 309.

227 D. Greenhill, 'Philby – The Aftermath', 26 October 1967, LSE WIGG 4/154.

228 Andrew, *MI5*, p. 326.

229 'Extract from 24 Hours, 21:55, 19 October 1967', LSE WIGG 4/168.

230 'Note for the Record: Daily Express Report of 19 October 1967', LSE WIGG 4/168.

231 B. Trend to R. H. Melville, 7 November 1967, TNA CAB 164/520.

232 Ibid.

233 'Paper for the Official Committee on Security Procedure for Inquiries into Leakages', 13 February 1968, TNA CAB 164/847.

234 'Leak Procedure', W. Armstrong to B. Trend, 7 April 1970, TNA CAB 164/847.

235 D. Greenhill, 'Philby – The Aftermath', 26 October 1967, LSE WIGG 4/154.

236 D. White to D. Greenhill, 31 October 1967, LSE WIGG 4/154.

237 M. Furnival Jones to D. Greenhill, 27 October 1967, LSE WIGG 4/154.

238 B. Trend to P. H. Gore-Booth, 3 November 1967, LSE WIGG 4/154.

239 Ibid.

240 N. Davies, *Flat Earth News* (London: Vintage Books, 2009), p. 295.

241 G. Wigg to B. Trend, 3 November 1967, LSE WIGG 4/154.

242 H. Kerby to G. Wigg, 7 June 1967, LSE WIGG 4/119.

5 Publish and be damned

1 Knowles, cited in 'The Press: Roadblocks on Fleet Street', *Time*, 14 March 1977.

2 'D-Notices and Press Freedom: Lecture Given by Chapman Pincher in the Harcourt Room, House of Commons, 21 July 1969', *Freedom First* (Autumn 1969), LSE WIGG 4/159.

3 C. Pincher, 'Haul Down Report', *Daily Express*, 12 November 1971.

4 'Report on Questionnaires', TNA DEFE 68/145; H. E. Davies, 30 December 1971, TNA DEFE 68/145.

5 J. L. A. Macafee to H. E. Davies, 21 December 1971, TNA DEFE 68/145.

6 J. M. Wilson, 22 November 1971, TNA DEFE 68/145.

7 For a more detailed account of the Scott Report Affair see J. Aitken, *Officially Secret* (London: Weidenfeld & Nicolson, 1971), esp. pp. 79–205.

8 A. Friendly, 'British Legal Monstrosity Is Stirring New Controversy', *Washington Post*, 21 March 1970.

9 Aitken, *Officially Secret*, p. 1.

10 Ibid., p. 206.

11 Cited ibid., p. 198.

12 K. Theakston, *The Civil Service Since 1945* (Oxford: Blackwell, 1995), p. 84.

13 Heclo and Wildavsky, *Private Government*, p. 12.

14 *The Civil Service, Report of the Committee 1966–68*.

15 Ibid., p. 91.

16 Ibid., paras. 277–80.

17 E. Shackleton to H. Wilson, 27 September 1968, TNA PREM 13/1972.

18 'The Secrecy of Official Information', W. Armstrong, 16 May 1968, TNA PREM 13/1970.

19 B. Trend, 21 May 1968, TNA CAB 164/640.

20 M. Halls to G. Walker, 26 November 1968, TNA PREM 13/1970.

21 'Prime Minister's Personal Minute', H. Wilson, TNA PREM 13/2528.

22 A. Part to W. Armstrong, 4 February 1969, TNA CAB 164/640.

23 'The Release of Official Information', 5 March 1969, TNA PREM 13/2528.

24 *Information and the Public Interest*, Cmnd. 4089 (London: HMSO, June 1969).

25 E. A. Shackleton to B. Trend, 27 September 1968, TNA CAB 164/1640.

26 *Information and the Public Interest*, Cmnd. 4089, p. 11.

27 *Departmental Committee on Section 2 of the Official Secrets Act*, Volume 1, Preface.

28 M. Halls to H. Wilson, 21 February 1969, TNA PREM 13/2528.

29 A. Danchev, *Oliver Franks: Founding Father* (Oxford: Clarendon Press, 1993).

30 A. Danchev, 'Franks, Oliver Shewell, Baron Franks (1905–1992)', *Oxford Dictionary of National Biography*, Oxford University Press, September 2004; online edn (www.oxforddnb.com/view/article/51039, accessed 31 August 2010).

31 *Departmental Committee on Section 2 of the Official Secrets Act*, Volume III, pp. 324–5.

32 Ibid., Volume II, p. 316.

33 Ibid., p. 314.

34 Ibid., Volume III, p. 249.

35 Ibid., Volume II, p. 316; Vincent, *Culture of Secrecy*, p. 250.

36 *Departmental Committee on Section 2 of the Official Secrets Act*, Volume III, p. 121.

37 Ibid., Volume I, p. 37.

38 J. Jaconelli, 'The Franks Report on Section 2 of the Official Secrets Act 1911', *Modern Law Review*, 36:1 (January 1973), 71.

39 Vincent, *Culture of Secrecy*, p. 251.

40 *Departmental Committee on Section 2 of the Official Secrets Act*, Volume III, p. 36.

41 Ibid., p. 90.

42 'Record of a Meeting to Discuss the Report of the Departmental Committee on Section 2', 8 March 1973, TNA CAB 130/661.

43 *Hansard*, 6th Series, 21 December 1988, col. 460.

44 Rogers, *Secrecy and Power*, pp. 78–9.

45 D. Campbell, 'When the Press Must Publish', *The Times*, 4 January 1984, p. 9.

46 G. Robertson, *The Justice Game* (London: Chatto & Windus, 1998), p. 104.

47 D. A. Phillips, 'Intelligence Literature', David Atlee Phillips Papers, Library of Congress, MMC 3579, Box 5.

48 Aldrich, *GCHQ*, p. 356.

49 R. J. Aldrich, *Espionage, Security and Intelligence in Britain 1945–1970* (Manchester University Press, 1998), p. 216.

50 Aldrich, *GCHQ*, p. 358.

51 D. Campbell and M. Hosenball, 'The Eavesdroppers', *Time Out*, 21 May 1976.

52 Ibid.

53 'Three-Month Sentence on "Isis" Case Undergraduates', *The Times*, 19 July 1958.

54 'Police See Students about Isis Article', *The Times*, 20 March 1958.

55 'The Aubrey/Berry/Campbell Case', 30 June 1977. Appendix, TNA DEFE 47/34.

56 See P. Richardson, *A Bomb in Every Issue: How the Short, Unruly Life of Ramparts Magazine Changed America* (New York: New Press, 2009).

57 Hooper, *Official Secrets*, p. 105.

58 CIA Records Search Tool (hereafter CREST), National Archives II, College Park, Maryland, cia-rdp99–00498R000100020024–6.

59 B. D. Nossiter, 'Outcasts of the Island', *New York Review of Books*, 14 April 1977.

60 'The Press: Back Out in the Cold', *Time*, 29 November 1976.

61 Rogers, *Secrecy and Power*, p. 79; S. Dorril and R. Ramsay, *Smear: Wilson and the Secret State* (London: HarperCollins, 1992), p. 314.

62 'Detention under the Official Secrets Act: Ex Corporal John Berry', Director of Security (Army), 24 February 1977, TNA DEFE 47/34.

63 Hooper, *Official Secrets*, p. 107.

64 'Bail Refused for Three on Secrets Act Charge', *The Times*, 22 February 1977.

65 'Note of a meeting between the MoD and the Security Services to discuss procedures and action on the forthcoming prosecution of Messrs Campbell, Aubrey and Berry. Held on Friday 27 May 1977', TNA DEFE 47/34.

66 'The Aubrey/Berry/Campbell Case', 30 June 1977. Appendix, TNA DEFE 47/34.

67 'Statement by Major-General Henry Arthur John Sturge', TNA DEFE 47/34.

68 'Note of a meeting between the MoD and the Security Services to discuss procedures and action on the forthcoming prosecution of Messrs Campbell, Aubrey and Berry. Held on Friday 27 May 1977', TNA DEFE 47/34.

69 Ibid.

70 Ibid.

71 'J. A. Berry – Charges Under the Official Secrets Act', A. J. Hockaday, 20 June 1977, TNA DEFE 47/34.

72 Robertson, *Justice Game*, p. 113.

73 Hooper, *Official Secrets*, p. 110.

74 Ibid.

75 'Colonel B is Named Three Times at NUJ Conference', *The Times*, 20 April 1978.

76 Hooper, *Official Secrets*, p. 111.

77 Robertson, *Justice Game*, p. 128.

78 G. Robertson, 'Against Secrets and Lies', *Guardian*, 12 January 1999.

79 'Man in Secrets Case "Ferret, Not Skunk"', *The Times*, 18 November 1977.

80 Robertson, 'Secrets and Lies'.

81 Cited in Aldrich, *GCHQ*, p. 360.

82 Hooper, *Official Secrets*, p. 119.

83 P. Hain, *Political Trials in Britain* (London: Allen Lane, 1984), p. 210.

84 See D. Campbell, 'Official Secrecy and British Libertarianism', *Socialist Register*, 16 (1979), 75–87.

85 Ibid., p. 76.

86 Robertson, *Justice Game*, p. 131.

87 Ibid., p. 109.

88 'ABC Case', A. Duff, 9 November 1978, TNA DEFE 13/1303.

89 Hooper, *Official Secrets*, p. 113.

90 Robertson, *Justice Game*, p. 119.

91 Some of these flyers can be found in TNA DEFE 13/1303.

92 'Cheltenham Picket-nic', *ABC Newsletter*, TNA DEFE 13/1303.

93 H. Noyes, 'Tapped Telephones Allegations Denied by Both Mr Whitelaw and Mr Rees', *The Times*, 1 February 1980, p. 2.

94 Wilkinson, *Secrecy and the Media*, p. 377.

95 P. Hennessy, 'Editor Calls for D-Notice Review', *The Times*, 2 April 1980, p. 3.

96 P. Hennessy, 'D-Notice System Is an Anachronism, Editor Tells MPs', *The Times*, 23 July 1980, p. 4.

97 Cited in Wilkinson, *Secrecy and the Media*, p. 380.

98 Ibid.

99 Cited in 'Chronicle: Government Censors', *Third Way*, March 1988, 4.

100 D. Campbell, 'The Parliamentary Bypass Operation', *New Statesman*, 23 January 1987.

101 See P. Gill, 'Allo, Allo, Allo, Who's in Charge Here Then?', *Liverpool Law Review*, 9:2 (1987), 189–201.

102 See A. Milne, *DG: Memoirs of a British Broadcaster* (London: Hodder & Stoughton, 1988).

103 Interview with Chapman Pincher.

6 Cabinet confessions: from Churchill to Crossman

1 M. Hankey, 'The Banned Book: The Supreme Command 1914–1918', 30 May 1957, CCC HNKY 25/1.

2 Precisely this problem was the subject of a 2005–6 House of Commons Public Administration Select Committee. See *Whitehall Confidential? The Publication of Political Memoirs*, HC 689-I (London: HMSO, 25 July 2006).

3 H. Shawcross, 7 January 1948, TNA LCO 2/3219.

4 B. Trend to E. Heath, 18 June 1971, TNA CAB 164/1332. Also see B. Trend to D. Allen, 10 July 1970 in 'Harold Macmillan Publication', J. M. Moss, 13 May 1975, TNA CAB 164/1295.

5 Hennessy, *Whitehall*, p. 352.

6 J. Murray to M. Hankey, 30 June 1954, CCC HNKY 25/2.

7 Cited in Reynolds, 'Official History'.

8 Ibid.

9 Reynolds, *Command of History*.

10 S. Hoare, *Ambassador on Special Mission* (London: Collins, 1946); S. Hoare, *Nine Troubled Years* (London: Collins, 1954); Viscount Halifax, *Fullness of Days* (New York: Dodd, Mead, 1957); J. Simon, *Retrospect: The Memoirs of*

the Rt Hon. Viscount Simon (London: Hutchinson, 1952); C. Attlee, *As It Happened* (New York: Viking Press, 1954); H. Dalton, *Call Back Yesterday: Memoirs 1887–1931* (London: Muller, 1953).

11 'Disclosure of Official Information', N. Brook to H. Macmillan, 8 February 1960, TNA PREM 11/4660.

12 M. Hankey to N. Flower, 20 June 1946, CCC HNKY 25/2.

13 Ibid.

14 M. Hankey to Viscount Adison, 29 May 1946, CCC HNKY 25/1.

15 Ibid.

16 M. Hankey to N. Flower, 20 June 1946, CCC HNKY 25/2.

17 M. Hankey to Viscount Adison, 29 May 1946, CCC HNKY 25/1.

18 N. Brook to W. Churchill, 28 May 1953, TNA CAB 21/3743.

19 'Objectionable Passages', E. Bridges, 20 July 1953, TNA CAB 21/3743.

20 Ibid.

21 Ibid.

22 W. Churchill to N. Brook, 2 July 1953, TNA CAB 21/3743.

23 'Objectionable Passages', E. Bridges, 20 July 1953, TNA CAB 21/3743.

24 Ibid.

25 W. Churchill to E. Bridges, 4 August 1953, TNA CAB 21/3743.

26 N. Brook to T. Jones, September 1953, TNA CAB 21/3743.

27 Ibid.

28 T. Jones, *Whitehall Diary*, ed. K. Middlemas, 3 vols. (Oxford University Press, 1969–71).

29 T. Padmore to E. Bridges and N. Brook, 11 October 1956, TNA T 215/504.

30 N. Brook to H. Bunbury, 22 October 1956, TNA T 215/504.

31 Ibid.

32 Ibid.

33 E. Bridges to T. Padmore, 1 October 1956, TNA T 215/504.

34 W. Braithwaite, *Ambulance Wagon: Being the Memoirs of William J. Braithwaite*, ed. H. Bunbury, (London: Methuen, 1957).

35 H. Macmillan to M. Hankey, 31 March 1957, CCC HNKY 25/3.

36 M. Hankey to H. Macmillan, 1 May 1957, ibid.

37 Ibid.

38 Ibid.

39 H. Macmillan to M. Hankey, 23 May 1957, CCC HNKY 25/3.

40 Ibid.

41 M. Hankey, 'The Banned Book: The Supreme Command 1914–1918', 30 May 1957, CCC HNKY 25/1.

42 Ibid.

43 L. Heald to M. Hankey, 13 January 1958, CCC HNKY 25/3.

44 Roskill, *Hankey*, p. 616.

45 'Extracts from Reports on Supreme Command from Hutchinson', CCC HNKY 25/4.

46 Ibid.

47 Ibid.

48 Ibid.

49 Ibid.

50 Naylor, *A Man and an Institution*, p. 289.

51 H. Macmillan to L. Heald, 30 April 1958, CCC HNKY 25/3.

52 Roskill, *Hankey*, p. 618.

53 Ibid.

54 Ibid.

55 Ibid., p. 619.

56 Naylor, *A Man and an Institution*, p. 290.

57 A. Hodge to A. Eden, 28 November 1957, Cadbury Research Library, Special Collections, University of Birmingham, Avon Papers (hereafter UBL), AP 33/3/2/32.

58 This is the main argument of D. Dutton, *Anthony Eden: A Life and a Reputation* (London: Arnold, 1997).

59 *Hansard*, 5th Series, 332, 21 February 1938, col. 42.

60 W. Churchill, *The Gathering Storm* (Boston: Houghton Mifflin, 1948), p. 190; Dutton, *Eden*, p. 4.

61 R. R. James, *Anthony Eden* (London: Weidenfeld & Nicolson, 1986), p. 404.

62 Margach, *Abuse of Power*, p. 100.

63 Dutton, *Eden*, p. 5.

64 P. Johnson, *The Suez War* (London: MacGibbon & Kee, 1957).

65 R. Churchill, *The Rise and Fall of Sir Anthony Eden* (London: MacGibbon & Kee, 1959).

66 Thorpe, *Eden*, p. 602.

67 A. Eden, *The Memoirs of Sir Anthony Eden: Full Circle* (Boston: Houghton Mifflin, 1960), Foreword.

68 Ibid.

69 R. Lamb, *The Failure of the Eden Government* (London: Sidgwick & Jackson, 1987), p. 310.

70 Eden, *Full Circle*, p. 437.

71 *Hansard*, 5th Series, 502, 20 December 1956, col. 1,457.

72 A. Nutting, *No End of a Lesson: The Story of Suez* (London: Constable, 1967); C. Pineau, *Suez 1956* (Paris: R. Laffont, 1976); M. Dayan, *Story of My Life* (New York: Morrow, 1976); S. Lloyd, *Suez 1956: A Personal Account* (London: Cape, 1978).

73 P. L. Hahn, 'Suez', *Reviews in American History*, 20:4 (December 1992), p. 567.

74 James, *Eden*, p. 603.

75 Ibid.

76 Ibid., pp. 603–4.

77 Ibid., pp. 604, 613.

78 M. and S. Bromberger, *The Secrets of Suez* (London: Pan Books, 1957).

79 'The Eden Memoirs', J. M. Moss, 18 June 1975, TNA CAB 164/1297.

80 Thorpe, *Eden*, p. 553.

81 M. Amory (ed.), *The Letters of Ann Fleming* (London: Collins Harvill, 1985), p. 217.

82 'Disclosure of Information', N. Brook to H. Macmillan, 8 February 1960, TNA PREM 11/4660.

83 W. Edwards to R. Furneaux, 9 December 1959, UBL AP 33/3/3/47.

84 Naylor, *A Man and an Institution*, p. 294; N. Brook to H. Macmillan, 1 January 1958, TNA PREM 11/332.

85 'The Eden Memoirs', J. M. Moss, 18 June 1975, TNA CAB 164/1297.

86 A. Eden to N. Brook, 18 May 1958 cited ibid.

87 'The Eden Memoirs', J. M. Moss, 18 June 1975, TNA CAB 164/1297.

88 Ibid.

89 S. Lloyd to N. Brook, 8 August 1959 cited ibid.

90 Ibid.

91 Ibid.

92 Ibid.

93 R. Blake to A. Eden, 2 March 1959, UBL AP 33/3/1/33.

94 Ibid.

95 Ibid; R. Blake to A. Eden, 14 April 1959, UBL AP 33/3/1/45.

96 R. Blake to A. Eden, 2 March 1959, UBL AP 33/3/1/33.

97 R. Blake to A. Eden, 14 April 1959, UBL AP 33/3/1/45.

98 R. Blake to A. Eden, 2 March 1959, UBL AP 33/3/1/33; R. Blake to A. Eden, 14 April 1959, UBL AP 33/3/1/45.

99 Ibid.

100 Lord Chandos to A. Eden, 29 September 1959, UBL AP 23/17/37.

101 A. Eden to Lord Chandos, 1 October 1959, UBL AP 23/17/37.

102 'Comments on Memoirs', N. Brook, TNA PREM 11/4234; 'Comments on Books II and III of Volume II. The Period of Premiership', Brook, 20 July 1959, TNA PREM 11/4234; 'The Eden Memoirs', J. M. Moss, 18 June 1975, TNA CAB 164/1297.

103 Ibid.

104 Ibid.

105 Ibid.

106 A. Hodge to A. Eden, 20 October 1959, UBL AP 33/3/2/314.

107 David Reynolds makes exactly the same argument for Winston Churchill's war histories.

108 'The Eden Memoirs', J. M. Moss, 18 June 1975, TNA CAB 164/1297.

109 Cited in M. Jones, 'Operation Musketeer', *Sunday Times*, 6 September 1998; E. Heath, *The Course of My Life* (London: Hodder & Stoughton, 1998).

110 Reynolds, *Command of History*, pp. 57–8.

111 Ibid., p. 58.

112 Ibid.

113 See E. B. Childers, *The Road to Suez: A Study of Western–Arab Relations* (London: MacGibbon & Kee, 1962); A. J. Barker, *Suez: The Seven-Day War* (New York: Praeger, 1964); L. Epstein, *British Policy in the Suez Crisis* (Urbana: University of Illinois Press, 1964).

114 H. Azeau, *Le Piège de Suez* (Paris: R. Laffont, 1964); M. Bar-Zohar, *Suez Ultra Secret* (Paris: Fayard, 1964); D. Eisenhower, *The White House Years: Mandate for Change 1953–6* (Garden City: Doubleday, 1963); D. Eisenhower, *The White House Years: Waging Peace 1956–61* (Garden City: Doubleday, 1966).

115 H. Macmillan to N. Brook, 9 February 1960, TNA PREM 11/4660.

116 Policy regarding the transmission of secret documents is catalogued in TNA CAB 21/2839 and TNA CAB 21/2407.

117 A. Eden to A. Hodge, 10 September 1957, UBL AP 33/3/2/1.

118 A. Hodge to A. Eden, 28 November 1957, UBL AP 33/3/2/32.

119 Ibid; A. Hodge to A. Eden, 9 December 1957, UBL AP 33/3/2/40.

120 H. Macmillan, July 1961, TNA PREM 11/4660.

121 Eden, *Full Circle*, p. 64.

122 Ibid., p. 499.

123 Ibid., p. 484; Lamb, *Eden Government*, p. 307.

124 A. Eden to N. Brook, 27 August 1959 cited in 'The Eden Memoirs', J. M. Moss, 18 June 1975, TNA CAB 164/1297.

125 N. Brook to H. Macmillan, 2 November 1959, cited ibid.

126 'The Eden Memoirs', *The Times*, 11 January 1960, p. 4; 'Note for the Record', N. Brook, 3 November 1959, TNA PREM 11/4234; H. Macmillan to D. Eisenhower, 5 January 1960, TNA PREM 11/4234.

127 H. Macmillan to D. Eisenhower, 5 January 1960, TNA PREM 11/4234.

128 'Note for the Record', N. Brook, 3 November 1959, TNA PREM 11/4234. Guidance was also given to the press explaining that, 'These are the personal memoirs of Sir Anthony Eden and Her Majesty's Government are not responsible for the views expressed in them.' ('Note: Guidance to the Press', TNA PREM 11/4234.)

129 Thorpe, *Eden*, p. 559.

130 R. Blake to A. Eden, 9 February 1960, UBL AP 33/3/1/158.

131 Using the Retail Price Index, where £1,000 in October 1957 is the equivalent of £17,575 in December 2007, one might speculate that Eden earned a sum equal to £2.8 million in present-day terms.

132 D. Middleton, 'The Clash of Two Men', *The Times*, 29 February 1960, p. 11.

133 Ibid.

134 'The Eden Memoirs', J. M. Moss, 18 June 1975, TNA CAB 164/1297.

135 M. Wight, 'Brutus in Foreign Policy: The Memoirs of Sir Anthony Eden', *International Affairs*, 36:3 (July 1960), 309.

136 Ibid.

137 'Redefining That Special Relationship', *Time*, 2 February 1970.

138 Wight, 'Brutus in Foreign Policy', 300.

139 'Two Views of the Eden Memoirs: I Randolph Churchill', *New Statesman*, 5 March 1960, pp. 335–6.

140 F. N. Baker to H. Macmillan, 11 August 1963, TNA PREM 11/4660; Dutton, *Eden*, p. 11.

141 Eden, *Full Circle*, pp. 178, 184; Wight, 'Brutus in Foreign Policy', 299.

142 'Two Views of the Eden Memoirs: II Paul Johnson', *New Statesman*, 5 March 1960, pp. 335–6.

143 'Two Views of the Eden Memoirs: I Randolph Churchill'.

144 Eden, *Full Circle*, p. 543.

145 Gaitskell, cited in 'The Unhappy Memory', *Time*, 14 March 1960.

146 'Two Views of the Eden Memoirs: I Randolph Churchill'.

147 T. Jones to B. Trend, 4 January 1964, TNA PREM 11/4660.

148 Ibid.

149 B. Trend to S. Lloyd, 1 May 1963, TNA PREM 11/4938.

150 B. Trend to H. Macmillan, 19 November 1963, TNA CAB 21/5848.

151 'The Kilmuir Memoirs', J. M. Moss, 7 May 1975, TNA CAB 164/1295; 'Note for the Record', T. Bligh, 5 December 1963, TNA CAB 21/5848.

152 B. Trend to H. Macmillan, 19 November 1963, TNA CAB 21/5848.

153 B. Trend to Lord Kilmuir, 12 December 1963, TNA PREM 11/4115.

154 Ibid.

155 W. Deedes to B. Trend, 8 April 1964, TNA CAB 21/5848.

156 H. Finer, *Dulles Over Suez: The Theory and Practice of His Diplomacy* (Chicago: Quadrangle Books, 1964); R. Scott, 'Joint Plan over Suez Admitted', *Guardian*, 6 May 1964.

157 C. Tickell to C. Lush, 9 November 1966, TNA FO 371/190241.

158 E. Monroe, 'Suez Secrets: The Jigsaw Continues', *Observer*, 24 July 1966.

159 'Note to B. Trend', 29 July 1966, TNA CAB 103/628.

160 Miscellaneous Note, B. Trend, TNA CAB 103/628. Also see 'Cabinet Still Undecided on Suez Inquiry', *Daily Telegraph*, 8 November 1966; 'Inquiry into Suez Affair Denied', *Guardian*, 12 December 1966.

161 H. Thomas, *The Suez Affair* (London: Weidenfeld & Nicolson, 1967);
P. Calvocoressi, *Suez: Ten Years On* (London: British Broadcasting
Corporation, 1967).

162 N. Nicholson, 'Nutting, Sir (Harold) Anthony, third baronet (1920–1999)',
Oxford Dictionary of National Biography, Oxford University Press, 2004;
online edn, (www.oxforddnb.com/view/article/72010, accessed 11 February
2008); D. R. Thorpe, 'Obituary: Sir Anthony Nutting', *Independent*, 3 March
1999.

163 Nutting, *No End*, pp. 14, 96.

164 'No End of a Lesson by A. Nutting', J. M. Moss, 6 May 1975, TNA CAB 164/
1295.

165 *Independent*, 3 March 1999.

166 Ibid.

167 'No End of a Lesson by A. Nutting', J. M. Moss, 6 May 1975, TNA CAB
164/1295.

168 Ibid.

169 Nutting, *No End*, pp. 91–3.

170 Cited in James, *Eden*, p. 614.

171 A. Eden to Lord Normanbrook, 25 April 1967, UBL AP 20/49/41.

172 A. Eden to Lord Normanbrook, 20 April 1967, UBL AP 20/49/19.

173 A. Eden to Lord Normanbrook, 24 April 1967, UBL AP 20/49/21.

174 Ibid.

175 Ibid.

176 Ibid.

177 'No End of a Lesson by A. Nutting', J. M. Moss, 6 May 1975, TNA CAB 164/
1295.

178 Ibid.

179 Ibid.

180 See P. Murphy, 'Telling Tales out of School: Nutting, Eden and the Attempted
Suppression of *No End of a Lesson*', in S. C. Smith, *Reassessing Suez 1956:
New Perspectives on the Crisis and Its Aftermath* (Aldershot: Ashgate, 2008),
pp. 195–214.

181 Ibid.

182 Castle, *Diaries*, p. 246.

183 'No End of a Lesson by A. Nutting', J. M. Moss, 6 May 1975, TNA CAB 164/
1295.

184 Crossman, *Diaries*, Volume II, pp. 343–4.

185 'No End of a Lesson by A. Nutting', J. M. Moss, 6 May 1975, TNA CAB 164/
1295.

186 H. Wilson to B. Trend, 10 April 1967, TNA PREM 13/1556.

187 D. Carlton, *Anthony Eden: A Biography* (London: Allen Lane, 1981), p. 472.

188 E. Stock, 'Reviewed Work: *No End of a Lesson* by Anthony Nutting', *Political Science Quarterly*, 84:1 (March 1969), 136–7.

189 H. Macmillan, *Memoirs*, 6 vols., Volume IV *Riding the Storm 1956–1959* (London: HarperCollins, 1971).

190 Lloyd, *Suez 1956*; G. Watson to H. Evans, 18 April 1978, Selwyn Lloyd Papers, Churchill College, Cambridge, CCC SELO 9/89.

191 B. Trend, cited in H. Harcombe to B. Cheeseman, 30 May 1973, TNA FCO 12/155.

192 A. Eden to N. Brook, 24 April 1967, UBL AP 20/49/21.

193 'No End of a Lesson by A. Nutting', J. M. Moss, 6 May 1975, TNA CAB 164/1295.

194 'Transcript of the programme "The Editors", Recorded and Transmitted BBC1, Sunday 22 June 1975', TNA PREM 16/466.

195 Naylor, *A Man and an Institution*, p. 1.

196 A. Howard, 'The Decline and Fall of the August Cabinet Secretary', *Guardian*, 13 February 2001.

197 B. Trend to D. Allen, 10 July 1970, cited in 'Harold Macmillan Publication', J. M. Moss, 13 May 1975, TNA CAB 164/1295.

198 G. Gordon to J. Bray, 7 February 1969, Jeremy Bray Papers, Churchill College, Cambridge, BRAY 97/13, Churchill College, Cambridge, CCC BRAY 97/13.

199 B. Trend to H. Wilson, 4 March 1969, TNA CAB 164/587.

200 'Notes of a Meeting between the Prime Minister and the Secretary of State for Economic Affairs and the Minister of Technology, 13 March 1969', TNA CAB 164/587.

201 Ibid.

202 Ibid.

203 T. Benn to H. Wilson, 2 May 1969, CCC BRAY 97/13.

204 Ibid.

205 H. Wilson to J. Bray, 24 September 1969, CCC BRAY 97/13.

206 Ibid.

207 J. Bray to H. Wilson, 24 September 1969, TNA CAB 164/587.

208 Cited in T. Dalyell, 'Jeremy Bray: Obituary', *Independent*, 5 June 2002.

209 See 'Publish and Be Fired', *The Times*, 26 September 1969; 'Minister Quits in Dispute over Publication of Book', *Financial Times*, 26 September 1969.

210 'Jeremy Bray: Obituary', *Daily Telegraph*, 5 June 2002.

211 B. Trend to H. Wilson, 12 February 1971 in '*The Labour Government 1964–1970: A Personal Record*', J. M. Moss, 12 May 1975, TNA CAB 164/1295.

212 B. Trend to E. Heath, 2 May 1971, ibid.

213 H. Wilson to B. Trend, 12 February 1971, in '*The Labour Government 1964–1970: A Personal Record*', J. M. Moss, 12 May 1975, TNA CAB 164/1295.

214 B. Trend to H. Macmillan, 2 March 1973, TNA CAB 164/1332.

215 G. Wigg to B. Trend, 14 April 1971 in '*The Labour Government 1964–1970: A Personal Record*', J. M. Moss, 12 May 1975, TNA CAB 164/1295.

216 Interview with Anne Crossman.

217 Crossman, *Diaries*, Volume I, p. 11.

218 Crossman, 'Real English Disease', *New Statesman*, 24 September 1971, p. 1.

219 T. Dalyell, 'Anne Crossman: Widow and Literary Executor of the Labour Minister Dick Crossman', *Independent*, 1 November 2008.

220 Castle, *Diaries*, p. 361.

221 Crossman, *Diaries*, Volume I, p. 304.

222 Crossman, *Diaries*, Volume II, p. 210.

223 R. Crossman to B. Trend, 13 May 1971, TNA PREM 15/902.

224 B. Trend to R. Crossman, 1971, MRC MSS 154/3/LIT/33/1–26. See also 'Advice to B. Trend', TNA PREM 16/24.

225 R. Crossman to B. Trend, 20 May 1971, TNA PREM 16/24; R. Crossman to E. Heath, 22 July 1971, TNA PREM 16/24. The case of George Brown's memoir is documented in TNA CAB 164/588.

226 'Crossman Picks Girl Diary Editor', *The Times*, 13 September 1971.

227 Crossman, *Diaries*, Volume I, p. 12.

228 J. Morgan to R. Crossman, 21 November 1971, MRC MSS 154/3/LIT/32/1–58.

229 T. Dalyell, 'Michael Foot: The Last of a Dying Breed', *Telegraph*, 17 March 2011.

230 C. Walker, 'Labour MP Seeking Corruption Inquiry', *The Times*, 16 May 1974. See also PREM 16/465.

231 H. Evans, *Good Times, Bad Times* (New York: Atheneum, 1984), p. 18.

232 C. J. Child to J. Hunt, 'The Crossman Diaries', 31 May 1974, TNA CAB 164/1256.

233 I. P. Bancroft to W. Armstrong, 'The Crossman Diaries', 7 June 1974, TNA CAB 164/1256.

234 Ibid., p. 19.

235 Naylor, *A Man and an Institution*, p. 306.

236 Evans, *Good Times, Bad Times*, p. 21.

237 Cited in B. Fenton, 'How Whitehall was Beaten to the Punch by the Crossman Diaries', *Daily Telegraph*, 2 January 2006.

238 J. Hunt to H. Wilson, 17 March 1975, TNA PREM 16/466.

239 For a vivid portrait of Sharp's career see K. Theakston, 'Evelyn Sharp', *Contemporary British History*, 7:1 (Summer 1993), 132–48.

240 Crossman, *Diaries*, Volume I, p. 48.

241 For a detailed discussion of the alleged rise of command premiership see M. Foley, *The Rise of the British Presidency* (Manchester University Press, 1993).

242 C. J. Child to J. Hunt, 'The Crossman Diaries', 31 May 1974, TNA CAB 164/1256.

243 'Public Presentation of Government Policy', Note by the Prime Minister, CP (72) 70, 3 July 1972, TNA PREM 15/1682.

244 'Open Government', R. T. Armstrong, 1972, TNA PREM 15/1682.

245 Ibid.

246 'Press Comments and Regulations with the Press', General Secretary to E. Sugden, 18 December 1975, MRC MSS 415, Box 90.

247 Evans, *My Paper Chase*, p. 364.

248 Ibid., p. 23.

249 Cited in B. Fenton, 'How Whitehall Was Beaten to the Punch by the Crossman Diaries', *Daily Telegraph*, 2 January 2006.

250 W. Armstrong, May 1975, TNA PREM 16/466.

251 Evans, *Good Times, Bad Times*, p. 24.

252 Cited in 'Drafts: Report of the Committee of Privy Councillors on Ministerial Memoirs', TNA CAB 164/1294.

253 D. G. T. Williams, 'Case and Comment: The Crossman Diaries', *Cambridge Law Journal*, 35:1 (April 1976), 1.

254 Ibid., 2.

255 'Anne Crossman: Obituary', *Daily Telegraph*, 8 October 2008.

256 B. Trend to G. Wigg, 2 April 1971 cited in 'The Memoirs of George Wigg', J. M. Moss, 30 May 1975, TNA CAB 164/1296.

257 B. Levin, 'The Light that Mr Crossman Lets in Can Never Again be Shut Out', *The Times*, 3 June 1976, p. 14.

258 Interview with Mrs Anne Crossman.

259 Leigh, *Frontiers of Secrecy*, p. 71.

260 J. Naylor, 'British Memoirs and Official Secrecy: From Crossman to Thatcher', in Egerton (ed.), *Political Memoir*, p. 332.

261 *Report of the Committee of Privy Councillors on Ministerial Memoirs*.

262 Ibid.

263 Ibid.

264 H. Wilson, January 1976, TNA PREM 16/904.

7 Keeping the secrets of wartime deception: Ultra and Double-Cross

1 P. Calvocoressi, *Top Secret Ultra* (New York: Littlehampton, 1980), p. 14.

2 JIC (45) 223 (o) Final, 'Use of Special Intelligence by Official Historians', 20 July 1945, TNA CAB 103/288.

3 R. Bennett, 'FORTITUDE, ULTRA and the "Need to Know"', *Intelligence and National Security*, 4:3 (July 1988), 498; R. Bennett, 'ULTRA and Some Command Decisions', *Journal of Contemporary History*, 16:1 (January 1981), 131–52.

4 Cited in F. W. Winterbotham, *The Ultra Secret* (London: Weidenfeld & Nicolson, 1974), p. 18.

5 H. Hinsley, 'The Enigma of Ultra', *History Today*, 43:9 (September 1993), 15–20.

6 M. Howard, *Captain Professor: A Life in War and Peace* (London: Continuum, 2006), p. 188.

7 Andrew, *Secret Service*, p. 125.

8 Calvocoressi, *Top Secret Ultra*, p. 14.

9 D. Kahn, 'The Ultra Secret: Enigma Unwrapped', *New York Times*, 29 December 1974, p. 5.

10 Aldrich, *Hidden Hand*, p. 2.

11 'JIC: General Directive to Chief Historians for Safeguarding Special Intelligence Sources in Compiling Official Histories', 20 July 1945, TNA CAB 103/288.

12 See J. Keegan, *Intelligence in War: Knowledge of the Enemy from Napoleon to Al-Qaeda* (London: Key Porter Books, 2003), pp. 190–6; C. Andrew, 'Churchill and Intelligence', *Intelligence and National Security*, 3:3 (July 1988), 181–93.

13 'Security of Deception: Development up to Mid-January 1946', London Controlling Section, TNA DEFE 28/28; M. Vyvyan to H. Jenkinson, 3 August 1944, TNA FO 371/39171; Anon. to Major Cave G2 Division Supreme Headquarters Allied Expeditionary Force, 10 August 1944, TNA FO 371/39171.

14 Miscellaneous Notes, 12 April 1941, TNA HW 50/22.

15 R. A. Butler, 'Preliminary Histories of the War', Head of Military Branch, 10 November 1944, TNA ADM 116/5558.

16 M. Hankey to R. Howorth, 21 July 1941, TNA CAB 21/2165.

17 'Report: Progress of the Official Histories', K. Hancock, 18 February 1942, TNA FO 370/692.

18 Telegram, Cabinet Office to JSM (Washington), July 1945, TNA CAB 103/288.

19 JIC (45) 223 (o) Final, 'Use of Special Intelligence by Official Historians', 20 July 1945, TNA CAB 103/288.

20 'Security of Deception', Memorandum by Controlling Officers, 17 February 1946, TNA DEFE 28/28.

21 'JIC: General Directive to Chief Historians for Safeguarding Special Intelligence Sources in Compiling Official Histories', 20 July 1945, TNA CAB 103/288; 'Special Order', E. Travis, 7 May 1945, TNA HW 3/29.

22 Ibid.

23 Cited in S. Schoenherr, 'Code Breaking in World War Two', 13 March 2007. http://history.sandiego.edu/gen/ww2timeline/espionage.html.

24 Miscellaneous Notes, 17 November 1943, TNA HW 50/22.

25 Ibid.; 'Compromise of Co-belligerents by Cypher Communications', May 1953, TNA HW 50/22.

26 JIC (45) 223 (0) Final, 'Use of Special Intelligence by Official Historians', 20 July 1945, TNA CAB 103/288; 'JIC: General Directive to Chief Historians for Safeguarding Special Intelligence Sources in Compiling Official Histories', 20 July 1945, TNA CAB 103/288.

27 Telegram, Cabinet Office to JSM (Washington), July 1945, TNA CAB 103/288.

28 JIC (45) 223 (0) Final, 'Use of Special Intelligence by Official Historians', 20 July 1945, TNA CAB 103/288; 'JIC: General Directive to Chief Historians for Safeguarding Special Intelligence Sources in Compiling Official Histories', 20 July 1945, TNA CAB 103/288.

29 'Summary: London Signals Intelligence Board Meeting. No. 13', 18 July 1945, TNA WO 208/5126.

30 Cited in A. Cave Brown, *Bodyguard of Lies* (London: HarperCollins, 1976), p. 826.

31 Aldrich, *Hidden Hand*, pp. 3–4.

32 E. G. Hastings, 3 February 1948, TNA CAB 104/282.

33 'Proposal for an Official History of Intelligence Activities in World War Two', The Intelligence Co-ordinator, 19 June 1969, TNA CAB 163/133; J. R. Deane, *The Strange Alliance: The Story of Our Efforts at Wartime Co-operation with Russia* (London: John Murray 1947); 'Exasperation in Moscow', *Time*, 13 January 1947.

34 Director of Military Intelligence to London Controlling Section, 17 January 1946, TNA DEFE 28/28; 'Security of Deception', Memorandum by Controlling Officers, 17 February 1946, TNA DEFE 28/28.

35 Ibid.

36 R. Lewin, *Ultra Goes To War* (London: Book Club Associates, 1978), p. 183.

37 Aldrich, 'Policing the Past', 927. See also L. Johnson, *Strategic Intelligence*, Volume 1 (Westport: Greenwood, 2007), p. 53.

38 N. Brook, 28 January 1948, TNA CAB 104/282.

39 E. G. Hastings, 3 February 1948, TNA CAB 104/282.

40 Ibid.

41 Ibid.

42 'W. Churchill's *Second World War* Volume II, Book IV: Points for Consideration', N. Brook, 7 April 1948, TNA CAB 21/2176.

43 N. Brook to W. Churchill, 1 June 1948, TNA CAB 21/2176.

44 D. Reynolds, 'The Ultra Secret and Churchill's War Memoirs', *Intelligence and National Security*, 20:2 (June 2005), 211.

45 N. Brook to W. Churchill, 1 June 1948, TNA CAB 21/2176.

46 Anon. to N. Brook, 27 April 1948, TNA CAB 104/282; N. Brook, 12 July 1949, TNA CAB 21/2187.

47 J. A. Drew to G. Liddell, 3 November 1952, TNA CAB 21/3759.

48 See Reynolds, 'Ultra Secret'; Reynolds, *Command of History*, p. 499.

49 D. Petrie to J. Masterman, 11 December 1945, John Masterman Papers (hereafter JMP), Worcester College (hereafter WC), Oxford, 10/1/128/1.

50 D. Petrie, 6 December 1950, WC JMP 10/1/128/1.

51 J. Masterman to Lord Swinton, 20 April 1961, WC JMP 10/1/128/1.

52 J. Masterman to D. White, 2 December 1954, WC JMP 10/1/128/1.

53 J. P. Campbell, 'An Update on the Interpretation of the Ultra Documentation', *Archivaria*, 26 (September 1988), 184.

54 N. Annan, *Our Age: Portrait of a Generation* (London: Weidenfeld & Nicolson, 1990), p. 5.

55 D. White to J. Masterman, 10 December 1954, WC JMP 10/1/128/1.

56 As MI5 had predicted, the Spanish General Staff forwarded the information to the German High Command, who, 'having regarded [it] as being worthy of the most urgent attention' and spread-eagled their defensive force right across Europe, were blinded to the true Allied objective – an invasion of Italy through Sicily. T. R. Rawer, 22 October 1945, TNA WO 208/3163.

57 D. Petrie to J. Masterman, 19 February 1953, WC JMP 10/1/75.

58 Ibid.

59 See Aldrich, 'Policing the Past', 929–31.

60 For more information on Chapman's wartime activities see N. Booth, *ZigZag: The Incredible Wartime Exploits of Double Agent Eddie Chapman* (London: Piatkus, 2007); B. Macintyre, *Agent ZigZag: The True Wartime Story of Eddie Chapman: Lover, Traitor, Hero, Spy* (London: Bloomsbury Publishing, 2007).

61 'Edward Arnold Chapman', 6 May 1953, TNA DEFE 28/137.

62 Private information. See also Booth, *ZigZag*, p. 302.

63 'Edward Arnold Chapman', 6 May 1953, TNA DEFE 28/137.

64 Ibid.

65 D. White to J. Drew, 15 May 1953, TNA DEFE 28/137.

66 J. Drew to H. Palmer, 14 September 1953, TNA DEFE 28/137.

67 B. Hill to J. Drew, 14 September 1953, TNA DEFE 28/137.

68 M. Richardson, 'Top Secret Agent', *Observer*, 1 November 1953.

69 J. Drew, 7 October 1953, TNA DEFE 28/17.

70 J. Masterman to D. White, 3 October 1967, WC JMP 10/1/128/1.

71 D. White to J. Masterman, 5 October 1967, WC JMP 10/1/128/1.

72 M. F. Jones to J. Masterman, 1 December 1967, WC JMP 10/1/128/1.

73 'Notes for Meeting', 1968, WC JMP 10/1/128/1.

74 J. Masterman to M. F. Jones, 12 December 1967, WC JMP 10/1/128/1.

75 Ibid.

76 H. Hart to J. Masterman, 9 June 1968, WC JMP 10/1/128/1.

77 J. Butler to J. Masterman, 29 December 1967, WC JMP 10/1/128/1.

78 T. Robertson to J. Masterman, 31 March 1968, WC JMP 10/1/128/1.

79 P. Allen to J. Masterman, 2 April 1970, WC JMP 10/1/128/2.

80 P. Fleming to J. Masterman, 5 July 1968, WC JMP 10/1/128/1.

81 L. Farago to J. Masterman, 18 August 1971, Ladislas Farago Papers (hereafter LFP), Howard Gotlieb Archival Research Center (hereafter HGARC), Boston University, Box 51, Folder 1; L. Farago to R. Denniston, 18 March 1972, HGARC LFP, Box 68; L. Farago, *Burn after Reading: The Espionage History of World War II* (New York: Macfadden-Bartell, 1963).

82 L. Farago to J. Masterman, 17 August 1971, HGARC LFP, Box 51, Folder 1.

83 J. Masterman to J. Osborn, 27 October 1970, WC JMP 10/1/128/3.

84 G. Watson to J. Masterman, 9 April 1970, WC JMP 10/1/128/2.

85 L. Farago, 7 July 1971, HGARC LFP, Box 51, Folder 1.

86 Ibid; A. D. Peters & Co. Literary Agents to J. Masterman, 23 June 1971, WC JMP 10/1/128/3.

87 C. Kerr to L. Farago, 7 July 1971, HGARC LFP, Box 51, Folder 1.

88 L. Farago to R. Denniston, 11 August 1971, HGARC LFP, Box 51, Folder 1.

89 Ibid.

90 Ibid.

91 L. Farago to C. Kerr, 1971, LFP, Box 51, Folder 1.

92 'Book by Sefton Delmer', JIC Addendum to JIC (A) (70) (SSC) 157, 22 September 1970, TNA CAB 163/194. See also: N. Denning to JIC (A), 21 January 1969; 'Note: Ladislas Farago', P. Allen, 2 August 1971, TNA FCO 73/158.

93 'Comments by GCHQ', TNA CAB 163/194.

94 Kent to Wolf, 14 March 1972, TNA CAB 163/194.

95 N. Denning to JIC (A), 21 January 1969, TNA CAB 163/194; 'Book by Sefton Delmer', JIC Addendum to JIC (A) (70), 4 November 1970, TNA CAB 163/194.

96 L. Farago to J. Masterman, 17 August 1971, HGARC LFP, Box 51, Folder 1.

97 N. West (ed.), *The Guy Liddell Diaries Volume I: 1939–42* (London: Routledge, 2005), p. 3.

98 Cited in M. Howard, 'Reflections on Strategic Deception', in W. R. Louis (ed.), *Adventures with Britannia* (Oxford: I. B. Tauris, 1994), p. 237.

99 M. F. Jones to A. Douglas-Home, TNA FCO 73/158.

100 M. F. Jones to J. Masterman, 4 August 1971, WC JMP 10/1/128/4.

101 Ibid.

102 C. Kerr to L. Farago, 18 October 1971, HGARC LFP, Box 51, Folder 1.

103 L. Farago to J. Masterman, 23 October 1971, HGARC LFP, Box 51, Folder 1; C. Kerr to J. Masterman, 15 November 1971, WC JMP 10/1/128/5.

104 R. Denniston to G. Thomson, 11 February 1972, HGARC LFP, Box 51, Folder 2.

105 L. Farago to R. Denniston, 18 March 1972, HGARC LFP, Box 68.

106 L. Farago to R. Denniston, 20 February 1972, HGARC LFP, Box 51, Folder 2.

107 C. Kerr to J. Masterman, 1 June 1972, WC JMP 10/1/128/7.

108 J. P. Campbell, 'Masterman, Sir John Cecil (1891–1977), *Oxford Dictionary of National Biography*, Oxford University Press, September 2004; online edn, October 2009 (www.oxforddnb.com/view/article/31420, accessed 24 November 2009).

109 L. Farago to R. Denniston, 18 March 1972, HGARC LFP, Box 68.

110 C. T. Anthony to A. Waghaler, 8 February 1972, HGARC LFP, Box 68.

111 R. Mansbridge to J. Masterman, 9 February 1972, WC JMP 10/1/128/6.

112 P. Beesly to Guy Hughes, 3 November 1975, Patrick Beesly Papers, Churchill College, Cambridge, CCC MLBE 2/15.

113 D. Kahn, *The Codebreakers: The Story of Secret Writing* (New York: Macmillan, 1967); W. Kozaczuk, *Bitwa o Tajemnice. Sluzby wywiadowcze Polski i Rzeszy Niemieckiej 1922–1939* (Warsaw: Ksiazka i Wiedza, 1967); K. Philby, *My Silent War: The Soviet Master Spy's Own Story* (New York: Grove Press, 1968); 'Published Material on Intelligence in World War Two', GCHQ to Intelligence Co-ordinator, 27 May 1969, TNA CAB 163/134.

114 D. McLachlan, *Room 39: Naval Intelligence in Action 1939–45* (London: Atheneum, 1968).

115 R. Bublitz, 'Review: Room 39: A Study in Naval Intelligence by D. McLachlan', *Military Affairs*, 33:1 (April 1969), 278.

116 'The Release of SIGINT Records', JIC (58) 46, 13 November 1968, TNA PREM 13/3252.

117 Ibid.

118 Ibid.

119 Ibid.

120 Ibid.

121 Ibid.

122 'Release of SIGINT Records', B. Trend to E. Heath, 9 November 1970, TNA DEFE 31/8.

123 Ibid; 'Release of Official Records', B. Trend to H. Wilson, 25 March 1969, TNA DEFE 13/615.

124 Ibid.

125 L. Farago, *The Game of the Foxes: The Untold Story of German Espionage in the United States and Great Britain During World War II* (New York: David McKay, 1971), p. 664.

126 'Book Reviews: The Cryptologists who Briefly Came in from the Cold', G. F. Goodhall, 15 May 1974, TNA HW 25/16; G. Bertrand, *Enigma ou la plus grande enigma de la guerre* (Paris: Libraire Plon, 1973).

127 J. Roper to J. H. Robertson, 8 February 1963, TNA CAB 21/5865; British Defence Staffs (Washington) to the Ministry of Defence, 19 March 1963, TNA CAB 21/5865.

128 'Biography of Anthony Cave Brown', 9 November 1962, TNA CAB 21/5865; I. Adams to R. W. Ford, 4 December 1962, TNA CAB 21/5865.

129 R. J. Aldrich, 'The Secret State', in P. Addison and H. Jones (eds), *A Companion to Contemporary Britain* (Oxford: Wiley-Blackwell, 2005), p. 336.

130 See Aldrich, 'Never-Never Land and Wonderland?'

131 W. McIndoe to S. Lohan, 19 November 1966, TNA CAB 21/5865.

132 M. Wyeth, Jr, to M. Jaffe, 18 February 1972, Anthony Cave Brown Papers (hereafter ACBP), Georgetown University Special Collections (hereafter GU), Second Accession, Box 1.

133 Ibid.

134 Ibid.

135 'British Ear at the German Keyhole', *Christian Science Monitor*, 3 December 1974.

136 P. Tompkins, 'War Between the Machines', *New Republic*, 1 February 1975.

137 E. Montagu, *Beyond Top Secret Ultra* (London: Coward, McCann & Geoghegan, 1977); P. Beesly, *Very Special Intelligence: The Story of the Admiralty's Operational Intelligence Centre 1939–45* (London: Doubleday, 1977).

138 R. Bennett, *Ultra in the West: The Normandy Campaign 1944–45* (London: Charles Scribners, 1979).

139 G. Hughes to P. Beesly, 30 October 1975, CCC MLBE 2/15.

140 C. Loehnis to P. Beesly, 6 November 1975, CCC MLBE 2/30.

141 Ibid.

142 C. Andrew, 'Intelligence, International Relations and Under-Theorisation', *Intelligence and National Security*, 19:2 (Summer 2004), 170–84.

8 SOE in France

1 Gaitskell is cited in J. Masterman to D. White, 16 May 1968, WC JMP 10/1/128/4.

2 M. R. D. Foot, *SOE in France* (London: HMSO, 1966), pp. ix–x.

3 See, for example, Dame I. Ward, 'Letter to the Editor', *Daily Telegraph*, 29 April 1966.

4 P. Howarth, *Undercover: The Men and Women of the Special Operations Executive* (London: Routledge, 1980), p. 162. See also N. West, *Secret War* (London: Hodder & Stoughton, 1992), p. 4.

5 C. J. Murphy, 'The Origins of *SOE in France*', *Historical Journal*, 46:4 (2003), 935–52.

6 This turn of phrase was coined by Foot himself in a private correspondence with Dame Irene Ward in 1966. See M. R. D. Foot to Dame I. Ward, 21 March 1966, Oxford, Bodleian Library, Dame Irene Ward Papers, MS. Eng.c.6980, folder 190.

7   'The History of the Special Operations Executive in France', B. Trend, 26 March 1964, TNA CAB 103/572; B. Trend, 11 May 1960, TNA PREM 11/5084.

8   A. Cadogan to L. C. Hollis, 13 November 1945, TNA CAB 121/305.

9   M. Seaman, 'A Glass Half Full – Some Thoughts on the Evolution of the Study of the SOE', *Intelligence and National Security*, 20:1 (March 2005), 29.

10 'Publicity of SOE Matters', C. Gubbins, August 1945, TNA HS 8/863.

11 'SOE Publicity. Minutes of Meeting held at Air Ministry on 19 September 1945', TNA HS 8/863.

12 See N. Wylie, 'SOE and the Neutrals', in M. Seaman (ed.), *Special Operations Executive: A New Weapon of War* (London: Routledge, 2006), pp. 157–78; R. Bickers, 'The Business of a Secret War: Operation "Remorse" and SOE Salesmanship in Wartime China', *Intelligence and National Security*, 16:4 (December 2001), 11–36.

13 'Publicity of SOE Matters', C. Gubbins, August 1945, TNA HS 8/863.

14 Ibid.

15 S. Berg, 'Churchill's Secret Army Lived On', *BBC Today*, 13 December 2008.

16 'SOE Publicity. Minutes of Meeting held at Air Ministry on 19 September 1945', TNA HS 8/863.

17 For a more detailed treatment of post-war OSS films see J. I. Deutsch, '"I Was a Hollywood Agent": Cinematic Representations of the Office of Strategic Services in 1946', *Intelligence and National Security*, 13:2 (1998), 85–99.

18 'Suggested Screen Treatment for: Cloak and Dagger', Lt-Colonel Corey Ford and Major Alastair Macbain, 1 October 1945, University of Southern California (USC), Warner Bros Archives, Cloak and Dagger Papers, 2:1.

19 Ibid.

20 'The Question of BBC Broadcast on Resistance. Minutes of Meeting held on 18 September 1945', TNA HS 8/863.

21 Bromley to H. N. Sporborg, 8 October 1945, TNA HS 8/863.

22 A. Cadogan to L. C. Hollis, 13 November 1945, TNA CAB 121/305.

23 H. Caccia, 9 November 1945, TNA HS 8/863.

24 L. C. Hollis to Chief of the Air Staff, 27 November 1945, TNA CAB 121/305.

25 See L. Valero, 'We Need Our New OSS, Our New General Donovan, Now . . .: The Public Discourse over American Intelligence, 1944–53', *Intelligence and National Security*, 18:1 (Spring 2003), 91–118.

26 Undated Correspondence, USC, Warner Bros Archives, Cloak and Dagger Papers, Folder 15.

27 'Synopsis: *13 Rue Madeleine*', Harry Brand, Academy of Motion Picture Arts and Sciences (AMPAS), Los Angeles, Production Code Administration Records for *13 Rue Madeleine*; J. Parish and R. Pitts, *The Great Spy Pictures*, (Metuchen: Scarecrow Press, 1974), p. 358.

28 Deutsch, '"I Was a Hollywood Agent"', 85–99.

29 W. J. Donovan to L. de Rochement, 3 July 1946, J. Russell Forgan Papers, Hoover Institute, Stanford University, 73089–8.36, Box 1.

30 J. R. Forgan to W. J. Donovan, 1 March 1946, J. Russell Forgan Papers, Hoover Institute, Stanford University, 73089–8.36, Box 1.

31 Ibid.

32 20th Century Fox to W. Casey, 19 March 1946, J. Russell Forgan Papers, Hoover Institute, Stanford University, 73089–8.36, Box 1.

33 The first wave of post-war SOE publications included: G. Millar, *Horned Pigeon* (London: William Heinemann, 1946), I. Morrison, *Grandfather Longlegs: The Life and Gallant Death of Major H. P. Seagrim* (London: Faber & Faber, 1947); J. Amery, *Sons of the Eagle: A Study in Guerrilla War* (London: Macmillan, 1948); S. Moss, *Ill Met By Moonlight* (London: George G. Harrap, 1950).

34 M. Seaman, 'Good Thrillers, But Bad History', in K. G. Roberston (ed.), *War, Resistance and Intelligence: Essays in Honour of M. R. D. Foot* (London: Pen & Sword Books, 1999), pp. 119–33.

35 'History of Secret Organisations 1939–45', N. Brook, May 1947, TNA CAB 103/256.

36 D. White to D. Hubback, June 1947, TNA CAB 103/356.

37 N. Brook to S. Luke, 22 October 1947, TNA CAB 103/256.

38 R. Walton to S. Luke, 24 June 1947, TNA CAB 103/256.

39 N. Brook to S. Luke, 22 October 1947, TNA CAB 103/256.

40 F. Newsam to P. Sillitoe, August 1952, TNA HO 287/1415.

41 See M. J. Buckmaster, *Specially Employed: The Story of British Aid to French Patriots of the Resistance* (London: Batchworth, 1952); B. Marshall, *The White Rabbit* (London: Evans Bros., 1952); P. Churchill, *Of Their Own Choice: An Account of the Author's Secret Mission to France During the Second World War* (London: Hodder & Stoughton, 1952); P. Churchill, *The Spirit in the Cage: An Account of the Author's Experiences as a Prisoner of War* (London: Hodder & Stoughton, 1954).

42 P. Sillitoe to E. Bridges, 24 September 1952, TNA HO 287/1415; E. Bridges to D. M. Fyfe, 28 November 1952, TNA HO 287/1415.

43 Ibid.

44 I. Fleming, *The Diamond Smugglers* (London: Jonathan Cape, 1957).

45 A. Simkins, 'Sillitoe, Sir Percy Joseph (1888–1962)', first published September 2004, 1,180 words, with portrait illustration. http://dx.doi.org/10.1093/ref: odnb/36092.

46 E. Bridges to F. Newsam, 13 October 1952, TNA HO 287/1415; F. Newsam to Bridges, 17 October 1952, TNA HO 287/1415; E. Bridges to D. M. Fyfe, 28 November 1952, TNA HO 287/1415.

47 F. Newsam to E. Bridges, 17 October 1952, TNA HO 287/1415.

48 E. Bridges to D. M. Fyfe, 28 November 1952. TNA HO 287/1415

49 D. M. Fyfe to E. Bridges, 16 January 1953, TNA HO 287/1415.

50 E. Bridges to F. Newsam, 29 January 1953, TNA HO 287/1415.

51 P. Sillitoe, 'The War against Crime: My Answer to Critics of MI5', *Sunday Times*, 22 November 1953.

52 A. Boyle, 'Obituary: Sir Dick White', *Independent*, 23 February 1993.

53 Miscellaneous Note, 23 November 1953, TNA HO 287/1415.

54 D. White to F. Newsam, 26 November 1953, TNA HO 287/1415; F. Newsam to P. Sillitoe, 4 January 1954, TNA HO 287/1415.

55 Miscellaneous Note, 23 November 1953, TNA HO 287/1415.

56 D. White to F. Newsam, 26 November 1953, TNA HO 287/1415.

57 Ibid.

58 For more information on MI5–FBI animosity see M. Goodman, 'Who Is Trying to Keep What Secret from Whom and Why? MI5–FBI Relations and the Klaus Fuchs Case', *Journal of Cold War Studies*, 7:3 (2005), 124–46.

59 P. Sillitoe to F. Newsam, 11 December 1953, TNA HO 287/1415; P. Sillitoe to F. Newsam, 29 January 1954, TNA HO 287/1415.

60 P. Sillitoe to F. Newsam, 29 January 1954, TNA HO 287/1415.

61 E. Bridges to F. Newsam, 10 March 1954, TNA HO 287/1415.

62 Booth, *ZigZag*.

63 R. Pape, *Boldness Be My Friend* (London: Elek, 1953).

64 H. T. Smith to Director of Public Prosecutions, 14 November 1953, TNA TS 28/568.

65 See C. J. Murphy, *Security and Special Operations: SOE and MI5 during the Second World War* (Basingstoke: Palgrave, 2006).

66 TNA HO 287/1415, F. Newsam to P. Sillitoe, 3 November 1954, TNA HO 287/1415.

67 Hooper, *Official Secrets*, p. 193.

68 P. Wilkinson to Trend, 24 January 1962, TNA CAB 103/571.

69 '*The Hole in the Ground* (Later renamed *War at the Top*) by J. Leasor', J. Hollis to N. Brook, 27 February 1958, TNA CAB 21/3773.

70 *Hansard*, 22 February 1956, cols. 363–6.

71 I. Ward to S. Lloyd, 20 October 1958, TNA PREM 11/5084.

72 M. Buckmaster, *They Fought Alone: The Story of British Agents in France* (London: Odhams, 1958); 'Monstrous Assertion about British Agents', *The Times*, 1 December 1958, p. 6; 'SOE and Dame Irene Ward', TNA PREM 11/5084.

73 I. Ward to S. Lloyd, 29 October 1958, TNA PREM 11/5084; I. Ward to H. Macmillan, 31 October 1958, TNA PREM 11/5084.

74 'SOE and Dame Irene Ward', TNA PREM 11/5084.

75 Howarth, *Undercover*, p. 161.

76 I. Ward to S. Lloyd, 29 October 1958, TNA PREM 11/5084.

77 'SOE and Dame Irene Ward', TNA PREM 11/5084.

78 Ibid.

79 P. Dean to B. Trend, 3 May 1960, TNA PREM 11/5584.

80 'Official History of SOE: Further Report by a Working Party', 22 May 1959, TNA T220/1388.

81 Ibid.

82 E. Hale to N. Brook, 22 May 1959, TNA T 220/1388.

83 N. Brook to P. Dean, 31 July 1959, TNA T 22/1388.

84 F. A. Bishop to N. Brook, 25 May 1959, TNA T 220/1388.

85 Aldrich, 'Policing the Past', 937.

86 'Study of the Pros and Cons of Publication of Further Histories of SOE', B. Salt, July 1969, TNA CAB 103/570.

87 'History of SOE in France', B. Trend to A. Douglas-Home, 26 March 1964, TNA PREM 11/5084.

88 'SOE History: Notes of a Meeting', 18 May 1960, TNA PREM 11/5084.

89 P. Dean to B. Trend, 3 May 1960, TNA PREM 11/5084.

90 E. Heath to I. Ward, 2 September 1960, Dame Irene Ward Papers, Bodleian Library, MS.Eng.c.6976.

91 Ibid.

92 P. A. Wilkinson to M. R. D. Foot, 7 November 1960, TNA 11/5084; 'A Biography: M. R. D. Foot', P. A. Wilkinson, September 1960, TNA CAB 103/571; E. G. Boxshall, 23 September 1960, TNA CAB 103/571. For further details about Foot's appointment, see C. Andrew and R. J. Aldrich, 'The Intelligence Services in the Second World War', *Contemporary British History*, 13:4 (Winter 1999), 130–69, esp. 145.

93 In his most recent publication, the excellent and moving *Memories of an SOE Historian* (Barnsley: Pen & Sword Military Books, 2008), Foot explains that he is not and never has been a revisionist. The Second World War was a just cause against an evil foe. Even the firebombing of Dresden was right and proper. (P. J. Conradi, 'Review: Memories of an SOE Historian, M. R. D. Foot', *Independent*, 18 November 2008.)

94 'SOE History: Working Arrangements', E. G. Boxshall, 23 September 1960, TNA CAB 103/571.

95 Ibid.

96 'Some Lessons from the First Publication', M. R. D. Foot, 19 July 1966, TNA CAB 103/576.

97 Helen Jones, 'Smith, (Margaret) Patricia Hornsby-, Baroness Hornsby-Smith (1914–1985)', *Oxford Dictionary of National Biography*, Oxford University Press, Sept 2004; online edn, May 2007 (www.oxforddnb.com/view/article/39178, accessed 20 February 2010).

98 P. Hornsby-Smith to J. Profumo, 25 September 1962, TNA WO 32/17807.

99 See *Daily Mail*, 1 March 1957.

100 F. Feldcamp to G. Thomson, 8 November 1960, TNA WO 32/17807.

101 Ibid.

102 M. Hyde, *The Quiet Canadian: The Secret Service Story of Sir William Stephenson* (London: H. Hamilton, 1962).

103 'C' to B. Trend, 7 November 1962, TNA CAB 21/5864.

104 A. Wyatt, 2 November 1962, TNA CAB 21/5864.

105 'Note for the Record: The Quiet Canadian', A. W. Wyatt, 2 November 1962, TNA CAB 21/5864.

106 'Promotional Material: The Quiet Canadian', Montgomery Hyde Papers, Churchill College, Cambridge, CCC HYDE 1/9.

107 I. Fleming, 'Intrepid: Silhouette of a Secret Agent', *Sunday Times* Magazine, 21 October 1962.

108 *Hansard*, 5th Series, 8 November 1962, 666, cols. 1,153–4.

109 'Minute of Conversation between I. Ward and H. Macmillan', 13 December 1962, TNA CAB 21/5864.

110 Ibid.

111 W. Deakin to B. Trend, 8 June 1962, TNA CAB 103/571.

112 Ibid.

113 *European Resistance Movements 1939–1945: Presentations at the First International Conference on the History of the Resistance Movements* (London: Pergamon Press, 1964).

114 www.cia.gov/csi/kent_csi/docs/v05i4a14p_0001.htm.

115 W. Deakin to B. Trend, 8 June 1962, TNA CAB 103/571.

116 www.cia.gov/csi/kent_csi/docs/v05i4a14p_0001.htm.

117 Ibid.

118 P. Wilkinson to B. Trend, 24 January 1962, TNA CAB 103/571.

119 Murphy, *Security and Special Operations*, pp. 4–5.

120 N. Mott, 4 June 1963, TNA CAB 103/571.

121 Ibid.

122 P. Wilkinson to B. Trend, 16 December 1963, TNA CAB 103/571.

123 E. G. Boxshall to P. Wilkinson, 10 October 1963, TNA CAB 103/571.

124 Ibid.

125 C. Gubbins to M. R. D. Foot, 5 February 1964, TNA CAB 103/572.

126 E. G. Boxshall to P. Wilkinson, 10 October 1963, TNA CAB 103/571; C. Gubbins to M. R. D. Foot, 5 February 1964, TNA CAB 103/572; P. Wilkinson to B. Trend, 22 May 1963, TNA CAB 103/571.

127 M. Buckmaster to E. Boxshall, 11 November 1964, TNA CAB 103/572.

128 Ibid.

129 Ibid.

130 'Lieutenant-Colonel Buckmaster's Objections and Comments', Principal Assistant Solicitor, 22 January 1965, TNA CAB 103/573.

131 Ibid.

132 M. Buckmaster to E. Boxshall, 11 November 1964, TNA CAB 103/572.

133 D. Dodds-Parker to B. Trend, 28 November 1964, TNA CAB 103/572.

134 'Historical Note: Decision to Write History', J. E. Jackson, 26 October 1965, TNA PREM 13/949; D. D. Parker to E. Boxshall, 21 April 1964, TNA CAB 103/572.

135 D. D. Parker to E. Boxshall, 21 April 1964, TNA CAB 103/572.

136 M. R. D. Foot to E. Boxshall, 16 November 1964, TNA CAB 103/572.

137 Ibid.

138 'Record of Meeting', 29 October 1963, TNA CAB 103/571.

139 M. Buckmaster to E. Boxshall, 20 April 1965, TNA CAB 103/753.

140 'Resistance History to Be Published', *Daily Telegraph*, 14 April 1964.

141 A. Goodenough to J. Adams, 21 October 1966, TNA FO 146/4635.

142 J. E. Jackson to D. Logan, 25 October 1966, TNA FO 146/4635.

143 B. Trend to the Prime Minister, 26 March 1964, TNA CAB 103/572.

144 'Resistance History to Be Published'.

145 P. Wilkinson to B. Trend, 2 January 1963, TNA CAB 103/571.

146 'Frozen Secrets Start to Thaw', *Sunday Telegraph*, 3 October 1965.

147 'My Cloak and Dagger Book May Shock Top Brass Says Historian', *Daily Mail*, 17 April 1964.

148 S. E. Ambrose, 'Reviewed Work: SOE in France: An Account of the Work of the Special Operations Executive in France, 1940–44', *American Historical Review*, 74:3 (February 1969), p. 1,006.

149 Ibid.

150 J. Bross, 'Review: SOE in France', *Studies in Intelligence*, 11:2 (Spring 1967).

151 Ibid.

152 L. D. Grand to H. Wilson, 26 April 1966, TNA PREM 12/949.

153 Ibid.

154 E. Behr, 'La guerre secrète des services secrets', *Le Nouvel Observateur*, TNA FO 146/4634.

155 Solicitor to G. Wigg, 3 May 1966, TNA CAB 103/575; 'Threat of Libel Action by Odette Sansom', E. G. Boxshall, 14 April 1966, TNA CAB 103/575.

156 O. Nickson to HMSO, 24 June 1966, TNA CAB 103/575; 'Writ between Peter Morland Churchill and M. R. D. Foot/HMSO', 10 August 1966, TNA CAB 103/576.

157 R. J. Minney, 15 July 1966, TNA CAB 103/576; 'Writ Minney vs HMSO and Foot', TNA CAB 103/577.

158 R. Pitman, 'I Call This a Shocking Attack on a Brave Woman', *Sunday Express*, 3 May 1966; 'Agents Who Survived the SOE', *Sunday Times*, 1 May 1966;

J. E. Jackson, 29 April 1966, TNA CAB 103/575; 'Statement to the Editor, M. R. D. Foot, *The Times*, 11 July 1966; B. Salt to G. Jones, 24 January 1969, TNA CAB 103/599; T. Johnson, 'Secret Agent Gets Libel Settlement', *Evening News*, 27 January 1969; 'Minney Case: Terms of Settlement', TNA CAB 103/579.

159 'Note of Meeting held at Cabinet Office', 18 May 1967, TNA CAB 103/569.

160 'The Salt Report', July 1969, Annexe A, TNA CAB 103/570.

161 Miscellaneous Note, January 1967, TNA CAB 103/569.

162 'Study of the Pros and Cons of Publication of Further Histories of SOE', B. Salt, July 1969, TNA CAB 103/570.

163 Ibid.

164 Ibid.

165 Ibid.

166 Ibid.

167 Ibid.

168 Ibid.; 'Note of Meeting between B. Trend and B. Salt', 6 October 1969, TNA CAB 103/569.

169 'Some Lessons Learnt from First Publication', M. R. D. Foot, 19 July 1966, TNA CAB 103/576.

170 'Note of Meeting between B. Trend and B. Salt', 6 October 1969, TNA CAB 103/569.

171 D. O'Sullivan, *Dealing with the Devil: Anglo-Soviet Intelligence Cooperation in the Second World War* (New York: Peter Lang, 2009).

172 'SOE: Pros and Cons. Notes of Meeting', 16 September 1969, TNA CAB 103/569.

173 This argument is made in Aldrich, 'Policing the Past', 944.

9 Counterblast: official history of British intelligence in the Second World War

1 'Policy on Official Histories', T. M. P. Stevens, Defence Secretariat (DS 22), 18 August 1972, TNA DEFE 11/567.

2 K. Philby, *My Silent War: The Soviet Master Spy's Own Story* (New York: Grove Press, 1968).

3 'Philby Offers to Withdraw Book', *New York Times*, 19 December 1967.

4 'The Significance of British Naval Intelligence during World War Two, and Postwar Security', J. H. Godfrey, 1965, CCC MLBE 6/3.

5 See C. Cabell, *The History of 30 Assault Unit: Ian Fleming's Red Indians* (London: Pen & Sword, 2009).

6 N. Denning to I. Fleming, 19 January 1961, L. Russell MSS, Manuscripts Department, Lilly Library, Indiana University, Bloomington.

7 I. Fleming to N. Denning, 12 January 1961, L. Russell MSS, Manuscripts Department, Lilly Library, Indiana University, Bloomington.

8 Cited in 'The Significance of British Naval Intelligence during World War Two, and Postwar Security', J. H. Godfrey, 1965, CCC MLBE 6/3.

9 P. Smithers to J. Pearson, 25 January 1966, J. Pearson MSS, Manuscripts Department, Lilly Library, Indiana University, Bloomington, Indiana.

10 'The Significance of British Naval Intelligence during World War Two, and Postwar Security', J. H. Godfrey, 1965, CCC MLBE 6/3.

11 Interview: Admiral John Godfrey', 3 March 1965, J. Pearson MSS, Manuscripts Department, Lilly Library, Indiana University, Bloomington.

12 Ibid. For debates about the origins of the CIA, see: R. Jeffreys-Jones, 'Why Was the CIA Established in 1947', *Intelligence and National Security*, 12:1 (1997), 21–40; R. Jeffreys-Jones, 'The Role of British Intelligence in the Mythologies Underpinning the OSS and Early CIA', *Intelligence and National Security*, 15:2 (2000), 5–19.

13 'Interview: Admiral John Godfrey', 3 March 1965, J. Pearson MSS, Manuscripts Department, Lilly Library, Indiana University, Bloomington.

14 Ibid.

15 J. Pearson, *The Life of Ian Fleming* (London: Companion Book Club, 1966).

16 Ibid., pp. 128–9.

17 B. Trend to A. Douglas-Home, 22 November 1963, TNA CAB 21/5230.

18 D. White to A. Dulles, 14 November 1963, Allen Dulles Papers, Folder 30, Box 57, Seely G. Mudd Manuscript Library, Princeton University.

19 'Intelligence Activities 1939–45', minutes of meeting, 26 February 1969, TNA DEFE 24/656.

20 Trend, cited in P. Gore-Booth, 19 April 1966, TNA FO 370/2913.

21 'Proposal for an Official History of British Intelligence Activities in World War II', Report by the Intelligence Co-ordinator, D. G. White, 4 July 1969, TNA DEFE 13/615.

22 Ibid.

23 'Record of a Meeting between D. White and M. Oldfield', 12 March 1969, TNA DEFE 31/8.

24 'Proposal for an Official History of British Intelligence Activities in World War II', Report by the Intelligence Co-ordinator, D. G. White, 4 July 1969, TNA DEFE 13/615.

25 Ibid.

26 Ibid.

27 Ibid.

28 B. Trend to H. Wilson, 25 March 1969, TNA DEFE 13/615.

29 See note 24.

30 Ibid.

31 B. Trend to N. Denning, 24 July 1969, TNA DEFE 13/615.

32 B. Trend to H. Wilson, 29 July 1969, TNA DEFE 23/107.

33 Trend, loose minute, 1 August 1969, TNA DEFE 23/107.

34 E. Heath to H. Wilson, 17 April 1970, TNA DEFE 23/107.

35 T. Powers, *The Man Who Kept the Secrets: Richard Helms and the CIA* (New York: Alfred Knopf, 1979).

36 R. Helms, 15 November 1961, The Richard Helms Papers, Part I, Lauinger Library, Georgetown University, 4/22/327.

37 W. Pforzheimer, 'Memorandum for the Assistant Deputy Director for Intelligence: The OSS Archives', 28 January 1970, CREST CIA-RDP72–0031R000200290016–8.

38 'Memorandum for the file', 14 January 1970, CREST CIA-RDP84–00780R003600140018–1.

39 P. Fleming to A. Douglas-Home, 8 October 1970, TNA CAB 164/1230.

40 B. Trend to E. Heath, 'Official History of Intelligence in the Second World War', 16 November 1970, TNA PREM 15/424.

41 B. Trend to E. Heath, 1 March 1971, TNA DEFE 23/107.

42 B. Trend to E. Heath, 10 February 1970, TNA DEFE 23/107.

43 'Official History of Intelligence: Meeting at Burke Trend's Room', 26 February 1969, TNA DEFE 24/656.

44 H. Butterfield, *History and Human Relations* (London: Longman, 1951), p. 186.

45 Ibid.

46 B. Trend to H. Wilson, 25 March 1969, TNA DEFE 13/615.

47 For more biographical information on F. W. Hinsley see: P. Linehan, 'Obituary: Professor Sir Harry Hinsley', *Independent*, 19 February 1998; R. Langhorne, 'Professor Sir Harry Hinsley: An Appreciation', *Diplomacy and Statecraft*, 9:2 (July 1998), 212–21.

48 R. Langhorne, 'Hinsley, Sir (Francis) Harry (1918–1998), *Oxford Dictionary of National Biography* (Oxford University Press, 2004).

49 'Record of a Meeting between D. White and M. Oldfield', 12 March 1969, TNA DEFE 31/8.

50 H. Hinsley to P. Beesly, 28 May 1976, CCC MLBE 2/12.

51 Private information.

52 J. Hunt to J. Callaghan, 22 May 1978, TNA DEFE 13/1304.

53 Aldrich, 'Policing the Past', 950.

54 M. Thatcher to J. Callaghan, 17 July 1978, TNA DEFE 13/1304.

55 Ibid.

56 Ibid.

57 Ibid.

58 J. Callaghan, 14 July 1978, TNA DEFE 13/1304.

59 J. Hunt to J. Callaghan, 28 July 1978, TNA DEFE 13/1304.

60 Cited in K. Boyd, *Encyclopedia of Historians and Historical Writing: Volume 1* (London: Fitzroy Dearborn, 1999), p. 592.

61 Reviews of Hinsley's histories can be found at http://intellit.muskingham.edu/uk_folder/ukwwii_folder/ukwwiihinsley.html.

62 Cited in P. Hennessy, 'Ultra's Shadowy Secrets Emerge', *The Times*, 9 September 1981, p. 5.

63 'A Corner of the Veil: British Intelligence in the Second World War', *Economist*, 2 June 1979.

64 See William Bundy Papers, Seely G. Mudd Manuscript Library, Princeton University, MC 189, Series 1, Boxes 4 and 5, as well as Series 2, Boxes 6, 7 and 8.

65 M. R. D. Foot, *SOE in the Low Countries* (London: St Ermin's Press, 2001); Sir B. Richards, *Secret Flotillas: Clandestine Sea-Lines to France and French North Africa* (London: HMSO, 1996).

66 W. J. Mackenzie, *The Secret History of SOE: Special Operations Executive, 1940–1945* (London: St Ermin's Press, 2000).

67 J. Curry, *The Security Service 1908–45* (London: Public Record Office Publications, 1999).

68 Aldrich, 'Policing the Past', 952.

69 Ibid., 953.

70 A. Dulles, *The Craft of Intelligence* (New York: Harper & Row, 1963), p. 39.

71 L. Scott and P. Jackson, 'The Study of Intelligence in Theory and Practice', *Intelligence and National Security*, 19:2 (Summer 2004), 152.

72 Liddell Hart, cited in R. Lowe, 'Official History'. www.history.ac.uk/makinghistory/resources/articles/official_history.html.

73 Private information.

74 A. Grafton, *The Footnote: A Curious History* (Harvard University Press, 1999).

75 Higham, cited in J. Grey, 'Introduction', in J. Grey (ed.), *The Last Word? Essays on Official History in the US and British Commonwealth* (Westport: Praeger, 2003).

Epilogue

1 S. Rimington, *Open Secret: The Autobiography of a Former Director-General of MI5* (London: Hutchinson, 2001), p. 286.

2 www.fco.gov.uk/en/news/latest-news/?view=Speech&id=23107618.

3 W. E. Schmidt, 'Britain's Spy Agencies Begin to Come out from the Cold', *New York Times*, 22 August 1993.

4 Cited in K. Robertson, 'Recent Reform of Intelligence in the UK: Democratisation or Risk Management?' *Intelligence and National Security*, 13:2 (Summer 1998), 145.

5 'The Secret's Out: Top British Spy Identified', *New York Times*, 7 May 1992.

6 Wark, 'In Never-Never Land?', 195–203.

7 www.mi5.gov.uk/output/retention-and-destruction-of-files.html; S. Rayment, 'MI5 Brings to Light the Faceless Figures Who Built the Service', *Telegraph*, 11 December 2005.

8 G. Brook-Shepherd, *Iron Maze: The Western Secret Services and the Bolsheviks* (Basingstoke: Macmillan, 1998).

9 A. Judd, *The Quest for Mansfield and the Founding of the British Secret Service* (London: HarperCollins, 1999).

10 C. Andrew and O. Gordievsky, *KGB: The Inside Story of Its Foreign Operations from Lenin to Gorbachev* (London: Hodder & Stoughton, 1990).

11 C. Andrew and V. Mitrokhin, *The Mitrokhin Archive: The KGB in Europe and the West* (London: Allen Lane, 1999).

12 C. Andrew and V. Mitrokhin, *The Mitrokhin Archive II: The KGB and the World* (London: Allen Lane, 2005).

13 *Lords Debates*, 9 December 1993, col. 1,028.

14 K. Robertson, 'Recent Reform of Intelligence in the UK', 144–58.

15 P. Gill, 'Reasserting Control' 313–31.

16 See C. Pincher, *A Web of Deception: The Spycatcher Affair* (London: Sidgwick & Jackson, 1987); M. Turnbull, *The Spycatcher Trial* (London: William Heinemann, 1988).

17 T. Bower, 'Obituary: Peter Wright', *Independent*, 28 April 1995.

18 Andrew, *Defence of the Realm*, p. 761.

19 Ibid., p. 762.

20 Ibid.

21 C. Ponting, *The Right to Know: The Inside Story of the Belgrano Affair* (London: Sphere Books, 1985).

22 Andrew, *Defence of the Realm*, p. 763.

23 [Anon.], 'Of Moles and Molehunters: A Review of Counterintelligence Literature, 1972–92', *Studies in Intelligence* (1995), 17.

24 R. C. Austin, 'The Wright Affair – The Wrong Response: Constitutional Aspects of the Wright Affair', *Parliamentary Affairs*, 40:3 (1987), 319–24.

25 P. Hennessy, 'Profile: Sir Robert Armstrong', *Contemporary Record*, 1:4 (Winter, 1988), 28.

26 C. Pilkington, *The Civil Service in Britain Today* (Manchester University Press, 1999), p. 59.

27 Andrew, *Defence of the Realm*, p. 764.

28 Cited in 'Spycatcher: A Diverting Obsession', *Times Literary Supplement*, 21 October 1988.

29 E. McDowell, 'Bestsellers from 1987's Book Crop', *New York Times*, 6 January 1988.

30 R. Norton-Taylor, 'Press Wins Spycatcher Battle', *Guardian*, 14 October 1988.

31 Andrew, *Defence of the Realm*, p. 765.

32 'Moles and Molehunters', p. 51.

33 Cited in Andrew, *Defence of the Realm*, p. 563.

34 Cited in A. Boyle, 'Obituary: Sir Dick White', *Independent*, 23 February 1993.

35 T. G. Carpenter, *The Captive Press: Foreign Policy Crises and the First Amendment* (Washington, DC: Cato Institute, 1995), p. 124.

36 A. Temple, 'The Spy Who Loved Me', *Guardian*, 2 October 2002; A. Barnett and M. Bright, 'Jackie Stewart Teamed Up with MI6 Renegade', *Guardian*, 27 August 2000.

37 D. Leppard, 'MI6 Tempts Rebel Ex-Spy Back Home', *Sunday Times*, 31 May 2009.

38 Speech by the Rt. Hon. Tony Blair MP, Leader of the Labour Party, at the Campaign for Freedom of Information's Annual Awards Ceremony, 25 March 1996.

39 A. Bevins, 'Freedom of Information Proposal Gets High Praise', *Independent*, 12 December 1997.

40 Cited in A. Roberts, *Blacked Out: Government Secrecy in the Information Age* (Cambridge University Press, 2006), p. 15.

41 T. Blair, *A Journey* (London: Hutchinson, 2010), p. 516.

42 Roberts, *Blacked Out*, p. 20.

43 Ibid.

44 www.mi5.gov.uk/ouput/director-generals-richard-dimbleby-lecture-1994.html.

45 C. Mullin, 'A Spy Like Us', *Guardian*, 29 September 2001.

46 Ibid.

47 D. Rose, 'Mission Implausible', *Guardian*, 16 September 2001.

48 P. Murphy, 'Review – The Defence of the Realm: The Authorised History of MI5', *Journal of Imperial and Commonwealth History*, 38:2 (2010), 34.

49 *Iraq's Weapons of Mass Destruction: The Assessment of the British Government* (London, 24 September 2002); *Iraq: Its Infrastructure of Concealment, Deception and Intimidation* (London, 7 February 2003).

50 A. Glees and P. Davies, *Spinning the Spies: Open Government and the Hutton Inquiry* (London: Social Affairs Unit, 2004).

51 R. J. Aldrich, 'Whitehall and the Iraq War: The UK's Four Intelligence Enquiries', *Irish Studies in International Affairs*, 16:1 (2005), 73–88.

52 B. Kovach, T. Rosensteil and D. Halberstam, *Warp Speed: America in the Age of Mixed Media* (London: Brookings Institution, 1999).

53 C. Arthur, 'They've Got Your Number', *Guardian*, 13 April 2009.

BIBLIOGRAPHY

Archives of unpublished government documents

Modern Records Centre, University of Warwick (MRC).
The National Archives (*formerly the Public Record Office*), Kew, Surrey (TNA).
US National Archives, College Park, Maryland.
West Sussex Record Office, Chichester.

Private papers: Great Britain

Amery, Julian. Liddell Hart Centre for Military Archives, King's College London.
Beesly, Patrick. Churchill College, Cambridge (CCC MLBE).
Bray, Jeremy. Churchill College, Cambridge (CCC BRAY).
Childers, Erskine. Trinity College, Cambridge.
Eden, Anthony. Cadbury Research Library, University of Birmingham (UBL AP).
Hankey, Maurice. Churchill College, Cambridge (CCC HANKEY).
Hart, Liddell. Liddell Hart Centre for Military Archives, King's College London (KCL LH).
Hyde, Montgomery. Churchill College, Cambridge (CCC HYDE).
Lloyd, Selwyn. Churchill College, Cambridge (CCC SELO).
Lloyd George, David. House of Lords Records Office, London (HLRO LG).
Masterman, John. Worcester College, Oxford (WC JMP).
Pincher Chapman. (not yet open to the public).
Suez Oral History Project, Liddell Hart Centre for Military Archives, King's College London.

Sylvester, Albert James. National Library of Wales, Aberystwyth (NLW).
Ward, Dame Irene. Bodleian Library, Oxford.
Wigg, George. London School of Economics, London (LSE WIGG).

Private papers: United States

Atlee Phillips, David. Library of Congress, Washington, DC.
Bundy, William. Seely. G. Mudd Manuscript Library, Princeton University.
Cave Brown, Anthony. Lauinger Library, Georgetown University Special Collections, Washington, DC (GU ACBP).
De Courcy, Kenneth. Hoover Institution, Stanford University.
Dulles, Allen. Seely G. Mudd Manuscript Library, Princeton University.
Farago, Ladislas. Howard Gotlieb Archival Research Center, Boston University (HGARC LFP).
Forgan, J. Russell. Hoover Institution, Stanford University.
Helms, Richard. Lauinger Library, Georgetown University, Washington, DC.
King, Cecil. Howard Gotlieb Archival Research Center, Boston University.
Mailer, Norman. Harry Ransom Center, Austin, Texas.
Pearson, J. Manuscripts Department, Lilly Library, Indiana University, Bloomington.
Production Code Administration Records, Academy of Motion Picture, Arts and Sciences, Los Angeles.
Russell, L. Manuscripts Department, Lilly Library, Indiana University, Bloomington.
Warner Bros. Archives, University of Southern California, Los Angeles.

Published documents, reports, diaries and autobiographies

Amery, J., *Sons of the Eagle: A Study in Guerrilla War* (London: Macmillan, 1948).
Amory, M. (ed.), *The Letters of Ann Fleming* (London: Collins Harvill, 1985).
Annan, N., *Our Age: Portrait of a Generation* (London: Weidenfeld & Nicolson, 1990).
Attlee, C., *As It Happened* (New York: Viking Press, 1954).
Azeau, H., *Le Piège de Suez* (Paris: R. Laffont, 1964).
Baden-Powell, B. F. S., *War in Practice: Some Tactical and Other Lessons of the Campaign in South Africa 1899–1902* (New York: Kessinger Publishing, 1903, reprinted 2007).
Barnes, J., *The Great War Trek: With the British Army on the Veldt* (New York: D. Appleton, 1901).
Bar-Zohar, M., *Suez Ultra Secret* (Paris: Fayard, 1964).

Beesly, P., *Very Special Intelligence: The Story of the Admiralty's Operational Intelligence Centre 1939–45* (London: Doubleday, 1977).

Bertrand, G., *Enigma ou la plus grande enigma de la guerre* (Paris: Libraire Plon, 1973).

Blair, T., *A Journey* (London: Hutchinson, 2010).

Blunt, W. S., *My Diaries: Being a Personal Narrative of Events 1888–1914 Part Two* (New York: Alfred A. Knopf, 1921).

Braithwaite, W., *Ambulance Wagon: Being the Memoirs of William J. Braithwaite*, ed. H. Bunbury (London: Methuen, 1957).

Bromberger, M. and S., *The Secrets of Suez* (London: Pan Books, 1957).

Buckmaster, M., *Specially Employed: The Story of British Aid to French Patriots of the Resistance* (London: Batchworth, 1952).

  They Fought Alone: The Story of British Agents in France (London: Odhams, 1958).

Castle, B., *The Castle Diaries 1964–70* (London: Macmillan, 1984).

Churchill, P., *Of Their Own Choice: An Account of the Author's Secret Mission to France During the Second World War* (London: Hodder & Stoughton, 1952).

  The Spirit in the Cage: An Account of the Author's Experiences as a Prisoner of War (London: Hodder & Stoughton, 1954).

Churchill, W., *Ian Hamilton's March* (New York: Longmans, Green and Co., 1900).

  The Gathering Storm (Boston: Houghton Mifflin, 1948).

Clark, W., *From Three Worlds: Memoirs* (London: Sidgwick & Jackson, 1986).

Crossman, R., *The Diaries of a Cabinet Minister*, 3 vols., Volume I: *Minister of Housing* (London: Jonathan Cape, 1975).

  The Diaries of a Cabinet Minister, 3 vols., Volume II: *Lord President of the Council and Leader of the House of Commons* (London: Hamish Hamilton, 1976).

Dalton, H., *Call Back Yesterday: Memoirs 1887–1931* (London: Muller, 1953).

Davies, N., *Flat Earth News* (London: Vintage Books, 2009).

Dayan, M., *Story of My Life* (New York: Morrow, 1976).

Deane, J. R., *Departmental Committee on Section 2 of the Official Secrets Act 1911*, Cmnd. 5104 (4 vols. London: HMSO, September 1972).

  The Strange Alliance: The Story of Our Efforts at Wartime Co-operation with Russia (London: John Murray 1947).

Dulles, A., *The Craft of Intelligence* (New York: Harper & Row, 1963).

Eden, A., *The Memoirs of Sir Anthony Eden: Full Circle* (Boston: Houghton Mifflin, 1960).

Eisenhower, D., *The White House Years: Mandate for Change 1953–6* (Garden City: Doubleday, 1963).

The White House Years: Waging Peace 1956–61 (Garden City: Doubleday, 1966).

European Resistance Movements 1939–1945: Presentations at the First International Conference on the History of the Resistance Movements (London: Pergamon Press, 1964).

Evans, H., *Good Times, Bad Times* (New York: Atheneum, 1984).

My Paper Chase (London: Abacus, 2009).

Firmin, S., *Crime Man: Experiences as a Crime Reporter* (London: Hutchinson, 1950).

Foot, M. R. D., *Memories of an SOE Historian* (Barnsley: Pen & Sword Military Books, 2008).

Gleichen, E., *A Guardsman's Memories* (London: William Blackwood, 1932).

Halifax, Viscount, *Fullness of Days* (New York: Dodd, Mead, 1957).

Hankey, M., *The Supreme Command: Volume II* (London: George Allen, 1961).

Heath, E., *The Course of My Life* (London: Hodder & Stoughton, 1998).

Hoare, S., *Ambassador on Special Mission* (London: Collins, 1946).

Nine Troubled Years (London: Collins, 1954).

Howard, M., *Captain Professor: A Life in War and Peace* (London: Continuum, 2006).

Information and the Public Interest, Cmnd. 4089 (London: HMSO, June 1969).

Iraq: Its Infrastructure of Concealment, Deception and Intimidation (London, 7 February 2003).

Iraq's Weapons of Mass Destruction: The Assessment of the British Government (London, 24 September 2002).

Jones, T., *Whitehall Diary*, ed. K. Middlemas, 3 vols. (Oxford University Press, 1969–71).

King, C., *The Cecil King Diaries 1965–70* (London: Jonathan Cape, 1972).

Le Queux, W., *Spies of the Kaiser* (Abingdon: Routledge, new edn. 1996).

Things I Know about Kings, Celebrities and Crooks (London: Eveleigh Nash and Grayson, 1923).

Lloyd, S., *Suez 1956: A Personal Account* (London: Cape, 1978).

Lloyd George, D., *War Memories*, 6 vols. (London: Odhams, 1938).

Mackenzie, C., *My Life and Times: Octave Seven, 1931–8* (London: Chatto & Windus, 1968).

Macmillan, H., Memoirs, 6 vols., Volume IV: *Riding the Storm 1956–1959* (London: HarperCollins, 1971).

Marshall, B., *The White Rabbit* (London: Evans Bros, 1952).

Marvin, C., *Our Public Offices* (2nd edn, London, 1880).

McLachlan, D., *Room 39: Naval Intelligence in Action 1939–45* (London: Atheneum, 1968).

Meyer, C., *Facing Reality: From World Federalism to the CIA* (New York: Harper & Row, 1980).

Millar, G., *Horned Pidgeon* (London: William Heinemann, 1946).

Milne, A., *DG: Memoirs of a British Broadcaster* (London: Hodder & Stoughton, 1988).

Montagu, E., *Beyond Top Secret Ultra* (London: Coward, McCann & Geoghegan, 1977).

Morrison, I., *Grandfather Longlegs: The Life and Gallant Death of Major H. P. Seagrim* (London: Faber & Faber, 1947).

Moss, S., *Ill Met by Moonlight* (London: George G. Harrap, 1950).

Nutting, A., *No End of a Lesson: The Story of Suez* (London: Constable, 1967).

Paget, A., 'Some Experiences of a Commandant: Prisoners of War at Deadwood Camp', *Longman's Camp* (October 1901).

Pape, R., *Boldness Be My Friend* (London: Elek, 1953).

Philby, K., *My Silent War: The Soviet Master Spy's Own Story* (New York: Grove Press, 1968).

Pineau, C., *The Civil Service, Report of the Committee 1966–68*, Cmnd. 3638 (London: HMSO, 1968).

Report of the Committee of Privy Councillors on Ministerial Memoirs, Cmnd. 6386 (London: HMSO, December 1975).

Suez 1956 (Paris: R. Laffont, 1976).

Rimington, S., *Open Secret: The Autobiography of a Former Director-General of MI5* (London: Hutchinson, 2001).

Robertson, G., *The Justice Game* (London: Chatto & Windus, 1998).

Security Procedures in the Public Service, Cmnd. 1681 (London, April 1962).

Final Report of the Senate Select Committee to Study Government Operations with Respect to Intelligence Activities, United States Senate: Together with Additional, Supplemental, and Separate Views, 6 vols. (Washington: GPO, 1976). 23 April 1976.

Simon, J., *Retrospect: The Memoirs of the Rt Hon. Viscount Simon* (London: Hutchinson, 1952).

Smyth, H., *Atomic Energy for Military Purposes: The Official Report on the Development of the Atomic Bomb under the United States Government, 1940–1945* (Princeton, 1945).

Stead, W. T., 'Government by Journalism', *Contemporary Review* (1886).

Stevenson, F., *The Years That Are Past* (London: Hutchinson, 1967).

Third Report from the Defence Committee, Session 1979–80, The D-Notice System, HC 773 (August 1980).

Thomas, J., *No Banners: The Story of Alfred and Henry Newton* (London: W. H. Allen, 1955).

White Paper on the D-Notice System, Cmnd. 3312 (1967).
Whitehall Confidential? The Publication of Political Memoirs, HC 689-I (London: HMSO, 25 July 2006).
Whitwell, J., *British Agent* (London: Frank Cass, 1996).
Williams, M., *Inside Number 10* (London: Weidenfeld & Nicolson, 1972).
Wilson, H., *The Labour Government 1964–70: A Personal Record* (London: Weidenfeld & Nicolson, 1971).

Secondary literature

Addison, P. and Jones, H. (eds.), *A Companion to Contemporary Britain* (Oxford: Wiley-Blackwell, 2005).
Aitken, J., *Officially Secret* (London: Weidenfeld & Nicolson, 1971).
Aldrich, R. J., *Espionage, Security and Intelligence in Britain 1945–1970* (Manchester University Press, 1998).
  GCHQ: The Uncensored Story of Britain's Most Secret Intelligence Agency (London: Harper Press, 2010).
  The Hidden Hand: Britain, America and Cold War Secret Intelligence (London: Overlook Press, 2002).
  'Never-Never Land and Wonderland? British and American Policy on Intelligence Archive', *Contemporary Record*, 8:1 (Summer 1994), 132–50.
  'Policing the Past: Official History, Secrecy and British Intelligence since 1945', *English Historical Review*, 119: 483 (September 2004), 922–53.
  'The Secret State', in Addison, P. and Jones, H. (eds), *A Companion to Contemporary Britain* (Oxford: Wiley-Blackwell, 2005), pp. 333–50.
  'Whitehall and the Iraq War: The UK's Four Intelligence Enquiries', *Irish Studies in International Affairs*, 16:1 (2005), 73–88.
Ambrose, S., 'Reviewed Work: SOE in France: An Account of the Work of the Special Operations Executive in France, 1940–44', *American Historical Review*, 74:3 (February 1969), 1,005–6.
Andrew, C., 'Churchill and Intelligence', *Intelligence and National Security*, 3:3 (July 1988), 181–93.
  The Defence of the Realm: The Authorised History of MI5 (London: Allen Lane, 2009).
  'Intelligence, International Relations and Under-Theorisation', *Intelligence and National Security*, 19:2 (Summer 2004), 170–84.
  Secret Service: The Making of the British Intelligence Community (London: Heinemann, 1985).
Andrew, C. and Aldrich, R. J., 'The Intelligence Services in the Second World War', *Contemporary British History*, 13:4 (Winter 1999), 130–69.

Andrew, C. and Dilks, D. (eds.), *The Missing Dimension: Governments and Intelligence Communities in the Twentieth Century* (London: Palgrave Macmillan, 1984).

Andrew, C. and Gordievsky, O., *KGB: The Inside Story of Its Foreign Operations from Lenin to Gorbachev* (London: Hodder & Stoughton, 1990).

Andrew, C. and Mitrokhin, V., *The Mitrokhin Archive: The KGB in Europe and the West* (London: Allen Lane, 1999).

The Mitrokhin Archive II: The KGB and the World (London: Allen Lane, 2005).

Austin, R. C., 'The Wright Affair – The Wrong Response: Constitutional Aspects of the Wright Affair', *Parliamentary Affairs*, 40:3 (1987), 319–24.

Bagehot, W., *The English Constitution* (3rd edn, London, 1882).

Barker, A. J., *Suez: The Seven-Day War* (New York: Praeger, 1964).

Baston, L., 'The D-Notice Affair', *Labour History*, 1 (Autumn 2003), 21–2.

Baylen, J., 'George Moore, W. T. Stead, and the Boer War', *Studies in English*, 3 (1962), 49–60.

Bennett, R., 'FORTITUDE, ULTRA and the "Need to Know"', *Intelligence and National Security*, 4:3 (July 1988), 482–502.

'ULTRA and Some Command Decisions', *Journal of Contemporary History*, 16:1 (January 1981), pp. 131–52.

Ultra in the West: The Normandy Campaign 1944–45 (London: Charles Scribners, 1979).

Bernstein, C. and Woodward, B., *All the President's Men* (New York: Simon & Schuster, 1974).

Bickers, R., 'The Business of a Secret War: Operation "Remorse" and SOE Salesmanship in Wartime China', *Intelligence and National Security*, 16:4 (December 2001), 11–36.

Bond, B., *The Unquiet Western Front: Britain's Role in Literature and History* (Cambridge University Press, 2002).

Booth, N., *ZigZag: The Incredible Wartime Exploits of Double Agent Eddie Chapman* (London: Piatkus, 2007).

Boston, R., 'From Inkwells to Computers', *British Journalism Review*, 5:63 (1994), 63–5.

Boyd, K., *Encyclopedia of Historians and Historical Writing: Volume I* (London: Fitzroy Dearborn, 1999).

Brien, J., 'Sir Arthur Conan Doyle and W. T. Stead: The Novelist and the Journalist', *Albion: A Quarterly Journal Concerned with British Studies*, 2:1 (1970), 3–16.

Brook-Shepherd, G., *Iron Maze: The Western Secret Services and the Bolsheviks* (Basingstoke: Macmillan, 1998).

Bross, J., 'Review: SOE in France', *Studies in Intelligence*, 11:2 (Spring 1967).

Bublitz, R., 'Review: Room 39: A Study in Naval Intelligence by D. McLachlan', *Military Affairs*, 33:1 (April 1969), 278.

Bunyan, T., *Political Police in Britain* (London: Quartet Books, 1976).

Burke, P., *What Is Cultural History?* (London: Polity Press, 2004).

Butterfield, H., *History and Human Relations* (London: Longman, 1951).

Cabell, C., *The History of 30 Assault Unit: Ian Fleming's Red Indians* (London: Pen & Sword, 2009).

Calvocoressi, P., *Suez: Ten Years On* (London: British Broadcasting Corporation, 1967).

Top Secret Ultra (New York: Littlehampton, 1980).

Campbell, D., 'Official Secrecy and British Libertarianism', *Socialist Register*, 16 (1979), 75–87.

Campbell, J. P., 'An Update on the Interpretation of the Ultra Documentation', *Archivaria*, 26 (September 1988), 184–8.

Carlton, D., *Anthony Eden: A Biography* (London: Allen Lane, 1981).

Carpenter, T. G., *The Captive Press: Foreign Policy Crises and the First Amendment* (Washington, DC: Cato Institute, 1995).

Cave Brown, A., *Bodyguard of Lies* (London: HarperCollins, 1976).

Chester, N., *The Administrative System 1780–1870* (Oxford University Press, 1981).

Childers, E. B., *The Road to Suez: A Study of Western–Arab Relations* (London: MacGibbon & Kee, 1962).

Churchill, R., *The Rise and Fall of Sir Anthony Eden* (London: MacGibbon & Kee, 1959).

Clare, J. D., 'Interpretation of Haig', www.johndclare.net/wwi3_HaigHistoriography.htm.

Clarke, I. F., *Voices Prophesying War* (Oxford University Press, 1966).

Conboy, M., *The Press and Popular Culture* (Gateshead: Sage, 2001).

Craddock, P., *Know Your Enemy: How the Joint Intelligence Committee Saw the World* (London: John Murray, 2002).

Cranfield, G. A., *The Press and Society: From Caxton to Northcliffe* (London: Longman, 1978).

Creevy, M., 'A Critical Review of the Wilson Government's Handling of the D-Notice Affair 1967', *Intelligence and National Security*, 14:3 (Autumn 1999), 209–27.

Crossman, R., 'The Real English Disease', *New Statesman*, 24 September 1971, p. 1.

Cullather, N., *Secret History: The CIA's Classified Account of Its Operations in Guatemala, 1952–54* (Stanford University Press, 1999).

Curry, J., *The Security Service 1908–45* (London: Public Record Office Publications, 1999).

Danchev, A., *Oliver Franks: Founding Father* (Oxford: Clarendon Press, 1993).

Deutsch, J., '"I was a Hollywood Agent": Cinematic Representations of the Office of Strategic Services in 1946', *Intelligence and National Security*, 13:2 (1998), 85–99.

Dorril, S. and Ramsay, R., *Smear: Wilson and the Secret State* (London: HarperCollins, 1992).

Drewry, G. and Butcher, T., *The Civil Service Today* (Oxford: Wiley-Blackwell, 1988).

Dutton, D., *Anthony Eden: A Life and a Reputation* (London: Arnold, 1997).

Egerton, G., 'The Lloyd George "War Memoirs": A Study in the Politics of Memory', *Journal of Modern History*, 60:1 (March 1988), 55–94.

(ed.), *Political Memoir: Essays on the Politics of Memory* (London: Frank Cass, 1994).

Emmott, B. (ed.), *Changing Times: Leading Perspectives on the Civil Service in the 21st Century and Its Enduring Values* (London: Palgrave, 1999).

Epstein, L., *British Policy in the Suez Crisis* (Urbana: University of Illinois Press, 1964).

Farago, L., *Burn after Reading: The Espionage History of World War II* (New York: Macfadden-Bartell, 1963).

The Game of the Foxes: The Untold Story of German Espionage in the United States and Great Britain During World War II (New York: David McKay, 1971).

Finer, H., *Dulles over Suez: The Theory and Practice of His Diplomacy* (Chicago: Quadrangle Books, 1964).

Fleming, I., *The Diamond Smugglers* (London: Jonathan Cape, 1957).

Foley, M., *The Rise of the British Presidency* (Manchester University Press, 1993).

Foot, M. R. D., *SOE in France* (London: HMSO, 1966).

SOE in the Low Countries (London: St Ermin's Press, 2001).

Fraser, P., 'Cabinet Secrecy and War Memoirs', *History*, 70:230 (1985), 397–409.

French, D., 'Sir Douglas Haig's Reputation, 1918–1928: A Note', *Historical Journal*, 28:4 (1985), 953–60.

'Spy Fever in Britain, 1900–1915', *Historical Journal*, 21:2 (June 1978), 355–70.

Furedi, F., 'Wikileaks: This Isn't Journalism – It's Voyeurism', www.spiked-online.com/index.php/site/article/9953.

Gerth, H. H. and Mills, C. W., *Essays in Sociology* (London: Routledge, 1946).

Gill, P., 'Allo, Allo, Allo, Who's in Charge Here Then?', *Liverpool Law Review*, 9:2 (1987), 189–201.

'Reasserting Control: Recent Changes in the Oversight of the UK Intelligence Community', *Intelligence and National Security*, 11:2 (1996), 313–31.

Glees, A. and Davies, P., *Spinning the Spies: Open Government and the Hutton Inquiry* (London: Social Affairs Unit, 2004).

Goodman, M., 'Who Is Trying to Keep What Secret from Whom and Why? MI5–FBI Relations and the Klaus Fuchs Case', *Journal of Cold War Studies*, 7:3 (2005), 124–46.

Goodman, M. and Pincher, C., 'Research Note: Clement Attlee, Percy Sillitoe and the Security Aspects of the Fuchs Case', *Contemporary British History*, 19:1 (2005), 67–77.

Ferguson, N., *Virtual History: Alternatives and Counterfactuals* (New York: Basic Books, 1998).

Grafton, A., *The Footnote: A Curious History* (Harvard University Press, 1999).

Grey J. (ed.), *The Last Word? Essays on Official History in the US and British Commonwealth* (Westport: Praeger, 2003).

Hahn, P. L., 'Suez', *Reviews in American History*, 20:4 (December 1992), 567–74.

Hain, P., *Political Trials in Britain* (London: Allen Lane, 1984).

Hart, P. and Steel, N., *Passchendaele: The Sacrificial Ground* (London: Cassell, 2001).

Heclo, H. and Wildavsky, A., *The Private Government of Public Money* (Basingstoke: Palgrave, 1981).

Hedley, P. and Aynsley, C., *The D-Notice Affair* (London: Michael Joseph, 1967).

Hennessy, P., *Hidden Wiring: Unearthing the British Constitution* (London: Weidenfeld & Nicolson, 1995).

  The Prime Minister: The Office and Its Holders since 1945 (London: Penguin, 2000).

  'Profile: Sir Robert Armstrong', *Contemporary Record*, 1:4 (Winter, 1988).

  The Secret State: Whitehall and the Cold War (London: Penguin, 2003).

  Whitehall (London: Secker & Warburg, 1989).

Hiley, N., 'Decoding German Spies: British Spy Fiction 1908–18', *Intelligence and National Security*, 5:4 (October 1990), 55–79.

Hinsley, H., 'The Enigma of Ultra', *History Today*, 43:9 (September 1993), 15–20.

Hooper, D., *Official Secrets: The Use and Abuse of the Act* (London: Secker & Warburg, 1987).

Howard, M., 'Reflections on Strategic Deception', in Louis, R. W. (ed.), *Adventures with Britannia* (Oxford: I. B. Tauris, 1994), pp. 235–46.

Howarth, P., *Undercover: The Men and Women of the Special Operations Executive* (London: Routledge, 1980).

Hoy, H., *40 OB: Or How the War Was Won* (London: Hutchinson, 1932).

Hyde, M., *The Quiet Canadian: The Secret Service Story of Sir William Stephenson* (London: H. Hamilton, 1962).

Inglis, F., *Culture* (London: Polity Press, 2004).

Jaconelli, J., 'The Franks Report on Section 2 of the Official Secrets Act 1911', *Modern Law Review*, 36:1 (January 1973), 68–72.

James, R. R., *Anthony Eden* (London: Weidenfeld & Nicolson, 1986).

Jeffery, K., *MI6: The History of the Secret Intelligence Service* (London: Bloomsbury, 2010).

Jeffreys-Jones, R., 'The Role of British Intelligence in the Mythologies Underpinning the OSS and Early CIA', *Intelligence and National Security*, 15:2 (2000), 5–19.

'Why Was the CIA Established in 1947', *Intelligence and National Security*, 12:1 (1997), 21–40.

Jenks, J., *British Propaganda and News Media in the Cold War* (Edinburgh University Press, 2006).

Johnson, L., *Strategic Intelligence*, Volume 1 (Westport, CT: Greenwood, 2007).

Johnson, P., *The Suez War* (London: MacGibbon & Kee, 1957).

Jones, G., 'The Lloyd George War Memoirs', *Transactions of the Honourable Society of Cymmrodorion*, 14 (2008), 127–43.

Jones, R. V., 'Alfred Ewing and Room 40', *Notes and Records of the Royal Society of London*, 34:1 (1979), 65–90.

Judd, A., *The Quest for Mansfield and the Founding of the British Secret Service* (London: HarperCollins, 1999).

Kahn, D., *The Codebreakers: The Story of Secret Writing* (New York: Macmillan, 1967).

Keegan, J., *Intelligence in War: Knowledge of the Enemy from Napoleon to Al-Qaeda* (London: Key Porter Books, 2003).

Kellner, P., 'The Lobby, Official Secrets and Good Government', *Parliamentary Affairs*, 36:1 (1983), 275–81.

Kellner, P. and Hunt, C., *The Civil Servants: An Inquiry into Britain's Ruling Class* (London: Macdonald, 1980).

Kimball, W. F., 'Openness and the CIA', *Studies in Intelligence*, 44:2 (2000), 63–7.

Kovach, B., Rosensteil, T. and Halberstam, D., *Warp Speed: America in the Age of Mixed Media* (London: Brookings Institution, 1999).

Kozaczuk, W., *Bitwa o Tajemnice. Sluzby wywiadowcze Polski i Rzeszy Niemieckiej 1922–1939* (Warsaw: Ksiazka i Wiedza, 1967).

Lamb, R., *The Failure of the Eden Government* (London: Sidgwick & Jackson, 1987).

Langhorne, R., 'Professor Sir Harry Hinsley: An Appreciation', *Diplomacy and Statecraft*, 9:2 (July 1998), 212–21.

Lashmar, P., 'Mr. Waldegrave's Need to Know', *History Today*, 44 (August 1994).

Leigh, D., *The Frontiers of Secrecy* (London: Junction Books, 1980).

Leigh, D. and Harding, L., *Wikileaks: Inside Julian Assange's War on Secrecy* (London: Guardian Books, 2011).

Lewin, R., 'Sir Basil Liddell Hart: The Captain Who Taught the Generals', *International Affairs*, 47:1 (January 1971), 79–86.

Ultra Goes to War (London: Book Club Associates, 1978).

Lowe, R., 'Official History', www.history.ac.uk/makinghistory/resources/articles/official_history.html.

Macintyre, B., *Agent ZigZag: The True Wartime Story of Eddie Chapman: Lover, Traitor, Hero, Spy* (London: Bloomsbury Publishing, 2007).

Mackenzie, W. J., *The Secret History of SOE: Special Operations Executive, 1940–1945* (London: St Ermin's Press, 2000).

Mandler, P., 'Reviewed Work: *The Culture of Secrecy: Britain 1832–1998* by D. Vincent', *American Historical Review*, 105:3 (June 2000), 1,013–14.

Margach, J., *The Abuse of Power: The War between Downing Street and the Media from Lloyd George to Callaghan* (London: W. H. Allen, 1978).

Marsh, D., Richards, D. and Smith, M. J., *Changing Patterns of Governance in the United Kingdom: Reinventing Whitehall?* (London: Palgrave, 2001).

Middlemas, R. K., 'Cabinet Secrecy and the Crossman Diaries', *Political Quarterly*, 47:1 (January 1976), 39–51.

Morley, J., *The Life of Gladstone* (London: Macmillan, 1908).

Mowat, C., *Britain Between the Wars 1918–1940* (London: Methuen, 1955).

Moynihan, D. P., *Secrecy: The American Experience* (New Haven: Yale University Press, 1999).

Murphy, C. J., 'The Origins of *SOE in France*', *Historical Journal*, 46:4 (2003), 935–52.

Security and Special Operations: SOE and MI5 during the Second World War (Basingstoke: Palgrave, 2006).

Murphy, P., 'Review – The Defence of the Realm: The Authorised History of MI5', *Journal of Imperial and Commonwealth History*, 38:2 (2010), 340–4.

'Telling Tales Out of School: Nutting, Eden and the Attempted Suppression of *No End of a Lesson*', in Smith, S. C. (ed.), *Reassessing Suez 1956: New Perspectives on the Crisis and Its Aftermath* (Aldershot: Ashgate, 2008), pp. 195–214.

Naylor, J., *A Man and an Institution: Sir Maurice Hankey and the Cabinet Secretariat* (Cambridge University Press, 1984).

O'Sullivan, D., *Dealing with the Devil: Anglo-Soviet Intelligence Cooperation in the Second World War* (New York: Peter Lang, 2009).

Palmer, A., 'The History of the D-Notice Committee', in Andrew, C. and Dilks, D. (eds), *The Missing Dimension: Governments and Intelligence Communities in the Twentieth Century* (London: Palgrave Macmillan, 1984), pp. 227–49.

Parish, J. and Pitts, R., *The Great Spy Pictures* (Metuchen: Scarecrow Press, 1974).

Pearson, J., *The Life of Ian Fleming* (London: Companion Book Club, 1966).

Pilkington, C., *The Civil Service in Britain Today* (Manchester University Press, 1999).

Pincher, C., *The Giant Killer* (London: Weidenfeld & Nicolson, 1967).

Inside Story: A Documentary of the Pursuit of Power (London: Sidgwick & Jackson, 1978).

Not With a Bang (London: Four Square, 1965).

Treachery: Betrayals, Blunders and Cover-ups: Six Decades of Espionage against America and Great Britain (New York: Random House, 2009).

A Web of Deception: The Spycatcher Affair (London: Sidgwick & Jackson, 1987).

Piper, L., *The Tragedy of Erskine Childers: Dangerous Waters* (London: Hambledon and London, 2003).

Ponting, C., *The Right to Know: The Inside Story of the Belgrano Affair* (London: Sphere Books, 1985).

Secrecy in Britain (Oxford: Wiley-Blackwell, 1990).

Powers, T., *The Man Who Kept the Secrets: Richard Helms and the CIA* (New York: Alfred Knopf, 1979).

Reynolds, D., *In Command of History: Churchill Writing and Fighting the Second World War* (London: Penguin, 2005).

'Official History: How Churchill and the Cabinet Office Wrote *The Second World War*', *Historical Research*, 78:201, 400–22.

'The Ultra Secret and Churchill's War Memoirs', *Intelligence and National Security*, 20:2 (June 2005), 209–24.

Richards, B., *Secret Flotillas: Clandestine Sea-Lines to France and French North Africa* (London: HMSO, 1996).

Richardson, P., *A Bomb in Every Issue: How the Short, Unruly Life of Ramparts Magazine Changed America* (New York: New Press, 2009).

Robbins, K., *Politicians, Diplomacy and War in Modern British History* (London: Hambledon Continuum, 1994).

Roberts, A., *Blacked Out: Government Secrecy in the Information Age* (Cambridge University Press, 2006).

Public Secrets: A Study in the Development of Government Secrecy (London: Macmillan, 1982).

'Recent Reform of Intelligence in the UK: Democratisation or Risk Management?', *Intelligence and National Security*, 13:2 (Summer 1998), 313–31.

(ed.), *War, Resistance and Intelligence: Essays in Honour of M. R. D. Foot* (London: Pen & Sword Books, 1999).

Rogers, A., *Secrecy and Power in the British State: A History of the Official Secrets Act* (London: Pluto Press, 1997).

Roseveare, H., *The Treasury: The Evolution of a British Institution* (London: Allen Lane, 1969).

Roskill, S., *Hankey: Man of Secrets*, 3 vols. (London: Collins, 1970–74), Volume III: *1931–1963*.

Rowat, D. C. (ed.), *Administrative Secrecy in Developed Countries* (New York: Columbia University Press, 1979).

Rubin, M., 'What Is Cultural History Now?', in Cannadine, D. (ed.), *What Is History Now?* (London: Palgrave, 2002), pp. 80–94.

Ryan, W. M., 'The Invasion Controversy of 1906–08: Lieutenant-Colonel Charles à Court Repington and British Perceptions of the German Menace', *Military Affairs*, 44:1 (February 1980), 8–12.

Sampson, A., *The New Anatomy of Modern Britain* (London: Hodder & Stoughton, 1971).

Scott, L. and Jackson, P., 'The Study of Intelligence in Theory and Practice', *Intelligence and National Security*, 19:2 (Summer 2004), 139–69.

Seaman, M., 'A Glass Half Full – Some Thoughts on the Evolution of the Study of the SOE', *Intelligence and National Security*, 20:1 (March 2005), 27–43.

'Good Thrillers, But Bad History', in Robertson, K. G. (ed.), *War, Resistance and Intelligence: Essays in Honour of M. R. D. Foot* (London: Pen & Sword Books, 1999), pp. 119–33.

(ed.), *Special Operations Executive: A New Weapon of War* (London: Routledge, 2006).

Seed, D., 'Erskine Childers and the German Peril', *German Life and Letters*, 45:1 (January 1992), 66–73.

Shils, E., *The Torment of Secrecy: The Background and Consequences of American Security Policies* (London: Heinemann, 1956).

Smith, S. C. (ed.), *Reassessing Suez 1956: New Perspectives on the Crisis and Its Aftermath* (Aldershot: Ashgate, 2008).

Spufford, M., *Contrasting Communities: English Villagers in the Sixteenth and Seventeenth Centuries* (Cambridge University Press, 1974).

Stafford, D., *Churchill and Secret Service* (London: Abacus, 1997).

The Silent Game: The Real World of Imaginary Spies (Athens, GA: University of Georgia Press, 1989.

Stock, E., 'Reviewed Work: *No End of a Lesson* by Anthony Nutting', *Political Science Quarterly*, 84:1 (March 1969), 136–7.

Suttie, A., *Rewriting the First World War: Lloyd George, Politics and Strategy* (Basingstoke: Palgrave Macmillan, 2005).

Taylor, A. J. P., *English History, 1914–1945* (Oxford University Press, 1965).

Theakston, K., *The Civil Service Since 1945* (Oxford: Blackwell, 1995).

'Evelyn Sharp', *Contemporary British History*, 7:1 (Summer 1993), 132–48.

The Labour Party and Whitehall (London: Routledge, 1992).

Thomas, H., *The Suez Affair* (London: Weidenfeld & Nicolson, 1967).

Thomas, R. M., *Espionage and Secrecy: The Official Secrets Act 1911–1989 of the United Kingdom* (London: Routledge 1991).

Thompson, E. P., *Customs in Common* (New York: New Press, 1993).

'The Secret State', *Race and Class*, 20 (1979), 219–42.

Writing by Candlelight (London: Merlin Press, 1980).

Thorpe, D. R., *Eden: The Life and Times of Anthony Eden* (London: Random House, 2003).

Thurlow, R., *The Secret State: British Internal Security in the Twentieth Century* (Oxford: Wiley-Blackwell, 1994).

Travers, T., 'The Relativity of War: British Military Memoirs from the Campaigns of Marlborough to the First World War', in Egerton, G. (ed.), *Political Memoir: Essays on the Politics of Memory* (London: Frank Cass, 1994), pp. 151–66.

Trotter, D., 'The Politics of Adventure in the Early British Spy Novel', *Intelligence and National Security*, 5:4 (October 1990), 30–54.

Turnbull, M., *The Spycatcher Trial* (London: William Heinemann, 1988).

Valero, L., 'We Need Our New OSS, Our New General Donovan, Now ...: The Public Discourse over American Intelligence, 1944–53', *Intelligence and National Security*, 18:1 (Spring 2003), 91–118.

Vincent, D., *The Culture of Secrecy: Britain 1832–1998* (Oxford University Press, 1997).

'The Origins of Public Secrecy in Britain', *Transactions of the Royal Historical Society*, 6th series, 1 (1991), 229–48.

Warber, G., '"Collusion" and the Suez Crisis of 1956', *International Affairs* (April 1979), 226–39.

Wark, W., 'In Never-Never Land? The British Archives on Intelligence', *Historical Journal*, 35:1 (March 1992), 195–203.

'"Our Man in Riga": Reflections on the SIS Career and Writings of Leslie Nicholson', *Intelligence and National Security*, 11:4 (October 1996), 625–44.

Weber, M., *From Max Weber: Essays in Sociology*, ed. and trans. H. H. Gerth and C. W. Mills (London: Routledge, 1991).

West, N., *Secret War* (London: Hodder & Stoughton, 1992).

(ed.), *Faber Book of Espionage* (London: Faber & Faber, 1993).

(ed.), *The Guy Liddell Diaries* Volume I: *1939–42* (London: Routledge, 2005).

(ed.), *The Guy Liddell Diaries* Volume II: *1942–45* (London: Routledge, 2005).

Wight, M., 'Brutus in Foreign Policy: The Memoirs of Sir Anthony Eden', *International Affairs*, 36:3 (July 1960), 209–309.

Wilkinson, N., *Secrecy and the Media: The Official History of the D-Notice System* (London: Routledge, 2009).

Williams, D. G. T., 'Case and Comment: The Crossman Diaries', *Cambridge Law Journal*, 35:1 (April 1976), 1–3.

'Official Secrecy in England', *Federal Law Review*, 3 (1968–9), 20–50.

Wilsnack, R. W., 'Information Control: A Conceptual Framework for Sociological Analysis', *Urban Life*, 8:4 (January 1980), 467–99.

Wilson, D. (ed.), *Secrets File: The Case for Freedom of Information in Britain Today* (London: Heinemann, 1984).

Winterbotham, F. W., *The Ultra Secret* (London: Weidenfeld & Nicolson, 1974).

Wylie, N., 'SOE and the Neutrals', in Seaman, M. (ed.), *Special Operations Executive: A New Weapon of War* (London: Routledge, 2006), pp. 157–78.

INDEX